INTRODUCTION TO THE COUNSELING PROFESSION

Introduction to the Counseling Profession is a comprehensive overview of the history and foundational concepts of counseling, offering the most current and relevant breadth of coverage available. Students will gain insight into the myriad issues that surround not only the process of counseling and its many populations but also the personal dynamics that have an impact on this process. The contributed-author format provides state-of-the-art information from experts in their respective fields while maintaining a consistent structure and message.

This edition has been brought in line with the 2009 Council for the Accreditation of Counseling and Related Educational Programs (CACREP) standards and includes chapters on each of the CACREP specializations. Topics rarely treated in other introductory texts are addressed, such as research and writing in counseling, technology and counseling, and self-care and growth.

This edition includes new pedagogical features such as sidebars and more case studies to expand on key topics, as well as new chapters on:

- Cross-Cultural Counseling
- Self-Care and Self-Growth
- Individual Counseling
- Diagnosis and Treatment Planning
- Addictions Counseling
- Student Affairs and College Counseling

A collection of supplemental resources are available online to benefit both instructors and students. Instructors will find PowerPoint slides and test banks to aid in conducting their courses, and students can access chapter summaries, exercises, and other tools to questions for thought and reflection to supplement their review of the material in the text. These materials can be accessed at http://www.routledgementalhealth.com/cw/Capuzzi

David Capuzzi, PhD, NCC, LPC, is a professor emeritus at Portland State University and a counselor educator at both Walden University and Canisius College. He is a past president of the American Counseling Association.

Douglas R. Gross, PhD, NCC, is a professor emeritus at Arizona State University, Tempe, where he served as a faculty member in counselor education for 29 years. He is a past president of the Arizona Counselors Association and the Western Association for Counselor Education and Supervision.

INTRODUCTION TO THE COUNSELING PROFESSION

Sixth Edition

Edited by

David Capuzzi
Walden University
Canisius College

and

Douglas R. Gross
Arizona State University

Routledge
Taylor & Francis Group

NEW YORK AND LONDON

First published 2013
by Routledge
711 Third Avenue, New York, NY 10017

Simultaneously published in the UK
by Routledge
27 Church Road, Hove, East Sussex BN3 2FA

Routledge is an imprint of the Taylor & Francis Group, an informa business

Library of Congress Cataloging-in-Publication Data
Introduction to the counseling profession / [edited by] David Capuzzi and
Douglas R. Gross. — 6th ed.
    p. cm.
Includes bibliographical references and index.
ISBN 978-0-415-66051-8 (hardback : alk. paper) —
ISBN 978-0-415-52496-4 (pbk. : alk. paper) 1. Counseling–Vocational
guidance. I. Capuzzi, Dave. II. Gross, Douglas R.
BF636.64.I58 2013
158.3–dc23   2012029734

ISBN: 978-0-415-66051-8 (hbk)
ISBN: 978-0-415-52496-4 (pbk)
ISBN: 978-0-203-12006-4 (ebk)

Typeset in Garamond
by Cenveo Publisher Services

SFI® Certified Sourcing
www.sfiprogram.org
SFI-00453

Printed and bound in the United States of America
by Edwards Brothers, Inc.

CONTENTS

CONTENTS

PREFACE

The profession of counseling is best described as one through which counselors interact with clients to assist them in learning about and dealing with themselves and their environment and the roles and responsibilities inherent in this interactive process. Individuals exploring counseling as a career choice need to be aware of the personal, professional, and societal demands placed on the professional counselor. The role of the professional counselor calls for individuals who are skilled and knowledgeable in the process and theory that undergird the profession, who are able and willing to reach deeper levels of self-understanding, and who are able to integrate this skill, knowledge, and self-understanding to provide the effective counseling interaction to which clients are entitled. Individuals attempting to decide whether this is the right career choice for them will find the information contained in the text helpful in the decision-making process.

The book is unique both in its format and in its content. The contributed author format provides state-of-the-art information by experts in their respective fields. The content provides readers with areas not often addressed in introductory texts. Examples of these areas include chapters devoted to self-care and self-growth, research and writing in counseling, and the use of technology in counseling. The book is designed for students who are taking a preliminary course in the counseling field and who are trying to determine if they are well matched to the profession of counseling. The book presents a comprehensive overview of the major aspects of counseling as a profession and provides its reader with insight into the myriad of issues that surround not only the process of counseling and its many populations, but also, the personal dynamics of the counselor that have an impact upon this process.

OVERVIEW OF THE SIXTH EDITION

This sixth edition of our text is congruent with the 2009 standards of the Council for the Accreditation of Counseling and Related Educational Programs (CACREP) and addresses core curricular areas specified by CACREP so that beginning counselors can obtain overviews of the knowledge and skills they must master as they progress through their graduate programs of study. In addition, the last six chapters of the sixth edition overview all the specializations CACREP now accredits: addictions counseling, career counseling, mental health counseling, marriage, couple, and family counseling, school counseling, and student affairs and college counseling. More discussion of the implications of counseling with diverse populations, additional case studies, sidebars, and a number of new authors add freshness and dimension to this new edition. Both format and content enhance the readability of the book and should increase student interest in the material.

We know that one text cannot adequately address all the factors that make up this complex profession. We have, however attempted to provide our readers with a broad perspective on the profession of counseling. The text is divided into the following three sections: Counseling Foundations, Counseling Skills, and Counseling Specializations. Part One—Counseling Foundations (chapters 1 through 7)—begins with an introduction to the *Therapeutic Alliance and the Helping Relationship*. This first chapter is followed by a chapter dealing with *The Counseling Profession: Historical Perspectives and Current Issues and Trends* that serves as the foundation of the counseling profession; it builds on this foundation providing the reader with current information regarding legislation, professional associations, certification, licensure, accreditation and current issues and trends related to counseling. Chapters entitled *Cross Cultural Counseling, Ethical and Legal Considerations in Counseling, Self-Care and Self-Growth: A Professional Responsibility, Research and Writing in Counseling*, and *Technology and Counseling* follow. Part Two, Counseling Skills (chapters 8 through 12), presents information relative to the skills counselors must acquire through a combination of education, supervision and practice. These chapters include *Individual Counseling: Traditional and Brief Approaches, Group Counseling, Creative Approaches to Counseling, Assessment Practices in Counseling*, and *Diagnosis and Treatment Planning*. All of these chapters provide overviews and introduce readers to roles that cut across a variety of work settings. Part Three—Counseling Specializations (Chapters 13 through 18)—presents information relative to the six specializations now accredited by CACREP. These chapters, *Addictions Counseling, Career Counseling, Counseling in Clinical Mental Health and Private Practice Settings, Marriage, Couple, and Family Counseling, School Counseling, and Student Affairs and College Counseling* include discussions of the content outlined in the 2009 standards for those specializations.

New to this Edition

This edition of our text is based on both post publication reviews of the fifth edition and the desire of the co-editors to update content, enhance reader interest by using sidebars and additional case studies, and make the reading even more user friendly.

Chapter 1 (*Therapeutic Alliance and the Helping Relationship*) contains updated references, new case studies, and sidebars that were not part of the fifth edition. It is placed first in the book since the establishment of a therapeutic alliance forms the basis for all aspects of the helping relationship and is foundational and a prerequisite to any role the counselor might be engaged in with a client or clients.

Chapter 2 (*The Counseling Profession: Historical Perspectives and Current Issues and Trends*) provides historical and updated information about the profession, major professional organizations, and new developments that inform the reader about current issues and trends.

Chapter 3 (*Cross Cultural Counseling*) is a newly written chapter for this sixth edition. Since it is the co-editors' philosophy that all counseling is cross cultural in nature, it is a critical component of the education and supervision of a counselor.

Chapter 4 (*Ethical and Legal Considerations in Counseling*) has been rewritten and updated and contains a number of interesting sidebars and case studies that will be of high interest to the reader.

Chapter 5 (*Self-Care and Self-Growth: A Professional Responsibility*) was written at the request of the editors and is new to the sixth edition. This chapter provides information that is crucial to the beginning counselor entering a profession that places huge responsibility on its members that often precipitates burnout, impairment, or both. It is the hope of the editors that readers will view this chapter as preventive in intent and will periodically review its content.

Chapter 6 (*Research and Writing in Counseling*) is a very unique chapter since the information it contains is not usually part of the textbooks used for required courses in Counselor Education programs and departments. Since professional counselors are encouraged to use research to inform their practices with clients and to write up the results of their own research for dissemination to members of the profession, the editors requested this information update for the benefit of the reader.

Chapter 7 (*Technology and Counseling*) is critical to the successful functioning of the 21st century counselor. The updated information, addition of sidebars and case studies, and expertly written and organized content provides the most up-to-date information possible to prepare the counselor for the crescendo in the use of technology in the counseling profession.

Chapter 8 (*Individual Counseling: Traditional and Brief Approaches*) is a newly written chapter for the sixth edition. Readers are introduced to traditional theoretical frameworks for individual counseling and how they may be used in brief counseling. Case studies and interesting sidebars make this a very user-friendly chapter that is easy to assimilate.

Chapters 9, 10, and 11 (*Group Counseling, Creative Approaches to Counseling, and Assessment Practices in Counseling*) have all been updated with sidebars and case studies and current information that make each of them even more useful to the beginning professional counselor.

Chapter 12 (*Diagnosis and Treatment Planning*) is newly written for this edition. We think readers will find the author's approach to the topic current, refreshing, and congruent with the emphasis on resilience and health and wellness inherent in the counseling profession.

Chapters 13 through 18 (*Addictions Counseling, Career Counseling, Counseling in Clinical Mental Health and Private Practice Settings, Marriage, Couple, and Family Counseling, Professional School Counseling,* and *Student Affairs and College Counseling*) contains two chapters (*Addictions Counseling* and *College Counseling and Student Affairs*) that are new to the sixth edition of our text. Each of the six chapters have been organized to be congruent with the 2009 CACREP Standards and follow the CACREP specified content that counselors must receive if the specializations are to be CACREP accredited. The co-editors believe that this is the only introductory textbook containing chapters organized in such manner to address the 2009 CACREP Standards.

Finally, this sixth edition provides faculty members with a comprehensive set of ancillary materials that can be used for instructional purposes. They include power points for each chapter, test items, chapter summaries, and exercises that can be used as assignments, etc. We think these ancillaries are a welcome addition to our textbook and will enable faculty to use their time and expertise to develop other ways to enhance the instructional experience for students.

Every attempt has been made by the editors and contributors to provide the reader with current information in each of the eighteen chapters. It is our hope that *Introduction to the Counseling Profession* (6th ed.) will provide the neophyte with the foundation needed to make a decision regarding future study in the professional arena of counseling.

ACKNOWLEDGMENTS

We would like to thank the twenty-nine authors who contributed their time, expertise, and experience to the development of the sixth edition of this textbook for the new professional. We would also like to thank our families, who provided the support to make our writing and editing efforts possible. Our thanks are also directed to Christopher Tominich and other staff of Routledge Publishing for their creativity, encouragement, and editing skills.

ABOUT THE EDITORS

David Capuzzi, PhD, NCC, LPC, is a professor emeritus at Portland State University, a core faculty member in Mental Health Counseling at Walden University and a counselor educator and consultant for the Department of Counseling and Human Services at Canisius College in Buffalo, New York. Previously, he served as an affiliate professor in the Department of Counselor Education, Counseling Psychology, and Rehabilitation Services at Pennsylvania State University and Scholar in Residence in counselor education at Johns Hopkins University. He is past president of the American Counseling Association (ACA), formerly the American Association for Counseling and Development, and past Chair of both the ACA Foundation and the ACA Insurance Trust.

From 1980 to 1984, Dr. Capuzzi was editor of *The School Counselor*. He has authored a number of textbook chapters and monographs on the topic of preventing adolescent suicide and is coeditor and author with Dr. Larry Golden of *Helping Families Help Children: Family Interventions with School Related Problems* (1986) and *Preventing Adolescent Suicide* (1988). He coauthored and edited with Douglas R. Gross *Youth at Risk: A Prevention Resource for Counselors, Teachers, and Parents* (1989, 1996, 2000, 2004, and 2008); *Introduction to the Counseling Profession* (1991, 1997, 2001, 2005, and 2009); *Introduction to Group Work* (1992, 1998, 2002, 2006, and 2010); and *Counseling and Psychotherapy: Theories and Interventions* (1995, 1999, 2003, 2007, and 2011). Other texts are *Approaches to Group Work: A Handbook for Practitioners* (2003), *Suicide Across the Life Span* (2006), and *Sexuality Issues in Counseling,* the last coauthored and edited with Larry Burlew. He has authored or coauthored articles in a number of ACA-related journals.

A frequent speaker and keynoter at professional conferences and institutes, Dr. Capuzzi has also consulted with a variety of school districts and community agencies interested in initiating prevention and intervention strategies for adolescents at risk for suicide. He has facilitated the development of suicide prevention, crisis management, and postvention programs in communities throughout the United States; provides training on the topics of youth at risk and grief and loss; and serves as an invited adjunct faculty member at other universities as time permits.

An ACA fellow, he is the first recipient of ACA's Kitty Cole Human Rights Award and also a recipient of Leona Tyler Award in Oregon. In 2010, he received ACA's Gilbert and Kathleen Wrenn Award for a Humanitarian and Caring Person. In 2011, he was named a Distinguished Alumni of the College of Education at Florida State University.

Douglas R. Gross, PhD, NCC, is a professor emeritus at Arizona State University, Tempe, where he served as a faculty member in counselor education for 29 years. His professional work history includes public school teaching, counseling, and administration. He is currently retired and living in Michigan. He has been president of the Arizona Counselors Association, president of the Western Association for Counselor Education and Supervision, chairperson of the Western Regional Branch Assembly of the ACA, president of the Association for Humanistic Education and Development, and treasurer and parliamentarian of the ACA.

Dr. Gross has contributed chapters to seven textbooks: *Counseling and Psychotherapy: Theories and Interventions* (1995, 1999, 2003, 2007, 2011), *Youth at Risk: A Resource Guide for Counselors, Teachers and Parents* (1989, 1996, 2000, 2004, 2008), *Foundations of Mental Health Counseling* (1986, 1996), *Counseling Theory, Process, and Practice* (1977), *The Counselor's Handbook* (1974), *Introduction to the Counseling Profession* (1991, 1997, 2001, 2005, 2008), *Introduction to Group Work* (1992, 1998, 2002, 2006, 2010). His research has appeared in the *Journal of Counseling Psychology, Journal of Counseling and Development, Association for Counselor Education and Supervision Journal, Journal of Educational Research, Counseling and Human Development, Arizona Counselor's Journal, Texas Counseling Journal,* and the *AMHCA Journal.*

During the past 15 years, Dr. Gross has provided national training in bereavement, grief and loss.

ABOUT THE AUTHORS

Anne-Laure Bourgois, BA, is an international student from France who is a graduate student in Community Counseling at the University of Texas at El Paso. She is currently doing her internship at a community agency and a homeless shelter. Mrs. Bourgois specializes in serving marginalized and underserved populations. Currently, she is working with low income Hispanic populations. After graduation, Mrs. Bourgois would like to focus on providing therapy to children and adolescents.

Elizabeth Christensen, PhD, LPC, NCC was a Registered Nurse for 15 years prior to entering the counseling profession. She is often amazed at the parallels between the two types of helping, especially in noting that the resilience of the patient/client, nurtured and supported by the helper, lies at the core of the healing process in both physical and emotional healing. Dr. Christensen's clinical and research interests are in the process of healing from childhood sexual abuse. She received the Outstanding Graduate and Outstanding Intern awards upon completion of her master's degree at Lady of Holy Cross College, and the Outstanding Graduate and College of Education and Human Development Faculty Award upon completion of her doctoral degree at the University of New Orleans. She has given professional presentations at the local, regional, and national levels, primarily on the use of the creative arts in counseling, resilience in the face of trauma, and in psychopharmacology.

Teresa M. Christensen, PhD, is a full professor of Counselor Education and Chair of the Master of Arts in Counseling program at Regis University in Denver, Colorado. Teresa is also a Licensed Professional Counselor (LPC) and Registered Play Therapist-Board Approved Supervisor who has practiced for over 20 years, most recently in a part-time private practice in Colorado. Prior to this, Teresa was an associate professor of Counseling at Old Dominion University in Virginia and the University of New Orleans in Louisiana. At these universities, Teresa taught courses specific to qualitative research methods and served as the chair/methodologist for over 45 dissertations. Teresa has published in a variety of books and peer refereed journals in areas specific to her specializations in: qualitative research methods, play therapy, group work, clinical supervision, and counselor education.

J. Kelly Coker, PhD, is the Program Director for the Counselor Education and Supervision program at Walden University. She is a Licensed Professional Counselor in North Carolina, and maintains a small private practice focusing on work with children and adolescents. Dr. Coker has worked as a drug prevention and intervention school counselor in North Carolina and as a counselor in an art therapy department for a residential adolescent treatment facility in Nevada. She has been a counselor educator in CACREP accredited programs since 1998. She also serves on the editorial board for the *Journal of Counseling and Development* and the *Journal of International Counselor Education*, and as a CACREP site team reviewer.

Tamara E. Davis, EdD, EdS, is a professor in the counseling program at Marymount University in Arlington, Virginia. Before coming to Marymount in 1999, Dr. Davis was an elementary and high school counselor for nine years in Manassas, Virginia. Her professional positions have included being Past President of the Virginia Association for Counselor Education and Supervision and of the Virginia School Counselor Association. She is the Counselor Educator Vice-President for the American School Counselor Association (2010–2013). Dr. Davis has presented over 100 workshops locally, regionally, and nationally on a number of topics in school counseling including developing resilience and positive thinking in students. Her publications include books and articles in school counseling as well as book chapters on counseling suicidal children and group counseling in schools. She was named the 2007 Counselor Educator of the Year by the American School Counselor Association. She teaches courses at Marymount in both the School and Mental Health Counseling programs and serves as the coordinator for the Northern Virginia School Counseling Leadership Team. She resides in Manassas, Virginia with her husband Ken (an assistant principal) and their three Siberian Huskies.

Savitri Dixon-Saxon, PhD, is the Associate Dean for the School of Counseling and Social Service at Walden University. She has over twenty years' experience in higher education. She is a Licensed Professional Counselor in North Carolina, and had worked as a university counselor and as an agency counselor providing out-patient counseling for children and adults. She was the first director of the CACREP accredited master's degree program in the Mental Health Counseling program at Walden University.

Meredith Drew MS, LPC, NCC, ACS, holds a Master's of Science in Education from Fordham University with a concentration in counseling. She is currently working towards her Ph.D. in Counselor Education and Supervision at Walden University. She is a Licensed Professional Counselor in New Jersey, a National Certified Counselor and an Approved Clinical Supervisor. Meredith is an Assistant Professor of Psychology at Centenary College and teaches in the undergraduate and graduate counseling program. She is the Internship Coordinator for the Graduate Program. She has extensive experience as a school counselor and previously worked with the homeless, substance abuse and adolescent populations. Her areas of interests include examining the role of personal counseling with emerging students from graduate programs, supervision of counselors and wellness counseling for the counselor and client.

Cass Dykeman, PhD, received his masters in Counseling from the University of Washington and his doctorate in Counseling from the University of Virginia. Prior to his work in higher education, he worked as both an elementary school and high school counselor in Seattle. As a counselor educator, Dr. Dykeman has worked at Eastern Washington University (1993–1997) and Oregon State University (1997-present). At the university level, he has served in the following roles: School Counseling Program Lead, PhD Program Lead, Counseling Academic Unit Lead, and Department Chair. Dr. Dykeman has published two books and is in double-digits in peer-reviewed articles and book chapters. In addition, he has received over 1.2 million in federally sponsored external funding. He has served in the following professional roles: President-Washington Association for Counselor Education and Supervision, President-Western Association for Counselor education and Supervision, *Journal for Counseling and Development*, Editorial Board, and Member-CACREP On-site Accreditation Team. In terms of professional certification, Dr. Dykeman possesses the following: National Certified Counselor, National Certified School Counselor, Master Addiction Counselor, and Washington State Certified School Counselor.

Jeannie Falkner, PhD, LCSW, is Core faculty for the Mental Health Counseling Program at Walden University. Dr. Falkner holds an MSSW from the University of Texas at Arlington and a PhD in Counselor Education from the University of Mississippi. A Licensed Certified Social Worker, she has over 30 years' experience in private practice working with individual, families, and groups. Dr. Falkner's clinical interests are in redecision therapy, multicultural counseling, integrated mental health, and supervision. Dr. Falkner has co-authored book chapters on counseling gay, lesbian, and bisexual clients and multiracial adolescents. She has presented numerous national and regional workshops on the role of money in group counseling and has research interests in financial wellness for counselors and integrative mental health. Dr. Falkner is a member of NASW, ACA, and ACES.

Linda H. Foster, PhD, Dr. Foster is an Assistant Professor at Troy University Montgomery and received her undergraduate degree from Samford University, master's and education specialist degrees in Community Counseling from the University of Alabama in Birmingham and a Ph.D. in Counselor Education at Mississippi State University in 2003. Dr. Foster worked as a school counselor for over 10 years at the elementary, middle and high school level and is now entering her fifth year as a counselor educator. She has served on local, state, national and international counseling boards and editorial boards. Her research interests include professional identity of counselors, clinical supervision of school counselors, counselor education faculty dynamics, personal development, leadership styles and personality types among counselor educators and the use of single subject research methods by counselors. Dr. Foster has presented on various topics at the state, national and international level and has published numerous articles in peer reviewed journals, as well as several book chapters.

Jessica C. Gelgand, BS, is pursuing her master's degree in Counseling at the University of Texas at El Paso. She received her BS in Biology at the University of Texas at San Antonio. Currently, Jessica is working on research within her field and is about to start her internship in a community setting. In pursuing a master's degree in Counseling, Jessica wants to work with children, adolescents, adults and military personnel and their families. In the future, Jessica hopes to become a licensed professional counselor and aspires to continue her education.

Harriet L. Glosoff, PhD, LPC, NCC, ACS, is a professor of Counseling and Doctoral Program Director at Montclair State University. Her professional background includes teaching, research, and extensive experience in providing clinical supervision and counseling services in community, inpatient, school (K–higher education), and private practice settings. She has published and presented in the areas of ethics, spirituality and cultural issues, advocacy, preparing counselors as social justice advocates, and clinical supervision. In addition, she has held numerous leadership positions on the national, regional, and state levels. Recent examples include serving as a board member of the Association for Ethical, Spiritual and Religious Values in Counseling, president and secretary of the Association for Counselor Education and Supervision, co-chair of the American Counseling Association (ACA) Ethics Committee, and member of the ACA Code of Ethics 2005 Revision Task Force.

Matthew V. Glowiak, MS, NCC, LPC, is a second year doctoral student in Walden University's Counselor Education and Supervision program. As an active member of the university, Mathew has already co-authored a qualitative study in *ACA Vistas* (2011), assisted in a textbook revision of *Career Counseling: Foundations, Perspectives, and Applications* (Capuzzi & Stauffer, 2011), serves as a committee member of the Chi Sigma Iota newsletter, and is a teaching assistant for Dr. David Capuzzi. Significant goals as a professional are to achieve tenure as a professor of Counselor Education and Supervision, run a private practice focused on counseling children and adolescents, continue publishing, and serve on various state and national organizational committees.

Melinda Haley, PhD, received her doctorate in Counseling Psychology from New Mexico State University in Las Cruces, New Mexico and is currently an Assistant Professor at the University of Texas, El Paso. Dr. Haley has written numerous book chapters and multimedia presentations on diverse topics related to counseling and psychology. She has extensive applied experience working with adults, adolescents, children, inmates, domestic violence offenders, and culturally diverse populations in the areas of assessment, diagnosis, treatment planning, crisis management, and intervention. Dr. Haley's research interests include multicultural issues in counseling, personality development over the lifespan, personality disorders, the psychology of criminal and serial offenders, trauma and posttraumatic stress disorder, bias and racism, and social justice issues.

Melanie M. Iarussi, PhD, is an assistant professor in the Counselor Education program at Auburn University. Melanie earned her master's degree in Community Counseling and her PhD in Counselor Education and Supervision from Kent State University. Melanie's clinical background is in substance abuse counseling, college counseling, and private practice. Prior to taking her current faculty position, Melanie was a full-time counseling practitioner in Virginia where she is a Licensed Professional Counselor and a Certified Substance Abuse Counselor. She is also a member of the Motivational Interviewing Network of Trainers. Melanie's research interests include counselor training in substance abuse counseling, college student substance use, and applications of motivational interviewing.

Courtland C. Lee, PhD, is a professor of Counselor Education at the University of Maryland, College Park. He is the author, editor, or co-editor of five books on multicultural counseling and two books on counseling and social justice. He is also the author of three books on counseling African American males. In addition, he has published numerous book chapters and articles on counseling across cultures.

Rochelle Moss, PhD, is currently an associate professor of Counselor Education at Henderson State University in Arkadelphia, Arkansas. She has experience as a school counselor, as well as working in private practice. Dr. Moss is also a supervisor for licensed associate counselors. Her research interests include the use of creative techniques in supervision and the power of mindfulness in treating PTSD symptoms.

GoEun Na, MA, NCC, is a doctoral student at the University of Maryland, College Park. She has presented at a number of local and national conferences on cross-cultural counseling and supervision. She was awarded the 2011 Leadership Fellowship of Chi Sigma Iota and has served as the Webmaster of the Maryland Association for Counseling and Development. Her research interests include multicultural counseling, supervision, and acculturation issues among immigrants and international students.

Ann M. Ordway, JD, MA, EdS, is a doctoral student in the Counselor Education and Supervision Program at Walden University and an adjunct professor in the Psychology and Counseling Department at Farleigh Dickinson University in New Jersey. She has been an attorney for more than 20 years, with a practice focusing exclusively on family law. Ann is the co-founder of Little Voices, Inc., where she practices parenting coordination, mediation, child advocacy, and supervision for parenting time.

Cynthia J. Osborn, PhD, is professor of Counseling and Human Development Services (CHDS) at Kent State University. She earned her PhD degree in Counselor Education and Supervision from Ohio University after several years in pastoral ministry. Her clinical background is with persons with co-occurring disorders (mental health and substance use disorders). She is licensed in Ohio as a Professional Clinical Counselor and a Chemical Dependency Counselor, and she is a member of the Motivational Interviewing Network of Trainers. She teaches both addictions counseling courses (theories of addiction and treatment planning and evidenced-based practices) along with practicum, internship, and an advanced case conceptualization/treatment planning course. Publications, research, and presentations are in the areas of addiction, motivational interviewing, solution-focused counseling, counselor supervision, and leadership in the counseling profession.

Laura Owen, PhD, is a full time faculty member in the Department of Counseling and Human Services at Johns Hopkins University. She is a passionate advocate for increasing programs that provide equity and access for all students and has presented nationally and at the state level on the transformed role of school counseling. Prior to joining the faculty at Johns Hopkins, she was the district school counseling manager for Albuquerque Public Schools where she spearheaded the implementation of several innovative programs aimed at helping all students graduate college and be career ready. Laura's dissertation was a joint project with Stanford and Harvard Universities and the U.S. Department of Education. Funded partially by the Gates Foundation, the dissertation looked at the impact school counselor outreach has on FAFSA completion and college enrollment.

Roxanna N, Pebdani, MS, CRC, is a fourth year doctoral student in Counselor Education at the University of Maryland. Rosanna holds a master's degree in Rehabilitation Counseling from Syracuse University and a bachelor's degree in Psychology from the American University of Paris. Roxanna's research interests include multicultural counseling, sexuality and disability, the reasonable accommodation process for people with disabilities, and the transition process for youth with disabilities to work or to post-secondary education.

Abby Platt, MS, NCC, acquired her BA in Art Therapy from Arcadia University. She lives in Chester Springs, PA, a small suburb outside of Philadelphia. She received her master's degree in Mental Health Counseling from Walden University in 2010. She is a Nationally Certified Counselor currently working on her PhD in Counselor Education and Supervision through Walden University. Abby currently works as a part-time counselor for Gwynedd Mercy College and as a part-time counselor for Adolescent Advocates, a private practice in Bryn Mar, Pa. One of her areas of interest is examining the social-emotional experience for college students with learning disabilities. Additionally, she is interested in how having a learning disability affects treatment outcomes with individuals with substance abuse issues.

Theodore P. Remley, Jr., PhD, holds the Batten Endowed Chair in Counseling at Old Dominion University in Norfolk, Virginia, were he is director of the CACREP-accredited counseling master's and Ph.D. degree programs. In the past, he has coordinated counseling graduate programs at George Mason University, Mississippi State University, and the University of New Orleans. He holds a Ph.D. in Counselor Education from the University of Florida and a law degree (J.D.) from Catholic University in Washington, D.C. He is licensed as a Professional Counselor in Virginia, Louisiana, and Mississippi, and is a member of the bar in Virginia and Florida. He is licensed as a Marriage and Family therapist in Louisiana. Dr. Remley has served on the counselor licensure boards in Virginia, Mississippi, the District of Columbia, and Louisiana. He chaired the boards in Virginia and Mississippi. He has served as a school counselor, college counselor, U.S. Army officer, and has had a private practice in both counseling and law. Dr. Remley frequently takes counseling students and professionals to Italy where he is actively involved in professional counseling activities. He is an author of three textbooks focused on legal and ethical issues in counseling. Dr. Remley is a former Executive Director of the American Counseling Association.

Jill E. Schwarz-Whittaker, MA, NCC, is a doctoral fellow and student at Montclair State University. She also serves as an adjunct instructor and supervisor at other colleges and universities. In addition, Jill has taught graduate courses internationally in Asia and Europe. Prior to pursuing her doctoral studies, she was a professional school counselor and served as a site supervisor for practicum and internship students. Jill's scholarly activities include a co-authored published book chapter on utilizing supervision to prepare counselors as leaders and social justice advocates, as well as national and regional presentations in the areas of multicultural competencies, feminist teaching and counseling, school counseling, bullying and conflict resolution, and spirituality in counseling, counselor education, and supervision. She also has provided professional development workshops for school counselors as well as workshops for master's graduate assistants and doctoral fellows. She currently serves on the executive board of Montclair State University's chapter of Chi Sigma Iota.

Brian M. Shaw, PhD, received his PhD in Counselor Education from Old Dominion University and his Master's of Arts in Counseling from Wake Forest University. Currently, he works as a counselor and coordinator of clinical services at Georgia College and State University in Milledgevillle, Georgia. His research interests include college counseling and integrating spirituality into counseling.

Laura R. Simpson, PhD, LPC-S, NCC, ACS, is a core faculty for Counselor Education and Supervision at Walden University. Dr. Simpson has been a counselor educator since 2005, supported by 21 years as a mental health clinician. She is a Licensed Professional Counselor, National Certified Counselor and an Approved Clinical Supervisor. Dr. Simpson is an active counseling professional and has served on the Mississippi Licensed Professional Counselors Board of Examiners and the executive boards for Mississippi Counseling Association and Mississippi Licensed Professional Counselors Association. Dr. Simpson routinely presents research on the state, national, and international levels and publishes scholarly writings for professional counseling journals and textbooks. Her research interests include counselor wellness and secondary trauma, spirituality, crisis response, cultural diversity, and supervision.

Mark D. Stauffer, PhD, NCC, specialized in couples, marriage, and family counseling at Portland State University and in Counselor Education and Supervision at Oregon State University. He has worked in the Portland Metro Area in Oregon at crises centers and other non-profit organizations working with individuals, couples and families, often with homeless and at-risk populations. Dr. Stauffer was a Chi Sigma Iota International Leaders in Counselor Education Fellow and currently is a CSI faculty representative for the CES doctoral program at Walden University where he is a core-faculty member. He has co-edited three textbooks: *Introduction to Group Work* (2006–2010); *Career Counseling: Foundations, Perspectives, and Applications* (2006–2012); and *Foundations of Addictions Counseling* (2008–2012).

Ann Vernon, PhD, is Professor Emerita, University of Northern Iowa, where she served as Professor and Coordinator of the School and Mental Health Counseling Programs for 25 years. During her tenure there, she primarily taught courses related to counseling children and adolescents and also maintained a very successful private practice where she specialized in working with children and adolescents, and parents. Dr. Vernon has published 19 books, including *What Works When With Children and Adolescents: A Handbook of Individual Counseling Techniques, Thinking, Feeling, Behaving: An Emotional Education Curriculum* for *Children and Adolescents, The Passport Program,* and *More What Works When.* She is the editor of 4 editions of *Counseling Children and Adolescents,* a popular textbook used in many counselor education programs, is the co-editor of *Counseling Theories: Practical Applications for Children and Adolescents in School Settings,* and is presently writing a book on creative counseling techniques. In addition, she is the sole author of numerous journal articles dealing primarily with counseling children and adolescents, developmental counseling and applications of REBT with children and adolescents. Dr. Vernon is the recipient of various professional awards and has assumed many leadership roles within the counseling profession. She is President of the Albert Ellis Board of Trustees, was one of the first two to receive Diplomate status at the Albert Ellis Institute, and is internationally recognized as the leading expert on applications of REBT with children and adolescents. She currently conducts workshops on a variety of topics related to counseling children and adolescents in Holland, Australia, Latin America, and the United States. She also teaches school counseling courses in Romania and Singapore.

Part I

COUNSELING FOUNDATIONS

1

THERAPEUTIC ALLIANCE AND THE HELPING RELATIONSHIP

Rochelle Moss and Matthew V. Glowiak

What is it that separates the helping profession from other professions? And what is it that separates counselors from other helping professionals? Hotel housekeepers help people by making sure the room is just right. Florists help people by creating beautiful floral arrangements to make that special day. The weatherman (or woman!) gives us notice about whether we should equip ourselves with an umbrella or throw on our flip-flops. If one really wants to get philosophical about it, any job that provides any type of service or information in any way is a helping profession. Is it not? Yes and no. What "helping profession" really refers to is those responsible for promoting the well-being of humankind.

The helping professions require a special type of individual. Those who choose to take on one of these roles are taking on a significant responsibility that cannot be taken lightly. This is why professionals require extensive study, training, and experience before they can perform their work. But what about mental health professionals? What sets apart the social worker from the counselor from the psychiatrist? We all diagnose by the DSM-IV-TR. We all base our theoretical knowledge upon the same principles. And we must all obey the same legal doctrines. The key is the therapeutic alliance.

More often than not it is safe to say that people enjoy working with those with whom they feel warmth, genuineness, and respect. The therapeutic alliance takes this every day social phenomenon and makes it work in the clinical setting. Clients are able to open up to counselors on a level that they cannot with others. Counselors take the time to truly listen to and openly discuss issues without passing judgment or responding with discrimination. The relationship is one of mutual respect. It is a team built upon trust—one that requires hard work on both ends. If successful, the client (or clients) will leave each session feeling equal to or better than a period of life when well-being was highest. Establishing this relationship is not necessarily easy and soaking in some of the clients' horrible stories takes a toll on the counselor's personal well-being, but it is this truly compassionate nature for humankind combined with professional knowledge and skills that makes the counselor more than just a counselor. It makes the counselor an advocate for positive social change. And it all begins with the therapeutic alliance.

Examples of the Relationship at Work

A counselor waits outside a social services office with her 15-year-old client who is holding her infant son, helping her through the emotions of giving up her baby for adoption. Another counselor processes the joy his 24-year-old male client is feeling, who has successfully controlled his panic attacks for the past year and has just received word that he has gotten his first job. Somewhere else, a different counselor sits with a husband and wife of 30 years who are contemplating divorce after an extramarital affair and helps them to realistically examine their relationship and deal with their current feelings of anger and betrayal. In a playroom across the country, a counselor reflects the mixed emotions of a five-year-old as he plays out his family welcoming a new baby sister into his world.

Imagine yourself as the client in each of these scenarios. Think of the importance and hope you have placed upon the counseling process. Although you may have felt apprehension and uncertainty, the critical need for help has motivated you to reach out for assistance. In each of the above scenarios, the therapeutic relationship is essential. A sense of safety and trust in the counseling process allows you the courage to freely express your thoughts and feelings and to work on the most difficult of life's issues.

When you place yourself in the position of the client, you can understand the importance most clients place on their decision to seek counseling and the apprehension they often feel about the counseling process. This chapter focuses on the characteristics, knowledge, and skills needed by the counselor to build effective counselor–client helping relationships. The first section describes the helping relationship and its importance. The following sections review what research has shown to be the characteristics of effective counselors and the skills needed to help clients move toward positive change. Also, a case study is provided in the skills section where you will find examples taken from conversations between the counselor and client; these examples demonstrate specific techniques you might use when working with clients.

What is a Helping Relationship?

There are many informal helping relationships in our lives in which we seek assistance, including friends, family members, and co-workers. These relationships meet the mutual needs of those involved. Unlike these relationships, the counselor–client helping relationship—more commonly referred to as the therapeutic alliance—is unique in that it is established as a one-way relationship with the purpose of resolving a concern and/or fostering the personal growth of one person—the client. The counselor is designated as the helper and is assumed to have the knowledge and training to assist the client in an intentional and systematic way. Rogers (1961) defined this relationship as one "in which at least one of the parties has the intent of promoting the growth, development, maturity, improved functioning and improved coping with life of the other (party)" (p.39).

The goals of any counselor–client relationship, whether in educational, career or personal counseling, can be placed into four basic goal areas: changes in behavior and lifestyle, increased awareness or insight and understanding, relief from suffering, or changes in thoughts and self perceptions (Brammer & MacDonald, 1996). An important aspect of the therapeutic alliance is that it is a process that enables a person to grow in directions chosen by that person. It is the counselor's job to make the client aware of possible alternatives and encourage client acceptance of responsibility for taking action on one or more of these alternatives.

The therapeutic alliance minimally can be broken down into three phases—that of relationship building, that of challenging the client to find ways to change, and that of facilitating positive client action (Egan, 2010). In the first phase, the goal is to build a foundation of mutual trust that promotes the client's exploration of the presenting issues. In the second phase, the client has a deeper level of awareness and understanding regarding the issues, and the helper then challenges the client to "try on" new ways of thinking, feeling and behaving. In the final phase, the counselor facilitates client actions that lead toward change and growth in the client's life outside the counseling relationship.

Seligman (2004) suggests that a positive helping relationship has the following characteristics:

- It provides a safe and protective environment for clients.
- It encourages collaboration, with both clients and counselors playing an active role in the counseling process.
- It has mutuality or a feeling of shared warmth, caring, affirmation, and respect.
- Clients can identify with their counselors, perhaps using them as role models.
- Client and counselor have an agreement on goals and procedures; sessions are structured in such a way as to clearly move toward accomplishment of these goals.
- Client and counselor view themselves as engaged in a shared endeavor that seems likely to succeed. (p. 212)

Studies repeatedly show that these qualities of the alliance are the most important predictors of positive counseling outcomes (Assay & Lambert, 1999; Horvarth & Symonds, 1991; Orlinksy, Grawe, & Parks, 1994; Sexton & Whiston, 1994). The contributions of the therapeutic alliance are independent of the theoretical orientation or type of treatment (Norcross, 2001). Specific procedures and techniques have been proven to be much less important than the alliance between counselor and client (Assay & Lambert, 1999).

It is the counselor's responsibility to begin establishing this vital relationship as quickly as possible. Researchers have found that there are several essential elements that make the relationship more favorable for client growth. In this next section, we will take a look at these relational elements.

Essential Components of the Therapeutic Alliance

Several decades ago Carl Rogers was instrumental in determining the core conditions necessary for a beneficial relationship in counseling. Rogers (1957) believed that congruence, unconditional positive regard for the individual, and empathic understanding needed to be present for the relationship to be therapeutic.

When describing *congruence*, Rogers (1961) emphasized the importance of being genuine and real in the relationship. He explained that counselors should strive to have congruence between what they are feeling on the inside and what they are outwardly communicating. When a counselor is congruent, interactions with the client are characterized by honesty, transparency, and openness. Rogers believed that "it is only by providing the genuine reality which is in me, that the other person can successfully seek for the reality in him" (p. 33).

When Rogers (1961) explained the condition of having *warm, unconditional regard* for the person, he stressed the importance of accepting the client without evaluation or judgment. He stated that this acceptance "makes for him (the client) a relationship of warmth and safety, and the safety of being liked and prized as a person seems a highly important element in a helping relationship" (p. 33). This attitude of valuing the client and showing positive regard is referred to as nonpossessive warmth by more recent writers (Cormier & Hackney, 2008).

Rogers (1961) described the condition of *empathy* as being necessary for the client to feel the counselor's acceptance. Empathy is often defined as the understanding of the client's experiences and feelings as if they were your own but without losing the "as if" quality (Rogers, 1957; Bozarth, 1997). When a counselor effectively communicates empathy, it assures clients that they are understood; it also can provide a sense of safety and can encourage clients to begin exploring oftentimes difficult issues (Bohart, Elliott, Greenberg, & Watson, 2002). Rogers (1961) described this process:

> It is only as I understand the feelings and thoughts which seem so horrible to you... it is only as I see them as you see them, and accept them and you, that you feel free to explore all the hidden nooks and frightening crannies of your inner and often buried experiences. (p. 34)

Rogers' core conditions have proven to be essential in establishing and maintaining effective helping relationships and are now considered to be basic helping skills used in the majority of counseling approaches. Additional elements have been found to be necessary for a therapeutic relationship including commitment, respect, trust, confidentiality, and benevolent power (Kottler & Shepherd, 2008).

- *Respect* describes the helping attitude that communicates acceptance of the client as a person of worth and dignity (Rogers, 1957). In utilizing this skill, the counselor demonstrates a belief in the client's ability to deal with his or her problems in the presence of a facilitative person. Respectful counselors use communication skills to actualize the power, ability, and skills already possessed by the client. In other words, the counselor believes in the problem-solving ability of the client. These skills and attitudes are very important in facilitating an effective helping relationship. They communicate a willingness to work with the client and an interest and belief in the client as a person of worth (Cormier, Cormier, & Cormier, 1997).
- *Trust* is essential in a healthy, productive counseling relationship. Trust can be established by being genuine and by expressing respect and positive regard for the client's individual worth. Trust can be maintained by consistently following ethical standards and always remembering to put the needs of the client first and foremost.
- *Confidentiality* assures clients that whatever they tell counselors will remain private (within certain limits; see chapter 4). This promise allows the client to feel safe and promotes the telling of information that would otherwise remain hidden.
- The *use of benevolent power* refers to using the interpersonal influence one has as a counselor in a careful manner. According to Strong and Claiborn (1982), counselors are influential due to their perceived levels of expertness, attractiveness, and trustworthiness and must use this power responsibly in facilitating change for the client.
- *Commitment* to carry out respective responsibilities in the helping relationship is important for both counselors and clients. Counselor responsibilities include delivery of specified services and following ethical guidelines; client responsibilities include a commitment toward working on his or her problems and investing energy in the counseling process.

Now that we have examined the components of this relationship, we will outline specific counselor characteristics and attitudes that are linked with being an effective and competent helper.

Personal Characteristics of Counselors

Effective counselors have specific personal qualities and are able to convey those qualities to the people they help. There is an increasing amount of evidence supporting the concept that helpers are only as effective as they are self-aware and able to use themselves as vehicles of change (Okun, 2008). Combs (1986) summarized 13 studies that looked at helpers in a variety of settings. These studies supported the view that there are differences in the beliefs of effective and ineffective person-centered helpers. Effective counselors are interested in and committed to an understanding of the specialized knowledge of the field and find it personally meaningful. As such, they are challenged to remain current in their knowledge and skills. They like people and have a feeling of oneness with others. Effective counselors use interventions that focus on the individual's perception of self and expand the individual's view of life rather than narrowing it. They are committed to freeing rather than controlling the client and are able to be objectively involved with, rather than alienated from, their clients.

In other studies, effective counselors have been found to be compassionate and believing of the client's world. In their own lives they are open to a full range of experiences and feelings, are spontaneous, and have a sense of humor. When interacting with others, they are able to be involved, yet remain somewhat detached (Cormier, et al., 1997). In the process of dealing with problems and issues, they are able to help clients clearly see their own worlds while adding a fresh perspective to the issues.

SIDEBAR 1.1 Self-Awareness: Which Helpful Characteristics Do You Possess?

Examine the checklist of desirable counselor characteristics in Table 1.1. The items have been compiled from numerous resources (Combs, 1986; Gladding, 2008; Rogers, 1957; Rogers, 1961; Seligman, 2004; Sexton & Whiston, 1994). The characteristics are listed in no particular order of importance. As you examine the list, check those which you believe you possess, and make note of those which you have not yet developed. Think of ways you might begin to acquire these qualities.

Table 1.1 Checklist of desirable counselor characteristics

Intelligent	Empathic
Energetic	Optimistic
Caring	Self-confident
Trustworthy	Self-aware
Genuine	Creative
Emotionally stable	Flexible
Resourceful	Hard-working
Unselfish	Insightful
Curious	Nonjudgmental
Good listener	Knowledgeable
Realistic	Ethical
Dependable	Friendly
Hopeful	Sense of humor
Respectful of individual differences	Comfortable with intimacy
Maintains balance in own life	Able to express oneself clearly

In the next section, the fundamental helping skills of counseling will be explained. We will begin with microskills and attending skills.

Fundamental Skills and Concepts

According to Ivey and Ivey (2009), the aim of counseling is personal and social development. They have described a hierarchy of microcounseling skills that define what the counselor does in an interview to achieve specific results. Ivey's hierarchy rests on a foundation of attending behaviors and basic listening skills. The list of skills presented here is based on Ivey's model with additional information taken from Cormier et al. (1997), Egan (2010), and Ivey and Ivey (2009).

Attending Skills

Attending behavior, including eye contact, body language, vocal quality, and verbal tracking, is one of the most powerful of the communication skills (Ivey, 2009). In the counseling relationship, counselors communicate through body language and words that their full attention is on the client's nonverbal and verbal behaviors. Eye contact, facial expressions, and body posture are the physical fundamentals that indicate to others that you are either carefully attending or not attending to them.

Eye Contact

Good eye contact is not an unwavering stare, but an intermittent yet frequent looking into the eyes of the client. It indicates to clients that you are interested in them and what they have to say. It also can signal understanding and provide feedback (Evans, Hearn, Uhlemann, & Ivey, 2008). Effective eye contact occurs more frequently when there is a comfortable distance between counselor and client and when topics being discussed are not too threatening. Cultural differences abound in what is considered appropriate eye contact (Ivey, 2009). For example, Anglo-Americans usually have more eye contact when listening and less when talking; the opposite is true of many African Americans. In some cultures, eye contact is avoided when discussing serious topics (Evans et al.). The counselor should first consider cultural differences if eye contact seems strained or awkward in the relationship.

Attentive Body Language

Body orientation can encourage or discourage interpersonal interactions. In Anglo-American culture, a slight forward body lean and a relaxed, comfortable posture are usually received favorably and indicate interest in the client. Egan (2010) uses the acronym SOLER to describe this attentive body posture. The letters stand for *S*quarely—face the client, *O*pen—body posture, *L*ean—forward slightly, *E*ye—contact, and *R*elaxed—manner. Facial expressions should fit the material being discussed.

Distance

The distance between counselor and client also affects communication. While most people feel uncomfortable with, intimidated by, or nauseated from the close-talker that enjoys nose-to-nose chit-chat, the conversation becomes just as awkward when there is so much distance that text or email seems more appropriate. There is an optimal "comfort zone" for conversing that is largely controlled by cultural influences. It is about an arm's length in American culture. It is imperative that the counselor be aware of the level of comfort or discomfort that the client is experiencing with the distance and adjust it if necessary.

While there are many things counselors can do to convey an interest in their clients, certain mannerisms are distracting. Behaviors such as checking one's phone, chewing gum, or continual change of body position may seriously affect any interpersonal interaction and convey a sense of counselor disinterest. After all, do these things not bother you in regular, everyday interactions?

SIDEBAR 1.2 Self-Awareness: What about Cell Phone Use?

Have you ever been talking with someone who continually looks at his or her cell phone for messages? Or answers his or her phone in the middle of the conversation? How do you feel? What does this behavior mean to you? Usually individuals may feel annoyed or may believe that what they have to say isn't important or perhaps even that **they** are not important to the other person. When you are in session, put your cell phone away or place it on silent or ask that your incoming calls be held. Your client should get 100 percent of your attention during the counseling session. (And you should ask the same of your clients.)

Vocal Tone

Another aspect of attending behavior is voice tone. A warm, pleasant, caring voice strongly indicates an interest and willingness to listen to the client. The pitch, volume, and rate of speech can convey much of one's feeling toward another person or situation. Scherer (1986) has shown that the use of specific paralinguistic cues can convey either high or low levels of self-confidence. High levels of confidence are conveyed when you speak in a caring voice that is neither hesitant nor rapid, but which projects inner qualities of warmth, respect and compassion for the client. These cues of self-confidence can affect client perceptions of counselor expertness, attractiveness, trustworthiness, and associated satisfaction with the counseling relationship (Barak, Shapira, & Fisher, 1988).

Verbal Tracking

Even when the client engages in long irrelevant discourses, the counselor often needs to remain relaxed and follow the client's topic and logic. The counselor can choose to either attend or ignore certain portions of the client's statements this is termed *selective attention*. The portions of the client's statements to which a counselor attends depend upon the counselor's theoretical orientation and professional beliefs. It is imperative that counselors be aware of their own patterns of selective attention, for the topics their clients focus on will tend to be partially determined by those topics to which the counselor unconsciously attends.

Silence

Silence is another important part of verbal attending behavior. The counselor's ability to remain silent while clients are silent facilitates clients listening to their inner voice (and also may give the counselor time to think of the most effective way to respond). Silence may give the client time to further contemplate or process the issues at hand, and a deeper level of understanding may be the result. Remaining silent is often an excellent tactic to start a reluctant client talking because silence is perceived by many clients as an uncomfortable condition that must be filled with a response. However, the meaning of silence is culturally based (Murphy & Dillon, 2008). The challenge for beginning counselors is learning to be comfortable enough with silence to use it effectively.

The following section begins with a case study, which will be used when giving specific examples of basic helping skills, as well as advanced skills in the latter part of the chapter.

Case Study

Melissa is a 16year-old female who was brought in to counseling after swallowing a bottle of Tylenol. She told her mother what she had done, and her mother rushed her to the hospital where the emergency staff pumped her stomach. She recovered and was referred for individual counseling.

During the first few sessions, the client explored several significant issues with the counselor. First of all, she emphasized the main issue behind the overdose was that her boyfriend broke up with her. She also said that she was very upset over the fact that a 19-year-old male friend was being deployed to the Middle East in a couple of months. She felt guilty and worried because she had not been on good terms with him and "had been mean to him." Melissa stated that these two stressors were behind her taking the overdose.

In addition, Melissa explained that she has few, if any, true friends. She believes that she does not belong in any group. She is not a "goody-two-shoes" nor is she a "nerd". She also has decided that her old group may have some behaviors that she does not want to get mixed up with, such as drug use. However, she later reveals that she does smoke a little marijuana from time to time.

Melissa's parents are divorced, and she lives with her mother. She is an only child. Melissa said that she wants to have a good relationship with her father and that they try to see each other about once a month. However, she added that if she has anything else to do, she will make an excuse and not see him. Her mother has a very busy work schedule with lots of job responsibilities but seems to pay attention to Melissa when there is a crisis situation.

The Basic Listening Skills

Active listening is an extremely important dimension of counselors' work (Egan, 2010). Counselors need to be sure that they are hearing the client accurately and clients must know that the counselor has fully heard them, seen their point of view, and felt the world as they experience it. The basic listening skills that facilitate active listening include client observation; noticing client nonverbal behavior; the use of encouraging, paraphrasing, and summarization statements; the reflection of client feelings; and the use of open and closed questions. The outcome of using these basic listening skills in combination is the establishment of an empathic relationship with the client (Carkhuff, 1969). The overall purpose of empathy is to "...understand the situation of another person from that person's perspective" (Berger, McBreen & Rifkin, 1996, p. 210).

Client Observation

Simply observing the client provides the counselor with a rich source of "silent information." Noticing and paying attention to the *physiological cues* expressed in another person's appearance and physique provide a way to identify the internal emotional responses of the other person. These physiological cues may include changes in skin color, pupil dilation, muscle tone, and/or breathing—that can reflect the internal emotional processes and the physiologic changes occurring within the client. These physiological messages are difficult to hide because they are generally involuntary reactions of the autonomic nervous system. Observing subtle changes in these areas can silently reveal the moments of emotional change for a client.

The points during the interview at which eye contact is broken, the voice changes, skin color changes, shifts in body posture occur, or when changes in muscle tension or facial expression take place may indicate moments when important information is being revealed.

Case Example

The counselor observes Melissa as she describes the break-up with her boyfriend. The client's voice tone drops, and she speaks more slowly. Eye contact is broken as she looks down, and her skin becomes pale. From these observations, the counselor is aware of the strong emotions connected with the break-up.

Verbal Behavior

In addition to nonverbal behavior, one can also learn a great deal from the client's verbal behavior. At the most basic level, the counselor should note *topic changes* or *topic exclusions* and any *key words* that appear again and again. For example, when the client continues to use "should" or "ought" statements, it may indicate a lack of control in those areas and should be explored further. Also, noticing topics the client avoids may give the counselor valuable information that can be explored later with the client.

Case Example

The counselor notes that Melissa often changes the topic when the relationship with her father is mentioned. Words that continue to resurface include "alone", "hurt" and "guilty", which may point toward themes in this client's current situation.

Sentence structure is an important clue to how the client views the world. Is the client the subject or the object of the sentence? Specifically, does the client feel he or she does the acting, or is acted on? Are concerns portrayed as being in the past, the present, or the future? Are there key words and descriptions that give a clue to the client's worldview? Hearing certain patterns of words and ideas gives clues to a client's typical thought processes and self-perceptions.

SIDEBAR 1.3 Case Study: Attending to Melissa's Verbal Patterns

Being Melissa's counselor, you are listening for themes in her verbal communication. You notice that Melissa uses mostly past tense, especially when describing relationships, and that she is the object of most sentences, meaning that she is being acted upon. You are aware that her voice lowers as she discusses her feelings—first, about her parents' divorce; then, concerning the friendships ending at school; next, about her best friend enlisting in the military; and finally, regarding the break-up with her boyfriend. What are some possible themes you might identify as you attend to her verbal patterns?

Incongruities, discrepancies, and *double messages* are nearly universal in counseling interviews. They are often at the root of a client's immobility and inability to respond creatively to difficult life situations (Egan, 2010). When counselors notice such incongruities, they may either choose to hold back and say nothing or try to bring the discrepancy into the client's awareness. The emotional state of the client and the impact upon the relationship should be the main consideration when making this decision. In time-limited counseling, or within certain theoretical frameworks such as Gestalt, immediate confrontation may be the preferred intervention. Confrontation skills will be discussed later in this section.

Case Example

The counselor notices a couple of incongruities in Melissa's communication. First, she said that she does not want to associate with her old friends because of the drug use but later revealed that she smokes marijuana from time to time. She also stated that she wishes to have a strong relationship with her father but makes excuses to avoid seeing him when possible.

Encouraging, Paraphrasing, and Summarizing

The skill of *encouraging* includes the use of both "encouragers" and "restatements," both of which punctuate the interview and provide a smooth flow. Using encouragers such as head nods, an interested facial expression, or verbal utterances such as "umm" or "uh-huh" is an active way to let clients know that they have been heard and understood. Encouragers can be used to influence the direction taken by the client and are part of selective attention as described above.

One powerful type of encourager is for the counselor to respond with a restatement of a "key word" or a short phrase from the client's statement, often in a questioning tone of voice.

Case Example

An example of a key word restatement follows:

MELISSA: I was at the end of my rope when my boyfriend broke up with me.
COUNSELOR: End of your rope?

The *paraphrase* is used to reflect the content of what the client has just said. It is not parroting the client (repeating back exactly what was said), but feeding back to the client the essence of what was said (Evans et al., 2008). It is an encapsulated rephrase of the content of the client's message in the counselor's words, sometimes containing key words and constructs used by the client. The strength of the paraphrase is that the counselor is giving of self, yet is paying primary attention to the client's frame of reference. The purpose of this skill is to let clients know that they have been heard accurately and to encourage them to continue discussing the issue in more detail.

Case Example

The counselor's response provides an example of a paraphrase:

MELISSA: I wish I could take back some of the mean, hurtful things I said to my friend, but now he's being deployed, and I don't have the chance. And who knows what will happen?

COUNSELOR: You wish you could talk to your friend and apologize for what you said in the past, but now you don't have that opportunity, and you think of the uncertainty of the situation with him going to fight in the war.

Summarizations are similar to paraphrasing, except that they "paraphrase" a longer period of conversation. These responses gather together a client's verbalizations—facts, feelings, meanings, and patterns—and restate them for the client as accurately as possible. Summarizations frequently give the client a feeling of movement as ideas and feelings are explored (Brammer & MacDonald, 1996).

Summarizations may be useful at the beginning of a session to warm up a client or at other times to bring closure to discussion on a theme. They can be used to add direction and coherence to a session that seems to be going nowhere (Egan, 2010). Also, summarizations are valuable to counselors as a check on the accuracy of their understanding of the information that has just been gathered.

Case Example

Here is an example of a summarization in an interview with Melissa:

COUNSELOR: You're feeling uncertain about lots of things in your life right now—your relationships with friends, relationships with parents, and trying to figure out who you are and where you fit.

Reflection of Feelings

In addition to hearing the words of the client accurately, the counselor must uncover and recognize the emotions underlying those words. The counselor listens and watches for both nonverbal messages and direct verbal communication to accurately determine the feeling(s) being expressed by the client. Reflection of feeling can help clients to feel understood, to sort out complex feelings, and to continue exploring their feelings at a deeper level (Evans et al., 2008; Egan, 2010). Seligman (2004) stated that a counselor's use of this tool is the most powerful way to communicate empathy.

It is also important for the counselor to know how to communicate the feeling accurately by recognizing and labeling the category of emotion (i.e. anger, gladness, sadness, fear, or uncertainty), as well as the correct intensity of the emotion (Carkhuff & Anthony, 1979).

Case Example

The counselor demonstrates a reflection of feeling in the following response:

MELISSA: I know that Dad had an affair while he and Mom were married, and I'll never get over that. And now he wants to just trade us in for his NEW family!

COUNSELOR: You're really angry with your dad and resent the fact that he's starting over with someone else.

Be careful, however, to not let behavior cloud one's interpretation of feelings. Take laughter for instance. People may let out sudden burst of laughter as a defense mechanism to mask anxiety, sadness, pain, confusion, and so on without even realizing this. In this respect, reflecting feeling requires attention to a combination of some of these previous components. When using reflection of feeling with clients of differing cultures, the counselor must be able to express culturally sensitive empathy by having knowledge of the client's culture and communicating respect and understanding of the culture while understanding the client's circumstances (Evans et al., 2008). Also, the counselor needs to have an awareness of how that specific culture views the open discussion of emotions.

Questions

The use of questions can open communication. In the helping relationship, effective, open communication is especially necessary from the counselor. It facilitates moving the client from self-exploration through increased understanding and finally commitment to appropriate action. By using specific verbal leads, the counselor is able to bring out the major facts, feelings, and self-perceptions that a client brings to the session. Effective use of open and closed questions can encourage the client to talk more freely and openly.

Asking *open-ended questions* is considered to be the most beneficial type of questioning because the client is encouraged to talk more freely and openly. Open questions usually begin with "what," "how," "could," or "would" and require the client to provide a longer, more expansive response than simply "yes" or "no". Open questions are used to begin interviews; to encourage clients to express more information; to elicit examples of particular behaviors, thoughts, or feelings; and to increase the client's commitment to communicate. Some examples might be:

COUNSELOR: What obstacles do you think might get in the way of you reaching your goal?
COUNSELOR: How do you plan to re-establish that friendship?

Sometimes a client is very talkative and rambles or jumps from topic to topic. In such a case, *closed questions* can be used to gather information, give clarity, gain focus, and narrow the area of discussion. These closed questions usually begin with the word "is," "are," "do," or "did." One must use caution though, because extensive use of closed questions can hinder conversation (Egan, 2010). A questioning counselor can appear to have all the power in the relationship, and this inequality can destroy the counselor–client alliance, especially during initial encounters. With too many closed questions, clients may feel as though they are being interrogated.

Clients from some cultures are rapidly turned off by counselor questions, as are those clients who have not developed trust in their counselors. Frequently, the same information can be obtained by asking the client what goals they have, how they feel about those goals, and how they plan to attain them. (Note that asking too many questions at once can confuse clients.) "Why" questions are especially troublesome because they may put clients on the defensive or leave them feeling they must provide a logical explanation for their behavior.

SIDEBAR 1.4 Case Study: Asking Open Questions to Melissa

You are Melissa's counselor, and she tells you that she regrets the mean things she said to her friend before he left for military duty. She explains that this is unlike her, and she is confused about her behavior. You want her to gain insight about her behavior and then to make an action plan to remediate the situation, if she chooses. What are some examples of open questions you might use to get her to better understand her behaviors? What are some open questions that might help her to devise an action plan?

Because questions may cause resistance with some clients, the skills of encouraging, paraphrasing, summarization, and reflection of feeling may be used to obtain similar information yet seem less intrusive to the client.

Counselors must be flexible and adapt their skills to accommodate the client's culture (see chapter 3 for information on culture-specific issues). To prevent counselors from making generalizations that lead to stereotyping, Hays (1996) developed a model for considering the multifaceted cultural influences that affect the helping relationship. These influences include gender, race and ethnicity, age and generation, social status, sexual orientation, religion, indigenous heritage, and national origin. Counselors must remember that the client's issues are developed in a cultural context, and it is important for the counselor to listen for family and cultural issues that affect the client in order that the issues can be resolved within that context.

Concreteness

In the process of exploring problems or issues, a client often presents an incomplete representation of what has happened. The goal of concreteness is to make the information and awareness gained through self-exploration more specific and concrete (Meier & Davis, 1993). It is the task of the counselor to help the client clarify the pieces of the puzzle and fit them together so that the whole makes sense to the client. This clarification increases the likelihood that an organized, specific, workable action plan can be implemented and accepted by the client. When encouraging concreteness, one attempts to focus very specifically on the situation at hand, and tries to make clear all facets of the issue, including the accompanying behaviors and feelings.

There are several ways to help clients become more concrete and focused. When a client makes a vague statement, the counselor can reflect in a more concrete way. At times, a rambling client may need to be focused. The effective use of concreteness in such situations may feel like interrupting, but should lead to increased counselor–client interaction. When clients need to be more definite and clear, leads such as "what" and "how" rather than "why" will usually produce more relevant and specific information (Egan, 2010).

Case Example

The following counselor's response demonstrates the concept of concreteness:

MELISSA: I just want to feel like I belong somewhere.
COUNSELOR: Describe for me a specific time or situation in your life when you remember feeling that way.

Effective use of concreteness keeps the counseling session productively focused and aims at making vague experiences, behaviors, and feelings more specific. The more specific the information, the better the understanding and the more effective future choices and actions will be.

Self-Attending Skills

Counselors who are aware of their own values, beliefs, and assets are much more likely to find it easier to "be with" clients, help clients explore personal issues, and facilitate client action. Take, for example, the case of the dentist with bad teeth. Not only does it make clients fear for their own sake, it is a clear indication that the dentist is missing some clearly important information about how to care for one's teeth. Therefore, the self-attending skills are extremely important for each person who wishes to be an effective counselor. There are several components to the self-attending process. Shulman (1979) referred to these counselor components as "tuning-in." The first component in the "tuning-in" process is self-awareness.

Self-Awareness

The personal knowledge and understanding that the counselor has of self and the counseling setting are extremely important to the self-attending process. Practically speaking, the counselor should not consciously rehearse how counselors are "supposed" to be. The effective counselor acts professionally, but does not put on a professional front, play acting some imaginary expert counselor. Effective counselors know their strengths as well as their weaknesses, and by understanding themselves are able to overcome self-consciousness and devote fuller attention to what the client is trying to disclose.

In the process of learning counseling skills, there may be times when using the skills seems awkward and uncomfortable. The learning cycle for trainees recognizes that learning counselor skills can sometimes be an unsettling process. Unlearning competing behaviors and relearning new ones in their place take time, a great deal of concentration, and practice. Counselor self-awareness is crucial throughout this process.

Centering and Relaxing

Centering, or getting "in touch" and then "in-tune" with one's person (Brammer & MacDonald, 1996) is an important skill for the counselor to develop. By becoming centered the counselor is able to show more social-emotional presence (Egan, 2010) in the counseling relationship and to give the client his or her undivided attention. With a keener focus than is common in most human interaction, the counselor is better able to empathically understand the client's problems and concerns. Similarly, a significant level of relaxation (both physical and psychological) in the counselor will help clients relax as they face the stress and challenges of the counseling process itself.

Nonjudgmental Attitude Toward Self

Counselors need to have a broad awareness of their own value positions. They must be able to answer very clearly the questions, "Who am I?" "What is important to me?" "Am I nonjudgmental?" (Brammer & MacDonald, 1996).

This awareness aids counselors in being honest with themselves and their clients and in being free from judgments about themselves. In addition it helps the counselor avoid unwarranted or unethical use of clients to satisfy personal needs. Although counselors may have opinions about traits of people they like and want to associate with, one characteristic of effective counselors is that they try to suspend personal judgments about their clients' lives. When they find that past events in their own lives prevent them from being as effective with clients as possible, they may need to seek counseling to resolve these issues.

SIDEBAR 1.5 Case Study: Melissa's Issues Affect Counselor's Effectiveness

As Melissa tells you about the details of her parents' divorce, you notice your body tightening. You attempt to relax but find it difficult. Her story parallels many of the same events in your own parents' divorce, and you are aware that you feel angry at her father. You have learned the importance of being nonjudgmental, and you question whether your unresolved issues might interfere with the effectiveness of the counseling process. What do you need to do to benefit Melissa, as well as future clients?

Nonjudgmental Attitude Toward Others

This attitude is one of respect for a client's individuality and worth as a person and is very similar to Rogers' (1961) concept of "unconditional positive regard." It allows clients to be open and to be themselves, because they know that the counselor will not be judging them or what they say. The counselor conveys this nonjudgmental attitude by being warm, accepting, and respectful toward the client; this is especially important in the early phases of the relationship.

Case Example

In the following response, the counselor attempts to express understanding without judgment:

MELISSA: I feel really awful. I had sex with my boyfriend, and then he broke up with me. I know my parents wouldn't approve, but I thought he really loved me. But I don't think they would understand.

COUNSELOR: You thought at the time it was the right decision because there were strong feelings involved. But you don't think that your parents could ever understand.

Respect is rarely found alone in communication. It usually occurs in combination with empathy and genuineness.

Communicating Genuineness

When counselors relate to clients naturally and openly, they are being genuine. Being a counselor is not just a role played by the individual. Instead, it is the appropriate revelation of

17

one's own feelings and thoughts and the full participation of being in a therapeutic alliance. The effective use of genuineness reduces the emotional distance between the counselor and client (Cormier, et al., 1997). It breaks down the role distance and links the counselor and client together, allowing the client to see the counselor as human, and a person similar to him or her. The genuine counselor is spontaneous, non-defensive, and consistent in relationships.

Case Example

The counselor gives a genuine response to the client's question:

MELISSA: Do you think I'm as crazy and weird as I feel?
COUNSELOR: You have been going through some difficult situations, and you're feeling confused about what to do. I don't experience you as being crazy and weird at all.

Cultural Competence

It is the counselor's responsibility to educate oneself about cultural diversity and to become culturally competent. This process enables the counselor to have increased levels of awareness and sensitivity for clients of different ethnicities. Daw (1997) emphasized several recommendations. First of all, become aware of your own cultural heritage and how it affects you as a counselor; also, become aware of your own biases and prejudices including racism. Next, seek opportunities to interact with people of different cultures and learn from these experiences. Finally, examine your understanding of poverty and how it affects those of different cultures; plus take an honest look at your own positions of power and privilege (see chapter 3 for a more thorough discussion).

Humor

The counselor who can enjoy and use humor effectively has an invaluable asset. The healing power of humor has long been valued and can be used in counseling as an emotional

Table 1.2 Multicultural considerations when establishing a therapeutic alliance

Beliefs	What are my beliefs about the client's culture and what impact has my culture had on my beliefs?
Attitudes	Do I value cultural diversity presented by my client?
Skills	What skills and strategies do I need to work effectively with this culturally diverse client?
Knowledge	
Acculturation	What is the client's level of acculturation or assimilation into the majority culture?
Perceptions	How does my client view seeking help from a counselor?
Social philosophy	Is this client from an individualistic or collectivist society?
Approach	Will a direct or subtle approach be more effective? Will the client respond better to an equal relationship or to an expert stance?
Distance	At what physical distance is this client most comfortable?
Communication	What are the cultural norms for eye contact, vocal tone, speech rate? How does this client view silence, questioning, confrontation?
Respect	How do I express politeness and respect to this client?

release. Although counseling is serious business, there are many truly humorous dimensions to the human condition and when humor appears as a natural outgrowth of the counselor–client relationship it should be attended to (Prochaska & Norcross, 2003). Humor can provide a means of connecting with clients, and counselors need to affirm any humor presented by their clients. Laughter and joking can release built-up tensions and laughing at one's self can be extremely therapeutic—since it requires seeing one's problems in a whole new perspective. A good laugh can even feel good to the most serious or depressed of individuals. For these individuals particularly, laughing is letting their guard down. If they are made to feel comfortable during this moment, the alliance may be strengthened.

When using humor with clients of a different ethnic background, the counselor needs to exercise particular caution (Maples, et al., 2001). Humor can be defined, interpreted, and valued differently by individuals from different cultures. For that reason, it is imperative to consider both the individual and cultural values of the client and tailor or customize the use of humor so that it is appropriate to the particular client.

Touch

Counselors need always be sensitive to the therapeutic value of touch. This involves a consideration of the client's issues and sensitivity to the role that touch has played in creating the problem; it is also important to know the recommendations for best practices from those who are considered to be experts. For example, counselors must use extreme caution when using touch with individuals traumatized by physical or sexual abuse.

Humanistic models suggest that touch which is genuinely felt may help create within the client a willingness to be open and share. Driscoll, Newman, and Seals (1988) found that college students observing videotapes felt that counselors who touched their college-age clients were more caring than counselors who did not. It must be emphasized, though, that touch without genuine feeling behind it may be more harmful than helpful.

The type of touch that is generally considered acceptable is one that is long enough (1–3 seconds) to make contact yet does not create uncomfortable feelings. Most professionals who do touch believe that appropriate touching is contact of the counselor's hand or forearm with the client's hand, arm, shoulder, or upper back, and recognize that gender differences may influence how such contact is interpreted. Alyn (1988) suggested that touch can reinforce the culturally prescribed unequal power relationship between genders and perpetuate the routine infringement upon women's boundaries.

There are no specific ethical standards concerning nonsexual touching; however, there are strict ethical guidelines regarding sexual contact with clients. Some counselors who are opposed to touch believe that nonsexual touching may lead to crossing boundaries and the gratification of the counselor's needs. The decision to touch must be based on ethical, clinical, and theoretical principles and must always be based on the client's needs (Durana, 1998).

Touch may be perceived differently from culture to culture. For example, in Hispanic and other Latin cultures, most individuals report being comfortable with touch while in casual conversation. In other cultures, people are more restrained. For instance, in the Asian/Vietnamese cultures, individuals are more comfortable standing far apart and do not engage in casual touching. Cultural views of appropriate touching may transfer into the alliance; however, individual personalities and levels of acculturation and assimilation always need to be taken into account and should take precedence over general norms.

Advanced Skills and Concepts

The first goal of helping is to help clients tell their story in an understandable way (Egan, 2010). This involves the facilitation of client self-understanding. Such exploration helps both the counselor and client understand the client's problems and concerns. Clients begin to focus and see more clearly the puzzles of their lives and are led skillfully to identify the missing pieces and blocks. This exploration involves a look at the real self and related issues. The process leads to insightful self-understanding that invites the client to change or take action.

Once the beginning counselor is adept at using the basic counseling skills, advanced skills and concepts can be added to the repertoire. These skills and concepts are more action oriented and allow the counselor to facilitate deeper client self-understanding, change, and eventual termination of the helping relationship. The advanced understanding and challenging skills include advanced empathy, self-disclosure, confrontation, and immediacy (Egan, 2010).

Advanced Empathy

Primary empathy forms the foundation and atmospheric core of the helping relationship (Gladding, 2008). It involves listening for basic or surface messages with frequent, but brief, responses to those messages. The skills of paraphrasing and reflection of feeling serve counselors well when they establish an empathic base of understanding (Carkhuff, 1969). The counselor sees the world from the client's frame of reference and communicates that it has been understood. The goal is to move the client toward identifying and exploring crucial topics and feelings. During this early self-exploration phase, the counselor must be sensitive to signs of client stress or resistance and try to judge whether these arise from lack of accurate response or from being too accurate too quickly. As the counselor moves the client beyond exploration to self-understanding and action, advanced skills become more necessary.

Primary empathy gets at relevant feelings and meanings that are actually stated; the skill of *advanced empathy* gets at feelings and meanings that are hidden or beyond the immediate reach of the client (Egan, 2010). The most basic form of advanced empathy is to give expression and understanding to what the client has only implied. It challenges the client to take a deeper look at self.

Advanced empathy includes the identification of themes presented by the client. Feeling, behavioral, experiential, or combined themes may occur. Once the counselor recognizes the themes, the task is to communicate the relevant ones to the client in a way that will be heard and understood. The themes must be based solidly on an accurate understanding of the client's feelings, experiences, and behaviors and communicated as concretely as possible using the client's experiences and communication style.

The act of bringing together and communicating relevant core material that the client has presented in only a fragmented way is part of advanced empathy. The counselor helps the client fill in the missing links in the information. When it becomes apparent that two aspects of client information are closely linked, this information should be shared, but the counselor must guard against premature speculation or unfounded linkages.

As the counselor explores the deeper, underlying meaning of an experience of the client, the skill of reflection of meaning can be used. It provides a way for the client to develop a new worldview and interpret old situations or information in new ways.

Because information is always subject to individual interpretation (Gelatt, 1989), the counselor needs to reframe the situation, belief, or experience to help the client view it from a different perspective and also check out that the interpretation is correct.

Advanced empathy gets at more critical, deeper, and delicate issues and, therefore, puts the client under additional stress. To avoid overwhelming the client and evoking resistances, the counselor's empathetic responses should be tentative and cautious. Leads such as "From what you have said...," "Could it be that...," or "It seems like...," may be most helpful.

Counselors may find it helpful to reflect back to clients what they see as the meaning of an experience.

Case Example

The counselor reflects the possible meaning of Melissa's behavior.

MELISSA: I believed everything my boyfriend told me and then he dumped me. It seems as though every time I trust someone, I get hurt.

COUNSELOR: You've had several situations in your life in which people that you trust have disappointed you. I'm wondering if that may be part of the reason that you're avoiding close relationships now. It seems like maybe you're becoming more guarded because you don't want to get hurt.

Self-Disclosure

Hendrick (1988) and Peca-Baker and Friedlander (1987) have found that clients want to have information about their counselors. Sharing oneself can be a powerful intervention for making contact with clients, but it should not be an indiscriminate sharing of personal problems with clients (Egan, 2010; Sexton, Whiston, Bleuer, & Walz, 1997). Take, for instance, the camaraderie that is developed by people that have gone through similar difficulties and undertaken similar challenges. Individuals in drug and alcohol rehabilitation programs are a prime example of this. Another example may include war veterans suffering from posttraumatic stress syndrome. People are able to relate with those who have undergone similar circumstances; they can appreciate one another.

Self-disclosure is defined as any information counselors convey about themselves to clients (Cormier et al., 1997; Cozby, 1973). It can generate a more open, facilitative counseling atmosphere, encourage client talk and additional trust, and create a more equal relationship. In some instances, a self-disclosing counselor may be perceived as more caring than one who does not disclose. At times, counselor self-disclosure can present a model for clients to increase their own levels of disclosure about events and feelings (McCarthy, 1982).

The use of self-disclosure as a skill involves consideration of timing, goals, genuineness, and appropriateness. Effective self-disclosure does not add another burden to an already burdened client (Egan, 2010), and it should not distract the client from his or her own problems (Sexton, Whiston, Bleuer, & Walz, 1997). The counselor must consider how the client will be able to benefit from the information shared.

Perhaps the most important type of self-disclosure is that which focuses on the relationship between you and your client. If you are having a difficult time listening to a client, for example, it could be useful to let them know that it is difficult. However, it helps to only describe your own feelings and reactions and not judge the client. It may be fairly easy for the counselor to self-disclose, but making the disclosure relevant to the client is the important and more complex task (Ivey & Ivey, 2009). The counselor's self-disclosure should be genuine and fairly close in mood and content to the client's experience. As a counselor, you must remember that self-disclosure is appropriate only when it is genuine, benefits the client, and adds to client movement or understanding, and does not interfere with the counseling process or contribute to raised levels of client anxiety (Cormier et al., 1997).

Case Example

The counselor gives a brief self-disclosure response to model desired behavior.

MELISSA: I can't believe I was so dumb and gullible.
COUNSELOR: It seems like you're being really hard on yourself. I've found when I get in these situations that it is easy to beat myself up. I've learned instead to think of ways to be gentle on myself. What might you tell yourself to reduce your self-blaming?

How willing are you to engage in appropriate and relevant self-disclosure? You become vulnerable when you share your own experiences, feelings, and reactions, yet can you expect your clients to become vulnerable in front of you if you rarely show them anything of yourself? Good self-disclosure is a kind of sharing that clients can use to grow, and it lets them know how you are perceiving and experiencing them (Sexton, Whiston, Bleuer, & Walz, 1997).

Most evidence indicates that a moderate amount of self-disclosure has more impact than too little or too much. Counselors who disclose very little risk being seen as aloof, weak, and role-conscious (Egan, 2010), whereas the counselor who discloses too much may be seen as lacking in discretion, being untrustworthy (Levin & Gergen, 1969), seeming preoccupied (Cozby, 1973), or needing assistance.

SIDEBAR 1.6 Self-Awareness: Do You Accept a Client's Request to be "Friends" on a Social-Networking Site?

You and your client, a young career woman in her early thirties, have established an excellent therapeutic relationship, and your client is actively working on her counseling goals. She has had problems in the past with establishing and keeping friendships but is currently working on these issues. You receive a "friend" request from her on one of the social-networking websites. What do you do? What factors do you consider?

Due to the rapid growth and extensive use of social-networking sites, there are no ethical guidelines specific to this issue. However, these sites may pose unique ethical and safety risks due to the importance of client confidentiality and counselor self-disclosure. Van Allen and Roberts (2011) suggest proactive measures such as having a written social media policy and reviewing it with your client during the first session as part of informed consent. Having a professional social-networking site where you share helpful information is one solution. Keeping close watch on privacy settings is another suggestion (Kolmes, 2010).

When considering the use of self-disclosure with clients of a different culture, be aware that disclosing personal information may be valued in some cultures, but not considered appropriate in others. Become knowledgeable about the meaning and use of self-disclosure in that culture, and use this information to help in deciding the benefit of using the skill (Evans et al., 2008).

Confrontation

Confrontation is a skill that is used when there are discrepancies, conflicts, or mixed messages being sent by the client. The mixed messages may occur between the verbal and nonverbal messages sent by the client or between two contradictory verbal messages. Egan (1975) describes confrontation as "the responsible unmasking of the discrepancies, distortions, games and smoke screens the client uses to hide both from self-understanding and from constructive behavioral change" (p. 158).

When confronting a client, the counselor must always exercise concern for the client's understanding of the challenge so that there will be client progress, not denial and flight. To do this effectively, the counselor must accurately reflect the situation. Using a tentative reflection is important, especially if it is early in the relationship. Consideration should also be given to the state of the client; an already distressed, confused, or disorganized client will not benefit from a confrontation. In fact, confrontation with such clients may add to their distress or confusion.

Case Example

· The counselor's response is an example of a gentle confrontation regarding a discrepancy in Melissa's message.

MELISSA: I want to have a close relationship with my dad. We have specific dates when we're supposed to meet for dinner and that's okay. But if I have anything else to do, I'll usually just make an excuse and not go.

COUNSELOR: On one hand I hear you saying that you want a close relationship with your dad, but on the other hand, you often make excuses so you don't have to meet him for dinner. Can you help me understand this?

Confrontation should be done with care and may be more effective if done gradually. A gradual confrontation will give the client time to assimilate information. Good counselor practice demands a careful balance between confrontation followed by support in the form of primary empathy, positive regard, and respect (Ivey, Ivey, & Simek-Downing, 1987).

When considering cultural implications, the counselor needs to be aware that some cultures may consider confrontation to be insensitive and disrespectful. These include Native North Americans, Canadian Inuit, and traditional Latino/Latina people. The counselor may need to choose alternate methods that are more culturally appropriate (Evans et al., 2008).

Immediacy

The phenomenon of immediacy involves the counselor's sensitivity to the immediate situation and an understanding of what is occurring at the moment with clients (Pietrofesa,

Hoffman, & Splete, 1984). It involves the ability to discuss directly and openly with another person what is happening in the "here and now" of an interpersonal relationship (Egan, 2010). This is sometimes referred to as "you–me" talk.

The use of immediacy combines the skills of confrontation and self-disclosure and requires the counselor to reveal feelings and/or challenge the client to deal more openly with his or her feelings. The purpose of immediacy responses is to help clients understand themselves more clearly, especially what is happening at that moment and how they are relating to the counselor in the session. The focus can be on the client, the relationship, or the counselor's own feelings and reactions (Murphy & Dillon, 2008). As interviews move more to the present tense, the counselor's presence in the interview becomes more powerful and important (Ivey & Ivey, 2009), and the counselor is modeling a kind of behavior that clients can use to become more effective in all their relationships.

Counselors usually know what is happening in a session, but do not always act on it. Acting on what is happening at the moment is part of the phenomenon of immediacy. When either counselor or client has unverbalized thoughts or feelings that seem to be getting in the way of progress, the counselor may believe it is advantageous to bring these issues to light.

Case Example

The counselor uses immediacy to expose the unverbalized thoughts Melissa may be having.

MELISSA: I'm not sure I should tell you about all the other stupid things I've done.
COUNSELOR: It sounds like something is getting in the way of your trusting me to understand everything that's happened in your life without judging you.

There are many areas or issues in which the skill of immediacy might be used: trust, differences in style, directionless sessions, dependency, counterdependency, and attraction are areas where "you–me" talk might pay off (Egan, 2010). Other areas might include concern for the client's welfare, lack of follow-through on homework, and the client questioning the value of counseling.

Carkhuff (1969) suggests that the counselor ask, during the course of the interview, "What is the client trying to tell me that he or she can't tell me directly?" The answer lies embedded in the verbal and nonverbal behavior of the client. The skilled helper can uncover it and make it an "immediacy" topic.

In considering whether to use immediacy, the counselor should decide whether it is appropriate to focus the relationship on here-and-now concerns at this specific time. If so, then counselor-initiated leads will focus on the identification and communication of feelings. The counselor must seriously consider word choice; as in many other cases, a tentative statement may be more inviting of a client response.

When considering multicultural implications in the use of immediacy, several points need to be considered (Evans et al., 2008). First of all, individuals from some cultures may need present concerns communicated in a way that permits the client to save face. Another issue of immediacy may come up if the client feels the counselor is culturally biased. The counselor should use immediacy to resolve these issues before continuing the session (Refer to chapter 3).

Table 1.3 Helping Skills

Attending skills	Description
Eye contact	Intermittent yet frequent looking into the eyes of the client*
Attentive body language	Having a comfortable, relaxed, open posture
Distance	Awareness of personal space; distance appropriate from client*
Verbal tracking	Attending to client's story; may involve selective attention*
Active Listening Skills	
Observing non-verbals	Noting physiological changes, facial expressions, body language*
Verbal behavior	Noticing key words, topic changes, topic exclusions, incongruities*
Minimal encouragers	Head nodding, "umm hmm", interested facial expressions
Paraphrase	Rephrasing the content of the client's message
Summarization	Restating overall meaning from a long period of conversation
Reflection of feelings	Accurately recognizing and communicating the client's emotions*
Questions	Using open-ended questions beginning with "what" and "how"
Concreteness	Helping to make feelings, experiences, and behaviors more specific
Advanced Skills	
Advanced Empathy	Communicating a deeper underlying meaning of client's experiences
Self-disclosure	Sharing personal information for specific reasons, i.e. modeling
Confrontation	Communicating to the client their discrepancies or mixed messages
Immediacy	Discussing what is happening in the moment or the "here and now"

Action Skills

The goal of counseling is to have a client come away from the process changed. This growth or change often entails the counselor and client working together on an action plan appropriate to the client's stated goals. These action plans should grow out of the counseling work itself and be based in part on the theoretical orientation of the counselor and what is considered the standards for practice in the profession. For instance, a behaviorally oriented counselor will be more inclined to use behavioral contracts, while a cognitive therapist may emphasize thought-stopping and thought-disputing exercises.

It is important for the counselor to remember that the theoretical orientation is secondary to the development of effective core helping skills. These skills seem to be shared by all effective helpers and really address the quality of the interaction between the counselor and the client. With respect to the action phase, for example, Egan (2010) has suggested that the counselor must have skills to help clients choose effective strategies for change and maintain action-based change programs.

Case Example

In the response that follows, the counselor helps the client to develop an effective strategy for reaching a goal:

COUNSELOR: One of your main goals is to establish new friendships. I'm wondering how you might begin. What are some ways you've made new friends in the past?
MELISSA: In the past, I usually became friends with people who have similar interests. I think I'll begin by accepting the invitation to go out Friday evening with the group from my journalism club. They seem pretty cool.

COUNSELOR: It sounds like you've thought this over, and you have a good idea about where to begin. I'll be interested in hearing about how the plan worked.

Termination Skills

"Goodbye" is not always the easiest thing to say. The ending of a helping relationship can be either one of the most gratifying or one of the most difficult and frustrating aspects of the relationship. Termination may occur either by mutual agreement or prematurely (that is, before all goals of counseling are met). When counselor and client agree that the goals of counseling have been accomplished, they may mutually agree that it is time to terminate. Sadness about parting and some client anxiety may be expected, but by exploring and sharing such feelings, each person is more likely to leave with a sense of growth and accomplishment because goals have been achieved. This process also gives them time to prepare for the future (Murphy & Dillon, 2008). It is important to leave time to discuss feelings about ending the therapeutic alliance and, for a smooth termination, it is important for both individuals to know when the last session will occur (Meier & Davis, 1993).

Either the counselor or the client may initiate premature termination. When counselor-initiated termination occurs, the client needs to be informed as early as possible or reminded that only a limited number of sessions are available. Frequently, counselors may be in the position of terminating counseling prematurely in schools and agencies with session limits. On rare occasions, it may occur because of irreconcilable differences or perceived lack of commitment by the client. When the counselor does terminate the sessions, the reasons must be specified to the client. Most counselors agree that early termination by the counselor violates the premise that clients are in charge of solving their own problems, and early termination may lead to feelings of personal rejection in the client. These feelings should be dealt with before termination is complete. Referring the individual to another agency and/or keeping the door open for future sessions are sometimes helpful.

SIDEBAR 1.7 Self-Awareness: I Enjoy This Client and Don't Want to Terminate the Counselor/Client Relationship.

An awareness of our feelings about certain clients is essential. Counselors have an ethical responsibility to keep the relationship with the client professional and to prevent a personal relationship from developing. If you notice hesitancy on your part to terminate the client although this client has completed all of his or her counseling goals, you need to examine your reasons for delaying termination. There may be clients that we enjoy seeing and talking with and perhaps even think that they would make a good friend. To keep a client active to meet our own needs is unethical. What would you do if your "favorite" client is ready to be terminated and you are hesitating because you will miss him or her?

When the client prematurely terminates the sessions, the counselor should try to explore with the client the reasons for termination. Letting clients know that they are in charge of the decision to return in the future can be beneficial, as is the exploration of possible referral resources.

When termination is mutual or initiated by the counselor, several steps can benefit the outcome of the relationship (Ward, 1984). There should be discussion and evaluation of the goals that have already been reached. Encouragement from the counselor may include a reminder of the client's strengths and new coping strategies, as well as who is included in his or her support system. Closure issues and feelings need to be discussed and clients need to be prompted to explain how they will transfer their new insights to future events. Clients should be prepared for self-reliance and continued self-help. Finally in the last session, discussion is likely to be lighter and more social. Okun (2008), for example, often shares a poster with the client that symbolizes the significance of the client's journey. The termination process should not focus on the generation of new problems or issues, but rather on an appreciation of the growth that has already occurred.

Summary

You began this chapter viewing yourself as the client, feeling apprehensive about seeking counseling, but motivated because of the critical problems in your life. Now imagine yourself as the counselor with each of the clients described in the introductory paragraph. You have learned the importance of establishing the counselor/client relationship and the conditions essential to a therapeutic alliance, including genuineness, empathy, and non-possessive warmth.

You know that developing the alliance consists of three relatively distinct phases: building the relationship, challenging the client to find ways to change, and facilitating positive action. Also important are the characteristics most effective counselors possess, including high levels of self-awareness, empathy, genuineness, and respect for others, and an ability to use themselves as vehicles of change.

You have learned that effective counselors use attending skills (eye contact, body language, and vocal tone) and basic listening skills (client observation, encouraging, paraphrasing, summarizing, reflection of feeling, and open/closed questions) throughout the alliance. Also vital is the use of self-attending skills, which emphasize the importance of the person of the counselor in mediating the communications skills necessary in the therapeutic alliance.

You have been introduced to primary and advanced empathy skills as well as the challenging skills of confrontation, self-disclosure, and immediacy. These skills strengthen the alliance and move the client toward therapeutic change. Counselor action skills facilitate behavior change around the client's stated goals for counseling. Finally, termination skills are needed to bring closure to, and end, the therapeutic alliance.

The following websites provide additional information relating to the chapter topics.

Useful Websites

http://www.carlrogers.info/aboutCarl-Farson.html
http://amhd.org/About/ClinicalOperations/MISA/Training/Therapeutic%20 Alliance%20Curriculum%20activity%20quiz.pdf
http://www.cacd.org/ACA_2005_Ethical_Code10405.pdf
www.wglasser.com/reality.html
http://drkkolmes.com/for-clinicians/social-media-policy/

References

Alyn, J. H. (1988). The politics of touch in therapy: A response to Willison and Masson. *Journal of Counseling and Development, 66,* 432–433.

Assay, T., & Lambert, M. (1999). The empirical case for the common factors in therapy; Quantitative findings. In M. A. Hubble, B. L. Duncan, & S. D. Miller (Eds.), *The heart and soul of change: What works in therapy* (pp. 23–55). Washington, DC: American Psychological Association.

Barak, A., Shapira, G., & Fisher, W. A. (1988). Effects of verbal and vocal cues of counselor Self-confidence on clients' perceptions. *Counselor Education and Supervision, 27,* 355–367.

Berger, R. L., McBreen, J. T., & Rifkin, M. J. (1996). *Human behavior: A perspective for the helping professions.* White Plains, NY: Longham Publishers.

Bohart, A. C., Elliott, R., Greenberg, L., & Watson, J. C. (2002). Empathy. In J. C. Norcross (Ed.), *Psychotherapy relationships that work* (pp. 89–108). New York: Oxford University Press.

Bozarth, J. (1997). Empathy from the framework of client-centered theory and the Rogerian hypothesis. In A. Bohart, & L. Greenberg (Eds.), *Empathy reconsidered* (pp. 81–102). Washington, DC: American Psychological Association.

Brammer, L. M., & MacDonald, G. (1996). *The helping relationship: Process and skills.* Needham Heights, MA: Allyn and Bacon.

Carkhuff, R. (1969). *Helping and human relations* (Vols. 1–2). New York: Holt, Rinehart & Winston.

Carkhuff, R. R. (1986). *The art of helping* (5th ed.). Amherst: MA: Human Resources Development Press.

Carkhuff, R. R., & Anthony, W. A. (1979). *The skills of helping.* Amherst: MA: Human Resources Development Press.

Combs, A. W. (1986). What makes a good helper? A person-centered approach. *Person-centered Review, 1*(1), 51–61.

Cormier, B., Cormier, L. S., & Cormier, W. H. (1997). *Interviewing strategies for helpers: Fundamental skills and cognitive behavioral interventions.* Pacific Grove, CA: Brooks/Cole.

Cormier, S., & Hackney, H. (2008). *Counseling strategies and interventions.* Boston, MA: Pearson Education.

Cozby, P. C. (1973). Self-disclosure: A literature review. *Psychological Bulletin, 79,* 73–91.

Daw, J. (1997). Cultural competence: What does it mean? *Family Therapy News, 28,* 8–9, 27.

Driscoll, M. S., Newman, D. L., & Seals, J. M. (1988). The effects of touch on perception of counselors. *Counselor Education and Supervision, 27,* 344–354.

Durana, C. (1998). The use of touch in psychotherapy: Ethical and clinical guidelines. *Psychotherapy: Theory, Research, Practice, Training, 35*(2), 269–280.

Egan, G. (1975). *The skilled helper.* Monterey, CA: Brooks/Cole.

Egan, G. (2010). *The skilled helper: A problem-management and opportunity development approach to helping* (9th ed.). Pacific Grove, CA: Brooks/Cole.

Evans, D. R., Hearn, M. T., Uhlemann, M. R., & Ivey, A. E. (2008). *Essential interviewing: A programmed approach to effective communication* (7th ed.). Pacific Grove, CA:Brooks/Cole.

Gelatt, H. B. (1989). Positive uncertainty: A decision-making framework for counseling. *Journal of CounselingPsychology, 36*(2), 252–256.

Gladding, S. T. (2008). *Counseling: A comprehensive profession* (6th ed.). Englewood Cliffs, NJ: Prentice-Hall.

Hays, P. (1996). Addressing the complexities of culture and gender in counseling. *Journal of Counseling &Development, 74,* 332–333.

Hendrick, S. S. (1988). Counselor self-disclosure. *Journal of Counseling and Development, 66*(9), 419–424.

Horvarth, A. O., & Symonds, D. D. (1991). Relation between working alliance and outcome in psychotherapy: A meta-analysis. *Journal of Counseling Psychology, 38,* 139–149.

Ivey, A. E., Ivey, M. B., & Zalaquett, C. P. (2009). *Intentional interviewing and counseling: Facilitating client development in a multicultural society* (7th ed.). Pacific Grove, CA: Brooks/Cole.

Ivey, A. E., Ivey, M. B., & Simek-Downing, L. (1987). *Counseling and psychotherapy: Integrating skills, theory and practice.* Englewood Cliffs, NJ: Prentice-Hall.

Kolmes, K. (2010). *Private practice social media policy.* Retrieved from http://drkkolmes.com/for-clinicians/social-media-policy/

Kottler, J. A., & Shepherd, D. S. (2008). *Introduction to counseling: Voices from the field* (6th ed.). Pacific Grove, CA: Brooks/Cole.

Levin, F. M., & Gergen, K. J. (1969). Revealingness, ingratiation, and the disclosure of self. *Proceedings of the 77th Annual Convention of the American Psychological Association, 4*(1), 447–448.

Maples, M. F., Dupey, P., Torres-Rivera, E., Phan, L. T., Vereen, L., & Garrett, M. T. (2001). Ethnic diversity and the use of humor in counseling: Appropriate or inappropriate? *Journal of Counseling and Development, 79,* 1, 53–61.

McCarthy, P. (1982). Differential effects of counselor self-referent responses and counselor status. *Journal of Counseling Psychology, 29,* 125–311.

Meier, S. T., & Davis, S. R. (1993). *The elements of counseling.* Pacific Grove, CA: Brooks/Cole.

Murphy, B. C., & Dillon, C. (2008). *Interviewing in action in a multicultural world* (3rd ed.). Pacific Grove, CA: Brooks/Cole.

Norcross, J. C. (2001). Purposes, processes, and products of the task force on empirically supported therapy relationships. *Psychotherapy, 38,* 345–356.

Okun, B. F. (2008). *Effective helping: Interviewing and counseling techniques* (7th ed.). Pacific Grove, CA: Brooks/Cole.

Peca-Baker, T. A., & Friedlander, M. L. (1987). Effects on role expectations on clients' perceptions of disclosing and nondisclosing counselors. *Journal of Counseling and Development, 66*(2), 78–81.

Pietrofesa, J. J., Hoffman, A., & Splete, H. H. (1984). *Counseling: An introduction.* Boston: Houghton-Mifflin.

Prochaska, J. O., & Norcross, J. C. (2003). *Systems of psychotherapy: A transtheoretical analysis* (5th ed.). Pacific Grove, CA: Brooks/Cole.

Rogers, C. R. (1957). The necessary and sufficient conditions of therapeutic personality change. *Journal of Counseling Psychology, 21,* 95–103.

Rogers, C. R. (1961). *On becoming a person.* Boston: Houghton-Mifflin.

Scherer, K. R. (1986). Vocal expression: A review and model for future research. *Psychological Bulletin, 99,* 143–165.

Seligman, L. (2004). *Technical and conceptual skills for mental health professionals.* Upper Saddle River, NJ: Pearson Education.

Sexton, T. L., & Whiston, S. C. (1994). The status of the counseling relationship: An empirical review, theoretical implications, and research directions. *The Counseling Psychologist, 22*(1), 6–78.

Sexton, T. L., Whiston, S. C., Bleuer, J. C., & Walz, G. R. (1997). *Integrating outcome research into counseling practice and training.* Alexandria, VA: American Counseling Association.

Shulman, L. (1979). *The skills of helping individuals and groups.* Itasca, IL: F. E. Peacock Publishers.

Strong, S. R., & Claiborn, C. D. (1982). *Change through interaction.* New York: Wiley Interscience.

Van Allen, J., & Roberts, M. C. (2011). Critical incidents in the marriage of psychology and technology: A discussion of potential ethical issues in practice, education, and policy. *Professional Psychology: Research and Practice, 42*(6), 433–439.

Ward, D. E. (1984). Termination of individual counseling: Concepts and strategies. *Journal of Counseling Psychology, 63*(1), 21–26.

2

THE COUNSELING PROFESSION

Historical Perspectives and Current Issues and Trends

Harriet L. Glosoff and Jill E. Schwarz-Whittaker[1]

Historical and Formative Factors

If one assumes that counseling is advising, counselors have existed since people appeared on earth. Mothers, fathers, friends, lovers, clergy, and social leaders all provide such counsel—whether sought after or not. The idea of professional counseling, defined by the American Counseling Association (ACA, 2010a), as "a professional relationship that empowers diverse individuals, families, and groups to accomplish mental health, wellness, education, and career goals" is relatively new. This idea did not, however, emerge because of the recognition of a "deep need within human development" (Stripling, 1983, p. 206). The counseling profession evolved in response to the demands made by the industrialization and urbanization of the United States. At the turn of the 20th century, America faced a confluence of social and economic problems, such as the proper distribution of a growing workforce, an increasingly educated population, the needs of immigrants, and the preservation of social values as family connections were weakened (Aubrey, 1982; Herr, 1985).

A representative democracy demands an educated citizenry taking responsibility for the government itself. As the new democracy developed, so did the ideal of education for all citizens. Toward the end of the 19th century, the curriculum of schools began to change, and choices among school subjects became available. Help with such choices was necessary. Jessie Davis, one of the pioneers in counseling, declared in his autobiography that he had graduated from school "fairly well prepared to live in the Middle Ages" (Davis, 1956, p. 57). His experiences led directly to the establishment of guidance and counseling services in schools. There were other societal factors that contributed to the evolution of requiring professional training for those in positions to help people. For example, the industrial revolution and its attendant job specialization and technological advances added pressure to understand how to best help people make career choices. There was also an increase in democracy after the Civil War ended in 1865. If the United States had continued to exist as a slave society or a closed class society, there probably would have been little need for the development of counseling services.

The population of the country was on the increase, and the census of 1890 revealed that the frontier was essentially closed. Larger cities were growing increasingly more crowded, and immigrants to the United States and other citizens could no longer move westward without regard for others. "Free" land was all but gone. It became necessary to remain near the cities to work, to live, and to get along with one's neighbors. Providing assistance in the choices necessary to live in the large industrially based cities became necessary.

During the 20th century, the development of professional counseling in the United States was influenced by a variety of factors. The newly developed science of psychology began, and continued, studying the differences among individuals. Instruments for appraising people were in their infancy but were known to pioneers in the field, who noted the need for counseling services. As these tools developed more sophistication, they were adapted and/or adopted by counselors. Other factors contributing to the evolution of counseling included the work of leaders of the early settlement house movement and other social reformers; the mental hygiene movement; the extent to which Americans value personal success; the emphasis placed on the awareness and use of one's talents, interests, and abilities; the ongoing industrialization of the country; the continued growth of career education and career guidance; the development of psychology as a profession; and the rapid changes in all fields due to increased availability of technology (Shertzer & Stone, 1986).

Pressures from various socioeconomic factors also led to the kaleidoscope we know as counseling today. The history of counseling has continued the thread of individual choice in a society that prizes freedom to choose as an ideal. Like a kaleidoscope, the form, emphasis, and brightness of various aspects of counseling have changed as society changes. This chapter examines the following select facets of that kaleidoscope that have shaped the counseling profession:

- The vocational guidance movement
- The mental health counseling movement
- The ongoing development of professional identity
- The influence of federal legislation
- The history of the American Counseling Association
- Credentialing and the "professionalization" of counseling

The chapter concludes with a brief review of current issues and trends in the counseling profession.

Beginnings of the Vocational Guidance Movement

Perhaps the earliest notion of professional counseling in response to societal pressures was that of Lysander S. Richards. In 1881, Richards published a slim volume titled *Vocophy*. He considered vocophy to be a "new profession, a system enabling a person to name the calling or vocation one is best suited to follow" (Richards, 1881). His work has been dismissed because there is no documented proof that he actually established the services he advocated. Nevertheless, his ideas foreshadowed what was to come. He called his counselors "vocophers" and urged that they study occupations and the people they counseled.

Richards (1881) included letters from various famous people of the day in his book *Vocophy*. He believed that aspirants to particular occupations should consider what successful people had to say about the qualifications for success in that field. Letters from Grant, Longfellow, Westinghouse, and others, which described the ingredients for success in their occupations, were included in the book.

Later, a series of pamphlets published by the Metropolitan Life Insurance Company in the 1960s and used widely by school counselors asked the question, "Should your child be a _____?" A famous person in a field would describe what was necessary for success in that field. Using successful people to provide career information is a technique employed by counselors today as well.

Richards also seemed advanced for his time regarding his views of women and youth and their work. He said that if a woman could do the work "though at present solely followed by man, there can be no objections, whether normally or religiously considered, to her following it" (Richards, 1881, preface). He deplored the drifting of youth from job to job without consideration of what would be best for them and for society.

Whether Richards influenced those who followed is speculative. Influence is the quicksilver of history. He was active in the literary societies in the Boston area, as was Frank Parsons. Did they meet? Did they debate? Richards's *Vocophy* was in the Harvard Library in the 1890s. In an article published in the later 1890s, Parsons (1894) expressed ideas similar to those of Richards. Brewer (1942) noted that Meyer Bloomfield, a colleague of Parsons at the Breadwinners Institute, mentioned Richards in his Harvard courses, as did Henry C. Metcalf of Tufts and Frank Locke of the YMCA in Boston.

* ON EXAM ⟶

Frank Parsons

Regardless of who influenced whom, the need for counseling about vocational choice seems to have permeated American society of the late 19th and early 20th centuries. There is no question of the credit given to Frank Parsons for leading the way to vocational guidance. Parsons had a long history of concern for economic and political reforms that would benefit people. He published books and articles on a wide variety of topics, including taxation, women's suffrage, and education for all people. Of all his endeavors, Parsons was most interested in social reform and especially in assisting people to make sound occupational choices. Other pioneers in the field credited him with being the first counselor (Davis, 1914; Reed, 1944), and he has often been referred to as the "father of guidance." Parsons alone, of those individuals who had some direct connection with the organization and extension of guidance services, had a definite, well-thought-out, and organized social philosophy, which he articulated often and at length (Rockwell, 1958).

Parsons was one of the many in the late 19th and early 20th centuries who were striving to make the world a better place in which to live. These people saw in the growth of large private fortunes, based on industrial might and the resultant political power, a clear danger to the realization of a more perfect society based on the comradeship of all humankind. They were each humanitarians, who sought ways for all individuals within our society to have the good things in life. Parsons found himself in the company of such notables of this movement as Henry D. Lloyd, Edward Bellamy, Phillip Brooks, and Benjamin O. Flower (Rockwell, 1958).

Parsons believed it was better to select a vocation scientifically than to drift through a variety of vocations, perhaps never finding one that would be best for the person and, thus, make society better. Meyer Bloomfield, director of the Civic Service House in Boston, asked Parsons to establish such a service within the Civic Service House. Thus, Parsons became director of what was called the Breadwinners Institute from 1905 through 1907 (Brewer, 1942).

Parsons developed a plan for individualized counseling and opened the Vocational Bureau of Boston in January 1908. He served as its director and vocational counselor. The primary goal of the bureau was to develop the potential of Boston's growing immigrant population. Although Parsons was but one of many who were seeking social reforms at this time, he was able to secure the support of the leaders of powerful groups in business, labor, education, and politics. His report to the members of the board controlling the Vocational Bureau was the first recorded instance of the use of the term *vocational guidance*. (Brewer, in 1942, published the report as an appendix to his *History*.) Parsons' report emphasized that counseling was not designed to make decisions for counselees. "No attempt is made, of course, to decide FOR [*sic*] the applicant what his calling should be; but the Bureau tries to help him arrive at a wise, well-founded conclusion for himself" (Brewer, 1942, p. 304). According to Williamson (1965), this was consistent with the moral and intellectual atmosphere of that time. He traced the growth of counseling before Parsons's work to the concept of "vocational freedom of choice" (p. 3). He noted that the climate of the late 1800s stimulated practical application of vocational choice or individuals' freedom to pursue choice in personal development.

Parsons also developed a plan for the education of counselors. His plan was outlined in his book *Choosing a Vocation* (1909), published posthumously. Parsons's prescriptions for how counselees should examine themselves and their lives reflected his political and social philosophy (Rockwell, 1958).

Early Ties Between Vocational Guidance and School Counseling

Many see educational settings as the first homes to the profession of counseling, especially in terms of vocational guidance. In 1898, at about the same time that Parsons opened the Vocational Bureau, Jesse Davis began advising students about educational and vocational matters (Aubrey, 1982). Jessie B. Davis had been unsure of what he wanted to do with his life throughout his educational career. He was questioned thoroughly by Charles Thurber, one of his professors at Cornell University, and that left a lasting impression on him. He began to use the professor's methods in his work with students at the Central High School in Detroit and attempted to incorporate guidance into the normal educational experience of students. In 1907, Davis became principal of the Grand Rapids, Michigan, Central School and was able to implement his ideas of self-study, occupational study, and examination of self in relation to the chosen occupation throughout the 7th through 12th grades (Brewer, 1942). This was done primarily through essays written in English classes. Essay topics varied from self-examination of values and ideals to the selection of a vocation by the 12th grade. Throughout the topics, social and civic ethics were emphasized (Davis, 1914). Just five years later (1912), Grand Rapids established a citywide guidance department.

Grand Rapids was not the only city in the early 1900s that housed newly developed vocational guidance services. Both Anna Y. Reed in Seattle and Eli Weaver in New York established counseling services based on Social Darwinian concepts (Rockwell, 1958). Similar to Darwin's biological theory of "survival of the fittest," Social Darwinism contends that certain groups in a society become powerful because they have adapted best to the evolving requirements of that society. Reed decided that counseling services were needed for America's youth through her study of newsboys, penal institutions, and charity schools. She emphasized that business people were the most successful and counseling should be designed to help youth emulate them. She equated morality and business ideals and was much concerned that whatever course of action was taken on any social question should be taken on the basis of social research, of economy, and of how it would be accepted by the business world. Reed urged that schools keep children focused on the potential for making money, which she believed every pupil could understand (Reed, 1916).

The guidance services that Reed developed were similar to those of modern placement agencies that focus on an individual's acceptability to employers. Other programs, she said, "savored too much of a philanthropic or social service proposition and too little of a practical commercial venture" (Reed, 1920, p. 62).

Eli Weaver also believed in working within the framework of the existing society and looked at counseling as a means of keeping the wheels of the social machinery well oiled. He was chairman of the Students' Aid Committee of the High School Teachers' Association of New York in 1905. In developing the work of his committee, Weaver concluded that the students were in need of advice and counsel before their entrance into the workaday world. He had no funds or active help from school authorities but was able to secure the volunteer services of teachers to work with young people in New York. By 1910, he was able to report teachers actively attempting to help boys and girls to discover what they could do best and how to secure a job in which their abilities could be used to the fullest advantage (Brewer, 1942; Rockwell, 1958).

Counselors in the school systems of Boston and New York during the 1920s were expected to assist students in making educational and vocational choices. It was during the 1920s that the certification of school counselors began in these two cities. It was also during that decade that the Strong Vocational Interest Inventory was first published (1928) and used by counselors, setting the stage for future directions in career counseling (Shertzer & Stone, 1986).

The Creation of the National Vocational Guidance Association

The early pioneers in counseling clearly reflected society's need for workers who were skilled and happy in what they did. A distinct influence in early counseling was the vocational education movement. In 1906, the National Society for the Promotion of Industrial Education (NSPIE) was formed. Advocates of vocational counseling served on its board and later on the board of the Vocation Bureau established by Parsons. Ralph Albertson, an employment supervisor at William Filene's Sons Company and confidant of Frank Parsons, became secretary of the board of trustees of the Vocation Bureau (Stephens, 1970). Frank Snedden, a vocational educator from Massachusetts, is given credit for suggesting that a vocational guidance conference separate from the NSPIE be held (Brewer, 1942). Such conferences were held in 1911 and 1912.

At a third national conference in 1913, the National Vocational Guidance Association (NVGA) was formed in Grand Rapids, Michigan (Norris, 1954). Frank Leavitt became the first president and noted the economic, educational, and social demands for guidance and the counseling it entailed. He also felt that it was necessary "for the very preservation of society itself" (Norris, 1954, p. 17). Counseling in regard to career choice remained an integral part of the movement.

Beginnings of the Mental Health Counseling Movement

The economic, educational, and social reform forces that led to the organization of NVGA also led to other movements, which were later incorporated into the kaleidoscope we call

ON EXAM

counseling today. In the early 1800s, American reformers such as Dorothea Dix advocated for the establishment of institutions that would treat people with emotional disorders in a humane manner. Although these reformers made great strides in accomplishing their goals, following the Civil War there was a rapid decline in the conditions related to the humane treatment of institutionalized individuals (Palmo & Weikel, 1986).

Clifford Beers, who had suffered harsh treatment for mental illness in several psychiatric institutions, published *A Mind That Found Itself,* an autobiography about his experience (Beers, 1908). Publication of this book served as a catalyst for the mental hygiene movement and studies of people with emotional and behavior problems. Early studies of children with emotional problems supported the concept of providing counseling for all children in schools. Beginning at about the same time as vocational guidance, the mental hygiene movement and the field of psychology have had equally strong influences on the development of professional counseling.

In 1908, the same year Frank Parsons opened the Vocational Bureau, William Healy, a physician, established the first community psychiatric clinic. The Juvenile Psychopathic Institute was founded to provide services to young people in Chicago who were having problems. The institute used testing, modified psychoanalysis, and involvement of family members. In 1909, leaders of Cook County, Illinois, deciding that counseling services would benefit children, established countywide child guidance clinics. During the same year, U.S. Congress founded the National Committee on Mental Hygiene.

Early Psychologists

Wilhelm Wundt is credited with establishing, in the late 1870s in Germany, the first experimental psychology laboratory. One way that Wundt endeavored to study the structure of the mind was by using a form of introspection in which he asked subjects to use self-reflection and verbalize what they were experiencing (Belkin, 1988).

In the United States, William James modified Wundt's approach and tried to discover the functions of the mind, rather than focusing primarily on its structure. James believed that individuals function as holistic beings who use thoughts, reasoning, emotions, and behaviors. James and his followers are referred to as "functionalists," and they developed experimental designs to facilitate understanding of why human beings' minds function as they do (Belkin, 1988). James's interest in the ideas of "adaptive functioning," "free will," and the conscious functioning of individuals is clearly pertinent to the development of the counseling profession.

A scientific approach to social problems had become popular in the late 19th and early 20th centuries. Granville Stanley Hall founded what many consider the first psychology laboratory in the United States in 1883 at Johns Hopkins University, where he focused on collecting data on the mental characteristics of children (Belkin, 1988). His study of the development of children's mental and physical abilities continued under his tenure as president of Clark University, where he emphasized graduate study and research. The scientific approach to social problems was based on the assumption that the answer to a social problem could be discovered through objective research. Many consider G. Stanley Hall the "father of American psychology" (Belkin, 1988, p. 15). Even though his work itself has not endured, in addition to founding one of the first psychology departments, G. Stanley Hall was also the primary person to organize the American Psychological Association (APA), and he bestowed the first doctorates in the field of psychology. Of course, the early behaviorists, such as John Watson and B. F. Skinner, and experimental psychologists, such as Max Wetheimer and Wolfgang Kohler, are also associated with the development of the field of psychology.

David Spence Hill, who organized the first guidance and counseling services in New Orleans, was a graduate of Clark University during the presidency of G. Stanley Hall. As director of research for the New Orleans schools, he discovered a need for guidance while researching whether there was a need for a vocational school in his district (Rockwell, 1958). He concluded that there was a need for such a high school, and he also believed it necessary to assist youth in assessing their abilities and in learning about the opportunities that would best help them use those skills. He was aware of Binet's appraisal work and attempted to use the Binet tasks in helping the students in the New Orleans schools. He realized the need for counseling because of his belief that the education of an individual must be of the highest order. Counseling based on scientific research would help secure the best education for each pupil.

If counselors were to help youth know themselves and match their characteristics with qualifications for jobs, some means of measuring individual characteristics was necessary. Counselors relied a great deal on questioning youth about their abilities and their desires, with the implicit assumption that counselees know themselves and can reason about their reported skills and their qualifications for jobs. A counselor's task was to help them in this process by using greater maturity and objective judgment. The development of tests and appraisal instruments lent a scientific air to the process.

During the late 1800s and early 1900s, the testing movement was also taking hold. In the 1890s, James Cattell was the first person in this country to focus on ways to measure intelligence. In 1894, he introduced the first mental abilities test, which was administered to freshmen entering Columbia University (Goldenberg, 1973).

In 1905, the Binet–Simon Test was introduced in France. In 1916, L. M. Terman of Stanford University released a revised version of the Binet–Simon Test he had developed, titled the Stanford–Binet Test. With the release of the Stanford–Binet Test, the term *intelligence quotient* or *IQ* was first used. Although the development of the Stanford–Binet certainly helped spearhead the testing movement in the United States, it was World War I that truly gave flight to the development and use of standardized instruments.

Influences of World War I and the Development of Testing

World War I influenced the counseling profession's roots in both the vocational guidance and mental health arenas. The Army, in order to screen personnel, commissioned the development of psychological instruments, including the Army Alpha and Beta IQ tests of intelligence. In the period following World War I, the number and variety of such instruments proliferated, and even though counselors were not the major creators of the instruments, they began to use standardized instruments as tools for use in military, educational, and clinical settings. These screening tools also supported the development of aptitude and interest tests used by counselors in business and educational settings (Aubrey, 1982). Quantifying a person's intelligence, aptitude, achievement, interest, and personality gave a great deal of credibility to a counselor's judgment about the person (Ginzberg, 1971).

After World War I, psychological testing became pervasive in industrial personnel classification, in education, and in counseling offices. Knowledge about and skill in using standardized tests became part of the education of a counselor. Data derived from appraisal instruments were used to make better judgments about counselees and to advise them about what decision was the wisest to make. Large commercial producers of psychometric devices emerged. The process of developing and marketing tests to industry, education, government, and counselors in private practice became quite sophisticated. Counselors were expected to be experts in selecting and using appropriate instruments from a myriad of those offered. Their use in the counseling process became such that testing and counseling were often considered synonymous.

The practice of using tests in counseling was not without controversy. Criteria for psychometric instruments used in decision-making were not published until 1954, with the publication of the American Psychological Association's *Technical Recommendations for Psychological Tests and Diagnostic Techniques* (Stephens, 1954). Publications such as *Testing, Testing, Testing* (Joint Committee on Testing, 1962), *The Educational Decision-Makers* (Cicourel & Kitsuse, 1963), and *The Brain Watchers* (Gross, 1962) are examples of many early voices questioning counselors and others' reliance on test data.

Beginnings of Professional Identity

The Great Depression and the Continuation of the Career Guidance Movement

There was continued progress in the development of career counseling during the 1930s. The Great Depression, with its loss of employment for millions of people, demonstrated the need for career counseling to assist adults as well as youth to identify, develop, and learn to market new vocational skills (Ohlsen, 1983). At the University of Minnesota, E. G. Williamson and colleagues modified the work of Frank Parsons and employed it in working with students. Their work is considered by some to be the first theory of career counseling, and it emphasized a directive, counselor-centered approach known as the "Minnesota point of view." Williamson's approach continued to emphasize matching individuals' traits with those of various jobs and dominated counseling during most of the 1930s and 1940s. The publication of the *Dictionary of Occupational Titles* in 1938 provided counselors with a basic resource to match people with occupations for which they were theoretically well suited (Shertzer & Stone, 1986).

The concept that society would be better if individuals and their occupations were matched for greater efficiency and satisfaction continued to shape the vocational guidance movement. There was a plethora of organizations dedicated to this end. In 1934, a number of them met to form the American Council of Guidance and Personnel Associations, or ACGPA (Brewer, 1942, p. 152), including the American College Personnel Association, the National Association of Deans of Women, the National Federation of Bureau of Occupations, the National Vocational Guidance Association, the Personnel Research Foundation, and the Teachers' College Personnel Association. By 1939, the name was changed to the Council of Guidance and Personnel Associations (CGPA), and other groups were added: the Alliance for the Guidance of Rural Youth, the International Association of Altrusa Clubs, the National Federation of Business and Professional Women's Clubs, the Western Personnel Service, the American Association of Collegiate Registrars (withdrew in 1941), the Institute of Women's Professional Relations, the Kiwanis International, and the Association of YMCA Secretaries met with the group from time to time.

Brewer (1942) stated that the October 1938 issue of *Occupations,* the publication of the NVGA, listed 96 organizations interested in furthering vocational guidance among the young people of the nation. Counseling per se was coming to the forefront of concerns within the vocational guidance movement. All groups seemed dedicated to placing "square pegs in square holes" through the use of tests.

The career guidance movement in the U.S. continued to grow after the Great Depression with an emphasis on helping young people plan for future careers. During the 1950s, the U.S. government was particularly interested in issues related to vocational guidance or career guidance. In response to the Soviet Union's successful space program (for example, the launching of *Sputnik*), the government became concerned with identifying young people with scientific and mathematical talent. To this end, they passed the National Defense Education Act (NDEA) in 1958. Some contend that the impact of NDEA goes well beyond funding of vocational guidance programs. Hoyt stated that NDEA "had a greater impact on counselor education than any other single force" (1974, p. 504). NDEA funded the training of guidance counselors at both the elementary and secondary levels, and NDEA training programs were established to produce counselors qualified for public schools (Herr, 1985). Although the legislation established counselor education programs specifically to train professionals to identify bright children and steer them into technical fields, these counselors were also trained in other domains of counseling as well.

Influence of World War II

World War II strongly influenced the confluence of the vocational guidance and mental health movements, along with that of rehabilitation counseling. The U.S. government continued to rely on standardized instruments and classification systems during World War II. The government requested that psychologists and counselors aid in selecting and training specialists for the military and industry (Ohlsen, 1983). Before and during World War II, millions of men and women were tested and assigned to particular duties according to their test scores and their requests. The armed forces stationed counselors and psychologists at many induction and separation centers. Picchioni and Bonk (1983) quote Mitchell Dreese of the adjutant general's office as saying that counseling "is essentially the same whether it be in the home, the church, the school, industry, business or the Army" (p. 54). The process was certainly an extensive use of the scientific approach to counseling. Society, through its representatives in government, had become embroiled in what counseling should be and what it should become. Society has not relinquished that sense of involvement through all the forms, shapes, and colors of the kaleidoscope counseling has become.

The use of standardized tests is not the only reason World War II had a tremendous influence on the counseling profession. Personnel were also needed on the front lines and in aid stations to help soldiers deal with "battle neuroses." This was accomplished through minimum training and what seemed to be an "overnight" credentialing of new medical school graduates and research-oriented clinical psychologists. Even though minimally trained, their interventions resulted in a significant reduction of chronic battle neuroses (Cummings, 1990).

SIDEBAR 2.1 Counselors Dealing with Trauma: The Need for Self-Awareness

All counselors will be called upon to help clients deal with trauma of some kind. When you consider your area of specialization (e.g., counseling in addictions, college, clinical mental health, rehabilitation, or school settings) where do you anticipate you might be confronted with issues of trauma? Write these down and consider the following questions.

- What areas or types of trauma might be especially challenging for you to encounter?
- How might your own life experiences impact you as a developing counseling professional?
- What are some ways you can proactively begin to deal with these challenges?

In 1944, the War Department established the Army Separation-Classification and Counseling Program in response to the emotional and vocational needs of returning soldiers. The Veterans Administration (VA) also established counseling centers within their hospitals (Shertzer & Stone, 1986). The VA coined the term *counseling psychology* and established counseling psychology positions and training programs to fill these positions. The National Institute of Mental Health (NIMH) was founded just after World War II and established a series of training stipends for graduate programs in professional psychology. By setting up Ph.D. training stipends, the NIMH reinforced the VA's standard of the doctorate being the entry level into professional psychology. The American Psychological Association (APA) was asked to set standards of training for the new programs in university graduate schools. Although the goal of the VA and NIMH was to train counseling psychologists for the public sector, more and more trained psychologists chose to enter private practice.

In addition, during the 1940s a trend toward working with the psychological problems of "normal people" emerged. In reaction to the Nazi movement and World War II, humanistic psychologists and psychiatrists came from Europe to the United States. Their work gradually influenced the strong quantitative leanings in counseling and contributed to the work of well-known psychologists such as Rollo May, Abraham Maslow, and Carl Rogers.

Carl Rogers and the Continuation of the Mental Health Movement

[handwritten annotation: ✱ ON EXAM]

In reviewing a history of what has happened, it is often difficult to know whether events have shaped a leader of an era or whether a person has influenced events. There seems little doubt that Carl R. Rogers, his ideas, and his disciples affected counseling from its core outward. Rogers idea was that individuals had the capacity to explore themselves and to make decisions without an authoritative judgment from a counselor. He saw little need to make diagnoses of client problems or to provide information or direction to those he called *clients*. He emphasized the importance of the relationship between the counselor and client. In his system, the client rather than the counselor was the most important factor. Because there was no persuasion used or advice given to follow a particular course, Rogers's system became known as *nondirective counseling*. Rogers became interested in the process of counseling and pioneered the electronic recording and filming of counseling sessions, an unheard-of idea at that time. Working in the academic environment of Ohio State University and the University of Chicago, Rogers published his ideas in *Counseling and Psychotherapy: Newer Concepts in Practice* in 1942 and *Client-Centered Therapy* in 1951.

It is not the purpose of this chapter to delineate all the postulates of what became known as *client-centered counseling* and, later, *person-centered counseling*. It is important to note, however, the impact that approach had on counseling has continued to the present day. The rise to prominence of Carl Rogers's theory was the first major challenge to the tenets of the Minnesota point of view. In fact, many programs at counseling conventions debated the issue of client-centered versus trait-factored counseling.

Rogers himself remained within the scientific approach to counseling. His concern was to learn what went on in the counseling process, to learn what worked (for him), and what did not. His was a search for necessary and sufficient conditions under which effective counseling could take place. Whenever Rogers reported research about client-centered counseling, it was supported by psychometric data. Certainly one of the effects of Rogers on the profession was to emphasize understanding the counseling process and the need for research. The ensuing debates about the primacy of feeling or rationality as a proper basis of counseling stimulated professional counselors to research their processes and techniques. Theories were refined, and new instruments for determining their efficacy were developed. Counselors in training became as familiar with recording devices as they were with textbooks.

Aubrey (1982) noted that "without doubt, the most profound influence in changing the course and direction of the entire guidance movement in the mid and late 1940s was Carl Rogers" (p. 202). Rogers built on the humanistic and individualistic foundations of the education guidance movement in which he was trained at Columbia University by formulating the nondirective client-centered approach to counseling. He brought a psychologically oriented counseling theory into the guidance movement, thus grounding the counseling profession in the broad disciplines of education and psychology (Weikel & Palmo, 1989).

**SIDEBAR 2.2 Case Study: Identifying Significant Pioneers
in the Counseling Profession**

We highlighted several pioneers, such as Frank Parsons, Clifford Beers, Jesse Davis, and Carl Rogers, who have influenced the profession of counseling. Marcus, Jessica, and Emilio are in a learning team in their introduction to counseling class. The teams were asked to identify the pioneers members thought were most important to the profession of counseling, to articulate reasons for their selection, and to try to come to consensus as to the top two pioneers. Marcus and Jessica are specializing in school counseling and Emillo in clinical mental health counseling. Jessica states that she believes Clifford Beers was the most important as he "began the mental hygiene movement." Marcus believes that Jesse Davis was most influential and Emilio identifies Carl Rogers as being the most instrumental person in the development of counseling as we know it today. What reasons would you give for each of the choices noted? Of the four pioneers, who do you think was most important to the profession of counseling? Why?

Federal Legislation and Its Influence on the Counseling Profession

The Great Depression prompted the development of government-sponsored programs that included a counseling component with an emphasis on classification. Both the Civilian Conservation Corps (CCC) and the National Youth Administration (NYA) attempted to help youth find themselves in the occupational scene of the 1930s (Miller, 1971). In 1938, the George–Dean Act had appropriated $14 million for vocational education, and by 1938 the Occupational Information and Guidance Services was established. The federal government became influential in the field of counseling and remains so today.

The following list exemplifies how the federal government has influenced the development of the counseling profession over the years by offering *examples* of governmental actions and legislation. Primary sources of this information include ACA legislative briefing papers available from the ACA Office of Public Policy and Information; Barstow (personal communication, August 25, 2003, May 15, June 15, 2007, and February 24, 2012); and, Vacc & Loesch, 1994. This is not meant to be an exhaustive listing of all legislation that has influenced professional counseling and counseling services. In addition, many of these acts (e.g., Rehabilitation Act, No Child Left Behind) must be reauthorized on a regular basis. We have noted only major revisions to the original bills enacted, rather than listing each time an act was reauthorized. We also refer readers to the Current Issues and Trends in Counseling for additional information on recent legislative issues.

SIDEBAR 2.3 The Role of Federal Legislation in the Recognition of the Counseling Profession and its Specialties

As you read through federal legislation that has been passed over the years, consider the growth that occurred for the counseling profession as well as the challenges faced by professional counselors during each of the decades. Many of the acts are specific to areas of counseling specialization (e.g., career counseling, college counseling, mental health counseling, rehabilitation counseling, school counseling). Identify three laws in your specialty area(s) of interest to investigate further. Consider how each of these laws has influenced current practice in the counseling specialization area you chose. How do you think federal legislation has contributed to the recognition of counseling as a profession, as compared to specialties?

1900–1939

1917   *The Smith–Hughes Act* created federal grants to support a nationwide vocational education program.

1933   *The Wagner–Peyser Act* established the U.S. Employment Services.

1936   *The George–Dean Act* continued the support established by the Smith–Hughes Act.

1938   The U.S. Office of Education established the Occupational and Information Guidance Services Bureau that, among other things, conducted research on vocational guidance issues. Its publications stressed the need for school counseling.

1940s

1944   The Veterans Administration established a nationwide network of guidance services to assist veterans. The services included vocational rehabilitation, counseling, training, and advisement.

1944   The U.S. Employment Service was begun under the influence of the War Manpower Commission. Fifteen hundred offices were established, and employment "counselors" were used.

1946   *The George–Barden Act* provided government support for establishing training programs for counselors. The emphasis was on vocational guidance and established a precedent for funding of training for counselors.

1946   The National Institute of Mental Health (NIMH) was established and the National Mental Health Act was passed in 1946 authorizing funds for research, demonstration, training, and assistance to states in the use of effective methods of prevention, diagnosis, and treatment of people with mental health disorders.

1950s

1954   *The Vocational Rehabilitation Act* (VRA) recognized the needs of people with disabilities. The VRA was a revision of earlier vocational rehabilitation acts and was prompted, in part, by the government's attempts to meet the needs of World War II veterans. It mandated the development of counselors who specialized in assisting persons with disabilities and allocated funds for the training of these counselors.

1955   *The Mental Health Study Act* of 1955 established the Joint Commission on Mental Illness and Health.

1958   As noted previously, the emphasis of the National Defense Education Act (NDEA) was on improving math and science performance in our public schools; counseling in the schools was seen as an important function in helping students explore their abilities, options, and interests in relation to career development. Title V of this act specifically addressed counseling through grants to schools to carry out counseling activities. Title V-D authorized contracts to institutions of higher education to improve the training of counselors in the schools.

1960s

1962   *The Manpower Development Training Act* was enacted and established guidance services to individuals who were underemployed and/or economically disadvantaged.

1963   *The Community Mental Health Centers Act,* an outgrowth of the Mental Health Study Act, was passed. The act mandated the creation of more than 2,000 mental health centers and provided direct counseling services to people in the community as well as providing outreach and coordination of other services. The Community Mental Health Centers Act also provided opportunities for counselors to be employed outside of educational settings.

1964   *The Amendment to the National Defense Education Act* of 1958 continued to impact counseling through the addition of counselors in the public schools, especially elementary schools, aimed at reducing the counselor–student ratio.

1965   *The Elementary and Secondary Education Act* (ESEA) did much to develop and expand the role of the elementary school counseling program and the services provided by the elementary school counselor.

1970s–1980s

1972   Title IX of the Education Amendments to the 1964 Civil Rights Act mandated that no one be discriminated against or excluded from participating in any federally funded educational program or activity on the basis of sex. It also prohibited sex-biased appraisal and sex-biased appraisal instruments.

1975   *Public Law (P. L.) 94–142*, also known as the Education for All Handicapped Children Act, mandated that all children, regardless of their disabilities, were entitled to an appropriate free public education. Counselors became instrumental in designing, implementing, and evaluating the individualized education plans that were required for each student with special needs.

1976   *P. L. 94–482* was enacted, extending and revising the Vocational Education Act of 1963 and its 1968 amendments. P. L. 94–482 directed states to develop and implement programs of vocational education specifically to provide equal education opportunities to both sexes and to overcome sex bias and stereotyping. It also specified that funds must be used in vocational education for individuals who are disadvantaged, had limited English proficiency, and/or had handicapping conditions.

1977   Sections 503 and 504 were added to the civil rights law typically known as the Rehabilitation Act of 1973. Section 503 mandates all employers conducting business with the federal government (meeting specific criterion) to take affirmative action in the recruitment, hiring, advancement, and treatment of qualified persons with disabilities. This act was a precursor to what may be the more widely known Americans with Disabilities Act that was enacted in 1990.

1977   President Carter established the President's Commission on Mental Health.

1979   *The Veterans' Health Care Amendments* called for the provision of readjustment counseling and related mental health services to Vietnam-era veterans.

1980   *The Mental Health Systems Act* was passed, stressing the need for balancing services in both preventive and remedial mental health programs. The act required the development of new services for children, youth, minority populations, older people, and people with chronic mental illness. The act was repealed during the same year it was passed because of the severe federal budget cuts for social programs during the first year of President Reagan's term in office.

SIDEBAR 2.4 Balancing Proactive and Reactive Counseling Services: Budget Cuts, Policy, and Advocacy

In this chapter, we present information on the impact of some major historical events on the development of the counseling profession. Consider some of the modern-day events that have affected our world and nation in recent years. Which worldwide disasters or crises (natural or created by people) have influenced the profession of counseling? Consider events that have possibly impacted the lives of the clients or students with whom you will work. How do you think the counseling profession is still being shaped by societal events?

After reviewing materials on the ACA website (http://www.counseling.org/PublicPolicy/), as well as in the professional literature, discuss in teams: (a) how you think federal and state funding and budget cuts have influenced the balance in counseling services that are reactive to crisis and those that are more proactive or more preventive in nature; and (b) what actions counselors can take to advocate for funding for both prevention and remedial counseling services.

1984   *Carl D. Perkins Vocational Education Act* amended the Vocational Education Act of 1963. Its primary purpose was to help the states develop, expand, and improve vocational education programs. The act sought to include previously underserved people such as those with disabilities, adults in need of both training and retraining, and single parents, to name a few. The legislation indicated that career guidance and counseling functions should be performed by *professionally trained counselors*. In addition, the entire act was filled with language that showed how important legislators believed counseling and career development services to be.

1990s

1990   *Americans with Disabilities Act* (ADA) prohibited job discrimination against people with disabilities. It also mandated that individuals with disabilities have the same access to goods, services, facilities, and accommodations afforded to all others.

1990   *Carl D. Perkins Vocational Education Act* was reauthorized setting directions for state and local agencies to develop vocational and applied education programs. It targeted single parents, displaced homemakers, and single pregnant women, noting that states were to use a certain percentage of their funds to provide basic academic and occupational skills and materials in preparation for vocational education and training to provide these people with marketable skills. In addition, states were required to use funds to promote sex equity by providing programs, services, and comprehensive career guidance, support services, and preparatory services for girls and women.

1994   *The School-to-Work Opportunities Act* set up partnerships among educators, businesses, and employers to facilitate the transition of those students who plan on moving from high school directly to the world of work.

1995   *Elementary School Counseling Demonstration Act* allocated $2 million in grant money for schools to develop comprehensive elementary school counseling programs.

1996   *The Mental Health Insurance Parity Act* (enacted in 1996 and became effective January 1, 1998) prevents health plans which cover mental health services from placing unequal caps on the dollar amount covered (either annually or on a lifetime basis) for the provision of mental health services if these same caps are not placed on the coverage of other medical services. Although this act has several limitations (e.g., it does not require that health plans provide mental health benefits), it was a major step toward parity of insurance coverage for mental health services (ACA Office of Public Policy and Information, 1996).

1996   *Health Insurance Portability and Accountability Act* (HIPAA, Public Law 104–191) included language to promote "administrative simplification" in the administration of health care benefits by establishing national standards for the electronic transmission of health information, for the use and disclosure of personally-identifiable health information, and for the security of information. Although the standards do not contain any counselor-specific provisions, they have an impact on all counselors, both as providers of mental health services and as health care consumers.

1997   *The Balanced Budget Act* included provisions that prohibit Medicaid managed care plans from discrimination against providers on the basis of the type of license they hold. This did not extend to fee-for-service plans administered through Medicaid.

1998   *Higher Education Act* Amendments reauthorized higher education programs for another five years. In addition to dropping student loan interest rates and increasing Pell Grant awards, the act created the *Gaining Early Awareness and Readiness for Undergraduate Programs* (GEAR-UP), which provides grants for establishing partnerships between colleges, schools, and community organizations. The provisions included payment for counseling services to certain at-risk and low-income students and other elementary, middle, and secondary school students. In addition to advising and counseling services related to financial aid, and college admissions, the amendments allow for personal counseling, family counseling, and home visits for students with limited English proficiency (ACA Office of Public Policy and Information, 1998a).

1998   *The Health Professions Education Partnerships Act* (HPEPA) is a landmark piece of legislation. It recognizes professional counselors under health professional training programs. Specifically, education programs, counseling students and graduates, and counselor educators stand to be made eligible for a wide range of programs operated by the federal Health Resources and Services Administration (HRSA) and the federal Center for Mental Health Service (CMHS) to the same extent as other master's-level mental health professions (e.g., social workers). Where the term "graduate programs in behavioral and mental health practice" is referenced in these programs, the provisions passed in HPEPA include graduate programs in counseling (ACA Office of Public Policy and Information, 1998b).

1998   *The Workforce Investment Act* (WIA) revamped all job training programs in the country as well as reauthorized the Rehabilitation Act. According to the ACA Office of Public Policy and Information (1998c), the WIA streamlined requirements for the major federal grant programs which support training and related services for adults, dislocated workers, and disadvantaged youth. Under the WIA, all adults, regardless of income or employment status, became eligible for core services such as skills assessments, job search assistance, and information on educational and employment opportunities.

1998   *Reauthorization of the Rehabilitation Act.* As noted, the WIA reauthorized the Rehabilitation Act for another five years. The act funds state-administered vocational rehabilitation services for people with disabilities. In addition, the act funds research on rehabilitation and disabilities, training for rehabilitation counselors, independent living centers, advocacy services, and other initiatives that facilitate the employment of individuals with disabilities. The act upheld previous requirements that state agency professionals meet state or national certification or licensure requirements. This means that professional rehabilitation counselors need to hold a master's degree in rehabilitation counseling or a closely related field. The act extended this requirement to private contractors with state agencies.

1999   *Medicare, Medicaid, and SCHIP Balanced Budget Refinement Act* (Public Law 106–554) included a section requiring the Medicare Payment Advisory Commission (MedPAC) to conduct a study on the appropriateness of establishing Medicare coverage of licensed professional counselors and other non-physician providers, including marriage and family therapists and pastoral counselors. MedPAC issued a weakly written report recommending *against* covering licensed professional counselors, marriage and family therapists, and pastoral counselors in June of 2002. Although MedPAC came to a negative conclusion, the language in P.L. 106–554 calling for the report marked the first time that Congress and the president had enacted legislation referencing licensed professional counselors with respect to Medicare.

1999   *The Elementary School Counseling Demonstration Act* was approved as part of the Omnibus Spending Package for FY 2000. The act allocates $20 million for schools to hire *qualified* school counselors. These funds were made available to school districts that are awarded three-year grants by the Department of Education (ACA, 1999a).

1999   *The Work Incentives Improvement Act* (WIIA) may be considered the most significant federal law enacted for people with disabilities since the Americans with Disabilities Act passed in 1990 (ACA, 1999b). The WIIA removes many of the financial disincentives that have prevented millions of people with disabilities from working. For example, it changes outdated rules that ended Medicaid and Medicare coverage when people with disabilities entered or reentered the workplace. In addition, it extends Medicare Part A coverage for people on Social Security disability insurance who return to work for another four and a half years. It was estimated that this would result in a difference between monthly premiums of almost $350 (the cost of purchasing Part A and B coverage) and $45.50.

2000–2010

2001   *Department of Defense Authorization Act* (Public Law 106–398) included language requiring the Office of the Civilian Health and Medical Program of the Uniformed Services (known as TRICARE) Management Authority to conduct a demonstration project allowing mental health counselors to practice independently, without physician referral and supervision. In 2001, licensed professional counselors were the only nationally-recognized mental health professionals required by TRICARE to operate under physician referral and supervision.

2001   *No Child Left Behind Act* (NCLB, Public Law 107–110) was a massive reauthorization of the federal education programs contained in the Elementary and Secondary Education Act and included language renaming the Elementary School Counseling Demonstration Program the Elementary and Secondary School Counseling Program (ESSCP). This language both removed the "demonstration" tag from the program, and expanded it to secondary schools. Under the NCLB language, the first $40 million appropriated for the program in any year must be devoted to supporting counseling programs and services in elementary schools.

2006   *The Veterans Benefits, Healthcare, and Information Technology Act* (Public Law 109–461) includes language establishing explicit recognition of licensed mental health counselors as health care professionals within the Department of Veterans Affairs (VA) health care programs. In addition to allowing the hiring of licensed professional counselors in clinical and supervisory positions with VA health care facilities, enactment of this provision should lead to the development of a position description for counselors by the Federal Office of Personnel Management, which would be applicable to all federal agencies.

2008   *The Paul Wellstone and Pete Domenici Mental Health Parity and Addiction Equity Act* (included in Division C of Public Law 110–343) prohibits health insurance plans from placing financial requirements or treatment limitations on the use of mental health or substance use disorder benefits that are not also used for substantially all other medical/surgical benefits. The law aims to end the inequities in insurance coverage for the treatment of behavioral disorders, although insurance companies are allowed to continue to use standard care management practices such as utilization review and the use of medical necessity criteria. The law exempts policies covering fewer than 50 employees.

2010   *The Patient Protection and Affordable Care Act* (Public Law 111–148, as amended by Public Law 111–152) establishes, for the first time, a functioning health insurance system for the U.S., based on employer-provided private health insurance for Americans who are in the workforce combined with public health insurance coverage and support for those without affordable private sector coverage. Importantly for counselors, the legislation requires health insurance plans to cover mental and addictive disorder services—and to do so meeting the requirements of the Mental Health Parity and Addiction Equity Act. In addition, the law contains a provision prohibiting health plans from discriminating against providers on the basis of their type of license. The major coverage expansion provisions of the law, including the operation of state health insurance exchanges, take effect in 2014, as does the provider nondiscrimination provision.

Continuing Development of Professional Identity

History of the American Counseling Association

The mission of the American Counseling Association is "to enhance the quality of life in society by promoting the development of professional counselors, advancing the counseling profession, and using the profession and practice of counseling to promote respect for human dignity and diversity"(http://www.counseling.org/AboutUs/). Table 2.1 shows the divisional structure of ACA as of January 2012 along with the year in which each division was founded. It is beyond the scope of this chapter to provide a detailed description of each of the divisions and we strongly encourage students to review the information on all of the divisions that can be accessed through the ACA website (www.counseling.org).

Vacc and Loesch (1994) noted that one way to understand the evolution of a profession is to study the history of a representative professional organization. The American Counseling Association (ACA) has a rich history that exemplifies its representation of professional counselors. The philosophical development of the counseling profession can be seen by reviewing the three names by which ACA has been known, along with the times those name changes occurred. From its founding in 1952 until 1983, ACA was known as the American Personnel and Guidance Association (APGA). From 1983 until 1992, it was called the American Association for Counseling and Development (AACD). In 1992, the governing body of the association renamed it the American Counseling Association. For purposes of simplicity, the association will be referred to as ACA regardless of the time reference.

Although its official inception is noted as 1952, ACA can trace its organizational beginnings to the turn of the 20th century with the formation of one of its founding divisions, then the National Vocational Guidance Association. Its roots in vocational guidance, education, and psychology have made for an interesting, rich, and often rocky evolution of counseling as a profession unto itself, even before the founding of ACA. The NVGA had considered changing its name at least five times between 1922 and 1948 to better reflect the concern members had about the total adjustment of their clients (Norris, 1954).

Table 2.1 Divisions of the American Counseling Association as of January 2012

AACE	Association for Assessment in Counseling and Education (founded in 1965; formerly the Association for Measurement and Evaluation in Guidance).
AADA	Association for Adult Development and Aging (founded in 1986).
ACAC	Association for Child and Adolescent Counseling (organizational affiliate founded in 2011; at the time this chapter was written, this was listed on ACA membership brochures but had not yet achieved divisional status).
ACC	Association for Creativity in Counseling (founded in 2004).
ACCA	American College Counseling Association (founded in 1991).
ACEG	Association for Counselors and Educators in Government (founded in 1984).
ACES	Association for Counselor Education and Supervision (founded in 1938; one of the founding organizations of ACA; formerly the National Association of Guidance Supervisors and Counselor Trainers).
AHC	Association for Humanistic Counseling (founded in 1931; one of the founding ACA organizations; formerly the Student Association for Teacher Education [SPATE], Association for Humanistic Education and Development, and Counseling Association for Humanistic Education and Development [CHEAD]).
AGLBIC	Association of Lesbian, Gay, Bisexual, and Transgender Issues in Counseling (founded in 1996 as the Association of Gay, Lesbian, and Bisexual Issues in Counseling).
AMCD	Association for Multicultural Counseling and Development (founded in 1972 as the Association for Non-white Concerns in Personnel and Guidance).
AMHCA	American Mental Health Counselors Association (founded in 1976).
ARCA	American Rehabilitation Counseling Association (founded in 1958 as the Division of Rehabilitation Counseling).
ASCA	American School Counselors Association (founded in 1953).
ASERVIC	Association for Spiritual, Ethical and Religious Values in Counseling (founded in 1974 as the National Catholic Guidance Conference).
ASGW	Association for Specialists in Group Work (founded in 1973).
CSJ	Counselors for Social Justice (founded in 1999).
IAAOC	International Association of Addictions and Offenders Counselors (founded in 1972 as the Public Offender Counselor Association).
IAMFC	International Association of Marriage and Family Counselors (founded in 1989).
NCDA	National Career Development Association (founded in 1913 and was one of the founding ACA organizations; formerly the National Vocational Guidance Association).
NECA	National Employment Counseling Association (founded in 1966).

Members of the American Council of Guidance and Personnel Associations, a federation of associations, were also considering whether it was wise or efficient to attempt to belong to several organizations doing essentially the same thing. Groups belonging to the federation had the practice of meeting in conventions at the same time and place. By the late 1940s, groups had established their identities in work settings, and members had begun to see commonalities of purpose and function. The name of the federation had changed from the American Council of Guidance and Personnel Associations (ACGPA) to the Council of Guidance and Personnel Associations (CGPA) in 1939, so there was a precedent for a name change.

In 1948 Daniel Feder, as chair of CGPA and president of NVGA, urged forming a national organization to include individuals as well as associations. A committee on unification was appointed to develop a plan for such an organization. Its plan was presented at the 1950 convention and forwarded to the organizations concerned (McDaniels, 1964). Both the NVGA and the American College Personnel Association approved the plan and arranged their constitutions to join the new organization as divisions in 1951. At this time the Personnel and Guidance Association (PGA) was born. The following year, 1952, PGA changed its name to the American Personnel and Guidance Association (APGA) to avoid confusion with the Professional Golfers Association (PGA). APGA is now known as the American Counseling Association (ACA). Table 2.2 presents highlights of the ACA's development since its founding.

Table 2.2 Organizational Chronology of the American Counseling Association

Year	Division name	Event
1951	PGA	The Personnel and Guidance Association was formed.
1952	APGA	American Personnel and Guidance Association became the new name for PGA
1952		*The following divisions became founding partners of APGA:*
	ACPA	American College Personnel Association
	NVGA	National Vocational Guidance Association
	SPATE	Student Personnel Association for Teacher Education
	NAGSCT	National Association of Guidance Supervisors and College Trainers.
		The following divisions became part of ACA or changed their names:
1953	ASCA	American School Counselors Association became a division.
1958	DRC	ACA added the Division of Rehabilitation Counseling.
1961	ACES	Association for Counselor Education and Supervision replaced the former NAGSCT.
1962	ARCA	American Rehabilitation Counseling Association became the new name for the former DRC.
1965	AMEG	Association for Measurement and Evaluation in Guidance was established.
1966	NECA	National Employment Counselors Association became a division.
1972	ANWIC	Association for Non-White Concerns in Personnel and Guidance was formed.
1973	ASGW	Association for Specialists in Group Work was established.
1974	NCGC	National Catholic Guidance Conference became a division.
	POCA	Public Offender Counselor Association was established.
1975	AHEAD	Association for Humanistic Education and Development replaced the former SPATE.
1977	ARVIC	Association for Religious Values in Counseling replaced what had been known as NCGA.
1978	AMHCA	American Mental Health Counselors Association became a division.
1983	AACD	American Association for Counseling and Development became the new name for what had been called APGA.
1984	AMECD	Association for Measurement and Evaluation in Counseling became the new name for the former AMEG.
	NCDA	National Career Development Association became the new name of the former NVGA.
	AMCD	Association for Multicultural Counseling and Development replaced the former Association for Non-White Concerns in Personnel and Guidance.

Table 2.2 Continued

Year	Division name	Event
1984	MECA	Military Educators and Counselors Association became an organization affiliate of AACD.
1986	AADA	Association for Adult Development and Aging was formed.
1989	IAMFC	International Association of Marriage and Family Counselors was established.
1990	IAAOC	Association of Addiction and Offender Counselors replaced the former POCA.
1991	ACCA	American College Counselors Association was formed to replace ACPA, which was in the process of withdrawing from ACA.
1992	ACPA	American College Personnel Association disaffiliated from ACA.
	AAC	Association for Assessment in Counseling became the new name for AMECD.
1993	ASERVIC	Association for Spiritual, Ethical and Religious Values in Counseling became the new name for ARVIC.
1995	ACEG	Association for Counselors and Educators in Government became the new name for MECA.
1996	AGLBIC	Association of Gay, Lesbian, and Bisexual Issues in Counseling became an organizational affiliate.
1997	AGLBIC	AGLBIC achieved division status.
1998	ACEG	ACEG became a division.
1999	CSJ	Counselors for Social Justice became an organizational affiliate.
	C-AHEAD	AHEAD changed its name to the Counseling Association for Humanistic Education and Development.
2002	CSJ	CSJ became a division.
2004	ACC	Association for Creativity in Counseling became a division.
2003	AACE	AAC changed its name to the Association for Assessment in Counseling and Education.
2007	ALGBTIC	AGLBIC voted changed its name to the Association for Lesbian, Gay, Bisexual, and Transgender Issues in Counseling (anticipated effective date is 2008).
2010	AHC	Counseling Association for Humanistic Education and Development changed its name to the Association for Humanistic Counseling.
2011	ACAC	Association for Child and Adolescent Counseling became ACA's newest organizational affiliate.

Professionalism: A Developmental Perspective

A review of Table 2.2 indicates not only the developmental nature of the ACA but also the evolving diversity of its divisions and its membership. The concept of unification was a common theme in this country in the 1950s (Vacc & Loesch, 1994). This trend may have influenced the four independent founding organizations: NVGA (now NCDA), American College Personal Association (replaced as an ACA division now by ACCA), the National Association of Guidance and Counselor Trainers (NAGSCT, now ACES), and SPATE (now ACH; the Association for Humanistic Counseling) to come together to work as one federation. The basic format of autonomous divisions working within an umbrella organization has continued to the present time. Divisions have been added as members' interests or counselor work settings changed because of changes in the socio-economic milieu.

Change is very much reflected in the chronological evolution of ACA. For example, the parent organization, APGA, changed its name twice over a 40-year period. Before 1983, APGA began to feel pressures from its membership for a name change that would accurately reflect the purposes and work activities of its members. The terms *guidance* and *personnel* were onerous to some members. In addition to describing the profession better, the term *counseling* was more prestigious and better understood by the public. By 1983, several of the divisions already recognized the terms *counseling* or *counselor* in their titles (ASCA, ARCA, ACES, ARVIC, POCA, NECA, and AMHCA). To appease its growing and diverse membership, to have a clearer identity with counseling, and to attract new members in a changing society, APGA became the American Association for Counseling and Development (AACD). Nine years later in 1992, the name was again changed to the American Counseling Association, removing the word *development* from its title.

Beginning in 1952 with four divisions, the first new division to join the parent organization was the American School Counselors Association (ASCA) in 1953, which quickly became one of the two largest ACA divisions. After World War II, there was a growing recognition in America that people with disabilities had counseling needs. At the same time that the Veterans Administration was attempting to meet the needs of returning World War II servicemen and women, a number of ACA members were becoming involved in rehabilitation counseling. These factors resulted in the organization of the second new division to join ACA, the American Rehabilitation Counseling Association (ARCA) in 1957 (known as the Division of Rehabilitation Counseling from 1957 to 1962). From that time until the present, divisions were created and revised to reflect changes in society and to meet the professional needs of ACA members. Following are just a *few examples*:

- During the 1960s and early 1970s there was increasing concern about minority representation with the structure of ACA. That concern, along with the general social consciousness movement in the 1960s and early 1970s, prompted the development of an interest-based division entitled the Association for Non-White Concerns in Personnel and Guidance (ANWIC), which was added in 1972.
- The formation of the Public Offender Counselor Association (POCA) in 1974 brought into the organization people involved with an increasing juvenile and probation population and those who worked with or within our prison systems. During the 1980s, the correlation between addictive and criminal behaviors became quite clear. Many POCA members became interested in broadening the focus of POCA, and it became the International Association of Addictions and Offenders Counselors (IAAOC) in 1990.
- The founding of the Association of Gay, Lesbian, and Bisexual Issues in Counseling (AGLBIC; which later became the Association of Lesbian, Gay, Bisexual and Transgender Issues in Counseling) in 1996 demonstrated the recognition of the growing numbers of counselors who serve clients dealing with issues associated with their sexual orientation.
- Counselors for Social Justice (CSJ) was formed as an organizational affiliate in 1999 to address issues related to social justice, oppression, and human rights within the counseling profession and the community at large. CSJ became an ACA division in 2002.

It is important to understand that the American Counseling Association is more than a collection of divisions. There is also a geographical regional structure: (1) North Atlantic (Connecticut, Delaware, the District of Columbia, Maine, Maryland, Massachusetts, New Hampshire, New Jersey, New York, Pennsylvania, Rhode Island, Vermont, and the Virgin Islands); (2) Southern (Alabama, Arkansas, Florida, Georgia, Kentucky, Louisiana, Mississippi, North Carolina, South Carolina, Tennessee, Texas, Virginia, and West Virginia); (3) Midwest (Illinois, Indiana, Iowa, Kansas, Michigan, Minnesota, Missouri, Nebraska, North Dakota, Ohio, Oklahoma, South Dakota, and Wisconsin); and (4) Western (Alaska, Arizona, California, Colorado, Hawaii, Idaho, Nevada, Montana, New Mexico, Oregon, Washington, Wyoming, and Utah). Each region, representing ACA state branches, was established to provide leadership training, professional development, and continuing education of branch members following the strategic plan adopted by the association.

Through its ACA Press, the association provides its membership with a plethora of books, scholarly journals, and monographs on topics of interest to counselors. Its workshop and home study program and regional and national conventions provide intensive training opportunities that keep members up-to-date and provide the continuing education units necessary to maintain licensure or certification. Its *Code of Ethics* (ACA, 2005) provides members and the public with both professional direction and guidance. Its legislative arm not only alerts members to current legislation that is either helpful or harmful to counseling but also gives members a voice in policy development at the federal, state, and local levels.

SIDEBAR 2.5 Belonging to Professional Associations: Are there Benefits or Just Costs?

Carefully explore ACA's website and take note of the resources available to students and professionals. Start to gather more information about specific divisions that interest you (go to http://www.counseling.org/AboutUs/DivisionsBranchesAnd Regions/TP/Divisions/CT2.aspx). Ask your professors, supervisors, and advisors about their professional involvement. What do you think are the benefits of professional membership in ACA and/or its divisions? Consider how you might become involved as a student.

Credentialing and the "Professionalization" of Counseling

The most commonly noted criteria used to evaluate whether an occupation has evolved to the status of a profession include (1) a specialized body of knowledge and theory-driven research, (2) the establishment of a professional society or association, (3) control of training programs, (4) a code of ethics to guide professional behavior, and (5) standards for admitting and policing practitioners (Caplow, 1966). Given these criteria, no historical perspective of the counseling profession can be considered complete without a discussion of the development of standards related to the preparation and practice of professional counselors.

The counseling profession has met the majority of conditions just noted. There is an evolving body of knowledge and systematic theories and a body of literature to provide a forum for such information. ACA serves as the primary professional association for counselors. There are standards for training programs, professional preparation, and ethical behavior (see Chapter 4). Accredited counselor-training programs have been established, and credentials are granted to individuals demonstrating professional competencies, and some form of licensure and/or certification for professional counselors now exists in all states, legally validating the profession.

SIDEBAR 2.6 Case Study: Understanding Counseling as a Profession

Alma is a graduate student in the first semester of her master's counseling program. At a family gathering, Alma's cousin Hector asks why she needs a master's degree to learn how to listen to people. He explains his belief that being a counselor is basically the same thing as being a good friend. You just have to listen to people and give good advice. He tells Alma that she is already good at those things and does not understand why she cannot just start her private counseling practice now. After all, she already went to college and was even a "peer counselor" in her residence hall! Explain how Alma could respond to her cousin about the profession of counseling. How is counseling different than "being a good friend?" Have you encountered similar situations or questions from friends or family members? How did you respond? How might you respond differently after reading this chapter?

The term *credentialing* was created to represent a broad array of activities pertaining to the establishment of professional training standards and regulations for practice (Bradley, 1991) such as accreditation of academic programs, national board certification, and state licensure. Following is an overview of each of these areas as relates to the counseling profession.

Accreditation

Accreditation is one means of providing accountability. The licensed professions in this country began the process of regulation and quality control by developing standards for training programs. According to the Council for Higher Education Accreditation (CHEA, 2008, para.1),

> Accreditation is a process of external quality review used by higher education to scrutinize colleges, universities and educational programs for quality assurance and quality improvement. In the United States, accreditation is carried out by private, nonprofit organizations designed for this specific purpose. Institutions and educational programs seek accredited status as a means of demonstrating their academic quality to students and the public and to become eligible for federal funds.

The development of standards of preparation for counselors began approximately 50 years ago when a joint committee of the ACES and ASCA, divisions of ACA, began two major studies in 1960. More than 700 counselor educators and supervisors and 2,500 practicing counselors participated in the studies over a 5-year period (Altekruse & Wittmer, 1991). The results facilitated the creation of the "Standards for Counselor Education in the Preparation of Secondary School Counselors," the first set of standards sanctioned for counselor education, in 1964. After a 3-year trial, they were officially adopted by ACES in 1967 (Association for Counselor Education and Supervision, 1967). Shortly thereafter,

"Standards for Preparation of Elementary School Counselors" (APGA, 1968) and "Guidelines for Graduate Programs in the Preparation of Student Personnel Workers in Higher Education" (APGA, 1969) were established.

The Council on Rehabilitation Education (CORE), incorporated as a specialized accrediting body with a focus on rehabilitation counseling in 1972, was a forerunner in setting educational standards and graduate program accreditation in counseling (Sweeney, 1991). The leaders responsible for the creation of the Council for Accreditation of Counseling and Related Educational Programs (CACREP) used CORE as a model. Both councils require similar generic counseling curricula (not focused on specialties) and standards. In addition, CORE focuses on rehabilitation counselor education (RCE) curricula while CACREP addresses program area curricula and standards in other specialty areas but does not include specific RCE curricula.

Council on Rehabilitation Education (CORE)

In addition to ARCA, the following four professional organizations were represented on the first CORE board: Council of Rehabilitation Educators (now the National Council on Rehabilitation Education, NCRE), Council of State Administrators of Vocational Rehabilitation (CSAVR), International Association of Rehabilitation Facilities (now American Rehabilitation Association, ARA), and the National Rehabilitation Counseling Association (NRCA). CORE's current membership has two public members, the chair of the Commission on Standards and Accreditation, and individuals appointed from the following sponsoring organizations: NRCA, ARCA, NCRE, CSAVR, and the National Council of State Agencies for the Blind (NCSAB).

As of February 2012, CORE had accredited 92 master's programs offering a degree in rehabilitation counseling (CORE, 2012). Since its creation, CORE has reviewed and revised the standards for the accreditation of master's programs in rehabilitation counselor education on a regular basis. The first major standards revisions in 1981 were followed by revisions in 1988, 1997, 2004, and 2011. The most recent revisions in the CORE standards can be reviewed on the CORE Web site (www.core-rehab.org). According to the 2011 standards all CORE-accredited programs are expected to address the following 10 curricular areas of study: professional identity and ethical behavior; psychosocial aspects of disability and cultural diversity; human growth and development; employment and career development; counseling approaches and principles; group work and family dynamics; assessment; research and program evaluation; medical, functional, environmental aspects of disability; and rehabilitation services, case management, and related services (CORE, 2011). Supervised practicum and internship experiences are required under the 1997, 2004, and 2011 standards. These experiences are very similar to the current (2009) CACREP standards.

Council for Accreditation of Counseling and Related Educational Programs (CACREP)

According to Altekruse and Wittmer (1991), ACES developed "Standards for Entry Preparation of Counselors and Other Personnel-Service Specialists" in 1973. This document, which merged earlier guidelines, was officially adopted by the ACA governing body in 1979. At that time, ACES was the only association using the standards of training. Not until 1981 did ACA's board of directors (governing council) adopt a resolution to formally oversee the responsibilities of the ACES National Committee on Accreditation.

This led to the establishment of the Council for Accreditation of Counseling and Related Educational Programs (CACREP), which was formed as an independently incorporated accrediting body, separate from but affiliated with ACA (CACREP, 1987). Since its inception, CACREP has conducted reviews of its accreditation standards. After the initial flurry of changes to the 1981 standards, CACREP declared a 5-year time period during which only minor changes would be allowed (Altekruse & Wittmer, 1991). There have been four significant revisions made to the 1981 standards adopted by CACREP, in 1988, 1994, 2001, and 2009. These revisions are necessary to keep up with the continually evolving field of counseling and, at the time this chapter was written, CACREP had begun its fifth review process.

In addition to providing for accreditation of doctoral-level programs in counselor education and supervision, the 2001 CACREP standards (CACREP, 2001) also provided for the accreditation of master's degree programs in the following specialty areas: career counseling (separate from community counseling); college counseling (no longer listed as an emphasis area under student affairs); community counseling; gerontological counseling (accredited separately from community counseling); marital, couple, and family counseling/therapy (instead of "marriage and family counseling/therapy"); mental health counseling; school counseling; and student affairs. A major revision in the 2009 standards involved combining the community counseling and mental health program areas into one clinical mental health counseling program area and combining the college counseling and student affairs program areas into one student affairs and college counseling program area. Under the most current CACREP standards (CACREP, 2009), however, the specialty areas are listed as: addiction counseling; career counseling; clinical mental health counseling; marriage and family counseling/therapy; school counseling; and student affairs and college counseling.

As of February 2012, CACREP had 601accredited programs (Jenny Gunderman, CACREP staff, personal communication, February 22, 2012). Of these 601 programs, 60 were doctoral level, and 541 master's level programs in 266 institutions. The majority of the master's programs were in the areas of school counseling (218) and community counseling (156). In addition, there were 32 clinical mental health (accredited under the 2009 standards) and 55 mental health accredited programs (accredited under the 2001 standards), 34 college counseling or student affairs accredited programs (11 college counseling and 19 student affairs accredited under the 2001 standards and 4 programs accredited as "student affairs and college counseling" under the 2009 standards), 36 accredited marriage and family counseling/therapy programs, 9 accredited career counseling programs, and 1 accredited gerontological counseling program (which is no longer included in the 2009 standards) (Jenny Gunderman).

All academic programs accredited by CACREP, regardless of specialty designation, share a common core of curricular requirements. According to the 2009 CACREP Accreditation Procedures Manual (CACREP, 2009), all accredited programs must address the following eight curricular areas: professional orientation and ethical practice, social and cultural diversity, human growth and development, career development, helping relationships, group work, assessment, and research and program evaluation. Supervised practica and internships also are required across all program areas. In addition to these common core areas, CACREP-accredited programs must also offer specific types of curricular experiences related to the program accreditation, such as clinical mental health, school counseling, and student affairs and college counseling.

In addition to shifts in the areas of specialization that are accredited by CACREP, the 2009 standards represent a significant shift from knowledge-based to outcome- or performance-based standards. Under the current standards, students are required to demonstrate the ability to implement their knowledge in the core and program or concentration areas, and departments are required to document these outcomes. An additional major change in the 2009 standards is that new full-time faculty hired after 2013 will be required to have earned a doctoral degree in counselor education (rather than counseling psychology or other related disciplines) if they have not already taught in counselor education programs.

Certification

Certification is one of the most confusing of the credentialing terms (Brown & Srebalus, 1988). It is used in reference to (1) the process of becoming qualified to practice in public schools, (2) state laws passed in the same ways as licensure laws, and (3) recognition bestowed on individuals by their professional peers (such as certified public accountants). Certification most typically grants recognition of competence by a professional group or governmental unit and allows for the use of certain titles (e.g., National Certified Counselor) but does not confer authority to the holder to practice a profession or restrict others who are not certified from practicing a profession (Forrest & Stone, 1991. An exception to this is that professional counselors holding positions in public schools must be certified by the state to do so.

Types and Purposes of Certification

Certification in Schools

As noted, state boards or departments of education, by authority of state legislatures, establish certification standards for teachers, counselors, administrators, and other school personnel. Certification of school counselors first began in Boston and New York in the 1920s, but not until the National Defense Education Act (NDEA) was passed in 1958 did this type of certification take hold nation-wide. By 1967 more than 24,000 guidance counselors were trained under NDEA funding. The NDEA also mandated the establishment of criteria that would qualify schools to receive funds for the services of school counselors, which led to the rapid growth of certification (Sweeney, 1991).

National Board Certification

Many professional groups have initiated credentialing efforts at the national and the state levels to encourage excellence by promoting high standards of training, knowledge, and supervised experience. These standards promulgated by professional organizations may or may not be considered by governmental agencies, such as state departments of education or mental health, in relation to hiring and promotion requirements (Sweeney, 1991).

The first counseling-related national certification addressed the specialty of rehabilitation counseling. During the late 1960s, rehabilitation counselors belonging to the National Rehabilitation Counselors Association and American Rehabilitation Counselors Association (an ACA division) began to work together toward establishing certification for rehabilitation counseling specialists (Forrest & Stone, 1991). Their efforts came to fruition in 1973, when the Commission on Rehabilitation Counselor Certification, known as CRCC, began to certify rehabilitation counselors (Forrest & Stone, 1991;

Sweeney, 1991). More than 16,600 rehabilitation counselors were designated as CRCs as of February 2012 (Susan Stark, CRCC staff, personal communication, February 10, 2012). Until recently, in addition to the general certification in rehabilitation counseling (CRC), CRCC offered specialty certification in addictions counseling and in clinical supervision. CRCC is no longer accepting new applications for certification in these specialties; however, individuals currently certified in these specialties who meet the continuing education requirements may apply for certification renewal.

CRCC divides the criteria for certification as a CRC into several categories. Depending on the category under which the applicant is seeking certification, requirements include either a minimum of a master's degree in counseling (non-specified) or a master's degree specifically in rehabilitation counseling. In addition to the requirement of a master's, CRCs are required to have relevant supervised professional experience as a rehabilitation counselor (if the applicant did not graduate from a CORE-accredited program) and successful completion of the CRCC examination (CRCC, 2012). The supervised experience requirement varies, depending on the type of degree earned by the applicant.

As previously noted, graduates of CORE-accredited programs are not required to have post-master's employment experience before applying to become a CRC. They do, however, need to complete an internship of 600 clock hours supervised by an on-site CRC or a faculty member who is a CRC. The internship must be in rehabilitation counseling. Those who graduate with a master's in rehabilitation counseling from a non-CORE-accredited program must demonstrate the completion of an internship comparable to that in CORE-accredited programs and must have 12 months of acceptable employment experience under the supervision of a CRC (or complete a provisional contract). If applicants have a degree in rehabilitation counseling but do not have 600 hours of internship in rehabilitation counseling, they must have 24 months of acceptable employment experience, including a minimum of 12 months under the supervision of a CRC; if lacking the supervision by a CRC, they must complete a provisional contract (CRCC, 2012).

There also are eligibility criteria for individuals with master's degrees in counseling with an emphasis other than rehabilitation counseling who have had a minimum of one graduate course with a primary focus on theories and techniques of counseling. CRCC staff reviews applicants' transcripts to determine that they have had required courses. The employment requirements vary for these applicants, depending on the number of required courses they have taken. Readers are referred to the CRCC website, http://www.crccertification.com, for additional information about specific requirements for individuals with master's degrees in counseling with a concentration other than rehabilitation counseling.

CRCC also offers certification to graduates of doctoral programs offering degrees in counseling or rehabilitation counseling. The doctoral transcript must include a minimum of one graduate-level course in theories and techniques of counseling, one graduate-level course in medical or psychosocial and cultural aspects of disabilities, and 600 hours of internship at the doctoral level in a rehabilitation setting supervised by a CRC or 12 months of acceptable employment experience under the supervision of a CRC. In all these situations (master's and doctoral level), if applicants meet the employment criteria but lack supervision by a CRC, they must complete a provisional contract (CRCC, 2012).

In 1979, the National Academy of Certified Clinical Mental Health Counselors (NACCMHC) was the next national counselor certifying body to be established. The NACCMHC merged with the National Board for Certified Counselors (NBCC) in 1992. Basic requirements to become a Certified Clinical Mental Health Counselor (CCMHC) include (1) completion of a minimum of 60 graduate semester hours, (2) graduation with a master's or higher degree from an accredited counselor-preparation program encompassing at least 2 years of post-master's professional work experience that included a minimum of 3000 client-contact hours and 100 clock hours of individual supervision by a CCMHC or a professional who holds an equivalent credential, (3) submission of an audio recording or video recording of a counseling session, and (4) successful completion of the CCMHC's Mental Health Counselor Examination for Specialization in Clinical Counseling (NBCC, 1995). Weikel and Palmo (1989) noted that the stringent requirements to become a CCMHC may be one reason that there were only slightly more than 1000 National Certified Clinical Mental Health Counselors (NCCMHCs) in 1985.

At the time this chapter was written, NBCC was probably the most visible and largest national counselor-certifying body. As of February 2012, NBCC had certified more than 49,800 National Certified Counselors, or NCCs (Kristi McCaskill, NBCC staff, personal communication, February 16, 2012). The founding of NBCC offered the public a way to identify professional counselors who meet knowledge and skills criteria set forth by the counseling profession in the general practice of counseling. This was especially important given the paucity of counselor licensure laws at that time. The concept of a general practice of counseling is in line with CACREP's belief that there is a common core of knowledge that is shared by all professional counselors, regardless of any specific area of specialization.

To be certified by NBCC as a National Certified Counselor (NCC), applicants must: (1) hold a master's degree or higher with major study in counseling, including a minimum of 48 semester hours or 72 quarter hours in graduate coursework; (2) demonstrate that their graduate coursework was from a regionally accredited institution and includes at least one course (carrying at least two semester/three quarter ours) in each of the required coursework areas; (3) have successfully completed two academic terms of supervised field experience in a counseling setting or 1 additional year of post-master's supervised experience (1,500 additional hours of counseling experience including 50 extra hours of face-to-face supervision) beyond the required 2 years of post-master's supervised experience; (4) provide two professional endorsements; and (5) pass the National Counselor Examination (NCE) (or another NBCC examination depending on the application) (Kristi McCaskill, NBCC staff, personal communication, February 16, 2012). Counselors who have not graduated from a CACREP-accredited program must also document the completion of a minimum of 3,000 hours of work as a counselor over at least 24 months since the date an advanced degree with a major study in counseling was conferred. In addition, these individuals need to document that they received at least 100 hours of face-to-face counseling supervision over a minimum of 2 years, provided by a supervisor who holds an advanced degree in counseling or mental health field (social work, psychology, or marriage and family therapy). NBCC offers specialty certifications in addictions, clinical mental health, and school counseling. Of the current specialties, as of January, 2012, there were more than 1,100 Certified Clinical Mental Health Counselors (CCMHC), more than 700 Master Addictions Counselors, (MAC) and more than 2,600 National Certified School Counselors (NCSC) (Kristi McCaskill, NBCC staff, personal communication, February 16, 2012).

NBCC and CRCC are not, however, the only bodies that certify specialists in counseling and counseling-related specialties. For example, the National Board for Professional Teaching Standards (NBPTS) offers certification in school counseling in addition to teaching. NBCC participated in negotiations with NBPTS for quite some time to arrive at joint standards (similar to the MAC standards adopted by both NBCC and the National Association of Alcoholism and Drug Abuse Counselors). Negotiations apparently broke down, and NBPTS moved forward with plans. One major problem in developing mutually agreed upon standards was that the NBPTS had proposed certifying school counselors who do not hold a master's degree in counseling. This has been a core criterion for all NBCC credentials. As of February 2012, NBPTS had certified 2246 school counselors at the early childhood/young adult level (Jasmine Green, NBPTS, personal communication, February 21, 2012). It is unclear what this may mean for how school counselors perceive themselves in regard to being counselors or educators first and how having national certification offered by both NCCC and NBPTS will influence the public's perceptions of counselors.

Licensure

According to the ACA (2010), licensure is a credential granted or sanctioned by governmental bodies such as state legislatures that regulates either the title, practice, or both of an occupational group. Although states enact licensure laws as a means to protect the public from incompetent practitioners, such laws also provide benefits for the profession being regulated. The very fact that a state considers a profession important enough to regulate may lead to an enhanced public image and increased recognition for that profession. In addition, more and more, being licensed has become necessary to be recognized and reimbursed by insurance companies and government and private mental health programs.

Just as certification can be confusing, so, too, can the concept of licensure. There are two primary types of licensure laws for counselors; title and practice acts (ACA, 2010b). States with practice acts require people to be licensed or to meet criteria for exemption from licensing noted in those laws to engage in specified counseling activities. Individuals in states with title acts must be licensed to refer to themselves as "licensed professional counselors" or use other counseling-related titles, but counselors may engage in the practice of counseling without being licensed. The majority of states have adopted practice acts for professional counselors (please see the section on Current Trends and Issues in this chapter for additional information). Sweeney (1991) pointed out that it is essential to examine specific state laws and their accompanying regulations to determine the implications for practice. ACA assists counselors in this process by providing information about licensure requirements in each state and the District of Columbia on its Website (http://www.counseling.org). In addition to using resources provided by ACA, we strongly encourage practitioners to directly contact the regulatory boards in their states to determine if they need a license to practice counseling and what they may and may not call themselves.

1970s in Virginia: The Beginning of Licensure for Counselors

Licensure of counseling practitioners, separate from psychologists, can be traced to the early 1970s. Before 1976, no state law defined or regulated the general profession of counseling. This left the profession in a state of legal limbo—although counseling was not expressly forbidden (except where the laws regulating psychology specifically limited activities of professional counselors), it was not legally recognized as a profession, either (Brooks, 1986). At that time, the American Psychological Association began to call for stringent psychology licensure laws that would preclude other professionals from rendering any form of "psychological" services. In Virginia, this resulted in a cease-and-desist order being served to John Weldon, a counselor in private practice, in 1972 (Hosie, 1991;

Sweeney, 1991). The Virginia State Board of Psychologist Examiners obtained a court order restraining Weldon from rendering private practice services in career counseling (Weldon v. Virginia State Board of Psychologist Examiners, 1972). The board claimed that Weldon was in fact practicing psychology, even though he presented himself as providing guidance and counseling services. In October 1972, Weldon was found to be practicing outside the law, but the court also ruled that the Virginia legislature had created the problem by violating his right to practice his chosen profession of counseling. The court proclaimed that personnel and guidance was a profession separate from psychology and should be recognized and regulated as such (Hosie, 1991). In response to the Weldon case, the Virginia legislature passed a bill certifying personnel and guidance counselors for private practice in March 1975 (Swanson, 1988). This law was amended by the Virginia legislature in 1976 and became the first general practice act for professional counselors.

At about the same time, Culbreth Cook, an Ohio counselor, faced a challenge similar to that of Weldon. Cook, well known and respected in his community, was employed at a 2-year college and provided private educational assessment on a part-time basis. Cook's education and training qualified him to offer the assessment services he rendered, but he was arrested on the felony charge of practicing psychology without a license (Hosie, 1991; Swanson, 1988). Carl Swanson, an attorney, counselor educator, and ACA Licensure Committee cochair testified on Cook's behalf (Sweeney, 1991). The Cleveland Municipal Court judge refused to provide a restraining order against Cook, noting that even attorneys used the tools of psychology (City of Cleveland, Ohio v. Cook, 1975).

ACA has focused on licensure since the 1970s. In 1973, the first ACA licensure committee was created by the Southern Association for Counselor Education and Supervision (SACES) (Hosie, 1991; Sweeney, 1991). The next year ACA published a position statement on counselor licensure and, in 1975, appointed a special licensure commission. The commission distributed an action packet in 1976, including information about counselor licensure, the fourth draft of model state legislation, and strategies to pursue licensing (APGA, 1976). Model legislation offers a prototype for counselors in states that do not have licensure laws, in states that are in the process of revising their current laws, and where credentialing laws face sunset or legislative review (Glosoff, Benshoff, Hosie, & Maki, 1995). It also facilitates the development of uniform standards for the preparation and practice of professional counselors across the United States.

Progress Continues

Since the first model legislation for licensed professional counselors was created, ACA has revisited and amended its model to reflect changes in standards within the profession and experiences in states that have implemented counselor licensure laws. An underlying philosophy of ACA's model legislation is that state licensure laws legalize the general practice of counseling within each state, whereas the credentialing of counseling specialists remains under the purview of professional credentialing organizations such as CRCC and NBCC.

The rate of licensure for counselors during the two decades between the time Virginia passed the first counselor licensure law and the endorsement of ACA's 1994 model legislation is seen by some to be painstakingly slow and by others as quite rapid. Brooks (1986) noted that "legislative successes were distressingly slow in the years following 1974" (p. 253). During the early 1980s, licensure took off when 15 states passed some form of credentialing acts between 1981 and 1986, 14 passed laws between 1987 and 1989; and 7 passed laws between 1990 and 1994 (Glosoff et al., 1995). Having counseling licensure laws enacted at that rate of progress is exceptional when compared with the 20 years it took the first 18 state psychology laws to be passed (Brooks, 1988). Since 1994, licensure has been achieved in the remainder of all states, the District of Columbia, and Puerto Rico, and a number of states have passed amendments that have brought existing credentialing laws more into line with ACA's model legislation (for example, changing title acts to practice laws, expanding the scope of practice of professional counselors to include diagnosis and treatment of people with mental disorders, and increasing educational and experience requirements). This is further discussed in the next section on "Current Issues and Trends in Counseling."

Current Issues and Trends in Counseling

In 2012, ACA celebrated its 60th anniversary, making the profession of counseling still relatively young as compared to other mental health professions. Professional counselors continue to respond to both the needs of society and the pressures from various socioeconomic factors—some of which led to the kaleidoscope we know as counseling today and others that will shape the future of the profession. These needs and pressures cut across the various specialty areas of counseling and cannot be categorized or delineated as neatly as in a historical review of the profession. For example, counselors continue to deal with issues related to: the ongoing struggle for professional identity (including serving diverse clientele and providing services across a continuum of wellness to pathology); licensure, the recognition and reimbursement of professional counselors both through private and governmentally-based providers; multicultural counseling and social justice issues (see Chapter 3); and technology (see Chapter 7).

Professional Identity

The American Counseling Association

In 2012, with 19 national divisions, 1 organizational affiliate, 56 state and territorial branches, 4 regional assemblies, a myriad of divisional affiliates in each of the branches, and a membership of approximately 50,225 (Rae Ann Sites, personal communication, March 15, 2012) the American Counseling Association remains the strongest organization representing counselors on the national scene. It is not, however, without its problems. ACA developed from a "group of groups" and has been faced with ongoing organizational challenges that stem from the groups continued desire to have independence while working under an umbrella structure. In October 1997, the governing council voted to amend the ACA bylaws so that, effective July 1, 1998, ACA members were no longer required to also belong to a division and division members were no longer required to also belong to ACA. This freedom of choice for members has led to some interesting developments. As of December 1999, 14 of the then 18 divisions (77.8%) opted to require their *professional members* (typically defined as members with a master's degree in counseling) to belong to ACA in addition to their division. As of June 2012, only 9 of the divisions (47.4%) required *professional members* to also join ACA. Do members consider themselves professional counselors first and specialists second or the other way around? Issues related to divisional and ACA membership may certainly be influenced by professional identity and at the same time, may be influenced by finances and what counselors can afford to pay for association membership.

Although fewer divisions in 2012 as compared to 2000 require members to join ACA in order to be professional members of the division, at the time this chapter was written, approximately only 30% of all ACA members belonged to a division. It is difficult to discern how policy makers (e.g., legislators) view the structure of ACA. To date, a "strength in numbers" philosophy has facilitated passage of legislation that has been important to the provision of counseling services and the recognition of professional counselors. It seems that all ACA entities, regardless of whether ACA membership is required, have managed to work together to have a positive influence on the passage of some key pieces of legislation since 1997, as noted in this chapter. When examining the many laws that have been enacted, it is easy to see that professional counselors serve clients in a wide variety work settings. The types of persons being served as well as the role and function of counselors may differ based on the work settings. This, in turn, may lead to confusion about professional identity as perceived by the public. Who are counselors and who do they serve?

Diverse Clientele

Professional counselors provide services to people who exhibit a full range of functioning from healthy adaptation to pathology—from those seeking assistance with self-exploration to those individuals who are dysfunctional enough to require hospitalization. There is not enough space to comprehensively explore all of those work settings and types of services, but we will attempt to briefly review some of the major trends related to types of clients being served by counselors in a variety of work settings. The types of clients served by professional counselors are as diverse as the work settings in which counselors are employed. Following are a *few* examples of the types of clients receiving increasing attention from professional counselors.

INCARCERATION

According to the U.S. Department of Justice (Bureau of Justice Statistics, 2005), of the more than 2.1 million individuals incarcerated in state and local facilities in the United States, approximately 16.9% have a mental illness. Glaze and James (2006), however, reported that in 2005, closer to one half of individuals incarcerated in Federal and state prisons and local jails had reported mental health problems. It seems that our jails and prisons often are alternatives to mental health facilities for people who are homeless and have mental disorders and that individuals with substance abuse disorders are often being incarcerated rather than treated in the community. Mental health services clearly are needed in our jails and prisons. In addition, there are often significant implications for the children and other family members of persons who have been incarcerated. Counselors have been active in providing these services as well as advocating for effective treatment for many years (note the IAAOC was established in 1974).

VETERANS

A similar training issue exists in regards to counselors being adequately prepared to provide services to veterans. As previously discussed, the counseling profession has been strongly influenced by U.S. involvement in wars. Sadly, this continues today. Posttraumatic stress disorder (PTSD) and other mental health effects of combat can be seen in veterans years after they return home. Clawson (2007), testifying before the President's Commission on the Care of Wounded Warriors, noted that approximately one in eight soldiers who fought in Iraq reported symptoms of PTSD and that more than one in three soldiers who served in combat in Iraq, Afghanistan, and other locations later sought help for mental health problems. These numbers may increase as military personnel have been required to serve for longer periods than ever before without significant breaks. In addition, although veterans do not seek service only through the Department of Veterans Affairs (VA), many do—and the need to include processional counselors as among those qualified to provide such services was recognized by the Federal government with the enactment of the Veterans Benefits, Healthcare, and Information Technology Act of 2006, which recognized LPCs as mental health specialists within all health care programs operated by the Department of Veterans Affairs (VA) (ACA, 2007). Of course, the mental health needs of military personnel also have implications for their families and loved ones. In turn, this has implications for counselor education programs.

TRAUMATIC EVENTS

Military personnel are clearly not the only individuals to experience trauma. In addition to the more typical developmental types of crises with which clients often present, counselors are likely to come across clients who are dealing with trauma as a result of crises created by people or by nature. It is difficult to read a paper or listen to the news without hearing about violent crimes, car accidents, domestic violence, terrorist attacks, school shootings, and natural disasters (e.g., hurricanes, earthquakes, tornadoes). Cavaiola and Colfold (2006) note how common it is for individuals to feel overwhelmed and unable to cope with either being directly or indirectly affected by such types of events. It is not uncommon for survivors of major traumatic events such as the 9/11 attacks, Hurricane Katrina, and school/college shootings to suffer from symptoms of PTSD many years later, especially if they did not receive crisis counseling at the time of the event. Counselors need to be adequately prepared to provide crisis intervention as well as to work with long term effects of trauma. In fact, the 2009 CACREP standards specific that counselors must demonstrate both knowledge and skills related to crisis intervention, including psychological first aid.

OLDER POPULATIONS

There also has been a marked increase in counseling services targeted to older individuals. This makes sense, given the "graying of America" shown by the steadily increasing average age of the population. In 2010, approximately 13% of the U.S. population was 65 years and older (U.S. Administration on Aging, 2011) and the Federal Interagency Forum on Aging-Related Statistics (2010) projects that by 2030, approximately 20% of the total U.S. population will be 65 years and older. In 2008, a large percentage of older Americans were still in the labor force: more than 50% of men and 42% of women ages 62–64; 36% of men (up from 25% in 1993) and 26% of women (up from 17% in 1993) (Federal Interagency Forum on Aging-Related Statistics). Although a large number of older Americans are still in the labor force, we must consider that a number of these individuals are ready or will be ready to retire and some would prefer to retire but remain in the labor force only because of economic needs. Given our strong roots in the career development area, this seems to be an excellent market for professional counselors. In addition to work-related issues, older adults are faced with mental health and substance abuse problems. For example, according to the Federal Interagency Forum (2010), in 2006 approximately 18% of women and 10% of men in the U.S. ages 65 and older reported clinical symptoms of depression. In addition, individuals 65 and older account for 14% of all completed suicides in the U.S. although only 12. 4% of the U.S. population is 65 or older (Centers for Disease Control and Prevention [CDC], 2009). The CDC reported depression as one of the leading risk factors in older adults, along with chronic illnesses and pain, experiencing significant losses and a sense of social isolation, and losing a sense of meaning or purpose in life. Further, according to Han, Gfroerer, Colliver, and Penne (2009), admissions for substance abuse treatment for people who were 50 or older increased by almost 50% between 2004 and 2009, yet the number of facilities offering specialized services to older adults decreased.

ADDICTIONS

Older adults are certainly not the only ones in the U.S. who struggle with addictions of some kind. According to a report made by the SAMHSA (2009) to congress, more than 23 million Americans age 12 and older required treatment for substance-related problems and that large numbers of individuals do not have access to such services because of lack of adequately trained mental health professionals. In fact, Kaplan (2003) predicted that 5,000 new mental health professionals will be needed each year to replace those who leave positions in the field of substance abuse. These data do not begin to address the need of adolescents and adults with process addictions such as internet, gambling, and sexual addictions. The expansion of services in the addictions area can be seen in the numbers of states that offer certification to people who specialize in the delivery of addictions counseling as well as professional associations such as the National Board for Certified Counselors, the Commission on Rehabilitation Counselor Certification, and the National Association for Addictions Professionals to name a few.

SERVING INDIVIDUALS WHO ARE GAY, LESBIAN, BISEXUAL, OR TRANSGENDER (GLBT)

We have seen estimates that between 4 and 18% of the U.S population are bisexual, gay, lesbian or transgendered. This variance indicates the difficulty in obtaining accurate demographic information on sexual orientation. Sexual orientation and gender identification are not easily measured constructs, and individuals who are gay, lesbian, bisexual, or transgendered (GLBT) may be reluctant to identify themselves as such in surveys. Regardless, the results of several studies have strongly indicated that many individuals who are GLBT experience bullying and discrimination in their schools while growing up and in their workplaces as adults. For example, according to the Williams Institute (2007), since the mid-1990s, there have been 15 studies in which 15% to 43% of GLBT respondents experienced discrimination in the workplace (e.g., being fired or denied employment based on their sexual orientation, being verbally or physically abused). In addition, 15% to 57% of people who identified as transgendered reported experiencing employment discrimination. The 2009 National School Climate Survey conducted by the Gay, Lesbian, and Straight Education Network (GLSEN, 2010) indicated that of the 7,261 middle and high school students who responded to a survey, 9 out of 10 reported experiencing some form of harassment in schools in the past year due to their sexual orientation, and over 60% of the participants reported feeling unsafe in schools due to their sexual orientation. More than 72% of student participants have heard derogatory remarks and name-calling such as "faggot" or "dyke" frequently in their schools, 84.6 % were verbally harassed, 40.1% experienced physical harassment at school on the bases of sexual orientation, and 18.8% were physically assaulted. The results of the 2009 study further indicate that having supportive staff, such as counselors, makes a difference to students and is correlated with positive indicators such as a greater sense of safety, reports of missing fewer days of school, and a higher incidence of planning to attend college.

Counselors are likely to work with a client (child, adolescent, or adult) who is gay, lesbian, bisexual, transgender, or questioning her or his identity. Although clients may or may not be open about their sexual orientation, and their sexual orientation may or may not be a primary counseling issue, counselors must be prepared to work effectively with individual clients who are GLBT and to advocate for the affirmation, respect, and equal opportunity for all individuals, regardless of sexual orientation or gender identity. To assist counselors, ALGBTIC developed "Competencies for Counseling Transgender Clients" ((http://www.algbtic.org/resources/competencies), which were endorsed by the ACA Governing Council in 2009. In addition, in 2012 the ALGBTIC published "Competencies for Counseling with Lesbian, Gay, Bisexual, Queer, Questioning, Intersex and Ally Individuals (LGBQQIA)" (ALGBTIC LGBQQIA Competencies Taskforce, 2012; http://www.algbtic.orga/resources/competencies).

Wellness Orientation and Diagnosis

Another issue related to professional identity is what some perceive to be a tension because the roots of the counseling profession are in constructs of both wellness and pathology. Counselors are often thought of as traditionally working with well-functioning individuals and a "wellness" orientation not only remains the basis for many counselors' work, but also has been promoted in recent years (Lawson, Venart, Hazler, & Kottler, 2007). At the same time, counselors increasingly have been serving people with severe and chronic mental illness and addictions in hospital and community settings. Counselors working in community or clinical mental health agencies, rehabilitation facilities, substance or addictions treatment in- and out-patient facilities, and hospitals are expected to provide a variety of assessment, diagnostic, and counseling services with clients who exhibit a wide range of clinical disorders. There has been much discussion amongst professional counselors about the benefits and drawbacks to providing diagnostic services. For example, Seligman (2009) offers that the use of a diagnostic system provides for shared language or a framework for describing mental disorders. In addition, this framework offers counselors a way to make sense of symptoms presented by individuals and to make decisions about the most effective ways to work with those individuals. Conversely, the use of diagnostic labels can add to the stigma faced by people dealing with mental health issues, which were endorsed by the ACA Governing Council in 2009. Further, the concept of diagnosis has traditionally been associated with a medical model that is inconsistent with wellness-based and developmental approaches to counseling that focus more on individuals' strengths and contextual and cultural influences in their lives (Seligman, 2009). This raises the question of whether counselors can diagnose individuals while maintaining a wellness orientation: can we assess and diagnose without using a medical model?

There are models of wellness that focus on working with clients holistically; attending to mind, body, and spirit and all aspects of their lives. For example, Myers, Sweency, and

Witmer (2000) offer a model of wellness that focuses on five life tasks: spirituality, self-direction, work and leisure, friendship, and love. Such models, coupled with clinical observations, provide a framework for describing the condition or symptoms of individuals. Most typically, however, counselors working in mental health, addictions, rehabilitation facilities as well as others who tend to rely on insurance reimbursement, are required to use provide diagnoses or diagnostic impressions about clients using the Diagnostic and Statistical Manual of Mental Disorders (DSM), which is published by the American Psychiatric Association.

The DSM is currently in its fourth edition (DSM-IV-TR). According to the American Psychiatric Association (2000), the DSM attempts to use evidence-based criteria to present objective definitions for a wide variety of mental disorders. The authors further contend that the reliability of diagnoses made using the multi-axes DSM-IV-TR is increased because, most typically, individuals must present a specific number of symptoms before a clinician assigns a diagnosis. The authors, however, also note that there are several limitations to the DSM-IV-TR and proponents of the DSM as the primary diagnostic system to be used by mental health professionals support the revising of the manual. The American Psychiatric Association has been working on such as revision and the DSM-V is scheduled for publication in 2013. Several aspects of the revision process, including a perceived lack of an empirical foundation for the DSM categories, remain a topic of concern for many mental health professionals at the time this chapter was written. Several associations, including the ACA, have called on American Psychiatric Association to consider identified problems in methodology used to construct the revised manual.

As professional counselors continue to make strides in being recognized as qualified providers of services to individuals with diagnosable disorders, they will be hired in a broader array of community and hospital-based settings that will require them to use the DSM. Because of this, we anticipate that there will be on-going discussions regarding if it is possible to or how to balance the profession's roots in wellness and multiculturalism with marketplace and employment realities. As counselors serve an ever increasingly diverse clientele and as many counselors adopt post-modern theories of counseling, we believe the use of the DSM as the primary diagnostic system will be seen as an issue of ethical advocacy and alternative diagnostic systems will be proposed. Regardless of what diagnostic system counselors choose to use, it has been important that licensure laws include assessment, diagnosis, and treatment of persons with mental and emotional disorders as part of the scope of practice of licensed counselors.

Continued Progress in Licensure

In the 36 years since the passage of the Virginia certification law, all 50 states, the District of Columbia, and Puerto Rico have enacted some form of counselor credentialing legislation. It appears that counseling has made great progress in gaining recognition as a profession. For example, in 2010, 86.5% of the 52 jurisdictions with counselor credentialing laws were practice acts (ACA, 2010b), as compared to 53% of 43 jurisdictions in 1996. Another example of progress is that as of 2010, the majority of state licensing laws include language specifying that counselors who are licensed (at the highest level in those states with tiered licensure) can assess, diagnosis, and treat persons with mental disorders. A number of states include a caveat when discussing "assessment" in their licensure laws, noting that assessment by licensed counselors does not include the use of projective tests or individually administered tests of intelligence. It is critical to note that scope of practice requires an interpretation of state licensing laws; this is not always an easy task as legislative language can be difficult to interpret at times. Because of this, readers should check with the licensing boards in their states to determine what services they may and may not provide.

The model legislation endorsed by ACA's governing body in 1994 is clearly a practice act and establishes a comprehensive scope of practice for licensed professional counselors (LPCs), including that assessment, diagnosis, and treatment of persons with mental and emotional disorders. This scope of practice represents the broad continuum of services provided by professional counselors in the general practice of professional counseling and across specialty areas (Glosoff et al., 1995). The broadness of the scope is not meant to imply that all LPCs are experts in providing all services. Including a comprehensive scope of practice does, however, legally protect LPCs who are practicing within their scope of expertise. Without this protection, LPCs practicing within their scope of training (for example, career counseling, crisis intervention, or assessment) may find themselves, like John Weldon, legally prevented from rendering the very services for which they have been trained (Glosoff et al., 1995). Readers are referred to Glosoff et al. (1995) for details of the ACA's model licensure law.

Although a great deal has been achieved in the licensing arena, the state of licensure is confusing to many because the requirements vary from state to state. For example, 16 states and the District of Columbia have one tier of licensure. Other states have tiered licensing, with different scopes of practice and different criteria for eligibility. Twenty-five states have two tiers of licensure (e.g., licensed professional counselor as a "basic license" and licensed clinical counselor as a more "advanced" license), six states have three tiers, and three states have four tiers of licensure (ACA, 2010b). Following are a few other examples of variances in licensing laws, as reported in the 2010 ACA report that may be confusing to both counselors and policy makers:

- Educational requirements ranged from a master's degree with no specified number of hours to 60 semester hours including a master's degree, with 47 states and the District of Columbia requiring between 48 and 60 graduate semester hours (ACA, 2010b).
- There was a wide range of post-master's supervised counseling experience required to become licensed as a professional counselor, from 500 (one jurisdiction) to 4,500 hours (six jurisdictions required between 4,000–4,500 hours) with the majority of states (36) requiring between 3,000 and 3,600 hours of post-master's supervised counseling experience, to be completed in no less than two years (ACA, 2010b).
- The titles granted to professional counselors by the regulatory boards vary. "Professional Counselor" is the most frequently used title, followed by "Mental Health Counselor," "clinical professional counselor," and "clinical counselor." We believe a lack of uniformity in titles used by state-credentialed counselors has proven to be detrimental to credentialed counselors in their ongoing efforts to gain the same recognition afforded to psychologists and clinical social workers (ACA, 2010b).
- Continuing education requirements for licensed counselors vary from state to state. The majority of jurisdictions (47 or 90%) specifically include continuing education credits as a requirement for licensure renewal with the number of continuing education hours required ranging from 10 to 55 every two years (ACA, 2010b).

In addition to lack of uniformity, or maybe because of it, there have been legal challenges regarding what professional counselors can and cannot do as part of their scope of practice.

For example, although approximately 85% of state licensure laws include that licensed counselors can assess individuals with mental disorders, licensed counselors in several states have found themselves embroiled in legal battles over their ability to use standardized assessment instruments. This is ironic, given the strong roots that the counseling profession has in testing and assessment. The challenges are driven by efforts on the part of state psychological associations to proclaim that the use of most tests comes under the sole purview of doctoral-level psychologists. The tests noted by psychologists as requiring a doctorate in psychology to administer and interpret run the gamut from personality tests to psychoeducational and career-related measures.

Counselors will continue to fight for their right to administer and interpret those tests based on their education and training rather than on the name of the degree they earned. Legislation proposed by several state psychological associations may serve to bring together master's- and doctoral-level counselors, social workers, marriage and family therapists, and speech therapists, who may all find themselves unable to legally provide testing services for which they are trained. Professional organizations such as the ACA, NBCC, CRCC, and several ACA divisions have taken an active role in challenging proposed and enacted legislation and in defending mental health professionals who are charged with practicing psychology without a license based on their use of standardized instruments for which they have been adequately trained.

Portability of licensure is another issue. There is clearly a great deal of variance in licensure laws, often making it difficult for counselors licensed in one state to easily move to another state and become licensed. Many states that have practice licensure laws in place include a provision to obtain licensure through a review of credentials or endorsement. This, however, is often cumbersome and time-consuming and still does not allow counselors to simply take their license with them from state-to-state. To assist with the portability of credentials, the American Association of State Counseling Boards (AASCB), which was founded in 1986, established the National Credentials Registry (AACSB, 2004). This registry allows licensed counselors, for a fee, to deposit or store information relevant to licensure (e.g., their education, work history, supervised experience). Once this information is "banked," counselors who want to apply for licensure in another state can ask that AASCB send all of that information to that licensing board.

Another effort that may yield positive results in the long run for licensure portability is the 20/20 Future of Counseling Oversight Committee established by ACA and AASCB. This committee is comprised of representatives from a total of 29 counseling organizations, including all ACA divisions. In addition to creating a definition of counseling (as presented earlier in this chapter), its charge included creating licensure portability by the year 2020. The committee's charge, however, went far beyond this and addressed other issues that have been discussed in this chapter, such as to clearly define the profession of counseling, to examine how to present counseling as one profession rather than a group of groups, to improve recognition and public perception of counseling, and to expand and promote the research base of the counseling profession.

Recognition and Reimbursement of Professional Counselors

Credentialing has far-reaching ramifications for the hiring and reimbursement of professional counselors. Contrary to popular belief, credentialing affects the reimbursement of those professionals in settings other than private practice. Administrative rules used by several federal, state, and local agencies specify that only state-licensed practitioners can be employed by these agencies. These same rules often stipulate that only licensed workers can supervise mental health services, and call specifically for licensed psychologists. In the late 1970s, Alabama eliminated all counselor position titles because of this type of thinking. This is also true at many university counseling centers that will only hire licensed psychologists. These are just a few examples of how credentialing has become strongly related to employment opportunities for counselors.Reimbursement for services rendered has played a strong part in the licensure movement for all mental health practitioners. A motivating force in psychological licensing of the late 1960s and early 1970s was to secure third-party reimbursement and to be included in national health insurance (Hosie, 1991). To facilitate these two goals, in 1975 APA established the *National Register for Health Service Providers in Psychology* as a means of identifying qualified practitioners of psychological services. Since January 1, 1978, to be listed in the *National Register* one was required to have obtained a doctoral degree in psychology from a regionally accredited educational institution. Even though it has been argued that proficiency can be developed just as well in a counselor education department as in a psychology department, criteria for inclusion in the *National Register* clearly do not allow anyone who was trained outside of a psychology department to take the examinations for licensure or certification as psychologists in most states (Rudolph, 1986). This had direct economic consequences for many doctoral-level professional counselors who were previously eligible to be licensed as psychologists. Having licensure laws for professional counselors in all states and the District of Columbia has been critical in influencing federal legislation and regulations that increase the likelihood of the hiring and reimbursement of professional counselors in a wide variety of settings.

Federal Legislation

As we previously discussed, legislation has greatly influenced the development of the counseling profession. In addition to achieving the enactment of licensure laws in all 50 states and the District of Columbia, counselors have made great strides in being recognized as providers of mental health services in many pieces of legislation enacted over the past fifteen years. At the same time, the struggle and the need for ongoing advocacy in this area continues. Following are example of current issues related to some key laws.

HEALTH PROFESSIONS EDUCATION PARTNERSHIPS ACT

Professional counselors are included in some federal legislation and federally funded programs. For example counselors were successful in their efforts to be recognized as qualified providers under the Health Professions Education Partnerships Act (HPEPA). According to the American Counseling Association Office of Public Policy and Information (1998b), HPEPA revised the Public Health Services Act (PHSA) by including counselors under the definition of mental health professionals. In addition, the HPEPA provisions directly influence the ability of counselor education programs to compete for clinical training grants by having graduate programs in counseling included in the HPEPA termed "graduate program in behavioral and mental health practice." The act did not include a specific authorization level for any programs. Therefore, the passage of HPEPA does not, in itself, guarantee that counselors will be made eligible for any specific program. For example, although HPEPA added "counseling" to the current list of mental health professionals who are eligible for the Center for Mental Health Services (CMHS) clinical traineeship program, at the time HPEPA was enacted the staff of the CMHS indicated that they did not expect any new clinical traineeships to be granted.

The passage of HPEPA resulted in counselors being included in the National Health Service Corps loan repayment program (ACA Office of Public Policy and Information, 1998b). This program provides financial assistance in repaying student loans in exchange for working in health professions in underserved areas for two to four years following graduation (for example, serving in public inpatient mental institutions or federal or state correctional facilities or as members of the faculties of eligible health professions). Other programs authorized by HPEPA provide for grants to schools to identify, recruit, select, and financially support people from disadvantaged backgrounds for education and training in health and behavioral and mental health fields, and grants to aid in the establishment of centers of excellence in health education for underrepresented minority individuals.

MEDICARE AND THE FEDERAL EMPLOYEES HEALTH BENEFITS PROGRAM

As of 2012, counselors were not yet included as recognized providers of Medicare except when providing services "incident to" the services of a physician or psychologists. This means that professional counselors are not recognized to practice independently, which has indirectly had a negative impact on counselors being included as reimbursable to provide services under other public and private insurance programs. This may change in the near future. From 2003 through 2009, the Senate and House each twice approved legislation that would establish LPCs as mental health providers directly reimbursable under Medicare. Although establishing Medicare coverage of counselors is no longer a new or controversial idea, deep concerns regarding federal budget deficits and the steep rise in Medicare spending projected over the coming years have made it difficult to win support for even modest increases in program spending. Counselor recognition under Medicare, when achieved, should go a long way toward evening the playing field for counselors in the health care provider marketplace.

Because professional counselors are not included as independent Medicare providers in the federal statute, they have been unable to "sign off" on the delivery of mental health services through Medicare. This, in turn, may deter administrators from hiring professional counselors.

TRICARE

Another area which has been a focus of advocacy work is the coverage policies of TRICARE with respect to mental health counselors. TRICARE is the health services program operated by the Department of Defense for active duty military service members, retirees, and their family members, and covers more than 9 million beneficiaries. For years, TRICARE regulations have required that licensed professional counselors practice only under physician referral and supervision. These limitations are not placed on services provided by clinical psychologists, clinical social workers, psychiatric nurses, and marriage and family therapists. ACA and AMHCA have been working for several years to enlist Congressional support for parity between counselors and other TRICARE mental health service providers. This work culminated in the adoption of language, included in the National Defense Authorization Act for Fiscal Year 2011, requiring that the Department of Defense (DoD) adopt regulations to allow licensed mental health counselors to practice independently (Scott Barstow, personal communication, February 24, 2012). At the time this chapter was written, the DoD had issued an interim rule spelling out criteria which counselors must meet in order to be TRICARE providers and practice independently, and adoption and implementation of a final version of this regulation was expected by the end of 2012 (Scott Barstow).

VETERANS AFFAIRS

Public Law 109–461, the "Veterans Benefits, Healthcare, and Information Technology Act of 2006," includes language that clearly recognizes LPCs and licensed marriage and family therapists as mental health specialists within all health care programs operated by the Department of Veterans Affairs (VA) (ACA, 2007). In September of 2010, the VA finally issued a qualification standard establishing the occupation of "licensed professional mental health counselor" within the agency. The occupational standard establishes these positions at the same salary and responsibility levels as for clinical social worker positions. Rehabilitation counselors had long been employed by the VA but the VA had not, until the enactment of this law, recognized counselors as mental health specialists. Unfortunately, since the occupational standard was adopted, very few licensed professional mental health counselor positions have been instituted at VA facilities, with the majority of mental health clinician positions continuing to be filled by clinical social workers (Scott Barstow, personal communication, February 24, 2012). At the time this chapter was written, the Office of Personnel Management (OPM) was expected to develop and adopt an occupational standard for mental health counselors, based on the VA's standard, which will be applied to other federally operated programs, which will in turn hopefully increase the actual hiring of professional counselors.

MEDICAID

Medicaid, a federal program, is implemented through state regulations. The enactment of the 1997 Balanced Budget Act included provisions that prohibit Medicaid managed care plans from discriminating against providers on the basis of the type of license they hold. The act, however, did not extend to fee-for-service plans regulated through Medicaid and most states have traditionally used fee-for-service programs. This is changing, however, and many states have moved to managed Medicaid care plans. The battle to include professional counselors as recognized Medicaid providers continues to be fought at the state level.

A number of states have passed legislation that requires that providers of health insurance recognize LPCs as providers or vendors of mental health care services. Such laws increase consumers' choice of providers, thereby expanding the markets for mental health providers, including professional counselors. As of 2010, 22 states had enacted such laws. It is important to note, however, that although such laws require the reimbursement for services provided by specific professionals, such as LPCs, the regulations apply only *if* these services are covered by a health plan (ACA, 2010b). In addition, the vast majority of the vendorship laws do not typically regulate managed care companies, employers that set aside money to pay for the medical claims of their employees, or publicly funded (state or federal) insurance programs.

Multicultural Counseling and Social Justice Issues

One of the most significant trends in relation to professional counselors' clients is that they reflect the diversity seen in today's society in terms of age, race, ethnicity, gender, and sexual orientation. It is more likely than not that counselors will work with clients who have different cultural backgrounds than their own. Although people from all cultures may encounter problems that counselors are trained to address, these problems are experienced within a cultural context that counselors may not understand. The profession must determine the applicability of traditionally taught theories to diverse clientele, as well as explore the effectiveness of *how* services are delivered (for example, 50–minute sessions, in counselors' offices, that focus on intrapsychic phenomena).

The ACA *Code of Ethics* (2005) requires counselors to develop and maintain cross-cultural effectiveness. Standards related to diversity and cross-cultural counseling are apparent throughout the code. For example, the preamble states that we "recognize diversity and embrace a cross-cultural approach in support of the worth, dignity, potential, and uniqueness of people within their social and cultural contexts." In addition, the majority of introductory statements speak specifically to ethical obligations of counselors to consider cultural contexts related to the standards in the related sections. Further, many sections of the ACA Code speak specifically to the need for counselors to address diversity and multiculturalism, and to demonstrate not just cultural competence but also competence in the ability to advocate with and on behalf of clients to address societal barriers. This is beyond the scope of this chapter, however, and is covered in Chapter 4.

SIDEBAR 2.7 Case Study: Social Justice in Counseling

The week before the semester begins, Daryl receives the syllabi for his counseling courses. As he eagerly reads through them, he notices that the term social justice is mentioned several times. Daryl is not entirely sure what social justice means and what it has to do with counseling, so he decides that he will ask one of his classmates about it. If you were Daryl's classmate, how would you begin to explain your understanding of the counseling profession's roots in social justice? Consider some of the legislation you read about in this chapter and identify laws that demonstrate the profession's commitment to social justice. Revisit these questions while reading Chapter 4.

Summary

The roots of counseling are deeply embedded in a variety of disciplines that have come together and created different emphases at various points in time. These emphases have led to the development of counseling specialties, counselors working in a wide variety of settings and offering a broad range of services, and the profession struggling with the formation of an identity.

Counselors in the United States, regardless of work setting or theoretical orientation, are linked by the common belief that a person has the capacity and right to choose directions and activities that are most personally satisfying. Choices must be made within the bounds of social and moral value systems that will not bring harm to self or to others. The counselors who were pioneers and the counselors who work now are dedicated to helping individuals find their way in an increasingly complex society.

Counselors are active in dealing with a great number of social problems that affect the populations with which they work. Society is in turmoil, trying to deal with the use of illegal drugs, changing family structures; the effect of technology on education, occupations and employment; immigration issues; and complex pluralism; leading to the development of special populations at risk of being inundated by the majority. There is not space here to discuss each issue and the role of counselors in addressing these. Counselors must work to ensure that through their systematic, scientific, and professional efforts, individuals and groups will be served well. The following websites provide additional information relating to the chapter topics.

Useful Websites

American Association of State Counseling Boards: http://www.aascb.org/aws/AASCB/pt/sp/stateboards

American Counseling Association: www.counseling.org

American Counseling Association Public Policy Information: http://www.Counseling.org/public policy/

Chi Sigma Iota: http://www.csi.net

National Board for Certified Counselors: http://www.NBCC.org

Commission on Rehabilitation Counselor Certification: http://www.crccertification.com

Note

1   We would like to extend our gratitude and appreciation to Perry Rockwell, Jr., PhD, and professor emeritus of Counselor Education at the University of Wisconsin at Platteville. His pioneer work in the historical underpinning of guidance and counseling in the United States formed the bases for the first edition of this chapter. We also would like to thank Scott Barstow, director of public policy for the American Counseling Association, for information on federal legislation enacted since the last edition of this chapter.

References

Altekruse, M., & Wittmer, J. (1991). Accreditation in counselor education. In F. Bradley (Ed.), *Credentialing in counseling* (pp. 53–62). Alexandria, VA: American Association for Counseling and Development.

American Association of State Counseling Boards. (2004). AASCB portability policy and procedure. Retrieved October 10, 2004, from www.aascb.org/pdfs/AASCB%20Portability%20document1–9–04.pdf.

American Counseling Association. (1999a). Special message: Congress approves $20 million for school counseling as part of Omnibus Spending Package for FY2000. Retrieved March 20, 1999, from http://www.counseling.org/urgent/special112299a.html.

American Counseling Association. (1999b). Special message: WIIA passes house and senate. Clinton to sign bill into law. http://www.counseling.org/urgent/special112299a.html.

American Counseling Association (ACA). (2007). *New Veterans Affairs law recognizing counselors to be implemented*. Retrieved June 1, 2007, from http://www.counseling.org/PublicPolicy/PositionPapers.aspx.

American Counseling Association (ACA). (2005). *Code of ethics*. Alexandria, VA: Author.

American Counseling Association (ACA). (2010a). *Definition of counseling*. Retrieved from http://www.counseling.org/Resources/.

American Counseling Association (ACA). (2010b). *Licensure requirements for professional counselors. A state-by-state report*. Alexandria, VA: Author.

American Counseling Association Office of Public Policy and Information. (1996). *Briefing paper: Mental Health Insurance Parity Act passed*. Alexandria, VA: Author.

American Counseling Association Office of Public Policy and Information. (1998a). *Briefing paper: Higher education programs updated*. Alexandria, VA: Author.

American Counseling Association Office of Public Policy and Information. (1998b). *Briefing paper: Congress passes bill recognizing counselors under health professional training programs*. Alexandria, VA: Author.

American Counseling Association Office of Public Policy and Information. (1998c). *Briefing paper: Workforce Investment Act signed into law. Legislation revamps job training, reauthorizes the Rehabilitation Act*. Alexandria, VA: Author.

American Personnel and Guidance Association (APGA). (1968). *Standards for preparation of elementary school counselors*. Washington, DC: Author.

American Personnel and Guidance Association (APGA). (1969). *Guidelines for graduate programs in the preparation of student personnel workers in higher education*. Washington, DC: Author.

American Personnel and Guidance Association (APGA). (1976). *Model for state legislation concerning the practice of counseling, 1976, draft no. 4*. Alexandria, VA: Author.

American Psychiatric Association. (2000). *Diagnostic and statistical manual of mental disorders* (4th ed.). Washington, DC: Author.

Association for Counselor Education and Supervision (ACES). (1967). Standards for the preparation of secondary school counselors. *Personnel and Guidance Journal, 46*, 96–106.

Association for Lesbian, Gay, Bisexual, and Transgender Issues in Counseling LGBQQIA Competencies Taskforce. (2012). *Competencies for counseling with lesbian, gay, bisexual, queer, questioning, intersex and ally individuals*. Retrieved from http://www.albgtic.org/resources/competencies.

Aubrey, R. F. (1982). A house divided: Guidance and counseling in 20th century America. *The Personnel and Guidance Journal, 61*, 198–204.

Beers, C. W. (1908). *A mind that found itself*. NY: Doubleday.

Belkin, G. S. (1988). *Introduction to counseling* (3rd ed.). Dubuque, IA: Wm. C. Brown Publishers.

Bradley, F. (1991). *Credentialing in counseling*. Alexandria, VA: American Association for Counseling and Development.

Brewer, J. M. (1942). *History of vocational guidance*. NY: Harper.

Brooks, D. K. (1986). Credentialing of mental health counselors. In A. J. Palmo, & W. J. Weikel (Eds.), *Foundations of mental health counseling* (pp. 243–261). Springfield, IL: Charles C. Thomas.

Brooks, D. K., Jr. (1988). Finishing the job. In R. L.Dingman (Ed.), *Licensure for mental health counselors* (pp. 4–7). Alexandria, VA: American Mental Health Counselors Association.

Brown, D., & Srebalus, D. (1988). *An introduction to the counseling profession*. Englewood Cliffs, NJ: Prentice Hall.

Bureau of Justice Statistics. (2005). *Prison statistics: Summary of findings*. U.S. Department of Justice, Office of Justice Programs. Retrieved March 9, 2007, from www.ojp.usdoj.gov/bjs/prisons.thm.

Caplow, T. (1966). The sequence of professionalization. In H. M. Vollmer, & D. L. Mills (Eds.), *Professionalization*. Englewood Cliffs, NJ: Prentice Hall.

Cavaiola, A. A., & Colford, J. E. (2006). *A practical guide to crisis intervention*. Boston, MA: Lahaska Press.

Centers for Disease Control and Prevention. (2009). *Web-based injury statistics query and reporting system (2007 Data)*. Retrieved from www.cdc.gov/ncipc/wisqars.

Cicourel, A. V., & Kitsuse, J. I. (1963). *The educational decision-makers*. Indianapolis, IN: Bobbs-Merrill. *City of Cleveland, Ohio v. Cook, Municipal Court,* Criminal Division, No. 75–CRB 11478, August 12, 1975. (Transcript dated August 19, 1975).

Clawson, T. W. (2007). *Written testimony by Dr. Thomas W. Clawson before the President's commission on the care of wounded warriors*. Retrieved June 3, 2007, from http://www.nbcc.org/home/newspage/nbccnews/dr.-thomas-clawson-submits-written-testimony-before-the-presidents-commission.

Commission on Rehabilitation Counselor Certification (CRCC). (2012). *CRC Certification guide*. Retrieved February 10, 2012, from http://www.crccertification.com/.

Council for Accreditation of Counseling and Related Educational Programs (CACREP). (2001). *Accreditation procedures manual for counseling and related educational programs.* Alexandria, VA: Author.

Council for Accreditation of Counseling and Related Educational Programs (CACREP). (2009). *Accreditation procedures manual for counseling and related programs.* Alexandria, VA: Author.

Council for Higher Education Accreditation. (CHEA). (2008). *Informing the public about accreditation.* Retrieved from http://www.chea.org/public_info/index.asp.

Council on Rehabilitation Education (CORE). (2012). *Master's programs in rehabilitation counselor education.* Retrieved March 6, 2012, from http://www.core-rehab.org.

Council on Rehabilitation Education. (2011*). Accreditation manual.* Retrieved March 6, 2012 from http://www.core-rehab.org.

Cummings, N. A. (1990). The credentialing of professional psychologists and its implication for the other mental health disciplines. *Journal of Counseling and Development, 68*(5), 485–490.

Davis, J. B. (1914). *Moral and vocational guidance.* Boston: Ginn.

Davis, J. B. (1956). *Saga of a schoolmaster: An autobiography.* Boston: Boston University Press.

Federal Interagency Forum on Aging-Related Statistics. (2010). *Older Americans 2010: Key indicators of well-being.* Washington, DC: U.S. Government Printing Office. Retrieved from http://www.agingstats.gov/agingstatsdotnet/Main_Site/Data/2010_Documents/Docs/OA_2010.pdf.

Forrest, D. V., & Stone, L. A. (1991). Counselor certification. In F.Bradley (Ed.), *Credentialing in counseling* (pp. 23–52). Alexandria, VA: American Association for Counseling and Development.

Gay, Lesbian, and Straight Education Network (GLSEN). (2010). The 2009 national school climate survey: The experiences of lesbian, gay, bisexual and transgender youth in our nation's schools. Retrieved from http://www.glsen.org/binary-data/GLSEN_ATTACHMENTS/file/000/001/1675–2.pdf.

Ginzberg, E. (1971). *Career guidance.* New York: McGraw-Hill.

Glaze, L. E., & James, D. J. (2006, September). *Mental health problems of prison and jail inmates.* (Report: NCH 213600). Retrieved from Bureau of Justice Statistics: http://bjs.ojp.usdoj.gov/content/pub/pdf/mhppji.pdf.

Glosoff, H. L., Benshoff, J. M., Hosie, T. W., & Maki, D. R. (1995). The 1994 ACA model legislation for licensed professional counselors. *Journal of Counseling and Development, 74*(2), 209–220.

Goldenberg, H. (1973). *Contemporary psychology.* Belmore, CA: Wadsworth.

Gross, M. L. (1962). *The brain watchers.* NY: Random House.

Han, B., Gfroerer, J. C., Colliver, J. D., & Penne, M. A. (2009). Substance use disorder among older adults in the United Sates in 2020. *Addiction, 104,* 88–96. doi: 10.1111/j.1360–0443.2008.02411.x

Herr, E. (1985). *Why counseling?* Alexandria, VA: American Association for Counseling and Development.

Hosie, T. W. (1991). Historical antecedents and current status of counselor licensure. In F. Bradley (Ed.), *Credentialing in counseling* (pp. 23–52). Alexandria, VA: American Association for Counseling and Development.

Hoyt, K. B. (1974). Professional preparation for professional guidance. In E. Herr (Ed.), *Vocational guidance and human development* (pp. 502–527). Boston: Houghton Mifflin.

Kaplan, L. (2003). *Substance abuse treatment workforce environmental scan.* Washington, DC: Department of Health and Human Services. Retrieved from http://partnersforrecovery.samhsa.gov/docs/Environmental_Scan.pdf.

Lawson, G., Venart, E., Hazler, R., Kottler, J. A. (2007). Toward a culture of counselor wellness. *Journal of Humanistic Counseling, Education & Development, 46,* 5–19.

McDaniels, C. O. (1964). *The history and development of the American Personnel and Guidance Association, 1952–1963.* Unpublished doctoral dissertation. Charlottesville, VA: University of Virginia.

Miller, C. H. (1971). *Foundations of guidance* (2nd ed.). New York: Harper & Row.

Myers, J. E., Sweeney, T. J., & Witmer, J. M. (2000). The wheel of wellness counseling for wellness: A holistic model for treatment planning. *Journal of Counseling & Development, 78,* 251–265.

Norris, W. (1954). *The history and development of the National Vocational Guidance Association*. Unpublished doctoral dissertation. Washington, DC: George Washington University.

Ohlsen, M. M. (1983). *Introduction to counseling*. Itasca, IL: F. E. Peacock.

Palmo, A. J., & Weikel, W. J. (1986). *Foundations of mental health counseling*. Springfield, IL: Charles C. Thomas.

Parsons, F. (1894). The philosophy of mutualism. *The Arena, 9,* 738–815.

Parsons, F. (1909). *Choosing a vocation*. Boston: Houghton-Mifflin.

Picchioni, A. P., & Bonk, E. C. (1983). *A comprehensive history of guidance in the United States*. Austin, TX: Texas Personnel and Guidance Association.

Reed, A. Y. (1916). *Vocational guidance report 1913–1916*. Seattle, WA: Board of School Directors.

Reed, A. Y. (1920). *Junior wage earners*. New York: Macmillan.

Reed, A. Y. (1944). *Guidance and personnel services in education*. Ithaca, NY: Cornell University Press.

Richards, L. S. (1881). *Vocophy*. Marlboro, MA: Pratt Brothers.

Rockwell, P. J., Jr. (1958). *Social concepts in the published writings of some pioneers in guidance*. Unpublished doctoral dissertation. Madison, WI: University of Wisconsin.

Rogers, C. R. (1942). *Counseling and psychotherapy*. Boston: Hougton Mifflin.

Rogers, C. R. (1951). *Client-centered therapy*. Boston: Hougton Mifflin.

Rudolph, J. (1986). Third-party reimbursement and mental health counselors. In A. J. Palmo, & W. J. Weikel (Eds.), *Foundations of mental health counseling* (pp. 271–284). Springfield, IL: Charles C. Thomas.

Seligman, L. (2009). Diagnosis in counseling. In D. Capuzzi, & D. R. Gross (Eds.), *Introduction to the counseling profession* (5th ed., pp. 373–394). Needham Heights: MA: Allyn & Bacon.

Shertzer, B., & Stone, S. C. (1986). *Fundamentals of counseling*. Boston, MA: Houghton Mifflin.

Stephens, W. R. (1954). *Technical recommendations for psychological tests and diagnostic techniques*. Washington, DC: American Psychology Association.

Stephens, W. R. (1970). *Social reform and the origins of vocational guidance*. New York: Harper & Row.

Stripling, R. O. (1983). Building on the past- A challenge for the future. In G. R. Walls, & L. Benjamin (Eds.), *Shaping counselor education programs in the next five years: An experimental prototype for the counselor of tomorrow* (pp. 205–209). Ann Arbor: ERIC/CAPS.

Substance Abuse and Mental Health Services Administration (SAMHSA). (2009). *Report to Congress: Addictions treatment workforce development*. Retrieved from http://www.partnersforrecovery.samhsa.gov/docs/report_to_congress.pdf.

Swanson, C. (1988). Historical perspective on licensure for counselors. In R. L. Dingman (Ed.), *Licensure for mental health counselors* (pp. 1–3). Alexandria, VA: American Mental Health Counselors Association.

Sweeney, T. J. (1991). Counselor credentialing: Purpose and origin. In F. Bradley (Ed.), *Credentialing in counseling* (pp. 23–52). Alexandria, VA: American Association for Counseling and Development.

U.S. Administration on Aging. Profile of older Americans: 2011. Retrieved from http://www.aoa.gov/AoARoot/Aging_Statistics/Profile/2011/2.aspx.

Vacc, N., & Loesch, L. (1994*). A professional orientation to counseling* (2nd Ed.). Muncie, IN: Accelerated Development.

Weldon v. Virginia State Board of Psychologist Examiners. Corporation Court Opinion (Court Order). Newport News, VA: October 4, 1972.

Weikel, W. J., & Palmo, A. J. (1989). The evolution and practice of mental health counseling. *Journal of Mental Health Counseling, 11*(1), 7–25.

Williamson, E. G. (1965). *Vocational counseling: Some historical, philosophical, and theoretical perspectives.* NY: McGraw-Hill.

Williams Institute. (2007). Bias in the Workplace: Consistent Evidence of Sexual Orientation and Gender Identity Discrimination. Retrieved March 2, 2007 from http://www.law.ucla.edu/williamsinstitute//publications/bias%20in%20the%workplace.pdf.

3

CROSS CULTURAL COUNSELING

Courtland C. Lee, GoEun Na, and Roxanna N. Pehdani

Among the contemporary issues facing professional counselors, addressing the mental health and educational needs of the growing number of clients from culturally diverse backgrounds are, perhaps, the most challenging. Counseling theory and practice has been greatly impacted by the changing demographics and social dynamics that characterize the 21st century. As an example, data from the 2010 Census underscore the scope of the nation's changing racial and ethnic diversity. A review of racial and ethnic group distributions nationally shows that while the non-Hispanic White alone population is still numerically and proportionally the largest major race and ethnic group in the United States, it is also growing at the slowest rate. During the past 10 years, it has been the Hispanic population and the Asian population that have grown considerably, in part due to relatively higher levels of immigration (Humes, Jones, & Ramirez, 2011).

Significantly, the 2000 Census marked the first time that people could describe themselves by selecting more than one racial category (Root & Kelley, 2003). According to 2010 Census data, 9 million people—or 2.9 percent of the population—chose more than one race on the census form, a change of about 32 percent since 2000 (Humes, et al., 2011).

Importantly, while changes in the racial/ethnic makeup of the country are occurring, it is important to note that there are other aspects contributing to a new awareness of cultural diversity. Data indicate that groups of people long marginalized or disenfranchised along dimensions other than race or ethnicity are being increasingly recognized. As an example, an estimated 3.5% of adults in the United States identify as lesbian, gay, or bisexual and an estimated 0.3% of adults are transgender. This implies that there are approximately 9 million LGBT Americans, a figure roughly equivalent to the population of New Jersey (Gates, 2011). In addition, individuals with disabilities make up a notable portion of the United States population. According to the 2010 census, there were 36 million people who had some type of disability (U.S. Bureau of the Census, 2010).

Significantly, while the United States continues to be the most affluent country in human history, there are still large numbers of individuals who experience socioeconomic disadvantage and the "culture of poverty" has long been recognized (Lewis, 1971; Valentine, 1968). Underscoring this notion of poverty as culture are census data that indicate that the official poverty rate in 2010 was 15.1 percent—up from 14.3 percent in 2009. This was the third consecutive annual increase in the poverty rate. Since 2007, the poverty rate has increased by 2.6 percentage points, from 12.5 percent to 15.1 percent. In 2010, 46.2 million people were in poverty, up from 43.6 million in 2009—the fourth consecutive annual increase in the number of people in poverty (DeNavas, Proctor, & Smith, 2011).

As marginalized or oppressed groups have gained greater awareness and made significant strides towards social inclusion, other social movements have changed the fabric of American life. For instance in the last several decades we have seen significant changes in the roles of men and women (Collins, 2009; Freedman, 2003; Pease & Pringle, 2001; Rabinowitz & Cochran, 1994). In addition, the needs and challenges of older Americans are becoming more apparent. Data from the 2010 Census indicate that the number of Americans 60 years and older increased by over 20 million people in the period 2000–2010. This represented a 79 percent increase in the number of persons in this population group (U.S. Bureau of the Census, 2010).

In concrete people terms, data and issues such as these mean that, perhaps as never before, the United States has become a social arena where individuals who represent truly diverse behavioral styles, attitudinal orientations, and value systems interact on a daily basis. Cultural pluralism, therefore, has become widely recognized as a major factor deserving increased understanding on the part of individuals in all professions. Within this context, professional counselors must provide services that help people to solve problems or make decisions in the midst of such sweeping demographic and sociological change.

The past several decades have seen a growing realization that counseling services often do not have broad applicability across the range of cultural backgrounds represented by clients (Katz, 1985; P. B. Pederson, Lonner, & G., 1976; Sue, 1977; Sue, Arredondo, & McDavis, 1992; Sue & Sue, 2012; Vontress, 1969, 1981). With this awareness has come frustration that in attempting to promote human development, the values inherent in counseling and those of culturally diverse clients often come into conflict within the helping process. In order to resolve this conflict and the frustration which often accompanies it, cultural differences must be effectively addressed in the provision of counseling services. It is evident that professional counselors need new direction if they are going to insure that clients from culturally diverse backgrounds have access to competent services.

The purpose of this chapter is to explore cross cultural counseling and the development of cross cultural counseling competence. Cross cultural counseling is first defined. Next the basic principles which underlie counseling across cultures are discussed. A conceptual framework for developing cross cultural counseling competency is then presented. The cross cultural counseling encounter and its inherent challenges are then introduced. The chapter concludes with an overview of some important concepts for consideration when counseling with culture in mind.

SIDEBAR 3.1 "Can a Counselor from One Culture Effectively Counsel a Person who is from Another Cultural Background?"

This is a question that is often debated in the counseling profession. It is also a question that is often asked by graduate students in a multicultural counseling course. This question characterizes the confusion and skepticism students often experience as they grapple with the often complex issue of culture.

How would you answer this question?

What is Cross Cultural Counseling?

Cross cultural counseling can be defined as the working alliance between a counselor and client(s) that takes the personal dynamics of the counselor and client(s) into consideration alongside the dynamics found in the cultures of both of these individuals. As a process, therefore, cross cultural counseling takes into consideration the cultural background and individual experiences of clients from diverse backgrounds and how their unique psychosocial needs might be identified and met through counseling (Lee, 2006b; Sue & Sue, 2012). Given this definition, there are six basic principles that are foundational to the process of counseling across cultures:

1. Culture refers to any group of people who identify or associate with one another on the basis of some common purpose, need or similarity of background.
2. Cultural differences are real and they influence all human interactions.
3. All counseling is cross cultural in nature.
4. Cross cultural counseling places an emphasis on human diversity in all its many forms.
5. Culturally competent counselors develop awareness, knowledge and skills to intervene effectively into the lives of people from culturally diverse backgrounds.
6. Culturally competent counselors are globally literate human beings.

SIDEBAR 3.2

Cross Cultural Principle #4: Cross cultural counseling places an emphasis on human diversity in all its many forms.

How would you describe yourself along each of these dimensions of cultural identity?

- Age?
- Gender?
- Place of Residence?
- Socioeconomic Status?
- Educational Level?
- Ability Status?
- Formal Affiliations?
- Informal Affiliations?
- Nationality?
- Sexual Orientation?
- Language?
- Religion/spirituality?
- Ethnicity?

Reflecting on the definition and principles of cross cultural counseling, it is important to note that the American Counseling Association (ACA) has recently adopted the following definition of counseling:

> Counseling is a professional relationship that empowers diverse individuals, families, and groups to accomplish mental health, wellness, education, and career goals.
>
> (American Counseling Association, 2010)

This definition makes explicit the idea that counselors will encounter individuals from diverse cultural backgrounds in helping relationships. Implicit in this idea is the importance of counselors having the awareness, knowledge, and skill to help empower individuals, families, and groups in ways that are sensitive to and inclusive of their cultural realities.

Counseling across Cultures: A Conceptual Framework

Within the context of the definition and principles of cross cultural counseling a set of professional competencies have been developed which form the basis for best practice when counseling across cultures (Arredondo, et al., 1996; Sue, et al., 1992). These competencies describe the awareness level, knowledge base, and skill-set that enables a counselor to provide culturally sensitive service to clients. The following is a conceptual framework for understanding the components required to develop the competencies deemed necessary for counseling across cultures.

This conceptual framework focuses on the development of culturally competent counselors who apply their practice in a diverse society. Cross cultural counseling competency can be defined as a set of attitudes and behaviors indicative of the ability to establish, maintain, and successfully conclude a counseling relationship with clients from diverse cultural backgrounds (Lee & Park, 2013).

The framework is comprised of three areas: the foundational dimension, the cross cultural dimension, and cross cultural counseling competency. There are eight themes imbedded in these three areas.

The Foundational Dimension

The foundational dimension consists of four themes: self-awareness, global literacy, foundational knowledge of traditional counseling theory, and ethical knowledge and aspirations. While these themes are the foundation of multicultural counseling competency, they can also be considered the essence of competent counseling in general.

Self-awareness

The basis for culturally competent counseling practice is counselor self-awareness. It is important that counselors fully experience themselves as cultural beings. An individual who expects to work cross-culturally must first be anchored in his or her own cultural realities. This process should start with explorations of how one's own cultural background has influenced one's psychosocial development. It is of critical importance that a person considers the role that cultural heritage and customs play in shaping his or her personality characteristics. It is also crucial that a person assess his or her own process of cultural identity development (Lee & Na, 2011). The significant questions that one must ask in this regard are "How do I experience myself as a member of Cultural Group X?" "How do I experience others members of Cultural Group X?" and "How do I experience people of other cultural backgrounds?"

As part of this self-exploration process, it is also important that a counselor evaluate the influences that have shaped the development of his or her attitudes and beliefs about people from different cultural backgrounds. It is important to evaluate the explicit, as well as the often subtle, messages one has received throughout his or her life about people who are culturally "different." A counselor must evaluate how his or her personal attitudes and beliefs about people from different cultural groups may facilitate or hamper counseling effectiveness.

Cross cultural counseling competency begins with an exploration of personal issues and questions, no matter how uncomfortable, in an attempt to discern how one's own cultural heritage, values and biases might impact upon the counseling process. Self-exploration leads to self-awareness, which is crucial in developing a set of personal attitudes and beliefs to guide culturally competent counseling practice. Culturally competent counselors are sensitive to cultural group differences because they are aware of their own identity as cultural beings.

SIDEBAR 3.3

All people are products of the dynamics of their own cultural background. Do an analysis of your cultural heritage within the context of the following questions:

- What generation in the United States do you represent?
- If you are an international student, what would you describe as some of the major cultural characteristics of your country?
- Does your family practice cultural customs that you or they value or identify with?
- What role has religion/spirituality played in your family?
- How is sexual orientation regarded within your family?
- What prejudices or stereotypes does your family have about other cultural groups?
- What was your parents' main advice to you about people from other cultural groups?
- To what extent do you regularly interact with members of other cultural groups?

How do you think your cultural background and attitudes will affect your work with culturally diverse clients?

Global Literacy

Global literacy is the breadth of information that extends over the major domains of human diversity. It consists of basic information that a person needs to know in order to successfully navigate life in the technologically sophisticated, globally interconnected world of the 21st century—a world in which people from diverse cultural backgrounds interact in ways that were inconceivable in previous centuries. It is impossible, therefore, to be a culturally competent counselor in a globally interconnected world without a passing knowledge of the historical, sociological, political, and economic dynamics that form the foundation of diverse cultural contexts.

Ideally, then, in order to be truly culturally competent as a professional counselor, one should spend time studying history, anthropology, sociology, economics, religion, politics, and any number of other social science disciplines in an attempt to develop the knowledge base to truly understand the cultural dynamics of diverse groups of people.

In lieu of this, however, one could commit oneself to living a life that is truly open to experiencing cultural diversity in all its many facets.

Global literacy implies an understanding of the contemporary world and how it has evolved over time. It encompasses important knowledge of cultural variations in areas such as geography, history, literature, politics, economics and principles of government. Global literacy is the core body of knowledge that an individual gains over a lifetime about the world in which he or she lives. The driving force behind the development of global literacy is the commitment one makes to ensure that openness to cultural diversity is the cornerstone of his or her life. While cross cultural competency is the goal for professional counseling practice, global literacy is the goal for a life lived in a culturally competent manner. It logically follows, therefore, that one cannot be a culturally competent counselor if he or she is not a globally literate person.

The development of global literacy is a lifelong process that is rooted in a commitment to living one's life in a manner that makes cultural diversity a core principle. A globally literate person exhibits ongoing cultural curiosity that is characterized by openness to engaging in new cultural experiences whenever possible. He or she embraces and celebrates cultural difference as opposed to fearing the fundamental distinctions in worldviews that underlie human diversity. A globally literate individual approaches diverse lifestyles from a position that transcends tolerance and promotes mutual respect and understanding. Embracing a globally literate life style also involves a commitment to social justice and social responsibility. In modern society a globally literate person, for example, would be one who has a knowledge of cultural variations in history, has domestic/international travel experience, and is knowledgeable about current national and international events (Lee, 2013).

SIDEBAR 3.4 Global Literacy

One cannot be a culturally competent counselor if he or she is not a globally literate person.

- Identify 5 major events from the past year that had an impact at the national or international level.
- Why is it important for a counselor to have knowledge about these events?
- What possible implications does each of these events have for mental health and psychosocial development?

Foundational Knowledge of Traditional Counseling Theory

The concept of cross cultural counseling competency must also rest on an understanding of traditional counseling theory. Although there have been criticisms of the Eurocentric nature of these theories (Sue, Ivey, & Pederson, 1996), each has important aspects that contribute to best practice in counseling. Therefore, it is important that the foundation of counseling practice constructed by pioneering thinkers and practitioners such as Freud, Adler, Rogers, Perls, and the behaviorists are incorporated into culturally diverse concepts and approaches to helping.

Ethical Knowledge and Aspirations

Another crucial foundational aspect of multicultural counseling competency is knowledge of ethical standards. Indeed, the integrity of the counseling profession rests on ethical practice. Importantly, the ethical standards of the American Counseling Association call on counselors to actively attempt to understand the diverse cultural backgrounds of the clients they serve (American Counseling Association, 2005). Best practice in counseling, therefore, is putting ethics in the forefront of all professional activity. It is safe to assume then that counselors who are culturally competent aspire to high ethical standards.

SIDEBAR 3.5 The Case of Mrs. Ogawa

Mrs. Ogawa, a recent immigrant from Nigeria, has been in counseling with Ms. Diaz for the last two months. The sessions have been very helpful to Mrs. Ogawa. At the end of the most recent session, Mrs. Ogawa presents Ms. Diaz with a small wooden elephant that was carved in her country as a token of appreciation. Ms. Diaz explains to Mrs. Ogawa that while she is very appreciative, for professional reasons she cannot accept the gift. Due to this rejection, Mrs. Ogawa leaves the session very upset with her counselor.

In thinking about your answers to these questions, please refer to Section A.10.e of the *2005 ACA Code of Ethics:*

- From an ethical perspective, do you think Ms. Diaz handled this situation appropriately?
- If you were the counselor in this situation, would you have accepted the gift?

The Cross Cultural Dimension

The cross cultural dimension of the conceptual framework consists of three themes: cross cultural counseling theoretical knowledge, cross cultural encounters, and cross cultural counseling skill development. These themes reflect the theory and practice cross cultural counseling.

Cross Cultural Counseling Theoretical Knowledge

In addition to knowledge of traditional counseling theory, it is imperative that counselors have a knowledge base which includes culturally diverse ideas on the nature of helping and its impact on human development from which to plan, implement and evaluate services in a cross cultural context. Significantly, Sue, Ivey, and Petersen (1996) proposed a theory of multicultural counseling and therapy. The basic assumption of this theory is that it is a metatheory of counseling that recognizes that both counselor and client identities are embedded in multiple levels of experience and context. It posits that cultural identity development is a major determinant of both counselor and client attitudes, which are also influenced by the dominant and subordinate relationships among groups. Cultural identity refers to an individual's sense of belonging to a cultural group and the part of one's personality that is attributable to cultural group membership. Cultural identity may be considered as the inner vision that a person possesses of himself or herself as a member of a cultural group and as a unique human being. It forms the core of the beliefs, social forms, and personality dimensions that characterize distinct cultural realities and world-view for an individual. Cultural identity development is a major determinant of a person's attitudes toward himself or herself, others of his or cultural group, and those of different cultural groups (Sue, et al., 1996).

Cross cultural theoretical knowledge must also include an understanding that counseling is most likely enhanced when modalities and goals are consistent with the life experiences and cultural values of the client. Such knowledge must, therefore, also include an awareness of the importance of multiple helping roles of culturally diverse groups of people (Sue, et al., 1996).

Another crucial aspect of cross cultural knowledge is an understanding of how social systems operate with respect to their treatment of culturally diverse groups of people (Lee, 2007; M. J. Ratts, Toporek, & Lewis, 2010). Culturally competent counselors must have an understanding of the impact that systemic forces such as racism, sexism, heterosexism, classism, and ableism can have on psychosocial development and wellness.

Cross Cultural Encounters

Cross cultural competency must be predicated on one's ability to acquire working knowledge and information about specific groups of people. This should include information about the histories, experiences, customs, and values of culturally diverse groups. However, the acquisition of such knowledge must not be limited to books, classes, and workshops. A crucial way to acquire such knowledge is through on-going professional, and perhaps more importantly, personal encounters with people from diverse cultural backgrounds. Such encounters may entail getting outside of the familiarity of one's own cultural realities and experiencing diversity first hand. An important component of any cross cultural encounter is the ability to get beyond stereotypes and ensure that one sees people as individuals within a cultural context.

Cross Cultural Counseling Skill Development

It is imperative that counselors enter a cross cultural helping relationship with a repertoire of skills. They should develop counseling strategies and techniques that are consistent with the life experiences and cultural values of their clients. Such skill development should be based on the following premises. First, cultural diversity is real and should not be ignored in counseling interactions. Second, cultural differences are just that—differences. They are not necessarily deficiencies or pathological deviations. This suggests having the ability to meet clients where they are, despite obvious cultural gaps between counselor and client. Third, when working with clients from culturally diverse groups, it is important to avoid stereotypes and a monolithic perspective. It is crucial that counselors consider clients as individuals within a cultural context.

In developing culturally competent counseling skills, a number of theoretical approaches should be included in a helping repertoire. It is important that one's counseling approach be eclectic enough that one can use a variety of helping interventions. Any counseling approach should incorporate diverse worldviews and practices.

Upon actually encountering a client from a different cultural context, a counselor's skill set must proceed from important answers to the following questions, "What 'buttons,' if any, does this client push in me as a result of the obvious cultural difference between us?"; "What are some cultural blind spots I may have with respect to this client?"; "As a result of my cultural realities, what strengths do I bring to this counseling relationship?"; "As a result of my cultural realities, what limitations do I bring to this counseling relationship?"

Cross Cultural Counseling Competency

The apex of this conceptual framework is cross cultural counseling competency. This is a construct that has received significant attention in the cross cultural literature (Arredondo, et al., 1996; Roysircar, Arredondo, Fuertes, Ponterotto, & Toporek, 2003; Sue, et al., 1992). Cross cultural counseling competency defines a set of attitudes and behaviors indicative of the ability to establish, maintain, and successfully conclude a counseling relationship with clients from diverse cultural backgrounds. Therefore, counselors who are culturally competent have heightened awareness, an expanded knowledge base, and use helping skills in a culturally responsive manner.

In the developmental process that has been described in this conceptual framework, three important questions summarize the essence of the evolution of cross cultural counseling competency. First, those counselors who demonstrate cross cultural competency possess self-awareness that is grounded in an exploration of the question, "Who am I as a cultural being?" Second, in addition to knowledge of counseling theory and ethical principles, cross culturally competent counselors consider the question, "What do I know about cultural dynamics?" Third, the counseling practice of counselors who exhibit cross cultural competency is predicated on the question, "How do I promote academic, career, and personal-social development in a culturally competent manner?"

The Challenge of the Cross Cultural Counseling Encounter

Entering a counseling relationship with a person from a different cultural background brings with it certain unique challenges and inherent opportunities. Engaging in such a relationship involves entering an important and potentially problematic zone of helping (Lee & Diaz, 2009). This helping space can be conceptualized as the cross cultural encounter. In much of the cross cultural counseling literature this helping space has been traditionally conceptualized as a White counselor engaging in a helping relationship with a client of color (Atkinson, Morten, & Sue, 1993; Lee, 1997b; Locke, 1990; McFadden, 1993; Vontress, 1971). However, the cultural gaps that exist between counselor and client in a cross cultural encounter may also consist of distinct differences in aspects such as gender, religion, social class, sexual orientation, ability status, and age. In addition, it has been argued by Pedersen (1991) that multiculturalism is a basic aspect of all counseling and that every counselor–client relationship is in effect a cross cultural encounter.

Regardless of how it is perceived, what has been clearly evident in cross cultural encounters is that the cultural differences between counselor and client, when not fully appreciated or understood, can be a significant impediment to the counseling process. Metaphorically, these counselor–client differences in a cross cultural encounter can be perceived as a wall that impedes or negates counseling. This wall underscores the cultural distance between the counselor and the client. In many instances, the cultural differences in a cross cultural encounter are ignored or misunderstood thereby widening the distance between helper and helpee.

Given this metaphorical wall, a cross cultural counseling encounter can produce one of two possible outcomes. The first of these is underscored by multicultural incompetence on the part of a counselor which can spawn unintended cultural disregard, or worse, cultural disrespect. Such cultural insensitivity may result in early termination of the relationship on the part of the client. With respect to ethical guidelines such an outcome would be considered unethical counseling practice (American Counseling Association, 2005). The second possible outcome, however, reflects cross cultural competence on the part of the counselor which should result in a working alliance between counselor and client. Respect and validation of a client's culture through culturally competent counseling practice increases the likelihood of problem resolution or effective decision making. Cultural competence also promotes ethical counseling practice.

The goal, therefore, when entering a cross cultural encounter is to acknowledge the wall and decrease the cultural distance between counselor and client. It is important that cultural differences are acknowledged and factored into the counseling relationship as appropriate. In order to accomplish this and increase counseling effectiveness in a cross cultural encounter important issues must be considered. Competent counseling practice in a cross cultural encounter must be predicated on an understanding of these issues.

SIDEBAR 3.6 The Case of Margaret

Margaret is a client with a visual impairment who has come to you for career counseling. In a session in which you and Margaret have been exploring career options you make the following statement, "Margaret, it is really important that you see the differences between a career in financial management and one in accounting." Margaret's response to you is, "I can't see anything."

- How does Margaret's response underscore the inherent challenges in a cross cultural encounter?
- What would be your response to Margaret's statement?
- How could this response impact the counseling relationship?

Issues to Consider When Entering a Cross Cultural Encounter

The Cultural Characteristics of Counseling

It has been long been noted that the theoretical and practical traditions of counseling reflect European–American middle class culture (Atkinson, et al., 1993; P. Pederson, 1987; Sue, 1977; Vontress, 1971). In many respects the counseling process is uniquely reflective of major North American culture, class, and language values (Sue & Sue, 1981). Some of these culture-bound characteristics of counseling have been identified as the individual-centered nature of the helping process, openness and intimacy between counselor and client, long-range goal setting, and the use of Standard English and verbal communication in the counselor–client interaction (Sue & Sue, 1981).

Significantly, for people whose cultural, class, or language values, may not be consistent with those found in counseling, an encounter with a counselor can often be an alienating and dissonant experience. This difference in values between counselor and client, while having the potential to enhance a working alliance between helper and helpee, far too often it has become an impediment to problem-resolution or decision-making (Sue, 1977; Vontress, 1981; Whaley, 2001).

Sociopolitical Nature of Counseling

It is important to point out that a cross cultural encounter in counseling can be a sociopolitical process related to a power differential between counselor and client (Katz, 1985; Lee, 2006b, 2007; M. J. Ratts, et al., 2010). This is particularly true if, because of race/ethnicity, religion, gender, sexual orientation, age, or ability status, a client occupies a subordinate cultural position in society. Such a position is usually characterized by forces of racism, sexism, ageism, classism, heterosexism, or ableism that impact negatively on academic, career, or personal-social development. Significantly, in many instances, counseling practice has been perceived as a tool of power, oppression, or social control among many groups of people. Often a cross cultural counseling encounter is a forced, as opposed to a voluntary experience, with a counselor perceived as a culturally insensitive or unresponsive agent of the broad and repressive social welfare system. Therefore, rather than being an empowering process, counseling can become disenfranchising, contributing to social marginalization for scores of client groups (Lee & Diaz, 2009).

Power and Privilege

Given the often sociopolitical nature of counseling two pervasive concepts that underlie the helping process in the cross cultural encounter must be considered: power and privilege. Power is a major theme in any counseling relationship. However often counselors tend to conceal or deny the fact, there is an inequality of power in the helping relationship. Individuals needing help with problem resolution or decision-making voluntarily come, or are referred (often by a powerful other), to a counselor for that assistance. By default therefore, that individual places the counselor in a power position. It is therefore crucial, when entering a cross cultural encounter, that a counselor acknowledges his or her power and ensure it is competently directed to help a client become empowered (Lee & Diaz, 2009). The dynamics of power, therefore, must be acknowledged in a cross cultural counseling encounter. This is particularly the case for those clients whose counseling issues relate to the stress of prejudice, discrimination, or social injustice (Cartenuto, 1992; Lee, 2006a; Lee & Diaz, 2009).

With respect to the concept of privilege, it is important that counselors reflect on the nature of the cultural privilege they may possess due to the color of their skin, gender, sexual orientation, age, socioeconomic status, ability status, or other social or cultural characteristic. Privilege can be conceived along several dimensions. First, it is generally unearned. In most cases individuals are born with it and their privilege tends to be innate. This is certainly the case with skin color or gender, for example. Second, individuals with privilege generally tend to be unaware of the unearned benefits that accrue from their privileged status. Third, privilege gives the individual who has it distinct cultural, social, and economic advantages. Individuals with privilege are generally seen to be in a position of social dominance when compared with those who lack these advantages (McIntosh, 1989). Significantly, in the United States, privilege generally comes with race/ethnic background (White), gender (Male), religion (Christian), sexual orientation (Heterosexual), ability status (Able Bodied), and socioeconomic status (Degree of Accumulated Wealth).

SIDEBAR 3.7 What is Your Degree of Privilege?

1. Were you ever called names because of your race/ethnicity, socioeconomic status, gender, religion, or sexual orientation?
2. Did you attend a private elementary or secondary school?
3. Were you ever discouraged from going to college because of your race/ethnicity, or socioeconomic status?
4. Did you ever go to school speaking a language other than English?
5. Have you ever encountered physical barriers to entering a building?

Your answers to these will give you an idea of what level of privilege you possess in society.

How will your level of privilege impact a cross cultural counseling encounter?

Significantly, the prerequisite for entering a cross-cultural encounter must be that counselors consider the nature of the possible power differential between counselor and client. Equally as important is an understanding of the extent of cultural privilege distinctions between counselor and client. Both the dynamics of power and privilege may significantly impact the counseling process.

Social Justice

Counselors who are aware of the sociopolitical nature of counseling and acknowledge their potential power and privilege in a cross cultural encounter must appreciate the importance of social justice to culturally competent counseling. In an attempt to address issues of equity, power relations, and institutionalized oppression, social justice seeks to establish a more equitable distribution of power and resources so that all individuals can live with dignity, self-determination, and physical and psychological safety. Social justice creates opportunities for people to reach their full potential within a mutually responsible, interdependent society (Goodman, 2001; Lee & Hipolito-Delgado, 2007; Rawls, 1971).

Social justice places a focus on issues of oppression, privilege and social inequities. For counselors, social justice implies professional conduct that opposes all forms of discrimination and oppression. Counseling practices that are rooted in social justice seek to challenge inherent inequities in social systems. Such practices are often of great importance in cross cultural counseling encounters when the etiology of client problems is ultimately linked to oppressive social, economic or cultural environments which serve to negatively impact academic, career or personal-social development (Lee, 2007).

A culturally competent counselor must also be an agent of social justice who possesses the awareness, knowledge and skill to intervene not only at an individual client level, but at a system-wide level as well. Whether in partnership with or on behalf of disempowered clients, a culturally competent counselor challenges cultural, social, historical, or economic barriers that stifle optimal human development and wellness (Lee, 2012).

Social justice is a foundational aspect of the cross cultural counseling encounter. Significantly, from a theoretical perspective, social justice is now considered the "fifth force" in the counseling field, following the paradigms of the psychodynamic approach, the cognitive/behavioral approach, humanism, and multiculturalism (Lee, 2012; M. Ratts, D'Andrea, & Arredondo, 2004, September 13; M. J. Ratts, et al., 2010).

SIDEBAR 3.8 The Case of Ms. Butler

Ms. Butler is a 35-year-old African American woman who has been referred to counseling for depression. She is a wage-reliant worker who holds down two jobs. Ms. Butler's 12-year-old son recently passed away from a bacterial infection in his brain. The infection had spread to his brain from an abscess in his tooth. She states that she had no health insurance and her Medicaid coverage had temporarily lapsed when her son's toothache started. Because of this, she could not afford to pay the $80.00 that it would have cost for a visit to the dentist. She is now trying to cope with the loss of her son and continue to provide for his younger brother.

If you were Ms. Butler's counselor, how would you address her issue in a culturally competent manner that reflected an understanding of the concept of social justice? What would you consider doing at a systemic level that could benefit Ms. Butler?

Counseling with Culture in Mind

If counselors are to exhibit competence in cross cultural encounters, then they must approach the counseling process with culture in mind (Vontress, 2009). This means that cultural factors must be considered in any counseling interaction. It is important to consider that cultural differences between counselor and client are just that, differences. These differences are not necessarily deficiencies or pathological deviations. Counseling with culture in mind entails working from a perspective that simultaneously acknowledges human similarity and celebrates human difference. Counselors must adopt a philosophy that views each client as a unique individual while, at the same time, taking into consideration the client's common experiences as a human being (i.e., the universal developmental challenges that face all people regardless of cultural background) and the specific experiences that come from his or her cultural background. It is important that counselors consider each client within a cultural group context and a broader global human perspective (Lee, 2006a, 2013).

The following are important concepts that should be considered when attempting to facilitate a working alliance between counselor and client in a cross cultural encounter. An understanding of these concepts is a reflection of counseling with culture in mind in a cross cultural counseling encounter.

Cultural Identity Development

Cultural identity refers to an individual's sense of belonging to a cultural group and the part of one's personality that is attributable to membership in that group. Cultural identity may be considered as the inner vision that a person possesses of himself or herself as a member of a cultural group and as a unique human being. It forms the core of the beliefs, social forms, and personality dimensions that characterize distinct cultural realities and worldview for an individual (Lee & Na, 2011).

Over the past several decades a number of cultural identity development models have emerged in the psychological literature which suggests that cultural identity formation is an important part of the psychosocial developmental process for people (Cass, 1979; Cross, 1971; Gill, 1997; Poston, 1990).

How a person views him or herself as a cultural being can have a profound impact on the counseling relationship. One of the basic components of a cross cultural counseling working alliance is an understanding of how the inner vision of the client impacts the counseling process (Cokley, 2007; Fischer & Moradi, 2001; Helms, 2007; Lee & Na, 2011; Ponterotto & Park-Taylor, 2007).

The perceptions people develop about themselves as cultural beings have important implications for the counseling process. Therefore, cultural identity must be factored into the working alliance between counselor and client. An understanding of cultural identity development is a fundamental aspect of the cross cultural counseling encounter.

Language Preference

Counseling is an activity that relies on communication between counselor and client. It is known as the "talking cure." Language, therefore, is an important variable in all counseling interactions, but it can assume complex dimensions in cross cultural counseling encounters. This is because the practice of counseling is predicated on an understanding of Standard English, while many clients from diverse cultural backgrounds may not necessarily value this language tradition as a primary means of communication.

Language is culture. It is a cornerstone of cultural identity. Language structures meaning, determines perception, and transmits culture. It communicates thought and subjective cultural experiences at deep and subtle levels (Westwood & Ishiyama, 1990). Acquisition and use of language is a primary aspect of psychosocial development and socialization in all cultures. Mastery of language generally implies mastery of culture.

Verbal and nonverbal communication is a cultural phenomenon involving the use of symbols of meaning that are culturally defined. The same words or gestures can have different meanings depending on the cultural context in which they are used (Gudykunst & Kim, 1984; Westwood & Borgen, 1988).

Culturally competent counseling, therefore, must be based on an appreciation of and sensitivity to possible language differences between counselor and client. These include differences in language fluency, accent, dialect, and the use of non-verbal communication (e.g., eye contact, body language, facial expressions, and emotional expressions). Failure to respect language differences in a counseling relationship invariably leads to misunderstanding and the possible alienation of clients.

An appreciation for language dynamics must be a central theme in the cross cultural zone. Clients must be able to tell their story in a manner that is most comfortable and appropriate for them (Roysircar, et al., 2003; Westwood & Ishiyama, 1990).

SIDEBAR 3.9 The Case of Mr. Kim

Mr. Kim, a recent immigrant from Korea, has been mandated for counseling due to charges of driving under the influence of alcohol. Mr. Kim begins to explain to his counselor, Mr. Harris, the frustrations that have led to his drinking. He has had difficulty finding a job, his children are experiencing problems at school, and he is having difficulty obtaining a green card. Midway through his explanation, Mr. Kim sighs and says, "I cannot explain any further in English."

If you were Mr. Harris, what would you do at this point?

Help-seeking Attitudes and Behavior

Counselors must recognize the fact that there is great variability among cultural groups with respect to help-seeking attitudes and behaviors. Not all cultural groups traditionally value or understand the nature of formal counseling as a source of help. It might be necessary, therefore, to step outside the confines of the traditional helping setting to offer counseling services. A culturally competent counselor may need to think creatively in terms of how he or she provides services to clients for whom the counseling process might be a totally alien experience.

As an example of help-seeking behavior, within the cultural traditions of many groups of people, religious institutions or spiritual centers are important sources of psychological support. Likewise, religious or spiritual leaders have been expected to not only provide for spiritual needs, but also offer guidance for physical and emotional concerns. These institutions and their leaders have been an important indigenous source of help for decision-making and problem resolution in many cultures for generations (Bond, et al., 2001). As appropriate, it might be necessary to form consultative relationships with religious/spiritual leaders or other indigenous helpers/healers for the benefit of clients.

Involving Key Others in the Counseling Process

Immediate and extended kinship networks must be considered as primary sources for promoting mental health and normal development among many cultural groups. Such networks may include immediate and extended family, friends, or community cultural resources. Within these support networks can be found hierarchical structures and cultural roles that promote a collective unity among groups of people. This collective unity provides the basis for a worldview which emphasizes communalism rather than individualism (Lee, 1997a).

Kinship and other collective support networks are crucial in providing resolutions to both situational and developmental problems related to educational, career, or personal-social issues. In many instances, the supportive dynamics of these indigenous networks may keep an individual from needing to seek outside decision-making or problem-resolution assistance. Culturally competent counseling practice, therefore, must include an understanding of and appreciation for the role of collective dynamics in mental health and well-being. As appropriate, counselors should find ways in which to make use of the kinship system and involve key others in the counseling process (Lee, 1997b, 2001).

Historical Hostility

Counseling across cultures often requires sensitivity to a dynamic that can be labeled "historical hostility" (Lee & Diaz, 2009; Vontress, Johnson, & Epp, 1999). The essence of this dynamic can be observed anywhere in the world where there has been a long-term pattern of exploitation or oppression between one group of people who is favored on the basis of ethnicity, religion, gender, social class, politics, etc., and another who is devalued in a common relationship. In their collective experience, therefore, people from the devalued group harbor conscious and unconscious negative emotions produced by traditions of brutality and frustrations which they and their forbearers suffered at the hands of the group that is favored (Lee & Diaz, 2009; Vontress, et al., 1999).

This concept underscores the historical reality of intergroup relations in the United States. Sadly, the history of this country is replete with examples of negative social encounters between people from different cultural backgrounds—from the enslavement of Africans, to violence perpetuated against the GLBT population, to religious intolerance directed towards those of the Muslim faith. The motivating forces defining these encounters have generally been racism, heterosexism, xenophobia, or other forms of social and economic oppression. Over time, the social and political processes associated with these oppressive and intolerant forces have taken a collective physical and psychological toll on many cultural groups. This toll is often seen in intense negative feelings that members of cultural groups with minority status often possess, either overtly or covertly, towards members of majority cultural groups. Whether these feelings are justified or warranted at any given point in time is generally rendered moot by the nature of the often exploitative and destructive relationships that have existed between groups of people from diverse cultural backgrounds in the United States.

With respect to counseling, historical hostility can manifest itself in resistance to the helper and the helping process. It is important to note that counseling has often been a sociopolitical process for many members of cultural groups (Lee, 1997a; Sue & Sue, 2012). Mental health services have been perceived as a tool of oppression and social control in many communities (Lee, 1997a; Sue & Sue, 2012). Often counseling is a forced, as opposed to a voluntary experience with a culturally insensitive or unresponsive agent of some aspect of the broad social welfare system (Lee & Diaz, 2009).

Historical hostility is a concept that may need to be factored into a cross cultural counseling encounter. This is particularly the case for those clients whose counseling issues relate to the stress of prejudice, discrimination, or intolerance. Resistance to counseling might include: denial of problems, viewing counseling as something that is done to an individual rather than with them, distrust of the counselor and the process, silence, passive aggressive behavior, or premature termination. These phenomena may be symptomatic of generalized negative feelings about a dominant cultural group fostered by negative intergroup relations over time.

While this list of concepts is by no means exhaustive, they provide key points of reflection for understanding the importance of counseling with culture in mind. Although the relevance of these concepts may vary across clients, a working knowledge of them and how they may impact the helping process should frame the context of competent counseling intervention in a cross cultural encounter. Understanding concepts such as these will go far in helping counselors eliminate the brick wall and minimize the cultural distance often inherent in cross cultural encounter.

SIDEBAR 3.10 Entering a Cross Cultural Encounter

Reflect on the following two questions:

- Given your cultural identity and degree of cultural privilege, what feelings do you contemplate having when entering a cross-cultural encounter?
- Given your cultural identity and degree of cultural privilege, what issues/challenges do you contemplate dealing with when entering a cross-cultural encounter?

Summary

This chapter has presented an overview of the discipline of cross cultural counseling. Given the changing population demographics of the United States in the second decade of the 21st century, it is important that professional counselors develop the awareness, knowledge and skill to establish, maintain, and successfully conclude counseling relationships with clients from diverse cultural backgrounds. At a fundamental level, any counselor who enters into a cross cultural counseling encounter must have self-awareness, an awareness of the world in which or she lives, a foundational knowledge of traditional counseling theory, and must aspire to high ethical standards. In addition, such a counselor must possess knowledge of culturally diverse perspectives of counseling and engage in cross cultural encounters as a way to enhance counseling skill development in a culturally competent manner. The sum total of this knowledge and experience should be cultural competency and the ability to effectively enter a cross cultural counseling encounter with culture in mind.

The following websites provide additional information relating to the chapter topics.

Useful Websites

Multicultural Counseling Competencies: www.counseling.org/Resources/
Association for Multicultural Counseling and Development: www.amcd-aca.org
2005 ACA Code of Ethics: www.counseling.org/Resources/
Dimensions of Personal Identity: www.counseling.org/Resources/
U.S. Census Bureau: www.census.gov (2010 Census data related to racial/ethnic groups, socioeconomic status, disability issues, and ageing)

References

Arredondo, P., Toporek, M. S., Brown, S., Jones, J., Locke, D. C., Sanchez, J., et al. (1996). *Operationalization of the Multicultural Counseling Competencies*. Alexandria, VA.

Association, A. C. (2005). *Code of Ethics*. Alexandria, VA: Author.

Association, A. C. (2010). 20/20: A vision for the future of counseling. Retrieved 2/14/2012, 2012, from http://www.counseling.org/20–20/definition.aspx.

Atkinson, D. R., Morten, G., & Sue, D. W. (1993). *Counseling American minorities: A cultural perspective* (Vol. 4th Ed). Madison, WI: Brown and Benchmark.

Bond, T., Lee, C. C., Lowe, R., Malaypillay, A. E. M., Wheeler, S., Banks, A., et al. (2001). The nature of counselling: An investigation of counselling activity in selected countries. *International Journal for the Advancement of Counseling, 23*, 245–260.

Cartenuto, A. (1992). *The difficult art: A critical discourse on psychotherapy*. Wilmette, IL: Chiron.

Cass, V. (1979). Homosexuality identity formation: A theoretical model. *Journal of Homosexuality, 4*, 219–235.

Census, U. S. B. o. t. (2010). United States: Profile of general population and housing characteristics: 2010. Washington, D. C.: Author.

Cokley, K. O. (2007). Critical issues in the measurement of ethnic and racial identity: A referendum on the state of the field. *Journal of Counseling Psychology, 54*, 224–239.

Collins, G. (2009). *When everything changed: The amazing journey of American women from 1960 to the present*. New York: Little, Brown and Company.

Cross, W. E. (1971). The Negro-to-Black conversion experinece: Toward a psychology of Black liberation. *Black World, 20*, 13–27.

DeNavas, W. C., Proctor, B. D., & Smith, J. C. (2011). *Income, poverty, and health insurance coverage in the United States: 2010*. Washington, D. C.

Fischer, A. R., & Moradi, B. (2001). Racial and ethnic identity: Recent developments and needed directions. In J. G.Ponterotto, J. M. Casas, L. A. Suzuki, & C. M. Alexander (Eds.), *Handbook of multicultural counseling* (2nd ed.). Thousand Oaks, CA: Sage.

Freedman, E. (2003). *No turning back: The history of feminism and the future of women*. New York: Ballantine Books.

Gates, G. J. (2011). *How many people are lesbian, gay, bisexual, and transgender*. Los Angeles: The Williams Institute.

Gill, C. J. (1997). Four types of integration in disability identity development. *Journal of Vocational Rehabilitation, 9*, 39–46.

Goodman, D. J. (2001). *Promoting diversity and social justice: Educating people from privileged groups*. Thousand Oaks, CA: Sage.

Gudykunst, K. B., & Kim, K. Y. (1984). *Communicating with strangers: An approach to intercultural communication*. Reading, MA: Addison-Wesley.

Helms, J. E. (2007). Some better practices for measuring racial and ethnic identity constructs. *Journal of Counseling Psychology, 54*, 235–246.

Humes, K. R., Jones, N. A., & Ramirez, R. R. (2011). *Overview of race and Hispanic origin: 2010*. Washington, D. C.

Katz, J. H. (1985). The sociopolitical nature of counseling. *Counseling Psychologist, 13*, 615–624.

Lee, C. C. (1997a). Cultural dynamics: Their importance in culturally responsive counseling. In C. C. Lee (Ed.), *Multicultural issues in counseling: New approaches to diversity* (2nd ed.). Alexandria, VA: American Counseling Association.

Lee, C. C. (1997b). *Multicultural issues in counseling: New approaches do diversity* (2nd ed.). Alexandria, VA: American Counseling Association.

Lee, C. C. (2001). Defining and responding to racial and ethnic diversity. In D. C. Locke, J. E. Meyers, & E. L. Herr (Eds.), *The handbook of counseling*. Thousand Oaks, CA: Sage Publications.

Lee, C. C. (2006a). Entering the cross-cultural zone: Meeting the challenge of culturally responsive counseling. In C. C. Lee (Ed.), *Multicultural issues in counseling: New approaches to diversity* (3rd ed.). Alexandria, VA: American Counseling Association.

Lee, C. C. (2006b). *Multicultural issues in counseling: New approaches to diversity* (3rd ed.). Alexandria, VA: American Counseling Association.

Lee, C. C. (2007). *Counseling for social justice*. Alexandria, VA: American Counseling Association.

Lee, C. C. (2012). Social justice as the fifth force in counseling. In C. Y. Chang, A. L. Dixon, C. B. Minton, J. E. Meyers, & T. J. Sweeney (Eds.), *Professional counseling excellence through leadership and advocacy*. New York: Routledge.

Lee, C. C. (2013). Global Literacy: The foundation of culturally competent counseling. In C. C.Lee (Ed.), *Multicultural issues in counseling: New approaches to divesity* (4th ed.). Alexandria, VA: American Counseling Association.

Lee, C. C., & Diaz, J. M. (2009). Counseling People of Color. In D. Capuzzi, & D. R. Gross (Eds.), *Introduction to the counseling profession* (5th ed.). Columbus, OH: Pearson.

Lee, C. C., & Hipolito-Delgado, C. P. (2007). Counselors as agents of social justice. In C. C. Lee (Ed.), *Counseling for social justice*. Alexandria, VA: American Counseling Association.

Lee, C. C., & Na, G. (2011). Identity development and its impact on the therapy relationship. In C. Lago (Ed.), *The handbook of transcultural counseling & psychotherapy*. Berkshire, England: McGraw Hill.

Lee, C. C., & Park, D. (2013). A conceptual framework for counseling across cultures. In C. C. Lee (Ed.), *Multicultural issues in counseling: New approaches to diversity* (4th ed.). Alexandria, VA: American Counseling Association.

Lewis, O. (1971). The culture of poverty. In M. Pilisuk, & P. Pilisuk (Eds.), *Poor Americans: How the White poor live*. New York: Transaction, Inc.

Locke, D. C. (1990). A not so provincial view of multicultural counseling. *Counselor Education and Supervision, 30*, 18–25.

McFadden, J. (1993). *Transcultural counseling: Bilateral and international perspectives*. Alexandria, VA: American Counseling Association.

McIntosh, P. (1989). White Privilege: Unpacking the invisible knapsack. *Peace and Freedom, 2*, 10–12.

Pease, B., & Pringle, K. (2001). *A man's world?: Changing men's practices in a globalized world*. New York: St. Martin's Press.

Pederson, P. (1987). Ten frequent assumptions of cultural bias in counseling. *Journal of Multicultural Counseling and Development, 15*, 16–24.

Pederson, P. B. (1991). Multiculturalism as a generic approach to counseling. *Journal of Counseling & Development, 70*, 6–12.

Pederson, P. B., Lonner, W. J., & G., D. J. (1976). *Counseling across cultures*. Honolulu: University of Hawaii Press.

Ponterotto, J. G., & Park-Taylor, J. (2007). Racial and ethnic identity theory, measurement, and research in counseling psychology: Present status and future directions. *Journal of Counseling Psychology, 54*, 282–294.

Poston, W. S. C. (1990). The biracial identity development model: A needed addition. *Journal of Counseling & Development, 69*, 152–155.

Rabinowitz, F. E., & Cochran, S. V. (1994). *Man alive: A primer of men's issues*. Belmont, CA: Thomson Brooks/Cole Publishing Co.

Ratts, M., D'Andrea, M., & Arredondo, P. (2004, September 13). Social justice counseling: 'Fifth force' in field. *Counseling Today*.

Ratts, M. J., Toporek, R. L., & Lewis, J. A. (2010). *ACA advocacy competencies: A social justice framework for counselors*. Alexandria, VA: American Counseling Association.

Rawls, J. A. (1971). *A theory of justice*. Cambridge, MA: Harvard University Press.

Root, M. P., & Kelley, M. (2003). *Multicultural child resource book: Living complex identities*. Seattle, WA: MAVIN Foundation.

Roysircar, G., Arredondo, P., Fuertes, J. N., Ponterotto, J. G., & Toporek, R. L. (2003). *Multicultural counseling competencies 2003: Associatin for multicultural counsleing and development*. Alexandria, VA: American Counseling Association.

Sue, D. W. (1977). Barriers to effective cross-cultural counseling. *Journal of Counseling Psychology, 24*, 420–429.

Sue, D. W., Arredondop, P., & McDavis, R. J. (1992). Multicultural counseling competencies and standards: A call to the profession. *Journal of Counseling & Development, 70*, 477–486.

Sue, D. W., Ivey, A. E., & Pederson, P. B. (1996). *A theory of multicultural counseling and therapy*. Pacific Grove, CA: Brooks/Cole.

Sue, D. W., & Sue, D. (1981). *Counseling the culturally different: Theory and practice*. New York: John Wiley & Sons.

Sue, D. W., & Sue, D. (2012). *Counseling the culturally diverse: Theory and practice* (6th ed.). New York: John Wiley & Sons.

Valentine, C. A. (1968). *Culture and poverty: Critique and counter-proposals*. Chicago, IL: University of Chicago Press.

Vontress, C. E. (1969). Cultural Differences: Implications for counseling. *Journal of Negro Education, 37*, 266–275.

Vontress, C. E. (1971). Racial differences: Impediments to rapport. *Journal of Counseling Psychology, 18*, 7–13.

Vontress, C. E. (1981). Racial and ethnic barriers in counseling. In P. Pederson, J. G. Draguns, W. J. Lonner, & J. E. Trimble (Eds.), *Counseling across cultures*. Honolulu: University of Hawaii Press.

Vontress, C. E. (2009). A conceptual approach to counseling across cultures. In C. C. Lee, D. A. Burnhill, C. Butler, C. P. Hipolito-Delgado, M. Humphrey, O. Muñoz, & H. Shin (Eds.), *Elementis of culture in counseling*. Columbus, OH: Pearson.

Vontress, C. E., Johnson, J. A., & Epp, L. R. (1999). *Cross-cultural counseling: A casebook*. Alexandria, VA: American Counseling Association.

Westwood, M. J., & Borgen, W. A. (1988). A culturally embedded model for effective intercultural communication. *International Journal for the Advancement of Counseling, 11*, 115–125.

Westwood, M. J., & Ishiyama, F. I. (1990). The communication process as a critical intervention for client change in cross-cultural counseling. *Journal of Multicultural Counseling and Development, 18*, 163–171.

Whaley, A. L. (2001). Cultural mistrust and mental health services for African Americans: A review and meta-analysis. *Counseling Psychologist, 29*, 513–521.

4

ETHICAL AND LEGAL CONSIDERATIONS IN COUNSELING

Mark D. Stauffer, Ann M. Ordway, and Laura Owen

Counseling is a profession guided by ethics, laws, and professional standards. Professional counselors formed associations to provide support, increase visibility, and galvanize professional identity. In this process, ethical codes and standards were created for the field. Codes and standards are living documents that change with the needs of the public and the individual client. Equally important, counselors are subject to local, state, and federal laws. New and novice counselors often experience a variety of emotions as they begin practice. They are often overwhelmed by excitement, worry, confusion, doubt, and pride. While excited about a first counseling session and about being helpful to clients, there is much to learn about the skills, knowledge, and attitudes necessary for making good professional decisions based on ethical standards and state and federal laws. The purpose of this chapter is to introduce the basic ethical concepts and legal guidelines that influence one's behavior as a counselor. In the end, it is up to counselors to integrate new knowledge and insights into their counseling practice. In the end, the individual counselor is responsible for ethical practice that ensures that clients are not harmed, but also benefitted from counseling.

Background: Basic Concepts

First, it will help to clarify what the terms *Ethics* and *Professional Ethics* mean. According to MacKinnon (1998), ethics is a branch of philosophy, specifically moral philosophy, that "asks basic questions about the good life, about what is better and worse, about whether there is any objective right and wrong, and how we know it if there is" (p. 5). Remley and Herlihy (2010) suggested that although ethics and morality have overlapping meanings, morality is based on one's values while ethics is concerned with human behavior and moral decision making. "The term *professional ethics* refers to agreed-upon rules, principles, and standards that govern appropriate conduct and define acceptable practices in various professional fields, including the mental health professions" (Pack-Brown, Thomas, & Seymour, 2008). Whether spoken or unspoken, codified or not, individuals and groups have beliefs about what is right and wrong, about what is ethical and unethical. These beliefs motivate day-to-day behaviors. On personal, familial, communal, and societal levels, ethics exist as part of the complex way humans create interpersonal boundaries and make choices. Ethical dilemmas arise that are not easily solved because of the multifaceted nature of life. If one considers the current debate on life and death issues such as abortion, capital punishment, and euthanasia, it is easy to understand that ethical practice is not a formula for behavior carved in stone but rather is an arena in which dilemmas arise.

As suggested by the dictionary definition of ethics, joining and identifying as a member of a group usually signifies that a member agrees to adhere to the ethical standards established by the group. In the mental health profession, that group could be the American Counseling Association (ACA), the American Psychological Association (APA), or the National Board of Certified Counselors (NBCC), to name just a few. In this chapter, the discussion of ethics will be based on the guidelines provided by professional codes of ethics such as the ACA *Code of Ethics* (2005), the APA *Ethical Principles of Psychologists and Code of Conduct* (2010) (hereafter referred to as APA *Ethical Principles*), and the American School Counselor Association (ASCA, 2010) *Ethical Standards*. Please refer to *Useful Web Resources* at the end of this chapter for links to these professional codes and standards.

Remley and Herlihy (2010) discussed the difference between mandatory ethics and aspirational ethics. Mandatory ethics are influenced and shaped in conjunction with legal standards. Aspirational ethics, as the name implies, promote ethical behavior based on broad-spectrum aspirations such as justice and respect for the rights and dignity of persons. Two important elements of aspirational ethics are virtues and principles. Virtue ethics focus on internal moral processes and on "who one is." Principle ethics are concerned with "what one does" and implies a certain level of obligation to act in certain ways (Sim, 1997, p. 31). Meara, Schmidt, and Day (1996) suggested that integration of both virtue and principle ethics into professional ethical standards improves counselor competency, especially in multicultural settings in which flexibility is a necessity.

When individual rights are compromised or when public safety, health, and general welfare are jeopardized in some way, law also factors into the decision-making process and guides the actions of the counselor. "Laws are the agreed-on rules of a society that set forth the basic principles for living together as a group" (Remley & Herlihy, 2007, p. 3). Laws are divided into two primary categories: criminal and civil. Criminal laws generally govern and pertain to behaviors which are crimes, such as statutory rape, fraud, and acts of violence. In some states, domestic violence is governed by criminal law, while in other states it is considered quasi-criminal or civil. Civil laws govern or pertain to individual and group interests and rights which are non-criminal in nature, such as contract, personal injury/tort, divorce and custodial rights, and property interests. Laws can be created as a result of an extrapolation of rights as defined by the United States or local Constitutions; as Statutes created by legislative bodies of government; or through case law, which represents the refinement or definition of law created through interpretations of pre-existing laws by the court systems. Such situational interpretations found in court verdicts become a type of guidepost or precedent for future cases. The creation, interpretation, and enforcement of laws are not separate from cultural values and biases and fluctuate with political tides. Law and judicial interpretation on the federal, state, district, and territorial level are most often in agreement with one another, but in some situations they do not agree. While it is helpful for counselors to have some basic familiarity with law that is most relevant to their area of practice so as to avoid giving a client inappropriate advice, it is especially important that counselors do not give legal advice. Specifically, when a client faces legal implications connected to issues presented in counseling, the counselor should strongly suggest that the client confer with a licensed attorney with expertise in the relevant area.

SIDEBAR 4.1

Jason, a newly licensed counselor working in a Community Mental Health Center, works with UK-born mother of one Juliet, who has come to counseling without her American husband to figure out how to leave her husband. She reports domestic violence and that her husband will not let her and her 3-year-old daughter move back to the UK. Juliet has been talking with Jason for awhile about feeling homesick and missing her family in England. As it is apparent from many signs and symptoms that Juliet is telling the truth related to domestic violence, Jason, as a counselor, advises her to leave her husband, and return to her home country with her 3-year-old daughter for safety reasons.

In this case, three specific laws are important: The Uniform Child Custody Jurisdiction and Enforcement Act (UCCJEA, 1997), Parental Kidnapping Prevention Act (28 U.S.C. 1738A), and The Hague Convention ("Hague"). According to these laws, the parent who removes and transports a child from one State to another may be subject to criminal prosecution for kidnapping. Pursuant to the PKPA and Hague Convention (to which the US and England are both signatories), Juliet could be transported back to the United States, criminally prosecuted for kidnapping, and lose custody of the child to her husband. What do you see as the ethical and legal dilemmas of this case? What would you do differently, if anything, from what the counselor did in this story?

Malpractice torts can be particularly important to professional counselors. Tort law pertains to the careless, reckless, negligent, and sometimes even intentional behavior of a third party when that behavior is the proximate cause of injury to another. An example is a ruling that allows an individual to receive compensation for injury inflicted by others. Based on a general principle that holds professionals responsible for practices that harm clients, a malpractice tort empowers judicial systems to establish what is unacceptable conduct for the professional (Remley & Herlihy, 2010). The connection between the actions of a counselor and injury to a client is linked to foreseeability (the predictability that certain behavior is likely to cause a specific result), but also consideration of whether the counselor "should have known" that certain practices would likely lead to specific injury or trauma, for example, to the client. Counselors must be acutely aware of the nuances of the potentially fragile populations of clients with whom they work—with special attention to the core tenet of ethics—"Do No Harm."

SIDEBAR 4.2

Marissa, an LPC starting a private practice in a new location, has an appointment with Doug, an 18-year-old college freshman who is grappling with his sexual orientation, and is considering telling his parents that he is gay. Marissa holds certain conservative Christian beliefs about homosexuality being an "unacceptable lifestyle." As far as she knows, she has never worked with, or even befriended, someone from the LGBT population. At first, she is concerned that her personal beliefs might interfere with her ability to work with Doug, but in the end, she decides to work with Doug for the following reason: to develop a greater client base, to help him make better choices, to gain greater experience helping this population, and to improve her "cultural competence." She agrees to begin seeing him as a client, and immediately suggests that Doug tell his parents about his dilemma and solicit their support in helping him change. Doug does tell his parents about his sexual orientation. Unbeknownst to Marissa as she has worked with Doug for only a short time, Doug's parents hold Marissa's conservative beliefs about being gay, but unlike Marissa, they believe in "strong punishment for homosexual activity." Doug's parents reject him and order him out of their home, then and there, leaving Doug with nowhere to go. In what ways could Marissa's actions cause Doug harm? What would you do differently, in anything, from what the counselor in this story did? If you were a counselor stepping in to support Doug after this event, what would you need to do in your counseling sessions?

Dilemmas often arise because differences exist between ethical standards and law. Counselors need to understand the relationship between what is ethical and what is legal; however, should one follow or break a law that is unethical by one's personal and professional standards? Counselors are sometimes forced to answer such questions with immediate action and then bear the consequences of their choices. At other times law and ethics do not interact directly, for example, such as when an ethical standard is alegal, or such that it is not specifically covered by any law. This is true because law establishes the minimum requirements for counselor behavior. Examine the following categorical graph as an exploration of the possible interplay between law and ethics. Can you add a few of your own examples?

	Legal	*Illegal*	*Alegal*
Unethical	Advertising as having unusual talents	Unwarranted disclosure of confidential information	Attempts to enhance "professional" skills at the expense of the client
Ethical	Reporting child abuse	Refusing to testify to prevent client harm	Providing some service to the profession without profit

It is noteworthy that ignorance of the law is not a defense for a violation of the law. This concept can be complicated during the interplay between the law and cultural values, especially when a counselor is working with a client whose cultural beliefs and practices violate an existing law. For example, as child abuse is illegal and counselors are legally bound to report child abuse, counselors are required to break confidentiality to adhere to the law. However, there are distinct cultures which consider corporal punishment, sometimes severe corporal punishment, as normative parenting practice. In such cases, the counselor is faced with mandatory reporting requirements, possible advocacy for family members, while also applying cultural sensitivity in approaching the situation.

It is best to stay current about state and federal laws, state licensing board requirements, and the ethical standards of professional counseling organizations. For new practitioners, this may seem daunting and perhaps threatening; however, these standards exist to protect both the counselor and the client. They foster higher standards for the practice of counseling. Familiarity with relevant laws serves as an additional protection for the counselor. However, familiarity with the law is not a license to give client's legal advice; nor is it a valid replacement for seeking legal advice from an expert when a dilemma based in law arises. In fact, it is best for the client to seek direct legal advice, rather than the counselor merely repeating the advice the counselor solicited on behalf of a client. Too much can be lost in the translation of the information, which could open the counselor to potential liability resulting from misunderstanding or miscommunication.

Decision Making (STEPS)

With so many things to consider, how does a counselor move forward to make a decision with confidence? Koocher and Keith-Spiegel's (1998) problem-solving model provides guidelines for establishing the existence of ethical violations as well as outlining the steps to resolve them. The ASCA Ethical Standards (2010) also address the decision making process by including the Solutions to Ethical Problems in the Schools (STEPS) as a standard (G.3).

1. Define the problem emotionally and intellectually
2. Apply the ASCA Ethical Standards and the law
3. Consider the students' chronological and developmental levels
4. Consider the setting, parental rights and minors' rights
5. Apply the moral principles
6. Determine your potential courses of action and their consequences
7. Evaluate the selected action
8. Consult
9. Implement the course of action

These sequential problem solving models provide decision makers with a set of tools in a step-by-step approach helping facilitate the decision making process. Collaborative consultation is a key component of most ethical decision making models and provides the opportunity for multiple views when addressing difficult issues. Following the guidelines in ethical decision making models may protect the counselor from potential pitfalls that would otherwise not be seen when working in isolation.

SIDEBAR 4.3 Ethical Decision Making Cases

Using the ACA or ASCA Code of Ethics as a guide, write down the actions you would take if you were the counselor asked to respond to the following situations.

1. A teacher reports that one of her 9th grade students, Nicole, just disclosed that her best friend Katie has been "cutting" and she is worried that Katie will die

---

without some intervention. Nicole believes that Katie has a razor in her backpack at school today. The teacher also shares that Nicole is a responsible student and she trusts that she is not overreacting, but Nicole asked the teacher to please keep this confidential. Using a decision making model (i.e. STEPS), outline your next steps. What do you say to the teacher? How do you respond to Nicole's request to keep this information confidential? Do you speak with Katie? What about Nicole? Do you contact either or both girl's parents?

2. You are a female African American graduate student currently receiving supervision from a white male counselor and notice that your supervisor is uncomfortable addressing issues of gender and diversity. Whenever you broach the topic of gender, racial identity or white power the supervisor quickly changes the subject. You are uncomfortable with his response and are concerned that the supervisor is not equipped to provide multiculturally sensitive supervision. What are your next steps?

Choosing to Be a Counselor and Ethical Motivations

What are your motivations for being a counselor? Motivations are often the root sources of a counselor's behavior, whether or not such behavior is legal or ethical. In 1972, Max Hammer discussed motivations for entering the helping profession in his classic chapter entitled "To Students Interested in Becoming Psychotherapists." He believed that persons often had wrong reasons, such as the need to be dominant, to be needed and loved, to be a voyeur on other's lives, to be an omnipotent healer, to escape one's own life, and to cure themselves by curing others. Corey, Corey, and Callahan (2011) also indicated that the therapeutic process could be blocked when therapists use clients to fulfill their own needs to nurture others, to feel powerful or important, or to win acceptance, admiration, respect, or awe.

It is unethical when counselors are primarily meeting their own needs and imposing personal values in the counseling relationship. Without bringing awareness to our motivations a counselor may miss the subtle ways our underlying motivations enter the counseling relationship. ACA's (2005) *Code of Ethics* specifically states under A.4.b. Personal Values that "counselors are aware of their own values, attitudes, beliefs, and behaviors and avoid imposing values that are inconsistent with counseling goals." Additionally, Standard A.4.a. states that "counselors act to avoid harming their clients. . . ." The APA *Ethical Principles* (2010) encourage one to, "exercise reasonable judgment and take precautions to ensure that their potential biases, the boundaries of their competence and the limitations of their expertise do not lead to or condone unjust practices" (Principle D: Justice).

Multiple Relationships

Clients are harmed by counselors who meet their personal needs through "multiple relationships" with their clients. Multiple relationships occur when a counselor relates to a client in a professional role and concurrently or sequentially occupies one or more other professional or nonprofessional roles with the client (e.g. friend, intimate partner, peer, financial partner, etc.). While not all multiple relationships are harmful or unethical, some can be devastating.

The most devastating of these occurs when a counselor engages in a sexual relationship with a client, a multiple relationship unequivocally considered unethical in the counseling profession and deemed illegal in many states (Hermann & Robinson Kurpius, 2006). Having a sexual relationship with a client is the most consistently violated ethical standard among psychologists and the second most frequently claimed violation against counselors (Herlihy & Corey, 1992; ASPPB, 2001). All ethical codes ban sexual intimacies with clients. "Sexual or romantic counselor—client interactions or relationships with current clients, their romantic partners, or their family members are prohibited" (ACA, 2005, A.5.a. Current Clients). Furthermore, counselors cannot engage in "sexual or romantic counselor—client interactions or relationships with former clients, their romantic partners, or their family members . . . for a period of 5 years following the last professional contact" (ACA, 2005, A.5.b Former Clients). Counselors who engage in such a relationship after five years following the last professional contact have the responsibility to "demonstrate forethought and document (in written form) whether the interactions or relationship can be viewed as exploitive in some way and/or whether there is still potential to harm the former client" (ACA, 2005, A.5.b. Former Clients).

A client advocacy website posted the following comments from a client who was victimized by a therapist: "It's really hard to explain how powerful the therapist seems to the client. He is supposed to be the expert, the trusted person who knows what is best for you. I wish I hadn't ignored my uneasiness and confusion when he started touching me. I guess I wanted him to take my pain away and to take care of me. It turned out that I was taking care of his needs most of the time. I was someone for him to confide in, to hold, to be flattered by" (Public Education Work Group, 1988, p.1). When sexual contact becomes part of a therapeutic relationship, the expectation of trust that is essential to the process of therapy is violated (Thoreson, Shaughnessy, Heppner, & Cook, 1993).

Research has demonstrated that a therapeutic alliance, also known as a working alliance, is one of the preeminent factors in therapeutic efficacy and outcome (Lustig, Strauser, Rice, & Rucker, 2002). An effective therapeutic alliance rests on the personal well-being and mental health of the counselor, which allows for bonding, collaborative goal setting, and task accomplishment. Discussing the personhood of the counselor, Hammer (1972) noted,

> [. . .] to be really effective, the therapist needs to know from *personal experience* what the "path" is that leads from internal conflict and contradiction to liberation. If you do not know how to liberate yourself from an internal conflict, fear or pain, then you are not in a position to help others do it either. . . . What right does the therapist have to ask the patient to face his [her] rejected truths and anxiety and to take risks in terms of exposing himself [herself] and making himself [herself] vulnerable, if the therapist is not willing or able to do so? (p. 12)

Therefore, a counselor's first ethical responsibility is to be as emotionally healthy as possible, to be aware of "unfinished business" that could potentially influence attempts to be helpful to others, and to seek professional help as soon as one is aware that some aspect of one's own life may be infringing on one's work as a counselor. When counselors have ongoing mental health challenges that need to be managed to provide counseling for others, additional supports and safeguarding habits need to be in place. Your competence is limited by your own self-awareness and psychological health and maturity (Robinson, 1988; Corey et al., 2011).

Moral Principles

Counselors integrate and use ethical principles as a way to monitor and reflect upon internal motivations and to guide their behaviors, especially when difficulties arise. The professional literature as well as professional organizations, suggest that certain principles serve as guideposts for counselor behavior. Synthesizing the literature, Remley and Herlihy (2007) suggested six principles for counselors to consider:

1. Beneficence—do good, promote well-being and health.
2. Nonmaleficence—do no harm, prevent harmful actions and affects.
3. Autonomy—recognize and respect independence and self-determination.
4. Justice—promote fairness and equality in dealings.
5. Fidelity—be responsible to clients and honor agreements.
6. Veracity—be truthful and honest in dealings.

The APA *Code of Ethics* (2010) incorporated these principles into its ethical code: *Principle A: Beneficence and Nonmaleficence; Principle B: Fidelity and Responsibility; Principle C: Integrity; Principle D: Justice; and Principle E: Respect for People's Rights and Dignity.*

Professional Responsibility

Counselors have a fiduciary *trusty* responsibility to their clients and must be accountable for client welfare and rights. A breach of fiduciary responsibility, including a breach of confidentiality without appropriate justification, can evoke legal considerations and the potential for a malpractice claim. Furthermore, counselors have a responsibility to the public, to other professionals, to agencies and institutions in which they work, as well as to the counseling profession. In addition to respecting differences among clients, counselors must be competent, respect client rights, maintain confidentiality, and promote client welfare.

The Importance of Multiculturalism in Ethics

Professional Ethical standards and the application of these standards are increasingly reflecting the importance of multiculturalism and social justice. However, there is much that can be improved. To start, the adept counselor understands that ethics and culture are inseparable. "Culture affects counselors' ethical thinking as well as the decisions practitioners make about what they consider to be good and appropriate professional conduct. In short, cultural issues affect all aspects of the counseling process, including ethical considerations that emerge from the time the counselor first meets a client to termination of the helping endeavor" (Pack-Brown, Thomas, & Seymour, 2008).

A challenge in creating ethical standards is finding standards that are specific enough to highlight proper behavior and yet broad enough so that the codes are not unrepresentative or myopic. Ibrahim (1996) suggested a universalistic approach to ethical standards, that is, having ethical codes that reflect what is common across cultures while honoring the ethics of each individual culture (as cited in Atkinson, 2004). This is not an easy task, especially since terminology and the meaning of assigned words may vary from culture to culture. Most codes have broad aspirational goals related to multiculturalism that require counselors to act from what the code implies rather than from specific behavioral guidelines. Cottone and Tarvydas (2007) noted that "implied ethical standards are not enforceable in grievance processes, which limits the profession's ability to protect consumers from being harmed by incompetent multicultural practices" (p. 220).

SIDEBAR 4.4

Nida is a 14-year-old female student of Pakistani heritage. Though she is forbidden in her family's culture from dating as arranged marriage is expected, she is secretly dating. One day, Nida divulges her secret to her female counselor, who shares the same ethnic background. The counselor understands that severe punishment (e.g., beating) is not uncommon for such infractions. Nonetheless, in keeping with her interpretation of ACA and ASCA ethical guidelines, the counselor honors Nida's confidentiality and right to "Autonomy." Furthermore, the counselor also believes it would be wrong for her to interfere with Nida's parents' response. Accordingly, when the counselor hears in the community about Nida's dating, before Nida hears of it, the counselor remains silent. What dilemmas come to mind from this story related to culture and counseling ethics? What would you do differently, if anything, from what the counselor in this story did?

Almost all beginning counselors understand that cultural insensitivity, racism, oppression, and discrimination are *wrong*. However, what often remains unclear is how such problems manifest in subtle ways in ordinary activity. For example, microaggressions may go unnoticed by White counselors, but picked up by African American clients, which may directly affect therapeutic alliance and client satisfaction (Constantine, 2007). Beginning counselors often fail to realize how much effort is truly necessary to be a culturally competent counselor.

There are several passages in both the APA (2010) Ethical Principles and ACA (2005) Ethical Codes that stress that it is unethical to discriminate, harass, or demean clients on the basis of culture, including but not limited to race, ethnicity, religion, gender, sexual orientation, or socioeconomic status, as well as a host of other unspoken cultural identities. Ethical codes have made it clear that discrimination is not acceptable for any reason. Counselors are challenged to consider their own individual biases, and experiences with specific cultural groups, and how those biases and experiences have affected them as individuals and as counselors (McAuliffe, 2008). For example, we can recognize pain as a human phenomenon, but we also need to understand how specific groups and individuals experience pain differently. Ethics codify bases by which counselors must not discriminate, but counselors should continue to strive to understand and validate the variation, complexity, and severity of the underlying issues, including but not limited to the imbalance of power that often accompanies the concept of white privilege even as it potentially manifests in the counseling context (Pinderhughes, 1989). There are individuals and groups who are yet to be acknowledged in their need for social justice. What other forms of discrimination are not listed? For example, one form of discrimination that is often unrecognized is discrimination based on body fat/size. The following exemplifies why respect and awareness of differences are important:

Sandy McBrayer, the 1995 national Teacher of the Year, tells of visiting an elementary school that was proud of its ethnic diversity and the integration achieved within the school's social milieu. The principal walked her to the newly built multipurpose 'cafetorium' and ceremoniously pulled open the doors to reveal children of all colors eating, talking, and laughing together. As she entered, a contrasting scene near the door caught her eye. Separated from the rest of the student body were two large children who sat at a table eating their lunches in silence, staring directly ahead. They were not laughing. They were not talking. They were just bringing their forks to their mouths and down again, trying to be inconspicuous and to finish quickly. This day, they were too slow. As other children finished their meals and exited the cafetorium, they threw their uneaten food at the two children.

(Loewy, 1998)

Based on a study of 52 professionals, Loewy (1994/1995) found that mental health counselors were no less biased than the general public in that they stereotyped "fat" persons negatively and "thin" people positively (as cited in Loewy, 1998). One task of the counselor is to stop malevolent action and take responsibility for harmful behavior, whatever it is.

Beginning in the late 1960s, concern was raised over counselor competence to counsel someone who was of a different ethnicity. According to Atkinson (2004), professional competence is still the quintessential ethical issue regarding multicultural counseling. Sue and Sue (2003) noted, "From our perspective, mental health professionals have seldom functioned in a culturally competent manner. Rather, they have functioned in a monoculturally competent manner.... We submit that much of the current therapeutic practice taught in graduate programs derives mainly from experience and research with middle-to upper-class White folks" (pp. 9–10). The above criticism is not new to the field of counseling and comes from within the community of counselors. It is a statement that we hope challenges all to improve.

Multicultural counseling competence involves three main components: (a) An awareness of one's cultural values and biases; (b) cultural awareness of your client's worldview; and (c) using culturally appropriate counseling practices (ACA, 2002). To become more skilled at meeting the needs of diverse clients, a competent counselor will proactively evolve through study, training, and supervision. Part of a counselor's job is to become secure with his/her own ethnic identity, which correlates with greater openness and acceptance of different cultural backgrounds (as noted in Semans & Stone Fish, 2000). Self-examination and accepting the many facets of one's heritage are steps toward a self-awareness that requires accountability for one's intolerance, oppression, racism, and elitism. A counselor is also called on to be "aware of and respect, cultural, individual, and role difference ..." (APA 2010, Principle E: Respect for People's Rights and Dignity). In order to move from being unaware to aware, it is important to have didactic and experiential knowledge of individual and group differences.

Is it ethical to apply counseling theories, techniques, and even ethical standards without consideration of a client's cultural background? Although the easy answer is "no," to make the necessary adaptations is more than a simple task. For example, would your personal religious convictions or conceptualization of "appropriate" counseling prevent you from collaborating with a client's traditional healer?

The client's culture may also influence the boundaries of the counseling relationship. In some cultures, for example, sharing food or small gifts are signs of respect. The APA Code of Ethics (2010) states, "A psychologist refrains from entering into a multiple relationship if the multiple relationship could reasonably be expected to impair the psychologist's objectivity, competence, or effectiveness in performing his or her functions as a psychologist, or otherwise risks exploitation or harm to the person with whom the professional relationship exists. Multiple relationships that would not reasonably be expected to cause impairment or risk exploitation or harm are not unethical" (3.05a Multiple Relationships). The important point is that a skilled counselor should consider client welfare and culture when using counseling interventions and apply consistent efforts to be competent while still respecting the culture of the client.

Counselor Competence

This naturally brings us to the topic of counselor competence. The notion that it is unethical to practice beyond the limits of one's competence is widely accepted. Here are some important points drawn from the 2005 ACA *Code of Ethics* (C.2. Professional Competence), regarding competence:

(1) Boundaries of Competence:
   (a) Provide only those services for which you are qualified.
   (b) Represent accurately your professional qualifications.
(2) New Specialty Areas of Practice: Practice in new specialty areas only after appropriate education, supervision and experience.
(3) Qualified for Employment:
   (a) Only accept employment for which you are qualified.
   (b) Hire for professional counseling positions only those that are qualified.
(4) Monitor Effectiveness: Make continual efforts to monitor and improve efficacy and outcomes.
(5) Consultation on Ethical Obligation: Consult with colleagues and other relevant professionals regarding ethical issues.
(6) Continuing Education:
   (a) Grow professionally through involvement in continuing education.
   (b) Take steps to insure nonmalefecience in using the new specialty area.
(7) Impairment:
   (a) Seek assistance in solving personal issues.
   (b) Refrain from your professional services if a client may be harmed by your physical, mental or emotional problems.
(8) Counselor Incapacitation or Termination of Practice: Counselors prepare a written plan for the transfer of clients to an identified colleague in the case of incapacitation, death, or termination of practice.
(9) When counselors leave a practice, they follow a prepared plan for transfer of clients and files. Counselors prepare and disseminate to an identified colleague or "records custodian" a plan for the transfer of clients and files in the case of their incapacitation, death, or termination of practice.

For a student, it is your professors' responsibility to foster your learning of these aspects of competence and to provide ongoing "evaluation and appraisal" to "address the inability of some students to achieve counseling competencies that might impede performance" (ACA, 2005, F.9.b. Limitations). Counselor educators "assist students in securing remedial assistance when needed" (ACA, F.9.b. Limitations) and "recommend dismissal from training programs . . . when those supervisees are unable to provide competent services" (ACA, F.5.b. Limitations). For students, competence is a shared responsibility between you and your training program. However, after graduation and entering the professional world, it is the graduate's professional and ethical responsibility to remain competent.

The ACA *Code of Ethics* (2005) clearly states that "Counselors practice only within the boundaries of their competence, based on their education, training, supervised experience, state and national professional credentials, and appropriate professional experience" (C.2.a. Boundaries of Competence). The ethical standards are quite clear regarding what a counselor should do when they are not competent to treat a certain client problem. Here is a rough step-by-step procedure to assist you when you recognize your competency is insufficient.

1) Limit services and refer clients to other helping professionals who can meet the needs of one's client in the given area and then consider expanding one's competence base. (NOTE: Refer to more than one professional so that the client has options and does not feel obligated to receive services from a specific professional.)
2) Suspend services and refer to several appropriate professionals while you receive sufficient training and supervision in the specialty area,
3) Terminate professional responsibilities and make appropriate referrals,
4) If there is no one to whom the counselor can refer (which would be an exception rather than a common occurrence), the counselor should seek education on the presenting problem and seek supervision of the work with the client.

To be competent, continuing education is a never-ending requirement that does not stop upon graduation. One area of training for which students often need additional preparation is in diagnosis. Typically, insurance companies will not pay for service unless the client has a DSM-IV-R diagnosis (or DSM-V after May 2013–see http://www.dsm5.org/Pages/Default.aspx). Counselors must know when to provide a diagnosis and also when to refrain from providing a diagnosis. The ACA ethical Standard E.5.d. states, "Counselors may refrain from making and/or reporting a diagnosis if they believe it would cause harm to the client or others." The ability to diagnose has been the subject of debate and court proceedings. In Arizona, a social worker diagnosed a client as paranoid, a diagnosis which was confirmed by a consulting psychiatrist (*Cooke v. Berlin*, 1987). When the client later killed a man and was diagnosed with atypical psychosis, the social worker was sued by the victim's widow. Although the case was eventually settled out of court, it left several questions unanswered. What is the appropriate scope of practice of various mental health professionals? Had there been competent diagnosis, would there have been an assessment of dangerousness resulting in a duty to warn? When can one professional, especially an unlicensed one, provide information to another without the risk of malpractice? These questions all center on knowing the limits of one's competence and behaving within the boundaries of professional training and experience.

A final area of professional competence is ethically presenting one's services and credentials to the public. The Federal Trade Commission has granted considerable freedom for advertising as a result of the *Goldfarb v. Virginia State Bar* (1975) ruling. However, most codes of ethics have strict ethical standards about advertising; for example, they warn professionals against making false claims regarding expertise and qualifications and hold the professional responsible for correcting misrepresentation of their qualifications by others (ACA, 2005, C.4.a. Accurate Representation). So to be called a "doctor," one should hold a doctoral degree in counseling or a related field. If there is a misunderstanding, a counselor must correct this misrepresentation immediately. In advertising services, counselors "identify their credentials in an accurate manner that is not false, misleading, deceptive, or fraudulent" (ACA, 2005, C.3.a. Accurate Advertising). One cannot claim that he or she is a "candidate for" a degree. When trying to build a practice, client testimonials must be avoided as well as implying unusual or one-of-a-kind abilities (Koocher & Keith-Spiegel, 1998). The ACA *Code of Ethics* (2005, C.6.c. Media Presentations) requires that media presentation statements be appropriate and consistent with the *Code of Ethics*. Additionally, the APA *Principles* (2010) state that a paid advertisement must be acknowledged or "clearly recognizable" as such (5.02c Statements by Others).

Client Rights and Welfare

When clients enter a counseling relationship, they assume the counselor is competent. In addition, they have certain rights, known as client rights. Foremost of these are confidentiality, privileged communication, and informed consent, which are based on the Fourth Amendment, established to guarantee privacy. Privacy is defined as "the constitutional right of an individual to decide the time, place, manner, and extent of sharing oneself with others" (Corey et al., 2011, p. 212).

Privacy and Confidentiality

Confidentiality and Privileged Communications

The concept of privacy is the foundation for the client's legal right to privileged communication and the counselor's responsibility to hold counseling communications confidential. Confidentiality is a professional concept. Privileged communication is a legal term referring to a right held by clients to prevent therapeutic information from entering into a legal proceeding. Clients, not counselors, have control over who has access to what they have said in therapy, and clients are protected from having their communication disclosed in a court of law. However, a client's confidential communications may not be privileged in a court of law unless the mental health professional is legally certified or licensed in the state in which he or she practices.

Most states grant the clients of state certified or licensed mental health professionals (i.e., psychologists, professional counselors, marriage and family therapists) the right of privileged communications source. On a federal level, in 1996, the U.S. Supreme court ruled in *Jaffee v. Redmond* that communication was indeed privileged communication for clients of licensed social workers, which has important implications for master's level mental health professionals. Since then, privileged communication was recognized for a client of a licensed clinical social worker (see Cottone & Tarvydas, 2007). HIPAA defines the term "psychotherapy notes" as "notes recorded (in any medium) by a health care provider who is a mental health professional documenting or analyzing the contents of conversation during a private counseling session or a group, joint, or family counseling session and that are separated from the rest of the individual's medical record" (USDHHS, 2003, p. 9). Much is still uncertain regarding privileged communication for clients who seek services from certain mental health professionals in various states.

Outside of eligibility concerns, in order for communication to be privileged, four conditions must be met:

1) Communication must originate in confidence that it will not be disclosed.
2) Confidentiality must be essential to the full and satisfactory maintenance of the relationship.
3) In the opinion of the greater community, the relationship must be one that should be sedulously fostered, or in other words, noted by care and persistent effort.
4) Injury to the relationship by disclosure of the communication must be greater than the benefit gained by the correct disposal of litigation regarding the information (Schwitzgebel & Schwitzgebel, 1980).

If, as a counselor, you can claim these four conditions and your professional licensure makes your clients eligible, your clients' communications are not only confidential, but also they are privileged and, thus, are protected from being disclosed in a court of law, unless the client specifically waives privilege or consents to the testimony. However, once the client waives privilege as to one issue, the door is potentially unlocked for testimony by the professional as to any and all interactions between that client and that professional. One must remember, however, that there is always a balance between a client's right to privacy and society's need to know. This is often referred to as the "doctor's dilemma" (Koocher & Keith-Speigel, 1998). Due to the delicate nuances associated with confidentiality and the heightened potential that a counselor can be subpoenaed to turn over records or provide court testimony, a counselor who encounters a request or requirement to participate in a legal proceeding should consult with an attorney regardless of whether the request comes from the counselor's own client or a party adverse to the position of the client, such as in a divorce or custody proceeding.

SIDEBAR 4.5

A subpoena is a legal document usually issued by an attorney. Through a subpoena, an attorney can seek to obtain the release of a counselor's confidential documents or to compel a counselor's testimony. While the counselor may assert the client's "privilege" and should seek to honor the confidentiality of the client if the client does not consent to the release of documents or to a counselor's testimony, the counselor may not simply ignore the subpoena, nor may they simply refuse to respond without legal ramifications. Most often the best practice is for the counselor to consult with an attorney in the specific jurisdiction where the legal proceeding is occurring. Rather than simply turning over requested information, there are options a counselor's lawyer may find available. One option is to move to *quash* the subpoena, essentially asking the Court to rule that the subpoena is invalid. For example, subpoenas are sometimes deficient (meaning not prepared correctly), and additionally, attorneys are not always familiar with the parameters of privilege as it applies to counselors. Moreover, your attorney may be able to ascertain whether the other attorney is even entitled to the information. The confidential records of a client should never be released until the counselor is sure that the release is warranted and appropriate. When possible, the counselor should seek and/or obtain an authorization from the client before releasing documents.

In spite of the importance given to confidentiality and privileged communication, Pope, Tabachnick, and Keith-Spiegel (1987) reported that 62 percent of psychologists in a national survey indicated that they had unintentionally violated a client's confidentiality and 21 percent had intentionally violated a client's confidentiality. These alarming statistics suggest that mental health professionals are at risk for violating this core ethical principle. Therefore, adept mental health professionals are acutely aware of the professional standards regarding confidentiality and of their state's laws governing privileged communication. For example, in most states, if staff working in the mental health professional's office breach a client's confidentiality, the professional is potentially liable for the breach by the employees of the agency/office. The extent of the liability may vary from State to State. Office administrators and other staff who have access to client records are considered extensions of certified/licensed mental health professionals.

HIPAA and the "Privacy Rule"

In the late 1990s, concern over the privacy of health services consumers increased because of advances in technology and shift to managed health care. For example, the electronic transfer of or faxing entire health records from service providers to insurance agencies pose threats to the privacy of insured patients. The U.S. Department of Health and Human Services (USDHHS) created the Health Insurance Portability and Accountability Act (HIPAA) to insure privacy of consumers while at the same time allowing for efficient transfer of information. As a division of the Department of Health and Human Services, the Office of Civil Rights (OCR) has the responsibility for HIPAA implementation through the encouragement of voluntary compliance and enforcement through civil monetary penalties (USDHHS, 2003). This Act also sought to improve how consumers understand and manage their use of personal health information (USDHHS, 2003). HIPPA affects the job task requirements of both mental and physical health care providers, especially those working with health insurance companies.

The USDHHS's "Privacy Rule," formally titled *Standards for Privacy of Individually Identifiable Health Information*, focused on the use and disclosure of client information termed, "protected healthcare information (PHI)." This is information on any past, present, or future mental or physical health of clients, including payment information. Certain health service providers are declared "covered entities," if they must abide by HIPAA. Often helping professionals such as counselors, psychologists and social workers fall into this category when "they hold or transmit [PHI] . . . in any form or media, whether electronic, paper, or oral." (USDHHS, 2003, p. 3). The nuances involved in operationalizing HIPPA are extensive; for this reason a detailed and thorough explanation is beyond the scope of this chapter.

The Privacy Rule addresses protected information related to counseling. The privacy rule applies to information that might identify or could be used to identify a person. Except in unusual circumstances, individuals have the right to review and obtain a copy of their protected health information in a counselor's "designated record set." The designated record set is that group of records that is "used to make decisions about individuals" (USDHHS, 2003, p. 12). The rule makes an exception for "psychotherapy notes." Descriptive of a relatively smaller portion of most mental health records, a psychotherapy note does not include: "medication prescription and monitoring, counseling session start and stop times, the modalities and frequencies of treatment furnished, results of clinical tests, and any summary of the following items: diagnosis, functional status, the treatment plan, symptoms, prognosis, and progress to date" (USDHHS, p. 9). Agencies should have policies to distinguish a psychotherapy note from other records and should have separate storage for each type of record. A counselor must obtain client authorization for specific uses and disclosures of psychotherapy notes. Some important exceptions exist: for use in treatment whereby the originator of the note is the sole user; to conduct training programs in order to instruct and supervise students, interns and other trainees; to defend oneself in legal proceedings activated by a client; to facilitate HHS checks for compliance; to avert a "serious and imminent threat to public health or safety;" and for lawful oversight of a counselor by a health oversight agency (USDHHS, p. 9).

The privacy rule requires professionals to inform, if not educate, clients about their privacy rights and privacy procedures and practices used by the counseling agency. They inform clients by notice, which explains and provides examples of how protected information is used, disclosed, amended, inspected, and copied, including exceptions and prohibitions. Notices also inform clients regarding their rights to restrict, revoke and receive an accounting of disclosures. For example, a client may request that an authorization be valid for only 10 days and that he or she be informed if the transmission is completed. A general notice is also posted in reasonably clear view on counseling premises. Furthermore, notices are given to clients upon intake, promptly mailed to clients when initial communications are by phone and sent electronically (in a proper format) when providing services online. Agencies should post a notice of their privacy practices on their website. Furthermore, counselors should make a "good faith" effort to obtain written acknowledgement from clients that they received a privacy notice, and should document efforts made when this acknowledgement is not possible (USDHHS, 2003).

Authorization forms for use and disclosure of information should be in specific terms and allow clients to understand their privacy rights. "All authorizations must be in plain language, and contain specific information regarding the information to be disclosed or used, the person(s) disclosing and receiving the information, expiration, right to revoke in writing, and other data" (USDHHS, 2003, p. 9). In keeping with both APA and ACA ethical guidelines, when clients give authorization, they should be informed about what exact information is being released, to whom, for what purpose, and the time period for which the signed consent for release is valid (Robinson Kurpius, 1997). Under the privacy rule, an agency providing covered health services must also set up procedures for the use of forms for routine disclosure and create criteria to follow when unusual, non-routine disclosures of information are required. Counselors may not demand that clients give authorization for the release of information in order to receive treatment, except in certain limited circumstances (USDHHS, 2003).

HIPAA stipulates that training on privacy practices should be an ongoing procedure for the entire agency *workforce*. This covers how and who handles protected information. The privacy rule requires that classifications of personnel related to information access be clarified on the basis of workplace role and then operationalized. For example, an agency database should not allow an office manager access to psychotherapy notes; he/she should only be able to access the minimum information necessary to perform his or her job (e.g. schedule clients, bill insurance). Agencies should also appoint or identify a "privacy officer," incorporate privacy protocol and safeguards, and instruct clients on grievance procedures (USDHHS, 2003, p. 14).

Exceptions to Confidentiality

There are three global issues that require one to breach confidentiality. In cases of minors, we have both a legal and ethical responsibility to protect them from ". . . future harm of continued abuse or neglect and to protect children who are insufficiently autonomous to act on their own behalf" (Sattler, 1990, p. 105). In New Jersey, for example, the duty to report known child abuse or neglect is not limited to a professional responsibility, but rather is a mandate for all citizens who become aware of a situation potentially dangerous for a child. Moreover, failure to do so can result in various penalties, including monetary fine or even jail time in extreme circumstances. Minors are usually all individuals under the age of 18; however, some states recognize emancipated minors who are 16 or older. Counselors should know their state laws that apply to minors and breaching confidentiality (Lawrence & Robinson Kurpius, 2000). Every state has passed a law mandating the reporting of child abuse. Regardless of the counselor's personal feelings about helping a client to overcome his or her abusive behavior, the abuse must be reported. Society has deemed that knowing of and stopping child abuse outweigh the abuser's right to privacy. Differences exist among states, so counselors should check with their state protective service for information on what is specifically meant by abuse.

Many states also require that counselors report abuse, neglect, or exploitation of incapacitated and vulnerable adults. For example, in Arizona, incapacitated is defined as "an impairment by reason of mental illness, mental deficiency, mental disorder, physical illness or disability, advanced age, chronic use of drugs, chronic intoxication, and other causes to the extent that the person lacks sufficient understanding or capacity to make or communicate responsible decisions" and a vulnerable adult is defined as, "an individual who is eighteen years of age or older who is unable to protect himself from abuse, neglect or exploitation by others because of a physical or mental impairment" (Arizona Revised Statute 46–451).

Finally, privilege is automatically waived when a client presents with a "serious and forseeable harm" to self or others (ACA, 2005, B.2.a. Danger and Legal Requirements). A well-known court case that established such mandatory disclosure was *Tarasoff v. Board of Regents of the University of California* (1974, 1976). A young graduate student, Prosenjit Poddar, had been working with a university psychologist regarding his depression and anger resulting from being rejected by a female peer, Tatiana Tarasoff. He told the psychologist about his intent to buy a gun. The psychologist notified the campus police both verbally and in writing about his concerns that Poddar was dangerous and should be taken to a community mental health facility. The police interviewed Poddar and released him from custody. The psychologist's supervising psychiatrist decided that the letter to the police and selected case notes should be destroyed. Shortly thereafter, Poddar shot and stabbed Tatiana to death. The California Supreme Court held that "Once a therapist does in fact determine, or under applicable professional standards reasonably should have determined, that a patient poses a serious danger of violence to others, he bears a duty to exercise reasonable care to protect the foreseeable victims of that danger" (Tarasoff, 1976). This has been interpreted as the duty to protect or the duty to warn. In these instances, it is the counselor's overriding responsibility to protect an intended, identifiable victim from harm that could result from a client's actions. The duty to warn is incorporated in Section B.2.a. of the ACA Code of Ethics, which permits a breach of confidentiality when there is an existing threat of "serious and foreseeable harm." The amended language is designed to broaden the circumstances under which a counselor has a legal duty to warn.

Other instances when the privilege is typically lost include when clients introduce their mental condition as an element in a court case, when the mental stability of either spouse is introduced in a child custody case, when the counselor is working for the court such as in conducting a court-ordered evaluation examination, when the client is suing the counselor, and when the counselor believes that the client is in need of immediate hospitalization. There is a significant difference between a client seeking to have their own therapist testify on their behalf, and a counselor being subpoenaed by the adverse party. The client must be made to understand that a waiver of confidentiality as to one topic opens the door to testimony by the counselor as to other issues which the client may not want the counselor to disclose. While a subpoena by an adverse party does not automatically pierce the veil of confidentiality, a subpoena should never be ignored, since doing so presnts a risk that the counselor will be held in contempt of court. It is best to consult with an attorney as to how to respond appropriately, while also maintaining the confidentiality of a client who did not waive that right. It is strongly suggested that at the onset of therapy, counselors inform clients about the limits of confidentiality and the specific instances when confidentiality must be breached. Clients can then make informed decisions about what they say in therapy.

Confidentiality and HIV

Counselors with HIV-AIDS clients may face a delimma between protecting their clients' right of confidentiality and a duty to warn when clients do not inform their sexual partners of their medical condition. The ACA *Code of Ethics* (2005 B.2.b. Contagious, Life-Threatening Diseases) addresses this issue, "When clients disclose that they have a disease commonly known to be both communicable and life threatening, counselors may be justified in disclosing information to identifiable third parties, if they are known to be at demonstrable and high risk of contracting the disease. Prior to making a disclosure, counselors confirm that there is such a diagnosis and assess the intent of clients to inform the third parties about their disease or to engage in any behaviors that may be harmful to an identifiable third party." Robinson Kurpius (1997) pointed out that "unless there is an identifiable victim and the client refuses to behave in a manner that protects this person, the covenant of confidentiality should not be broken" (p. 10). As Koocher and Keith-Spiegel (1998) noted, good clinical judgment is essential in making decisions regarding duty to protect. Furthermore, two-thirds of the states have legislation regarding limits to confidentiality of a client's HIV status (Corey et al., 2007); therefore, counselors should be aware of the legislation in the state where they practice. Finally, ACA standard B3.f states, "counselors protect the confidentiality of deceased clients, consistent with legal requirements and agency or setting policies."

Informed Consent

This brings us to a discussion of informed consent. According to Everstine et al. (1980) three elements must be present for informed consent to be legal.

1. Competence—requires that the person granting the consent is able to engage in rational thought to a sufficient degree to make competent decisions about his or her life. Minors cannot give informed consent, and consent must be sought from their parents or legal guardian. Minors give informed assent.

2. Informed—requires that the individual is given the relevant information about the procedures to be performed in a language that he or she can understand.
3. Voluntariness—requires that consent is given freely by the client.

Counselors should "appropriately document written or oral consent, permission, and assent." (APA, 2010, 3.10d Informed Consent). Legal minors can only give assent; parents must provide consent. The ACA (2005) *Code of Ethics* is very specific with respect to what should be disclosed to clients in order for them to give informed consent: "Counselors explicitly explain to clients the nature of all services provided. They inform clients about issues such as, but not limited to, the following: the purposes, goals, techniques, procedures, limitations, potential risks, and benefits of services; the counselor's qualifications, credentials, and relevant experience; continuation of services upon the incapacitation or death of a counselor; and other pertinent information. Counselors take steps to ensure that clients understand the implications of diagnosis, the intended use of tests and reports, fees, and billing arrangements. Clients have the right to confidentiality and to be provided with an explanation of its limitations (including how supervisors and/or treatment team professionals are involved); to obtain clear information about their records; to participate in ongoing counseling plans; and to refuse any services or modality change and to be advised of the consequences of such refusal" (A.2.b. Types of Information Needed).

If a counselor is asked by a client to disclose to a third party information revealed in counseling, the client should sign an informed consent form before a disclosure is made. New counselors may be surprised to learn that counselors are not even permitted to respond to inquiries about whether they are seeing a person in therapy—even the client's name and status in counseling are confidential, unless the client has granted permission for this information to be released. This is true even after the client is deceased.

Right to Treatment

Having clients sign informed consent forms implies that they have a right to receive or refuse treatment. Several court cases have been based on the right-to-treatment issue. In the early 1970s, *Wyatt v. Stickney* (1974) was the first case in which the right to treatment was ruled a constitutionally protected right. The case was filed against the state of Alabama on behalf of mentally disabled institutionalized patients who were being kept confined under conditions of psychological and physical deprivation. There was one physician for every 2000 patients, making adequate care impossible. The court ruled that involuntarily committed patients have a constitutional right to receive "such individual treatment as will give each of them a realistic opportunity to be cured or to improve" (*Wyatt v. Stickney*, 1974). In addition, the court required the institution to have individualized treatment plans developed by qualified mental health professionals for each patient. Furthermore, committed patients have the right to their own clothing, to receive minimal pay for labor performed, to receive mail, to exercise several times per week, and to have an appropriate physical environment in which to live.

In *Rogers v. Orkin* (1980) and in *Rennie v. Klein* (1981), courts ruled that clients have the right to refuse treatment. In *Roger v. Orkin*, the court ruled that the "power to produce ideas was fundamental to our cherished right to communicate." The court indicated that the right to refuse medication and seclusion was a Fourth Amendment right, but cited several state interests that can overrule a person's right to this privacy: police power—the right of the state to protect others from harm; *parens patriae*—the duty of the state to prevent the patient's condition from deteriorating; and consideration of the financial costs of operating facilities that may result from extended hospitalization (Levenson, 1989). In *Rennie v. Klein,* the Court held that the right to refuse medication could only be overruled under due process, except in an emergency. All of these court cases have provided us with parameters for client rights with respect to treatment issues. Counselors should be constantly alert to the legal issues surrounding this very important client right.

Variations of Counseling and Counselor Ethics

The preceding discussion rests on the premise that the counselor's primary obligation is to protect the welfare of the client. The ACA (2005) *Code of Ethics* states that "the primary responsibility of counselors is to respect the dignity and to promote the welfare of clients" (A.1.a. Primary Responsibility). However, the setting, type of counseling, and the method by which counseling is conducted leads to variations in application. The type of counseling and the media by which counseling is conducted all impact client welfare and ethical practice. In this section we will cover an introductory explanation of some key ethical issues related to couples and family counseling, counselor groupwork, and technology assisted counseling.

SIDEBAR 4.6 A Taxonomy of Face-To-Face and Technology-Assisted Distance Counseling
From http://www.nbcc.org/Assets/Ethics/internetCounseling.pdf

In examining this taxonomy, what variation of ethical considerations might arise for these types of Counseling?

1. Face-To-Face Counseling
    a. Individual Counseling
    b. Couple Counseling
    c. Group Counseling
2. Technology-Assisted Distance Counseling
    a. Telecounseling
        i. Telephone-Based Individual Counseling
        ii. Telephone-Based Couple Counseling
        iii. Telephone-Based Group Counseling
    b. Internet Counseling
        i. E-Mail-Based Individual Counseling
        ii. Chat-Based Individual Counseling
        iii. Chat-Based Couple Counseling
        iv. Chat-Based Group Counseling
        v. Video-Based Individual Counseling
        vi. Video-Based Couple Counseling
        vii. Video-Based Group Counseling

Couples and Family, and Groupwork Counseling Ethics

Thus far, the discussion has focused on individual clients. An additional set of guidelines impact the counselor when they work with more than one person in a session. The International Association of Marriage and Family Counselors' (2003) *Ethical Codes* and the Association for Group Workers' *Best Practices* are useful and should be followed by the counselor (Thomas & Pender, 2007). Please view these two documents at the associations' websites or at the Ethics links for IAMFC (http://www.iamfconline.com/PDFs/Ethical%20Codes.pdf) and for ASGW (http://www.asgw.org/PDF/Best_Practices.pdf) respectively.

There are some key differences when working with couples and families. Often they relate to ensuring group confidentiality and appropriate treatment of the family as a group as well as the members of the group. As examples, counselors are not to disclose confidences or secrets provided by one member in an individual session to other members of the couple of family without consent (SECTION II.a.3), the counselor must be clear that the primary client is the family (SECTION I.j.), and counselors must take care to get informed consent from each client (SECTION II.d.3).

In group work some of the distinguishing ethical requirements for the counselor relate to group types, group management, and communication of group parameters. As examples, the purpose and goals of the group should be clear and then the group worker must monitor progress of the group goals; counselors cannot assure that group members will maintain group confidentiality; and "group workers apply and modify knowledge, skills and techniques appropriate to group type and stage, and to the unique needs of various cultural and ethnic groups" (Thomas & Pender, 2007, Section B3a). Unlike individual counseling, clients who want to be involved in a group experience need to be screened before being accepted into a group. This screening not only ensures that the client is appropriate for the group but also protects other group members from a potentially dysfunctional group member.

School Counseling Ethics

School counselor ethics reflect the particular challenges and needs of the school counseling environment. First, school counselor ethics are impacted by federal laws related to academics and education; for example, the Family Educational Rights and Privacy Act (FERPA, 2002) guarantees certain rights to parents of students to protect and have access to their child's information (see http://www2.ed.gov/policy/gen/guid/fpco/ferpa/index.html). Second, counselors working in school may have additional challenges around maintaining and breaching confidentiality as they have greater student caseloads, they have to coordinate their work with other school-based professionals, they do not share the same ethical mandates as other professionals in the school environment, and they are often held accountable to more community stakeholders (i.e., parents, administrators) than other types of counselors (Moyer, Sullivan, & Growcock, 2012). Third, counselors working in schools mostly work with minors, requiring parent buy-in and support, which can be an aid as well as a complication. Finally, counseling and groupwork sessions may happen in the classroom environment or at times, environments that are not designated specifically for counseling. In addition to adhering to the ASCA (2010) *Ethical Standards for School Counselors,* school counselors must work with supervisors, consultants, as well as counseling peers and mentors to practice ethically in the school setting.

Technology-Assisted Distance Counseling Ethics

The increasing use of the technology to provide counseling requires new and continually unfolding ethical requirements of the counselor or e-counselor (Finn & Barak, 2010). Indeed, the "information highway" poses many ethical concerns that were not present just a decade ago (Cottone & Tarvydas, 2007). The ACA Governing Council (1999, 2005) and the National Board of Certified Counselors (2007) published ethical standards to guide counselors. Here are a few important points conveyed in their document:

1. Counselors consider the appropriateness of online counseling and addresses potential limitations of such services. For example, counselors provide ways to cope with and address misunderstandings.
2. Counselors explain the limits of confidentiality particular to online counseling.
3. Counselors explain and notify clients about certain aspects of how confidential information is handled (e.g.-who has access to the counselor's computer).
4. Counselors use security technology, software, and "secure" sites to protect client information and communications such as encryption, firewall technology, digital shredders, password protection for computers and files, HIPAA compliant web conferencing tools, etc.
5. "Professional counselors identify foreseeable situations in which confidentiality must be breached in light of the law in *both* the state in which the client is located and the state in which the professional counselor is licensed" (ACA, 1999, A4).
6. "Professional counselors identify clients, verify identities of clients, and obtain alternative methods of contacting clients in emergency situations" (ACA, 1999, B3). This includes local alternative professional help in the case of a crises.
7. There are certain circumstances in which a client must waive a right to priviledged communication because of the nature of online services.
8. Find cost free sites for clients when possible, be aware of the client's local environment and culture as well as provide a barrier-free environment for clients with disabilities.

Client Rights—Summary

The rights of your clients are many and varied. Perhaps one of the best statements regarding client rights can be found at the National Board for Certified Counselors Web Site. The NBCC (2001b) listed the following client rights and responsibilities:
"Your Rights As a Consumer

- Be informed of the qualifications of your counselor: education, experience, professional counseling certification(s), and license(s).
- Receive an explanation of services offered, your time commitments, fee scales, and billing policies prior to receipt of services.
- Be informed of the limitations of the counselor's practice to special areas of expertise (e.g. career development, ethnic groups, etc.) or age group (e.g. adolescents, older adults, etc.).
- Have all that you say treated confidentially and be informed of any state laws placing limitations on confidentiality in the counseling relationship.
- Ask questions about the counseling techniques and strategies and be informed of your progress.

- Participate in setting goals and evaluating progress toward meeting them.
- Be informed of how to contact the counselor in an emergency situation.
- Request referral for a second opinion at any time.
- Request copies of records and reports to be used by other counseling professionals.
- Receive a copy of the code of ethics to which your counselor adheres.
- Contact the appropriate professional organization if you have doubts or complaints relative to the counselor's conduct.
- Terminate the relationship at any time.

Your Responsibilities as a Client

- Set and keep appointments with your counselor. Let him or her know as soon as possible if you cannot keep an appointment.
- Pay your fees in accordance with the schedule you pre-established with the counselor.
- Help plan your goals.
- Follow through with agreed upon goals.
- Keep your counselor informed of your progress towards meeting your goals.
- Terminate your counseling relationship before entering into arrangement with another counselor."

Notice that the consumer/client responsibilities require the counselor to have provided the client with informed consent at the beginning of therapy. Also note that the client cannot behave unethically—only counselors can make that mistake.

Summary

Unethical treatment causes harm to clients and leaves the counselor open to malpractice suits and loss of credibility. This may leave the counselor and client in vulnerable positions which minimize or negate the benefits of counseling and damage the credibility of counselors and the counseling profession. A counselor's best defense is to behave as ethically as possible while doing everything to promote the best interests of clients.

Most have entered this profession in order to help others while also earning a living and reaping the fruits of a rewarding career. For both to occur, counselors must keep the ethical codes in mind at all times; must strive to be as mentally, emotionally, spiritually, and physically healthy as possible; must obtain a thorough graduate education that emphasizes both knowledge and practice; and must seek continuing education, advanced training and supervision when in the "real world."

Useful Websites

American Association for Marriage and Family Therapists' (Ethical and legal information page): http://www.aamft.org/iMIS15/AAMFT/MFT_Resources/Legal_and_Ethics/Content/Legal_Ethics/Legal_Ethics.aspx?hkey=2e3ddff7–9dff-45f6–9344–a8f152c91681
American Counseling Association (ACA Code of Ethics): http://www.counseling.org/Resources/CodeOfEthics/TP/Home/CT2.aspx

American Psychological Association (Ethics page): http://www.apa.org/ethics/

American School Counselor Association (Ethics page): http://www.schoolcounselor.org/content.asp?pl=325&sl=136&contentid=136

Association of Specialist in Group Work (Best practices page): http://www.asgw.org/best.htm

National Association of Social Workers (Ethics page): https://www.socialworkers.org/pubs/code/default.asp

National Board for Certified Counselors (Client rights and ethics page): http://www.nbcc.org/About/Advocacy

National Center on Elder Abuse-state laws page: http://www.ncea.aoa.gov/NCEAroot/Main_Site/Find_Help/APS/Analysis_State_Laws.aspx

U.S. DHHS-ACF-Child Welfare Information Gateway: http://www.childwelfare.gov/

U.S. DHHS-Office of Civil Rights-Information on HIPAA: http://www.hhs.gov/ocr/hipaa/

References

American Counseling Association. (2005). *Code of ethics and standards of practice*. Alexandria, VA: Author.

American Counseling Association. (1999). *Approved by the ACA governing council, October 1999.* Retrieved September 1, 2003 from http://www.counseling.org/site/PageServer?pagename=resources_internet.

American Counseling Association. (2002). *Cross cultural competencies and objectives*. Alexandria, VA: Author. Retrieved April 27, 2012 from http://www.counseling.org/Resources/Competencies/Cross-Cultural_Competencies_and_Objectives.pdf.

American Psychological Association. (2010). *Ethical principles of psychologists and Code of Conduct*. Washington, DC: Author.

American School Counselor Association. (2010). *Ethical standards for school counselors*. Alexandria, VA: Author. Retrieved May 1, 2012 from http://www.schoolcounselor.org/files/EthicalStandards2010.pdf.

Association of State and Provincial Licensing Psychology Boards. (2001). Ethics, law, and avoiding liability in the practice of psychology. Montgomery, AL: Author. Arizona Revised Statute 46–451.

Atkinson, D. R. (2004). *Counseling American Minorities* (6th ed.) NY: McGraw Hill.

Cooke v. Berlin, 153 Ariz.220 (1987); 735 P.2d 830 (App. 1987).

Constantine, M. G. (2007). Racial microaggressions against African American clients in cross-racial counseling relationships. *Journal of Counseling Psychology*, *54*(1), 1–16. doi:10.1037/0022–0167.54.1.1

Cottone, R. R., & Tarvydas, V. M. (2007). *Counseling ethics and decision making* (3rd Ed.). Columbus, OH: Pearson Merrill/Prentice Hall.

Corey, G., Corey, M. S., & Callanan, P. (2011). *Issues and ethics in the helping professions*. (8th Ed.). Belmont, CA: Brooks/Cole.

Everstine, L., Everstine, D. S., Geymann, G. M., True, R. H., Frey, D. H., Johnson, H. G., & Seiden, R. H. (1980). Privacy and confidentiality in psychotherapy. *American Psychologist*, *35*, 828–840.

Family Educational Rights and Privacy Act. (FERPA). (20 U.S.C. § 1232g; 34 CFR Part 99).

Finn, J., & Barak, A. (2010). A descriptive study of e-counsellor attitudes, ethics, and practice. *Counselling & Psychotherapy Research*, *10*(4), 268–277. doi:10.1080/14733140903380847

Goldfarb v. Virginia State Bar 421 U.S. 773 (1975).

Hammer, M. (1972). To students interested in becoming psychotherapists. In M.Hammer (Ed.), *The theory and practice of psychotherapy with specific disorders* (pp. 1–23). Springfield, IL: Charles C. Thomas.

Hermann, M., & Robinson Kurpius, S. E. (2006, December). New guidelines on dual relationships: A review of revisions to the ACA Code of Ethics. *Counseling Today*, 8–9.

Herlihy, B., & Corey, G. (1992). Dual relationships in counseling. Alexandria, VA: American Association for Counseling and Development.

Jaffee vs. Redmond. 518 U.S. 1 (1996).

Koocher, G. P., & Keith-Spiegel, P. (1998). *Ethics in psychology: Professional standards and cases.* (2nd ed.). New York: McGraw-Hill.

Lawrence, G., & Robinson Kurpius, S. E. (2000). Legal and ethical issues involved when counseling minors in a non-school setting. *Journal of Counseling and Development.* 78(2), 130–136.

Levenson, M. (1989). Right to accept or refuse treatment: Implications for the mental health profession. Unpublished manuscript. Arizona State University.

Loewy, M. I. (1998). Suggestions for working with fat children in the schools. *Professional School Counseling, 1*(4), 18–22.

Lustig, D. C., Strauser, D. R., Rice, N. D., & Rucker, T. F. (Fall, 2002). The relationship between working alliance and rehabilitation outcomes. *Rehabilitation Counseling Bulletin*, 46, 25.

MacKinnon, B. (1998). *Ethics: Theory and contemporary issues.* (5th ed.). Belmont, CA: Wadsworth.

McAuliffe, G. (2008). Culturally Alert Counseling. Los Angeles, CA: Sage Publications.

Meara, N. M., Schmidt, L. D., & Day, J. D. (1996). Principles an virtues: A foundation for ethical decision making, policies and character. *The Counseling Psychologist*, 24, 4–77.

Moyer, M. S., Sullivan, J. R., & Growcock, D. (2012). When is it ethical to inform school administrators about at-risk behaviors? Perceptions of school counselors. *Professional School Counselor*, 15(3), 99–109.

National Board for Certified Counselors. (2001a). *National counselor Exam.* Alexandria, VA: Author. Retrieved on September 1, 2003 from http://www.nbcc.org/exams/nce.htm.

National Board for Certified Counselors. (2001b). *What can I expect from a counselor.* Alexandria, VA: Author. Retrieved September 1, 2003 from http://www.nbcc.org/admin/clientrights.htm.

National Board of Certified Counselors and Center for Credentialing and Education. (2007). The practice of internet counseling. Greensboro, NC: Author. Retrieved April 22, 2012, from http://nbcc.org/Assets/Ethics/internetCounseling.pdf.

Pack-Brown, S. P., Thomas, T. L., & Seymour, J. M. (2008). Infusing professional ethics into counselor education programs: A multicultural/social justice perspective. *Journal of Counseling & Development*, 86(3), 296–302. doi:10.1002/j.1556–6678.2008.tb00512.x

Pinderhughes, E. (1989). Understanding race, ethnicity, and power: The key to efficacy in clinical practice, New York: The Free Press.

Pope, K. S., Tabachnick, B. G., & Keith-Spiegel, P. (1987). Ethics of practice: The beliefs and behaviors of psychologists as therapists. *American Psychologist*, 42, 993–1006.

Public Education Work Group of the Task Force on Sexual Exploitation. (1988). *It's never ok!* Advocate Web. Retrieved September 1, 2003 from http://www.advocateweb.org/hope/itsneverok/.

Remley, T. P., and Herlihy, B. (2007). *Ethical, legal, and professional issues in counseling* (2nd Ed.). Saddle River, NJ: Pearson Merrill/Prentice Hall.

Remley, T. P., and Herlihy, B. (2010). *Ethical, legal, and professional issues in counseling* (3rd Ed.). Saddle River, NJ: Pearson Merrill/Prentice Hall.

Rennie v. Klein, 462 F. Supp. 1131 (D.N.J. 1978) (modified 653 F.2d 836, (1983, Ct. of App 3rd; 720 F.2d 266, 1983 Ct of App. 3rd).

Robinson, S. E. (1988). Counselor competency and malpractice suits: Opposite sides of the same coin. *Counseling and Human Development*, 20, 1–8.

Robinson Kurpius, S. E. (1997). Current ethical issues in the practice of psychotherapy. *The Hatherleigh Guide to Ethics in Therapy* (pp. 1–16). New York: Hatherleigh Press.

Rogers v. Orkin, 634 F. 2nd 650 (Ct. of App. 1st Cir, 1980); 738 F2d 1. (Ct. of App. 1st Cir. 1984).

Sattler, H. A. (1990). Confidentiality. In B. Herlihy, & L. Golden (Eds.), *ACD Ethical Standards Casebook* (4th ed). Alexandria, VA: American Association for Counseling and Development.

Schwitzgebel, R. L., & Schwitzgebel, R. K. (1980). *Law and psychological practice*. New York: John Wiley & Sons.

Sim, J. (1997). *Ethical decision making in therapy practice*. Oxford: Butterworth-Heinemann.

Semans, M., & Stone Fish, L. (2000). Disecting life with a Jewish scapel: A qualitative exploration or Jewish families. *Family Process*, 39(1), 121–139.

Sue, D. W., & Sue, D. (2003). *Counseling the culturally diverse* (4th ed.). New York: John Wiley and Sons.

Tarasoff v. Board of Regents of the University of California, 17 Cal.3d 425, 551 P.2d 334, 131 Cal Rptr 14 (1976).

Thoreson, R. W., Shaughnessy, P., Heppner, P. P., & Cook, S. (1993). Sexual contact during and after the professional relationship: Attitudes and practices of male counselors. *Journal of Counseling and Development*, 71, 429–434.

U.S. Department of Health and Human Services. (2003). *OCR privacy brief: Summary of the HIPAA privacy rule*. Retrieved September 1, 2003 from http://www.hhs.gov/ocr/privacy summary.pdf.

Wyatt v. Stickney, 325 F. Supp. 781 (M.D.Ala. 1971); 334F.Supp. 131 (M.D. Ala. 1971); 344 F. Supp. 373 (M.D. Ala. 1971); SUB NOM Wyatt v. Aderholt, 503 F.2D 1305 (5th CIR. 1974).

5

SELF-CARE AND SELF-GROWTH

A Professional Responsibility

Laura R. Simpson and Jeannie Falkner

Beyond ethical and competent practice, counselors are charged with fostering personal development. Personal development includes attention to self awareness, self care, and personal growth. However, many counselors find that maintaining a positive balance between personal development and professional standards can be challenging. Sadly, this seems to be grounded in the fact that many counselors tend to invest much more time and energy in taking care of others than in taking care of self. The cost of this lack of self care has many potential implications for counselors including burnout and professional impairment. A lack of counselor wellness can also have a direct impact on the quality of services that clients receive. As a result, counselors are challenged to learn the skills necessary to practice as a counselor, as well as making personal self care a priority.

Illuminating the significance of these issues, many professional counseling organizations have placed an emphasis on the wellness of counseling professionals. The American Counseling Association (ACA) has a longstanding commitment to counselor self care. A little over two decades ago, ACA confirmed their allegiance to counselor wellness when ACA, formerly the American Association for Counseling and Development (AACD), developed a strategic plan which included "…the Governing Council of AACD declares a position for the profession as advocates for policies and programs in all segments of our society which promote and support optimum health and wellness" (AACD, 1991). In addition, ACA developed a Task Force on Counselor Wellness and Impairment in 1993 which demonstrates ACA's commitment to "identifying and developing intervention strategies and resources to help impaired counselors" (ACA, 2010). The emphasis on counselor self care has been reinforced by research which asserts the need for attention to professional development (Furr & Carroll, 2003; Schwitzer, Gonzalez, & Curl, 2001). This chapter will explore counselor wellness, including emotional, physical, cognitive and spiritual self care. In addition, we will examine challenges to wellness and the ethical implications related to a lack of self care including burnout and impairment.

Counselor Wellness and Impairment

Most days counselors go to work and interact with people who are struggling. We listen to clients' painful stories, offer support for our clients' feelings, and sustain our clients throughout their despair. The work can be demanding, isolating, sometimes devalued, require attention to ethics and asks that we remain empathically attuned to clients' stories which may have a powerful impact on us. We give of ourselves physically, cognitively, emotionally and spiritually and at what cost? It is critical to remember that counselors are human too. We are not exempt from stress, adversity, or shortcomings. Yet this human side of counselors receives much less attention than the professional side. There is so much emphasis on the knowledge and skills of counselors that we often overlook that we have all the same need for balance as everyone else. Remembering that "Mental and physical health are essential to maintaining competence as much or more than knowledge and skills" (Lawson, Venart, Hazlet, & Kottler, 2007, p. 7) would serve us well.

SIDEBAR 5.1

With a partner, review the ACA Code of Ethics (2005). Identify one code which specifically addresses counselor wellness or impairment. Answer the following questions:

1. In your own words, describe what the code you selected prescribes for counselors in relation to self care.
2. Identify one strategy that you will employ in order to comply with the identified code.

Because we cannot stop the current of life, our state of being tends to ebb and flow in response to the ups and downs of life and work. Melancholy, fear of inadequacy, isolation and disappointment are common components of the internal experience. Fortunately, these feelings are typically balanced by feelings of pleasure, success, connection to others, and being needed and helpful. As counselors, we must work to keep these personal ups and downs away from those we serve, and neglecting our own needs can have consequences on our health, thoughts, feelings and behaviors. Wellness is not simply the absence of illness, but rather an outcome of consistently acknowledging and resolving life challenges throughout the life span. Myers, Sweeney, and Witmer (2000) defined wellness as

> a way of life oriented towards optimal health and well-being in which body, mind and spirit are integrated by the individual to live life more fully withinthe human and natural community. Ideally, it is the optimum state of healthand well-being that each individual is capable of achieving. (p. 252)

Similarly, there are definitions of impairment that imply the opposite of wellness, suggesting that impairment and wellness are situated along the same continuum. For example, Gladding (2006) defined impairment as being "unable to function adequately or at the level of one's potential or ability" (p. 72). In general, this suggests that wellness is a result of living life with purpose and achieving one's potential, whereas being impaired means being unable to attain one's potential or to perform to the best of one's ability. The American Counseling Association Task Force on Exemplary Practices for Promoting Wellness for Counselors (ACA, 2010) utilizes the following definition for impairment:

> Therapeutic impairment occurs when there is a significant negative impact on a counselor's professional functioning which compromises client care or poses the potential for harm to the client. Impairment may be due to
>
> • Substance abuse or chemical dependency
> • Mental illness

- Personal crisis (traumatic events or vicarious trauma, burnout, life crisis)
- Physical illness or debilitation.

Impairment in and of itself does not imply unethical behavior. Such behavior may occur as a symptom of impairment or may occur in counselors who are not impaired.

Counselors who are impaired are distinguished from stressed or distressed counselors who are experiencing significant stressors, but whose work is not significantly impacted. Similarly, it is assumed that the impaired counselor has at some point had a sufficient level of clinical competence, which has become diminished as described above.

All counselors fall somewhere on this continuum between well and impaired, which means that all counselors have the potential to be well, the potential to be impaired, and the potential to fall somewhere in between.

SIDEBAR 5.2 *Elizabeth*

Elizabeth works for a community mental health center. Six months ago, Elizabeth's husband asked her for a divorce. She was devastated and has not shared the information with her friends or family because she is embarrassed and fears they will judge her. She feels unattractive so she has been dieting and exercising to lose 10 pounds. Elizabeth has started being late 3 out of 5 work days. She has double booked clients because she has neglected to write appointments on her schedule. Her supervisor mentions that her session notes are a little behind but isn't too concerned because Elizabeth has always been extremely conscientious about documentation. Elizabeth continues to see all of her clients but finds that her mind wanders during sessions and sometimes she has to ask client's to repeat themselves due to her inability to concentrate. She has not missed one day of work or cancelled any appointments.

The case study of Elizabeth was intended to illustrate this point. She is getting up, going to work, and functioning adequately by appearances. However, there are also signs of cognitive distortion, emotional instability, and spiritual crisis. And though we don't know the details, she is clearly at risk for transference issues and legal liability. Now don't panic! Having a bad day, making a poor choice, or having a less than satisfactory outcome with a client does not necessarily suggest you are impaired. Remember, we all have bad days, make poor decisions occasionally, and don't always come in first. The key is to be mindful and self aware in recognizing that life stressors are affecting work performance.

Unfortunately, counselors often miscalculate the possibility of becoming impaired and fail to recognize the importance of routine wellness practice. Today, personal wellness is a holistic and systematic paradigm which goes "…beyond the physical body to target particular behavioral, psychological and social factors" (Peterson, 2006 as cited in Miller et al., 2007, p. 5). Roach and Young (2007) suggested, "By achieving and maintaining a greater sense of wellness, counseling students may enhance their personal growth and development, experience more satisfaction, and as a result, remain better able to meet the demands of their training…" (p. 31).

Finally, the focus on the personal wellness of the counselor is rooted in a long tradition in counseling that suggests the personal characteristics of counselors are crucial to their capacity to help others (Rogers, 1961). It has been argued that counselor effectiveness depends more on the personal characteristics of the counselor that on school, training or theory (Hanna & Bemak, 1997). As Corey (2000) noted, "It is not possible to give to others what you do not possess" (p. 29).

Holistic Approach to Wellness

As previously mentioned, there are endless definitions of wellness. However, one common thread that tends to run among and between the various definitions is a holistic theme. One straightforward definition that illuminates this idea is the work of Archer, Probert, and Gage (1987), who stated that wellness is "the process and state of a quest for maximum human functioning that involves the body, mind and spirit" (p. 311). Specific to counselors, Witmer and Young (1996) stated that wellness includes professional proficiency and personal growth that is reached through cognitive, emotional, physical, and spiritual well being. Let's consider it another way. Each of us is a system made up of many parts. If any one of those parts is not working adequately, all of the parts suffer. Think about it: when you aren't feeling well physically, do you think as clearly? When you are grieving, do you find yourself questioning the meaning and purpose of your life? These examples illustrate the concept of holistic wellness. Thus, we will take a closer look at these dimensions in relation to promoting wellness and self care.

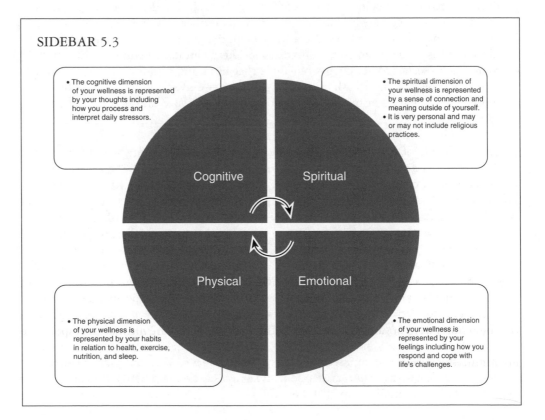

SIDEBAR 5.3

- The cognitive dimension of your wellness is represented by your thoughts including how you process and interpret daily stressors.

- The spiritual dimension of your wellness is represented by a sense of connection and meaning outside of yourself.
- It is very personal and may or may not include religious practices.

Cognitive   Spiritual

Physical   Emotional

- The physical dimension of your wellness is represented by your habits in relation to health, exercise, nutrition, and sleep.

- The emotional dimension of your wellness is represented by your feelings including how you respond and cope with life's challenges.

Cognitive Wellness

Counselors must examine their own thought processes that underlie assumptions about their professional identity. Counselors are, by nature, helpers and with this mindset come both benefits and risks. This desire to help combined with heavy workloads and sometimes inadequate resources can be a formula for counselor exhaustion. Learning to set limits on what one can and cannot do is often juxtaposed to the desire to offer our time and energy to those in need. We challenge you to intentionally adopt an attitude which provides a balance of your personal resources and enhances, rather than depletes, your professional energy. In addition to your counseling practice, you will be invited to join multiple committees, attend workshops, present workshops, provide training, and volunteer in your community. Your time and talent as a counselor will be a much sought after commodity. Necessary preservation of your time and energy requires a cognitive component of self-talk which serves as your internal Global Positioning System (GPS). Your guidance command might sound something like this, "Alert, your schedule is really full. It is OK to say *no* to this committee invitation. If you are stretched too thin, you will not be able to serve the committee or yourself well. I care for you and you deserve to be healthy and rested." For those of us who routinely say, "Yes" before we think, a good rule of thumb is to incorporate a personal rule to never say "Yes," until you have waited 24 hours. "Let me think about your invitation and get back to you tomorrow" may serve as your mantra. Counselors must realize they cannot be all things to all people.

Saying no to the demands of a busy work schedule may not be so easy. Nevertheless, an important part of maintaining an effective counseling practice is time management. Learn to end your sessions on time. This is good for the counselor and models structure and healthy limits for your clients. Schedule time for paperwork and respect the important role paperwork plays in good counseling. Make purposeful decisions about how many clients to see (when possible within agency standards). Leave room in your schedule for breaks and take them! Even in the face of busy and emotionally challenging caseloads, you must learn to reserve your emotional and physical resources. Like the flight attendant instructions in case of a loss of air pressure, "Please place your oxygen mask on before attempting to assist those around you." We must attend to our needs in order to help our clients.

Our attitude is another cognitive component of a healthy lifestyle. Optimism and hope are attributes which come from positive thinking. Optimistic people were found "... to be physically healthier and to possess immune systems that work more effectively than pessimistic individuals" (Carr, 2004, as cited in Miller, Gilman, & Martens, 2007, p. 6). Griping about our work may actually make us sick! Optimism is not, however, a Pollyanna perspective which denies the severity of problems clients bring to us. A realistic perspective of the changes our clients can and will make is healthy. Shovholt (2001) offers us the concept of "normative failure," which reminds counselors that not all clients will grow or change to meet their full potential. In some cases, small changes are all we can expect. We never really know the final impact our time with our clients in the trajectory of their lives. We may not see positive results quickly or at all. That does not mean that our efforts were in vain. A gentle reminder that our clients are ultimately responsible for their lives can help to keep us grounded. A healthy dose of humility helps to keep our grandiosity in check!

Because you care, you will find that you sometimes carry the weight of your clients' pain long after the session has ended. For those times when our hearts are heavy and our minds are overloaded, cluttered with the business of our daily lives, we need skills to clear the mental chatter. "Be in the moment," we are told. "Don't take your work home with you." This is hard to do when our thoughts are racing. "Did I do my best?" "Did I make a difference?" "What if…?" Counselors need a way to calm their thoughts. A simple and effective stress reducing exercise is meditation.

Meditation

One of the most well researched self-care stress management tools is mindfulness-based stress reduction (MBSR) (Schure, Christopher, & Christopher, 2008). Meditation has shown positive results in reducing anxiety and depression, mediating substance abuse treatment, reducing chronic pain, and multiple other health concerns (Finger & Arnold, 2002; McCollum & Gehart, 2010; Miller, Fletcher, Kabat-Zinn, 1995). Meditation may also provide a buffer for the risks of the counseling profession. Schure, Christopher, and Christopher (2008) suggest that meditation seemed to provide space for addressing the complex emotions that are triggered during counseling. As such, mindfulness may be a useful tool in minimizing burnout and vicarious trauma and enhancing stamina. At the very least, a counselor who practices mindfulness takes time to acknowledge and honor their personal experience in mind, body, and spirit.

"OK, I'll give it a try, but what is mindfulness meditation?" "How long does it take?" Is it a religious practice?" You may have many questions at this point. Meditation may include an Eastern worldview of spirituality, but does not ascribe to any particular religious doctrine. Mindfulness is a meditation practice that involves bringing attention and awareness to the present moment without judgment or evaluation (Kabat-Zinn, 1993). Sitting quietly and concentrating on the "self" is in contrast to the many hours a counselor spends in the active involvement focused on the life and experiences of our clients. A meditation practice usually consists of a 10 to 20 minute session. Adding a journaling exercise at the end of the meditation can provide the counselor with further self-reflection. You may find that the "clutter" in your mind has a theme or a pattern which you may want to address in your own counseling or supervision. Do you routinely hassle yourself? If so, Stop! Replace any negative "mental chatter" with loving affirmations. Many people think that meditation is complex or that one should have an "empty" mind to be successful with their meditation. Nothing could be further from the truth!

We suggest you try this simple exercise which may help you center and focus.

Meditation Practice

1. Find a comfortable place to sit. You may want to include some relaxing music.
2. Pick a thought, word, or phrase which will be the base of your meditation today. Peace, comfort, joy, love, or acceptance is often used as a focal point.
3. Begin to simply breathe! Notice your breath. Do not try to change or alter your breath, just become aware of your breathing for five rounds of inhalation and exhalation. Count them. Now, take a deep inhalation and blow out gently through slightly parted lips. Take in another full cleaning breath, exhale, and return to your normal breath for three rounds. Simply notice how this feels. Make a mental note of any differences you may experience.

4. During this exercise, when thoughts enter your mind (and most of us have long "to do" lists cluttering up our thoughts), just label them "thoughts" and return to a focus on your breath. Sometimes it helps to count the inhalation and exhalation. Inhale, 1, 2, 3 and exhale 1, 2, 3.

5. Notice the weight of your body in the chair and sink deeper. Give thanks to the world for the support you now feel—your body in the chair, the chair on the floor, the floor on the solid earth. Breathe deeply.

6. Begin at the top of your head for a brief body scan and notice where you might be holding tension. You may find it helpful to first tighten the muscle group in that area and then release the tension. For example, tighten all of your facial muscles as if you taste something sour. Hold the tension for a count of 3 and then *release* the tension. Continue this from the top of your head to the tip of your toes. There is no goal but to notice and become aware of where your may hold tension. Notice each part of your body, one at a time: your neck, shoulders, spine, hips, legs, feet, arms, and hands. When your mind wanders, return to your breath.

7. After you have completed your body scan, return again to the breath. Inhale and exhale. Notice any new experiences, your feelings, and your thoughts. Label the thoughts as such and repeat your word or phrase. Thank yourself for taking time to honor your life and your work with your attention to being in the moment.

You may begin to lengthen the time you spend in your meditation or add other types of breath work to the practice. You will discover what is right for your meditation. In our busy lives and work, time out to appreciate and center is a gift we give to ourselves, to our clients, and to our profession.

Financial Wellness

Financial wellness is an area which has received little attention in counselor education. We were not even sure where to include this section in our chapter and settled on financial wellness as a sub-set of cognitive wellness. Wherever this section is included, we are resolute that financial wellness deserves serious counselor consideration! Counselors often hear complaints or tell jokes about the lack of financial reward in the counseling profession. "I'm not in it for the money," is the battle cry for the counselor who embraces their altruistic nature. There appears to be cognitive dissonance between the counselor's unselfish mission of service to the client and the business aspect of being paid for counseling. This disconnect is compounded by a societal taboo against discussing money matters. We have heard counselors say that they would much prefer to talk about sex than to talk about money! To avoid the discussion of money as a vital counselor resource, however, is to neglect a reality in the life and work of the counselor. Yet, there is little mention in counselor education about the need to budget our money wisely and set aside funds for health, leisure, and other supportive professional activities (Falkner, 2007).

Students are often burdened with student loans and reduced income while they pursue their professional goals. This leads one to wonder, "What role does financial stress play in the overall health and wellness of the counseling student and the professional counselor?" Is there such a thing as counselor financial impairment?" Can the lack of attention to one's finances impact the quality of the counseling services to the client?" And finally, "What is financial wellness?"

SIDEBAR 5.4 Case Study: Misha

Misha is exhausted after turning in her final paper for the term and completing her last hour of internship. "I'm so tired," she sighs. As Misha leaves campus, she drives past her favorite store and stops after she notices they are having a sale. As Misha begins to browse through the sale items, she begins to feel her spirits lift. She tries on several items and thinks "What a deal!" Misha pulls out her credit card and heads home with her new purchase and then decides to just run though and pick up some Chinese food to go.

As Misha settles in to watch TV, a dread begins to dampen her mood. "What have I done?" "That credit card is maxed out and why did I eat all that fattening food?" As she heads to bed she thinks, "Great, I've blown it again."

Joo and Badgewell (2003) explain that personal financial wellness can be viewed as "a concrete concept of personal financial health" (Joo & Badgwell, 2003, p. 41). The single most powerful direct determinant of financial satisfaction was found to be an individual's financial behavior (e.g. cash management, credit management, budgeting, financial planning, and general money management) (Joo & Grable, 1999, as cited in Joo & Badgwell, 2003). As you read this section, begin to think to yourself, "Where do I spend my money?" "Am I comfortable with my overall financial lifestyle?" Does my money management really reflect my personal values and career goals? Garman and Forgue (1997) found a lack of knowledge about personal finance, the complexities of financial life, and a lack of time to learn about personal finance often lead individuals into making poor financial decisions. Many of us have laid awake nights wondering how we are going to pay the bills this month, buy the new tires for the car, or save enough to pay our professional dues and buy the text books for next term. While there is a normal amount of "money worry" for the typical counseling student, serious financial debt can lead to poor decisions and lead toward financial impairment. When a counselor overspends and runs up debt on high interest credit cards, they may be forced to take a second or third job to meet their financial obligations. Over time the added work hours, lack of sleep, and anxiety may begin to show up in their work. Nodding off when a client is talking, preoccupation with mounting bills, and phone calls or garnished wages may become overwhelming and lead to behaviors indicative of impaired practice. For those counselors who have entered private practice, ethical issues of client billing and inaccurate diagnosis for insurance reimbursements clearly indicate financial impairment.

In contrast to poor financial behaviors, Tang and Kim (1999) found that people who "budgeted money carefully tended to display a high level of altruism, conscientiousness, and intrinsic job satisfaction" (¶ 23), values which are inherent in the counseling profession. Cole and Reese (2004) suggest that conscious financial choices "involves defining your values, your goals, and your priorities and living a lifestyle that supports them" (p. 71). Financial wellness allows one to make use of money to create a life that is whole and one in which "all the pieces-work, spending, relationships, and values—fit together" (Cole & Reese, 2004, p. 72). Some simple suggestions can get the counseling student on the path to money management which enhance, not hinder their journey into self-care and self- growth. I encourage you to take the initial suggestions and see if your money practices are in line with your wellness plan! Happy budgeting!

SIDEBAR 5.5 Strategies for Cognitive Wellness

Befriend your thoughts. Cultivate good thoughts and use bad ones self-inquiry into old constructs that constrict you.

Be proactive about seeking supervision. Supervision is your lifeline for keeping in balance and talking out your thoughts and feelings relating to cases and support.

Live each day as if it was your last. Don't forget to laugh! Slow down and embrace the day, whatever it may bring.

Make a realistic budget. Know what money you have and create a budget.

Don't use credit cards. People spend more when using credit cards. Pay off high interest cards and cut them up or put them in the freezer to avoid impulse shopping!

Create an emergency fund. Most experts tell us we need a savings of a minimum of 3–6 months of income as a crisis safety net.

Budget for your wants. Even if it is a new magazine, we all need to have a discretionary fund to treat ourselves.

Emotional Wellness

Emotional wellness can also be called mental health. In the most basic sense, it refers to your ability to handle emotions in a constructive way in order to enable you to maintain a positive emotional state. Good mental health leads to positive self-image and in turn, satisfying relationships with friends and others. Emotional wellness helps a person achieve positive self-esteem, providing resilience to meet life's challenges. Having good mental health helps you make good decisions and deal with life's challenges at home, work, or school. But what about when we are stressed? We've all felt stress. Sometimes it's brief and highly situational, like being in heavy traffic. Other times, it's more persistent and complex. Emotional wellness is not an end stage but a continual process of change and growth and our emotional stability is critical to our sense of wellbeing. But even daily stress, the kind we think we can handle, can eventually overwhelm you, throwing your life out of balance and affecting your emotional wellness.

Emotional Stability

Emotional stability is the force of your emotions and represents your ability to handle difficulties in your life and to understand and have empathy for others. Emotional stability is not something we are born with. As children, our emotional stability is very fragile, requiring nurturing and growth. As we develop, we have the ability to work on our emotional stability the same way we do physical exercise. Emotional stability is a vital and constructive state of being. With emotions managed and under control, yet still having the ability to feel intense emotion and understand the reason for the emotions, an important balance is achieved.

Simply put, emotions are the ability to assess and appreciate or interpret what is happening at any given moment. That does not mean that the understanding and interpretation of your emotions is correct. Emotions are the responses you make to situations, whether that response is an accurate interpretation of events around you or not. Your emotions are both positive and negative. Positive and negative emotions are essential in life in order to understand how things are going. With a well rounded life, you will have better emotional stability, allowing you to correctly interpret situations. This is critical not only to your own well-being, but also to the well-being of your clients.

One author of this chapter has a cat named "Oliver". He is a good cat. He hangs out with the kids, tolerates the dog and sleeps at the foot of the bed. However, if Oliver is not in the mood for love, he narrows his eyes and backs away and has even been known to nip you with his teeth. While we might wish that this cat could gain some emotional stability and maturity, our best bet is to be mindful of the cues he sends when he is not happy. We as humans are sometimes not too far from Oliver, the moody cat. How often do we have a disproportionate response if something does not go our way? A great deal can be determined about how you are controlling your emotions by examining how you react to things on any given day. Did your supervisor tell you to hurry up and you still brooding over it? Did you get a $20 tax return instead of $40, and now you are ill-tempered? Emotional maturity is our ability to control our emotions and recognize the things in life that we can change, accept those things we cannot change and successfully avoid investing too much time in the things we cannot change. Let's do an emotional stability self check and answer the questions in the side bar below.

SIDEBAR 5.6

Ask yourself the following questions and see how you respond:

- When someone criticizes me, how do I feel?
- When something seems to be going well, how do I feel?
- Do I judge people frequently? If so, is my judgment related to trying to make myself feel better?
- Do I get angry and irritated easily?
- Am I accepting of other people?
- Have I ever noticed others behaving in a way that suggests I am not easy to be around?

Personal Counseling

We have already established that counselors are not exempt from life's challenges. They are also not exempt from experiencing emotional distress that may sometimes become debilitating. Remember the case study of Elizabeth at the beginning of the chapter? She was going through a divorce, feeling like a failure, not getting support from colleagues or family. Would counseling have been a reasonable option for her? It is fair to assume that counselors believe there is value in the practice of counseling. Yet studies suggest that counselors are incredibly reluctant to participate in counseling (Richards, Campenni, & Muse-Burke, 2010). When they do elect to participate, there is a much greater incidence among women counselors (Neukrug & Williams, 1993). However, research has proven many benefits of participation in personal counseling including the alleviation of symptoms of distress and impairment (Richards, Campenni, & Muse-Burke, 2010).

Personal counseling supports personal development by facilitating insight into how to take care of oneself and to develop self awareness regarding personal boundaries and limitations (Macran, Stiles, & Smith, 1999). Personal counseling has also been shown to elevate professional development and enhance counselors' empathic skills. And we would be remiss not to mention that participating in the counseling process as the client is also an opportunity to enrich our empathy for the experience of our clients. After all, they enter our offices each day and we expect them to share their innermost thoughts and feelings with us. Remaining sensitive to the experience of being the client could facilitate an even stronger therapeutic alliance.

Support Network

The support of others can benefit personal and professional development much like personal therapy (Koocher & Keith-Spiegel, 1998). Studies have shown that communication with professional colleagues can reduce the possibility of burnout and consultation, and supervision can assist in recognizing and understanding complicated clinical cases (Richards, Campenni, & Muse-Burke, 2010). Research also indicates that personal support satisfies the need to belong because it establishes relationships outside of the professional world (Walen & Lachman, 2000). Counselors should be mindful to ensure that supportive personal relationships are reciprocal in nature. Once again, helping professionals are routinely the first ones to volunteer to bake cookies for fund raisers or lend a hand with a friend's project. However, when it comes to our own needs, we often choose to handle those ourselves without asking for help. Counselors must be mindful to avoid only participating in relationships that require them to give of themselves without receiving help or support in return. This attention to balance assists in preventing or alleviating symptoms of burnout and mental exhaustion, suggesting that personal support enhances psychological well-being such as life satisfaction and elevated mood (Richards, Campenni, & Muse-Burke, 2010). Finally, this discussion allows for another opportunity to demonstrate the relationship between our dimensions of wellness. For example, adequate hydration is important for proper functioning of the brain. When we are well hydrated, brain cells are better supplied with fresh, oxygen-laden blood, and the brain remains alert. Mild dehydration can impair the ability to concentrate. Loss of more than 2% body weight due to dehydration can affect the brain's processing abilities and impair short-term memory (Bennett, 2000). Any of these issues can have an impact on your emotional reaction to situations or the way you interpret events. Hopefully this helps illuminate the importance of initiating a holistic approach to self care in an effort to keep all of your systems up and running!

When seeking strategies for coping with the emotional stress of personal and professional challenges, it is important to remember that there is no "one size fits all" option. Every coping strategy that you have used has worked at some point; otherwise you would not have used it. However, no single coping strategy is going to be effective all the time. This is why it is necessary to have a repertoire of stress relief techniques. The purpose of the strategies is to decrease the stress response and induce the relaxation response. In a calm state, you will have the capacity to think more clearly and solve problems more effectively, and have a greater capacity to manage your emotions. After all, you are not really coping with stress if you simply distract yourself and do not deal with the issues!

SIDEBAR 5.7 Strategies to Promote Emotional Wellness

Carve out time for yourself. No matter how busy your schedule is, remember that an empty cup cannot fill other cups.

Cultivate reciprocal friendships. Friends can make all the difference in how you experience the inevitable ups and downs of life. Friendships should be a safe and comfortable space to take as well as give.

Pay attention to your dreams. Give yourself permission to be hopeful or plan towards the future.

Enlist help from a professional. A counselor can offer you a safe place to feel, process your thoughts and encourage growth beneficial to you in a variety of ways.

Don't take life too seriously. Cut yourself (and others) some slack. Make room for imperfection. Relax and laugh. Perfection is an impossible goal!

Cultivate gratitude. Notice all that is given to you, even the small things, and say thanks.

Engage your creativity. You need not be an artist to be creative and play!

Physical Wellness

At first glance, an obvious ingredient of overall wellness is physical wellness; yet, little has been offered in the way of expectation for the counselor's physical health as a factor in overall counselor wellness (Roscoe, 2009). Rarely does a counseling student hear an instructor address the benefits of physical wellness as an important element in the personal growth and development of a well rounded professional counselor. In a study of a counselor education's impact on student wellness, only 5 [N = 204] students mentioned physical wellness related to exercise or nutrition (Roach & Young, 2007). This is consistent with the findings by Wie, Kilpatrick, Naquin and Cole (2006) that physical exercise is an underutilized coping strategy for college students. In contrast to the positive impact of maintaining one's physical fitness, about 400,000 preventable deaths each year are attributed to poor diet and lack of physical activity (Mokdad, Marks, Stroup, & Gerderding, 2004).

SIDEBAR 5.8 Sandy: A Case of Physical Wellness

"I am so nervous!" Sandy has returned to graduate school to pursue her dream of becoming a counselor. She has raised two children and is excited to focus on her career. Sandy has gained 30 pounds. Recently her doctor prescribed a blood pressure medication and warned her to manage her diet and add exercise as she is showing signs of Type 2 diabetes. "I'm just getting older," Sandy states firmly. Sandy is both excited and worried about returning to college. "Can I keep up with the younger students?" "Can I learn all of the technology?" "How am I going to manage using a computer to write all of those papers?" At times Sandy feels light headed and short of breath. "Maybe I'm having anxiety issues?" "If it continues, I'll ask my doctor for something to help, just until I get used to this new routine."

Physical health is, however, more than simply attention to diet and exercise. Roscoe (2009) suggests physical wellness goes beyond the mere absence of illness toward personal choices which encourage proactive healthy behaviors. "Physical wellness is the active and continuous effort to maintain the optimum level of physical activity and focuses on nutrition, as well as self-care and maintaining healthy lifestyle choices..." (Roscoe, 2009, p. 219).

You may be thinking at this point, "Where do I begin with what seems to be an overwhelming task of including physical activity and exercise into everything else I am supposed to do to become a counselor?" No doubt, the typical counseling student has likely been exposed the latest exercise phenomenon. From the early days of Jane Fonda's high impact aerobic workout to the popular P90X®, we are exposed to the latest exercise miracle workout promising total transformations and beautiful bodies. Most of us do not resemble athletic supermodels with six-pack abs and perfect muscle tone. You may be wondering, "How physically fit do I really have to be?" "Can I be considered physically healthy if I have a chronic illness?" "Can physical fitness really make me a better counselor?" If so, "How do I go about balancing the demands of school and counseling and my need for including a physical fitness plan?"

For a start, counselors are encouraged to make an assessment of their current physical health. A check up with your physician is always a good idea before beginning any new fitness routine. A visit to your doctor or to a community health center can provide a baseline of health factors to in order to establish realistic goals for overall physical well being. "I don't have the time or money to see a doctor," is not an acceptable excuse. Most universities have a student health center and communities frequently provide health fairs that can offer the counseling student personalized basic fitness information. Durlak (2000) described a range of specific physical markers to indicate fitness including cardiovascular fitness, lung capacity, muscle tone, cholesterol level, and blood pressure. Regular medical attention to and a general knowledge of one's fitness markers provides the counselor with necessary baseline indicators of physical wellness.

Once you have your baseline health indicators and are cleared to begin a new physical fitness routine, you are ready to go to the next step. Competencies in physical wellness naturally include physical exercise (Durlak, 2000; Renger et al., 2000). Multiple studies have extended the 1996 U.S. surgeon general's landmark report which detailed the benefits of physical activity and exercise (U.S. Department of Health and Human Services, 1996). Counseling, however, is usually done in a sedentary environment, with counselors sitting for long periods of time attending classes, workshops, and counseling clients. Our sedentary work environment is further confirmation of the value of physical exercise into an already busy schedule. Before you become discouraged with another *to do list* activity, let's consider some of the possibilities which improve overall physical fitness through exercise and physical activity. You might be pleasantly surprised!

For those who struggle with scheduling regular exercise routines, the good news is that even single periods of exercise, regardless of the participant's physical wellness, may offer a release of built up tension and a rejuvenation of mental acuity (Hansen, Stevens, & Coast, 2001). A simple brisk walk at the beginning and end of the day can provide the counselor a needed transition, a time to reflect on the day's activities, and provide physical activity to an otherwise physically inactive day. Dubbert (2002) reported that moderate-to-high levels of physical exercise fitness were associated with a longer lifespan. Even moderate activity such as walking provided protection against cardiovascular disease and some types of cancer. Park your car a few blocks from work on a sunny day. Take the stairs in your building. Make your daily physical activity a way to break up the routine. Add positive self-talk for encouragement. "I can do this! I don't have to do a whole routine. Ten minutes at a time." Before you know it, you have developed a healthy habit!

Let's take a look at some other fitness options. For those who enjoy vigorous exercise and are physically able to do so, running, weight lifting, bicycling and other vigorous aerobic activities can provide improved health outcomes. If you are one who enjoys (or needs) group support, attending an organized exercise class may provide another option. Consider a dance class. Zumba (a Latin dance fitness program which includes samba, salsa, mambo, and some belly dancing) or ballroom dancing can be fun, social, and a great stress reducer.

Options for fitness activities may include a combination of culturally diverse mind–body practices adapted from ancient Eastern influences. The National Institutes of Health established the National Center for Complementary and Alternative Medicine (NCCAM) in 1998, thereby validating the growing interest in integrated health and fitness practices. Americans are increasingly introducing complementary and alternative medicine (CAM) fitness alternatives into their lifestyles (Barnes, Powell-Griner, McFann, & Nahin, 2004, as cited in Caldwell, Winek, & Becvar, 2006). True to the Eastern tradition of a universal holistic perspective, many of these integrated wellness practices combine both physical fitness and mental well-being.

CAM practices are categorized into 5 categories: (1) Alternative Medical Systems (e.g., Ayurvedic, traditional Chinese medicine); (2) Mind–Body Interventions, (e.g., meditation, prayer); (3) Biologically Based Therapies, (e.g., herbs, vitamins); (4) Manipulative and Body-Based methods, (e.g., chiropractic, massage); and (5) Energy Therapies, (e.g. qigong, therapeutic touch). Many CAM or *mind–body* integrated wellness practices have demonstrated positive health and mental health outcomes (Finger & Arnold, 2002). While some of these practices may be novel for the counseling student, consideration as a component of an overall fitness plan for counselors appears to be worth further examination. We have provided a general overview of some of the leaders in the field of CAM that may pique your interest and enhance your pursuit of enhanced physical wellness.

Much of the initial research in the use of ancient mind–body practices in modern Western medicine evolved from attempts to enhance the healing of patients with serious medical concerns. Research has demonstrated the importance of meditation, relaxation, positive thinking, as well as social support to healing. For example, Spiegel's et al. (1989) landmark study found that support groups extended the lives of women with advanced stage breast cancer. Simonton and Matthews-Simonton (1992) initiated the use of guided imagery for improved healing and recovery of cancer patients. Dr. Herbert Benson, a cardiologist, and pioneer in mind–body medicine, discovered that through relaxation practices, patients with high blood pressure were able to slow their breathing and produce positive metabolic changes. Benson and his colleagues called this the "relaxation response" (Benson, Beary, & Carol, 1974). Dr. Benson's pivotal work has continued and can be investigated through the Mind/Body Medical Institute at Massachusetts General Hospital in Boston.

Another leader in the use of mind–body practices is Jon Kabat-Zinn. A microbiologist educated at MIT, and founder of the Stress Reduction Clinic and Professor of Medicine at the University of Massachusetts Medical School, Kabat-Zinn adapted a Buddhist meditation approach to an 8–week classof meditation and body awareness to treat patients who otherwise did not seem to be improving (Kabat-Zinn, 1993). Multiple empirical studies on Mindfulness Based Stress Reduction (MBSR) have produced reduced symptoms and/ or improved healing in health concerns including anxiety disorders (Miller, Fletcher, & Kabat-Zinn, 1995), carpel tunnel syndrome (Garfinkel et al., 1998), and chronic pain, just to name a few (Bruckstein, 1999, as cited in Finger & Arnold, 2002).

Dr. Dean Ornish, an internist, developed a highly successful multi-faceted intervention incorporating life-style, group support, meditation, diet, and exercise to treat and reverse severe coronary heart disease (Ornish, 1992). Ornish's work underscores the power of the body to sustain and heal itself. Today Dr. Ornish continues his work with remarkable success and has served as a medical consultant to former President Bill Clinton since 1993.

While the initial discovery of the healing benefits of these mind–body practices evolved from interventions with more serious medical conditions, certainly the incorporation of a variety of empirically-based mind body practices should be considered for counselor self-care to enhance the overall physical and mental fitness of counseling students and seasoned counselors as well! We have provided some examples of mind–body practices for your consideration. While many of these activities could fall under either the physical, cognitive, and/or spiritual sections in this chapter, most students will discover the immediate systemic benefits. Improvement in one area of our lives tends to lead to improvement in other areas as well.

SIDEBAR 5.9 Strategies to Promote Physical Wellness

Take care of your body. Healthy body is good for happy heart and healthy mind.

Exercise: You don't have to run a marathon. Start slow, set realistic goals, and do something fun! Ride a bike, fly a kite, dance in your den! Just get moving. You will feel better and have more energy.

Eat well: Diets don't work. Instead eat well. Become an educated shopper. Read food labels. Eat your favorite meals, simply practice portion control. Just by making three 100–calorie changes per day you can lose 30 pounds over a year.

Get enough sleep: Estimates are that 25% of us experience sleep deprivation. For a more restful sleep, turn off all electronics before bedtime. Cut out late night caffeine and foods that can cause heartburn. Meditation can help to quiet the mind for a more restful sleep.

Refrain from intoxicants: No smoking! Watch the overuse of over-the-counter medications. Limit your intake of alcohol.

Yoga

Yoga is becoming increasing more popular in the Westernized world. While some who may consider yoga for the first time have images of a lean and flexible body contorted in pretzel like poses, the reality is that yoga has applications for almost any population. Most Westernized yoga such as Iyengar or hatha yoga focuses on less movement and more precise alignment in poses which can provide strength and endurance benefits by safely stretching your muscles enabling you to develop your flexibility, strength, and balance. Yoga stretches not only your muscles but all of the soft tissues of your body. That includes ligaments, tendons, and the fascia sheath that surrounds your muscles (Ross & Thomas, 2010).

Perhaps one of the most studied areas of the health benefits of yoga is its effect on heart disease (Ornish, Scherwitz, & Billings, 1998). Yoga has long been known to lower blood pressure and slow the heart rate. A slower heart rate can benefit people with high blood pressure, heart disease, and stroke. With the growing body of evidence of the multiple physical health benefits from yoga, the inclusion of a yoga practice for counselors seems logical. A daily yoga practice can be as simple as purchasing an inexpensive yoga mat and checking out an instructive DVD from your college or community library. Most yoga practices end in a *shavasna* or *quieting pose* with a meditation. The practice ends by chanting *Namaste* which means "I salute and honor our mutual existence in society and the universe." What could be better for centering before or after our busy days as students and counselors? For those students who desire more information on yoga, a list of resources is provided in the web links of this chapter. *Namaste!*

Whatever choice of a physical activity you make, you are encouraged to incorporate physical fitness, which is enjoyable and promotes overall well being into your daily lives. Not only will these practices build a foundation for healthy physical fitness, but regular physical activity may enhance your resilience to burnout and compassion fatigue. In the words of First Lady, Michelle Obama's national fitness campaign, "Let's Move"!

Nutrition

No discussion of physical wellness would be complete without a conversation about nutrition. Most of us are aware that the number of persons classified as overweight or obese has been increasing steadily in all age groups throughout the industrialized world (Freedman, Khan, Serdula, Galuska, & Dietz, 2002). Everyone knows someone who is on a diet. We laugh at ourselves as we order a diet soda with our cheeseburger and fries. Just the mention of the word 'diet' brings to mind tiny portions of boring and bland food. Nevertheless, one is hard pressed to suggest a health regimen of exercise without attention to diet. Rather than looking at our eating habits from a deficit model, we would like to suggest that you instead imagine yourselves intentionally *eating well.* If one considers the mental acuity, energy, and stamina needed to function in our profession, then like a well trained athlete, we need to provide our bodies with the needed nutrients for our best performance.

In our Westernized culture of hustle and bustle, food rituals can bring people together; sharing a meal represents warmth and hospitality. Food can be an immediate comfort and is often associated with family. While this is a positive aspect of food, too much of a good thing is not! In the past 20 years, we have seen a dramatic increase in obesity rates. The Center for Disease Control (CDC) found that no state in the US had a prevalence of less that 20% obesity, with 12 states showing over 30% of their population as obese (CDC, 2012).

We all know that emotional issues have long been associated with obesity (Grant & Boersma, 2005). When individuals are stressed, they tend to eat diets high in fat and sugar and low in nutrition. Evidence suggests that chronic stress can actually trigger food cravings. These food cravings may parallel other addictive behaviors. Many people who are overweight crave food, lose control over eating, and experience negative health effects that should, but don't, serve as a deterrent (Oliver, Wardel, & Gibson, 2000). Foods high in fat and high in carbohydrates then trigger reward neural pathways, and restricting these foods can induce a cyclical stress-like response. The more I eat, the more I want! With a choice of high fat, processed foods, the body does not receive the nutritional value it needs and this can lead to vitamin deficiencies, added pounds or obesity. Certainly a counselor cannot be at their best, and may be impaired, if they are so underweight or overweight as to be a medical risk to themselves. Obviously serious eating disorders as anorexia or bulimia require immediate medical intervention.

Most of us are not at immediate risk, but may nevertheless be at risk for negative effects of improper nutrition. How can we expect our clients to grow and change if we are not in balance with our nutritional needs? So what does this mean for the counseling student? Pause for a moment and consider the case study of Sandy. How would you rate Sandy's health? How might her health impact her ability to complete her degree? To counsel others? As you reflect on these questions, consider your physical health and wellness. How is my health? Do I know my fitness markers? Are there health concerns that require attention? If so, what steps will I take to begin my physical wellness plan?

Spiritual Wellness

Spirituality is a complex, multidimensional concept that is difficult to define. To operationalize a topic that is both developmental and highly personal is tricky (Simpson. 2010). So, articulating what constitutes spiritual wellness is fraught with challenge. It is further complicated by the tendency of some to equate the topic with religion. For many, spirituality includes religion and for others it is highly unstructured. Spirituality is typically represented by a broad perspective that reflects the need for transcendence and connectedness, while religion is a view which incorporates the tenets of specific faith traditions. It has been suggested that spirituality is "what individuals find sacred in their lives, what is most important to them at the essence of their being. It is a context for understanding things" (Gange-Fling & McCarthy, 1996). This suggests that spirituality is individualized by each person's meaning system and values, and further complicates any efforts to define spiritual wellness.

As a concept, spirituality includes an ongoing search for meaning and purpose in life; an individualized belief system (Chandler, Holden, & Kolander, 1992), a profound sense of oneness, wholeness, and connectedness or belonging in the universe (Pargament, 1997; Ryan, 1998). Wiggins-Frame (2005) concludes, "...spirituality includes one's beliefs, awareness, values, subjective experience, sense of purpose and mission, and an attempt to reach toward something greater than oneself. It may or may not include a deity" (p. 13). An individual's spirituality is considered personal and private and may not involve religious practice in any way. When considering how that translates into spiritual wellness, it means examining "...willingness to seek meaning and purpose in human existence, to question everything, and to appreciate the intangibles which cannot be explained or understood readily" (Chandler, Holden, & Kolander, 1992, p. 168). Spirituality allows individuals to define and understand occurrences in their lives and provides them with a sense of meaning and purpose in their existence. Although a simplistic answer to a complex concept, the idea of spiritual wellness will be represented by the presence of this sense of meaning and purpose. Absence of this meaning, frequently results in confusion, sadness and lack of direction. Clearly any of these spiritual maladies can impact our sense of wellness and consequently, our work with clients (Simpson, 2010).

Regardless of an individual's position with regard to spiritual or religious practice, our quality of life is deeply affected by the degree of purpose and engagement we feel at any given time (Cherniss, 1995). Research suggests that individuals who have a sense of meaning and well being in their lives cope with stress in more healthy ways

(Pargament, 1997). "Thus, there is value in conscious, periodic consideration of what we find significant, what has priority, and what most deserves care and protection in our lives..." (Baker, 2003, p. 64). Ryan (1998) theorized that individuals who lack spiritual beliefs are at risk to experience unbearable pain and feelings of rejection as they search for meaning in the world. It can be suggested that spirituality is potentially a source of hope, meaning and purpose, particularly during difficult times. As suggested by Bullock (2002), "a person's spiritual needs are inextricably related to their growth, development, and healing" (p. 4). This brings us right back around to the question of how we can give to others what we do not possess.

SIDEBAR 5.10

When making a personal exploration of spirituality and religion, self reflection has been suggested to have importance (Fukuyama & Sevig, 1997; Miller, 2003; Curry & Simpson, 2010). Ask yourself the following questions.

1. What is my personal definition of spirituality?
2. Do I identify myself as spiritual?
3. Did the spiritual values of my parents influence my current beliefs and values?
4. What were the major spiritual influences outside of my immediate family, including the beliefs common to my peers?
5. How have my religious beliefs changed through my personal growth process? How has the practice of these beliefs changed?
6. Have there been any significant turning points, crises, or transitions that have affected the development of my spiritual beliefs and values?
7. Has spirituality or religion ever frightened or confused me? Made me feel joyful or energized?
8. Recall a situation, event, or moment which felt spiritual and describe it.

It is good practice to be aware of our own spiritual and religious beliefs, values, and spiritual journey. Counselors are not exempt from having their own biases and views when it comes to religion or spirituality. As a result of education, training, or supervision, counselors may view religious behavior with theoretical bias. Personal life experience may also play a role in a counselor's ability to receive and process a client's issues with neutrality. These personal or professional experiences have the potential to impact the counselor and result in biases towards religion or spirituality, either positively or negatively. Counselors may not pick up on concerns of their clients due to their own biases, or may pick up on these themes too readily to the exclusion of other issues. Counselors and clients benefit from the helpers' self awareness related to their perspective on spirituality and the inherent biases of that perspective. Without sensitivity toward personal bias, counselors may inadvertently neglect the welfare of the client and potentially cause harm. Having an awareness of bias may assist a counselor in addressing issues within spiritual domains while maintaining an emphasis on respect and care for the client's well being. Ultimately, counselors can facilitate a helping relationship that includes spiritual issues simply by being aware of their own perspective. Therefore, it is critical for counselors to be aware of their own personal perspectives within spiritual and religious domains.

We challenge you to pause and consider what spiritual self awareness actually includes. We offer that it begins with an examination of your personal value system. "Understanding one's own value system also increases sensitivity to the value system of others. Without self-awareness, ignoring others' value systems is unfortunately a potential consequence" (Hagedorn, 2005, p. 70). This is of utmost importance because the personal values of the counselor become a part of the counseling process and there is a risk that a helper will impose their values on clients. Being aware of one's own values assists counselors in avoiding making value judgments or invalidating client's feelings. Values also assist counselors in conceptualizing client issues and in the choice of theoretical orientations. Without self-awareness, counselors may inadvertently impact the conditions necessary for the counseling alliance or invalidate the client's experiences resulting in harm to the client or the counseling relationship (Simpson, 2010).

SIDEBAR 5.11 Strategies to Promote Spiritual Wellness

Trust your intuition. You are in charge of determining what is important, meaningful or gives you a sense of purpose.

Pay attention to your feelings and thoughts. Listening to your inner voice will often help you find direction when you are feeling challenged or lost.

Seek to understand your beliefs. This includes where they came from, why you have them and why you value them.

Continually seek purpose in your life. Having purpose and meaning in your life can offer you hope, joy, courage and gratitude.

Seek peace and balance in your life. Conduct routine self checks to examine if your values and ethics match your actions.

Challenges to Counselor Wellness

According to the American Counseling Association Code of Ethics (2005) and the American Mental Health Counselors Association (2010), counselors have a responsibility to refrain from causing hurt, strive to help others, and to pursue professional excellence. The susceptibility to impairment in their professional lives that can undermine their therapeutic efficacy includes the crisis of counselor impairment, which is often a result of secondary trauma, occupational stress, and burnout (Emerson & Markos, 1996; Hazler & Kottler, 1996; Herlihy, 1996; O'Halloran & Linton, 2000; Olsheski & Leech, 1996; Sheffield, 1998; Young & Lambie, 2007). We have firmly established that counselors should incorporate self care into daily living. This is only reinforced by the ethical mandate found within the ACA Code of Ethics (2005). The code spells out that "counselors engage in self care activities to maintain and promote their emotional, physical, mental and spiritual well being to best meet their professional responsibilities" (ACA Code of Ethics, 2005, Sec. C). Additionally, the ACA Code of Ethics (2005) states:

> Counselors are alert to the signs of impairment from their own physical, mental or emotional problems and refrain from offering and providing professional services when such impairment is likely to harm a client or others. They seek assistance for problems that reach the level of professional impairment, and if

necessary, they limit, suspend, or terminatetheir professional responsibilities until such time it is determined that theymay safely resume their work. (ACA Code of Ethics, Sec C..2.g.)

As our ethics codes are not suggestions for consideration, these codes command that counselors must actively seek wellness to be ethical. Unfortunately, counselors' major indicators of problems are often ignored or neglected. In addition to the personal components that make up an individual's sense of well being, there are additional concepts that warrant investigation.

Personal Susceptibility to Pain

An unresolved history of trauma, ongoing personal issues, and daily life stressors all have the potential to influence a counselor's ability to manage stress (Figley, 2002). Counselors who have a trauma or abuse history may develop burnout or vicarious trauma, or may be at risk for setting poor boundaries with clients (Pearlman & Mac Ian, 1995). Any of these issues can increase susceptibility to impairment.

Burnout

Burnout has been defined as "physical and emotional exhaustion, involving the development of negative self-concept, negative job attitudes and loss of concern and feelings for clients" (Pines & Marslach, 1978, p. 234). The American Counseling Association Taskforce on Counselor Wellness and Impairment utilizes Figley's (2005) definition: "A state of physical, emotional, and mental exhaustion caused by long-term involvement in emotionally demanding situations." It is characterized by emotional exhaustion, depersonalization and reduced feelings of personal accomplishment (Maslach, 2003). Burnout is an "occupational hazard that not only affects the counselor but also could contribute to a diminished ability to act in a manner that promotes the well being of others" (Roach & Young, 2007, p. 30). In other words, when you are feeling burned out you could stop being as effective with your clients. Maybe you will start showing up to work late or your mind will wander while you are in session. You may lose the capacity to relate to your clients on a personal level and instead just view them as items on your "to do" list. Counselors are vulnerable to burnout due to the demanding nature of the work and due to the empathically intimate relationships counselors' experience with clients (Skovholt, 2001). Making matters worse, counselors are often reluctant to admit they have a problem and do not seek help for this condition but simply continue to work even when impaired (Kottler, 1993). Although burnout shows up within the counselor, it is grounded in the environment, specifically the work environment. Maslach (2003) has identified a number of variables that may contribute to burnout, which include ineffective supervisors, excessive workloads, and unsupportive colleagues. This places the clients at risk for being affected as the counselor may demonstrate diminished empathy or decreased professional comportment such as frequent cancellations or tardiness.

Vicarious Trauma

The process of connecting with clients who are in pain has an impact on the counselor. Vicarious trauma is one of the personal risks of counseling work. The concept of vicarious trauma means that hearing the details of the traumatic experiences of your clients may affect you on a personal level. For example, it can impact your perspective on the world (Figley, 2002; Pearlman & Saakvitne, 1995). You may have always been the type of individual that looks for the good in all people and now you find that you have become cynical and lose faith that people are good by nature. Changes in interpersonal relationships are also common in counselors suffering from vicarious trauma. The ACA Taskforce on Counselor Wellness and Impairment (ACA, 2010) defines vicarious traumatization as "A cumulative process of change in the helpers' inner experience that happens through empathic connection with clients. The concept is applicable even when clients are not disclosing personal histories of trauma; in the process of connecting with clients, we are connecting with their pain, and our empathy with that pain has an impact".

This could mean that you become withdrawn within the relationships in your personal life, but it could also mean that you are no longer capable of meaningful therapeutic connection with your clients. When counselors begin to experience this phenomenon, it is common for them to miss appointments with clients, decrease communication within supervision or isolate themselves (Dutton & Rubinstein, 1995). All of these issues can take a toll on the counselor on a personal level and certainly has the potential to have dramatic impact on the effectiveness of the counselor within the counseling environment.

Work Environment

Another area that may affect counselor wellness is work related issues such as the counselors' job satisfaction. Mental health counselors report that when there is confusion about their role or really large caseloads, this has a negative impact (Walsh & Walsh, 2002). The type of caseload that a counselor has can also play a role in whether they are happy with their job. For example, counselors that work with large numbers of clients with a trauma history may be a greater risk for decreased job satisfaction (Trippany, Wilcoxin, & Satcher, 2003).

On a positive note, there are things that can help counselors function effectively and maintain a positive attitude about their work. These behaviors are knows as career-sustaining behaviors (CSBs) (Kramen-Kahn & Hansen, 1998). These behaviors include "maintaining a balance between professional and personal lives, maintaining objectivity about clients, reflecting on positive experiences, participating in continuing education and avoiding undue responsibility for clients' problems" (Lawson, 2007, p. 22). Counselors that participate in these behaviors may decrease their risk for burnout or vicarious trauma.

Anna: A Case Study of Ethics and Counselor Wellness

"What a morning!" Anna thinks as she heads back down the hall towards her office after returning from lunch. "I have got to get caught up on these session notes!" Concentrating on recalling each of her back-to-back clients from the morning, Anna initially doesn't hear her office phone beeping for her to pick up. She is startled when she hears her name on the office intercom, "Anna, you have a call on line 1". Irritated because she is behind on her case notes and needs to catch up, Anna snatches up the phone and answers with a harsh tone, "Anna Smith, how may I help you?" A voice that matches her own tone responds back to her. "Anna, this is Mr. Jones from Child Protective Services. We are still waiting on your report regarding the child we referred to you for evaluation. This family is scheduled for court tomorrow and we do not have your recommendations." Anna closes her eyes and silently sighs with frustration. One more thing that she is behind on. "How can I let this happen?" She offers a quick explanation to Mr. Jones and assures him that the report will be in his hands by the end of the business day. No sooner than she hangs up and sits down in her desk chair, the phone rings again. Anna reluctantly answers and this time it is the office receptionist. "Anna, there is a hospital consult for a 49-year-old female that is displaying psychotic symptoms." Anna responds and explains "I am swamped. I really don't have time to stop and go across town to the hospital right now." The receptionist informs her that she has no choice as she is the one on call for consults this week and there is no one else at the mental health center that can substitute for her. Anna hangs up the phone and simply stares at the stack of client files on her desk. Panicked, Anna thinks of the overdue report for Child Protective Services and the client sessions that took place this morning that have not been properly documented. "It doesn't really matter what I put in that report, they will probably just send that child right back into that terrible situation anyway." She knows that she is becoming chronically late with paperwork but she persistently blames an overbooked schedule on her poor time management. She has also lost faith that her work can make a difference in the lives of her clients. Additionally, she is feeling trapped between her work responsibilities and her professional obligation to report to the court and neither task is optional. "How am I going to get this all done?" Anna thinks as she feels irritated and tears welling up. "Just take a deep breath," she tells herself. Almost overcome with panic and frustration, she realizes that she is breathing rapidly and her face is beginning to feel numb. "I need a cola and a peanut butter cup." Although she just finished a large lunch, she thinks "I need a boost to get me through this. There are just not enough hours in the day!" She walks out of her office and heads for the vending machine. She purchases a 20-ounce caffeinated cola and a 4-pack of peanut butter cups. "Thank goodness for chocolate" she utters sarcastically as she heads back down the hall to get her car keys and head to the hospital. "I am just one person! How am I going to get all this done?"

Although this is a fictional case, there are similar situations occurring on a daily basis in mental health centers all over the country. The incidence of counselors being highly stressed and anxious is occurring with increasing frequency. Research suggests that regardless of work setting, counselors report high level of work related anxiety and stress (Hendricks, Bradley, Brogan, & Brogan, 2010; Knudsen, Ducharme, & Roman, 2008; Roscoe, 2009; Tanigoshi, Kantos, & Remley, 2008; Wadsworth, Harley, Smith, & Kampfe, 2008). Research tells us that counselors are experiencing role confusion, frustration with workloads and emotional exhaustion (Ducharme, Knudsen, & Roman, 2008; Rosenberg & Pace, 2006). In addition, insecurity about complex case conceptualization adds stress to the concerns of counselors (Ducharme, Knudsen, & Roman, 2008).

Developing a Wellness Treatment Plan for Anna

Let's take a moment to consider Anna's experience. How would you answer the following questions?

1. Based on the information that you have, do you believe that Anna is an impaired professional? Why or why not?
2. Does Anna demonstrate characteristics of burnout? Why or why not?

3. From a holistic perspective, does Anna display a lack of self care in the following areas: Emotional Wellness, Physical Wellness, Cognitive Wellness or Spiritual Wellness?
4. What would you recommend for Anna to assist her with her situation?

Conclusion

Counselors are faced with many exciting challenges as they traverse this unique professional helper's journey. Personal growth and development require the counselor to continually pursue a life of health and wellness in their personal and professional lives. Attunement to your cognitive, spiritual, physical, and emotional parts is vital to achieve your goal of help clients and doing no harm.

There will be times when you find yourself on the spectrum of wellness toward wholeness and fulfillment in most areas of your life. Enjoy and be mindful of the simple things. Be good to yourself and to those you love. These are the times when you will have the energy and resources to give to your best to your clients, to your profession and to yourself. At other times, you will naturally find that the complexities of life have moved you toward the less desirable end of the wellness spectrum. You may have an unexpected illness, family concerns, changes in jobs, or any combination of these normal crises of life. You may find yourself in need of additional resources. Do not hesitate to seek the support you need! Personal counseling, supervision, and time spent in spiritual practices may be needed to restore the equilibrium of life and help you achieve balance. It is important to monitor the impact these trying times may have on our work. Feedback from trusted colleagues, supervisors, and spiritual leaders can provide you with valuable insights and help you negotiate through the rough times. Remember, life has an ebb and flow and that these times, as we often tell our clients, are not permanent.

If you should find yourself with symptoms of impairment, seek professional help. After all, we are human and may, at times, need to take a sabbatical from our work to refresh, renew, recover or heal. As counselors, both authors have at one time or another felt burned out, worn out and used up. One author quit counseling children for 5 years in response to a trauma heavy caseload that became so heavy that she broke under the pressure. Realizing that her values for finding the good in people and giving the benefit of the doubt had been compromised, she made this drastic decision in an effort to salvage her ability to stay in a profession that she loved. Both of us have heard countless stories from professional colleagues that illuminate the need for self care. For example, one author's very good friend found herself burned out to the point of impairment. She described her experience like this: "One day I went in to the office and knew I simply could not sit through another counseling hour. 'What is wrong with me?', she asked. 'I have a successful practice, a beautiful office, and a supportive supervision group'. Today none of this was enough. I was spent and I knew it. I had to take drastic action to save myself and protect my clients. I cancelled my appointments, made arrangements for emergency calls, and left town for three weeks. I could not really afford this time from work, but I could not afford not to take the break! When I returned, I realized three weeks was not enough. After six weeks of rest and recovery, I was able to return to work and begin again, humbled and appreciative of the care and concern expressed by my clients and colleagues."

You may never experience this level of impairment, but know that some of us will. Even in the worst of times, there is hope for rejuvenation and repair. We hope to have raised your awareness and offered knowledge and skills that can assist you in practicing good counselor self-care. The following Websites provide additional information relating to the chapter topics.

Useful Websites

National Center for Complementary and Alternative Medicine: http://nccam.nih.gov/
The NCCAM is the Federal Government's lead agency for scientific research on diverse medical and health care practices.

Center For Disease Control on Sleep: http://www.cdc.gov/sleep/
The CDC provides helpful information on sleep and sleep disorders. Sufficient sleep is increasingly being recognized as a vital component of health.

American Dietetic Association: eatright.org
This helpful resource will provide you with science-based food and nutrition information needed to maintain our healthy bodies.

Duke Center for Spirituality, Theology, and Health: http://www.spiritualityandhealth.duke.edu/
This provides you with research and scholarly activities to encourage dialog between researchers, clinicians, theologians, clergy and others interested in the intersection of spirituality, theology, and health.

The Mayo Clinic for Stress Management: http://www.mayoclinic.com/health/stress-management/MY00435
This web site provides information on stress, stress management, and practices to reduce stress.

Jon Kabat Zinn's Mindfulness Meditation: http://www.mindfulnesscds.com/author.html
This web site will introduce you to the work of Joh Kabat-Zinn and provide you with multiple resources to develop a meditation practice. The author's books are listed as well as questions and answers about meditation.

Steven Halpern Inner Peace Music: http://www.innerpeacemusic.com/
Halpern's web site offers resources for a range of stress and personal growth topics. Professional CD's which enhance sleep, stress reduction, and many more professionally composed healing musical resources are available.

References

American Association for Counseling and Development. (1991). *AACD strategic plan*. Alexandria, VA: Author.

American Counseling Association. (2005). *The ACA code of ethics*. Alexandria, VA: Author.

American Counseling Association. (2010). ACA's Taskforce on Wellness and Impairment Definitions. Retrieved from http://www.counseling.org/wellness_taskforce/tf_definitions.htm.

American Mental Health Counselors Association. (2010). *Principles for AMHCA code of ethics*. Retrieved on January 12, 2012, from https://www.amhca.org/assets/content/AMHCACodeOfEthics2010 Final.pdf.

Archer, J., Probert, B.S., & Gage, L. (1987). College students' attitudes toward wellness. *Journal of College Student Personnel*, 28, 311–317.

Baker, E. K. (2003). *Caring for ourselves: A therapist's guide to personal and professional well-being*. Washington, DC: American Psychological Association.

Bennett, J. A. (2000). Dehydration: Hazards and benefits. *Geriatric Nursing, 21*(2), 84–88.

Benson, H., Beary, J. F., & Carol, M. P. (1974). The relaxation response. *Psychiatry, 37*, 37–46.

Bullock, L. E. (2002). The role of spirituality in the personal and professional lives of clinical social workers: An examination of coping and well-being. *Dissertation Abstracts International* (UMI no. 1410136).

Caldwell, K. L., Winek, J. L., & Becvar, D. S. (2006). The relationship between marriage and family therapists and complementary and alternative medicine approaches: A national survey. *Journal of Marital and Family Therapy, 32*(1), 101–114.

Chandler, C. K., Holden, J. M., & Kolander, C. A. (1992). Counseling for spiritual wellness: Theory and practice. *Journal of Counseling & Development, 71,* 168–175.

Center for Disease Control. http://www.cdc.gov/obesity/data/trends.html.

Cherniss, C. (1995). *Beyond Burnout.* New York: Routledge.

Cole, P. H., & Reese, D. (2004). *Mastering the financial dimension of your practice.* New York: Brunner-Routledge.

Corey, G. (2000). *Theory and practice of group counseling* (5th ed.). Elmont, CA: Wadsworth/Thompson Learning.

Curry, J., & Simpson, L. (2011). Communication about spirituality in counseling. In C. Cashwell, & J. S. Young (Eds.), *Integrating Spirituality and Religion Into Counseling: A Guide to Competent Practice.* American Counseling Association.

Dixon, W. A., Mauzey, E. D., & Hall, C. R. (2003). Physical activity and exercise: Implications for counselors. *Journal of Counseling & Development, 81*(4), 502–505. doi: 10.1002/j.1556–6678.2003. tb00278.x

Dubbert, P. M. (2002). Physical activity and exercise: Recent advances and current challenges. *Journal of Consulting and Clinical Psychology. 70*(3), 526–536. doi: 10.1037//0022–006X.70.3.526

Ducharme, L. J., Knudsen, H. K., & Roman, P. M. (2008). Emotional exhaustion and turnover intention in human service occupations: The protective role of coworker support. *Sociological Spectrum, 28,* 81–104.

Durlak, J. A. (2000). Health promotion as a strategy in primary prevention. In D. Cicchetti, J. Rappaport, I. Sandler, & R. P. Weissberg (Eds.), *The promotion of wellness in children and adolescents* (pp. 221–241). Washington, DC: CWLA Press.

Dutton, M. A., & Rubinstein, F. L. (1995). Working with people with PTSD: Research implications. In C. R. Figley (Ed.), *Compassion fatigue: Coping with secondary traumatic stress disorder in those who treat the traumatized* (pp. 82–100). Philadelphia: Brunner/Masel.

Emerson, S., & Markos, P. A. (1996). Signs and symptoms of the impaired counselor. *Journal of Humanistic Education and Development, 43,* 108–118.

Falkner, J. (2007). *A study to investigate counselor financial wellness as a predictor of counselor money practices among counseling professionals in private practice.* Dissertation Abstracts International: Section A, 67.

Figley, C. R. (2002). Compassion fatigue: Psychotherapists' chronic lack of self care. *Journal of Clinical Psychology, 58*(11), 1443–1441.

Figley, C. R. (1995). *Compassion fatigue.* New York: Brunner/Mazel.

Finger, W., & Arnold, E. M. (2002). Mind-body interventions: Applications for social work practice. *Social Work in Health Care, 35*(4), 57–78.

Freedman, D. S., Kahan, L. K., Serdula, M. K., Galuska, D. A., & Dietz, W. H. (2002). Trends and correlates of class 3 obesity in the United States from 1990–2000. *Journal of the American Medical Association, 288,* 1758–1761.

Fukuyama, M. A., & Sevig, T. D. (1997). Spiritual issues in counseling: A new course. *Counselor Education and Supervision, 36,* 233–245.

Furr, S. R., & Carroll, J. J. (2003). Critical incidents in student counselor development. *Journal of Counseling & Development, 81*(4), 483–489.

Gange-Fling, M. A., & McCarthy, P. (1996). Impact of childhood sexual abuse on clients spiritual development: Counseling implications. *Journal of Counseling & Development, 74*(3), 253–258.

Garfinkel, M. S., Singhai, A., Katz, W. A., Allan, D. A., Reshetar, R., & Schumacher, H. R. (1998). Yoga-based intervention for carpal tunnel syndrome. *Journal of American Medical Association, 280,* 1601–1603.

Garman, E. T., & Forgue, R. E. (1997). *Personal finance* (5th ed.). Boston: Houghton Mifflin.

Gladding, S. T. (2006). *The counseling dictionary* (2nd ed.). Upper Saddle River, NJ: Prentice.

Grant, P. G., & Boersma, H. (2005). Making sense of being fat: A hermeneutic analysis of adults' explanations for obesity. *Counselling and Psychotherapy Research, 5*(3), 212–220.

Hagedorn, W. B. (2005). Counselor self awareness and self exploration of religious and spiritual beliefs: Know thyself. In C. Cashwell, & S. Young (Eds.), *Integrating Spirituality and Religion into Counseling: A Guide for Competent Practice*. Alexandria, VA: American Counseling Association.

Hanna, F. J., & Bemak, J. (1997). The quest for identity in the counseling profession. *Counselor Education & Supervision, 36*(3), 194–207.

Hansen, C. J., Stevens, L. C., & Coast, R. J. (2001). Exercise duration and mood state: How much is enough to feel better? *Health Psychology, 20*, 26–275.

Hazler, R. J., & Kottler, J. A. (1996). *The emerging professional counselor: Student dreams to professional realities* (2nd ed.). Alexandria, VA: American Counseling Association.

Hendricks, B., Bradley, L. J., Brogan, W. C., & Brogan, C. (2010). Shelly: A case study focusing on ethics and counselor wellness. *The Family Journal, 17*(4), 355–359. doi:10.1177/1066480709348034

Herlihy, B. (1996). When a colleague is impaired: The individual counselor's response. *Journal of Humanistic Education and Development, 34*, 118–128.

Joo, S., & Bagwell, D. C. (2003). A tool for the financial professional: Personal financial wellness. *Journal of Personal Finance, 2*(1), 39–53.

Kabat-Zinn, J. (1993). Mindfulness meditation: Health benefits of an ancient Buddhist practice. In D. Goleman, & J. Gurin (Eds.), *Mind-body medicine* (pp. 259–275). Yonkers, NY: Consumer Reports Books.

Kabat-Zinn, J. (2005). *Coming to our senses: Healing ourselves and our world through mindfulness.* New York: Hyperion.

Koocher, G. P., & Keith-Spiegel, P. (1998). *Ethics in psychology: Professional standards and cases* (2nd ed.). New York: Oxford University Press.

Kottler, J. (1993). *On being a therapist.* San Francisco: Jossey-Bass.

Kramen-Kahn, B., & Hansen, N. D. (1998). Rafting the rapids: Occupational hazards, rewards, and coping strategies of psychotherapists. *Professional Psychology: Research and Practice, 29*, 130–134.

Lambie, G. (2007). Wellness in school and mental health systems: Organizational influences. *Journal of Humanistic Counseling, Education and Development, 46*, 98–113.

Lawson, G. (2007). Counselor wellness and impairment: A national survey. *Journal of Humanistic Counseling, Education and Development, 46*, 20–34.

Lawson, G., Venart, E., Hazler, R. J., & Kottler, J. A. (2007). Toward a culture of counselor wellness. *Journal of Humanistic Counseling, Education, and Development, 46*, 5–19.

Macran, S., & Stiles, W. B. (1999). How does personal therapy affect therapists' practice? *Journal of Counseling Psychology, 46*(4), 419–432.

Maslach, C. (2003). *Burnout: The cost of caring.* Cambridge, MA: Malor Books.

McCollum, E. E., & Gehart, D. R. (2010). Using mindfulness meditation to teach beginning therapists therapeutic presence: A qualitative study. *Journal of Marital and Family Therapy, 36*(3), 347–360. doi: 10.1111/j.1752–0606.2010.00214.

Miller, D. N., Gilman, R., & Martens, M. P. (2007). Wellness promotion in the schools: Enhancing students' mental and physical health. *Psychology in the Schools, 45*(1), 5–15. doi: 10.1002/pits.20274

Miller, G. (2003). *Incorporating Spirituality in Counseling and Psychotherapy.* Hoboken, NJ: John Wiley & Sons, Inc.

Miller, J. J., Fletcher, K., & Kabat-Zinn, J. (1995). Three-year follow-up and clinical implications for a mindfulness meditation-based stress reduction intervention in the treatment of anxiety disorders. *General Hospital Psychiatry, 17*, 192–200.

Mokdad, A. H., Marks, J. S., Stroup, D. F., & Gerberding, J. L. (2004). Actual causes of death in the United States, 2000. *Journal of the American Medical Association, 291*, 1238–1245.

Myers, J. E., Sweeney, T. J., & Witmer, J. T. (2000). The wheel of wellness counseling for wellness: A holistic model for treatment planning. *Journal of Counseling & Development, 78*, 251–266.

Neukrug, E. S., & Williams, G. T. (1993). Counseling counselors: A survey of values. *Counseling and Values, 38*(1), 51–63.

O'Connor, M. F. (2001). On the etiology and effective management of professional distress and impairment among psychologists. *Professional Psychology: Research and Practice, 32*, 345–350.

O'Halloran, T. M., & Linton, J. M. (2000). Stress on the Job: Self-care resources for counselors. *Journal of Mental Health Counseling, 22*(4), 354–364.

Oliver, G., Wardle, J., & Gibson, L. (2000). Stress and food choice: A laboratory study. *Psycosom Medicine, 62*, 853–865.

Olsheski, J., & Leech, L. L. (1996). Programmatic interventions and treatment of impaired professionals. *Journal of Humanistic Counseling, Education, and Development, 34*(3), 128–140.

Ornish, D. (1992). *Dr. Dean Ornish's program for reversing heart disease*. New York: Ballantine.

Ornish, D., Scherwitz, L. W., & Billings, J. H., et al. (1998). Intensive lifestyle changes for reversal of coronary heart disease. *JAMA, 280*, (2001–2007), 128–141.

Pargament, K. I. (1997). *The psychology of religion and coping*. New York: Guilford Press.

Pearlman, L. A., & Mac Ian, P. S. (1995). Vicarious traumatization: An empirical study of the effects of trauma work on trauma therapists. *Professional Psychology: Research and Practice, 26*, 558–565.

Pearlman, L. A., & Saakvitne, K. W. (1995). *Vicarious traumatization: The cost of empathy*. Ukiah, Ca: Cavalcade Productions.

Pines, A. M., & Maslach, C. (1978). *Characteristics of staff burnout in mental health setting*. Hospital Community Psychiatry, *29*, 233–237.

Renger, R. F., Midyett, S. J., Mas, F. G., Erin, T. E., McDermott, H. M., Papenfuss, R. L., Eichling, et al. (2000). Optimal Living Profile: An inventory to assess health and wellness. *American Journal of Health Promotion, 24*, 403–412.

Richards, K. C., Campenni, C. E., & Muse-Burke, J. L. (2010). Self-care and well-being in mental health professionals: The mediating effects of self awareness and mindfulness. *Journal of Mental Health Counseling, 32*(3), 247–264.

Roach, L., & Young, S. (2007). Do counselor education programs promote wellness in their students? *Counselor Education and Supervision, 47*, 29–45.

Rogers, C. R. (1961). *On becoming a person: A therapist's view of psychotherapy*. New York: Houghton Mifflin.

Roscoe, L. (2009). Wellness: A review of theory and measurement for counselors. *Journal of Counseling and Development, 87*, 216–226.

Rosenberg, T., & Pace, M. (2006). Burnout among mental health professionals: Special considerations for the marriage and family therapist. *Journal of Marital and Family Therapy, 32*(1), 87–99.

Ross, A., & Thomas, S. (2009). The health benefits of yoga and exercise: A review of comparison studies. *The Journal of Alternative and Complementary Medicine, 16*(1), 3–12. doi: 10.1089/acm.2009.0044

Ryan, P. (1998). Spirituality among adult survivors of childhood violence: A literature review. *The Journal of Transpersonal Psychology,* (30)1, 39–51.

Schiffman, S. S., Graham, B. G., Sattely-Miller, E. A., & Peterson-Dancy, M. (2000). Elevated and sustained desire for sweet taste in African-Americans: A potential factor in the development of obesity. *Nutrition, 16*, 886–893.

Schure, M. B., Christopher, J., & Christopher, S. (2008). Mind-body medicine and the art of self-care: Teaching mindfulness to counseling students through yoga, meditation, and Qigong. *Journal of Counseling and Development, 86*(1), 47–56.

Schwitzer, A. M., Gonzalez, T., & Curl, J. (2001). Preparing students for professional roles by simulating work settings in counselor education courses. *Counselor Education & Supervision, 40*(4), 308–320.

Sharkey, J. R., Johnson, C. M., & Dean, W. R. (2011). Food & Nutrition, *55*, 5819. doi: 10.3402/frm/v55i0.5819

Sheffield, D. S. (1998). Counselor impairment: Moving toward a concise definition and protocol. *Journal of Humanistic Education & Development, 37*(2), 96–107.

Skovholt, T. M. (2001). *The resilient practitioner: Burnout prevention and self-care strategies for counselors, therapists, teachers, and health professionals*. Needham Heights, MA: Allyn & Bacon.

Simonton, C., & Matthews-Simonton, S. (1992). *Getting well again*. New York: Bantam Books.

Simpson, L. R. (2010). Counseling and spirituality. In D. Capuzzi, & D. Gross (Eds.), *Introduction to the Counseling Profession*. Boston, MA: Allyn & Bacon.

Spiegel, D., Bloom, J. R., Kraemer, H. C., & Gottheil, E. (1989). Effect of psychosocial treatment on survival of patients with metastatic breast cancer. *The Lancet, 2*(8668), 888–891.

Tang, T. L. P., & Kim, J. K. (1999). The meaning of money among mental health workers: The Endorsement of money ethic as related to organizational citizenship, behavior, job satisfaction, and commitment. *Public Personnel Management, 28*(1).

Tanigoshi, H., Kantos, A. P., & Remley, T. P. (2008). The effectiveness of individual wellness counseling on wellness of law enforcement officers. *Journal of Counseling and Development, 86*, 64–75.

Trippany, R. L., Wilcoxin, S. A., & Satcher, J. F. (2003). Factors influencing vicarious traumatization for therapists of survivors of sexual victimization. *Journal of Trauma Practice, 2*, 47–60.

U.S. Department of Health and Human Services (USDHHS). (1996). Physical activity and health: A report of the Surgeon General. Atlanta: U.S. Department of Health and Human Services, Centers for Disease Control and Prevention, National Center for Chronic Disease Prevention and Health Promotion.

Wadsworth, J., Harley, D., Smith, S., & Kampfe, C. (2008). Infusing end-of-life issues into the rehabilitation counselor education curriculum. *Rehabilitation Education, 22*, 113–124.

Walen, H. R., & Lachman, M. E. (2000). Social support and strain from patner, family, and friends: Costs and benefits for men and women in adulthood. Journal of Social and Persoan Relationships, *17*, 5–30.

Walsh, B., & Walsh, S. (2002). Caseload factors and the psychological well-being of community mental health staff. *Journal of Mental Health, 11*, 67–78.

Wie, B., Kilpatrick, M., Naquin, M., & Cole, D. (2006). Psychological perceptions to walking, water aerobics and yoga in college students. *American Journal of Health Studies, 21*(3), 142–147.

Witmer, J. M., & Young, M. E. (1996). Preventing counselor impairment: A wellness approach. *The Journal of Humanistic Education and Development, 34*, 141–155.

Wiggins-Frame, M. (2005). Spirituality and religion: Similarities and differences. In C. Cashwell, & S. Young (Eds.), *Integrating Spirituality and Religion Into Counseling: A Guide for Competent Practice*. Alexandria, VA: American Counseling Association.

Young, M. A., & Lambie, G. W. (2007). Wellness in schools and mental health systems: Organizational influences. *Journal of Humanistic Counseling Education & Development, 46*(1), 98–113.

6

RESEARCH AND WRITING
IN COUNSELING

Teresa M. Christensen

What is research? How does research apply to counseling? How do I, as a beginning counseling student, incorporate research into what I am learning about counseling and my writing? What steps do I take to effectively search databases, construct literature reviews, and conduct research? At first glance, answers to these questions may seem rather simplistic and obvious; however, such issues often lead to high levels of anxiety, apprehension, and hours of wasted time spent by students who initially struggle with research and writing in their graduate studies (Galvan, 1999; Szuchman, 2002).

Numerous authors and presenters have addressed issues concerning how to conduct research in counseling (e.g., Creswell, 1994; Erford, 2008; Herman, 1997; Merchant, 1997; Stockton & Toth, 1997). Szuchman (2002) supplied a method for counseling students and professionals to follow when writing research papers in APA style and format (Publication Manual of the American Psychological Association, 2010). Szuchman's book provided hands on skills and instructions about how to construct papers that report research and incorporates concepts from recent literature that pertain to: selecting research topics, accessing resources, reviewing literature, critiquing research, and writing a litera-ture review in social sciences (e.g., Coelho & La Forge, 1996; Galvan, 1999; Nicol & Pexman, 1999; Nisenoff & Espina, 1999).

In the past decade, writers and researchers have directed more attention to the topics and populations being researched, researchers' different approaches to a variety of meth-odological designs, and procedures for program evaluation in professional journals within the field of counseling (Heppner, Wampold, & Kivlighan, 2008; Erford, 2008). Most recently, several researchers have focused attention on the meta-analysis of research find-ings and meta-study of publication patterns within professional journals affiliated with the field of counseling (Byrd, Crockett, & Erford, 2012; Crocket, Byrd, Erford, & Hays, 2010; Erford, Miller, Duncan, Erford, 2010; Erford, et al., 2011). Results from these meta-studies of various counseling journals affiliated with the American Counseling Association (ACA), have revealed consistent trends pertaining to: (1) increases in female and multiple author contributions; (2) increases in research based publications that uti-lized qualitative methodology and more sophistication statistical procedures; (3) increased focus on multicultural issues; (4) research participants continue to be predominantly graduate students and adults; and (5) declines in practitioner-author contributions. Such trends illustrate the continued evolution of research in the field of counseling and the responsiveness of researchers. However, as Byrd, Crocket, & Erford (2012) noted: "It is somewhat concerning that the voices of field-based practitioners are diminishing and the JSGW editorial board should encourage practitioner-scholar collaborations" (p. 67). Meta-studies such as those referenced illustrate researchers' attempts to compartmentalize, categorize, and summarize relevant themes, topics, and methodological designs currently implemented within the field of counseling. The increase in publications related to such topics further illustrate researchers' attempts to offer graduate students and practitioners with a review of relevant literature that further expands their understanding of research and writing.

Despite the continued effort by writers and researchers who detail plans about how to understand specific research designs and program evaluation models that apply to the field of counseling, many graduate students continue to struggle. In fact, both neophyte and advanced graduate students may be hesitant, anxious, defensive, and lack knowledge and confidence about their ability to understand, apply, and integrate research as a result of various factors (Nicol & Pexman, 1999; Rechtien & Dizinno, 1997; Szuchman, 2002). In fact, Bloomberg & Volpe (2008) noted, "We have witnessed and experienced many of the frustrations voiced by students confronted with the academic challenge of writing a dissertation" (p. 2). Such factors are multidimensional and include issues such as counseling students' confusion surrounding research designs, lack of familiarity with professional journals, and inadequate exposure to the utilization of APA guidelines.

**SIDEBAR 6.1 Self-Awareness: Setting up Your Own
Strategy for Success**

Think of conducting a literature review and writing a 20-page research paper on any topic you so choose. What reactions are you experiencing? How does this affect you? How would this interfere with your ability to initiate and complete this assignment? List 5 strategies that you can use to assist yourself in initiating the assignment.

Students often experience anxiety, fear, and apprehension when first broached with the assignment of conducting a literature review and writing a paper. Such reactions can inhibit students' ability to organize themselves. Accordingly, the best strategy is to relax and reach out to other resources and support systems.

Some students have difficulty distinguishing between literature that reports original empirical research with anecdotal reports, theoretical articles, literature reviews, and descriptions of programs, practice strategies, or standards (Galvan, 1999). In particular, Galvan (1999) attributed students' apprehensions to their lack of previous training regarding how to: (a) search databases for reports of original research and related theoretical literature, (b) analyze these particular types of literature, and (c) synthesize them into cohesive essays. Furthermore, novice students may find it difficult to conceptualize how research relates to the theory and practice of counseling. Szuchman (2002) added that beginning graduate students are in need of training specific to writing research papers in the style described by the APA publication manual.

Therefore, this chapter will attempt to incorporate various perspectives and ideas about: (1) the integration of research, practice, and theory; (2) the definition of and description of various research designs; (3) literature reviews and conducting research; (4) tips and techniques regarding how to compose and properly reference when writing; (5) legal and ethical considerations in research; and (6) program evaluations.

Integration of Research, Practice, and Theory

Many professionals in counselor education believe that research is the backbone of counseling practice and theory. Some authors go as far as to suggest that practice, research, writing, and publishing are the obligations of the professional counselor (Coelho & La Forge, 1996; Szuchman, 2002). Furthermore, advocates of research contend that it defines the profession of counseling, builds on old and generates new thinking and theory, sheds light on practice strategies that are effective and ineffective, and creates a forum for communication between various professionals in the field (Coelho & La Forge, 1996; Herman, 1997; Stockton & Toth, 1997). Essentially, many believe that counseling is informed and directed by research; hence the call by many researchers and professional journal editorial boards who continue to solicit practitioners to engage in field-based research and scholarship (Byrd et al., 2012).

Definition of Research

For the purposes of this chapter, attention is directed toward original research existing in academic journals and other professional resources. Research reports are considered to be original (primary sources) when they highlight initial results, including details about methodology, findings, implications, limitations and conclusions (Galvan, 1999). Whereas secondary sources of research are generated by someone other than the researcher and often include general descriptions of findings with only minor details about methodology. Some of the research found on the Internet, in summaries included in textbooks, magazines, newspapers, and on television and radio are examples of secondary sources of research. To avoid misinterpretation or distortion of research methodology and findings, it is wise to rely predominantly on primary research.

In terms of methodological procedures, research can be defined as quantitative or qualitative. Some researchers use a combination of the two (known as mixed methods design), but for the purposes of this chapter, each methodology will be explained separately. There have been many controversial discussions and open debates regarding the usefulness of quantitative and qualitative methodology in counseling. In the past two decades, many experts have contended and illustrated that both methodologies are important as the profession of counseling is in a constant state of transition in which the eclectic and subjective nature of humanity is appreciated (Herman, 1997). Accordingly, counseling students need to be familiar with the strengths and limitations of both types of research and must be able to accept quality research as informative and important, regardless of its methodological underpinnings. Continuous dialogue regarding quantitative and qualitative research is encouraged and essential; therefore, these two methodological approaches will be introduced and explored throughout the remainder of this chapter in terms of how they relate to each other, their unique attributes, and aspects related to the quality and credibility of each approach.

Quantitative research involves a systematic, logical, reductive, and empirically focused manner of interpreting information (Creswell, 1994). Researchers who use quantitative methodology utilize their worldview to develop hypotheses and test relationships of clearly defined variables that can be measured (Morse & Field, 1995). The goal is to gather information, reduce it through valid and reliable instrumentation, and produce numerical results in the form of statistics. Such numerical results possess differing meanings including averages, percentages, frequency of occurrence, and so on. The goal of many statistical operations is to test the hypotheses and determine whether there is a relationship between variables (Morse & Field, 1995). In general, quantitative researchers seek a statistical way to determine whether a cause and effect relationship exists between two or more variables (Lincoln & Guba, 1985).

In order to infer causal relationships, quantitative researchers believe that it is possible to extrapolate their personal values from the research process (Morse & Field, 1995). Furthermore, these researchers attempt to isolate specific factors, focus their investigations on predetermined variables, and control other variables that may interfere with the research process or alter researchers' hypotheses. When working with human beings and focusing on social sciences, it can be difficult to control for all factors of the human experience and isolate variables. However, many researchers and professional journals in the field of counseling prefer quantitative inquiry (Merchant, 1997; Sexton, 1996).

Coincidently, much of the training in research for undergraduate students in psychology and sociology and many graduate students in counseling rely primarily on the positivistic, linear, and reductionistic methods of quantitative research (Merchant, 1997). Meta-analysis of various professional journals illuminates the overall increased investment in research over the past several decades (Crocket et al., 2010). The prominence of quantitative methodology within the field of counseling continues to persist, with the implementation of various quantitative methodological designs. In a recent meta-study of publication patterns in the Journal for Specialists in Group Work (ASGW), it was noted that when quantitative methodology was used, there was a significant increase in the use of true experimental design (Byrd et al., 2012). According to Byrd et al., "True experimental designs use randomization procedures that allow greater generalizability and are higher valued in clinical trials and outcome research" (p. 68).

Qualitative Research Despite the efforts of Freud, Piaget, and other theorists in the early 1900s who used qualitative methods to construct developmental theories, research in counseling has predominantly neglected the use of naturalistic methodology (Merchant, 1997). In fact, Merchant offered the notion that reductionistic science or quantitative research is not always adequate to capture the richness and diversity of human experience; yet support for quantitative research persists.

However, this trend seems to be shifting as numerous counseling journals have consistently increased the prominence of qualitative research designs and related analytic techniques. In fact, Byrd et al. (2012) illustrated that significantly more qualitative research studies are published now as opposed to recent times. This trend has been unfolding for the past few decades as there have been several attempts to value and incorporate qualitative research into the field of counseling (Ambert et al., 1995; Erford et al., 2008; Lincoln & Guba, 1985; Merchant, 1997; Newsome, Hays, & Christensen, 2008; Sexton & Griffin, 1997; Strauss & Corbin, 1998). Flick (1998) stated, "Qualitative research is establishing itself in the social sciences and in psychology" (p. 1). Furthermore, Merchant (1997) devoted an entire monograph to the use of qualitative research in counseling and specifically highlighted the "relevance/fit of qualitative research" to many counselors' theoretical beliefs about human beings, ways of being with clients, and values about the process of counseling (p. 12). Most recently, Shank (2002) described how qualitative research is a "personal skills approach" (p. 1).

Probably most notable is the transition in accreditation standards about research in counseling. "Recent changes in academic standards (i.e., Council for Accreditation of Counseling and Related Educational Programs [CACREP], 2008) set forth a movement for counseling programs to promote knowledge about various research methodologies including qualitative approaches" (Newsome, Hays, & Christensen, 2008, p. 87). Qualitative research includes various non-numerical methods of investigating human experience and behavior (Denzin & Lincoln, 1994; Shank, 2002). Various terminologies such as naturalistic inquiry, ethnography, fieldwork, observation, and systematic inquiry into meaning often accompany qualitative research (Shank, 2002). Philosophically speaking, qualitative researchers believe that knowledge is contextual. Therefore, the researcher and reader must understand the overall process and see meaning in context (Lincoln & Guba, 1985; Sexton, 1996; Shank, 2002). Qualitative research is process-oriented, looks to explore why and how people behave, think, and make meaning as they do, and is conducted through an intense and/or prolonged contact with a life situation (Miles & Huberman, 1994). Such situations are commonly based on reflections of everyday life of individuals, groups, societies, and organizations.

Researchers attempt to capture data based on the perceptions of those being investigated. This is accomplished through a process of deep attentiveness, empathic understanding, and suspending or "bracketing" preconceptions about the topics under exploration (Miles & Huberman, 1994, p. 6). Qualitative data analysis is done primarily with words and entails a process through which information is explicated from narratives describing a particular setting, way of life, action, process, or manner of accounting for and managing one's life (Shank, 2002). Qualitative research is inductive in that researchers build on existing knowledge, discover and explore areas about which little is known, and construct concepts and theories as they emerge from the data (Lincoln & Guba, 1985; Strauss & Corbin, 1998).

In general, the objectives of qualitative research are to: (1) develop theory that is based on rich description resulting from documentation, description, and identification of patterns and relationships between concepts; (2) identify the essence of experience; (3) describe process; (4) understand meaning, context, and process; (5) develop causal explanations; (6) explore and identify phenomena; (7) create theoretical explanations of reality; and (8) describe theory and practice (Denzin & Lincoln, 1994; Lincoln & Guba, 1985; Maxwell, 1992; Miles & Huberman, 1994; Morse & Field, 1995; Shank, 2002). The overall purpose of qualitative research is to produce vivid, dense, full, and integrated descriptions in the natural language of an experience or situation under investigation (Polkinghorne, 1994). Such objectives are accomplished through exploring the phenomena under investigation in their natural setting. This includes using words, dialogue, narratives, journals, photographs, art, music, and personal reflections as data. Accordingly, the researcher is viewed as the primary instrument for data collection (Ambert et al., 1995; Strauss & Corbin, 1998; Shank, 2002). Qualitative research puts social science researchers in a position to design unique ways to explore and analyze concrete cases through the use of people's expressions and lived experiences (Shank, 2002).

Based on the assumption that significant contributions to the literature can be made by using any methodology that answers the research question, provided the methods are applied correctly, counseling courses must provide information about both forms of research. Furthermore, research and writing in counseling coursework should be designed to enhance students' understanding of human experience, thus producing exposure to diverse methodological procedures. Counseling students involved in reviewing and designing research projects are encouraged to seek meaningful answers to their questions through publications that inform them about human nature through both quantitative and qualitative research (Szuchman, 2002).

SIDEBAR 6.2 Case Study: Qualitative and Quantitative Research

Decide on one topic and obtain two research articles regarding virtually the same topic, one using primarily qualitative methods and the other quantitative. Carefully review each of the articles. Write a brief paper including: (a) a brief summary about what you learned from each article; (b) a discussion about how the results were similar or different; (c) a description of your perceptions of the articles (Did one enlighten you most about your specific topic? Which study did you prefer and why? Based on what you just reviewed, what are your perceptions about both qualitative and quantitative research?)

Meta-Analysis and Meta-Study Many researchers have moved to meta-analysis and meta-studies to explore trends and themes in research design over time. According to Erford et al. (2011), meta-studies involve the systematic exploration of studies published whereby researchers explore characteristics about the research design and the researchers, reveal trends that are emerging in the research and literature, and that are used to describe case-examples of how research is designed and implemented. Byrd et al. (2012) distinguish a meta-analysis as a specific set of procedures for statistically aggregating and evaluating effect size estimates from clinical trials on a topic of interest. Over the past few decades there have been significant increases in researchers who implement meta-studies to illuminate important information relevant to the field of counseling (Crocket et al., 2010; Erford et al., 2011). Both meta-studies and meta-analysis descriptive in nature, and can offer summaries and reviews of relevant literature and research; however, note that there can be limitations.

Literature Reviews and Conducting Research

Whether it be for a research paper, program evaluation, or thesis, intense anxiety can accompany students' thoughts about reviewing literature, planning and carrying out a research project, and producing a coherent essay (Galvan, 1999; Szuchman, 2002). Anxiety can be diminished and the task of conducting research can best be completed through a thorough review of existing literature and a careful plan for the project. Students' perceptions may change if they shift from conceptualizing research as a complicated and overwhelming project, to a process with various phases and tasks. As students expose themselves to literature, research becomes more manageable and less anxiety provoking. Based on these assumptions, this chapter provides a five-phased process for conducting a literature review and generating a plan for doing research. This process includes: (1) selecting a topic and searching for literature, (2) organizing and analyzing literature,

(3) structuring a written review of literature and developing an essay to illuminate findings, and (4) designing a plan for conducting research.

Many phases include steps that build from others and procedures that transfer to other parts of the writing and research processes. When doing projects, students are encouraged to carefully generate a timeline with a list of important due dates, specific guidelines, and any regulations that may affect their progress. These activities are designed to assist students in preparing themselves and in gaining a clear purpose for what they are attempting to accomplish. For example, if students are concerned with a thesis, they need to be aware of proposal and defense dates, university and departmental guidelines, and potential boundaries or resource issues that may interfere with their projects.

Specific guidelines to be aware of before beginning a project include, but are not limited to the instructions of the given assignment, as provided by the professor. For example, page limitations, focus on specific content, adherence to specific guidelines, and the use of specific journals. Other guidelines when conducting research or writing a paper may pertain to local, state, government, and university regulations regarding the use of human subjects in research. Other guidelines can be located through specific counseling departments, university research offices, and the appropriate publication manuals (i.e., the sixth edition of the Publication Manual of the American Psychological Association [2010]), as utilized by most counseling-related departments. Committee members, faculty advisors, and other instructors can also provide information about resources related to the processes of conducting and writing up research.

Phase One—Selecting a Topic and Searching for Literature

Obviously, the first step in conducting a search is to determine a specific topic about which to review and write. When doing research papers and sometimes in the case of master's theses, a topic is predetermined or limited by an instructor. If this is the case, students should clarify requirements regarding data searches and use of specific journals. For example, some instructors provide a list of detailed topics to choose from and specify the use of professional journals related to the field of counseling.

If not predetermined by course instructors, the selection of a topic can be difficult for beginning and advanced counseling students. Students are advised to pick a topic that can be kept narrow, is well defined, and within an area that sparks personal interest. Ideas can be generated from classroom lectures, discussions, textbooks, professional association newsletters and websites, or current issues prevalent in the field of counseling. Begin a search for literature immediately in order to clarify or report potential problems. Personal interest is important for those beginning a thesis or dissertation because they will spend time and energy on this topic and must be able to consistently maintain focus, desire, and interest to complete the project.

Choosing a topic, narrowing and broadening that topic, and searching for literature often coincide. Constructing a literature review begins with a thorough, yet manageable search of current publications in professionally prepared journals and database systems. It is wise to utilize resources related to other fields such as psychology, sociology, and education. Students are also encouraged to use information obtained from professional conferences, presentations, and organizational monographs.

Narrowing the Topic

A successful search for literature begins with a well-defined topic, yet often a topic cannot be defined until foundational information is known. Students are encouraged to start with an idea or concept that they are interested in learning more about. As students conduct searches of various databases related to their topics, they should attempt to narrowly define and specify exactly what they are exploring. Ways to limit the topic and search include using only those articles that are presented in professional journals, within a specified timeframe or era, related to a specific course, and within a particular theory or area of practice. Another way to limit the topic may be to conduct a preliminary search for literature related to a topic and then attempt to generate the first draft of a topic statement (Galvan, 1999; Szchman, 2002). A topic statement is a well-thought-out sentence that describes what a student is going to write about and/or research.

SIDEBAR 6.3 Case Study: Skylar's Topic Statement: Limiting Her Interests

Skylar is a 23-year-old second year counseling graduate student who is passionate about many topics within the field of counseling. Skylar has decided that she is most interested in counseling children, school counseling, social justice, child abuse/trauma, counselor values, group work, and legal and ethical issues. In her introduction to community counseling class, Skylar has been assigned to conduct a research review and write a brief reaction paper regarding her interests in the field of counseling. While Skylar has obvious interests in various areas within the field of counseling, she struggles with limiting her topic to a researchable and manageable project. What would you do if you were Skylar? How would you figure out which topics to cover as there is obviously NO way that Skylar can adequately research and write about such a wide array of topics? What could be a potential topic statement for Skylar's paper?

A potential solution—Skylar's topic can be limited by: (1) specifying the topic to counseling with children who have been abused, (2) using only journal articles published in the last five to seven years, (3) focusing on issues related to small group counseling with children who have been abused, and (4) focusing on articles that address cognitive-behavioral group counseling with children who have been abused. A topic statement could be: Implications of cognitive-behavioral group counseling with children who have been abused.

As previously inferred, defining a topic and conducting database searches work simultaneously. Based on information collected through searches of existing data, students may find themes that become interesting to them. They may think of questions for which they want answers. These are great reasons to narrow searches on topics where adequate literature exists and can be reviewed.

Searching Counseling Related Databases

Based on advances in the counseling profession, society, and technology, there are several methods to identify and utilize current literature. Reviewing literature in counseling can best be accomplished by searching varying databases and utilizing multiple methods to gather relevant information. Those interested in learning about a specific topic can gain a diversified and complete cluster of information by reviewing professional journals sponsored by or affiliated with the American Counseling Association (ACA) and the American Psychological Association (APA), searching the Internet, connecting to specific websites, accessing computerized database programs in counseling and other related fields, and attending professional conferences or seminars. Specific suggestions regarding database searching follow.

The word *database* refers to a constellation of information and resources arranged according to specialized topics and ease of retrieval. Each library has a unique organizational system that utilizes a multitude of on-line electronic database search options. Therefore, students must familiarize themselves with searching features and computer resources in their libraries. Many libraries provide workshops, handouts, and attendants that can inform others about effective ways to conduct electronic searches, yet many students can figure out how to operate computers and gain familiarity with electronic search devices and library resources on their own. With the abundance of database options, some students may struggle with how to access those that are specific to counseling.

On-line databases highlight abstracts from numerous publications including journal articles, doctoral dissertations, professional presentations/ papers, books, government documents, etc. Information about specific databases may be highlighted on professional association websites. Sample databases specific to counseling are (Bloomberg & Volpe, 2008; Szuchman, 2002):

> **ERIC** *(Educational Resources Information Center)*—information related to education, counseling, and related fields *Medline*—topics related to public health, medicine, and psychiatry.
>
> **PsycINFO®** —a comprehensive international database with numerous academic, research, and practice literature on topics related to psychology, counseling, criminology, social work, education, organizational behavior, medicine, and psychiatry.
>
> **PsycLit**—a subset of PsycINFO including only books and journals related to mental health.
>
> **SERLINE**—a subset of Medline with articles related to public health, medicine, nutrition, etc.
>
> **Social Work Abstracts**—provides information specific to the fields of social work and human services from 1977 to present.
>
> **Social Sciences Citation Index** *(SSCI)*—covers over 5,700 journals that represent every discipline in the social sciences.
>
> **Sociological Abstracts**—database that contains abstracts about articles in more than 2,500 journals and book reviews, including dissertations, from interdisciplinary research on social science issues and sociological perspectives.

SIDEBAR 6.4 Case Study: On-line Research & Resources

Jill is interested in the mind–body connection, in particular the neurobiological effects of counseling. She is also fascinated with current research specific to brain chemistry and the influence of psychotropic medications. As a previous Hospice nurse, Jill possesses a great deal of medical knowledge as well as an affinity for elderly. Because of a few bad experiences with the internet (catching a virus while surfing different sites and receiving false information from well-known site), Jill is very weary of on-line data bases and resources. Review the list of on-line databases provided in the chapter. Which databases would be best for Jill based on her interests? After accessing one or more of these databases, what could you say to Jill to provide some relief and reassurance about utilizing the internet? What other databases or on-line resources would you recommend?

The Internet

With recent advances in our technological capabilities, volumes of information can be accessed via the Internet. Specific websites and other on-line links offer a quick and cost-efficient means for gathering a multitude of information. While accessibility to great quantities of information is useful, it is pertinent to realize the shortcomings of such resources. In some situations, summaries and excerpts from journal articles or professional papers on web pages and listserves can be incomplete, even inaccurate. It is better to rely on original work created by primary authors and researchers, rather than secondary sources such as websites, which often include a mere synopsis of important information. Students cannot be cautioned enough to be mindful of the validity, content, and implications suggested by sources derived from the Internet. As adapted from Nisenoff and Espina (1999) and other experts in the field of mental health, a list of various websites and listserves focused on issues related to counseling and mental health can be found at the end of the chapter.

Professional Journals

In the hope of exposing students to professional publications in counseling, some instructors in counselor education require that students utilize journals supported by or affiliated with the ACA. Such professors may include a list of specific journals to be used or merely make reference to ACA-affiliated journals. These journals are numerous and cover a wide range of issues affiliated with counseling. Most notably is the *Journal of Counseling and Development* (JCD), the official publication for the American Counseling Association. This journal is printed quarterly and illuminates various areas related to research, theory, and practice in counseling.

Advances in technology have led many professional journals to move to on-line distribution by their professional organizations associated with ACA. Specialized divisions of ACA focus on a particular issue, population, or phenomenon related to counseling and, therefore, provide journals that illuminate information related to the specialized area at hand. Based on trends in the field of counseling and social sciences, divisions of the ACA sometimes split into independent associations, expand their focus, merge with other divisions, or cease to exist. Some of the ACA journals are selectively available and frequently change names. Thus, it can be quite difficult to provide a comprehensive list of all journals affiliated with the ACA. Consequently, the goal of this section is to introduce some, not all, of the most commonly utilized ACA journals.

1. *Adultspan*—Published twice a year, this is the official publication of the Association for Adult Development and Aging (AADA) which highlights current research, theory, and practice with respect to adult development & aging.

2. *Counseling and Values (CVJ)*—Published three times a year, this journal is the official publication of the Association for Spiritual, Ethical, and Religious Values in Counseling (ASERVIC). The focus is on relationships among psychology, philosophy, religion, social values, and counseling.

3. *Counselor Education and Supervision (CES)*—Official publication of the Association for Counselor Education and Supervision (ACES) published quarterly and focuses on research, theory development, and program applications re: counselor education and supervision.

4. *Measurement and Evaluation in Counseling & Development (MECD)*—Published quarterly, as the official journal of the Association for Assessment in Counseling and Education(AACE), this journal focuses on measurement specialists, counselors, or other personnel in schools, public and private agencies, businesses, industries, and government.

5. *Journal of Addictions and Offender Counseling (JAOC)*—Published twice, the official publication of the International Association of Addictions and Offender Counselors (IAAOC), theoretical/philosophical focus on specific problems and programs that address attitudes and behaviors of addictions and offender counselors.

6. *Journal of College Counseling (JCC)*—Published twice a year as the official journal of the American College Counseling Association (ACCA), and addresses issues specific to college counselors.

7. *Journal of Counseling and Development (JCD)*— Published quarterly, this is the official journal of the American Counseling Association (ACA), intended to publish archival material and research related to counseling.

8. *Journal of Employment Counseling (JEC)*—This journal is published four times a year and is the official publication of the National Employment Counseling Association (NECA). Articles highlight theory, research, and practice in employment counseling and vocational issues.

9. *Journal of Humanistic Counseling (JHC)*—This is the official journal of the Association of Humanistic Counseling (AHC), published twice a year, it focuses on educators and counselors interested in humanistic practices.

10. *Journal of Mental Health Counseling (JMHC)*—Published four times a year, this is the official publication of the American Mental Health Counselors Association (AMHCA), and addresses mental health counseling.

11. *Journal of Multicultural Counseling and Development (JMCD)*—Published quarterly in January, April, July, and October, official publication of the Association for Multicultural Counseling and Development (AMCD), and includes articles on multicultural and ethnic minority interests in counseling.

12. *Journal for Specialists in Group Work (JSGW)*—Published quarterly, this is the official publication of the Association for Specialists in Group Work (ASGW), thus focusing on research, practice, and theory in group work.

13. *The Career Development Quarterly (CDQ)*—Published quarterly, this is the official publication of the National Career Development Association (NCDA), and includes articles regarding career development and occupational resources.

Other Resources

In addition to the internet, electronic databases, books, journals, professional papers, and newspapers, students may also attain important information from monograms, video and audio productions, personal interviews, and professional presentations at conferences.

Students should start with the most recent publication and work backwards. If they find an article that is relevant to their topic, students are encouraged to focus on the article's reference list or bibliography. Many ideas and additional literature can be discovered through the review of articles previously used to explore any subject matter. Students are also encouraged to search for theoretical articles regarding their topic because these manuscripts often highlight key elements. Students should keep an eye out for existing reviews conducted on a topic relevant to theirs because previously published review articles are an excellent source for identifying additional information and expanding the scope of literature in a field of study. Finally, it is important that students identify the most prominent research and literature specific to their topic of interest.

SIDEBAR 6.5 Self-Awareness: Reviewing the Professional Organizations

Take some time to review your interests within the field of counseling. Review the American Counseling Organization Website and all of the different divisions. Explore the different publications supported by the different organizations. Since joining professional organizations can be an instrumental part of a counselors' professional development, which, if any of the ACA subdivisions speak to you? If you were going to join an ACA subdivision today, which one would it be and why? How could this professional organization be helpful to you? What, if any suggestions would you have for this organization to support you?

Phase Two—Organizing Literature

Once students have secured a significant amount of literature regarding a chosen topic, they are faced with the task of organizing various pieces of information into one comprehensive essay. This can seem overwhelming and impossible to beginning counseling students. In addition to designing a realistic timeline, students are encouraged to revisit the overall purpose of the project or paper. In many ways, students have already begun to unconsciously familiarize themselves with current topics during their perusal of titles, abstracts, and journals. The next step involves reading the first few paragraphs of each article in order to gain an overview of the research designs and writing styles. Students should note different researchers' perspectives, approaches to inquiry, purposes for conducting the research, and reasons for reporting their findings.

To become even more oriented to the literature, students should explore the hypothesis section of the article and focus on researcher hypothesis, research questions, and purpose. In the event that the article is not specifically related to research, readers are advised to scan the article for the conceptual framework or the author's rationale for creating the specific manuscript. Then students should continue to scan the remainder of the article, making note of salient information often introduced by headings, subheadings, or displays.

To group information into categories, cluster all articles into separate stacks that appear to correspond with common themes emerging from the information collected. Based on unique manners of organizing information, students may select any method that fits for them, but a common practice is to organize based on topics, subtopics, and chronological order (Galvan, 1999; Szuchman, 2002). Once students have loosely organized the articles, it is time to prepare for a thorough reading and analysis of the information.

Now students should revisit their organizational schema and begin to organize in greater detail. By reading the entire article, students can begin to summarize key points and become familiar with what the article is attempting to tell its readers. It might be helpful for students to construct a paragraph or two that summarize key articles. Students are encouraged to develop a personalized format for recording notes and build a conceptual map that highlights common themes throughout all of the articles. Being consistent and dogmatic about their personal system of review, students can prevent disorganized or repetitive procedures. This will pay off later when they start writing the literature review (Galvan, 1999; Szuchman, 2002).

When organizing, it is also important that students focus on explicit definitions and terms used by the authors. Questions about whether these definitions and terms match others' perceptions are important. Students are encouraged to note differences and similarities among various authors.

Next, it is time to explore methodological strengths and weaknesses in these terms: (1) Did the author provide enough information and clarify his or her purpose for conducting the study? (2) Why did the researcher utilize... quantitative or qualitative methodology? (3) How does the author use his or her findings to support or reject previous findings and perspectives? and (4) Does the research provide new insight regarding the topic? "Students must make sure that they understand the difference between the author's empirical evidence and his or her interpretations or assertions" (Galvan, 1999, p. 34). To avoid mistaking authors' assertions for actual findings, students should be aware of and avoid making statements that are not substantiated by the research they have reviewed unless they are clearly labeled as assertions.

Students should focus on major trends, themes, or patterns in the results of the literature that they review. They should identify and explore gaps that exist and highlight such discoveries in their write-ups, particularly when conducting a literature review for a thesis or dissertation. Due to human nature and the obstacles for researchers in the field of counseling, gaps in research can be catalysts to new and innovative approaches to practice, research, and theory. If there is a lack of relationship among studies on the same topic, discuss reasons for divergent thoughts. For example, two articles may focus on the same topic, but from different theoretical frameworks. Explanations and assertions as to why such differences exist are important.

Other issues to address in literature reviews include ways that specific manuscripts inform the reader about their topic. If students experience a complete lack of research directly related to their topic, they may need to explore other avenues of research or literature. For example, if a student was going to conduct a literature review of group supervision with child counselors, but found nothing on that topic, it would be permissible to explore publications on group supervision, training child counselors, individual supervision of child counselors, and so on. If an article is included that does not explicitly connect to the topic at hand, a writer must provide a clear rationale describing reasons for its inclusion.

Once information is read and organized, it is time to reevaluate references and ensure that a complete collection of timely, significant, and viable data exists with which to construct a well-thought-out review. As Galvan (1999) and Szuchman, (2002) contend, a literature review should represent the latest work done in the subject area, present an historical overview of the topic, and explicitly communicate reasons for including articles that are not directly related to the topic. Coelho and La Forge (1996) added that, "One should read extensively inside and outside the profession to ensure that the proposed contribution to the literature is a genuine one rather than merely repeating something that has already been written about" (p. 18).

At this point in the writing process, students should generate a preliminary list of references and citations. Oftentimes, throughout the writing process, students can get caught up in other organizational aspects and forget to keep track of references and appropriate citations. This can lead to extreme frustration near the end of the writing process, because students can easily find themselves in a desperate search for a specific article or citation that is missing from the volumes of information they have collected.

Phase Three—Analyzing Literature

During their organization of literature, students are encouraged to briefly explore the methodological section of the manuscripts collected. This includes an analysis of the methodology in terms of data collection and analysis procedures. As previously explored, methodological approaches utilized in counseling can be qualitative, quantitative, or a combination of these two methodologies. Based on philosophical and procedural differences between these two approaches, the following discussion will examine pertinent issues from each.

Quantitative Research

By reducing information to averages, percentages, and correlation coefficients, quantitative researchers utilize statistics and numbers to represent relationships. Readers can easily identify quantitative investigations by merely looking at the title of the article or exploring the results section of an article and noting whether or not the researchers used statistics and numbers to present findings of their study. Quantitative research has dominated social sciences for most of the 1900s; therefore, the majority of literature in the area of counseling illuminates quantitative rather than qualitative results (Galvan, 1999; Merchant, 1997).

To analyze a quantitative study, students are encouraged to orient themselves to common themes in the literature regarding effective use of quantitative methodology. Based on the following premises, students can explore methods sections in quantitative reports and determine whether researchers adhere to basic guidelines. According to Creswell (1994) and Galvan (1999), at a minimum, effective quantitative methodology should:

1. State a researcher's hypotheses at the onset of the investigation. Research hypotheses should not change throughout the study and should be evaluated only after all data are collected and analyzed.
2. Quantitative researchers serve as nonbiased individuals who can measure various aspects of human nature and counseling. Therefore, these researchers should remain objective throughout the entire investigation.
3. Use random selection in attaining research participants from a sample of the population that is said to represent the norm. This means that participants should be randomly picked from a larger group of representatives.
4. Include rather large sample sizes—between one to two hundred or a thousand, depending on the topic and resources of the researcher.
5. Indicate that specific variables of human nature, often referred to as confounding variables, were isolated, controlled for, and measured through quantifying procedures that produce numbers for data analysis.

6. Give detailed descriptions of data collection and analysis procedures. Measurements are taken with instruments that are believed to be scored objectively and deemed to be reliable and valid.
7. Present results using statistics. Use these statistical results to make inferences to correlations and relationships between variables and among groups of variables.
8. Indicate the reliability and validity of findings and address causality. Researchers must make generalizations between the study group and the general population. Researchers should never state results in terms of causes, but correlations.

Qualitative Research

Instead of adhering to the assumptions of the physical sciences as with quantitative researchers, qualitative researchers, much like counselors, focus on assumptions that address the complex nature of human experience (Sexton & Griffin, 1997). To understand the phenomenology of such naturalistic researchers, Hill and Gronsky (1984) proposed the following assumptions: (1) there is not one truth, but multiple truths or realities, depending on the perspective; (2) clinical phenomena are elusive and reactive; (3) clinical problems are deeply rooted and difficult to predict and manipulate in a controlled and rigid environment; (4) humans should be studied holistically and systematically rather than in isolated, restrictive, and incremental fashions; (5) systematic or circular models of causality may be more appropriate and useful than linear causality when exploring humans and their unique experiences.

Much like quantitative investigations, qualitative research can be identified by the titles of the articles. Titles often contain words such as naturalistic, exploration, or phenomenology and authors usually indicate that their study is qualitative in the abstract, introduction, or rationale for conducting the investigation. The results section of a qualitative article will be presented in terms of a narrative describing categories, themes, and trends that are usually supported by quotations and comments from the actual research participants.

Similar to quantitative research, good practice in qualitative research must address questions of reliability and validity; however these terms are replaced with parallel terms including dependability, trustworthiness, and authenticity in qualitative research (Lincoln & Guba, 1985; Shank, 2002). Literature on how to conduct qualitative research and how to ensure appropriate qualitative procedures emphasize several aspects. Students are encouraged to familiarize themselves with the following qualitative concepts. They can then compare such issues with methodological reports in the qualitative literature that they have collected. Denzin and Lincoln (1994), Lincoln and Guba (1985), Maxwell (1992), Newman et al., (2008), Shank, (2002), and Strauss and Corbin (1998) suggested that qualitative research include:

1. A statement of a general purpose without imposing rigid, specific goals and hypotheses to guide a study. Throughout the processes of data collection and analysis, this general purpose may emerge, and it is subject to change as additional data are collected.
2. Disclosure of the researcher's philosophical orientation and personal biases regarding the social and cultural context of the investigation.
3. Purposive and theoretical sampling procedures to select research participants who are accessible and appropriate for the research and topic. Purposive and theoretical sampling is a technique in which the sites, events, and participants being studied are deliberately chosen based on the purpose of the investigation and the phenomena

being explored. Participants can fluctuate greatly depending on the research question, population, and methodological approach. For example, the sample can be as low as one, as in a case study of Seung-Hui Cho, the college student who massacred several at Virginia Tech in 2007, or as many as 25 to 30, as in a phenomenological study of master's students in a multicultural counseling course. The researcher is the primary means of data collection by using relatively unstructured instruments such as interviews, observations, questionnaires, focus groups, existing documents, and so on to gather information.

4. Detailed descriptions of the internal process of the investigation as the researcher selects participants, gathers data, analyzes data, and reports their findings. A focus on "what and how" rather than "why" when analyzing data.

5. Prolonged engagement of the investigators with the material/people being studied. This includes spending extended periods of time with the participants to gain in-depth insights into the phenomena under investigation. Emphasis is often placed on how participants are experiencing themselves and the situation in which they are placed.

6. Results presented predominantly or exclusively in words, narratives, or stories with an emphasis on understanding research participants' experiences and perspectives.

7. Rich descriptions so that researchers are able to ground their interpretations in the data by illustrating concepts through interview excerpts or describing relationships of data to theoretical concepts.

8. Use of triangulation procedures to confirm and verify findings. Triangulation refers to utilizing multiple sources of information, interpretation, and theory to support, challenge, clarify, and verify findings. Such sources may include, but are not limited to, existing literature, more than one researcher, experts in the field being explored, and divergent theories.

Other Factors in Determining Quality of Research

Through exploring both quantitative and qualitative research and comparing the two methodologies, differences between the two seem blatant. Yet, both methodologies possess characteristics and procedures to ensure the credibility of findings. Differences between methodologies and unique measures to ensure trustworthiness of findings are important and must be understood in order to effectively evaluate the strengths and weaknesses of a study (Galvan, 1999).

Other important aspects to consider when addressing the quality of a quantitative or qualitative study include:

1. Determining if the study is experimental, meaning is the purpose of the study to assess the effectiveness of something, such as an innovative counseling technique or a new drug? If so, note how the researcher selected participants, assigned treatment conditions, and measured outcomes.

2. Note if the study is non-experimental (meaning that participants' traits are measured without attempting to change anything), and be conscious of attempts to extrapolate correlations between outcomes and findings.

3. Determine if researchers directly addressed issues related to measures of validity (Does the instrument or results seem accurate or correct?) and reliability (Would the instrument be consistent or would the same results occur over time?) for quantitative research. For qualitative research, are findings credible, trustworthy, thorough, and

comprehensive (Did researchers provide a detailed explanation or a brief description of what they did to ensure issues of validity, reliability, credibility, and trustworthiness?). Readers should attempt to make their own assessments regarding the findings and their accuracy.

4. Pay attention to the sampling procedures. In the case of a quantitative study, usually the more participants the better, and only through random sampling can researchers generalize their findings to the overall population. In qualitative investigations, participants are purposely selected and described in detail. The number of participants is directly related to the topic at hand and may not necessarily be a factor.

5. Understand that when quantitative researchers imply that there is statistical significance, they are suggesting that there is a difference between two variables, and that the difference is significantly greater than might be expected by chance alone. Since small differences can be classified as statistically significant in some studies, researchers should make note of the size of the differences.

6. Realize as Peshkin (1988) contends, "Beginning with the premise that subjectivity is inevitable, . . . researchers should systematically seek out their subjectivity, not retrospectively when data have been collected and analysis is complete, but while their research is actively in progress" (p. 17). Essentially, researchers should be aware of and communicate to the reader how their personal biases might have shaped their study and its outcomes (Peshkin, 1988).

7. Note (Galvan, 1999) that all empirical studies are subject to errors. Readers should refrain from assuming that an investigation provides absolute truths or definitive answers to a given research problem. Furthermore, researchers should examine and discuss flaws of their investigations. Limitations to specific studies can often shed light on important aspects related to the topic being explored, as well as serve as ideas for future research.

8. Consider that implications about how the study informs the profession about the topic being explored and suggestions for future research are also essential aspects in both quantitative and qualitative research. From a qualitative perspective researchers should discuss the transferability, and quantitative researchers should address the generalizeability, of their findings.

Phase Four—Structuring the Literature Review & Developing the Essay

It is finally time to explore ideas about how to conceptualize and synthesize review findings and writers' beliefs about the literature. Students are encouraged to look at the development of a literature review as a process with a planning phase, a construction phase, and a refining phase. This section serves as an overview of key aspects to consider when creating a literature review.

Structuring the Literature Review

Before integrating literature into the form of a literature review, students need to clarify their purpose, choice of voice, and the audience to whom they are writing. If the literature review is for a class assignment or research paper, it is important to re-review specific guidelines that instructors' provide. For example, instructors may provide an outline, specify page limitations, or determine the focus of the review. When choosing the voice in academic writing, many suggest that the first person, "I," be avoided and that third person or facts be allowed to speak for themselves (Galvan, 1999). Students must also take into consideration who will be reading their literature reviews. If the review is part of a thesis or dissertation, various committee members and reviewers will be reading students' work and in most cases, the relevant literature is used to establish a framework and build a rationale for a study. Accordingly, information regarding methodology, gaps in research, suggestions for future research, and other important details should be highlighted.

After clarifying the purpose and audience of the literature review, students are then faced with the task of organizing their ideas into an outline or structured plan. Such a plan gives direction to the information that students have obtained throughout their review of the literature. It also allows students a forum to creatively articulate their thoughts or judgments about the research that they have reviewed (Coelho & La Forge, 1996; Galvan, 1999). This means that students should have formed judgments about the topic based on their analysis and synthesis of the research literature (Galvan, 1999). The task of creating an outline that exhibits the integration of information and communicates students' thoughts and judgments can be accomplished in a few basic steps.

First, students must integrate various sources into a comprehensive summary and then clarify how all of this information is related. Next, students are encouraged to articulate their assertions, contentions, or propositions regarding the literature and research they have reviewed. Once students have established an argumentation for the reader, they should design their outlines around this set of beliefs. This includes reorganizing notes and ideas according to their assertions, contentions, or propositions.

Now that students have a detailed outline, they should begin connecting their beliefs to topic headings in the outline that emerged as they reviewed the literature. Students should focus on building a comprehensive and clear discussion of their line of argumentation under subheadings in the outline to define and describe each concept, clarify inter-relationships among concepts, discuss connections to the topic, and discuss relationships among various studies or sources. Subheadings also address obvious gaps or areas needing further attention, ideas about how individual studies relate to and enhance theory, and innovative concepts that clarify misconceptions about the topic.

Writing the Literature Review

Once students have developed a detailed outline including specific headings, subheadings, and concepts, they are ready to construct the first draft. This first draft is intended to serve as a rehearsal and an opportunity to explore initial attempts at articulating the context and arrangement of information and ideas (Coelho & La Forge, 1996). If students have done their work in formulating a well-organized and specific outline, they simply transfer concepts from that outline into a narrative with transitions, continuity, and appropriate grammar.

Students are encouraged to introduce their topic with the identification of the broad area under review. They should avoid global statements and instead move from a general topic to specific concepts and ideas. This includes giving details about what the topic is and how it relates to other aspects related to the field of counseling. For example, when discussing group counseling with children affected by abuse, it may be logical to begin with a brief introduction to research about group work with children. Then get more specific and address issues related to counseling children who have been abused. Finally, discuss the specific topic of group work with children who have been abused.

Students should indicate the importance of the topic and comment on the timeliness in terms of a specific context. They need to identify their reasons for conducting a review of the literature and discuss why it is being done at this time. For example, when conducting a literature review for a thesis or dissertation, students may indicate that their research will address a gap in existing research. In this example, students would also need to explain why the topic is important and issues currently faced by the field of counseling as a result of the topic. Students must remember to always justify their comments regarding how they determined a gap in literature and why they believe the topic is of importance.

When students are citing a classic or landmark study, attempting to replicate it, or hoping to elaborate on it, they should indicate this. Landmark studies are those that are pivotal and influential in the historical development of the published literature and topic under investigation (Galvan, 1999; Szuchman, 2002). Such studies stimulate additional research in many instances, and thus provide a solid foundation for students to build upon.

Students are also encouraged to discuss other literature reviews related to the topic being explored and make reference to reviews on issues related to the topic (Szuchman, 2002). In the case that earlier reviews were published about the same topic, writers are encouraged to incorporate a discussion about such reviews by focusing on how they are different, adequate, and worthy of readers' attention (Galvan, 1999). While students should cover their topic in great detail, they may find that related concepts printed in previous reviews are important, but not worthy of extended exposure. In this situation, students should simply make reference to other reviews when it may be useful to readers. On the other hand, if students locate research with an inconsistent or widely varying discussion, they should cite these manuscripts separately and indicate the effect on their topic and the field of counseling.

When writing a thesis, dissertation, or article for publication, students are encouraged to cite all relevant references in the literature review before they proceed to reporting original research. In this situation, students will use their review to justify and provide a rationale for conducting their studies. They should refrain from including long lists of nonspecific references within their text. Students are encouraged to cite only those references that provide direct quotations or essential facts needed for the text. Students should avoid the overuse of direct quotations and attempt to summarize whenever possible. Yet, it is vital that students give credit where credit is due. They should use references whenever they need to provide proper credit to an author or creator, and to demonstrate the coverage given in a manuscript (Galvan, 1999). A brief discussion of legal and ethical implications follows.

Multicultural Considerations

When writing and conducting research, students are encouraged to consider various multicultural considerations. Such considerations can include, but are not limited to the way researchers attend to gender, race, ethnicity, sexual orientation, etc.... Likewise, students should be mindful of multicultural considerations when they are writing their papers. For example, appropriate terminology must be utilized when describing gender, racial and ethnic groups, geographic locations, socioeconomic characteristics, etc.... It is essential that authors learn how to avoid the use of discriminatory language or gross generalizations when writing about any population. Likewise, students are responsible for ongoing awareness of cultural developments that emerge from professional organizations or through research in the field of counseling. For example, as of July 1, 2007 the American Counseling Association will stop referring to the Association for Gay, Lesbian, and Bisexual Issues in Counseling and begin using its new name: "the Association for Lesbian, Gay, Bisexual and Transgendered Issues in Counseling (ALGBTIC)" (ACAeNews, 2007).

Noting the Legal and Ethical Implications in Writing

Students must be aware that copyright protection begins at the creation of a work, regardless of registration with the U.S. Copyright Office. Copyright laws acknowledge that individuals own ideas once they have created them (Remley & Herlihy, 2009). Students must give credit to sources via proper referencing and citation when they use the words and creations of others. Due to the ethical and legal implications of proper referencing, when in doubt, students should review guidelines in the most recent edition of the American Counseling Association's (ACA) *Code of Ethics and Standards of Practice* (2005) and the American Psychological Association's (APA) style manual (currently 6th edition [APA], 2010). Depending on the source and the manner in which it is used, the APA manual (2010) specifies guidelines about how to properly cite the work of others. Published and unpublished sources that require citation include journal articles, books, professional presentations, personal interviews, videos, material from the Internet, and so on. Detailed descriptions and guidelines for appropriate citation and referencing are clarified and issues regarding manuscript organization, style, and format are included in the APA manual (2010).

Methods to Avoid Plagiarism

There has been a steady increase in research and literature specific to plagiarism in academia. Studies have addressed: (1) faculty members perceptions of and response to plagiarism (Robinson-Zanartu et al., 2005); (2) "Internet Plagiarism" (Howard, 2007); (3) how to help students avoid plagiarism (Landau, Druen & Arcuri, 2002); and (4) the role of librarians in helping students avoid plagiarism and other forms of academic dishonesty (Mundava & Chaudhuri, 2007).

"For decades, guidelines have defined plagiarism broadly as the public misrepresentations of work as original, or any activity in which a person knowingly or unknowingly and for some form of gain, represents the work of another as his/her own" (Robinson-Zanartu et al., 2005, p. 319). While the kinds of plagiarism can vary, the most common is word-for-word plagiarism which is easily detected and most frequently punished (Robinson-Zanartu et al.). The occurrence of plagiarism has steadily increased over the last several years. Howard (2007) contributed this increase in plagiarism to the internet and noted that the internet has increased students' accessibility to information and research. However, the overall lack of education about plagiarism as well as the inadequate preparation of many students continue to plague academia (Robinson-Zanartu et al.). Despite many professors' efforts to emphasize the importance of avoiding plagiarism and their adherence to "No Tolerance" policies, cultural and language barriers have lead to the increase of plagiarism in academia (Mundava & Chaudhuri, 2007).

Many experts have offered suggestions regarding how to address the problem of plagiarism in academia. In particular, Landau, Druen, and Arcuri (2002) illuminated that instruction regarding plagiarism identification and paraphrasing skills, followed by exercises to help students practice such skills, was the most effective way to assist students in avoiding plagiarism. According to Landau et al., written and oral warnings against plagiarism aren't effective; thus faculty members are encouraged to utilize exercises or feedback sessions to train students to avoid plagiarism. Since the majority of professors don't have or take the time to address plagiarism directly, students are encouraged to seek assistance via information and activities offered on websites and the internet. For example, http://www.plagiarism.org and the APA's publication guide offer details and examples of how to cite various resources correctly.

Overall students are encouraged to paraphrase information appropriately and utilize direct quotes only when necessary. If specific words are necessary to preserve the meaning of a passage, students should be tenacious about citing the author, year of publication, and page number or location.

SIDEBAR 6.6 Self-Awareness: Steps to Prevent Plagiarism

There has been a steady increase in research and literature specific to plagiarism in academia. Despite the increased attention, plagiarism is still a big concern. Students must give credit to sources via proper referencing and citation when they use the words and creations of others. Review the section regarding what to do to avoid plagiarism. What other steps can you take to avoid plagiarism? What else can be done to prevent plagiarism?

Creating a Comprehensive Essay

Since first drafts are seldom, if ever, complete, clear, and coherent, once students have completed the first draft, they must begin the process of refining their work. Although it is often easy to get discouraged, students should be prepared to rewrite at least two or three times after the first draft is finished. Szuchman (2002) indicated that the writing process inherently includes the following process of revision: (a) first draft, (b) first rewrite, (c) second rewrite, (d) third inspection, and (e) the final touches. At least two rewrites are required throughout the process of revising a research paper or manuscript. As Zinsser (1990) so appropriately commented, "Writing is hard work. A clear sentence is no accident"(p. 13).

When available, allowing peers or others to proof first and subsequent drafts can be extremely helpful. Students are encouraged to seek others who are willing and able to read and critique their work. Feedback is the most effective way for writers to gain perspective and enhance quality. If unable to receive feedback from others, students are encouraged to challenge themselves and their writing as they proofread their own manuscripts. During this self-editing process, students should compare their draft with their topic statement and outline; avoid using synonyms for recurring words; spell out all acronyms when they first appear in the text; avoid the use of contractions; set off coined terms in quotations; avoid slang expressions, colloquialisms, and idioms; and avoid plagiarism (Galvan, 1999). In addition, students must look for typical errors in typing, writing, spelling, and grammar. Students must edit and revise the first draft as many times as necessary to clarify, solidify, and edit flaws.

Since many authors understand that the writing process can be overwhelming, they have offered the following suggestions. Writers should develop a process of writing that is unique to them. A unique writing process takes into consideration writers' personalities and different writing styles. This can include the selection of a specific time of day to enable authors to write while they are fresh (Creswell, 1994). Coelho and La Forge (1996) stated that writers must avoid writing binges, but should focus on writing in small, yet regular amounts. Writers are also encouraged to understand that writing is a slow and tedious process requiring time, patience, and persistence. Writers may want to schedule daily writing tasks, generate goals for each day, keep daily charts of writing progress, select others to proofread who will provide supportive and corrective feedback, and try to work on two to three writing projects at once (Creswell, 1994). Coelho and La Forge (1997) asserted that writing is in a constant state of evolution; therefore, writers must be flexible and open to new ideas that occur while writing.

Phase Five—Designing a Plan for Conducting Research

At the conclusion of a literature review, those interested in conducting research need to consider their plans for carrying out research agendas (Bloomberg & Volpe, 2008; Cone & Foster, 1995). When writing a thesis or dissertation, this can be an ideal opportunity for students to solidify their research purposes and agendas and meet with faculty advisors. Students may find that they need to reexamine specific characteristics of their research plan, including the initial research question, hypotheses, and data collection and analysis procedures. This process can often lead to a revision of the initial research plan. For example, based on suggestions regarding methodology, students may find that they need to review and incorporate additional literature regarding the use of a specific methodological approach or alter their research plan to fit a particular mode of data collection and analysis.

This is also an excellent time for masters and doctoral students to coordinate with their advisors and develop detailed and specific plans for the remainder of their investigations. It is crucial that those embarking on theses or dissertations take ample time to decide how, when, where, and with whom they will conduct their research. Students must address specific details regarding the sample population, their research purpose, specific research questions, methodological procedures, and potential barriers. A tentative time line of events and procedures must be developed before the research process can be initiated.

Legal and Ethical Considerations in Research

According to ethical guidelines and CACREP (2008), studies must be rigorously and carefully designed or they may be considered to be unethical due to the waste of time and potential harm they can pose to participants and researchers (Remley & Herlihy, 2009). Therefore, students must take various legal and ethical considerations into account in the initial phases of planning their investigations. Of highest priority, researchers must protect research participants from harm. This includes voluntary participation, informed consent, ensuring confidentiality, and paying attention to issues of diversity.

Remley and Herlihy (2009) have discussed several of the ethical mandates pertaining to research that are supported by legal requirements. For example, any institution that receives federal funds must maintain a system to review research proposals with the intent to protect the welfare of research participants (Remley & Herlihy). Most universities and government affiliated organizations require that research including human subjects be reviewed and approved by a committee prior to the onset of data collection. Consequently, if students do not plan studies that integrate legal and ethical requirements, they will not receive approval from such review committees. This would more than likely delay students' research and could cause serious problems for students and research participants. For this and other reasons, students must familiarize themselves with ethical guidelines in conducting and reporting research prior to embarking on a research plan. A full discussion of such issues is provided in the ACA's *Code of Ethics and Standards of Practice* booklet (2005).

Program Evaluations

Up to this point, this chapter has been directed toward students concerned with constructing literature reviews and conducting research for a thesis or dissertation. However, there are other reasons that counseling students may do research, such as program evaluation. Program evaluations are based on whether the goals for implementation of a counseling program are being met and whether clients are getting what they need from the counseling experience. In many schools and agencies, counselors are asked to be accountable and produce evidence indicating the effectiveness of their practice. Novice and experienced counselors are faced with program evaluations and often struggle with how to accomplish this task. Such requests can be met by counselors if they begin gathering and recording data that illuminates their work and productivity.

Counselors are encouraged to utilize data collection procedures outlined in both quantitative and qualitative methodologies to attain various forms of information that testify to their effectiveness. Depending on the unique styles and settings of counselors, they should select methodological procedures that fit their individual, school, and agency needs. For example, a school counselor may simply begin keeping track of students they meet with on a weekly basis. They could develop a chart and tally specific issues that they address with various students and specific interventions or techniques that they used. At the end of a semester, these school counselors could analyze their data and produce a report highlighting numerical results of their efforts. Such research would provide a record of accountability regarding what school counselors have done over a specific period of time. This information would address issues of program effectiveness for principals, school board officials, and school-related personnel.

Summary

This chapter addressed issues related to writing and research in counseling. Concepts and ideas were directed toward novice and experienced counseling students who are currently encountering assignments ranging from essays, term papers, and literature reviews to theses and dissertations. Specific attention was placed on the role of research in the profession of counseling. Concepts included the importance of research, the definition of research, how to use research and literature in counseling, how to construct a comprehensive essay or literature review, legal and ethical implications for writing and research, and how to utilize research in program evaluations.

Useful websites

www.ishmo.org/webpsych—*WebSPIRS*—offers simultaneous searching of more than twenty periodical databases related to humanities and education.
www.counseling.org—American Counseling Association (ACA).
www.counseling.org/resources/bibliogrphies.htm—professional resource bibliographies regarding general or specialized topics, updated annually.
http://ericcass.uncg.edu/about.hitm—*counseling and student services.*
www.plagiarism.org/—plagiarism and appropriate referencing techniques.
www.plattsburgh.edu/projects/cnet—CounselorNet
www.cmhc.com—Mental Health Net

www.naswdc.org—National Association of Social Workers
www.nmha.org—National Mental Health Association
www.onlinepsych.com/index.html—On-Line Psychological Services
www.nimh.nih.gov—National Institute of Mental Health
www.samhsa.gov—Substance Abuse and Mental Health Services
listser@asuvm.inre.asu.edu—AERA-E American Educational Research
listserv@utkvm1.utk.edu—ICN—International Counselor Network
listserv@utkvm.utk.edu—CESNET-L (Counselor Ed & Supervision)

References

ACAeNews Vol. IX, No. 8, April 12, 2007.

ACA *Code of Ethics and Standards of Practice*. (2005). Annapolis Junction, MD: ACA Distribution Center.

American Psychological Association. (2010). *Publication manual*. (6th ed.). Washington, DC: Author.

Ambert, A., Adler, P. A., Adler, P., & Detzner, D. F. (1995). Understanding and evaluating qualitative research. *Journal of Marriage & Family, 57*, 879–893.

Bloomberg, L. D., & Volpe, M. (2008). *Completing your qualitative dissertation: A roadmap from beginning to end*. Thousand Oaks, CA: Sage.

Byrd, R., Crocket, S.A., & Erford, B.T. (2012). Journal for Specialists in Group Work (JSGW) publication pattern review: A meta-study of author and article characteristics from 1981–2010. *Journal for Specialists in Group Work, 37*(1), 56–70.

Coelho, R. J., & La Forge, J. (1996). Journal publication as a professional practice activity for rehabilitation counselors. *Journal of Applied Rehabilitation Counseling, 27*(1), 17–21.

Council for Accreditation of Counseling and Related Educational Programs [CACREP]. Revised Standards. (2008).

Creswell, J. W. (1994). *Research design: Qualitative & quantitative approaches*. Thousand Oaks, CA: Sage.

Crocket, S., Byrd, R., Erford, B. T., & Hays, D. G. (2010). Counselor Education and Supervision (CES) golden anniversary publication pattern review: Author and article characteristics from 1985–2009. *Counselor Education and Supervision, 50*, 5–20.

Denzin, N. K., & Lincoln, Y. S. (Eds.). (1994). *Handbook of qualitative research*. Thousand Oaks, CA: Sage.

Erford, B. T. (Ed.). (2008). *Research and evaluation in counseling*. Boston, MA: Houghton Mifflin/ Lahaska Press.

Erford, B. T., Miller, E. M., Schein, H., McDonald, A., Ludwig, L., & Leishear, K. (2011). Journal of Counseling and Development (JCD) submission patterns: Author and article characteristics from 1994–2009. *Journal of Counseling Development, 89*, 73–80.

Flick, U. (1998). *An Introduction to Qualitative Research*. Thousand Oaks, CA: Sage.

Galvan, J. L. (1999). *Writing literature reviews: A guide for students of the social and behavioral sciences*. Los Angeles, CA: Pyrczak.

Heppner, P. P., Wampold, B. E., & Kivlighan, D. M. (2008). *Research design in counseling*. (3rd ed.). Belmont, CA: Brooks/Cole.

Herman, K. C. (1997). Embracing human science in counseling research. *Counselor Education and supervision, 36*, 270–283.

Howard, R. M. (2007). Understanding "Internet plagiarism". *Computers and Composition, 24*, 3–15. ScienceDirect www.sciencedirect.com.

Landau, J. D., Druen, P. B., & Arcuri, J. A. (2002). Methods for helping students avoid plagiarism. *Teaching of Psychology, 29*(2), 112–115.

Lincoln, Y. S., & Guba, E. G. (1985). *Naturalistic inquiry*. Newbury Park: Sage.

Maxwell, J. A. (1992). Understanding and validity in qualitative research. *Harvard Educational Review, 62,* 279–299.

Merchant, N. (1997). Qualitative research for counselors. *Counseling and Human Development, 30*(1).

Miles, M. B., & Huberman, A. M. (1994). Qualitative data analysis. *An expanded sourcebook.* Newbury Park, CA: Sage.

Morse, J. M., & Field, P. A. (1995). *Qualitative research methods for health professionals.* (2nd ed.). Thousand Oaks, CA: Sage.

Mundava, M., & Chaudhuri, J. (2007). Understanding plagiarism: The role of librarians at the University of Tennessee in assisting students to practice fair use of information. *College and Research Libraries News, 68*(3), 1–5. http://www.ala.org/ala/acrl/acrlpubs/crlnews/backissues 2007/march07/plagiarism.htm.

Newsome, D., Hays, D. G., & Christensen, T. M. (In Press, 2008). Qualitative approaches to research. In B. T. Erford (Ed.), *Research and evaluation in counseling.* Boston: Houghton Mifflin / Lahaska Press.

Nicol, A. A. M., & Pexman, P. M. (1999). *Presenting your findings: A practical guide to creating tables.* Washington, D. C: American Psychological Association.

Nisenoff, S., & Espina, M. R. (1999, June). The a-b-c's of research in professional counseling. *Counseling Today,* p. 18.

Peshkin, A. (1988, October). In search of subjectivity-one's own. *Educational Research. (17–21).*

Polkinghorne, D. E. (1991). Qualitative procedures for counseling research. In C. E.Watkins, & L. J. Schneider (Eds.), *Research in counseling* (pp. 163–204). Hillsdale, NJ: Lawrence Erlbaum.

Polkinghorne, D. E. (1994). Reaction to special section on qualitative research in counseling process and outcome. *Journal of Counseling Psychology, 41*(4), 510–512.

Rechtien, J. G., & Dizinno, G. (1997). A note on measuring apprehension about writing. *Psychological Reports, 80,* 907–913.

Remley, T. P. Jr., & Herlihy, B. (2009). *Ethical, legal, and professional issues in counseling.* (3rd ed.). Upper Saddle River, NJ: Prentice Hall.

Robinson-Zanartu, C., Pena, E. D., Cook-Morales, V., Pena, A. M., Afshani, R., & Nguyen, L. (2005). Academic crime and punishment: Faculty members' perceptions of and response to plagiarism. *School Psychology Quarterly, 20*(3), 318–337.

Sexton, T. L. (1996). The relevance of counseling outcome research: Current trends and practical implications. *Journal of Counseling and Development, 74,* 590–600.

Shank, G. D. (2002). *Qualitative research A personal skills approach.* Upper Saddle River: NJ: Pearson Education.

Stockton, R., & Toth, P. L. (1997). Applying a general research training model to group work. *Journal for Specialists in Group Work, 22*(4), 241–252.

Strauss, A., & Corbin, J. (1998). *Basics of qualitative research: Techniques and procedures for developing grounded theory.* (2nd ed.). Thousand Oaks, CA: Sage.

Szuchman, L. T. (2002). *Writing with style: APA style for counseling.* Pacific Grove, CA: Brooks/Cole.

Zinsser, W. (1990). *On writing well* (4th ed.). New York: Harper Collins.

TECHNOLOGY AND COUNSELING

Melinda Haley, Anne-Laure Bourgois, and Jessica C. Gelgand

History

The use of technology in counseling has been apparent in some form or another for the last six decades. In the 1950s, Dr. Joyce Brothers used radio to reach millions of listeners and provide services to those in need (Dr. Joyce Brothers, 2007). Interactive video therapy, where client and therapist were connected by television for the counseling session, first began at the University of Nebraska during the same decade (Walker, 2007). Telephones have been used for suicide hot lines and 24-hour counseling services, and students and counselor educators have been using audiotape and videotapes in supervision for decades, while more recently webcams have been utilized. In the past decade technological applications for clients and counselors have flourished.

Technology has affected the way counselors perform their job tasks (Fields, 2011). Technologies used in counseling services are varied and include (a) software to aid in report writing, (b) Excel spreadsheets for recording client data, (c) statistical analysis packages for analyzing client data, (d) publishing software for marketing and client recruitment, and (e) software for assessment and testing (Murphy, 2003). E-mail and listservs are used for personal and professional communication as well as for consultation, supervision, referral, and professional development. The Internet has been used for client information (professional and informational web sites), advertising of services and provision of counseling services, marketing, and a host of other purposes. In fact, current estimates are that several thousand counselors use Internet Websites to advertise their counseling services (Rummell & Joyce, 2010).

The realization that the technological age has profound significance for counseling has spurred great debate and controversy within the profession regarding how technology will be used (Pelling, 2005). Professional associations and governing agencies have scrambled to provide counselors with guidelines, competencies, and ethics to regulate usage and provide protection to clients. This has been important for many new technological arenas such as Internet counseling, as there were no preceding laws, regulations, or codes of conduct to initially guide counselors (McAdams & Wyatt, 2010). This chapter will explore many of the current technological innovations counselors are using in their work today. An emphasis will be placed on discussing the benefits, consequences, considerations, and ethical implications of using these technologies in counseling.

Online Counseling/Distance Counseling

Online counseling is a growing modality for providing counseling services (Fields, 2011). It is estimated that over 100 million Americans have sought help or mental health information online (Chang, 2005). In addition, hundreds of websites exist offering mental health information or advice, and over a thousand counselors and mental health specialists provide some or all of their services online (Shaw & Shaw, 2006). Online counseling is one of the fastest growing health services on the Internet (Mallen, Vogel, Rochlen, & Day, 2005). Although online mental health services may never replace face-to-face psycho-therapy, it is clear that this modality is prolific and here to stay. Over the last few years, with all the technological developments, online counseling has changed significantly from being provided via e-mail to now utilizing such platforms as synchronous counseling through chat rooms and live session web-cam applications such as Skype or iChat (Boisvert, Lang, & Andrianopoulos, 2010). Both Skype and iChat videoconferencing applications can be downloaded for free from the Internet, which also makes it cost effective.

names for online counseling

Internet counseling services have been called by many names: cyber counseling, e-counseling, cyber-consultations, cyber psychology, cyber therapy, online counseling, virtual couch therapy, telehealth, and telecounseling to name just a few. In this chapter, this form of therapy will be referred to as online counseling. A further distinction needed for this section is that online counseling is counseling that is performed strictly with the use of computers via the Internet (e.g. e-mail, web sites, chat rooms, webcam), whereas distance counseling can use a variety of media in addition to the computer such as the telephone, television satellite hookup, or video and audiotape. Counseling utilizing both these forms is often utilized with individuals, couples, or groups.

When counseling is conducted online rather than in its traditional face-to-face form, it can be either synchronous or asynchronous. Synchronous counseling occurs when there is little or no gap between the responses of the counselor and the client and the interaction resembles a dialogue (Shaw & Shaw, 2006). Synchronous counseling might be delivered utilizing the telephone or Webcam. In contrast, asynchronous counseling occurs when there is a gap in time between the response of the counselor and the client (Efstathiou, 2009). Asynchronous counseling uses media such as e-mail. For example, the client asks the counselor a question through e-mail and the response might come back the next day rather than instantaneously as in face-to-face counseling or counseling done through a telephone line.

2 types

Discussion of each of these modes of cyber or distance counseling would be too lengthy and beyond the scope of this chapter. However, a brief discussion on videoconferencing will aid the reader in understanding the concept of this type of counseling service. Videoconferencing requires both counselor and client to have a webcam that can transmit images and sound via the Internet. In this way, counseling takes place synchronously and is the most similar to traditional face-to-face counseling although each participant may live in different geographical locations and time zones (NBCC, 2012).

Counselors have used videoconferencing and other technology to treat such issues as depression, suicidal ideation, eating disorders, attention deficit disorder, panic disorders, posttraumatic stress, and grief among others (Bradley, Hendricks, Lock, Whiting, & Parr, 2011; Zabinski, Wilfrley, Calfas, Winzelberg, & Taylor, 2004). In addition, video-conferencing has been utilized with a variety of client populations such as families, older adults, teenagers with seizure disorders, and psychiatric clients (Kirk & Belovics, 2005). Evidence reported from numerous studies suggest that counselors are just as effective at building rapport and a working relationship using videoconferencing as in face-to-face (F2F) counseling, and online counseling has been similarly effective as F2F in treating some disorders such as schizophrenia and obsessive-compulsive disorder (Rummell & Joyce, 2010).

Table 7.1 There are various forms of online counseling and distance counseling currently available. These include:

1   *Telephone Counseling*: These generally are crisis lines and 24-hour counseling lines, but also provide treatment for such issues as diet and exercise, disability services, addictions, and pain management (Cunningham et al., 2011; Mathias & Denson, 2011; Mohr, Ho, & Jin, 2010).
2   *E-mail Counseling*: The counseling experience consists of e-mails sent between counselor and client (Bradley et al., 2011).
3   *Bulletin Board Counseling*: Users post questions to an online bulletin board. Clients generally use an identity pseudonym for confidentially (e.g. Mickey Mouse). The mental health professional posts an answer for all users to see.
4   *Chat Room Counseling*: This allows for synchronous counseling as counselor and client(s) can engage in text communication in real time. Chat room counseling is popular for group counseling as several people can communicate at the same time (Cunningham et al., 2011).
5   *Web-Telephone Counseling*: This allows for real time speaking over the Internet using a microphone, speakers, and webcam via such applications as Skype and iChat.
6   *Videoconferencing*: This is real time (synchronous) counseling using audio and video technology and provides distance counseling but in a face-to-face manner via Skype or iChat.
7   *Computer assisted or simulated counseling*: These are generally computer generated answers to questions or concerns through software programs. The client does not receive help through a live person although a live person may oversee the program (Cunningham et al., 2011).
8   *E-coaching*: This is a human guided interactive module series for such issues as depression or anxiety. Each module might consist of eight or nine interactive applications that the client would complete on his or her own. Once finished, the client sends the completed application to an e-coach for process, feedback, and homework redirection.

Positives

Both online counseling and distance counseling are often more convenient for both counselor and client (Fields, 2011). This is especially true for asynchronous counseling using store it-and-forward technology such as e-mail. Store and forward systems take various types of data (e.g. text or psychological test data) and store it on a computer, which can then be forwarded to another computer to be seen by another person. Because the information is actually "stored" at both the sender and receiver ends, the parties need not be present simultaneously (Bradley et al., 2011). This can be beneficial as counseling can occur without a cumbersome synchronizing of counselor/client schedules.

This form of counseling can eliminate many barriers that might keep an individual from using or receiving counseling services such as inability to access a counselor's office due to geographical location or a disability (Cunningham, Kypri, & McCambridge, 2011; Mathias & Denson, 2011). When services are provided via e-mail, both counselor and client can respond at their own convenience rather than at a prescribed time (Bradley et al., 2011). In addition, while face-to-face counseling typically occurs no more than once per week, online counseling usually occurs with much greater frequency and is often less expensive than traditional "in the office" counseling (Mohr, Ho, & Jin, 2010).

One additional benefit to this type of counseling is all communication is written and, therefore, automatically documented. Both client and counselor can refer back to the communication at any time for clarification (Bradley et al., 2011). However, this written record also causes some ethical concerns regarding confidentiality, which will be discussed momentarily.

Distance counseling, whether via the computer or other technological means, also appears to reduce client anxiety or embarrassment toward the counseling process (Cunningham et al., 2011). This may be especially true for individuals who live in communities where there is a strong stigma against seeking mental health services (Zelvin & Speyer, 2003). This form of counseling has also been found to be as effective as face-to-face counseling (Mathias & Denson, 2011). Counseling performed via chat rooms also offers the client a measure of anonymity that cannot be found in face-to-face counseling (Fields, 2011). However, client anonymity can also produce profound problems for the counselor such as when a client discloses intentions of self-harm, harm to others, or child abuse.

Another benefit for the counselor is that distance counseling and online counseling circumvent the quagmire that has become managed care. A counselor can offer services as a provider without having to be governed by managerial systems. However, what is an advantage for the counselor is often a drawback for the client. These services are not usually covered by insurance.

Negatives

One major drawback to text based communication between the counselor and client is the relative lack of "presence" in the counseling situation. That is, it may be difficult to have a sense that another human being is "present" and communicating with you when using asynchronous communication (Efstathiou, 2009). It also may be difficult for the counselor to build rapport and show genuine positive regard with clients in the same manner that rapport is nurtured in face-to-face counseling (Bradley et al., 2011).

In addition, the counselor cannot assess a client's nonverbal behaviors, which gives a counselor additional data upon which to confer hypotheses and diagnoses as well as identify incongruent communication and behaviors (e.g. client says s/he is angry, yet is smiling) (Bradley et al., 2011). Using this medium, it is more likely that miscommunication will take place because visual and auditory cues are missing (Mathias & Denson, 2011).

Furthermore, there are many websites on the Internet that purport to be therapeutically inclined but are not regulated in any way. For many sites the service provided is by someone other than a mental health specialist (Rummell & Joyce, 2010). It is a "buyer beware" market. According to Shaw and Shaw (2006), online counselors should identify themselves and their credentials to their clients. Shaw and Shaw indicated that there are three levels of credentials: primary credentials (e.g., an earned degree from an accredited university and additional training), secondary credentials (e.g., any licensure or certification that the counselor holds), and tertiary credentials (e.g., professional associations to which the counselor belongs).

Only counselors that are certified or licensed can be held to ethical standards and guidelines. If a "counselor" is not a member of a regulating board (e.g. American Counseling Association, American Psychological Association or National Board of Certified Counselors, State Licensure Board), complaints for violations cannot be filed. There are online services that can help consumers find credentialed counselors.

Furthermore, not all client populations are appropriate for online counseling (Mathias & Denson, 2011). For example, suicidal clients or clients who are in crisis are not appropriate for online counseling. In some cases, depending on the therapist and mode of communication, there may be a significant delay in responding to clients after initial contact. This may especially be the case if the client did not provide accurate contact information (Rummell & Joyce, 2010). For a client seriously at risk for a suicide attempt, the delay in receiving any intervention may cost the client his or her life.

SIDEBAR 7.1 Case Study: Denzel

Denzel is a counselor who offers online counseling through his web page. Denzel uses several forms of synchronous counseling through the telephone, instant messaging, chat rooms, and Skype. During the course of one session when talking with a client who has struggled with chronic depression, the client stated he was suicidal. The client reported he had a plan, the means (a gun), and the intent to kill himself within the next few minutes to an hour. While Denzel routinely collected data on his clients such as address and phone number, to his dismay he discovered the information the client had given him about his physical location was incorrect. While Denzel has the client's correct name and billing address due to the client using a credit card to pay for Denzel's services, the billing address is a post office box and not a physical location. What do you think Denzel should do in this situation?

Ethical Issues

As can be imagined, there are a large number of ethical concerns with both online counseling and distance counseling. Confidentiality is certainly at the forefront of these, especially under the Health Insurance Portability and Accountability Act (HIPPA) of 1996, which dictates how electronic records can be stored and transmitted (Boisvert et al., 2010). How does a counselor who provides online services ensure client confidentiality? Currently, technology allows for the encryption of communication between computer systems and practitioners can use a Virtual Private Network (VPN). A VPN can help ensure confidentiality, because it offers data protection, verification of data, and admittance control to the site (Boisvert et al., 2010). A lengthy discussion about encryption techniques is beyond the scope of this chapter, but counselors can review the documents published by the National Institute of Standards and Technology, which has published guidelines to help counselors who provide online services remain in HIPPA compliance (Scarfone, Souppaya, & Sexton, 2007).

Other ethical concerns pertain to client safety. How can a client ascertain that the person on the other end of the telephone or computer is actually a counselor? How does a client find out the counselor's credentials? The National Board of Certified Counselors (2012) stipulates that a counselor's website have all the links necessary for a client to ascertain that counselor's certification and/or licensure.

If the client resides in a different state than the counselor and a problem does arise, which state has jurisdiction? For example, if elder abuse is disclosed by the client and the client's home state does not require the counselor to report it, but the counselor's home state does, then what? What if the client resides in a different country? How are multicultural concerns satisfied?

Counselors are obligated to fully disclose any risks associated with a counseling modality. Online counseling is no different. Counselors must allow clients to make informed choices, and, therefore, counselors providing this type of service need to be well versed in the benefits and costs to this type of counseling (Efstathiou, 2009).

The National Board of Certified Counselors, the American Counseling Association, the American Psychological Association, and the International Society for Online Mental Health all have provided standards for the ethical practice of Internet counseling (Efstathiou, 2009; ISOMH, 2010). These standards provide guidelines for services provided by telephone, web conferencing, and use of the Internet. Because technology is ever expanding these standards and codes should be reviewed frequently for changes and updates. In addition, different governing bodies have different rules and criteria for online or distance counseling in all its various forms, so counselors should be aware of which guidelines apply (McAdams & Wyatt, 2010).

Computer-Assisted Counseling

help couns plent collect data

Computer-assisted counseling utilizes computer software to provide assessment, intervention, and specific counseling techniques to clients (Hadjistavropoulos et al., 2011). Today, the category of computer-assisted counseling can include any computer-based application that aids the counselor in his or her work. This can include software packages for assessment or treatment planning, psycho-educational software packages to provide clients with information about disorders such as depression and anxiety, and computer-assisted counseling whereby the computer actually provides a type of counseling service to clients. An example of computer-assisted counseling would be a computer-tailored feedback system that uses what the client identifies as specific factors to generate tailored questions so that the client will begin to think more deeply about his or her topic.

use software to build questions for client

There are many ways computers can assist in counseling and supporting clients. For example, computerized virtual reality systems (VRS) have been used to help those with phobias, anxiety, or Posttraumatic Stress Disorder (PTSD) by providing a form of systematic desensitization (McKay et al., 2011; TerHeijden & Brinkman, 2011). The computerized VRS has advanced so much that there are prototypes of VRS having automatic free speech interaction (TerHeijden & Brinkman, 2011). The virtual caricature or avatar can even have a conversation with the client when they are in virtual reality. The VRS is programmed so that it has both manual and automatic speech responses to a client. Additionally, in the last two years there has been research on using robots in assisted living centers to conduct therapy for the elderly (Shibata & Wada, 2011).

Other assisted computer technology has emerged in recent years to help counselors with their job tasks. Some examples include the palm pilot, smart phone, and most recently the iPad. These devices are lightweight, easy to carry, and have most everything a full computer would have (e.g., internet capability, windows, Microsoft Office, a camera, USB drive). One drawback is that they have limited memory capacity.

However, since these devices have internet capabilities there are applications (apps) that can be put on a phone or iPad. Such capability gives a phone or iPad technology to help assist a counselor wherever the counselor goes. These apps can also help clients receive cognitive behavioral therapy (CBT) on their phone without even consulting a professional (Vivyan, 2010). This technology has been shown to help people with anxiety disorders, such as obsessive-compulsive disorder, social phobia, generalized anxiety disorder, and panic disorder (Vivyan, 2010).

Results of a review of studies exploring the use of computer software in cognitive behavioral applications indicate these software systems are just as efficacious as face-to-face therapy for treating anxiety disorders such as social phobia, panic disorder, or PTSD (Morland et al., 2011). Computer-assisted software is well suited for the treatment of depression and anxiety disorders because it gives the user an increased sense of mastery and control as well as instruction in relaxation techniques, cognitive restructuring, stress management, and systematic desensitization and exposure (Hadjistavropoulos et al., 2011).

programs

In addition, many counseling agencies and managed care organizations have set up online interactive consumer services including self-help and health education programs to aid clients. Some counseling centers now provide an interactive "coaching" program for plan participants who suffer from a variety of psychological problems such as anxiety, depression, and substance abuse (Rizvi, Dimeff, Skutch, Carroll, & Linehan, 2011). Participants are securely connected to a web-based series of exercises designed to offer confidential customized clinical feedback and can access these coaching tools through a website that the counseling center offers.

SIDEBAR 7.2 Self-Awareness: Multicultural Considerations

An online counselor must be aware of the diversity issues represented in online and distance counseling and use of media in interventions. Very little research has been devoted to diversity issues related to this modality of therapy. One issue that numerous studies have identified as a potential barrier to online counseling is the lack of cultural identifiers, such as skin color, age, and language when using asynchronous forms of communication (e.g., e-mail, message board) (Mallen, Vogel, Rochlen, & Day, 2005). Visual cues have been found important to both counselor and client in terms of building trust and rapport and therapeutic alliance (Sanchez-Page, 2005).

The possibility remains that the absence of these cues may increase some counselors' reliance on stereotypical information when relating to culturally different clients online (Mallen, Vogel, & Rochlen, 2005; Sanchez-Page, 2005). As suggested in Lee and Diaz's (2013) (chapter three of this text), there is danger in assuming individuals from an ethnic group are all the same.

In-group differences suggest a certain level of individuality within groups and individuals may have experiences that are distinct and hold different attitudes, behaviors, and values from the group. Counselor reliance on stereotypic thinking may alienate culturally different clients and ultimately do more harm to them than good. In addition, it is well documented that Hispanics and African Americans use the Internet less frequently than do other populations, especially affluent Whites, and there is little research regarding the efficacy of this modality of therapy with these populations (Chang & Kim, 2009). What thoughts do you have about using technology in counseling with diverse populations?

Positives

The use of computer-aided counseling can help clients when they cannot afford frequent sessions or can be used between sessions to supplement or reinforce the therapeutic gains made by face-to-face counseling. Supplementing face-to-face counseling by using computer-guided self-treatment can substantially cut therapy costs for the client. In addition, since some systems can be accessed by the telephone and are often voice-activated, so that clients do not necessarily need a computer. These systems can also be made available 24 hours a day.

Negatives

Computers are fallible and programs are only as good as the people who programmed them. Systems also have to be maintained and updated. This can sometimes be difficult,

computers need updates, maintenance, expensive.

time consuming, and expensive. In addition, computers cannot build a relationship with a client or notice the nuances of a client's speech. Computers are literal and can only process what is typed into them and cannot, at least at this time, respond in a spontaneous human way, show empathy, emotion, or understand non-verbal cues. Computers cannot assess and diagnose a client, create a treatment plan, or monitor a client's progress without human input, nor should they.

Ethical Concerns

The dangers come when a counselor uses computer assisted counseling as a primary means of intervention instead of using it as a counseling aid. Since many of the applications deal specifically with depression or severe anxiety, it would be unethical not to personally monitor a particular client and assess for suicidal ideation. With voice-activated systems, a client might be in serious trouble with no human counselor available to make an assessment. Computer-assisted counseling should, therefore, be used as a supplement and not as the main provision of services.

SIDEBAR 7.3 Self-Awareness: The Case of Denzel

So how can counselors protect themselves from having an emergency situation such as the one encountered with Denzel in the previous case study? The International Society for Mental Health Online (ISMHO) suggests several steps counselors can take, which can greatly mitigate the chances of such an occurrence happening. The ISMHO advocates that counselors should screen potential clients for suitability for online or distance counseling. They also advocate that the initial assessment should take place in a face-to-face format or at the very least over the phone. There are simply too many important non-verbal cues that can be missed when working online that may impact the assessment and treatment planning process (e.g. flat affect, motor retardation, degenerated physical appearance, slurred speech, tremors, etc). However, part of the assessment should also take place within the communication medium the counselor and client will be using to ascertain the client's ability to communicate within this modality (e.g., assess for the client's level of computer skills, assess for any access issues, or special software or services required) (ISMHO, 2010).

The ISMHO also suggests that counselors discuss with potential clients what procedures will be followed in the event of an emergency, and for counselors to verify the client's physical address prior to engaging in the counseling process. In addition, the counselor should have easy access to local resources within the client's community that can be called upon swiftly in the event of such an emergency (e.g., local emergency service numbers and the telephone number of the client's primary care physician) (ISMHO, 2010).

Technology in Assessment and Diagnosis

Assessment can be defined as the accumulation of knowledge about a person from a variety of sources for purposes of providing some kind of intervention, diagnosis, or treatment for individuals seeking services. Regardless of counselor specialty, technology can be used in the assessment process. One rapidly increasing technological innovation used for assessment is the Internet and Web-based assessment software, which provide professionals with continuously updated information about assessment procedures and assessment tools that may be used (de Beurs, van Rood, van Noorden, & Zitman, 2010).

Web-Based Assessment

Counselors have access to a wide variety of assessment instruments and Web-based applications through Internet sites that can be appropriate for a wide variety of purposes such as psychological evaluation, psychotherapeutic diagnostics, client self-exploration, and outcome assessment (Boisvert et al., 2010; de Beurs et al., 2010). These tests and assessments can measure specific factors such as IQ, aptitude, level of emotional intelligence, or client attitudes, while others are more general and evaluate various personality characteristics or provide help with vocational interests.

Technology has been used in the process of diagnosis with much success. McCarty and Clancy (2002) discussed a study conducted at the Medical Center of Central Massachusetts concerning the reliability and validity of conducting diagnoses through teleconferencing methods. The study compared diagnoses for acute psychiatric patients who were involuntarily admitted. Half the group was diagnosed in a face-to-face setting while the other half were diagnosed through teleconferencing. Results showed that the "telediagnoses" had a perfect correlation, one with another, and had a.85 correlation with the face-to-face diagnoses. Similar results were found between teleconferencing and face-to-face assessments using the Mini-Mental Status Exam, the Yale-Brown Obsessive-Compulsive Scale, the Hamilton Depression Scale, and the Hamilton Anxiety Scale (McCarty & Clancy, 2002).

Today, technology is routinely used for assessment and diagnosis in clinical settings. For example, Allen and Colleagues (2009) characteristically use technology for diagnosis and assessment at the Menninger Clinic. Upon arrival to the clinic, adults in inpatient care undergo a battery of computerized assessments, which they again undergo at biweekly intervals. This assessment data is then used for treatment planning, for tracking client progress, for discharge and follow-up care, and for client outcome assessment and general research. Use of technology for *routine outcome monitoring* (ROM) for client progress is an increasing part of professional counseling practice in today's environment. Counselors use ROM to identify the severity of client concerns at intake, to monitor the increase or decrease of symptoms over the course of therapy, and at periodic times during follow up with the client for outcome assessment (de Beurs et al., 2010).

Test Interpretation and Scoring Software

The role of computers in psychological assessment has dramatically increased in the last forty years (Litchenberger, 2006). Hundreds of these programs and services are available and include programs that can score and interpret the results of assessments for various evaluation purposes, such as personality traits and neuropsychological problems (de Beurs et al., 2010). Generally, these interpretations are a result of either data ensuing from the clinical experiences of many psychodiagnosticians, or from an accumulation of statistical data that define the relationships between questions answered on an inventory and a specific typology (Litchenberger, 2006).

Some paper-and-pencil assessments that previously entailed tedious hand scoring procedures, such as the Minnesota Multiphasic Personality Inventory (MMPI), provide answer sheets that can be directly scanned into a computer and, therefore, allow for quicker and more accurate scoring (Brooks, Iverson, Sherman, Roberge, 2010). These software packages can also provide narrative assessment reports for counselors and clients (Litchenberger, 2006). However, in spite of the convenience of computer based assessment interpretations, clinicians should take caution and not use computer generated reports as a replacement for clinical judgment (Litchenberger, 2006).

Databases

Databases can also be used in the assessment process. For example, *The Dangerous Assessment Database* contains information that aids experts in deciding whether to release potentially dangerous psychiatric patients (Davidson, 1991). This program consists of statistical information that is used to predict the likelihood that a released psychiatric patient would be a danger to society. The database system works by requiring input on 1000 different questions in such areas as family background, childhood behavior, and response to therapy. The information is then weighted for reliability on a scale from unconfirmed reports (at the low end) to certified reports where there have been attempts to corroborate evidence (at the high end). Bias is accounted for by requiring input from the expert assessors to ascertain any underlying factors that might influence judgment (Davidson, 1991). Similar databases are used for sexual offenders (Doyle, Ogloff, & Thomas, 2011).

Databases can be used for a variety of important concerns in addition to decision making in psychiatric release such as helping counselors assess for self-harm and suicidality. There are also computer programs that aid in clinical decision making, called Clinical Decision Support Systems (CDSSs). The CDSSs work by presenting a step-by-step sequence of decisions for diagnoses and symptomology (Decision Support Systems, 2011; Weinhardt, Mosack, & Swain, 2007).

Other uses of technology for assessment purposes include (a) databases for maintaining assessment results such as desktop spreadsheets programs (e.g. Excel or Lotus), (b) mainframe statistical packages (e.g. SAS or SPSS) for recording and analyzing information, (c) use of assessment programs that incorporate multiple computerized instruments, (d) electronically recorded patient tracking software with pre- and post-treatment measures, (e) computerized biofeedback assessment, (f) video, audio, USB, or CD-ROM to store data, and (g) e-mail and fax to transmit data.

Positives

Using computerized testing gains a counselor access to fast, accurate, highly accessible testing and scoring. Because the assessment is scored electronically, the process is nearly errorless. Data are accessible as soon as the respondent finishes the assessment and the data are stored in electronic form for easy transfer to a statistical package for analysis or to be incorporated into a databank. The counselor and client have immediate access to instructions, assessment items, and scoring techniques and these can be easily updated as needed. Data from testing can be electronically submitted to a central location so norms can be updated frequently. Testing can be convenient for both counselor and client as assessments can be taken nearly at any place, at any time. Assessment and testing can be conducted even when counselor and client are geographically separated by using electronic transfer of data or by using the Internet. Finally, there are no expendable materials as everything is done electronically.

SIDEBAR 7.4 Case Study: Fernando

Fernando just graduated from a Master's program in Counseling. He had diligently studied to take his licensure exam, but was apprehensive since he was to be given this exam at a testing center and the exam would be computerized. Fernando had never before taken an exam on a computer. He was worried that he would make mistakes and that he would not be assessed fairly due to using unfamiliar technology instead of uses the more familiar paper-and-pencil exam. However, Fernando learned that paper-and-pencil licensure exams were obsolete, at least for his geographical area. After seeking advice as to how best to prepare, Fernando purchased a study program, which came with online practice tests that simulated the content, process, and procedures he would use on the real exam. In this manner, Fernando was able to become familiar and comfortable with this computerized assessment technique and successfully passed his licensure exam.

Negatives

Many assessments put on the Internet may not meet the American Psychological Association's psychological assessment standards. Counselors using assessments from the Internet often cannot verify the validity or reliability of the assessments they are using. In addition, counselors may not be present when testing is conducted, and, therefore, cannot ascertain whether the client understood the test instructions. If the client did not understand, the entire assessment could be invalidated. Often assessment results and interpretations are not presented with clear explanations for the client. This could be problematic such as when a client receives a low IQ score or has been assessed in a negative way. The counselor also has no way to verify if the client actually took the assessment or had an accomplice take the test for him or her.

In addition, computer software packages that help with data collection, assessment, and interpretation of assessments are imperfect. Computer generated interpretations of assessment inventories may not be correct or may not consider individual client circumstances. Software can become corrupted and information can be lost. Counselors can become lackadaisical and become overly dependent upon computers to perform job tasks.

Ethical Concerns

Paper-and-pencil assessments formatted for the Internet may not retain their psychometric properties. Changing the assessment's format to fit electronic needs may compromise an otherwise acceptable assessment (Boisvert et al., 2010). Just because the original assessment had acceptable reliability and validity does not mean that its integrity is maintained when changes are made to provide the assessment in electronic form. It would be prudent for a counselor to seek information regarding these concerns for any assessment conducted electronically. Some assessments are available from large testing companies such as the Strong Interest Inventory, the Myers-Briggs Type Indicator and the Self-Directed Search. These companies provide counselors with the assessment's online validity and reliability information.

In addition, clients need to understand the limits of confidentiality when using Web-based assessments. The client should be informed when they are using assessments offered from unreliable sites. The client needs to know that these assessments are exploratory in nature and results should be presented as hypotheses due to the invalidated nature of most online assessments.

Lastly, the issue of security of data transmission and storage of electronic information is another commonly defined problem area. It may be difficult to verify the authenticity of electronic information (e.g. fraudulent transcripts or inaccurate Internet data). Assessments conducted via the Internet may have data collected by the website controlling the assessment. These website owners are not held to any ethical standards.

Technological Aids for Client Interventions

Computers and the Internet have become a widely used resource for counselors in many areas of their professional duties. With the technology available, counselors now have access to an array of tools that can improve their clinical interventions. Technological aids provide counselors endless possibilities to find new ways for clients to express themselves. For example, *Project Spectrum,* which was developed by the Internet giant Google, gives an opportunity for people with autism to express the images in their head in tangible ways through Google's modeling software (Google, 2011).

In today's 21st century counseling practice, technological devices such as Smartphones and digital cameras have gained an important place in therapeutic interventions. For instance, in the domain of expressive art therapy, video making has been successfully used to share stories and process client experiences (Alders, Beck, Allen, & Mosinski, 2011). *Audacity* and *Windows Movie Maker* are free software that can be used in these types of interventions to create and edit videos and sound recordings.

Eonta and Colleagues (2011) have presented therapeutic ways to use technology. They suggested that digital cameras (film or pictures) can document visual evidence of treatment progress, such as in an example of a case of compulsive hoarding. They also add that voice recorders have the capacity to create a personalized progressive muscle relaxation or guided imagery script that can be practiced beyond the session.

In cognitive and behavioral therapy, applications on mobile devices are designed to be an adjunct to interventions. The mobile device can aid therapy by providing clients with an easy way to practice therapeutic concepts between sessions. *E-CBT* (MindApps, 2010) and *CBT Referee* (CBTReferee, 2010) give clients the opportunity to track their thoughts and analyze them at the moment they occur, wherever they are. Counselors can also benefit from applications during the session. *Napuru.com* and *TMsoft.com* provide a large variety of ambient, calming sounds that a counselor can access with just a tap of a finger. These calming sounds can help create an ambiance propitious to client relaxation.

Tablets, computers, and electronic whiteboards can also support interventions by sharing hypermedia during sessions. Hypermedia includes numerous multimedia formats, such as video, music, and animation. For example, the therapist can use the electronic whiteboard to enhance his/her explanations through the use of diagrams and text, which the client would be able to see later on his/her computer screen. Websites from national agencies, such as the National Institute of Mental Health (NIMH at www.nimh.nih.gov) can be shared during the session and add to the intervention by educating the client in a friendly and visual manner. Counselors can also use the assistance of technological advances to give their clients homework as an addition to the therapy. For example, clients could be asked to review psycho-educational websites, listen to podcasts or write a blog (Barak, Klein, Proudfoot, 2009).

One only has to jump online to find endless resources, possibilities, and materials that can be used therapeutically. The Counseling Village (*http://ccvillage.buffalo.edu*) and the Center for Clinical Intervention (*http://www.cci.health.wa.gov.au/*) are reliable sources that provide downloadable handouts and worksheets for free and are tailored to specific client issues and interventions.

Positives

According to Eonta and Colleagues (2011), newer technologies can improve the personalization of treatment and provide clients with interventions tailored to their needs. Moreover, applications on portable devices and online services allow an increased exposure to therapy and can extend the intervention to outside the session. The Internet makes it possible for counselors to access many materials to use in their counseling practice for free that might otherwise be prohibitively costly. The possibilities are endless for the Internet's applicability for counseling work. All of these resources make the counseling experience richer and can be used to aid a child or adult in greater expression of emotion or concerns or actually aid in the practice of new skills.

SIDEBAR 7.5 Case Study: Using Technology to Help Duncan

Ayesha is a counselor who works with children. She works with one child named Duncan who has Asperger's. Ayesha wanted to use technology to strengthen Duncan's social skills and also help develop his family's support network. Ayesha conducted a survey of the Internet and found several useful tools that could be used to aid in Duncan's therapy. For example, Duncan's family was encouraged to go to Wrong Planet www.wrongplanet.net. This is a website for individuals (and their family and caregivers) who have Asperger's, autism, ADHD, or other neurological issues. The site provides a discussion board, a blog, and a chat room where members can communicate and share ideas and resources and give each other support. It also provides an article section so that members can educate themselves about their disorder, treatments, etiologies, prognosis, and resources.

Ayesha also ordered a DVD for Duncan called *Model Me Conversation Cues®* that shows middle school and high school children demonstrating social skills. Ayesha had Duncan watch the DVD between sessions and practice what he saw at school and in his neighborhood. She also helped him develop an avatar in *Second Life* so that he could practice these skills in virtual reality where Duncan felt safer. Finally, Ayesha had the family use an e-diary to record Duncan's symptoms and progress on a daily basis so that Ayesha could also access this information between sessions if needed.

Negatives

As these materials are all supplemental, there are not many negatives associated with them. Some software programs can be expensive; however it is often possible to find free software with similar functions. Counselors are cautioned to address possible issues that could occur when technology is integrated into therapy. For example, the client should be cautioned about loss of confidentiality if the client decides to make his or her e-diary or blog public (Alders et al., 2011).

Ethical Concerns

Counselors need to be careful that the materials they use fit the client's needs and that these materials will be therapeutically beneficial. If the counselor becomes adamant about using materials from the Internet, and selects materials that are not appropriate for the client's issue simply because the counselor is excited about using technology, or if the counselor insists upon using these materials even though the client does not want to use them, then ethical problems will exist. Counselors must be careful not to be blindsided by the excitement of using technology and use materials that do not therapeutically benefit the client.

Technologically Based Resources for Counselors and Clients

Today, research and informational resources are as close to the counselor and client as a mouse click. The Internet has created an increased number of sources from which counselors can access and learn about counseling research and obtain information in order to help their clients. Counselors can access professional journals, professional organizations, and electronic databases containing psychological research articles all from the comfort of their home or office.

Technology Based Resources for Counselors

This section explores those resources most utilized by counselors. As this section cannot be exhaustive the authors have decided to focus this section on a few examples of technology that can aid counselors in their work. These examples include electronic databases and journals, social networks, and technology to aid in case management.

Electronic Databases and Journals

Many counseling journals are offered through online databases either free or for a cost. A counselor can type in his or her search terms and gain access to every article listed within that database pertaining to that subject. Numerous online databases offer journals that provide hundreds of full-text articles available to be printed, saved on disc or hard drive, or e-mailed right to the counselor's computer. One example of such a database is PsycINFO, which contains over 3 million records and covers nearly 2,500 peer reviewed journal titles (APA, 2011).

Counselors can access the latest information on nearly any counseling topic. *Counseling Today* (http://ct.counseling.org/) is a journal published online by the American Counseling Association (ACA) and is partly accessible at no cost. *Counseling Today* addresses current issues and questions in the field of counseling. By using the newest technology, it is now possible to receive the latest news in the field directly onto a Smartphone or through applications such as *Psyc Explorer*, all for less than three dollars.

Most university or public libraries subscribe to databases that provide access to these professional journals, newsletters, or magazines at no cost to the user as long as that user belongs to that institution. If a counselor is not affiliated with an institution, he or she can usually subscribe to any number of databases for a fee or have access to some journals through an affiliation to a national association (see http://www.counseling.org/Publications/Journals.aspx for more information). Indeed, being a member of a national association such as the ACA provides access to a wide variety of resources ranging from podcasts on hot topics in the counseling field to access to ethical consultations.

Social Networks for Counselors

With the increasing expansion of social networking, mental health professionals are now finding a place they can connect to and network with one another. Barak and Grohol (2011) explain that blogs are now being designed to build an online network for therapist (e.g., Therapy Networking, at http:// marketing4therapists.ning.com). For example, the ACA Blog aims to connect mental health professionals by sharing their experiences and opinions as counselors (ACA Weblog, 2012).

Case Management Technology

In the current climate of accountability, it is important to add that the administrative functions of a counselor can now be facilitated by the use of fee-for-service websites and software. From the scheduling of appointments with *Fullslate* software (http://www.fullslate.com/) to managing electronic health records with the *e-record system* (http://www.carepaths.com/), technology is now integrating the managerial aspects of being a counselor.

Technology Based Resources for Clients

This section will explore those resources most utilized by clients. Again, this section cannot be exhaustive. Therefore, the authors have decided to focus this section on a few examples of technology that can aid clients in their therapy. These examples include psycho-educational websites and directories, interactive self-guided interventions, and online support groups and blogs.

Psycho-Educational Websites and Directories

Psycho-educational websites are web pages that provide information to clients about mental health in a relatively static manner (Barak et al., 2009; Merkel, 2010). Clients typically look for information on a specific condition to improve their understanding and awareness. The largest and oldest psycho-educational resource is *Psych Central*, which has been providing mental health information to its users since 1995 and currently has 1.5 million visits every month (Grohol, 2012). The National Institute of Mental Health (NIMH) is also widely visited; it is a reliable source that informs the user about a large array of mental health topics (See http://www.nimh.nih.gov/ for more information). Other websites are collection points of information to aid clients in finding counselors in their communities who specialize in that client's particular issue or concern. For example, sites such as *Good Therapy* (http://www.goodtherapy.org/) offer links to psychologists anywhere in the country.

Interactive Self-Guided Interventions

Interactive self-guided interventions take the benefits ascribed to psychoeducational websites one step further since the user has to be involved in the process (Barak & Grohol, 2011).

Self-guided interventions are specific to the user's problem. There are online interventions for a large variety of counseling and mental health issues. Contrary to computer-assisted therapy, self guided interventions do not involve a therapist and the treatment is completely provided by the computer. Those interventions are interactive and typically involve various multimedia formats. Depending on the complexity of the online intervention's programming, clients receive more or less elaborated and tailored feedback (Barak et al., 2009).

Some programs, such as *Beating the Blues* (http://www.beatingtheblues.co.uk/), have demonstrated a strong worth in symptom reduction for depression and have been approved for use and reimbursement by the UK government. *Mood Gym* (http://moodgym. anu.edu.au/welcome) has also shown positive effects in helping reduce symptoms of anxiety and depression for both adults and adolescents (Barak & Grohol, 2011). Other examples of self guided interventions are *Down Your Drink* (http://www.downyourdrink.org. uk) for problem drinking and *Fear Fighter* (http://fearfighter.com) for the treatment of panic and phobia.

Online Support Groups and Blogs

Barak and Grohol (2011) characterize online support group and blogs as "peer led" and "peer-focused" interventions. Support groups are considered to be" interactive" since there is an exchange between users, while blogs hold a more static dimension. In peer led support group or blogs, clients communicate with each other without professional inter-action, express themselves, and help each other (Barak & Grohol, 2011).

Blogs often take the role of a journal, letting the client express his or her thoughts and feelings publicly, usually free of charge. Status updates on social networks such as *Facebook* or *Twitter* can publically relate the emotional state of the client if he or she so chooses. This process is often referred to as micro-blogging. The feedback that clients get on their blog posts can be powerful and blogging has been shown to have a therapeutic effect (Barak & Grohol, 2011). Boniel-Nissim and Barak (2011) found that adolescent blog-ging over a period of 10 weeks significantly improved adolescent scores on scales of social–emotional difficulties and self esteem. The gains were stronger for participants who blogged about their difficulties.

Support groups can have a different level of structure from that of blogs. Support groups can be directed towards specific client goals (e.g., SparkPeople.com) or they can be more open like the *Big White Wall* (http://www.bigwhitewall.com). The latter encourages users to share whatever is on their minds and helps them work through their issues with the support of their peers. Online support groups are versatile and can be found in a large variety of formats such as discussion forums and bulletin boards, live chat rooms, or support groups that offer assistance, understanding, and emotional support (Barak et al., 2009).

Positives

There are numerous resources available online or through computer software that can be downloaded and printed. Internet research is easier than ever with easy-to-use search engines and hypertextual indexed links that allow counselors and clients to access information on nearly any topic, within seconds, at any time, and in relative privacy. Professional counseling and psychology information banks are generally an accurate, easily accessed, frequently updated resource that can be used by counselors and clients alike.

For example, Reavley and Colleagues (2011) explored the quality of information found on Wikipedia about depression and schizophrenia. Their findings showed that the information contained in Wikipedia on these two disorders was equal in quality to information provided by Encyclopedia Britannica or psychiatry textbooks. Counselors can research information on specific disorders, access the most current journal articles regarding treatment or theory, or converse with supervisors or colleagues, all from the convenience of home or office.

Negatives

It is not always easy to ascertain the accuracy of information found on the Internet. Many websites are individually owned and operated and are not peer reviewed or authenticated. The Internet is not a stable entity and is subject to rapid change and a lack of uniformity. Both counselors and clients are cautioned to use information from authentic sites such as the American Counseling Association (ACA) or the American Psychological Association (APA) in order to be certain the information is correct.

In addition, Internet material may fail to download or may not be trustworthy. The risk of misinformation deserves special attention in case of peer-led support groups. Users have to be particularly cautious of the information provided by their peers and the behaviors that are encouraged. For example, the case of the Pro-Ana group is the perfect counter-example of a healthy online support group. In the Pro-Ana group, users were guided to become anorexic (Barak & Grohol, 2011).

Websites with endings such as (gov., edu,.org) generally are more reliable since these endings denote government, educational, or professional organizational websites and are authorized by the Internet Corporation for Assigned Names and Numbers (Gale & McKee, 2002). Moreover, Barak and Grohol (2011) recommend searching for websites with the Health on the Net (HON) code label that indicate a higher quality content and accountability.

Online professional journal databases are generally reliable and accurate but unless a counselor has access to them for free through an organization, the cost for subscription could be prohibitive. Therefore, access to peer reviewed sources of counseling research may be limited. Even if the counselor belongs to the ACA and has access to that organization's database, access is limited to the ACA's journals. In comparison, many universities give students and faculty access to many different databases each of which provide access to 10–50 journals.

Ethical Concerns

Counselors must verify that information they receive or use is correct. It might be prudent to crosscheck information found on the Internet with other journal sources unless it is from a recognized professional source such as the ACA, PsychNet, or accessed through a University, or other reputable organization's database. Counselors are ethically responsible for the information they use with, or provide to, clients.

Technology in Counselor Supervision

Counseling students have long used means such as audio and videotapes to record their sessions for later perusal by their supervisor (Rosenberg, 2006). These forms of technology have been beneficial, but the counseling session is already over before the supervisor gets a chance to view the work that has been done. It is beneficial to the student to get immediate feedback either during or right after the session is complete; without technology this is only achieved through live supervision. Technology is expanding every day and there are new ways that students can obtain live supervision while their supervisor is at a different location. Such forms of technology are Skyping or Oovooing which give the supervisor and supervisee a real-time video conference while the session is occurring (Barnett, 2011). Many other types of technology can enhance the relationship and experience for both the supervisor and supervisee; however, there are pros and cons to this. Many universities like to use one-on-one live supervision so that the supervisee can get immediate feedback. Some systems use Instant Messenger (IM) on the trainee's computer so that the supervisor can type messages to the trainee during a session (Barnett, 2011).

If live supervision is not available for the student there are many new ways to get feedback on the session with a recording. The supervisor can use dual-track recording to record his or her own comments on the disc while the original soundtrack is playing (Apple Inc., 2009). The students record their sessions and the supervisor will use dual track recording to input their comments. Therefore, when the counselor in training plays back the enhanced version, the supervisor's comments are superimposed on the sound track over and above the students' and clients' voices (Apple Inc., 2009). This technique is especially useful in distance supervision where student and supervisor are not viewing the disc together.

One exciting innovation takes this concept one step further and uses webcams on the student trainee's computer. Counselors in training use these webcams to record counseling sessions or transmit the sessions live via the internet to the supervisor's office computer. This technology allows the student immediate feedback during and after a session as well as immediate intervention from the supervisor should client or counselor safety become compromised. In addition, these digitized images can be saved for later viewing with the student.

Computers are also used in training by providing counselors with interactive, multimedia simulations of counseling sessions in which the trainee can practice when a "live" client is not available or when counselors want to practice skills for crisis situations (Barnett, 2011). For example, the computer simulation could present the counselor with the scenario of a suicidal client. Students can then practice their skills without risking the safety of a real client. Apple's iMovie and Microsoft's Movie Maker 2 can easily be used to create these simulations (Barnett, 2011).

Blackboard can be used in counselor supervision for (a) posting course syllabi and calendars, (b) posting the Practicum Training Handbook, (c) posting supervision seminar topics and relevant readings, (d) providing access to many sources of information, (e.g., home pages of ACA, NBCC, and CACREP and mental health resources), (e) easy submission and review of student journals, (f) management of supervisor–student dialogues through the use of discussion threads and/or chat room, (g) enhance communication among students, (h) provide an electronic method for student evaluations of supervisors and sites, and (i) a format for submission and review of E-portfolios (Pulford, 2011). Digital counseling portfolios can consist of a variety of multimedia artifacts such as counselor-made materials, digital photographs, student assessments, videos of classroom experiences, guidance plans, and statements of philosophy, research projects, and any other artifacts that represent one's accomplishments (Willis & Wilkie, 2009).

Technology has also made supervision easier for counselors who are not in university training programs. Counselors who have already graduated from their counseling programs, and are licensed or certified, sometimes find themselves in need of supervision. Ethically, when working with a counseling issue or a diverse population for which the counselor has not previously worked, supervision or referral is warranted. If a counselor wants to add a specialization, counseling modality, or work with a diverse population the counselor will need someone trained in that area to supervise him or her until that counselor reaches a level of competence in the new area. These clinicians can use web training to become more familiar with a specialized population. Web training is becoming more available to clinicians with programs such as Escudero's e-SOFTA (Wolf, 2011).

Technology also allows for supervision to occur even when the supervisor and supervisee are not in the same location. There are many forms of telecommunications such as telephone, asynchronous email, and videoconferences to shorten the distance between a supervisor and supervisee (Wright & Griffiths, 2010). Wright and Griffiths (2010) looked at these forms of telecommunication to see how functional they were in using them on a day-to-day basis. They first looked at using only telephone supervision and found that not being able to view visual clues was problematic. Then they looked at using only email as a way of communicating and found that the supervisee would take out and edit all her emails. This was a problem because it was restricting her feedback and what she really wanted to say. Also the supervisor asked many questions that she would have not normally asked in face-to-face meetings. Finally, looking at videoconferencing they found this to be the most favorable and the closest to a face-to-face interaction. Overall, using only one form of communication creates a barrier that needs to be addressed; however, when using all the forms together the relationship can flourish even over great distances.

Positives

One benefit of using the internet and other technology for supervision is that the counselor and supervisor do not have to reside within the same geographical location. This opens up many possibilities for counselors when choosing a supervisor. The positive attributes for audio, video, or digital taping of sessions includes offering a high level of accuracy of observation, providing the supervisor a high level of objective detail regarding client / counselor interaction, as well as accessibility of reflection for the student (Barnett, 2011). In addition, telecommunication applications make it possible to offer students a variety of instructional formats (e.g., e-mail, web resources, and power point slides), which may serve to enhance the supervisee's learning experience (Wright & Griffiths, 2010).

Negatives

There may be instances when a counselor needs a supervisor to be accessible in person such as during a client crisis. Distance supervision would make this difficult. Supervisors must also be cognizant of how technology-mediated communication may differ from face-to-face supervision and how that might impact the work they do (Wright & Griffiths, 2010). Depending on the type of technology used, visual and social cues may be compromised or omitted from verbal exchanges (Wright & Griffiths, 2010).

Negatives associated with videotaping, audio taping, and digital recording of sessions is that equipment can fail. Discs can be accidentally scratched by the computer or DVD player and viruses can corrupt computers and compromise hard drives or discs (Apple Inc., 2009). Discs can also be misplaced or lost, which further compromises client confidentiality. Most states now have legal and ethical guidelines to follow when using telecommunication technology for supervision (McAdams & Wyatt, 2010). Moreover, some states prohibit these interactions and this may cause a problem when services are delivered across state lines (McAdams & Wyatt, 2010).

Ethical Concerns

Both counselor and supervisor need to exhibit extreme caution when communicating via e-mail or the internet so that identifying details of a client are not given in order to protect client confidentiality (Wolf, 2011). E-mail is often not secure although we might think that it is. When we have to provide a user identification and password to access it within our own office or home, we can become lulled into a false sense of security. Many counselors try to offset risk by providing a disclaimer on e-mail transmissions warning of the confidential nature of the communication such as the following:

> "The information contained in this email message may be privileged, confidential, and protected from disclosure. If you are not the intended recipient, any dissemination, distribution, or copying is strictly prohibited. If you think that you have received this email message in error, please reply to the sender to that effect."

However, such a disclaimer does not erase the damage done to a client. Also video communication, even done in real time, can be viewed by others by hacking the computer. Any type of communication, whether done in or out of the office setting, needs to be handled with extreme care and forethought.

SIDEBAR 7.6 Self-Awareness: Second Life as a Tool for Practicing Counseling Skills

Second Life is a free 3D virtual reality *multiple user virtual environment* (MUVE) that can be downloaded for free at http://secondlife.com/. You choose an avatar (on screen character that represents you). *Second Life* has different places you can visit and you can interact with people from all over the world. *Second Life* even has a translation program to help you communicate with others who do not speak your language.

In *Second Life*, it is possible for instructors to build a virtual counselor training faculty complete with a virtual classroom, training lab, student meeting areas and so forth that can be used in distance learning. Instructors can provide experiences that present an environment in which students can role-play and engage in simulated counseling experiences from the safety of their homes (Walker & Rockinson-Szapkiw, 2009). Students can even use their real voices in some *Second Life* locations to make the simulated counseling practice sessions more real. An example of avatars using their real voices can be seen in the You Tube video *Teaching Counseling Theories in Second Life* http://www.youtube.com/watch?v=g-Tm3JL_85M. There are even counselor education locations where counselors can attend classes and workshops in order to perfect or learn new skills such as Counselor Education in Second Life http://sl.counseloreducation.org/. Counselors can also do therapy in this virtual world http://www.youtube.com/watch?v=8Yen0TOeUiY&feature=related.

Counselor Education and Continuing Education

Online education is rapidly increasing and a shift has been identified regarding the use of technology in counseling education (Booth & Watson, 2009). Virtual schools are now present in the educational sphere and offer online distance learning programs. The Council for Accreditation of Counseling and Related Educational Programs (CACREP) currently accredits seven, graduate level, online learning programs. In addition, many websites, such as www.oedb.org and www.degreesearch.org, contain databases to find online programs.

More and more counselor education programs are using technology in the classroom or are considering using some aspect of distance learning to educate future counselors. Technology can be used in counselor learning for a variety of applications. E-learning platforms (WebCT and Blackboard), listserv program, blogs, wikis, multimedia presentation, email, and virtual environments are just examples of the diversity of applications that can be used in counselor education. Technology has changed the classroom. Indeed, many courses are now taught from a PowerPoint presentation exhibited on a screen and come with the lecturers' comments on the slides. It is not uncommon to see students take notes on a laptop or notebook computer instead of paper (Burt, Gonzalez, Swank, Ascher, & Cunningham, 2011).

Hayes (2008) claims that technology can be successfully included in a counselor's education. He describes three technological media that can improve a counselor's education: computer based simulation, synchronous electronic learning, and asynchronous learning. In computer based simulation, the student is confronted with a real life situation where he or she has to demonstrate the appropriate use of the therapeutic skills. Synchronous learning refers to a live, real time, interactive class led by an instructor, whereas asynchronous instruction is a self-paced learning process in which students access materials online wherever they are and whenever they want.

Hybrid courses, composed of an online component in addition to the traditional course, are not bound to one physical environment anymore and parts of the course can be completed from the comfort of one's home. Renfro-Michel, O'Halloran, and Delaney (2010) found in their study that students who took the hybrid section of a course got better results in the class than the students who took the traditional section of the course. The pedagogic tools used in their study were video podcast and virtual reality technology. Walker (2009) also showed positive results using the 3D virtual environment *Second Life*. Students who practiced their skills through role play activities in the virtual reality of *Second Life* reported significantly higher learning benefits. 3D virtual reality gives students an opportunity to apply the concepts learned in a traditional way.

Videos from a DVD, or directly from YouTube, can be shared with students to demonstrate a particular skill or to illustrate a topic. Warren, Stech, Douglas, and Lambert (2010) demonstrated that films can be used to improve the understanding of a case conceptualization for a counselor in training. *Psych Therapy*, an e-learning database created by the APA, can be purchased by educational institutions or by individuals included in their APA subscriptions. The database contains more than 300 videos demonstrating the work of clinicians with individuals, couples, and families.

Continuing education is now at the reach of counselors through their computer screens. The National Board of Certified Counselors (NBCC) provides access to credit for continuing education through accredited websites such as *I-counseling* (http://www.i-counseling. net/). Moreover, one just has to wander onto counseling websites to find multiple providers offering Continuing Education Units (CEUs) (Booth & Watson, 2009). The ACA, for example, has a whole section related to online learning and regularly presents new courses (see http://www.counseling.org/Resources/Portal.aspx for more information). Podcasts are another multimedia format that is used for continuing education and professional growth; they can be found, for instance, at www.counseloraudiosource.com, free of charge, or through the ACA website with a membership.

Positives

There are many benefits for counselors of engaging in distance learning, whether in fulfillment of their CEUs or to further their education. When the distance educational course offers asynchronous instruction, the counselor can then access materials, complete tests, send in papers etc., at any convenient time. This gives the counselor a lot of flexibility to work a class into his or her schedule. Sometimes counselors are in need of CEUs, but have tight schedules. They may be forced by time constraints to choose educational opportunities that fit a certain time frame or geographical location. Distance learning frees the counselor from these constraints and allows him or her to choose where and when he or she receives instruction.

Negatives

Technology is not foolproof. Internet servers go down. Computer viruses wreak havoc. While most students and instructors today are computer literate, some are not (Burt et al., 2011). Older students and instructors who did not grow up in the computer age might have a disadvantage, and in some cases, the educators may be forced to focus more on teaching technology and spend less time on critical thinking or counseling skills. Burt and Colleagues (2011) recommend that programs assess their student's self-efficacy about technology and provide remedial courses and workshops on basic technological skills if necessary.

Beyond the flexibility and independence that distance learning offers, there are serious drawbacks that should be considered. In distance learning courses, students are required to have access to a modern computer and the appropriate software. However, this is not always the case and distance learning is consequently reserved to those who can afford the technology. The lack of communication with the instructor and the student, as well as the absence of non-verbal cues, might hinder the learning process for some students (Leik & Govra, 2010).

Ethical Concerns

As always, it is a "buyer beware" market and counselors considering distance learning as a method of meeting educational goals should check with the appropriate licensing or credentialing board to make sure such classes meet their requirements. Many online classes will advertise if they meet CEU requirements, and if so, for which groups (e.g. social workers, psychologists, counselors etc). Do not make the assumption that just because CEUs are offered that they meet the criteria for your profession, licensure, or certification boards. While many professions require continuing education, not all credentialing or licensing boards agree on what is appropriate for continuing education.

Summary

Counselors need to build their technological knowledge and skills in order to use these tools in their work. The Association for Counselor Education and Supervision (ACES) has composed twelve counselor education technological competencies that graduates should master upon leaving any program (Haley & Carrier, 2010). Technology is advancing so fast that by the time this chapter is in print parts of what is talked about here may already be obsolete. There may also be innovations that are not covered in this chapter.

Counselor education programs need to train future counselors to use the technology currently available. Otherwise these counselors will fall behind other mental health service workers who are using this technology. There is no choice today as to whether a counselor will use technological advances in his or her practice. It is more a matter of which technology the counselor chooses. A new world has opened to counselors within the last few decades, a world that at times can be simultaneously frightening and exciting. There are so many choices from which to consider, as technology can be utilized in some form or another to aid in nearly every aspect of a counselor's work. Counselors need to think about the benefits, the drawbacks, and the ethical considerations when implementing technology into their work.

Useful Websites

ABC's of Internet Therapy: http://www.metanoia.org/imhs/issues.htm
ACES Technology Interest Network—ACES guidelines for online instruction in counselor education: http://files.acesonline.net/doc/1999_guidelines_for_online_instruction.htm
Counseling Center Village: http://ccvillage.buffalo.edu/ccv.html
John Grohol's Psych Central: http://psychcentral.com/
International Society for Mental Health Online (ISMHO): http://www.ismho.org
Internet Mental Health: http://www.mentalhealth.com/
Mental Help Net: http://www.mentalhelp.net
Mental Health Sourcebook Online: http://mentalhelp.net/selfhelp/
Mentonia: www.metanoia.org
National Institute of Mental Health (NIMH): http://www.nimh.nih.gov/
Resources for Mental Health Professionals: http://www.pohly.com/admin_mh.html
TelehealthNet: http://www.telehealth.net

References

Alders, A., Beck, L., Allen, P., & Mosinski, B. (2011). Technology in art therapy: Ethical challenges. *Art Therapy, 28*(4), 165–170. doi: 10.1080/07421656.2011.622683
Allen, J. G., Frueh, B. C., Ellis, T. E., Latini, D. M., Mahoney, J. S., Oldham, J. M., Sharp, C., & Wallin, L. (2009). Integrating outcomes assessment and research into clinical care in inpatient adult psychiatric treatment. *Bulletin of the Menninger Clinic, 73*(4), 259–295.
American Counseling Association Weblog. (2012). ACA blogs, written by counselors, for counselors. Retrieved from http://my.counseling.org.
American Psychological Association. (2011). PsycINFO database quick facts. Retrieved from http://www.apa.org/pubs/databases/psycinfo/index.aspx.
Apple Inc. (2009). *Dvd studio pro 4 user manual*. Retrieved from http://documentation.apple.com/en/dvdstudiopro/usermanual/index.html.

Barak, A., & Grohol, J. (2011). Current and future trends in internet-supported mental health interventions. *Journal of Technology in Human Service, 29*(3), 155–196. doi: 10.1080/15228835. 2011.616939

Barak, A., Klein, B., & Proudfoot, J. (2009). Defining internet-supported therapeutic interventions. *Annals of Behavioral Medicine, 38*(1), 4–17.

Barnett, J. (2011). Utilizing technological innovations to enhance psychotherapy supervision, training, and outcomes. *Psychotherapy, 48*(2), 103–108.

Boisvert, M., Lang, R., & Andrianopoulos, M. (2010). Telepractice in assessment and treatment of individuals with autism spectrum disorders: A systematic review. *Developmental Neurorehabilitation, 13*(6), 423–432.

Boniel Nissim, M., & Barak, A. (2011, December 12). The therapeutic value of adolescents' blogging about social–emotional difficulties. *Psychological Services.* Advance online publication. doi: 10.1037/a0026664

Booth, C., & Watson, J. (2009). Technology in counseling: Global implications for the 21st century. *NC Perspectives,* 3, 38–44. Retrieved from https://www.nccounseling.org/newsletters/NC Perspectives_Fall2009.pdf#page=40.

Bradley, L. J., Hendricks, B., Lock, R., Whiting, P. P., & Parr, G. (2011). E-mail communication: Issues for mental health counselors. *Journal of Mental Health Counseling, 33*(1), 67–79.

Brooks, B. L., Iverson, G. L., Sherman, E. M. S., & Roberge, M. (2010). Identifying cognitive problems in children and adolescents with depression using computerized neuropsychological testing. *Applied Neuropsychology 17,* 37–43. doi: 10.1080/09084280903526083

Burt, I., Gonzalez, T., Swank, J., Ascher, D., & Cunningham, L. (2011). Addressing the technology gap in counselor education: Identification of characteristics in students that affect learning in college classrooms. *Journal of Counselor Preparation and Supervision, 3*(1), 18–26. Retrieved from http://naraces.org/Resources/Documents/Journal/April_Journal_.04.11.2011.pdf.

CBTReferee. (2010). Cognitive behavioral therapy. Retrieved from http://www.cbtreferee.com/.

Chang, T. (2005). Online counseling: Prioritizing psychoeducation, self-help, and mutual help for counseling psychology research and practice. *The Counseling Psychologist, 33*(6), 881–890.

Chang, M., & Kim, S. (2009). Computer access and computer use for science performance of racial and linguistic minority students. *Journal of Educational Computing Research, 40*(4), 469–501.

Cunningham, J. A., Kypri, K., & McCambridge, J. (2011). The use of emerging technologies in alcohol treatment. *Alcohol Research & Health, 33*(4), 320–326.

Davidson, C. (1991). Will computers hold key to mental hospitals? *New Scientist, 22,* 16.

De Beurs, E., van Rood, Y. R., van Noorden, M. S., & Zitman, F. G. (2010). Routine outcome monitoring in the Netherlands: Practical experiences with a web-based strategy for the assessment and treatment outcome in clinical practice. *Clinical Psychology and Psychotherapy, 18,* 1–12. doi: 10.1002/cpp.696

Decision Support Systems. (2011). Retrieved from http://www.openclinical.org/dss.html.

Doyle, D. J., Ogloff, J. R., & Thomas, S. D. M. (2011). An analysis of dangerous sexual offender assessment reports: Recommendations for best practice. *Psychiatry, Psychology, and Law, 18*(4), 537–556.

Dr. Joyce Brothers. (2007). Information Please Database. Pearson Education Inc. Retrieved from http://www.infoplease.com/ipea/A0763051.html.

Eonta, A. M., Christon, L. M., Hourigan, S. E., Ravindran, N., Vrana, S. R., & Southam-Gerow, M. A. (2011). Using everyday technology to enhance evidence-based treatments. *Professional Psychology: Research and Practice, 42*(6), 513–520. doi:10.1037/a0025825.

Efstathiou, G. (2009). Students' psychological web consulting: Function and outcome evaluation. *British Journal of Guidance and Counseling, 37*(3), 243–255.

Fields, K. (2011). About online counseling. Retrieved from http://www.realpsychsolutions.com/uploads/About_Online_Counseling-Fields-rps.pdf.

Gale, A. U., & McKee, E. C. (2002). An information literate approach to the internet for counselors. *Journal of Technology in Counseling, 2*(2). Retrieved from http://scholar.googleusercontent.

com/scholar?q=cache:giSC3lBJxMEJ:scholar.google.com/+An+information+literate+approac
h+to+the+internet+for+counselor&hl=en&as_sdt=0,44.

Google. (2011). Project Spectrum: Strengths of autism shine through in 3D. Retrieved from
http://www.google.com/educators/spectrum.html.

Grohol, J. (2012). About psych central. Retrieved from http://psychcentral.com/about/.

Hadjistavropoulos, H., Thompson, M., Ivanov, M., Drost, C., Butz, C., Klein, B., & Austin, D.
(2011). Considerations in the development of a therapist-assisted internet cognitive behavior
therapy service. *Professional Psychology: Research and Practice, 42*(6), 463–471.

Haley, M., & Carrier, J. W. (2010). Psychotherapy groups. In D. Capuzzi, D. Gross, & M. Stauffer
(Eds.), *Introduction to group work, 5th ed.* Denver Colorado: Love Publishing Company.

Hayes, B. (2008). The use of multimedia instruction in counselor education: A creative teaching
strategy. *Journal of Creativity in Mental Health, 3*(3), 243–253. doi:10.1080/15401380802334614

International Society for Online Mental Health. (2010). Suggested principles for the online provision of mental health services. Retrieved from http://www.ismho.org/suggestions.asp.

Kirk, J. J., & Belovics, R. (2005). An unofficial guide to online resources for working with older
workers. *Journal of Employment Counseling, 42*, 42–66.

Lee, C. C., & Diaz, J. M. (2013). Cross cultural counseling. In D. Capuzzi, & D. R. Gross (Eds.),
Introduction to the counseling profession, 6th ed. London, England: Routledge.

Leik, S., & Govra, R. (2010). College distance education courses: Evaluating benefits and costs
from institutional, faculty and students' perspectives. *Education, 130*(4), 616–631.

Litchenberger, E. O. (2006). Computer utilization and clinical judgment in psychological assessment reports. *Journal of Clinical Psychology, 62*(1), 19–32.

Mallen, M. J., Vogel, D. L., & Rochlen, A. B. (2005). The practical aspects of online counseling:
Ethics, training, technology, and competency. *The Counseling Psychologist, 33*(6), 776–818.

Mallen, M. J., Vogel, D. L., Rochlen, A. B., & Day, S. X. (2005). Online counseling: Reviewing
the literature from a counseling psychology framework. *The Counseling Psychologist, 33*(6),
819–871.

Mathias, J. L., & Denson, L. A. (2011). Psychosocial outcomes of telephone-based counseling for
adults with an acquired physical disability: A meta-analysis. *Rehabilitation Psychology, 56*(1),
1–14.

McAdams, C. R., & Wyatt, K. L. (2010). The regulation of technology-assisted distance counseling and supervision in the United States: An analysis of current extent, trends, and implications. *Counselor Education & Supervision, 49*, 179–192.

McCarty, D., & Clancy, C. (2002). Telehealth: Implications for social work practice. *Social Work,
47*(2), 153–162.

McLay, R., Wood, D., Webb-Murphy, J., Spira, J., Wiederhold, M., Pyne, J., & Wiederhold, B.
(2011). A randomized, controlled trial of virtual reality-graded exposure therapy for posttraumatic stress disorder in active duty service members with combat-related post-traumatic
stress disorder. *Cyberpsychology, Behavior, and Social Networking, 14*(4), 223–229.

Merkel, P. (2010). *An inventory of web-based tools to support the developing field of online therapy.*
Retrieved from University of Oregon. Applied information management website: http://aim.
uoregon.edu/research/capstone/cap2010.php.

MindApps. (2010). Real time mental health solutions. Retrieved from http://www.mymindapps.com/.

Mohr, D. C., Ho, J., & Jin, L. (2010). Interest in behavioral and psychological treatments delivered face-to-face, by telephone, and by Internet. *Annals of Behavioral Medicine, 40*, 89–98. doi:
10.1007/s12160–010–9203–7

Morland, L., Greene, C., Grubbs, K., Kloezeman, K., Mackintosh, M., Rosen, C., & Frueh, C.
(2011). Therapist adherence to manualized cognitive-behavioral therapy for anger management delivered to veterans with PTSD via videoconferencing. *Journal of Clinical Psychology,
67*(6), 629–638.

Murphy, M. J. (2003). Computer technology for office-based psychological practice applications
and factors affecting adoption. *Psychotherapy: Theory, Research, Practice, Training, 40*(12), 10–19.

National Board of Certified Counselors (NBCC). (2012). The practice of Internet counseling. Retrieved from http://www.nbcc.org/Assets/Ethics/internetCounseling.pdf.

Pelling, N. J. (2005). A survey of career's counseling wants and needs: In person, by telephone, and via the internet. *Journal of Technology in Counseling, 4*(1). Retrieved from http://jtc.columbusstate.edu/Vol4_1/Pelling/Pelling.htm.

Pulford, B. D. (2011). The influence of advice in a virtual learning environment. *British Journal of Educational Technology, 42*(1), 31–39. doi:10.1111/j.1467–8535.2009.00995.x

Reavley, N., Mackinnon, A., Morgan, A., Alvarez-Jimenez, M., Hetrick, S., Killackey, E., Nelson, B., Purcell, R., Yap, M., & Jorm, A. (2011). Quality of information sources about mental disorders: A comparison of Wikipedia with centrally controlled web and printed sources. *Psychological Medicine, 1*(1) 1–10. doi: 10.1017/S003329171100287X

Renfro-Michel, E., O'Halloran, K., & Delaney, M. (2010). Using technology to enhance adult learning in the counselor education classroom. *Adultspan: Theory Research & Practice, 9*(1), 14–25. doi: 10.1002/j.2161–0029.2010.tb00068.x

Rizvi, S., Dimeff, L., Skutch, J., Carroll, D., & Linehan, M. (2011). A pilot study of the DBT coach: An interactive mobile phone application for individuals with borderline personality disorder and substance use disorder. *Behavior Therapy, 42*(4), 589–600.

Rosenberg, J. I. (2006). Real-time training transfer of knowledge through computer-mediated, real-time feedback. *Professional Psychology: Research and Practice, 37*(5), 539–546.

Rummell, C. M., & Joyce, N. R. (2010). So wat do u want to wrk on 2day? The ethical implications of online counseling. *Ethics and Behavior, 20*(6), 482–496. doi: 10.1080/10508422.2010.521450

Sanchez-Page, D. (2005). The online-counseling debate: A view toward the underserved. *The Counseling Psychologist, 33,* 891–899.

Scarfone, K., Souppaya, M., & Sexton, M. (2007). Guide to storage encryption technologies for end user devices: Recommendations of the National Institute of Standards and Technology. NIST Special Publication 800–111. Retrieved from http://csrc.nist.gov/publications/nistpubs/800–111/SP800–111.pdf.

Shaw, H. E., & Shaw, S. F. (2006). Critical ethical issues in online counseling: Assessing current practices with an ethical checklist. *Journal of Counseling and Development, 84,* 41–53.

Shibata, T., & Wada, K. (2011). Therapy: A new approach for mental healthcare of the elderly – a mini-review. *Gerontology, 57*(4), 378–386.

TerHeijden, N., & Brinkman, W. (2011). Design and evaluation of a virtual reality exposure therapy system with automatic free speech interaction. *Journal of CyberTherapy and Rehabilitation, 4*(1), 41–56.

Vivyan, C. (2010). Cognitive behavior therapy self-help resources get self help. Retrieved from http://www.get.gg/links2.htm.

Warren, J., Stech, M., Douglas, K., & Lambert, S. (2010). Enhancing case conceptualization through film: The addiction web. *Journal of Creativity in Mental Health, 5*(3), 228–242. doi:10.1080/15401383.2010.507663

Walker, M. (2007). Mental health treatment online. Retrieved from http://www.esd.org.uk/esd-toolkit/communities/DigitalInclusion/tools%5CMental+Health+Treatment+Online+elec+231107.pdf.

Walker, V. (2009). 3D virtual learning in counselor education: Using Second Life in counselor skill development. *Journal of Virtual World Research, 2*(1). Retrieved from http://Journals.tdl.org/jvwr/article/viewArticle/423.

Walker, V., & Rockinson-Szapkiw, A. (2009). Educational opportunities for clinical counseling simulations in Second Life. *Innovate, 5*(5). Retrieved from http://innovateonline.info/pdf/vol5_issue5/Educational_Opportunities_for_Clinical_Counseling_Simulations_in_Second_Life.pdf.

Weinhardt, L., Mosack, K., Swain, G. (2007). Development of a computer-based risk-reduction counseling intervention: Acceptability and preferences among low-income patients at an urban sexually transmitted infection clinic. *AIDS and Behavior, 11*(4), 549–556.

Willis, L., & Wilkie, L. (2009). Digital career portfolios: Expanding institutional opportunities. *Journal of Employment Counseling*, 46(2), 73–81.

Willis, L., & Wilkie, L. (2009). Digital career portfolios: Expanding institutional opportunities. *Journal of Employment Counseling*, 46(2), 73–81.

Wolf, A. (2011). Internet and video technology in psychotherapy supervision and training. *Psychotherapy*, 48(2), 179–181.

Wright, J., & Griffiths, F. (2010). Reflective practice at a distance: Using technology in counseling supervision. *Reflective Practice*, 11(5), 693–703.

Zabinski, M. F., Wilfrley, D. E., Calfas, K. J., Winzelberg, A. J., & Taylor, B. (2004). An interactive psychoeducational intervention for women at risk of developing an eating disorder. *Journal of Counseling and Clinical Psychology*, 72(5), 914–919.

Zelvin, E., & Speyer, C. M. (2003). Online counseling skills part 1: Treatment strategies and skills for conducting online counseling. In R. Kraus, J. Zack, & G. Stricker (Eds.), *Online counseling: A handbook for mental health professionals* (pp. 164–180). San Diego, CA: Academic Press.

Part II

COUNSELING SKILLS

INDIVIDUAL COUNSELING

Brief Approaches to the Use of Traditional Theories

Matthew V. Glowiak

I remember being humored as a little child by my parents' stories of "back in my day" this and "back in my day" that. Their stories were always of a simpler time. On special occasions where I would hear my grandparents stories of "back in their day" I also noticed a similar theme. With the technological revolution came a sort of psychosocial revolution where human beings began wanting everything faster. In the early 20th century (only 100 years ago) people would hand-write and mail letters that would take days or weeks for the recipient to receive. In the 1960s and 1970s a modernized version of the fax machine became commonplace in offices due to its ability to quickly transfer documents worldwide. Then in the 1990s email took over as it was even faster and saved on paper waste. Today people transfer documents via 3G and 4G data bands on their smart phones. Because communication is now so fast-paced, nearly every other aspect of the way mankind functions has sped up as well. Given that if a task that took 5 hours 50 years ago now takes 5 minutes, it is relative to be able to do the same task 100 times within the same 5-hour timespan. While the positive is that humans are now able to do significantly more than they had ever imagined, they may also be losing out on some of the important things in life—ones that are enjoyable, healthy, or both. Ironically enough, when I tell stories of "back in my day" to my younger cousins only 10 years younger than I, they look at me like I am even more ancient than I thought my grandparents were. *The times they are a-changin...* in the words of the famous Bob Dylan song.

In the days of Sigmund Freud it was relatively common for a therapist to work with the same client over multiple years. In fact, it was even suggested that longer therapeutic relationships yielded the most positive results. Logically this seems to be valid given that years of reinforcement should help an individual be able to function better in society. Whether duration of treatment is a significant factor in the overall therapeutic process or not, the reality is that with our contemporary fast-paced society came a plethora of reasons to modify some of the traditional ones. Take the story of Megan for instance:

> Megan is a 28-year old White single mother of two. After her husband Neil passed away three years ago she was left with very little financial support. Despite working a full-time and part-time job, Megan still requires minimal governmental support to help subsidize some of her expenses. Despite coping relatively well after the loss of her husband, she has been struggling with bouts of anxiety and depression. Megan feels anxious as a result of working two jobs, struggling financially, raising two girls on her own, and trying to do everything else possible to stay afloat. On the other hand, Megan feels depressed because she still laments the loss of her husband, cannot find any satisfaction at work, has given

up her social life, and feels as though she has no one to support her. To complicate matters of support even further, neither one of her jobs provides benefits. Therefore, in addition to the monthly stipend she receives from the state, she also receives basic healthcare. Having decided that she can no longer live like this, Megan decided to look into finding a counselor. After finding a good one she went to a state worker to try and solidify a schedule and payment plan. Too her surprise, however, the state advised her that they are only willing to fund a total of 12 sessions. Stressed out even further now with the thought that she may not be "fixed" in as little as 12 sessions, she begins seeing her counselor twice a month.

As a professional one should be wondering whether or not Megan has a legitimate reason to worry. With so much going on in the client's life is it possible to help treat her in as little as 12 sessions? Would it be possible to treat her in as little as 10 sessions? What number would be the bare minimum—5 sessions? Without more information on the client, the truth is that there is no black and white answer to this question. Unfortunately, though, with most insurance providers and state funding there are stipulations as to how many sessions will be provided to each individual. Therefore, if 12 sessions is what the state will provide, then it is up to the client to fully fund anything beyond that commitment. For Megan and many other clients like her this is the reality of seeking mental health services. Although in an ideal society people would be able to attend treatment until they feel mentally healthy enough to function again on their own, this is unrealistic in the real world. Because of this stipulation and others to be mentioned throughout this chapter, counseling professionals must be responsive in creating individualized treatment plans that fit within the relevant time constraints. Please note, however, that space restrictions in this chapter limit the amount of detail I may provide in a chapter devoted to theory. For more information, I encourage readers to conduct their own scholarly search.

The sections that follow will provide some general information on the brief theories along with traditional ones that may be modified to fit within this context. This is important, as most graduate programs include at least one course that specifically focuses on discussing the major theories of counseling and psychotherapy. Commonly discussed traditional theories include that of Freudian Psychoanalytic, Jungian, Adlerian, Gestalt, Reality, Person-centered, Cognitive-behavioral (CBT), Rational Emotive Behavior Therapy (REBT), Existential, and so on. Other major theories on the post-modern front include Narrative, Feminist, and Multicultural (MCT) to name a few. Due to the importance of multicultural factors in counseling, this exploration will also consider diversity across Hay's (2008) ADDRESSING format comprised of: a) age and generational influences, b) development disabilities, c) disabilities acquired later in life, d) religion and spiritual orientation, e) ethnic and racial identity, f) socioeconomic status, g) sexual orientation, f) indigenous heritage, g) national origin, and h) gender. These factors, in conjunction with environmental and situational considerations, should always be considered with each and every client in each and every case regardless of treatment modality selected.

In sum, the pages ahead review the basic concepts and proper use of selected theories as they apply in brief therapy. Although by no means comprehensive or exhaustive, these examples help the reader gain insight as to how brief therapy principles may be applied to many of the traditional theories commonly studied by students and practiced by professionals. For further reading, other popular textbooks that offer an excellent description of these theories include: *Counseling and Psychotherapy: Theories and Interventions* (5th *ed.*)

(Capuzzi & Gross, 2011), *Theory and Practice of Counseling and Psychotherapy* (8th *ed.*) (Corey, 2008), *Theories of Psychotherapy and Counseling: Concepts and Cases* (4th *ed.*) (Sharf, 2008).

SIDEBAR 8.1

As you read through this introduction you likely had some feelings either for or against the use and efficacy of brief theories and their subsequent methods. With strength in length being a traditional thought in psychotherapy (Halbur & Halbur, 2011), brief counseling sometimes receives criticism for having a predetermined end-date for treatment. Questions of moral conviction may arise when a client faces being cut-off from much needed additional treatment. With that being said, there is also evidence-based research that supports the notion that brief treatments are as—if not more—effective than their traditional, full-length counterparts (NIH, 1999). Therefore, if you are one that is opposed to brief theory, I challenge you to remove any negative feelings, challenge your biases, and keep an open mind throughout this chapter. If you are one that already believes in the efficacy of the brief modalities, then use the information in this chapter to guide yourself through various hypothetical scenarios that you may encounter in practice.

Brief Approaches

History

Although advancements and developments by way of research, theories, and approaches led toward the advent of brief therapy, Milton Erickson and Richard Bandler have been credited as its founding fathers. As a psychiatrist, Erickson specialized in the areas of hypnosis and family therapy. Although not necessarily something intentionally created by Erickson, brief therapy developed into a popular approach after Jay Haley (1973) published the book *Uncommon Therapy: The Psychiatric Techniques of Milton Erickson*. It was in the review and analysis of this work that professionals began piecing together what would come to be brief approaches to counseling and psychotherapy. Richard Bandler was one of these individuals. Primarily noted for his development of Neuro-linguistic programming (NLP) with John Grinder, Bandler used this text to develop the structure for this brief therapy.

Developments

Considering that the origin of brief theory as the profession knows it just recently made the scene in 1973, one might be amazed at how quickly it developed into a mainstream form of therapy that surpassed many other modalities as the preferred choice of treatment (Wells & Phelps, 1990). Resulting from internal advancements within the counseling profession including but not limited to decades of research, new theoretical knowledge, and experience in practice, brief counseling has been supported through:

- Reports that most client change occurs in the first 10 sessions of psychotherapy
- Follow-up evaluations concluding that more therapeutic sessions do not necessarily result in better outcomes (ISU, 2004)

Further, societal developments have also contributed toward the need for this form of counseling. This reality has grown out of the needs of:

- Managed healthcare organizations seeking more cost-effective treatments
- Client time constraints
- Increased numbers of individuals seeking treatment due to increased availability of these counseling (and related) services (NIH, 1999)

If a brief approach to counseling and psychotherapy is selected with the appropriate considerations in mind, it is a win-win-win situation for the client, therapist, and managed care organization. The client wins by receiving a proven treatment strategy that takes away very little from any other life obligations (Wells & Phelps, 1990), which in today's society is significant given the typical household works more hours than ever to make ends meet (Capuzzi & Stauffer, 2011). With so many positive highlights of this form of counseling, it is likely to continue to grow in popularity.

Efficacy of Brief Approaches

Contrary to the unlimited amount of time afforded to Freudian psychoanalysts in the early part of the 1900s, counselors using brief approaches are limited to a prescribed number of sessions prior to the onset of treatment, with six generally being the minimum (NIH, 1999). Therefore, the pressing issue of time becomes a significant factor for the members of the therapeutic alliance (ISU, 2004). This is not to say, however, that counselors will terminate the client or provide subpar treatment simply to fit within these time constraints. As aptly put by Aubuchon and Crosby (1999), "…it would be more accurate to assume that brief counseling is not so much about the number of sessions, but the establishment of a clear focus for the treatment." While the number of sessions may vary as a result of insurance stipulations, program structure, client schedule, and so on, the counselor is ethically responsible for providing an enriching therapeutic experience that promotes the welfare of the client (ACA, 2005, A.1.a). Even though a single shot of espresso is small in size, it usually provides the same level of caffeine as a Grande coffee. In fact, current evidence-based research supports the efficacy of placing a brief counseling spin on most of the traditional therapeutic models (Milner & O'Byrne, 2002; Shefler, 2001; Winston & Winston, 2002). At this point, then, brief theory and its ensuing applications may be viewed as an umbrella approach unto which the others may be modified (Hutchinson, 2010). As such, brief theories have been extended toward brief strategic solution-focused counseling brief cognitive-behavioral counseling, brief psychodynamic counseling, brief humanistic counseling, brief existential counseling, brief strategic family counseling, and time-limited group counseling.

By the same token, there are even some cases where a brief approach is more efficient than longer duration treatments. Research supports the notion that many problems common to those seeking therapy may actually be resolved within this brief context (Donovan, 2003; Goldring, 1997; Halford, 2001; Hudson-Allez, 1997). Take acrophobia (fear of heights), for instance. In this case it would be efficient to utilize a cognitive-behavioral desensitization approach. Although, yes, this approach will vary by client, it may likely take less than a year if that client is motivated to change. If counselors are expected to work within these limitations, then the approaches used within this modality must be highly strategic and solution-focused.

Principles of Brief Approaches

One major area of differentiation for brief approaches over others is the lack of interest in the client's history (NIH, 1999). There is no worry about the subconscious or inherited factors here. What happened yesterday has passed and what happens tomorrow may never come. All attention is placed on the here-and-now. By encouraging clients to focus on the present and create solutions to their own problems, they will likely undergo spontaneous and generative change (Hutchinson, 2010). This makes sense on several fronts. First, by focusing solely on the present, clients may experience less anxiety over past and future events they cannot change or control. Second, by removing this improper focus of attention, clients may allocate resources to the pressing problem at hand. Finally, by taking personal ownership of remediation it becomes that much more meaningful to the client. Table 1 provides a summary of these common to brief approaches:

Table 8.1 Brief approaches

Themes of brief approaches	*Those discouraged*
Sessions are solution-focused on a particular problem	Does not focus on pathology or understanding why the problem exists
Counselor is active and involved throughout the session	Passive, noninvolved counselors
Techniques, methods, and approaches used entail active involvement and are sometimes experimental	"Square peg in the round hole" technique whereby the client's situation is forced into a standard therapeutic format that does not work
Therapeutic goals are of utmost importance and continue to be the focus of the session	
Goals surround the concept of client empowerment and attaining change through personal achievement	
Developing an understanding of how these principles apply to general life situations	

(ISU, 2004)

SIDEBAR 8.2

This section provided a summary of brief theory, brief approaches, and the traditional theories that may be modified to fit within this contemporary approach. Although Wells and Phelps (1990) have coined this approach as the "treatment of choice for most patients," there are still plenty of examples and cases where treatments of longer duration are necessary. In thinking through this critically, what comes to mind? Even in these cases, would any of the methods or approaches found in brief theory be appropriate? How so?

Solution-Focused Counseling

The only difference between a problem and a solution is that people understand the solution.

—Charles F. Kettering

It was in the late 1970s after Haley's (1973) release of *Uncommon Therapy: The Psychiatric Techniques of Milton Erickson* that Steve de Shazer and Insoo Kim Berg began the development of what would be called solution-focused counseling. In harmony with the aforementioned characteristics of brief approaches, solution-focused counseling is "future-focused, goal-directed, and focuses on solutions, rather than on the problems that brought clients to seek therapy" (Dolan, 2012). With solutions in mind, the counselor uses talk therapy to facilitate the creation and achievement of goals by the client. Although this counseling is not one that has been modified from the traditional theories as discussed throughout the duration of this chapter, three principles are important toward understanding some of the basic concepts that have been infused into these corresponding therapies.

Techniques

Since many clients are in therapy because they struggle with appropriate behavior and decision-making, compliments that offer validation and encouragement serve as positive reinforcements for successes along the therapeutic journey (Dolan, 2012). It is important, however, that compliments offered are genuine so that they may be fully embraced by the client (Sharf, 2008). If the client perceives the compliment as mocking, infantilizing, or merely said as a push-off, there is a chance that the client will begin to emotionally withdraw from the therapeutic alliance. In some cases counselors must also watch the frequency at which they compliment the client. While some clients may thrive on compliments, others may find them awkward. This may be due to varying cultural standards (Sue & Sue, 2008), unfamiliarity with positive feedback (Wronka, 2008), or any other type of insecurity. In any case, an appropriate balance must be achieved for this technique to be effective.

Solution-focused counseling posits that the client holds the tools necessary for self-improvement (NIH, 1999). One of the therapeutic goals, then, is to help the client come to this understanding. The first means of doing this is by looking for previous solutions. Because it is common for people to consistently deal with the same issues time and time again, there is a type of learning curve that either: a) prepares the individual to deal with the same exact issue in the future, or b) allows the individual, through assimilation, to identify similar problems as they occur so that the same strategy may be employed. The issue here, however, is that some individuals do not have the mental capacity to extend toward this endeavor. Whether this is the result of a psychological disorder, trauma, learning disability, or anything else, the counselor's focus is to help clients make these connections. Therefore, one of the counselor's roles is to help the client focus on a time in the past when the problem was successfully resolved (Dolan, 2012). Questions the counselor may consider include but are not limited to: How did you resolve the problem last time? What was unique about that situation? What is preventing that solution not working now? What have you learned by making this analysis? The ability to assimilate a problem-solving strategy from one type of problem to the next is helpful in the therapeutic setting and offers the client an excellent skillset that may be used throughout life (Brookfield, 1986).

One relatively common theme with counseling clients is that they fall into dichotomous thinking—a pattern of thinking only in absolute (NIH, 1999). When these clients are happy, they are ecstatic; when they are upset, they are miserable. For instance, if one were apply the metaphor that of "when it rains, it pours" to these individuals, one would be faced with a hurricane of epic proportions. When individuals become so stuck on the negative that it becomes difficult to think about or even recall positive instances, there comes the need for a reminder that not all is bad. The reality is that most people deal with their fair share of good and bad in life. As such, another approach that focuses on previous knowledge and experience is looking for exceptions. The difference with this strategy is that it is effective even for those that have yet to find a solution to any of their problems. "An exception is something that happens instead of the problem, often spontaneously and without conscious intention" (Dolan, 2012). Let's take a look at the case of Jermichael:

> Jermichael is a 28-year old insurance salesman. Fed up with his performance, Jermichael's manager pulled him aside to give him one last chance to shape up before considering his termination from the company. Now feeling hated on by his employer, Jermichael has been experiencing bouts of anxiety and frustration and has decided to come to therapy to have an outlet to vent. In his discussions with the therapist, Jermichael—in a roundabout way—admits to his consistent tardiness, poor productivity ratings, and bad attitude. Despite acknowledging his poor work ethic, Jermichael still cannot seem to get past the misconception that his manager is out to get him. When asked by the therapist for exceptions to these negative interactions Jermichael then replied, "Well, three months ago when I created a new business model for our sales team I was taken out for a nice dinner and received a $1,000 bonus." Without saying a word the therapist merely watched Jermichael as he thought about what he just said. Within about a minute Jermichael came to understand where his logic was flawed and dedicated himself to performing at a higher level at his job.

Although some cases will be significantly more difficult to resolve than this simple example with Jermichael, the reality is that there are almost always exceptions to everyone's problems. Pointing them out and trying to figure out what it was that was done differently during these times may just be part of the overall solution.

Asking the Right Questions

When a client reaches a point of helplessness it becomes easy to lose sight of any hope that one's situation can ever become better (Murphy, Rosenheck, Berkowitz, & Marans, 2005). One's logic becomes so skewed that even realistic solutions that are attainable appear as big dreams not worth having. One way to put grand solutions into perspective is by asking the "miracle question". The miracle question will vary from case-to-case, but has a primary focus on what life would be like if the problem was removed (Dolan, 2012). For instance, in the case of a young mother who takes on the role of housekeeper, chef, part-time worker, wife, and other chores becomes so overwhelmed and defeated out of having no time to herself, having her imagine what life would be like without all of these tasks may help her focus on what she needs to do to get to this point. Perhaps splitting the household chores with her husband more evenly will free up some time for her to partake in some of the activities she enjoyed before taking on so many roles.

Scaling questions are another technique commonly used in solution-focused therapy. These questions are "useful in helping clients to assess their own situations, track their own progress, or evaluate how others might rate them on a scale of 0–10" (Dolan, 2012). Although these types of questions are not limited to any particular type of client, they are certainly more helpful with individuals that:

1) Struggle to think of the most appropriate words for their emotions
2) Speak English as a second language and struggle with word choice
3) Gain more out of visualizing things in numbers
4) Are lower on levels of intellect and struggle to think in abstract terms

The beauty behind scaling questions, as well, is that their applicability is nearly unlimited. Questions may include but are nowhere near limited to: On a scale of 1–10, would you be able to rate how happy you feel right now? Using a scale of 1–10, how angry were you last night? Let's say that you were asked to jump out of an airplane for the first time, how would you rate your potential anxiety from 1–10? With 10 being very helpful and 1 being not at all, how would you rate this counseling experience? One negative with this type of questioning, however, is that it is closed-ended. A suggestion here is to be sure to follow-up client ratings with an open-ended question that will encourage him or her to elaborate a bit further. As such, an entire therapeutic session based primarily off scaling questions would not go very far.

Brief Cognitive Behavioral Counseling

Except our own thoughts, there is nothing absolutely in our power.

—Rene Descartes

Deterministic in nature, behavior theory posits that an individual is ultimately shaped and determined through sociocultural conditioning (Halbur & Halbur, 2011). As such, behaviorists stress the significance of the specificity of goals to help alleviate the negative antecedents and consequences resulting from a progression of maladaptive behavior (Sharf, 2008). In the sense that behavior theory focuses on maladaptive behaviors, cognitive theory focuses on maladaptive thoughts. Cognitive theory evolves around the idea that "cognitive activity affects behavior" (Dobson & Dozioz, 2001, as cited in Prout & Brown, 2007). That is, less moments of impulse and loss of control, people usually have thoughts about a particular something before they act in a particular way. For instance, when one feels that it is cold outside the thought before the behavior is to put on something warm. Generally, maladaptive thoughts evolve around illogical representations of the self or irrational beliefs about the environment and those living in it "every body is out to get me!" or, "I can't do anything right!" are examples of this logic. In a world of over 8 billion people, not everybody knows you or cares enough to be out to get you. And if you're coming here to counseling to improve both your life and the one's of others around you, then you've likely made at least a good decision or two in your life. Therefore, central to the concept of Beck's cognitive theory is the belief that psychological dysfunction, or pathology, is a result of faulty logic in one's cognitions. "However, simple awareness of one's own thoughts and cognitions is not sufficient for change; ultimately people must choose and want to live life differently" (Halbur & Halbur, 2011, p. 68).

CBT continues further to rely on the premise of extinction and cue exposure procedures. CBT posits "if a behavior occurs repeatedly across time but is not reinforced, the strength of both the cue for the behavior and the behavior itself will diminish and the behavior will extinguish" (NIH, 1999, p. 2). It is important, however, to take a step back and think about the principles of classical conditioning in the various contexts that a CBT counselor may have to face. Take a moment to review Sidebar 8.3 and think about how you would address an issue of hoarding with client LeDanian:

SIDEBAR 8.3

LeDanian is a 24-year old male that has always been close with his father. Eight months ago his father passed away from a sudden heart attack. With no other close family members in the area, LeDanian's father left him every last bit of his money and property. After moving back into his father's house LeDanian became very possessive of everything his father left behind. Instead of selling, donating, or recycling items that were either broken or not needed, he started stockpiling. This habit extended from his father's items to his own life when he started buying random "collections" of items that he had never collected before or had any intention to sell. Now, spending more money than he is making on these items, he has become socially withdrawn and is more attached to his property than relationships with people. In what ways would CBT help this client?

Although CBT is a highly recommended treatment for a variety of pathologies, it is a leading approach for counselors working with substance abuse and addiction clients. As stated previously, the process of extinction generally occurs when a behavior is not reinforced. For instance, if a puppy learns that barking and crying all night will cause his masters to let him in the bedroom, then there is an excellent chance that this technique will likely continue on into adulthood. Now if that same puppy that barks and cries every night for attention does not receive it after several days or weeks, the likelihood is that it will give up and be able to sleep by itself. With addiction, however, things are a little bit different. For the more serious drugs, the case is that individuals are never able to recapture that first high. A term "chasing the dragon" has been coined for when addicts keep ingesting higher and higher amounts of a particular substance in attempt to achieve that first high one more time. Unfortunately, this quest may become so pervasive that people wind up overdosing. Therefore, CBT strategies must focus on removing the behaviors associated with the high. An ex-heroin addict that I used to work with would tell me how his trigger was driving through a particular neighborhood. He could be sober for 5 years but driving through this one neighborhood (which was the location where he would buy drugs) would make him relapse every time. So the first technique here was to have him avoid this neighborhood, and even some of the particular roads that would lead into it. Although removing himself from this location is not a direct treatment of the drug addiction per se, the behavioral component of staying away from this neighborhood helped with the psychological component of desiring the drugs. Individual triggers will vary person-to-person, but by using behavioral techniques to manipulate cognitions and vice versa, the client stands a much better chance of recovery than merely treating just one component or the other. Although general pathology addressed through CBT requires about 12–20 weeks of sessions, substance abuse—depending on the severity of the situation—may require anywhere from 6 months to several years worth of treatment (NIH, 1999). Those that struggle with addiction may even require a lifetime of therapy. In either case, similar strategies are applied. It's the frequency and intensity of treatment that vary most significantly.

REBT

"Rational emotive behavioral therapy (REBT) views human nature as including innate tendencies toward growth, actualization, and rationality as well as opposing tendencies toward irrationality and dysfunction" (Halbur & Halbur, 2001, p. 69). By adjusting one's irrational thoughts into more rational ones, positive adjustments at both the emotional and behavioral level will result (Vaida, Kállay, & Opre, 2008, p. 58). To address this, REBT counselors have adopted the A-B-C theory of personality as the preferred model for locating, assessing, and addressing these maladaptive cognitions and subsequent behaviors. "According to this model, people experience undesirable activating events (A), about which they have distorted (irrational) or undistorted (rational) beliefs or cognitions (B). These beliefs then lead to dysfunctional or functional emotional, behavioral, and cognitive consequences (C)" (Szentagotai, David, Lupu, & Cosman, 2008, p. 524). Therefore, Ellis' proposed A-B-C-D-E therapeutic approach utilizes a strong therapeutic alliance to help the client dispute (D) these irrational beliefs in order to elicit a new, socially appropriate effect (E) (Sharf, 2008).

> Vincent has a major issue with road rage—red lights in particular. After working a long ten-hour day, all he wants to do is get home and unwind. What used to be a 30-minute ride home has now been taking up to 45 minutes or in some cases even an hour due to four new traffic lights the community put up after complaints that residents living on off streets in the neighborhoods would struggle getting onto the main roads. Recently Vincent has been growing in rage to the extent that he has even committed traffic violations by running red lights and driving on the shoulder to get ahead of other drivers. In treatment Vincent's therapist has been focusing on the issue using an REBT approach. Here is an excerpt of their dialogue:

COUNSELOR: So what is it you had hoped to accomplish by committing those various traffic offenses?

VINCENT: Obviously, I was trying to make it home more quickly. I was tired, frustrated, and feel as though the mayor puts these lights in just to ruin my life—like he thinks he's better than me or something.

COUNSELOR: But didn't you say earlier that the community claimed to put them in due to complaints by residents living in the communities?

VINCENT: Yeah, that's what they claim.

COUNSELOR: Well, don't you live in one of these neighborhoods?

VINCENT: Well, yes....

COUNSELOR: And how long would you wait before you pulled onto the main road?

VINCENT: I mean, sometimes 5-10 minutes. One day it took 15 and I literally flipped out!

COUNSELOR: So if your ride was 30 minutes before and your wait to get on the road to 5, 10, or even 15 minutes, isn't that the same as what you are driving now?

VINCENT: Well, yes.

COUNSELOR: And isn't it safer?

VINCENT: I guess I suppose so.

COUNSELOR: OK, so I think we dawned on something here, Vincent. What we have found here, then, is that traffic that takes you longer to get home (A) infuriates you because you just want to get home. You think that the mayor put the lights up just to gloat in your face (B), so you commit traffic violations out of rage and the intention of making it home more quickly (C). Now that you realize that the lights actually do not take up any more time and are actually safer (D), you may feel better with the seemingly longer ride and practice some type of relaxation technique like creating a mixed tape of your favorite music to listen to while driving and waiting (E).

In all, REBT has proven to be an extremely effective modality that may be effectively used across a broad array of problems and pathology (Bishop, 2004).

Brief Theory in its Humanistic Form

You can talk with someone for years, everyday, and still, it won't mean as much as what you can have when you sit in front of someone, not saying a word, yet you feel that person with your heart, you feel like you have known the person for forever.... connections are made with the heart, not the tongue.

–C. Joybell C

The humanistic school of thought is phenomenological in the respect that it focuses on the here-and-now while believing that individuals possess the basic inclination to become fully functioning (Halbur & Halbur, 2011). Notable leaders of the humanistic movement include Abraham Maslow ("self-actualization"), Carl Rogers (person-centered therapy), and Fritz Perls (Gestalt therapy; NIH, 1999). Basic components include:

- Empathic understanding
- Respect
- Exploration of problems
- Exploration of goals and expectations
- Clarification of the helping role
- Assessment and enhancement of motivation
- Negotiation of a contract
- Demonstration of authenticity (NIH, 1999)

In sum, humanistic counselors must be genuine, warm, and have enough insight to help guide the client through his or her problem (Sharf, 2008). The rest of this section will continue to provide detailed information on person-centered and Gestalt therapies.

Person-Centered Counseling

Carl Rogers' vision of therapeutic intervention entailed a close observation of relationships between people (NIH, 1999). Individuals are unique and possess their own worldview.

That is, the client is the center of his or her universe. Therefore, the client is the center of this therapeutic approach (Sharf, 2008). He believed that abnormal behavior in relationships was an indicator of pathology that many clients exhibit. Viewing individuals in a positive light and as being experts on their own lives, person-centered therapy assists clients in their quest for self-actualization. The National Institutes of Health (1999) have provided three primary principles of client-centered counseling:

1. "Unconditional positive regard"
2. "A warm, positive, and accepting attitude that includes no evaluation or moral judgment"
3. "Accurate empathy, whereby the therapist conveys an accurate understanding of the client's world through skilled, active listening" (p. 5)

Self-actualization, then, is more of an ideal or journey than a destination. By pushing oneself to be the best one can, clients are encouraged to live the fullest, most meaningful lives possible (Halbur & Halbur, 2011). The goal then, is to help clients become more congruent and self-accepting. This is through a "genuine, accepting, and empathic relationship" where counselors are able to appraise "the individual's current awareness and experiencing" (Sharf, 2008, p. 193). The resulting positive relationship between the client and therapist results in newfound self-assurance and the tools needed for healthy functioning out in society.

Because the therapeutic alliance provides the core foundation upon which the rest of counseling is built, it is important that the therapist begins working on this from the very second the client is met. A study at Princeton University revealed that first impressions take as little as 1/10th second to create (APS, 2006). Unfortunately, it takes significantly longer than this to change that opinion. Being afforded limited resources on a time crunch, clients literally cannot afford to stay with a mismatched therapist. Additionally, with all of the adversity faced by multicultural clients, they are likely to terminate the relationship if they do not feel comfortable with the counselor, particularly as in many cases these individuals may have been reluctant to come to counseling in the first place (Sue & Sue, 2008). Once this relationship is solidified, it is the role of the counselor:

> To provide a safe climate conducive to clients' self-exploration, so that they can recognize blocks to growth and can experience aspects of self that were formerly denied or distorted. To enable them to move toward openness, greater trust in self, willingness to be a process, and increased spontaneity and aliveness.
>
> (Miller, 2005, p. 22)

Many blocks to growth result out of a fear of change. The reality is change is an extremely uncomfortable situation for many people (Zimmerman, Olsen, & Bosworth, 2000). By breaking one's routine, the individual must face a fear of the unknown, take risks, be faced with inconvenience, and perhaps even take on activities that are physically discomforting (i.e., a New Year's resolution to begin a workout regimen). Once these barriers are overcome, however, and the client begins to find excitement and novelty in the change (i.e., improved appearance and swagger from working out), the client may finally overcome some barriers that were at one time seemingly impossible.

Unfortunately, person-centered counseling is not without its limitations. One major limitation is in its lack of clearly defined techniques. This may make it extremely difficult for students, supervisees, and novice professionals to maintain direction in therapy. Another limitation is in its applicability across cultures.

> In cultures where individuals learn to respect and take direction from authority, the transition to a less directive person-centered approach may be difficult. Also, many cultures focus on familial and social decision making rather than individual empowerment, as does Rogers.
>
> (Sharf, 2008, p. 213)

Counselors must be cautious in their application of person-centered counseling with particular cultures as Rogers' idea of the importance of individual needs may actually go contrary to everything that person believes. If the counselor does not tread carefully, the ethical infraction of imposing personal beliefs may come into play (ACA, 2005, A.4.b.).

SIDEBAR 8.4

Depending on the client, context, and severity of use, any one of the brief approaches may prove as an excellent approach in working with substance abuse or addiction. One common issue with these clients is that they are either in denial that a problem exists or are lacking the motivation to actually fix a problem that they have been trying to avoid for however long. How many times do we hear the statements: "I don't have the time to deal with this right now," "Everyone has their issues and I am not hurting anyone with mine," or, "It's really not that big of a deal after all"? With the focus that person-centered counselors place on the use of motivation as an important therapeutic tool, research has shown that this technique may also be used to help clients overcome denial and move forward in therapy (NIH, 1999). Developed by Miller and Rollnick (1991, 2002), motivational interviewing utilizes Rogerian principles to help a client prepare and subsequently become engaged in a treatment program. Counselors utilizing this technique are strongly encouraged to: a) express empathy, b) develop discrepancy, c) roll with resistance, and d) support self-efficacy (Capuzzi & Stauffer, 2011). Once the client acknowledges the reality and severity of the substance abuse or addiction problem and wants to do something about it, it is then time to begin focusing on the problem.

Take a moment to consider the following:

Can you think of any other scenarios in which motivational interviewing may be appropriate?

What are the strengths of incorporating this approach into an eclectic professional development plan?

Are there any situations or types of clients where this approach may actually prove inappropriate? Why?

Gestalt Therapy

Founded in the 1940s by Fritz and Laura Perls, "Gestalt theory holds that the analysis of parts can never provide an understanding of the whole" (NIH, 1999, p. 9). It is a phenomenological-existential therapy that teaches "the phenomenological method of awareness, in which perceiving, feeling, and acting are distinguished from interpreting and reshuffling preexisting attitudes" (Yontef, 1993). The underlying premise of Gestalt is that the client is an individual and product of the environment. Therefore, this counseling focuses on the consequences of such interactions (Korb, Davenport, & Korb, n.d.). Because of the level of awareness required on behalf of the client for this counseling to work, the most appropriate clients are those with a moderate-to-higher level of functioning. Counseling is done through dialogue and conversation between the counselor and client. Similar to person-centered counselors, Gestalt counselors also maintain the centrality of the client in therapy, focus on the present, and ask more about the "how" than the "why" behind a particular phenomenon (NIH, 1999). As Yontef (1993) explains, the counselor is less interested in the client's interpretations than direct perceptions, because one's interpretations—especially if mentally unstable—are generally less reliable than the facts. The dialogue, then, delves into the inconsistencies between the client's interpretations and direct perceptions. By doing this, the therapist teaches the client how to become aware of their actions so that they may be changed. At the same time, however, the client must be comfortable with valuing and accepting oneself. This may prove important in pulling together the strength and determination needed to actually go through some of the difficult changes the client may face in treatment.

Dissimilar from the criticisms received by person-centered counseling for having a lack of any clearly directed techniques, Gestalt has plenty that generally work well in combination with the cognitive-behavioral approaches (Hutchinson, 2010). Table 8.2 provides a list and definition of commonly used techniques.

One of the key strengths of Gestalt counseling is that of awareness. It is through this discovery of awareness that unhealthy thoughts and behaviors are identified (O'Leary,

Table 8.2 List and definition of commonly used techniques

Commonly used gestalt techniques	
Unfinished Business	Uncomfortable feelings, repetitions of maladaptive behavior
Giving voice to physical sensation, nonverbal cues	Tenseness, sweaty palms, shaky hands, headache, increased heart rate
Dream Exploration	Immediate emotional dream work on current dreams the client is having
Empty chair	Clients speak their mind to an individual that they pretend is sitting in the chair
Top dog/underdog	Top dog strives for perfection while underdog attempts to resist external demands
Exaggerating feelings and actions	By exaggerating inner feelings and behaviors, the client is able to arrive to a clear understanding of them
Confrontation	Clients practice confronting tasks and individuals that they have been previously afraid to confront
Encouragement of awareness and responsibility	Through awareness comes ownership and responsibility—attributes needed for the client to have meaning behind making needed changes

(Hutchinson, 2010)

Sheedy, O'Sullivan, & Thoresen, 2003). Gestalt counseling also has strengths in the area of meeting the needs of both genders. Created by a team of male and female professionals, Gestalt theory has been found to be particularly empowering for women while offering great assistance in the area of awareness for both genders (Sharf, 2008).

Although Gestalt has relevance in work with diverse cultures, it has its limitations. One major criticisms within this realm is that it is problematic for cultures that discourage the expression of emotion (Sharf, 2008). Another limitation is in its exclusivity. Gestalt professionals tend to fear that this approach should not be intermixed into an eclectic approach due to "those who use a variety of techniques without a clear understanding of boundary disturbances and the need for an integrated approach to the patient" (Sharf, 2008, p. 246).

> Juanita is a 42-year old lawyer that has been working at the same law firm for the past fifteen years. Thinking nothing of the fact that all of the executive members were male, she found the workplace to be one of equal opportunity. It was not five years into working there that one of the executives had retired and an opportunity for promotion became available. Rather than open the floor for interviews, the executive merely appointed another male member to his position. Because the promoted individual was a highly valuable member of the firm, Juanita thought nothing of this and shrugged it off. Her next "opportunity" for promotion, like clockwork, came around 5 years later. Once again, another male member was appointed to the position. This time, however, Juanita was enraged because this individual was one that was consistently tardy, took short-cuts, and was disrespectful to other employees. Since this individual's promotion, three more males have been appointed to executive positions. In Juanita's opinion, she is much more qualified and experienced than all four of these individuals. In fact, employee data even confirms this claim. Feeling that her firm is discriminating against her for being a female of minority heritage, Juanita thinks it is time for her to stand up for herself and fight for an executive position. She wants to take caution, though, in throwing out allegations of discrimination because aside from a lack of promotion opportunities, she is treated in a respectful manner by her colleagues and has also been repeatedly recognized for her accomplishments.

The following dialogue between the therapist and Juanita represents an example of how a conversation between the client and therapist may occur:

COUNSELOR: So it sounds, Juanita, as though you have proven yourself at this company and think it is time that they recognize you by offering you a shot at promotion.

JUANITA: Exactly! And I think the only way I can do that is by standing up for myself andletting them know how I feel. That's just never been me, you know? I was raised to keep to my opinion to myself. I mean, as a lawyer I am very outspoken because I have to be, but it's much harder to speak up on my own behalf.

COUNSELOR: It sounds like you have a pretty great awareness as to what you need to do and as to what your needs and limitations are. How would you like to partake in a little exercise?

CLIENT: Sure, that sounds good.

COUNSELOR: Okay, now what I want you to do is sit face-to-face with this chair and say what you would like to say to your boss.

CLIENT: Okay, so this is something like talking into the mirror? Umm... All right. Thom, I've always wondered why none of the executives have given me—or any other woman for that matter—in the office an opportunity to be promoted. I feel as though I have the personality and experience to do it, and I also have the track record to prove that I have consistently performed at the top of my class. I know that Dante will be leaving soon and I would like a chance at his position.

By practicing her script before confronting her boss in a non-threatening manner, Juanita may feel more prepared and confident actually going into the situation in real life. Because this technique assists the client on multiple levels, it is a good approach to use when the situation warrants.

Existential Brief Counseling

...the individual is defined only by his relationship to the world and to other individuals; he exists only by transcending himself, and his freedom can be achieved only through the freedom of others. He justifies his existence by a movement which, like freedom, springs from his heart but which leads outside of himself.

–Simone de Beauvoir

Central to existential therapy is Frankl's concept of the existential vacuum. "If meaning is what we desire, then meaninglessness is a hole, an emptiness, in our lives. Whenever you have a vacuum, of course, things rush in to fill it" (Boeree, 2006). As a result, stressful life events such as job loss, divorce, or onset of a disability may lead the client to believe his life is meaningless. Consequentially, maladaptive behaviors may include anything from withdrawal from society, loss of appetite, passive behavior, or a complete and total loss of hope. Resulting pathology may include anything from major depression to alcohol dependence (NIH, 1999).

Existentialism is another phenomenological approach that focuses on the here and now. It "deals with the dynamic or ever-changing transitions that individuals encounter as they emerge, evolve, and become... Existentialism is concerned with how individuals relate to their objective world, to other human beings, and to their own sense of self" (Sharf, 2008, p. 151). In sum, an individual's reality is unique compared to that of anyone else's, it is something that no other human being in existence could ever fully experience. Although you and I may become angry about the same thing, it is highly unlikely that you and I will experience that anger to the *exact* same degree. In earlier philosophical inquiry philosophers like Rene Descartes would continually question whether one's interpretation of reality was enough to make it real. The same thought extends toward the construction of the labels society has placed on everything we have come to name. Just because humans perceive the color blue in one light does not mean that another organism does not perceive it differently. After all, the human eye goes through a series of instantaneous processes to process the color that we see; therefore, we can never really say that what we perceive as blue is completely accurate.

The National Institutes of Health (1999) have highlighted six underlying assumptions of existentialism:

1) "All persons have the capacity for self-awareness"
2) "As free beings, everyone must accept the responsibility the comes with freedom"

3) "Each person has a unique identity that can only be known through relationships with others"

4) "Each person must continually recreate himself. The meaning of life and of existence is never fixed, rather it constantly changes"

5) "Anxiety is part of the human condition"

6) "Death is a basic human condition that gives significance to life" (p. 11)

Because of the level of awareness and deeper-level thinking required of existentialism, it is generally reserved for clients of higher intellectual capacity (Sharf, 2008). The drawback, then, is that there will be clients that are either not cognitively able, uncomfortable with, unfamiliar with, or not accustomed to thinking on this type of level. Attempting to force a client into this mindset may also have negative consequences that include but are not limited to feelings of anger, frustration, confusion, and even belittlement (Sue & Sue, 2008). Therefore, counselors must work with clients during earlier sessions to get a feel as to their readiness for this type of therapy when creating appropriate counseling plans (ACA, 2005, A.1.c.).

SIDEBAR 8.5

Although it is important that counselors assess clients for best fit with brief existential counseling, it is even more important that the counselors themselves possess the tools in their own lives so that they, too, would be appropriate for this type of treatment. As such, being proficient in introspection and having the ability to think critically is key for counselor success in this modality. Take a moment to think how well you know yourself. Do you know when things are wrong in your life? Do you really know what you want and how to get there? How do you define meaning? By thinking through these questions you will better understand the pathway of thoughts needed to arrive at these conclusions, which will better help you help clients arrive at their own conclusions.

Under existential theory, the counselor's intent is therefore to help the client reestablish meaning while taking ownership of one's actions. Essentially the main question asked is "'How do I exist?' in the face of uncertainty, conflict, and death?" (NIH, 1999, p. 11). Common debilitating themes that may come out of this question include, but are certainly not limited to: fear of taking chances, fear of change, fear of confrontation, fear of being wrong, and fear of death. Therefore, the six assumptions of existentialism have led toward three important goals:

1) Achievement of awareness
2) Acceptance of the core human conditions
3) Find the discovery of meaning (Halbur & Halbur, 2011)

While existential counseling is not technique-specific, the most common techniques include: relationship development (therapeutic alliance), empathy, client understanding, and meaning identification (Halbur & Halbur, 2011). Therapists help clients achieve these goals by locating the "specific concerns rooted in the individual's existence" (NIH, 1999, p. 11). When the concern is pinpointed, it serves as a frame of reference for meaning, understanding, and progress. For instance, if a client that hates her job consistently passes up potentially promising opportunities, a notable theme is that she is likely afraid of change for some reason. Next the client and therapist may focus on why change is so difficult in this context along with others, if applicable. Once this is realized, it then becomes possible to actually develop remedies to work through the client's current roadblocks.

Brief Approaches to Psychoanalysis

> Freud has shown one thing very clearly: that we only forget our infancy by burying it in the unconscious; and that the problems of this difficult period find their solution under a disguised form in adult life.
>
> —Herbert Read

At the core of psychoanalysis is Freud's drive theory—the belief that individuals possess innate drives that express themselves through various unconscious processes. In the beginning, "Freud distinguished between self-preservative drives (including breathing, eating, drinking, and excreting) and species-preservative drives (sexuality)" (Sharf, 2008, p. 29). Taking it further, he "believed that people struggle[d] to balance complete animalistic and innate pleasure-seeking impulses with the challenges of social constraints" (Halbur & Halbur, 2011, p. 48). One of the primary motivators within this concept of pleasure seeking is that of sexual desires, or libido. As a result of this theory, Freud created a theory of personality (i.e. the id, ego, and superego) and the five psychosexual stages (i.e. oral stage, anal stage, phallic stage, latency stage, and genital stage) (Halbur & Halbur, 2011).

Setting everything else aside, a major strength of Freud's drive theory is that it was the first formal theory of its kind (Halbur & Halbur, 2011). It set the precedent for future research that would eventually lead toward many of the more advanced theories we have today. Unlike every other brief theory mentioned in this chapter, brief psychoanalysis relies on the unconscious. With that being said, rather than taking the "here and now" frame of reference, therapists are extremely concerned with past incidents and how they relate to the client's current functioning (NIH, 1999). Unconscious processes—although not visibly apparent on the surface—are significant in that they greatly affect one's behaviors and means of socialization (Sharf, 2008). By recognizing this, Freud was able to open a whole new door where mental health professionals could use unresolved unconscious conflicts to correct pathology.

Traditionally, psychoanalysis is one to take multiple years to complete "because the goal of therapy is often to change an aspect of one's identity or personality or to integrate key developmental learning missed while the client was stuck at an earlier stage of emotional development" (NIH, 1999, p. 2). Current evidence-based research on abbreviated methods, however, has proven brief psychoanalysis to be as effective, if not more-so, than its traditional format. Consequently, it is the most underprescribed of the brief treatments (Schuyler, 2000). Schuyler also states that evidence supports the notion that clients receiving this treatment have shown improvements over those who have not. Recommended clients for this treatment are those that suffer from anxiety, depression,

Table 8.3 Ten most popular models of brief psychodynamic counseling

Models of brief psychodynamic approaches	Goals
Mann's Time-Limited Psychotherapy (TLP)	To restore the client's self-esteem through resolution of one's most pressing issues
Sifneo's Short-Term Anxiety-Provoking Psychotherapy (STAPP)	Solution-focused, clients increase well-being by resolving problems through goal-setting
Davanloo's Intensive Short-term Dynamic Psychotherapy (ISTDP)	By bringing unresolved problems out of the subconscious, client issues are resolved by revisiting them in a more logical manner
SE Psychoanalytic Psychotherapy	Change results out of a positive helping relationship and increased self-awareness
The Vanderbilt Approach to Time-Limited Dynamic Psychotherapy (TLDP)	Positive change is constructed through improvement in interpersonal functioning
Short-Term Dynamic Therapy of Stress Response Syndromes	Dealing with recent crises, this therapy helps clients regain control of their lives by interpreting the traumatic event in relation to its meaning
Brief Adaptive Psychotherapy (BAP)	Mainly used for personality disorders, this form of therapy helps clients understand the meaning and operations of maladaptive behavior as reference for creating appropriate alternatives
Dynamic Supportive Psychotherapy	Serving more as support than therapy for the client, this approach does not require as many of the familiar techniques used in psychotherapy; this is done to foster client independence and growth
A Self-Psychological Approach	After selecting a couple goals early on in treatment, the client and therapist focus on the client's ability to use self-motivation to remove dysfunctional intrapsychic structures and replace them with healthy ones
Interpersonal Psychotherapy (ITP)	Primarily dealing with depressed clients (without bipolar or psychotic tendencies), this therapy focuses on symptom reduction and improved interpersonal functioning

(NIH, 1999)

PTSD, and perhaps substance abuse and dependence issues. Table 8.3 provides a brief description of the ten most popular models of brief psychodynamic counseling. Using the basic components of traditional theory, these models each provide a slightly different focus to assist clients along a continuum of issues.

With the impetus for change being the resolution of a past, unresolved conflict—or conflicts—psychodynamic approaches have been developed specifically to help in this aspect (Sharf, 2008). Because these conflicts generally stem from childhood and carry over into adulthood, clients may have low self-esteem and a pessimistic outlook on life. Therefore, it is important that counselors help clients regain (or in some case acquire for the first time) a positive self-image (NIH, 1999). Once this is acquired, the individual may become optimistic about potential improvements that may be gained through counseling while concurrently improving one's quality of life. For those that used to have a higher sense of well-being at one point, it is fruitful to help regain lost perspective. That is, if the client was much more satisfied with life at another time it would be helpful to know: What was different at that point? How can the client get back to this mindset? Is it possible? If not, the focus may then to shift toward helping the client reframe cognitions. Rather than think a particular event or series of events is the end-all, the client may be asked to view the opportunity as an end of one point but beginning of another—one where the client may regain control and acquire strength. As such, this theory also works well with clients suffering from PTSD. Another technique includes exposure. This may be done in either a real life setting or recreated through some type of simulation (Schuyler, 2000). By exposing the client to the issue, it may finally be confronted in a productive, meaningful way.

Stipulations for working with multicultural clients may exist when the counselor cannot access the root of the issue from the client's subconscious (Halbur & Halbur, 2011). Because some cultures are taught to not divulge information that may bring shame upon the family, multicultural clients may struggle to cooperate with this type of treatment (Sue & Sue, 2008). In these cases it may be best to opt for another primary theory in the therapeutic plan and select only the most appropriate approaches within the modality to use with the client. The psychosexual stages and their progression into adulthood may also prove misleading as far as female development goes. Because it has an affinity toward the male gender (Sharf, 2008), women may benefit from the insertion of principles from feminist theory (another approach which also works well with multicultural clients).

> Amanda is a 24-year old veteran that has been struggling both emotionally and behaviorally since returning from Iraq 2 years ago. Prior to leaving after high school graduation, Amanda was a happy-go-lucky girl that always wanted to be around family and friends. These days she is quiet, withdrawn, and very pessimistic about everything. On occasion she also breaks down—bawling about how there is no good in the world and that she is just as bad as those she was fighting. Reluctant to attend treatment, the V.A. office suggested that she go. The therapist she is seeing is a brief psychotherapist. In what ways can she help?

SIDEBAR 8.6

So far this chapter has described multiple brief approaches that have shared many of the same common traits as one another. Common traits include their phenomenological foundation, here-and-now focus, lack of interest in the meaning of the problem, and solution-focused attentiveness. Brief psychoanalysis, then, sets itself apart from the rest as everything is predicated upon unresolved conflicts stored in clients' subconscious.

Many of today's practicing professionals would state that they subscribe to an eclectic orientation (Halbur & Halbur, 2011). This is ideal considering the vast differentials amongst clients and their situations.

Summary

1. Although Milton Erickson and Richard Bandler have been credited as the founding fathers of brief theory, it did not become a popular approach until 1973 when Jay Haley published the book *Uncommon Therapy: The Psychiatric Techniques of Milton Erickson*.

2. Research supports the notion that many problems common to those seeking counseling may actually be resolved as well if not better using brief theory.

3. By encouraging clients to focus on the present and create solutions to their own problems, they will likely undergo spontaneous and generative change.

4. Solution-focused counseling has a focus that is on the future, specific goals, and the solutions toward achieving those goals.

5. In the sense that behavior theory focuses on maladaptive behaviors, cognitive theory focuses on maladaptive thoughts. Therefore, central to the concept of Beck's cognitive theory is the belief that psychological dysfunction, or pathology, is a result of faulty logic in one's cognitions.

6. The humanistic school of thought is phenomenological. It focuses on the here-and-now while believing that individuals possess the basic inclination to become fully functioning. In sum, humanistic counselors must be genuine, warm, and insightful.

7. Existentialism concerns the dynamic transitions that people encounter when they "emerge, evolve, and become..." In what way am I an important part of everything else?

8. The primary goal of brief psychoanalytic counseling is to either modify a maladaptive aspect of one's identity or integrate the learned and acquired skills missed during an earlier stage of emotional development.

Useful Websites

http://www.agpa.org/pubs/GS_0899.html
http://www.psychologicalscience.org/observer/getArticle.cfm?id=2010
http://teach.valdosta.edu/dtwasieleski/brief.htm
http://www.smartrecovery.org/resources/library/For_Family_Volunteers_Professionals/basics-of-rebt.pdf
http://webspace.ship.edu/cgboer/jung.html
http://psychology.illinoisstate.edu
http://www.afn.org/~gestalt/about.htm
http://www.ncbi.nlm.nih.gov/pmc/articles/PMC181103/
http://www.census.gov/
http://www.gestalt.org/yontef.htm

References

AGPA. (1999). Brief group psychotherapy and managed care: Integration or disconnection? Retrieved from: <http://www.agpa.org/pubs/GS_0899.html>.

American Counseling Association. (2005). Code of Ethics. Alexandria, VA: Author.

Association for Psychological Science. (2006). How many seconds to a first impression? Retrieved from: <http://www.psychologicalscience.org/observer/getArticle. cfm?id=2010>.

Aubuchon, J., & Crosby, C. (1999). Brief therapy resource and information page. Retrieved from: <http://teach.valdosta.edu/dtwasieleski/brief.htm>.

Bishop, F. M. (2004). Rational emotive behavior therapy: The basics. Retrieved from: <http://www.smartrecovery.org/resources/library/For_Family_Volunteers_Professionals/basics-of-rebt.pdf>.

Boeree, C. G. (2006). Personality theories: Carl Jung. Retrieved Dec. 26, 2010, from <http://webspace.ship.edu/cgboer/jung.html>.

Brookfield, S. D. (1986). *Understanding and facilitating adult learning.* San Francisco: Jossey-Bass.

Capuzzi, D., & Gross, D. R. (Eds.). (2011). *Counseling and psychotherapy: Theories and interventions* (5th ed.). Alexandria, VA: American Counseling Association.

Capuzzi, D., & Stauffer, M. (2011). *Career Counseling: Foundations, Perspectives, and Applications* (2nd. ed.). New York: Routledge.

Corey, G. (2008). *Theory and Practice of Counseling and Psychotherapy* (8th ed.). Belmont, CA: Thomson Brooks/Cole.

David, D., & Szentagatai, A. (2006). Cognitions in cognitive-behavioral psychotherapies; toward Dobson & Dozioz, 2001, as cited in Prout & Brown, 2007, an integrative model. *Clinical Psychology Review, 26*, 284–298.

Dolan, Y. (2012). What is solution-focused therapy? Retrieved from: <http://www.solutionfocused.net/solutionfocusedtherapy.html>.

Donovan, J. M. (2003). *Short-term object relations couples therapy: The five-step model.* New York: Brunner-Routledge.

Goldring, J. (1997). *A quick response therapy: A time-limited treatment approach.* Northvale, NJ: Jason Aronson.

Halbur, D. A., & Halbur, K. V. (2011). *Developing your theoretical orientation in counseling and psychotherapy* (2nd ed.). Boston: Pearson/Allyn and Bacon.

Halford, W. K. (2001). *Brief therapy for couples: Helping couples help themselves.* New York: Guilford Press.

Hays, P. A. (2008). *Addressing cultural complexities in practice* (2nd ed.). Washington, DC: American Psychological Association.

Hudson-Allez, G. (1997). *Time-limited Therapy in a General Practice Setting: How to help within six sessions.* London: Sage Publications.

Hutchinson, L. (2010). Study guide for the NCMHCE. (5th ed.). Winter Park, FL: Licensure Exams, Inc.

Illinois State University (ISU) Department of Psychology. (2004). Brief therapy. Retrieved from: <http://psychology.illinoisstate.edu/>.

Korb, P., Davenport, J., & Korb, J. P. (0000n.d.). The Gestalt approach: Basic Gestalt theory. Retrieved from: <http://www.afn.org/ gestalt/about.htm>.

Miller, G. (2005). *Learning the language of addiction counseling* (2nd ed., chap. 2, pp. 16–31). Hoboken, NJ: John Wiley & Sons, Inc.

Milner, J., & O'Bryne, P. (2002). *Brief counseling: Narratives and solutions.* New York: Palgrave.

Murphy, R. A., Rosenheck, R. A., Berkowitz, S. J., & Marans, S. R. (2005). Acute service delivery in a police mental-health program for children exposed to violence and trauma. *The Psychiatric Quarterly, 76*(2), 107–121.

National Institutes of Health. (1999). *Brief interventions and brief therapies for substance abuse.* Rockville, MD: Substance Abuse and Mental Health Services Administration (US).

O'Leary, E., Sheedy, G., O'Sullivan, K., & Thoresen, C. (2003). Cork older adult intervention project: Outcomes of a gestalt therapy group with older adults. *Counselling Psychology Quarterly, 16*(2), 131–143.

Schuyler, D. (2000). Prescribing brief psychotherapy. Retrieved from: <http://www.ncbi.nlm.nih.gov/pmc/articles/PMC181103/>.

Sharf, R. S. (2008). *Theories of psychotherapy and counseling: Concepts and cases* (4th ed.). Belmont, CA: Brooks/Cole, Cengage Learning.

Shefler, G. (2001). *Time-limited Psychotherapy in Practice.* New York: Brunner-Routledge.

Sue, D. W., & Sue, D. (2008). *Counseling the culturally diverse: Theory and practice.* (5th ed.). New York: John Wiley & Sons.

Szentagotai, A., David, D., Lupu, V., & Cosman, D. (2008). Rational emotive behavior therapy versus cognitive therapy versus pharmacotherapy in the treatment of major depressive disorder: Mechanisms of change analysis. *Psychotherapy: Theory, Research, Practice, Training, 45*(4), 523–538.

U.S. Census Bureau. (2008). Individuals and families below poverty level—Number and rate by state. Retrieved from: <http://www.census.gov/>.

Vaida, S., Kállay, É., & Opre, A. (2008). Counseling in schools. A rational emotive behavior therapy (REBT) based intervention — A pilot study — *Cognitie, Creier, Comportament/ Cognition, Brain, Behavior, 12*(1), 57–69.

Wells, R. A., & Phelps, P. A. (1990). *The brief psychotherapies: A selective overview.* In R. A. Wells & V. J. Giannetti (Eds.), *Handbook of brief psychotherapies* (pp. 3–26). New York: Plenum.

Winston, A., & Winston, B. (2002). *Handbook of integrated short-term psychotherapy.* Washington, D. C: American Psychiatric Publishing.

Wronka, J. (2008). *Human rights and social justice: Social action and service for the helping and health professions.* Thousand Oaks, CA: Sage Publications.

Yontef, G. (1993). *Awareness, Dialogue and Process.* Gouldsboro, ME: The Gestalt Journal Press, Inc. Retrieved from: <http://www.gestalt.org/yontef.htm>.

Zimmerman, G. L., Olsen, C. G., & Bosworth, M. F. (2000). A 'stages of change' approach to helping patients change behavior. *American Family Physician, 61*(5), 1409–1416.

9

GROUP COUNSELING

David Capuzzi and Douglas R. Gross

The twenty-first century poses challenges and possibilities that should be of high interest to the beginning counselor enrolled in a counselor education program and considering becoming a group work specialist. If we believe that the 1950s may have symbolized "the individual in society", the 1960s "the individual against society," the 1970s "the individual's conflict with self," and the 1980s "the individual's integration into the family," the society of the 1990s and 2000s may clearly be characterized as "the individual's integration with technology" (Greene, Lawson, & Getz, 2005). Much of the work in education, employment, and day-to-day living situations will be done by computers; connections between colleagues, friends, and family members will be maintained by the use of social media, skype, smart phones, etc. (The reader should review chapter seven for more information about technology and counseling.)

The replacement of consistent social contact with friends and coworkers via technology will create a much greater need for interpersonal communication on a person-to-person basis. Groups will provide an antidote to human isolation and more and more counselors and other human development specialists will be called upon to serve as group facilitators. The beginning counseling and human development specialist will experience an explosion of opportunities and escalating concomitant responsibilities as a group work specialist.

There are a number of reasons why the responsibilities of a group work specialist are so important. A facilitator must be skilled in catalyzing a therapeutic climate in a group and in monitoring therapeutic factors inherent in the group (Berg, Landreth, & Fall, 1998; Corey, 2012; Frew & Spiegler, 2013; Gladding, 2008; Ohlsen & Ferreira, 1994; Schimmel & Jacobs, 2011). Facilitators must also be able to assess which clients they can assist given the facilitators' level of skills, to describe their services and aspects of the group experience, to engender trust and confidence, and to answer questions about client rights and responsibilities, confidentiality, and expectations for change.

The purpose of this chapter is to provide an introduction to group work for those interested in pursuing follow-up education and experience in the context of master's and doctoral graduate preparation. The content of this chapter focuses upon the history of group work, types of groups, stages of group life, characteristics of group facilitators, responsibilities and interventions in groups, myths connected with group work, and issues and ethics of group work.

The History of Group Work

Beginnings

As noted by Vriend (1985), the first half of the twentieth century was characterized by lively interest, experimentation, and research in the promising new field of group dynamics.

Behavior in small groups, leadership styles, membership roles, communication variables, and so on were all examined and studied for their application to groups in a variety of settings (Corey, 2012; Hare, Borgatta, & Bales, 1967; Johnson & Johnson, 2000). J. H. Pratt (Boston), Jesse. B. Davis (Grand Rapids), J. L. Moreno, Alfred Adler, Samuel R. Slavson, Rudolf Dreikurs, Nathan Ackerman, Gregory Bateson and Virginia Satir were all well-known practitioners who pioneered early approaches to group work (Berg, Landreth, & Fall, 1998).

In 1947, a multidisciplinary group of researchers and practitioners attended a history-making conference in Bethel, Maine, from university and community settings throughout North America. The National Training Laboratory (NTL) in Group Development of the National Education Association held its first "laboratory session" at which T-groups (the "T" is for training) and the laboratory method were born (Bradford, Gibb, & Benne, 1964; Roller, 1997). First, using themselves as experimental subjects, participants at the conference created a laboratory situation in which the behavior of the participants was more important than any effort or technique employed. The situation created a safe place for group members to explore their own behavior, feelings, and the responses of others to them as people separate from social, work, and family roles. Under the direction of the NTL, such conferences continued each summer and the T-group movement grew and achieved national visibility.

As time passed, T-groups appeared on university campuses and in other settings. The T-group provided a fresh concept with tremendous appeal as opportunity was provided for group members to become more "sensitive," to "grow emotionally," and to "realize their human potential." The country began hearing about the "human potential movement" and of exciting developments in California, particularly at the Esalen Institute at Big Sur (Neukrug, 1999) and at the Center for the Studies of the Person founded by Carl R. Rogers and his colleagues. Soon there were a variety of marathon and encounter groups; it was an era of openness, self-awareness, and getting in touch with feelings.

SIDEBAR 9.1

As noted by Stockton (2010), although there was much enthusiasm about group work in the early days of its development as a specialization, "practice" was not evidence based and practioners had little access to research focused on either process or outcome. Group workers operated intuitively to develop the "art" of group counseling and its application to a variety of presenting issues and contexts.

The 1960s and 1970s

The 1960s were a time of social upheaval and questioning. There were riots on campuses and in cities as civil rights groups struggled to raise the consciousness of the nation about unfair discrimination and prejudice. Leaders such as John F. Kennedy and Martin Luther King, Jr., became the idolized champions and international symbols of a people's determination to change a society and to promote social responsibility.

The nation united in grief-stricken disbelief as its heroes were martyred and determination to counter the human rights violations of the decades escalated. As the 1960s ended, the encounter groups movement, emphasizing personal consciousness and connection with others, reached its zenith, then gradually waned as events such as the Charles Manson killings, the Watergate scandal, the first presidential resignation in the history of the United States, the group killings en route to the Munich Olympics, and the rise of fanatic cults made people in all parts of the country question the extent to which permissiveness and "human potential" should be allowed to develop (Janis, 1972; Rowe & Winborn, 1973).

For professionals in education and mental health, however, the 1960s and 1970s were decades of maintained interest in group work despite the highs and lows of societal fervor and dismay. Mental health centers conducted more and more group sessions for clients, and counselor education, counseling psychology, psychology, and social work departments on university campuses instituted more and more course work and supervised experiences in aspects of group work. In 1973, the Association for Specialists in Group Work (ASGW) was formed and by 1974 (Berg, Landreth, & Fall, 1998; Neukrug, 1999) it had become a division of the American Counseling Association (at that time named the American Personnel and Guidance Association). Similar developments took place in the context of other large professional groups such as the American Psychological Association and the National Association of Social Workers.

SIDEBAR 9.2

Initially, many practitioners who were called upon to facilitate groups, applied theoretical frameworks to group work that were really developed for use in individual counseling. Although some aspects of theories of individual counseling can be applied to group work, those theories (e.g., psychodynamic, REBT, Reality, CBT, Gestalt, etc.) were not originally conceptualized with group work in mind. Currently, many textbooks written for the education and supervision of group work specialiasts still devote an unusually large portion of the content to the application of theories for individual counseling to group work.

The 1980s

The 1980s witnessed increasing interest in group work and in working with special populations. Groups were started for alcoholics, adult children of alcoholics, incest victims, adults molested as children, persons who are overweight, under-assertive persons, and those who have been victims of violent crimes. Other groups were begun for the elderly, for those dealing with death and other losses, for people with eating disorders, smokers, and the victims of the Holocaust (Neukrug, 1999). This increasing specialization brought with it an increasing need for higher standards for preparation of the group work specialist, as evidenced by the development of training standards for group work specialists (ASGW, 1983, 1992) and the inclusion in the standards of the Council for Accreditation of Counseling and Related Educational Programs (CACREP, 1988) of specific group work specialist preparation guidelines for the graduate-level university educator to follow. At the same time, this increasing specialization has brought with it a reliance on self-help groups composed of individuals who share a specific affliction. Usually, such groups are not facilitated by a professional and this set of circumstances can be in conflict with the values and standards of professional group workers unless they have given some thought to how they might be involved (Corey, 2012).

The 1990s

The escalating interest in group work and in working with special populations so evident in the decade of the 1980s continued into the last decade of the century. The 1983 ASGW standards for training of group counselors was revised and a new set of standards was adopted in 1991 (ASGW, 1991). Although the 1991 standards built on the 1983 standards emphasizing the knowledge, skills, and supervised experience necessary for the preparation of group workers, the newer standards broadened the conception of group work, clarified the difference between core competencies and specialization requirements, defined the four prominent varieties of group work, and eliminated the previously made distinctions among different kinds of supervised field experience (Conyne, Wilson, Kline, Morran, & Ward, 1993). In addition, CACREP, in its 1994, 2001, and 2009 revisions of accreditation standards, reemphasized the importance of group work by identifying principles of group dynamics, group leadership styles, theories of group counseling, group counseling methods, approaches used for other types of group work, and ethical considerations as essential curricular elements for all counselor education programs (CACREP, 1994, 2001, 2009).

Groups in the 21st Century

Technology has taken the use of groups to computers through the use of chat rooms, live meeting rooms, list serves, etc. Support groups for recovering addicts, cancer survivors, individuals with eating disorders, Alzheimers care givers, and individuals interested in a variety of other theme focused topics that can be addressed in groups who connect through use of the internet, are becoming more and more common.

On-line courses offered by numerous counselor education programs and departments across the country often require course participants to engage in group work to complete course requirements. Sometimes this group work is experienced exclusively on an electronic basis; in most instances, graduate students are required to facilitate a group in their community while an on-site supervisor provides regular supervision.

SIDEBAR 9.3

Growing numbers of universities are offering courses such as group counseling, practicum, and internship on-line. Courses that are as "applied" and experiential as these, however, must include on the ground, supervised experiences if the university offering such on-line courses holds CACREP accreditation.

Although the issues and ethics of group work will be overviewed at the end of this chapter, it should be noted that the practice of the group work professional requires increasing levels of expertise and an enhanced ability to participate in and apply the results of needed research. The history-making national conference for group work specialists conceptualized and sponsored by ASGW in early 1990 in Florida and repeated during subsequent years and into the present in other parts of the country, symbolizes the importance of group work to the clients served by the counseling and human development professional.

Types of Groups

Most introductory textbooks for counselor education students begin the discussion of group work by attempting to make distinctions among group therapy, group counseling, and group guidance. In general, *group therapy* is described as being longer term, more remedially and therapeutically focused, and more likely to be facilitated by a facilitator with doctoral-level preparation and a more "clinical" orientation. *Group counseling* may be differentiated from *group therapy* by its more developmental focus on conscious problems, by the fact that it is not aimed at major personality changes, by an orientation toward short-term issues, and by the fact that it is not as concerned with the treatment of the more severe psychological and behavioral disorders (Corey, 2012; Gazda, Ginter, & Horne, 2001). The term *group guidance* usually is descriptive of a classroom group in a K through 12 setting in which the leader presents information or conducts mental health education. In contrast to a group therapy or group counseling situation involving no more than eight to ten group participants, a group guidance experience could involve twenty to forty group participants, lessening opportunities for individual participation, and facilitator observation and intervention.

For the purposes of this chapter ASGW's definitions of the four group work specialty types are presented next as a point of departure for classifying groups (Conyne et al., 1993). The reader may wish to do additional reading relative to group "types" from sources such as Capuzzi, Gross, and Stauffer, (2010), Corey (2012), Dinkmeyer and Muro (1979), Gazda (1984), Gladding (2008), Neukrug (1999), and Ohlsen (1977).

Task/Work Groups

The group worker who specializes in promoting the development and functioning of task and work groups seeks to support such groups in the process of improving their function and performance. Task and work group specialists employ principles of group dynamics, organizational development, and team building to enhance group members' skills in group task accomplishment and group maintenance. The scope of practice for these group work specialists includes normally functioning individuals who are members of naturally occurring task or work groups operating within a specific organizational context.

SIDEBAR 9.4

Being a member of a search committee in a work setting for the purpose of identifying, inteviewing, and hiring is a good example of a task group that many experience. The group is formed to carry out a specifically identified purpose (hiring a new employee) and it disbands once the goal or purpose has been achieved. It does not usually convene on a long-term basis as might be the case for a counseling or psychotherapy group.

It is important to note that graduate course work for specialists in task and work groups should include at least one specialization course in organizational management and development. Ideally, course work should be undertaken in the broad area of organizational psychology, management, and development to develop an awareness of organizational life and how task and work groups function within the organization. In addition, a task/work group specialist might also develop skill in organizational assessment, training, program development, consultation, and program evaluation.

Clinical instruction for training in working with task and work groups should include supervised practice in leading or co-leading a task/work group appropriate to the age and clientele of the group leader's specialty area(s) (such as school counseling, community counseling, mental health counseling, etc.).

Guidance/Psycho-educational Groups

The psycho-educational group specialist educates group participants. Such participants may be informationally deficient (Hall, Rushing, & Khurshid, 2011) in some area (e.g., coping with bullying, developmental transitions, or stress management). The scope of practice for facilitators of psycho-educational groups includes essentially normally functioning individuals who are "at risk" for, an environmental threat (e.g., AIDS, drug use or abuse, etc.), who are approaching a developmental transition point (e.g., new parents), or who are in the midst of coping with a life crisis (such as suicide of a loved one). The primary goal in psycho-educational group work is to prevent the future development of dysfunctional behaviors.

SIDEBAR 9.5

School counselors frequently conduct psychoeducational groups. The focus could be on any one of a number of topics such as refusal skills, bullying, or apprpriate use of social media. Membership in these groups is usually comprised of students in classroom settings and, although the information provided may faciliatate the health and wellness of the members, the individual agendas of members of the groups are not addressed in as much depth as would be the case in a counseling or psychotherapy group because of the larger size of such groups.

Course work for facilitators of psycho-educational groups should include at least one specialization course that provides information about community psychology, health and wellness promotion, and program development and evaluation. Ideally, psycho-educational group specialists would also undertake course work in curriculum design, group training methods, and instructional techniques. Psycho-educational group specialists should also acquire knowledge about the topic areas in which they intend to work (such as AIDS, substance abuse prevention, grief and loss, coping with transition, parent effectiveness training, etc.).

Clinical instruction for preparing to facilitate psycho-educational groups should include supervised practice in leading or co-leading a psycho-educational group appropriate to the age and clientele of the group leader's specialty area(s) (such as school counseling, community counseling, mental health counseling, etc.).

Counseling Groups

The group worker who specializes in group counseling focuses on assisting group participants to resolve the usual, yet often difficult, problems of living by stimulating interpersonal support and group problem solving (Steen, 2011). Group counselors support participants in developing their existing interpersonal problem-solving competencies so that they may become more able to handle future problems of a similar nature. The scope of practice for their group work includes nonsevere career, educational, personal, interpersonal, social, and developmental concerns of essentially normally functioning individuals.

Graduate course work for specialists in group counseling should include multiple courses in human development, health promotion, and group counseling. Group counseling specialists should have in-depth knowledge in the broad areas of normal human development, problem identification, and treatment of normal personal and interpersonal problems of living.

Clinical instruction for counseling groups should include supervised practice in leading or co-leading a counseling group appropriate to the age and clientele of the group leader's specialty area(s) (such as community counseling, mental health counseling, school counseling, etc.).

Psychotherapy Groups

The specialist in group psychotherapy helps individual group members remediate in-depth psychological problems or reconstruct major personality dimensions. The group psychotherapist differs from specialists in task/work groups, psychoeducational groups, or counseling groups in that the group psychotherapist's scope of practice is focused on people with acute or chronic mental or emotional disorders characterized by marked distress, impairment in functioning, or both.

Graduate course work for training in group psychotherapy should include multiple courses in the development, assessment, and treatment of serious or chronic personal and interpersonal dysfunction. The group psychotherapist must develop in-depth knowledge in the broad areas of normal and abnormal human development, diagnosis, treatment of psychopathology, and group psychotherapy. Clinical instruction for working with psychotherapy groups should include supervised practice in leading or co-leading a psychotherapy group appropriate to the age and clientele of the group leader's specialty area(s) (such as mental health counseling, community counseling, etc.).

SIDEBAR 9.6

It is interesting to note that, in the earlier days of the history of group work, a distinguishing characteristic of the difference between someone facilitating a counseling group and someone facilitating a psychotherapy group was the extent and depth of the training of the person doing the facilitation. Psychologists were considered to have completed superior coursework and supervised practice experiences; currently there is little difference in the preparation of a Ph.D. in Counseling and a Ph.D in psychology. Both degrees include course work and supervised practice in diagnosis and treatment planning, psychopathology, the psychopharmocological aspects of counseling and psychotherapy, etc.

Developmental Stages in Groups

Bruce Tuckman's stage model of group development (storming, norming, performing, and adjourning) was first published in 1965 and still remains one of the most commonly cited models for group program design and facilitation. In an outstanding article, David G. Zimpfer (1986) pointed out that much has been written about the developmental phases or stages through which a small group progresses over time (Capuzzi, Gross, & Stauffer, 2010; Corey, 2012; Bales, 1950; Braaten, 1975; Golembiewski, 1962; Hare, 1973; Hill & Gruner, 1973; Thelen & Dickerman, 1949).

He also noted that recent contributions to this topic range from descriptive, classificatory schemes (such as the stages presented by Corey in 2012) to detailed analyses of a single phase of group development. Zimpfer's recommendation to the group work specialist is to select the theory or model of small-group development that applies to the kind of group to be conducted. This recommendation was resubstantiated by Cassidy (2007). There are many additional resources that describe small group development that can be read as a follow-up to this chapter and as a follow-up to Zimpfer's recommendation (Donigan & Malanti, 1997; Gladding, 2008; Goldstein & Noonan, 1999; Jacobs, Masson, & Harvill, 1998; MacKenzie, 1997).

After studying a variety of models and conceptualizations of the developmental stages of groups and calling upon our own collective experience, we propose a composite conceptualization (Capuzzi, Gross, & Stauffer, 2010) of the stages of group life. In our view, the developmental process consists of four stages: (a) definitive stage, (b) personal involvement stage, (c) group involvement stage, and (d) enhancement and closure stage.

Definitive Stage

The length of time associated with this stage of group development varies with the group and is best explained in terms of the individual group member's definition of the purpose of the group, commitment, and involvement in it, and the degree of self-disclosure he or she is willing to do. Characterizing this stage of development are questions such as: Whom can I trust? Where will I find support? Will others knowing about me hurt me? How much of myself am I willing to share? These questions, and the lack of immediate answers, typify members in the definitive stage as increased anxiety, excitement, nervousness and self-protective dialogue increase. The dialogue during this stage tends to be of a social nature (small talk) as the members test the waters of group involvement. To help group members deal effectively with the definitive stage, the group leader needs skills in dealing with issues such as trust, support, safety, self-disclosure and confidentiality.

In the definitive stage in group development, individuals define, demonstrate, and experiment with their own role definitions; they "test" the temperament, personality, and behaviors of other group members; and they arrive at conclusions about how personally involved they are willing to become. The individual's movement through this stage can be enhanced or impeded by the group's makeup (age, gender, number, values, attitudes, socioeconomic status, and so on), the leadership style (active, passive, autocratic, democratic), the group's setting (formal, informal, uncomfortable, relaxed), the personal dynamics the individual brings to the group (shy, aggressive, verbal, nonverbal), and the individual's perceptions of trust and acceptance from other group members and from the group leader.

The definitive stage is crucial in group development because this stage can determine for the individual (and, therefore, for the group) future involvement, commitment, and individual, and group success or failure as the group progresses.

Personal Involvement Stage

Once individuals have drawn conclusions about their commitment and role in the group, they move into the personal involvement stage of group development. This stage is best described in terms of member-to-member interactions—the sharing of personal information, confrontation with other group members, power struggles, and the individual's growing identity as a group member. Statements such as "I am," "I fear," "I need," and "I care" are characteristic of this stage of group involvement. Through speech and behaviors, the individual member demonstrates the degree of personal sharing he or she is willing to invest and confirms the commitment made during the definitive stage.

The personal involvement stage is one of action, reaction, and interaction. Both fight and flight are represented in this stage as individuals strive to create a role within the group. This creating process often involves intense member-to-member interactions followed by a retreat to regroup and become involved again. The interactions that ensue not only enhance the member's place within the group but also aid in firmly establishing the group as an entity in its own right.

The personal involvement stage offers the individual the opportunity to try out various behaviors, affirm or deny perceptions of self and others, receive feedback in the form of words or behaviors, and begin the difficult process self-evaluation. Individual involvement in this stage of group development is critical to the eventual outcome of the group.

Group Involvement Stage

Because of the information about self gained in the personal involvement stage, group members move into the group involvement stage, characterized by self-evaluation and self-assessment of behavior, attitudes, values, and methods used in relating to others and by members' channeling their energies to better meet group goals and purposes. During this stage, the term *member* and the term *group* become synonymous. Degrees of cooperation and cohesiveness replace conflict and confrontation as members, now more confident in their role in the group, direct more of their attention to what is best for the group and all its members. This stage reveals increasing role clarification, intimacy, problem exploration, group solidarity, compromise, conflict resolution, and risk taking. The group, with its purposes and goals, is merging with the individual purposes and goals of its members. Individual agendas are being replaced by group agendas and the members are identifying more with the group. Bonding is taking place between members as they join forces to enhance the group and, in turn, enhance self in relation to the group. Members grow protective of other group members and of the group itself. The group and its membership take on a special significance unique to those who are part of the process. This melding of member and group purposes and goals is necessary to the group's ongoing success.

Enhancement and Closure Stage

The final stage in a group's life is often described as the most exhilarating but also the saddest aspect of group work. The exhilaration stems from the evaluation and reevaluation that are so much a part of the final stage. The evaluative aspect consists of reevaluation of the group process and individual and group assessment of change, in conjunction with individual and group reinforcement of individual member change, and a commitment to continue self-analysis and growth. Members have an opportunity to share significant growth experiences during the group tenure, and they receive feedback, generally positive, from other group members and the leader. Members are encouraged to review the process of the group and to measure changes that have taken place since their first entering the group to this period just before closure. Member statements at this stage of group development tend to be along the line of: "I was. . . now I am," "I felt. . . now I feel," "I didn't. . . now I do" and "I couldn't. . . now I can."

The sadness in this final stage centers on leaving an environment that provided safety, security, and support and individuals who offered encouragement, friendship, and positive feedback. A major concern seems to be whether the individual will ever be able to replace what he or she found in the group and be able to take what was learned in the group and apply it elsewhere. The answer to both questions is generally yes, but the individual is too close to the experience to have this self-assurance. Our experience indicates that this stage often ends with members' unwritten agreement to continue group involvement and, more specifically, to continue contact with members of the present group. Most group members find, after distancing themselves from the group, that neither of these activities is essential. The gains they made from the group experience will serve them well as they move into other facets of their lives.

The movement from group initiation to group termination varies. Groups differ in this movement process for a myriad of reasons, and no one conceptualization has all the answers or addresses all the issues inherent in the group process. This framework can provide, however, guidelines for working with groups.

SIDEBAR 9.7

The authors of this chapter realize that a stage theory, such as ours, conceptualizes the movement of a group from one stage to the next but a stage theory is not meant to imply a lock-step kind of progression. It is often the case that, because of something that happens during a group session or to an individual member of the group between sessions, a group can regress to an earlier stage of group development.

When this occurs, it is up to the counselor to initiate a discussion of what has happened to enable members of the group to understand what has occurred so members can regain the momentum, cohesion, and understanding of each other that had been achieved in previous sessions.

Characteristics of Group Facilitators

Many writers who are expert in group counseling have described the personal traits and characteristics of effective group counselors (Capuzzi, Gross, & Stauffer, 2010; Corey, 2012; Dinkmeyer & Muro, 1979; Gladding, 2008; Kottler, 1983). As expressed by Gerald Corey in 2004:

> Group leaders can acquire extensive theoretical and practical knowledge of group dynamics and be skilled in diagnostic and technical procedures yet be ineffective in stimulating growth and change in the members of their groups. Leaders bring to every group their personal qualities, values, and life experiences. To promote growth in the members' lives, leaders need to live growth-oriented lives themselves. To foster honest self-investigation in others, they need to have the courage

to engage in self-appraisal. If they hope to inspire others to break away from deadening ways of being, they need to be willing to seek new experiences themselves. In short, the most effective group direction is found in the kind of life the group members see the leader demonstrating and not in the words they hear the leader saying. (p. 25)

We believe that there are characteristics that the effective group leader must possess in order to do an effective job of facilitating group process. The reader is directed to sources such as Arbuckle (1975), Carkhuff and Berenson (1977), Jourard (1971), Truax and Carkhuff (1967), and Yalom (1975) for earlier readings on this topic. Corey's presentation is summarized here as a constructive point of departure for the beginning counselor.

Presence

The leader's ability to be emotionally present as group members share their experience is important. Leaders who are in touch with their own life experiences and associated emotions are usually better able to communicate empathy and understanding because of being able to relate to similar circumstances or emotions.

Personal Power

Personal power comes from a sense of self-confidence and a realization of the influence the leader has on a group. Personal power that is channeled in a way that enhances the ability of each group member to identify and build upon strengths, overcome problems, and cope more effectively with stressors is both essential and "curative."

Courage

Group facilitators must be courageous. They must take risks by expressing their reactions to aspects of group process, confronting, sharing a few life experiences, acting on a combination of intuition and observation, and directing the appropriate portion of the group movement and discussion.

Willingness to Confront Oneself

It takes courage to deal with group members; it is not easy to role model, confront, convey empathy, and achieve a good balance between catalyzing interaction and allowing the group to "unfold." It also takes courage on the part of the group leader to confront self. As Corey (2000) so aptly stated:

Self-confrontation can take the form of posing and answering questions such as these:
- Why am I leading groups? What am I getting from this activity?
- Why do I behave as I do in a group? What impact do my attitudes, values, biases, feelings, and behaviors have on the people in the group?
- What needs of mine are served by being a group leader?
- Do I ever use the groups I lead to satisfy my personal needs at the expense of the members' needs? (p. 30)

Sincerity and Authenticity

Sincerity on the part of a group counselor is usually considered to be related to the leader's genuine interest in the welfare of the group and each individual group member. Sincerity also relates to the leader's ability to be direct and to encourage each member to explore aspects of self that could easily be distorted or denied completely. Effective leaders are able to be real, congruent, honest, and open as they respond to the interactions in a group. Authenticity means that the leader knows who he or she really is and has a sense of comfort and acceptance about self. Authenticity results in an ability to be honest about feelings and reactions to the group in a way that is constructive to individuals as well as the group as a whole.

Sense of Identity

Group leaders often assist members of a group in the process of clarifying values and becoming "inner" rather than "outer" directed. If the leader of a group has not clarified personal values, meanings, goals, and expectations, it may be difficult to help others with the same process.

Belief in the Group Process and Enthusiasm

Leaders must be positive and enthusiastic about the healing capacity of groups and their belief in the benefits of a group experience. If they are unsure, tentative, or unenthusiastic, the same "tenor" will develop among members of the group. As will be noted in a subsequent discussion of myths, the outcome of a group experience is not totally dependent on the leader; however, the leader does convey messages, nonverbally as well as verbally, that do have an impact on the overall benefit of the experience.

Inventiveness and Creativity

Leaders who can be spontaneous in their approach to a group can often facilitate better communication, insight and personal growth than those who become dependent on structured interventions and techniques. Creative facilitators are usually accepting of members who are different from themselves and flexible about approaching members and

---

SIDEBAR 9.8

Sometimes when beginning graduate students read the discussion of the characterustics of group counselors, they wonder if they should really be thinking about the possibility of being trained to be a group work specialist since the listing may seem overwhelming. Although no one person may be able to be characterized by all of these charactreistics, the list certainly provides a base line for self-assessment. If most of these descriptions can be used to depict what a counselor could bring to group work, it is likely that such a counselor would be a successful facilitator. If the list seems like too much of a "stretch" then perhaps another specialization would be a better "fit".

groups in ways that seem congruent with the particular group. In addition, a certain amount of creativity and spontaneity is necessary to cope with the "unexpected"; in a group situation the leader will continuously be presented with comments, problems, and reactions that could not have been anticipated prior to a given session.

Group Facilitation: Responsibilities and Interventions

Responsibilities

One of the most important responsibilities of counselors interested in becoming group work specialists is to have a thorough understanding of what elements or factors are important in making groups effective in helping those who participate (Stockton, 2010). Even though the group approach is a well-established mode of "treatment," anyone interested in facilitating a group must ask and understand the question of what about groups makes them effective. One difficulty in answering such a question is that the therapeutic change that results from group participation is a result of a complex set of variables including leadership style, membership roles, and aspects of group process.

In a fascinating discussion of this topic, George and Dustin (1988) promote Bloch's (1986) definition of a therapeutic factor as "an element occurring in group therapy that contributes to improvement in a patient's condition and is a function of the actions of the group therapist, the patient, or fellow group members" (p. 679). Although this definition sounds somewhat "clinical," its application to all types of groups is apparent because it helps distinguish among therapeutic elements, conditions for change, and techniques.

Conditions for change are necessary for the operation of therapeutic elements but do not, in and of themselves, have therapeutic force. An example of this is the fact that a sense of belonging and acceptance—a therapeutic element that enhances personal growth in groups—cannot emerge unless the "condition" of the actual presence of several good listeners in the group exists.

Likewise, a technique, such as asking members to talk about a self-esteem inventory they have filled out, does not have a direct therapeutic effect but may be used to enhance a sense of belonging and acceptance (George & Dustin, 1988).

Group work specialists have a responsibility to understand the research that has been done on therapeutic elements of groups so they can develop the skills needed to create a group climate that enhances personal growth. Corsini and Rosenburg (1955) published one of the earlier efforts to produce a classification of therapeutic elements in groups. They abstracted therapeutic factors published in three hundred pre-1955 articles on group counseling and clustered them into nine major categories that are still applicable today:

1. *Acceptance:* a sense of belonging
2. *Altruism:* a sense of being helpful to others
3. *Universalization:* the realization that group members are not alone in the experiencing of their problems
4. *Intellectualization:* the process of acquiring self-knowledge
5. *Reality testing:* recognition of the reality of issues such as defenses and family conflicts
6. *Transference:* strong attachment to either the therapist or other group members
7. *Interaction:* the process of relating to other group members that results in personal growth

8. *Spectator therapy:* growth that occurs through listening to other group members
9. *Ventilation:* the release of feelings that had previously been repressed

In 1957, in an attempt to take the classification of therapeutic elements in groups further, Hill interviewed nineteen group therapists. He proposed the six elements of catharsis, feelings of belongingness, spectator therapy, insights, peer agency (universality), and socialization. Berzon, Pious, and Farson (1963) used group members rather than leaders as the source of information about therapeutic elements. Their classification included:

1. Increased awareness of emotional dynamics
2. Recognizing similarity to others
3. Feeling positive regard, acceptance, and sympathy for others
4. Seeing self as seen by others
5. Expressing self congruently, articulately, or assertively in the group
6. Witnessing honesty, courage, openness, or expressions of emotionality in others
7. Feeling warmth and closeness in the group
8. Feeling responded to by others
9. Feeling warmth and closeness generally in the group
10. Ventilating emotions

A very different set of therapeutic elements connected with group experience was proposed by Ohlsen in 1977. His list differs from earlier proposals in that it emphasizes client attitudes about the group experience. Ohlsen's paradigm included fourteen elements that he labeled as "therapeutic forces":

1. Attractiveness of the group
2. Acceptance by the group
3. Expectations
4. Belonging
5. Security within the group
6. Client readiness
7. Client commitment
8. Client participation
9. Client acceptance of responsibility
10. Congruence
11. Feedback
12. Openness
13. Therapeutic tension
14. Therapeutic norms

In what is now considered a landmark classification of "curative factors," Yalom (1970, 1975) proposed a list of therapeutic elements based on research he and his colleagues conducted:

1. Instillation of hope
2. Universality
3. Imparting of information
4. Altruism

5. The corrective recapitulation of the primary family group
6. Development of socializing techniques
7. Imitative behavior
8. Interpersonal learning
9. Group cohesiveness
10. Catharsis
11. Existential factors

SIDEBAR 9.9

Members of the American Counseling Association (ACA), were fortunate to be able to enjoy the comments of Irving Yalom as he gave the major keynote address during the 2012 annual conference. The interesting thing about his presentation was the fact that, even though he has been a prominent figure in the profession for decades, he still possesses the same ability to inspire counselors to want to be the best they can be for their clients. Although a group counselor cannot engender confidence and trust on the part of group members through charisma alone (deviod of the necessary knowledge and skills requirements for a successful group worker), inherent personal characteristics certainly enhance the healing power of the facilitator.

It is not possible to present all the possibilities for viewing the therapeutic elements of a positive group experience. It is possible, however, to encourage the beginning counselor to study the research and literature on group work (Akos et.al., 2007) relating to these elements prior to facilitating or co-facilitating groups under close supervision.

In an interesting discussion of facilitator responsibilities, Ohlsen and Ferreira (1994) discuss the topic from a very practical perspective. Understanding which clients can be helped through participation in a group; being able to describe a potential group experience to a client; understanding how to conduct an intake or pre-group screening interview; teaching group members how to be good clients and good helpers; mastering skills for structuring, norm setting, and feedback; and recognizing when to terminate a group and assist members to continue their growth after the group terminates are among the responsibilities Ohlsen and Ferreira (1994) address. We recommend further reading on this topic in textbooks focusing solely on group work and in the *The Journal for Specialists in Group Work* as the reader pursues information on the role of the group work specialist.

Just as the importance of understanding the responsibilities of a group facilitator cannot be stressed enough, the topic of interventions or techniques used by facilitators is important to consider.

Interventions

Numerous approaches to the topic of intervention strategies for groups can be found in the literature on groups. Corey (2012), in discussing the application of a variety of theoretical frameworks to group work, approached the topic by discussing active listening, restating, clarifying, summarizing, questioning, interpreting, confronting, reflecting feelings, supporting, empathizing, facilitating, initiating, setting goals, evaluating, giving feedback, suggesting, protecting, disclosing oneself, modeling, linking, blocking, and terminating and as well as numerous theory specific techniques. Dinkmeyer and Muro (1979) discussed the topic by focusing upon promoting cohesiveness, summarizing, promoting interaction, resolving conflicts, tone setting, structuring and limit setting, blocking, linking, providing support, reflecting, protecting, questioning, and regulating. Bates, Johnson, and Blaker (1982) emphasized confrontation, attending behavior, feedback, use of questions, levels of interaction, and opening and closing a session. They also presented the four major functions of group leaders as traffic director, model, interaction catalyst, and communication facilitator.

Individuals new to the profession of counseling may better relate to the topic of intervention strategies by becoming familiar with circumstances during which the group leader must take responsibility for intervening in the group's "process." A helpful model (and a favorite of ours) is that presented by Dyer and Vriend in 1973 in terms of ten occasions when intervention is required:

1. *A group member speaks for everyone.* It is not unusual for a member of a group to say something like, "We think we should . . . " "This is how we all feel," or "We were wondering why. . . ." This happens when an individual does not feel comfortable making a statement such as "I think we should . . ." or "I am wondering why. . ." or when an individual group member is hoping to engender support for a point of view. The problem with allowing the 'we' syndrome to operate in a group is that it inhibits individual members from expressing individual feelings and thoughts. Appropriate interventions on the part of the group leader might be, "You mentioned 'we' a number of times. Are you speaking for yourself or for everyone?" or "What do each of you think about the statement that was just made?"

2. *An individual speaks for another individual in the group.* "I think I know what he means" or "She is not really saying how she feels; I can explain it for her" are statements that one group member may make for another. When one person in the group speaks for another it often means that a judgment has been made about the capacity of the other person to communicate or that the other person is about to self-disclose "uncomfortable" information. Regardless of the motivation behind such a circumstance, the person who is allowing another group member to do the "talking" needs to evaluate why this is happening and whether the same thing occurs outside the group. In addition, the "talker" needs to evaluate the inclination to make decisions and/or rescue others.
   Appropriate interventions include saying, "Did Jim state your feelings more clearly than you can?" or "How does it feel to have someone rescue you?" Statements such as "Did you feel that June needed your assistance?" or "Do you find it difficult to hold back when you think you know what someone else is going to say?" might also be possible.

3. *A group member focuses on persons, conditions, or events outside the group.* Often group counseling sessions can turn into "gripe sessions." Complaining about a colleague, friend, or a partner can be enjoyable for group members if they are allowed to reinforce each other. The problem with allowing such emphasis to occur is that such a process erroneously substantiates that others are at fault and that group members do not have to take responsibility for aspects of their behavior.
   Possible interventions for the group leader include: "You keep talking about your wife as the cause of your unhappiness. Isn't it more important to ask yourself what

contributions you can make to improve your relationship?" Or "Does complaining about someone else really mean you think you would be happier if he or she could change?"

4. *Someone seeks the approval of the leader or a group member before or after speaking.* Some group members seek nonverbal acceptance from the leader or another group member (a nod, a glance, a smile). Such individuals may be intimidated by authority figures or personal strength or have low self-esteem and seek sources of support and acceptance outside themselves. One possible intervention is for the leader to look at another member, forcing the speaker to change the direction of his or her delivery. Another possibility is to say something like, "You always look at me as you speak, almost as if you are asking permission."

5. *Someone says, "I don't want to hurt her feelings so I won't say what I'd like to say."* It is not unusual for such a sentiment to be expressed in a group, particularly in the early stages. Sometimes this happens when a member thinks another member of the group is too fragile for feedback; other times such reluctance is because the provider of the potential feedback is concerned about being "liked" by other group members. The group leader should explore reasons for apprehension about providing feedback, which can include asking the group member to check with the person to whom feedback may be directed to determine whether such fears are totally valid.

6. *A group member suggests that his or her problems are due to someone else.* Although this item overlaps with item 3, this situation represents a different problem from a "group gripe" session. A single group member may periodically attribute difficulties and unhappiness to someone else. Interventions such as "Who is really the only person who can be in charge of you?" or "How can other people determine your mood so much of the time?" are called for in such a case. We are not suggesting a stance that would be perceived as lacking empathy and acceptance. It is, however, important to facilitate responsibility for self on the part of each group member.

7. *An individual suggests, "I've always been that way."* Such a suggestion is indicative of irrational thinking and lack of motivation to change. Believing that the past determines all one's future is something that a group member can believe to such an extent that his or her future growth is inhibited. The group leader must assist such a member to identify thinking errors that lead to lack of effectiveness in specific areas. Such a member needs to learn that he or she is not doomed to repeat the mistakes of the past. Possible statements that will stimulate examination of faulty thinking and assumptions are "You're suggesting that your past has such a hold over you that you will never be any different" or "Do you feel that everyone has certain parts of their life over which they have no control?"

8. *Someone in the group suggests, "I'll wait, and it will change."* Often, group members are willing to talk about their self-defeating behavior during a group session but are not willing to make an effort outside the group to behave differently. At times, they take the position that they can postpone action and things will correct themselves. A competent group leader will help members develop strategies for doing something about their problems outside the group and will develop a method of "tracking" or "checking in" with members to evaluate progress.

9. *Discrepant behavior appears.* Group leader intervention is essential when discrepancies occur in a member's behavior in the group. Examples of such discrepancies include a difference in what a member is currently saying and what he or she said earlier, a lack of congruence between what a member is saying and what he or she is doing in the

group, a difference between how a member sees himself or herself and how others in the group see him or her, or a difference between how a member reports feelings and how nonverbal cues communicate what is going on inside. Interventions used to identify discrepancies may be confrontational in nature because the leader usually needs to describe the discrepancies noted so that the group member can begin to identify, evaluate, and change aspects of such behavior.

10. *A member bores the group by rambling.* Sometimes members use talking as a way of seeking approval. At times, such talking becomes "over talk." The leader can ask other members to react to the "intellectualizer" and let such a person know how such rambling affects others. If such behavior is not addressed, other members may develop a sense of anger and hostility toward the "offender."

Johnson and Johnson (2000) also noted a number of situations that may require immediate intervention on the part of the group facilitator:

11. *A member responds with a rehearsed or often used statement.* Sometimes members do not know what to say after another member of the group has shared. This may be due to discomfort related to the speaker's topic, strong emotion precipitated by the sharing that has just taken place, "unfinished business" similar to that of speaker, or a number of other reasons. In an attempt to be responsive or fill a silence, the member may comment in a way that is similar to how he or she responds whenever discomfort or strong emotion is experienced. The comment may not fit the context and seem inappropriate, insensitive, or even unrelated. The leader may need to ask that member to clarify or respond differently so that the group can continue their work more effectively. This may even lead to some introspection and growth on the part of the member who misspoke.

12. *A member remains silent or non-participatory.* When a member remains silent while other group members actively participate in the group experience, it may encourage other group members to wonder why that member has chosen to be so inactive. Sometimes other members fantasize about what the silent member is like and begin to resent the silence and resent the group leader for allowing that member to be so non-participatory. Members can become so agitated that they may begin to make demands on the silent member and blame or scapegoat the member for things that occur in the group. It behooves the group leader to be invitational with such a member so that members of the group do not misinterpret the silence.

13. *A member's expectations for the group are not met.* Sometimes members enter groups with a preconceived idea of what the group will be like. When such expectations are not met, the member could respond in any number of ways: withdrawal, confrontation of the group leader, disagreements with other members of the group, ventilation of anger, etc. The group leader will need to encourage the member to share the reasons behind the discontent; sometimes doing so can lead to a resolution of the difficulties being experienced by the member and enhance the quality of the group experience for all concerned.

14. *A member of the group wants all the "air time".* There are instances in which a high need member of the group demands to be the sole focus of the attention of the group leader and the other group members. In such a circumstance, it may be difficult for anyone else to participate unless the facilitator intervenes. Such an intervention would need to be done in a way that communicates respect for the needs of the member and, at the same time, lets other members of the group know that they, too, are important. A statement such as "I know how important this is to you. Let me see

if I can accurately summarize so we can come back to this after other members have a chance to participate" may be necessary on the part of the group leader. Otherwise, members of the group will start wondering if one member will be allowed to take up all the time and question the value of the group experience.

15. *A group member blocks the expression of intense emotions by other members of the group.* Sometimes strong emotion makes a member feel uncomfortable and unsure of what to say. This could happen because of what the member has been taught about what emotions are appropriately shared or even if they should be shared. This could also occur when the emotion and experience mirrors similar unresolved issues of the member attempting to cut off such expression. The group leader would need to respond to such attempts and encourage the member to be introspective and aware of the tendencies and reasons for such "blocking".

SIDEBAR 9.10

The preceding list of suggestions about how to respond to members of a group is not an exhaustive listing; it is, however, typical of the kinds of skills a group work specialist has to have to be an effective facilitator. This skills set develops over time and can become second nature with experience and practice.

Berg, Landreth, and Fall (1998) and Jacobs, Masson, and Harvill (1998) are two sources of additional information on the topic of the leader's role in intervening in the group's "process" because of what individual members are doing or leaving unsaid.

In addition to the interventions described, the reader should be alerted to the necessity to be prepared to resolve the problem of resistance in groups. Clark (1992), Higgs (1992), Ohlsen and Ferreira (1994), Ormont (1993) and Schimmel and Jacobs (2011) provide some excellent guidelines on this aspect of the group leader's role.

Myths Connected with Group Work

Counselors who are group work specialists are usually quite enthusiastic about the benefits for clients of participation in a small group. Indeed, the outcomes of a competently facilitated group experience can be such that personal growth occurs. Often the memory of such an experience has an impact on clients well into the future. On the other hand, group work, as with other forms of therapeutic assistance (such as individual or family), can be for better or for worse (Carkhuff, 1969). Many group workers follow a belief system that can be challenged by empirical facts.

Beginning counselors are well advised to be aware of a number of myths connected with group work so they don't base their "practices" on a belief system not supported by research (Anderson, 1985; Capuzzi, Gross, & Stauffer, 2010; Kalodner & Riva, 1997).

Myth 1: "Everyone Benefits from Group Experience"

Groups do provide benefits. The research on the psychosocial outcomes of group work demonstrate that groups are a powerful modality for learning, which can be used outside the group experience (Bednar & Lawlis, 1971; Gazda & Peters, 1975; Parloff & Dies, 1978). There are times, however, when membership in a group can be harmful (Dykeman, 2010). Some research shows that one of every ten group members can be hurt (Lieberman, Yalom, & Miles, 1973). The research findings that seem to relate most to individuals who get injured in groups suggest some important principles for the beginning counselor to understand: (1) those who join groups and who have the potential to be hurt by the experience have unrealistic expectations, and (2) these expectations seem to be reinforced by the facilitator who coerces the member to meet them (De Julio, Bentley, & Cockayne, 1979; Lieberman, Yalom, & Miles, 1973; Stava & Bednar, 1979). Prevention of harm requires that the expectations members have for the group are realistic and that the facilitator maintains a reasonable perspective.

Myth 2: "Groups Can Be Composed to Ensure Effective Outcomes"

The fact is that we do not know enough about how to compose groups using the pregroup screening interview. In general, objective criteria (such as age, sex, socioeconomic status, presenting problem) can be used to keep groups homogeneous in some respects, but behavioral characteristics should be selected on a heterogeneous basis (Bertcher & Maple, 1977). The most consistent finding is that it is a good idea to compose a group in such a manner that each member is compatible with at least one other member (Stava & Bednar, 1979). This practice seems to prevent the evolution of neglected isolates or scapegoats in a group.

The essence of group process, in terms of benefit to members and effective outcomes is perceived mutual aid such as helping others, a feeling of belonging, interpersonal learning, and instillation of hope (Butler & Fuhrman, 1980; Capuzzi, Gross, & Stauffer, 2010; Long & Cope, 1980; Yalom, 1975).

Myth 3: "The Group Revolves around the Charisma of the Leader"

It is true that leaders influence groups tremendously, but there are two general findings in the research on groups that should be noted. First, the group, independently of the leader, has an impact on outcomes. Second, the most effective group leaders are those who help the group develop so that members are primary sources of help to one another (Ashkennas & Tandon, 1979; Lungren, 1971).

SIDEBAR 9.11

The topic of charisma as it realtes to the effectiveness of a group facilitator is an interesting one. Certainly, being perceived by group members as a personable communicator, an empathic personality, or a nice-looking person would all be advantages to the facilitator especially during initial and early sessions of the group. However, "charisma" is not a substitute for the knowledge and skills base needed to ensure that the group experience is one considered to be therapeutic from the beginning to the end of the group experience. Those aspiring to become group work specialiats need to be sure they have acquired the education and supervised practice needed to develop the needed expertise to be successful with groups.

As noted by Anderson (1985), research on leadership styles has identified four particular leader functions that facilitate the group's functioning:

1. *Providing:* This is the provider role of relationships and climate-setting through such skills as support, affection, praise, protection, warmth, acceptance, genuineness, and concern.
2. *Processing:* This is the processor role of illuminating the meaning of the process through such skills as explaining, clarifying, interpreting, and providing a cognitive framework for change or translating feelings and experiences into ideas.
3. *Catalyzing:* This is the catalyst role of stimulating interaction and emotional expression through such skills as reaching for feelings, challenging, confronting, and suggesting; using program activities such as structured experiences; and modeling.
4. *Directing:* This is the director role through such skills as setting limits, roles, norms, and goals; managing time; pacing; stopping; interceding; and suggesting procedures. (p. 272)

Providing and processing seem to have a linear relationship to outcomes: the higher the providing (or caring) and the higher the processing (or clarifying), the higher the positive outcomes. Catalyzing and directing have a curvilinear relationship to outcomes; too much or too little catalyzing or directing results in lower positive outcomes (Lieberman et al., 1973).

Myth 4: "Leaders Can Direct through the Use of Structured Exercises or Experiences"

Structured exercises create early cohesion (Levin & Kurtz, 1974; Lieberman et al., 1973); they help create early expression of positive and negative feelings. However, they restrict members from dealing with such group themes as affection, closeness, distance, trust, mistrust, genuineness, and lack of genuineness. All these areas form the very basis for the group process and should be dealt with in a way that is not hampered by a large amount of structure. The best principle around which to plan and use structured exercises to get groups started and to keep them going can best be stated as "to over plan and to under use."

Myth 5: "Therapeutic Change in Groups Comes about through a Focus on Here-and-Now Experiences"

Much of the research on groups indicates that corrective emotional experiences in the here and now of the group increase the intensity of the experience for members (Levine, 1971; Lieberman et al., 1973; Snortum & Myers, 1971; Zimpfer, 1967). The intensity of emotional experiences does not, however, appear to be related to outcomes. Members who develop "insight" or cognitive understanding of emotional experiences in the group and can transfer that understanding into their lives outside the group achieve higher level outcomes in groups. The Gestaltist's influence on groups in the 1960s and 1970s (Perls, 1969) suggested that members should "Lose your mind and come to your senses" and "stay with the here-and-now." Research suggests that members "use your mind and your senses" and "focus on the there and then as well as on the here and now."

Myth 6: "Major Member Learning in Groups Is Derived from Self-Disclosure and Feedback"

There is an assumption that most of the learning of members in a group comes from self-disclosure in exchange for feedback (Jacobs, 1974). To a large extent, this statement is a myth. Self-disclosure and feedback per se make little difference in terms of outcomes (Anchor, 1979; Bean & Houston, 1978). The use of self-disclosure and feedback appears to make the difference (Martin & Jacobs, 1980). Self-disclosure and feedback appear useful only when deeply personal sharing is understood and appreciated and the feedback is accurate (Berzon, Pious, & Farson, 1963; Frank & Ascher, 1951; Goldstein, Bednar, & Yanell, 1979). The actual benefit of self-disclosure and feedback is connected with how these processes facilitate empathy among members. It is empathy, or the actual experience of being understood by other members, that catalyzes personal growth and understanding in the context of a group.

Myth 7 "The Group Facilitator Can Work Effectively with a Group without Understanding Group Process and Group Dynamics"

Groups experience a natural evolution and unfolding of processes and dynamics. Anderson (1979) labeled these stages as those of trust, autonomy, closeness, interdependence, and termination (TACIT). Tuckman (1965) suggested a more dramatic labeling of forming, storming, norming, performing, and adjourning. We suggested a four-stage paradigm earlier in this chapter. Two reviews, which include over two hundred studies of group dynamics and group process (Cohen & Smith, 1976; La Coursiere, 1980), revealed remarkably similar patterns (despite differences in the labels chosen as descriptors) in the evolution of group processes as a group evolves through stages. It is extremely important for group facilitators to understand group processes and dynamics to do a competent job of enhancing membership benefits derived from participation.

Myth 8: "Change Experienced by Group Participation Is Not Maintained over Time"

Groups are powerful! Changes can be maintained by group members as much as six months to a year later even when groups meet for only three or four months (Dykeman, 2010; Lieberman et al., 1973).

Myth 9: "A Group Is a Place to Get Emotionally High"

Feeling good after a group session is a positive outcome but is not the main reason for being in a group in the first place. Some group members have periods of depression after group participation because they do not find elsewhere, on a daily basis, the kind of support they received from other members of the group. Group members should be prepared for this possibility and assisted in their ability to obtain support, when appropriate, from those around them.

Myth 10: "A Group's Purpose Is to Make Members Close to Every Other Member"

Although genuine feelings of intimacy and cohesiveness develop in effective groups, intimacy is the by-product and not the central purpose of the group. Intimacy develops as individual members risk self-disclosure and problem solving and other group members reach out in constructive ways.

Myth 11: "Group Participation Results in Brainwashing"

Professional groups do not indoctrinate members with a particular philosophy of life or a set of rules about how each member "should be." If this does occur in a group, it is truly a breach of professional ethics (Corey, 2012) and an abuse of the group. Group participation encourages members to look within themselves for answers and to become as self-directed as possible.

Myth 12: "To Benefit from a Group, a Member Has to Be Dysfunctional"

Group counseling is as appropriate for individuals who are functioning relatively well and who want to enhance their capabilities as it is for those who are having difficulty with certain aspects of their lives. Groups are not only for dysfunctional people.

Issues and Ethics: Some Concluding Remarks

Although a thorough discussion of issues and ethics in group counseling is beyond the scope of this chapter, it is important for the beginning counselor to be introduced to this topic. The *Professional Standards for Training of Group Workers* (ASGW, 1991, 2000), *Boundary Issues in Counseling* (Herlihy & Corey, 1997), and *Ethical, Legal, and Professional Issues in Counseling* (Remley & Herlihy, 2010) are all excellent points of departure for the counselor interested in groups, as well as *Principles for Diversity-Competent Group Workers*, published in 1999 by the Association for Specialists in Group Work (ASGW). In addition, these resources serve as useful adjuncts to the *Code of Ethics and Standards of Practice* of the American Counseling Association (2005).

ASGW (1991, 2000) recommends that the group work specialist acquire *knowledge competencies* (for example, understanding principles of group dynamics, the roles of members in groups, the contributions of research in group work), *skill competencies* (diagnosing self-defeating behavior in groups, intervening at critical times in group process, using assessment procedures to evaluate the outcomes of a group), and *supervised clinical experience* (such as observing group counseling, co-leading groups with supervision, participating as a member in a group). Interestingly, these very training standards have become an issue with some counselor preparation programs as they struggle to obtain a balance between the didactic and clinical components of the set of educational and supervisory experiences required to prepare an individual to do a competent job of group counseling. The clinical supervisory aspects of preparing the group work specialist are costly for universities, and often counselor educators are encouraged to abandon such efforts in favor of classroom didactics.

Another example of some of the issues connected with group counseling has to do with continuing education after the completion of masters and/or doctoral degree programs. Although the National Board for Certified Counselors (NBCC) requires those who achieve the National Certified Counselor (NCC) credential to obtain one hundred contact hours of continuing education every five years, there is no specification of how much of this professional enhancement activity should be focused on aspects of group work, if group work is the declared area of specialization of an NCC. In time, there may be a specific continuing education requirement for the group work specialist. Readers should refer to ACA's *Code of Ethics and Standards of Practice* (2005) for ethical guidelines pertaining to groups. An interesting earlier document, The *Ethical Guidelines for Group Leaders* (ASGW, 1991), initially helped clarify the nature of ethical responsibilities of the counselor in a group setting. These guidelines presented standards in three areas: (1) the leader's responsibility for providing information about group work to clients, (2) the leader's responsibility for providing group counseling services to clients, and (3) the leader's responsibility for safeguarding the standards of ethical practice. One of the greatest single sources of ethical dilemma in group counseling situations has to do with confidentiality. Except for the few exceptions delineated in ACA's *Code of Ethics and Standards of Practice* (2005) counselors have an obligation not to disclose information about the client without the client's consent. Yet, the very nature of a group counseling situation makes it difficult to ensure that each member of a group will respect the other's right to privacy.

Other issues such as recruitment and informed consent, screening and selection of group members, voluntary and involuntary participation, psychological risks, uses and abuses of group techniques, therapist competence, interpersonal relationships among the members of a group, and follow-up all form the basis for considerable discussion and evaluation. In addition, these issues emphasize the necessity of adequate education, supervision, and advance time to consider the ramifications and responsibilities connected with becoming a group specialist.

Group experiences can be powerful growth-enhancing opportunities for clients, or they can be pressured, stifling encounters to be avoided. Each of us has a professional obligation to assess our readiness to facilitate or cofacilitate a group. Our clients deserve the best experience we can provide.

Summary

The use of groups of all types is increasingly important to the role of the counselor in a variety of settings. As the decades have passed, emphasis has shifted from T-Groups to encounter groups to working with special populations. Self-help groups of all types are flourishing. The ASGW standards for the training of group counselors have received widespread acceptance. ASGW's definitions of the four group work specialty types (task/work, guidance/psychoeducational, counseling, psychotherapy groups), information about stages of group life, and research on the characteristics of group facilitators have also enhanced the ability of the group work specialist to function in the best interests of clients in groups. In addition, the more group work specialists know about their responsibilities and the interventions they need to master, myths connected with group work, and issues and ethics associated with groups, the more competent they will be as facilitators of group experiences. The importance of broad-based education and carefully supervised group practicum and other clinical experiences for group work specialists cannot be overemphasized.

The following Websites contain additional information relating to the chapter topics.

Useful Websites

Association for Specialists in Group Work (ASGW)
http://www.asgw.org/
American Group Psychotherapy Association (AGPA)
http://www.groupsinc.org

American Society of Group Psychotherapy and Psychodrama (ASGPP)
http://www.ASGPP.org
Group Psychology and Group Psychotherapy, Division 49 of APA
http://www.apadivisions.org/division-49/index.aspx

References

Akos, P., Hamm, J. V., Mack, S. G., & Dunaway, M. (2007). Utilizing the developmental influence of peers in middle school groups. *The Journal for Specialists in Group Work, 32*(1), 51–60.

American Counseling Association. (2005). *Code of ethics and standards of practice.* Alexandria, VA: Author.

Anchor, K. N. (1979). High-and-low-risk self-disclosure in group psychotherapy. *Small Group Behavior, 10,* 279–283.

Anderson, J. D. (1979). Social work with groups in the generic base of social work practice. *Social Work with Groups, 2,* 281–293.

Anderson, J. D. (1985). Working with groups: Little-known facts that challenge well-known myths. *Small Group Behavior, 16*(3), 267–283.

Arbuckle, D. (1975). *Counseling and psychotherapy: An existential-humanistic view.* Boston: Allyn & Bacon.

Ashkenas, R., & Tandon, R. (1979). Eclectic approach to small group facilitation. *Small Group Behavior, 10,* 224–241.

Association for Specialists in Group Work. (1991). *Ethical guidelines for group leaders.* Alexandria, VA: Author.

Association for Specialists in Group Work (ASGW). (1983). *Professional standards for training of group counselors.* Alexandria, VA: Author.

Association for Specialists in Group Work. (1992). Professional standards for training of group workers. *The Journal for Specialists in Group Work, 17*(1), 12–19.

Association for Specialists in Group Work. (2000). *Professional standards for the training of group workers.* Alexandria, VA: Author.

Association for Specialists in Group Work. (1991). Professional standards for training of group workers. *Together, 20,* 9–14.

Bales, R. F. (1950). *Interaction process analysis: A method for study of small groups.* Reading, MA: Addison-Wesley.

Bates, M., Johnson, C. D., & Blaker, K. E. (1982*). Group Leadership: A manual for group counseling leaders* (2nd ed.). Denver: Love Publishing.

Bean, B. W., & Houston, B. K. (1978*).* Self-concept and self-disclosure in encounter groups. *Small Group Behavior, 9,* 549–554.

Bednar, R., & Lawlis, G. (1971). Empirical research in group psychotherapy. In S. L. Garfield, & A. E. Bergin (Eds.), *Handbook of psychotherapy and behavior change* (2nd ed., pp. 420–439). New York: Wiley.

Berg, R. C., Landreth, G. L., & Fall, K. A. (1998). *Group counseling: Concepts and procedures* (3rd ed.). Philadelphia, PA: Taylor & Francis.

Bertcher, H. J., & Maple, F. F. (1977). *Creating Groups.* Newbury Park, CA: Sage.

Berzon, B., Pious, C., & Farson, R. (1963). The therapeutic event in group psychotherapy: A study of subjective reports by group members. *Journal of Individual Psychology, 19,* 204–212.

Bloch, S. (1986). Therapeutic factors in group psychotherapy. In A. J. Frances, & R. E. Hales (Eds.), *Annual Review,* (Vol. 5, pp. 678–698). Washington, DC: American Psychiatric Press.

Braaten, L. J. (1975). Developmental phases of encounter groups and related intensive groups. *Interpersonal Development, 5,* 112–129.

Bradford, L. P., Gibb, J. R., & Benne, K. D. (Eds.). (1964). *T-group theory and laboratory method: Innovation in re-education.* New York: John Wiley.

Butler, T., & Fuhriman, A. (1980). Patient perspective on the curative process: A comparison of day treatment and outpatient psychotherapy groups. *Small Group Behavior, 11*, 371–388.

Capuzzi, D., Gross, D. R., & Stauffer, M. D. (2010). *Introduction to group work* (5th ed.). Denver: Love Publishing.

Carkhuff, R. R. (1969). *Helping and human relations: A primer for lay and professional helpers.* Vol. 2: *Practice and research.* New York: Holt, Rinehart & Winston.

Carkhuff, R. R., & Berenson, B. G. (1977). *Beyond counseling and therapy* (2nd ed.). New York: Holt, Rinehart & Winston.

Cassidy, K. (2007). Tuckman revisited: Proposing a new model of group development for practitioners. *Journal of Experiential Education, 20*(3), 413–417.

Clark, A. J. (1992). Defense mechanisms in group counseling. *The Journal for Specialists in Group Work, 17*(3), 151–160.

Cohen, A. M., & Smith, D. R. (1976). *The critical incident in growth groups: Theory and techniques.* La Jolla, CA: University Associates.

Conyne, R. K., Wilson, F. R., Kline, W. B., Morran, D. K., & Ward, D. E. (1993). Training group workers: Implications of the new ASGW training standards for training and practice. *The Journal for Specialists in Group Work, 18*(1), 11–23.

Corey, G. (2000). *Theory and practice of group counseling* (5th ed.). Belmont, CA: Brooks/Cole.

Corey, G. (2004). *Theory and practice of group counseling* (6th ed.). Belmont, CA: Brooks/Cole.

Corey, G. (2012). *Theory and practice of group counseling* (8th ed.). Belmont, CA: Brooks/Cole.

Corsini, R., & Rosenberg, B. (1955). Mechanisms of group psychotherapy: Processes and dynamics. *Journal of Abnormal and Social Psychology, 51,* 406–411.

Council for Accreditation of Counseling and Related Educational Programs (CACREP). (1988). *Accreditation procedures manual and application.* Alexandria, VA: Author.

Council for Accreditation of Counseling and Related Educational Programs (CACREP). (1994, 2001, 2009). *CACREP accreditation standards and procedures manual.* Alexandria, VA: Author.

De Julio, S. J., Bentley, J., & Cockayne, T. (1979). Pregroup norm setting: Effects on encounter group interaction. *Small Group Behavior, 10,* 368–388.

Dinkmeyer, D. C., & Muro, J. J. (1979). *Group counseling: Theory and practice.* (2nd ed.). Itasca, IL: Peacock.

Donigan, J., & Malanti, R. (1997). *Systemic group therapy: A triadic model.* Pacific Grove, Ca: Brooks/Cole.

Dyer, W. W., & Vriend, J. (1973). Effective group counseling process interventions. *Educational Technology, 13*(1), 61–67.

Dykeman, C. (2010). The efficacy of group work. In D. Capuzzi, D. R. Gross, & M. D. Stauffer (Eds), *Introduction to group work* (5th ed., pp. 127–165). Denver: Love Publishing.

Frank, J., & Ascher, E. (1951). The corrective emotional experience in group therapy. *American Journal of Psychiatry, 108,* 126–131.

Frew, J., & Spiegler, M. D. (2013). *Contemporary psychotherapies for a diverse world* (1st rev. ed.). New York: Routledge.

Gazda, G. (1984). *Group counseling* (3rd ed.). Dubuque, IA: Brown.

Gazda, G. M., Ginter, E. J., & Horne, A. M. (2001). *Group counseling and psychotherapy: Theory and application.* Needham Heights, MA: Allyn & Bacon.

Gazda, G. M., & Peters, R. W. (1975). An analysis of human research in group psychotherapy, group counseling and human relations training. In G. M. Gazda (Ed.), *Basic approaches to group psychotherapy and group counseling* (pp. 38–54). Springfield, IL: Thomas.

George, R. L., & Dustin, D. (1988). *Group counseling: Theory and practice.* Englewood Cliffs, NJ: Prentice-Hall.

Gladding, S. T. (2008). *Groups: A counseling specialty.* (5th ed.). Upper Saddle River, NJ: Merrill/Prentice Hall.

Goldstein, E. G., & Noonan, M. (1999). *Short-term treatment and social work practice: An integrative perspective.* New York: The Free Press.

Goldstein, M. J., Bednar, R. L., & Yanell, B. (1979). Personal risk associated with self-disclosure, interpersonal feedback, and group confrontation in group psychotherapy. *Small Group Behavior, 9,* 579–587.

Golembiewski, R. T. (1962). *The small group: An analysis of research concepts and operations.* Chicago: University of Chicago Press.

Greene, R. T., Lawson, G., & Getz, H. (2005). The impact of the internet: Implications for mental health counselors. *Journal of Technology in Counseling, 4*(1). Retrieved May 3, 2007 from http://jtc.colstate.edu/Vol4_1/Lawson/Lawson.htm.

Hall, K. R., Rushing, J. L., & Khurshid, A. (2011). Using the solving problems together psychoeducational group counseling model as an intervention for negative peer pressure. *The Journal for Specialists in Group Work, 36*(2), 97–110.

Hare, A. P. (1973). Theories of group development and categories for interaction analysis. *Small Group Behavior, 4,* 259–304.

Hare, A. P., Borgatta, E. F., & Bales, R. F. (Eds.). (1967). *Small groups: Studies in social interaction* (Rev. ed.). New York: Knopf.

Herlihy, B., & Corey, G. C. (1997). *Boundary issues in counseling: Multiple roles and responsibilities.* Alexandria, VA: American Counseling Association.

Higgs, J. S. (1992). Dealing with resistance: Strategies for effective group. *The Journal for Specialists in Group Work, 17*(2), 67–73.

Hill, W. F. (1957). Analysis of interviews of group therapists' papers. *Provo Papers, 1*(1).

Hill, W. F., & Gruner, L. (1973). A study of development in open and closed groups. *Small Group Behavior, 4,* 355–381.

Jacobs, A. (1974). The use of feedback in groups. In A. Jacobs, & W. W. Spradline (Eds.), *The group as an agent of change* (pp. 31–49). New York: Behavioral Publications.

Jacobs, E. E., Masson, R. L., & Harvill, R. L. (1998). *Group counseling: Strategies and skills.* Pacific Grove, CA: Brooks/Cole.

Janis, I. L. (1972). *Victims of groupthink: A psychological study of foreign-policy decisions and fiascos.* Boston: Houghton-Mifflin.

Johnson, D. W., & Johnson, F. P. (2000). *Joining together: Group theory and group skills.* Boston: Allyn & Bacon.

Jourard, S. (1971). *The transparent self* (Rev. ed.). New York: Van Nostrand Reinhold.

Kalodner, C. R., & Riva, M. T. (1997). Group research: Encouraging a collaboration between practitioners and researchers: A conclusion. *Journal for Specialists in Group Work, 22*(4), 297.

Kottler, J. A. (1983). *Pragmatic group leadership.* Pacific Grove, CA: Brooks/Cole.

La Coursiere, R. (1980). *The life-cycle of groups: Group development stage theory.* New York: Human Sciences.

Levin, E. M., & Kurtz, R. P. (1974). Participant perceptions following structured and nonstructured human relations training. *Journal of Counseling Psychology, 21,* 514–532.

Leiberman, M. A., Yalom, I. D., & Miles, M. B. (1973). *Encounter groups: First facts.* New York: Basic Books.

Long, L. D., & Cope, C. S. (1980). Curative factors in a male felony offender group. *Small Group Behavior, 11,* 389–398.

Lungren, D. C. (1971). Trainer style and patterns of group development. *Journal of Applied Behavioral Science,* 689–709.

MacKenzie, K. R. (1997). *Time-managed group psychotherapy: Effective clinical applications.* Washington, DC: American Psychiatric Press, Inc.

Martin, L., & Jacobs, M. (1980). Structured feedback delivered in small groups. *Small Group Behavior, 1,* 88–107.

Neukrug, E. (1999). *The world of the counselor: An introduction to the counseling profession.* Pacific Grove, CA: Brooks/Cole.

Ohlsen, M. M. (1977). *Group counseling* (2nd ed.). New York: Holt, Rinehart & Winston.

Ohlsen, M. M., & Ferreira, L. O. (1994). The basics of group counseling. *Counseling and Human Development, 26*(5), 1–20.

Ormont, L. R. (1993). Resolving resistances to immediacy in the group setting. *International Journal of Group Psychotherapy, 43*(4), 399–418.

Parloff, M. B., & Dies, R. R. (1978). Group therapy outcome instrument: Guidelines for conducting research. *Small Group Behavior, 9,* 243–286.

Perls, F. (1969). *Gestalt therapy verbatim.* New York: Bantam.

Remley, T. P., Jr., & Herlihy, B. (2010). *Ethical, legal, and professional issues in counseling* (3rd ed.). Upper Saddle River, NJ: Pearson, Merrill/Prentice Hall.

Roller, B. (1997). *The promise of group therapy: How to build a vigorous training and organizational base for group therapy in managed behavioral healthcare.* San Francisco, Ca: Jossey-Bass.

Rowe, W., & Winborn, B. B. (1973). What people fear about group work: An analysis of 36 selected critical articles. *Educational Technology, 13*(1), 53–57.

Schimmel, C. J., & Jacobs, E. E. (2011). When leaders are challenged: Dealing with involuntary members in groups. *The Journal for Specialists in Group Work, 36*(2), 144–158.

Snortum, J. R., & Myers, H. F. (1971). Intensity of T-group relations as function of interaction. *International Journal of Group Psychotherapy, 21,* 190–201.

Stava, L. J., & Bednar, R. L. (1979). Process and outcome in encounter groups: The effect of group composition. *Small Group Behavior, 10,* 200–213.

Steen, S. (2011). Academic and personal development through group work: An exploratory study. *The Journal for Specialists in Group Work, 36*(2), 129–143.

Stockton, R. (2010). The art and science of group counseling. *The Journal for Specialists in Group Work, 35*(4), 324–330.

Thelen, H., & Dickerman, W. (1949). Stereotypes and the growth of groups. *Educational Leadership, 6,* 309–316.

Truax, C. B., & Carkhuff, R. R. (1967). *Toward effective counseling and psychotherapy: Training and practice.* Chicago: Aldine.

Tuckman, B. W. (1965). Developmental sequences in small groups. *Psychological Bulletin, 63,* 384–389.

Vriend, J. (1985). We've come a long way, group. *The Journal for Specialists in Group Work, 10*(2), 63–67.

Yalom, I. D. (1970). *The theory and practice of group psychotherapy.* New York: Basic Books.

Yalom, I. D. (1975). *The theory and practice of group psychotherapy* (2nd ed.). New York: Basic Books.

Zimpfer, D. G. (1967). Expression of feelings in group counseling. *Personnel and Guidance Journal, 45,* 703–708.

Zimpfer, D. G. (1986). Planning for groups based on their developmental phases. *The Journal for Specialists in Group Work, 11*(3), 180–187.

10

CREATIVE APPROACHES TO COUNSELING

Ann Vernon

Effective counseling establishes a therapeutic relationship to help clients think, feel, and behave in more self-enhancing ways. This relationship enables clients to work through difficulties (Nugent, 2000), empowering them to cope more effectively with life circumstances and to "enhance their present and future opportunities" (Welfel & Patterson, 2005, p. 1). Wagner (2003) stressed that counselors should not focus only on eliminating problems, but to also look for opportunities to facilitate optimal development. In effect, this occurs when the counselor helps clients develop more options for their lives and encourages them to accept more responsibility for their choices and actions (Kottler, 2004). Through counseling clients become more aware, conceptualize their experiences differently, and see themselves and their ways of being more constructively. According to Thompson, Rudolph, and Henderson (2004), counseling is "a process in which people learn how to help themselves and, in effect, become their own counselors" (p. 22). This implies that the counselor won't "fix it" so that the client will feel and act better, but rather, through a collaborative process, the client can be empowered to work through the dysfunctional aspects that interfere with her or his life in order to engage in more growth-producing activities.

Counseling has basically been a mental arena, characterized by a predominately verbal orientation, which according to Dunn and Griggs (1995) can be very limiting. Gladding (2011) concurred, noting that verbal techniques alone are not sufficient for reluctant or nonverbal clients. He emphasized that effective counselors "are aware of the multidimensional nature of the profession and are able to work with a variety of populations by using appropriate interventions" (preface). In his opinion, the creative arts, often referred to as the expressive arts, have been overlooked as one of the most effective approaches for helping clients. In effect, using dance and movement, the visual arts, music, imagery, literature and writing, drama and psychodrama, as well as play and humor enable clients to invest more in the counseling process, resulting in growth and development that helps them experience their world in different ways. Furthermore, expressive arts approaches, like verbal therapies, help clients see their goals more clearly (Allan, 2008), help them become better integrated, and increase clients' well- being (Robbins & Pehrsson, 2009).

Many practitioners are now recognizing that for many clients who seem relatively unaffected by the counseling process, standard techniques alone are inadequate. Consequently, there is more emphasis on expressive therapies (Malchiodi, 2005). While the goal is to facilitate change and problem solving, these approaches combine theory and practice in more flexible, creative ways, while at the same time focusing on the unique as well as universal qualities of clients (Gladding, 2011). Malchiodi (2005) noted that expressive therapies such as the use of the arts and play involve the "purposeful, active participation of the individual and are often complemented by verbal interventions" (p. xiv). According to Malchiodi, expressive therapies have been applied to many different client populations for a variety of issues such as trauma and loss, addictions, developmental and more serious psychiatric disorders, and relationship problems. Gladding (2011) stressed that this approach is emotionally sensitive and process oriented, making it applicable in numerous ways for clients throughout the life span, in remediation as well as prevention.

These non-traditional methods are especially relevant for children and adolescents, whose developmental needs are different and who may not be verbally proficient (Vernon & Clemente, 2005). These authors also emphasized that because reading, writing, and speaking can be difficult for some clients because of language differences, the expressive arts are more universal and culturally appropriate. Degges-White and Davis (2011) concurred, stating that because of the universal nature of the creative arts, they can be used with any client, "regardless of gender, ethnicity, ability, age, language, cultural identity, or physical functioning" (p. 5).

"Effective therapists understand both their clients' styles of communication as well as how to bring out the best in their clients within the helping relationship" (Malchiodi, 2005, p. xiv). The importance of understanding individual communication and learning styles, which refers to the way a person perceives and responds to the learning environment, began appearing in the literature in the 1980s and supported Nickerson and O'Laughlin's (1982) contention that verbal approaches to counseling are often ineffective (Griggs, 1985; Griggs, Price, Kopel, & Swaine, 1984). In the 1990s, Myrick stressed the importance of taking learning styles into account, noting that failure to do so may result in less success with some clients. According to Myrick (1997), counselors must be "flexible, adaptive, and learn how to use different counseling approaches" (p. 111).

The learning style approach assumes that individuals have unique learning patterns that should be accommodated in the counseling process. Because counseling is primarily a talking process, if this is not done, some clients may feel inundated with words, and feel overwhelmed, insecure, or lost (Myrick, 1997). Furthermore, the client may resist. Dunn and Griggs (1995) emphasized that this resistance is due in part to the "mismatch between the counseling interventions, strategies, and techniques used by the counselor and the learning-style preferences of the counselee" (p. 29). This mismatch may be more pronounced for clients from diverse cultures, particularly if they are not proficient in the language the counselor is using. Integrating the creative expressive arts into counseling has limitless possibilities for overcoming this mismatch because of the multidimentional aspects to this approach. As Malchiodi (2005) noted, the expressive arts engage clients in self-expression in their own creative and unique way that cannot always be accomplished verbally.

This chapter describes a variety of creative, expressive counseling approaches that may be used either as a complement to a predominately verbal orientation with a client, or as the primary therapeutic method. These approaches may be used with clients of all ages and in a variety of settings such as schools, hospitals, clinics, or mental health centers. As previously noted, these approaches are often more appropriate for clients from diverse cultures (Vernon & Clemente, 2005), as well as for nonverbal clients or anyone else who "needs to explore and to integrate their behavior in a comprehensive and effective fashion" (Nickerson & O'Laughlin, 1982, p. 7). Gladding (2011) concurred with Nickerson and O'Laughlin, noting that creative approaches help clients as well as counselors see things from a different, more positive, perspective. According to Gladding (1995)

"Clients from all backgrounds can benefit from using a creativity approach regardless of whether the form is fixed, such as with some creative exercises, or spontaneous" (p. 4). Gladding (2011) cited several compelling reasons for using the creative arts in counseling: they help clients become connected and integrated, they are participatory and involve energy and process, they are empowering, they enhance creativity for both the client and the counselor, they give clients a new way to experience themselves, they are very concrete which helps clients conceptualize more effectively, they promote insight, they focus on cooperation and socialization, and they are culturally sensitive.

SIDEBAR 10.1   Learning Style

Take some time to reflect on your own learning style. Are you an auditory learner or a visual learner, or do you learn best by doing? Think about why it is important to match interventions with learning styles as you read the following case study.

Kathy presented in counseling because of problems in her marriage. She shared with the counselor that she was very ambivalent about staying with her husband of 30 years. In recent years, they had grown apart and now the problems seemed insurmountable, especially since her husband was unwilling to attend counseling. Rather than probe further for what Kathy expected from counseling and how it could be most beneficial to her, the counselor enthusiastically gave Kathy a homework assignment at the end of the first session, which was to read *Can Your Relationship Be Saved?* (Broder, 2002). She told Kathy that so many other clients had found this book to be very helpful. At the next session, the counselor asked her client if she had read the book and if so, had she found it helpful. Kathy replied that she didn't like to read and wasn't a particularly good reader, but that she hadn't wanted to tell this to the counselor since she had been so enthusiastic about the assignment. This was an important lesson for the counselor who from then on did a more careful assessment of what types of interventions might be most appropriate for her clients.

The Visual Arts

According to Gladding (2011), the visual arts are defined as "those processes within the realm of art that focus on visually representing reality symbolically or otherwise" (p. 80). The visual arts include drawing, painting, photography, and sculpting. Gladding (2011) emphasized that the visual arts are effective in that they are perceived as non-threatening and can be used in conjunction with other creative arts, which makes them very flexible and widely applicable. In addition, "seeing" something visually is often more powerful than expressing it verbally (Nichols, 2010). Since art transcends cultural boundaries, it is especially effective with diverse populations. Brems (2002) stressed that the visual arts can be cathartic in that clients freely express their feelings and needs as they deal with current or past issues. In addition, visual arts techniques facilitate growth as clients explore problem-solving alternatives, skill development, and increased goal-directedness.

Malchiodi (2005) noted that "While art expression may be used as another form of language in therapy, the actual act of making art taps the universal human potential to be creative, a capacity that has been related to health and wellness" (p. 18). Citing it as being particularly effective with reluctant, nonverbal clients, Bush (1997) contended that painting and drawing can facilitate growth and change as the counselor helps the client focus on symbolic areas of pain and growth in an accepting, understanding manner. According to Gladding (2011), art provides an emotional outlet for people who have difficulty expressing their needs, feelings, and desires and is an effective way to help them begin to understand their confusion. Catharsis and growth, as well as assessment, are the three major purposes of art, according to Brems (2002).

Lev-Wiesel and Daphna-Tekoha (2000) noted that art therapy techniques allow the counselor to examine the client's inner language, which leads to increased insight, and Kwiakowska (2001) stressed that art helps clients perceive themselves more clearly. Malchiodi (2005) cited several other advantages of using art therapy, including the fact that it is experiential because it utilizes the senses; it is a "hands-on" activity (p. 19). In addition, it promotes catharsis and can alleviate stress by inducing relaxation. Silver (2001) noted that one of the advantages of using art in therapy is that it is a way for clients to articulate thoughts and express experiences that they cannot put into words. Another caveat is that using various forms of visual arts results in a tangible product which can help monitor progress in counseling (Vernon & Clemente, 2005).

Art in its many forms has been used since the beginning of history as a means of communication and healing, but it wasn't used in evaluation and treatment as a definable method of practice since the mid-20th century (Malchiodi, 2005). The American Art Therapy Association (as cited in Malchiodi, 2005) described art therapy as based on the belief that the "creative process of art making is healing and life enhancing" (p. 18). Vondracek and Corneal (1995) defined art therapy as "the use of art in a therapeutic setting to foster an individual's psychological growth and well-being" (p. 294). These authors referred to art within the therapeutic context as a means of bringing subconscious material into awareness, which in turn leads to perception and interpretation. Although the majority of research on art therapy has focused on making the unconscious material explicit, art therapy can also be used to increase understanding of conscious material. For example, a client can be encouraged to express his or her anger resulting from a loss in a drawing, and the client and therapist can discuss what the drawing symbolizes and the feelings it evokes.

An important distinction is made between art therapy, derived from art and psychology and literally means using art in a therapeutic way to facilitate communication and self-expression (Vick, 2003), and using the visual arts in counseling. Typically counselors use the visual arts as an adjunct to counseling, asking clients to draw or paint something, for example, and looking at what it represents rather than focusing on artistic eloquence which characterizes art therapy. Also, art therapy is a profession with specialized education and credentials, whereas counselors who are not credentialed art therapists use art as one of many mediums to help clients express themselves (Malchiodi, 2005).

According to Gladding (2011), counselors use art in therapy with children, adolescents, college students, adults, and the elderly. It has also been used with groups, couples and families, and with people from all ethnic backgrounds. Gladding noted that since art transcends cultural boundaries, it is especially effective with diverse populations.

Silver (2001) described using art with various client populations such as abused, emotionally disturbed, hearing-impaired, or brain-injured individuals. Malchiodi (2005) indicated that it is used to treat ADHD, autism, substance abuse, eating disorders, trauma and loss, domestic violence, physical and sexual abuse, and most forms of mental illness. Art is used in a variety of settings, such as schools, prisons, rehabilitation centers, day-treatment centers, hospitals, and clinics. It is now not only being used to work with people who have problem, but also it is more prevalent in helping "normal" clients, where the emphasis is on growth and self-development (Vondracek & Corneal, 1995).

The Process

Many art forms can be used to help clients gain self-awareness and work through emotional conflicts: painting, sculpting, modeling with clay, photography, drawing, printing/designing, collages, or graphic art. As Malchoidi (2005) pointed out, art making is experiential—a "hands-on activity" that involves physical action, as well as kinesthetic and perceptual experiences (p 19). Gladding (2011) suggested using already existing artwork as a means of introducing images that facilitate communication and understanding. In addition, he discussed the use of body outlines and serial drawing as visual art forms that can be used with clients to help uncover troublesome issues.

In using various forms of the visual arts, the goal is to facilitate communication between the helper and the client rather than mastery of art form or content (Kenny, 1987). In the process, the client is encouraged to express feelings symbolically through an art form. As Allan (1982) noted, the counselor's role is basically that of a listener who responds to the client and allows him or her time and space to initiate interaction. After a given interval, the counselor might invite the client to share by issuing a simple invitation such as "Would you like to tell me what's happening in your picture?" If working with a more seriously disturbed client with whom art media is used in each session, Allan indicated that the counselor's role may change. After several sessions, the counselor might become more active by relating the art to what is occurring in real life as well as emphasizing positive aspects that indicate growth.

Art can be an effective means of initiating contact with a client, as illustrated in the following example. Amanda, a third-grader, was referred by her teacher because she seemed preoccupied and unhappy. In the initial meeting, the counselor noted that Amanda seemed quite anxious and hesitant. To establish rapport and facilitate expression, the counselor put some modeling clay on the table and invited Amanda to play with it. At first, Amanda just rolled the clay around without molding it. The counselor made no comment, but simply communicated an attitude of acceptance. Presently Amanda began to shape the clay into a bridge. Next she made a car and attached small clay dots to the car. As she placed the car on the bridge, the bridge collapsed. At this point the counselor asked Amanda if she would like to tell her about what was happening. Amanda explained that the dots were people—her family. The counselor reflected that something must have happened to the family in the car, and Amanda began to talk about how her family had had an accident because her Dad and Mom were drunk. She shared her feelings of fright and how she took care of her brothers and sister after the accident. As she talked, she began to roll the clay and pound it, tears streaming down her cheeks. As the counselor supported her, it became apparent that the feelings Amanda needed to express would be more readily verbalized in future sessions as the counselor began to help Amanda deal with her painful situation.

Art media can be used in the manner previously illustrated, or in a more directed manner to facilitate a process. For example, clients could be instructed to draw their family, paint their life story or their dreams, or illustrate a book that describes a situation with which they are dealing. They could be asked to sketch and color themselves in moods that they have experienced recently, or be invited to draw a picture representing something that they need in their life. Designing a T-shirt, a banner, or a bumper sticker with a motto they feel describes them are good ways to encourage personal growth and sharing, particularly with resistant adolescent clients.

Photography can also be used effectively to elicit feelings and create awareness. "Photographs are footprints of our minds, mirrors of our lives, reflections from our hearts, frozen memories we can hold in silent stillness in our hands—forever, if we wish" (Gladding, 2011, p. 87). Stevens and Spears (2009) explained that photographs can be used with individuals, couples and families, as well as in groups, to improve understanding and perception. Photography can be active, meaning that clients take pictures to represent how they feel or what is significant to them, or it can be passive. Passive photography is when they gather together photos that have previously been taken that represent them in some way (Gladding (2011). Photographs can be used to help the elderly participate in a life review process or with families to increase awareness of their successes and challenges as a family unit. Vernon and Clemente (2005) explained how photographs were used with an adolescent to help her more realistically assess experiences with her peers, and the case of Mandy illustrates how it helped a teenager assess goals.

Mandy, a 17-year-old female, was referred for counseling by her parents who were concerned about her behavior, specifically her alcohol abuse, low grades, and her association with peers they felt were a bad influence. Although Mandy's parents felt that her behavior was very much out of control, Mandy did not share this same opinion. To the contrary, she did not want to be in counseling and saw nothing wrong with the way she was living her life. Because of her reluctance, the counselor felt that it would be more effective to use a variety of approaches to help her evaluate her goals and her current behaviors.

After establishing rapport by having her client share artifacts from her back pack that told something about her, as well as acknowledging her resistance, the counselor asked Mandy if she had any goals for these counseling sessions. Mandy's reply was that she wanted her parents to leave her alone and let her make her own decisions. The counselor replied that she thought one way of doing this would be for Mandy to "prove" to her parents that her present behaviors would help her achieve future goals. She suggested that Mandy take photographs of what her life would be like if she continued her present course of action (substance abuse, low grades, associating with peers who were encouraging her to drop out of high school, move away from home, etc.) and to take photos that represented a life she might like to have, in case it would be different from the one she would have if she continued along the same path.

This visual intervention proved to be very enlightening for Mandy, who took the task seriously. Her photographs depicting how her life would be if she continued her present lifestyle reflected working at fast food chains, living in substandard housing, and having her driver's license taken away for driving while intoxicated. Her pictures of how she wanted her life to be were considerably different: graduating from high school, getting a new car, and going to college. After discussing the differences between the two sets of pictures, Mandy and her counselor were able to set realistic goals for behavioral and attitudinal changes.

Implementation Considerations

In employing art, Rubin (2010) cautioned that experience and skill are necessary if working at a sophisticated level, but that specific training in art is not essential with simple expressive work and minimal interpretation. Brems (2002) emphasized that there are various approaches to the use of art and that it can be used exclusively or in combination with other strategies.

Rubin (2010) also noted that therapeutic work through art may be one way for clients to feel in charge when other parts of their life are overwhelming. As a trusting relationship is established, the counselor invites the client to share the meaning from his or her perspective. In essence, the counselor observes the client's work as it develops, attends to the nonverbal and verbal communication offered, and responds to clarify.

Kenny (1987) identified the following factors that may help the counselor understand clients' artwork by considering the larger context of their world:

1. In Western culture, dark colors or heavy shading generally indicate sadness, depression, or anger; excessive use of white may indicate emotional rigidity.
2. Small figures, particularly of self, may indicate insecurity, anxiety, or low self esteem.
3. Sadness, violence, aggression, or other emotional disturbances are often represented with dark images, storms, accidents, fighting, or murder.
4. Texture of materials can provide insight: aggressive, angry clients might select bold or tough materials, whereas a nonassertive client might choose watercolors or something softer.
5. Clients with emotional disturbances tend to depict figures more grotesquely, as stiff and rigid, or unintegrated, with some body parts being exaggerated. Excessive shading may indicate high anxiety.

Unless someone is a credentialed art therapist, counselors must use caution in over-interpreting their clients' creations, as illustrated in Sidebar 10.2.

SIDEBAR 10.2 Case Study: Interpreting a Picture Too Literally

I recall working with a young boy whose parents had recently been divorced. He was in a divorce group and seemed to be doing quite well, although I assumed there was still conflict between the parents based on what his mother had shared with me. During one of our sessions, I asked Ryan to draw a picture of how he was feeling about the divorce, which he finished just as the session was ending. Consequently, I didn't look at it until later in the day. When I did, I was very alarmed because there was so much violence depicted, including a figure holding a gun. I immediately chastised myself for not picking up on Ryan's inner turmoil sooner, and called him into the office. I explained that I had just looked at his picture and asked him to tell me more about it. "Oh," he said. "That's the television show I watched last night." I breathed a sigh of relief but did call his mother to verify that he had indeed seen this show and that what I had interpreted as significant inner conflict about the divorce was unfounded.

The basic function of the visual arts is to facilitate emotional expression from clients who do not communicate well verbally and to execute the counseling process more effectively through visual representation. The visual arts can be used to reduce resistance and put the client at ease during an initial session, can be used strategically in later sessions to help the client clarify and gain awareness, or can be used over a period of several sessions as the main vehicle to work through painful issues. Brems (2002) added that it is an effective means of introducing and discussing difficult topics or affects. Gladding (2005) emphasized that art helps awaken clients to "a new sense of self and deeper understanding of their intra- and interpersonal relationships" (p. 105). Bush (1997) noted that as clients liken themselves to artists who can repaint canvasses they do not like after the paint is dry, they can, in effect learn to paint over their problems to attain new solutions" (p. 4).

The *Handbook of Art Therapy* (Malchiodi, 2003) is an excellent resource for the professional interested in learning more about using art in a counseling relationship.

Music

Music has played an important role in healing and nurturing for centuries, and has been applied in many different ways to facilitate communication and expression of feelings (Silverman, 2008). Because of its universal, multicultural nature, it is an effective counseling approach to use with a variety of populations to help them gain insight and develop new behaviors (Horden, 2000; Silverman, 2008; Wigram, Pedersen, & Bonde, 2002). Music is a "therapeutic ally to verbal approaches to counseling" (Gladding, 2011, p. 23); it is a creative experience that can be used to initiate other counseling processes. The effectiveness of this intervention depends on the client's involvement with music, but because most clients enjoy singing, dancing, or listening to music, this can be an ideal approach for clients who have difficulty expressing themselves verbally (Gladding, 2011). It is important to distinguish between music therapy, which Peters (2000) described as "a planned, goal-directed process of interaction and intervention, based on assessment and evaluation of individual clients' specific needs, strengths, and weaknesses, in which music or music-based experiences are specifically prescribed to be used by specially trained personnel to influence positive changes in an individual's condition, skills, thoughts, feelings, or behaviors" (p. 2) and using music techniques in counseling. Gladding (2011) stated music therapy is more direct and implemented by therapists who are specialists in music and human behavior who must have technical skills such as playing various musical instruments and being able to sing and compose music. In contrast, counselors who use music in counseling engage clients in listening, improvising, performing, and composing that can be therapeutic but not as encompassing as music therapy.

Music has been used in individual as well as group settings to help geriatric clients with advanced Alzheimer's (Forinash, 2005), reduce depression and anxiety (Bradley, Hendricks, & Crews, 2009), and help people recall past events and work through painful memories (Duffey, 2007). Music can facilitate social interaction and self-expression in older adults (Rio, 2002), and help children deal with the trauma of abuse (Ostertag, 2002) or the pain when parents divorce (DeLucia-Waack & Gellman, 2007). Music also helps terminally ill clients reflect, refocus, and share their feelings (Duffey, 2007). Music can also increase wellness (Peters, 2000) and self-esteem (Hendricks, 2000).

Music has also been used successfully with the mentally challenged, institutionalized elderly, emotionally disturbed, sensory impaired clients, and with depressed clients in a hospital setting (Davis, Gfeller, & Thaut, 1999), as well as with physically and/or developmentally delayed clients (Wigram et al., 2002), with behaviorally disturbed or socially maladjusted children and adolescents (Peters, 2000), and with Alzheimer's patients to reduce their physical agitation (Jennings & Vance, 2002). Davis and colleagues (1999) stressed the importance of music therapy in treating individuals with psychological disorders, delinquent behavior, or drug addiction, and MacIntosh (2003) noted that it is an effective approach with victims of sexual abuse. Music can be energizing as well as calming and can be used as a catalyst for self-expression, resulting in a number of therapeutic changes, including heightened attention and concentration; stimulation and expression of feelings; and insight into one's thinking, feeling, and behavior (Thaut, 1990). It can be used to alleviate burnout (Peters, 2000), and plays an important role in preventive care and health maintenance (Guzzetta, 1991). Gladding (2011) noted that music is a versatile tool that can reduce anxiety, elicit memories, communicate feelings, develop rapport, and intensify or create moods. It is a very effective approach with children, adolescents, families and couples, and can be used in conjunction with other creative arts such as music and play, music and storytelling, and music and poetry.

Although music can be used as the primary method of treatment, it can also be incorporated into the counseling experience to facilitate the process more effectively. Or music may be used to introduce or convey messages in classroom guidance sessions and to clarify issues as a "homework" assignment. Song lyrics or CDs are perhaps the most accessible form of music, but for improvisation purposes, a guitar, drum, shakers, xylophone, or keyboard are useful.

Applications

Music can effectively establish rapport, particularly with teenagers, who are often not self-referred. Having the radio softly tuned into a popular rock station when the client walks into the office can help facilitate communication and relaxation. Generally, it is best left to the client to initiate conversation about the music, but if she or he doesn't, the counselor might comment on the song, inquire whether or not the client likes to listen to music, and then ease into the traditional get acquainted phase of the session. After a first session, one teenager commented to me that he was surprised to hear the music and that it didn't make it seem like he was "going to a shrink." This helped establish trust by communicating to the client that the counselor had some understanding of where he was coming from.

To help clients get more in touch with what they are thinking and feeling, music can be a useful homework assignment. The client is invited to bring in CDs or record songs that illustrate how she or he is thinking or feeling that week. Clients can also find songs that express who they are, their conflicts, or their hopes. This is effective especially for teenagers, since music is such an important part of their life experience.

This approach was used with 14-year-old Annette, a depressed, nonverbal client who asked to see a counselor because of conflicts at home. Despite the fact that she had initiated the counseling, it was difficult for Annette to express what was happening at home and why she was so upset. Annette was very willing to do the music assignment and came back the following week with several tapes. The counselor invited her to play the tapes, briefly reflected on what she thought was expressed through the music, and then encouraged Annette to share how the songs related to her experiences. She opened up some, which facilitated verbal exchange about the problems.

After several sessions of discussing and working through some of her difficulties, Annette was again asked to bring in songs that told more about her current feelings. This time the songs were less conflictual and more hopeful. The use of music homework had helped the counselor understand Annette's pain and confusion so they could begin dealing with it. The music also provided a useful way to determine therapy progress.

Vernon (2002) suggested using music in the counseling session and described having depressed adolescents "take a sad song and make it better," by selecting a song that conveyed elements of their own depression and rewriting the lyrics to convey a more hopeful outlook. She also developed the concept of "silly songs," where children take a familiar song and write silly lyrics to help them gain new perspective or insight about how to solve a problem. One such song, sung to the tune of *Three Blind Mice,* is as follows:

> Three sad kids,
> Three sad kids,
> See how they cry,
> See how they cry.
> They all got tired of crying so much,
> They ran around and made faces and such,
> You've never seen these kids laughing so much,
> The three happy kids, the three happy kids.

(Vernon, 2002, p. 129)

Newcomb (1994) described using songwriting to promote increased self-awareness and facilitate emotional release. She noted that song lyrics can be used to teach children about positive interpersonal relationships and suggested pairing children up and having them draw to music as a way to increase communication and cooperation. Peters (2000) indicated that music can be used to encourage team work.

Music can also be used with children in classroom guidance lessons (DeLucia-Waack, 2001). DeLucia Waack and Gellman (2007) created songs to help children learn how to cope with divorce, and Peter Yarrow (2000) wrote songs to promote acceptance of others. Dan Conley (1994) developed a series of children's songs to help children deal with typical problems such as anxiety, perfectionism, and guilt. Using the song *I Worry* from the Dan Conley album can introduce a lesson in classroom guidance about how everyone worries from time to time. After playing the recording, children can be invited to sing the song, and a discussion can follow about the main points in the song. Follow-up activities include making a "worry box," to contain the worries, writing advice columns about how to handle typical worries, or incorporating bibliotherapy.

Advantages

Because music is a popular medium and readily available, counselors are only limited by their creativity to specific applications. Music can easily be integrated into counseling sessions to help clients clarify issues, communicate problems, or monitor progress. It can also be used improvisationally to encourage risk taking, self-expression, spontaneity and playfulness, and creative expression (Forinash, 2005). Degges-White and Davis (2011) noted that clients may actively create their own music, experimenting with various musical instruments to create a piece of music that is meaningful to them. Putting words to the music adds yet another dimension. The counselor can also engage clients in musical activities they have developed to help them increase expression and awareness.

If clients respond to the use of music, it provides a pleasurable way to connect with them to stimulate personal awareness and growth. Music can readily be incorporated into drama, writing, the visual arts, and play, so it is a very versatile approach. Whether client listen, compose, or move to music, the benefits are multifaceted.

Writing or Scriptotherapy

According to Gladding, (2011), scriptotherapy is a term that is used to refer to writing in a therapeutic way and is very beneficial in diverse settings, according to Baikie and Wilhelm (2005). Writing, an effective self-help approach, offers a powerful way for clients to clarify feelings and events and gain a perspective on their problems. Bradley and colleagues (2009) noted that writing contributes to personal integration and provides a cathartic experience. For many clients, seeing something in writing has more impact than hearing it.

Writing as a therapeutic experience can take numerous forms, and the reader is encouraged to experiment with the variations later described to meet a client's needs most effectively. Obviously, for very young children writing must be more simplistic, or the counselor may choose to serve as the recorder. In addition, some clients don't find certain forms of writing helpful, and, therefore, it is important to gear the assignment to what the counselor deems will be most useful for achieving the therapeutic goals. Therapeutic writing approaches range from structured to more open-ended. Examples of each are described in the following sections.

Autobiographies

Autobiographies are generally written in one of two ways: describing a particular segment or aspect of one's life, or writing a chronicle that covers all of one's life history (Bradley et al., 2009). How the autobiography is used depends on which approach most effectively assists the client to clarify concerns, express feelings, and work toward resolution. In either case, once the client provides the written material, the counselor helps the client clarify the issues by asking questions, probing for feelings, confronting discrepancies in the writing, identifying specific concerns, and setting goals for change.

In one case in which this approach was used, the counselor determined that because the client was struggling with a relationship with her spouse, it would help her to chronicle all past significant relationships and indicate how these relationships were established, what was meaningful about them, how they were terminated, and how the client felt. Having done this assignment, the client and counselor identified some patterns in the way that the client reacted to significant others. In other instances, it might benefit the client to write a more detailed account of her or his life to see how perceptions and values change over time, and to thereby develop some perspective about the future.

Correspondence

We typically think of correspondence as appropriate when face-to-face contact isn't possible. However, correspondence can also help clarify concerns and expression in other ways. White and Murray (2002) noted that letter writing can allow for self-exploration and change. For example, clients can be encouraged to write letters to themselves to give themselves positive feedback about an accomplishment or some advice about how to handle a particular problem. Or, correspondence can occur between client and counselor to elaborate on important points that occurred during the session (White & Murray, 2002).

Clients may also find it useful to write a letter (probably unsent) to a person with whom they are in conflict to help them express thoughts and clarify issues. This approach was used with a woman who was having problems with her sister. Because the client wasn't very clear about what specifically was upsetting to her, the counselor asked her client to first put her thoughts on paper and then discuss these with him. The counselor helped her identify specific things that she was angry about: her belief that the sister must not care about the relationship because she never initiated contact and that she (the client) must be unimportant to her. She then asked her client to write a letter to herself from what might be her sister's perspective, which helped her gain some perspective. As a homework assignment, the client was asked to rewrite the letter to her sister, which incorporated some of her thoughts about what her sister's perspective might be and also how she felt about being ignored. When she brought it in the following week, the concerns were more succinctly expressed and the anger was more focused and less intense. The counselor showed the client ways to express the anger more assertively and how to dispute overgeneralizations and assumptions.

In this example, the client sent her letter, and it did not affect the relationship negatively, as the first letter might have. Instead, the first letter served as a valuable catharsis and a tool for the counselor to help the client clarify the problem and develop skills to address it more effectively.

In other cases, clients may not use the counselor as an editor, but may simply write a letter as a way of dealing with feelings. After they have written the letter, they may keep it, give it to the person with whom they are in conflict, or tear it up. It is important for clients to realize that an unedited letter that generally contains a lot of anger may create more problems when received. On the other hand, such a letter can serve as a springboard for getting problems out in the open.

Writing a letter to one's disease, such as cancer or Chron's disease, is an exceptionally helpful form of catharsis for clients who suffer from illnesses but often keep their feelings to themselves. Likewise, writing a letter to a deceased loved one, a hope or dream, or a major transition such as retirement or moving can be very therapeutic.

SIDEBAR 10.3 Writing a Letter

When I was a teenager, my mother and I communicated a lot through letters, airing our grievances in an attempt to arrive at new understandings. For me, it was very therapeutic to write these letters and it was an effective way for us to address typical mother–daughter conflict during adolescence. To this day, I still write letters when I am upset or need to clarify thoughts and feelings about something. Many of these letters are never sent, but the catharsis is very helpful.

Have you ever used correspondence as a way of expressing feelings, clarifying issues, or resolving conflict? Think of someone or something you could write a letter to. It could be a person or a pet who is living or dead, or it might be a disease or disability. You might write a letter to your house if you are moving, or to your job if you are leaving or retiring. After you finish the letter, list three feeling words that describe what that experience was like for you and think about how you might use this approach with clients.

Riordan and Ketchum (1996) discussed another form of writing which they called therapeutic correspondence, or the writing of notes in the form of letters after the session by the client and/or counselor. These letters can motivate the client to work on particular issues and help also serve as a good refresher of topics addressed during the counseling session. I adapted this technique with a 10-year-old whose mother had told me was very worried about coming to counseling. Therefore, prior to the first session, I wrote Larissa a short letter, telling her a bit about myself and how I routinely worked with boys and girls her age to help them work through problems they might be having. Larissa's mother had shared that her daughter's primary problem was that she was afraid her mother would be in a car accident and die. Because this was a relatively common concern for several of my young clients, I was truthfully able to tell Larissa that I had other clients with similar concerns and that I was quite sure we could find some ways to help her just as I had helped them. Larissa's mother called me shortly before the session to tell me that the letter had been very helpful and that she wasn't nearly as anxious about coming to the appointment.

Journaling

Journaling, either structured or unstructured, is a form of expressive writing that helps clients reflect on their personal experiences and identify where growth has occurred (Gladding, 2011). Journaling is particularly helpful with clients who are not very verbal because it can illuminate issues to encourage discussion. It is also an appropriate multi-cultural approach since there are some cultures where people are not openly encouraged to share their feelings. Parr, Haberstroh, and Kottler (2000) described the use of an inter-active journal in group work which allowed group members to share thoughts and feelings with others.

Journaling allows for self-expression and the acceptance of feelings, relieves emotional pain, and allows clients to start dealing with emotions on a cognitive and objective manner (Mercer, 1993). Recording thoughts and feelings enables both client and counselor to better understand the dimensions of the problem and monitor behavior. Another advantage of journaling is that clients are able to reflect on what they have learned and how they have grown over time.

When unstructured journaling is used, the client is invited to write down thoughts and feelings about events each day. The journal can then be used as catharsis. During each session, the counselor can invite clients to share anything from the journal that they felt was significant, anything they would like help with, or items they want to talk more about.

Journaling can also be more structured; for example, the counselor can present the client with a list of suggestions to guide the writing. These suggestions may include identifying events that were pleasurable or upsetting, goals that were accomplished, people whom they did or did not enjoy being with, and feelings about each of these topics. Often clients initially need these guidelines but don't generally rely on the structure for long. Regardless of the form, Gladding (2011) recommends reviewing the journal material on a regular basis to increase reflection and insight. He also suggests that an audiotaped journal may be an alternative for clients who process information auditorily or are not very adept at writing.

Structured Writing

Structured writing can be in the form of open-ended sentences, questionnaires, or writing in session. Hutchins and Cole (1992) cautioned that writing does not replace counselor–client interaction, but rather serves as a starting point for discussion as well as a way to help the client generate and synthesize data.

Open-Ended Sentences

Open-ended sentences may be used to establish rapport or to determine areas of concern to address during the counseling sessions. Children or adolescents, who are often more nonverbal, may readily respond to open-ended sentences, but they can also be very effective with adults, such as in couple counseling. Open ended sentences can provide a valuable source of information and set the client at ease with a structure to which she or he can respond. With very young children, the counselor can serve as the recorder so the child doesn't have to labor over writing.

Open-ended sentences can be general starters such as the following which are good to use in initial sessions to learn more about the client:

"I get upset when. . ."
"If I could change something in my life, it would be. . ."
"I am happiest when. . ."
"In my free time I like to. . ."

Or the starters may be geared more specifically to an area of concern the client previously expressed such as:

"I wish my spouse would…"
"Three things I consider important in our relationship are. . ."
"The biggest change in our relationship over the years has been…"
"The thing I most appreciate about my spouse is…"

Both strategies effectively collect information about thoughts and feelings that can be used as the counselor helps the client sort through concerns. In employing open-ended sentences, it is important to gear the starters to the client's developmental level. It is not necessary to have a long list of starters—the real purpose is to elicit information that can be used in the counseling session, not simply to collect data.

Stories

Writing personal stories with different endings is an effective way for clients of all ages make a decision when it is difficult to select an alternative. In using this strategy, the client is first invited to write the personal dilemma and is then encouraged to write several different endings to the same story. Dialogue between the counselor and client should focus on the advantages and disadvantages of each ending, as well as consequences. This technique facilitates problem resolution, as in the case of 18-year-old Enrique, who was struggling with what to do after high school. After writing about several alternatives including attending the community college, joining the armed forces, or working in the local factory, Enrique had a much clearer idea about his immediate and long-term future relative to each option.

Writing in Session

For many clients, seeing things in print has more impact than hearing them. For this reason, they might be encouraged to take notes during the counseling session and refer to these notes during the interim to work on aspects of the problem. In working with young children or clients who labor over writing, the counselor may opt to record key ideas that might be useful to the client.

Poetry

Poetry therapy is the use of various types of poetry in counseling, particularly by trained poetry therapists (Stepakoff, 2009), and involves five steps: entry, engagement, involvement, incorporation, and inititative. Gladding (2011) distinguished between trained poetry therapists and counselors who use poetry as a therapeutic tool, noting that certified poetry therapists use poetry in a more thorough way than do counselors who incorporate poetry into their work. Gorelick (2005) described poetry as speaking the "language of the heart" (p. 118), and Sloan (2003) noted that poetry helps clients "sift through the layers of their lives in search of their own truths" (p. 35). According to Gorelick (2005), poetry is a form of healing that began with shaman incantations many years ago. And, although poetry conjures up a negative reaction for some, it is more widely embraced now because it has returned to its lyrical roots.

With clients who are unsure about writing poetry, Woytowich (1994) suggested asking specific questions about the event. As clients tell their story, the counselor writes down what is shared and gives it back to them in the form of verses. It is also helpful with some clients to prescribe a specific poem related to their specific problem. Reading the poem helps the client understand she or he is not alone in experiencing this emotion. After reading the poem, the client is encouraged to do her or his own writing for further self-expression. It is critical that the poem be pertinent or relevant to the client's situation, age, and culture.

Poetry can be a form of catharsis and can also provide a liberating, therapeutic effect that increases understanding and contributes to more accurate self-perceptions. In addition, poetry enables clients to use words to reconstruct reality; it is "a way of seeing and ultimately, a way of knowing," (Bates, 1993, p. 155).

Poetry can be used to help clients understand themselves and others, improve interpersonal and communication skills, and promote change and coping skills (National Coalition of Creative Arts Therapies Associations, as cited in Gorelick, 2005). Counselors can use it themselves to prevent their own burnout and promote self-renewal (Gladding, 1987). It can also be used as a catalyst for growth and healing in hospitals, nursing homes, prisons, adult education centers, and chemical dependency units (Hynes, 1990). Robbins and Pehrsson (2009) found poetry therapy to be very effective in empowering anorexic women. Gladding (2011) described having elderly residents in long-term care facilities read poems aloud as a group and react to the content with their own opinions and emotions, which enhances self-concept and group cohesiveness.

Poetry can be used to facilitate healing for clients dealing with change and loss, substance abuse, and depression. The following poem was written by a 16-year-old girl who struggled with depression. It was often difficult for her to describe how she was feeling, so she accepted the invitation to write about her feelings through poetry, and this became the vehicle for discussing her pain.

Yesterday's Garbage

I wake up every day and force myself out of bed.
I know that every day holds a new adventure,

CREATIVE APPROACHES TO COUNSELING

That remains to be a complete mystery until I experience it.
I will take a shower and stand there forever,
Dreading what lies ahead.
I put some clothes on and walk out the door,
Not knowing how I will act that day.
I might be happy,
I might be sad,
I might just be pissed off.
Every day is something different,
Triggered by events that happen, things people say, the way people act.
I get to school and don't talk to anybody that much.
I sit in my classes where I am usually out of my mind.
But yet I am different.
They know about me and they know about my depression.
So when they look at me, they look at me like I am yesterday's garbage.

After a year of counseling, in which she typically described her feelings through her poetry, she began to feel better, as reflected in the following poem:

A Finalizing Day

A finalizing day has yet to arrive.
Everyday the same obstacles,
But now we can overcome.
The shadow upon me is slowly drifting away,
To where I can actually see myself, and all that lies around me.
So this will all end
And I will finally get my wish of happiness,
Now and forever.

Limericks

Limericks, a form of poetry written with precise rhythm (Sloan, 2003), can be a good way to help clients think "outside the box," discovering their own problem-solving or coping strategies. In writing limericks, the first and second lines rhyme, the third and fourth lines rhyme, and the last line rhymes with the first. The following is an example of a limerick developed for a young client with attention deficit hyperactivity disorder (Vernon, self-composed):

There once was a girl named Jill
Who had a very hard time sitting still
When the teacher would talk, Jill thought about playing
So she really never heard what the teacher was saying
Until she pretended she was still as a mouse sitting on the window sill.

Bibliotherapy

The term bibliotherapy refers to the use of literature as a therapeutic process (Vernon & Clemente, 2005). It is an interactive process designed to help individuals gain control over their lives as they solve problems, learn new skills, practice new behaviors (Jackson, 2001), and better understand themselves through their response to literature or media (Doll & Doll, 1997). Jackson (2001) noted that literature has been used to establish relationships with clients as well as to promote their insight. According to Pardeck (1998), the goals of bibliotherapy include (1) providing information and insight about problems, (2) communicating new values and attitudes, (3) creating an awareness of how others have dealt with similar problems, (4) stimulating discussion about problems, and (5) providing solutions.

Bibliotherapy has been used to increase academic and emotional development with children with serious emotional disturbances (Bauer & Balius, 1995), has been helpful for adolescents experiencing parental divorce (Pehrsson, Allen, Volger, McMillen, & Lowe, 2007), and for clients with anger management problems (Joshua & DiMenna, 2000). It has been used to assist adolescents in dealing with the transition from childhood to adulthood (Gladding, 2005), and for clients dealing with perfectionism (Nugent, 2000). Bradley and colleagues (2009) described it as beneficial for clients needing to work through grief, and Pardeck (1998) identified ways in which bibliotherapy increased socialization and self-actualization.

Bibliotherapy can be used to address a wide array of problems and has been implanted in various settings such as hospitals, schools, and outpatient clinics. Another advantage is that many different creative and experiential strategies can be used in conjunction with bibliotherapy (Pehrsson, 2006; Pehrsson & McMillen, 2007). It is also very empowering for ethnically diverse populations because clients feel empowered when they read about others from their culture who have overcome major challenges (Vernon & Clemente, 2005).

Bibliotherapy is especially effective for clients who process things visually as opposed to auditorily. I recall working with a couple experiencing relationship difficulties. I was attempting to stop the cycle of blame and increase this couple's understanding of their communication differences and ways of perceiving the world. Since verbal efforts had not been successful, I suggested they read a book as a homework assignment. When the couple arrived for the next session, they were eager to share their insights. The information they had learned provided them with new perspectives and information they needed to move to the next level of problem solving regarding their relationship issues.

In addition to literature in print, such as fiction, non-fiction, poetry, self-help books, autobiographies, and fairy tales, Caron (2005) described benefits of using movies as a bibliotherapy tool, otherwise known as cinematherapy (Shallcross, 2011). Just as with books, cinematherapy involves selecting a movie or movie clip that parallels issues the client is struggling with, requesting that he or she watch it, and then engaging the client in a guided discussion to promote insight and a deeper perspective on personal issues. According to Shallcross, movies are very effective because clients are "not processing it in their head; they're processing it in their heart" (p. 37), referring to how clients react to how the characters in the movie handle issues similar to their own.

This approach is particularly effective with adolescents who spend a great deal of time watching movies, but who may not pick up a book. Movies that depict events or emotions similar to those of the client can facilitate insight and emotional catharsis in addition to identification of coping strategies. Higgens and Dermer (2001) discussed having clients watch a movie as a homework assignment in order to gain insights they might not glean in face-to-face counseling sessions. Alternately, the counselor and client can view a movie together, stopping in key places to discuss insights and feelings.

The Process

Bibliotherapy is an interactive process that helps clients gain control over their lives as they develop greater self-awareness, learn new skills, practice new behaviors, and solve problems (Jackson, 2001). There are four stages to the bibliotherapy process, according to Kelsch and Emry (2003, as cited in Gladding, 2005): identification with the characters, situation, and setting; catharsis, which involves becoming emotionally connected with the characters; insight, which evolves from the emotional identification and catharsis and enables the client to apply concepts from the literature to his or her own life; and universality, in which clients are more empathic and sensitive, moving beyond their immediate situations.

The interactive format emphasizes guided discussion between the counselor and client to help integrate the client's thoughts and feelings relative to the literature. This is in direct contrast to the reactive format that involves asking clients to read a specific selection but there is no discussion; the counselor assumes that they will gain insight and release emotions through identifying with the literature (Gladding & Gladding, 1991). Clearly this approach is not as preferable as the more current interactive option that helps clients achieve therapeutic goals through guided discussion.

Bibliotherapy can be used individually as well as in small groups or classroom settings, and although it is often used in a remedial sense to help clients cope with problems, it can also be used for personal growth and problem prevention where the focus is on helping children cope with developmental needs and typical problems. Before using bibliotherapy, it is important to have a relationship built on trust and rapport.

In selecting books for treatment, it is important to consider the presenting problem. Also, the practitioner should select books that contain believable characters, situations that are relevant to the situation, and that offer realistic hope. The selections should be developmentally appropriate (Wagner, 2003) and reflect the client's culture, gender, and age (Vernon & Clemente, 2005).

SIDEBAR 10.4 Selecting Books for Bibliotherapy

In my clinical practice I found with some clients, both young and old, that using children's books was very effective. However, it is important to explain to the client that even though the book is written for children, the message has universal appeal. I recall working with a woman who suffered from depression and so often felt like just giving up. After talking about how difficult it was to tolerate this situation, I invited her to read a classic children's book, *The Little Engine That Could* (Piper, 1986), which described a train engine's persistent attempts to make it up the hill. Although it was a simple book, the message contained a powerful message of "I think I can, I think I can." Following some discussion, I asked the client to make a list of "I think I can" statements that she could use to remind herself that she could continue to fight her way through her depression. Other books with simple but profound concepts include *What If It Never Stops Raining* (Carlson, 1992), a book about dealing with anxiety, *Simon's Hook* (Burnett, 2000), a story about dealing with teasing and put-downs, and *The True Story of the Three Little Pigs* (Scieszka, 1989), with a good message about looking at situations from another person's perspective.

Play

"Play therapy is an approach to counseling young children in which the counselor uses toys and play as the primary vehicle for communication" (Kottman, 2009, p.111). Thompson, Rudolph, & Henderson (2004) noted that because play is the natural language for children, it is an ideal modality to help children work out problems and communicate with others. As Malchiodi (2005) noted, toys provide a way for children to "show" what has happened. Generally used with children ages 3–12, play provides a way for children to express their experiences and feelings through a natural, self-healing process (Kottman, 2009). Because children's experiences are often communicated through play, it becomes an important vehicle to help them know and accept themselves. Through play, children are able to act out confusing or conflicting situations, make choices (Thompson et.al., 2004), learn and practice problem-solving and relationship building skills (Kottman, 2009), master their fears (Kottman, 2001), explore alternative perceptions of problems and difficult relationships (Kottman, 2009), and learn to communicate more effectively (Brems, 2002). According to Brems, "play is perhaps one of the most common techniques utilized by child therapists" (p. 248).

Play Therapy Approaches

Kottman (2009) described four approaches to play therapy: Child-Centered, Adlerian, Cognitive-Behavioral, and Theraplay. Child-centered play therapy is based on the philosophy that children have an innate capacity for growth and maturity and that they are capable of being constructively self-directing. In this form of play therapy, the therapist builds a warm, genuine relationship with the child to facilitate a strong therapeutic bond. The therapist is totally accepting of the child and respects the child's ability to solve problems. Although the therapist maintains an active role, he or she does not manage or direct the experience. Rather, the child-centered play therapist believes that by communicating acceptance and belief in the child, the child will tap into his or her innate capacity for solving problems.

In Adlerian play therapy, the play therapist utilizes the principles and strategies of individual psychology along with the skills and concepts of play therapy. The Adlerian play therapist develops an egalitarian relationship with the client, then uses play to gain an understanding of the child's lifestyle and how the child conceptualizes his or her world. Next, the therapist helps the child gain insight into his or her lifestyle by using stories, artwork, metaphors, and metacommunication. Finally, the therapist provides reorientation and reeducation for the client, which can involve learning and practicing new skills.

Cognitive-behavioral play therapy combines play therapy approaches with cogntive and behavioral strategies. The cognitive-behavioral play therapist involves the child in the therapeutic process through play and examines the thoughts, feelings, and environment of the child. Next, the therapist helps the child develop more adaptive thoughts and behaviors, along with more effective problem-solving strategies. This form of play therapy is problem-focused, structured, and directive. Specific behavioral and cognitive interventions that have been proven to be successful for particular problems are employed.

Theraplay is directive, intensive, and brief. This type of play therapy is a treatment method that is modeled on the healthy interaction between parents and their children. It actively involves parents as observers and later as co-therapists. Play therapists use activities and materials that facilitate structure, challenge, intrusion/engagement, and nurture to remedy situations that create problems for children. The therapist is in charge of the session and the sessions are predictable and structured.

Ways of Using Play

Play can be used in several different ways to meet the developmental needs of all children. Orton (1997) identified the following uses of play:

1. To aid in the assessment process. The counselor notes the child's interactions, inhibitions, preoccupations, perceptions, and expressions of feelings and ideas.

2. To establish a working relationship. For children who may be fearful, nonverbal, or resistant, the use of play can help establish an accepting relationship, as in the case of Ryan. Ryan, age 6, was referred for inability to relate effectively to others. In the initial interview he sat as far away from the counselor as possible and only shook his head in response to questions. Instead of continuing to talk, the counselor got out a can of shaving cream and squirted some onto a large tray. Then she started playing with it, shaping it into different forms. Ryan watched for a few minutes and then hesitantly approached the table and began to play. The counselor added more shaving cream and some food coloring. Ryan's eyes widened, and he began making pictures out of the cream and chatting about what he was creating. By initiating the play that stimulated Ryan to interact, the counselor was able to establish a working relationship.

3. To help children express their concerns. Frequently children will not verbalize their concerns because they have been told not to (Malchiodi, 2005), or they are not able to articulate their feelings about events. Play can be used to facilitate verbalization as well as provide a means of dealing with the issue. In the following situation, the counselor used a dart game to elicit angry feelings.

   Dan was a behaviorally disordered third-grader who was hostile and aggressive with other children and adults. After an angry confrontation with the principal, the teacher requested that the counselor work with Dan. Knowing that he would be defensive, the counselor set up a dartboard equipped with rubber-tipped darts. When Dan entered the office, the counselor simply invited him to play darts. After several minutes of play, the counselor commented to Dan that he was really throwing the darts as if he were angry. Dan didn't comment, but simply continued to play. After a while he stopped and sat down. The counselor asked if there was anything he'd like to talk about, and he began to share situations in which other kids picked on him, he'd call them names and then got in trouble for name-calling. After discussing this for a while, the counselor asked Dan if he'd like to come back again to talk more about his anger and what he could do about it. He agreed to come, but expressed a desire to play darts again. Using the dartboard initiated verbalization and let Dan express his hostile, angry feelings.

4. To promote healing and growth. For example, 6-year-old Amelia was the youngest in her family. The teacher reported that several children had complained that every time Amelia played a game, she had to win. If she wasn't winning, she changed the rules. The counselor invited Amelia to play a board game, and when she tried to change the rules, the counselor commented on this. They discussed Amelia's need to win and what it said about her if she didn't win. After several sessions of this nature, the counselor invited several of Amelia's friends in to play. Amelia played the game without changing the rules. This experience seemed to successfully teach her alternative behaviors to help her interact more appropriately.

Regardless of how play is used, the therapeutic relationship is extremely important. Showing interest in what the child chooses to do and being patient and understanding are crucial. It is also imperative to be culturally sensitive when working with children from diverse cultures by becoming aware of the values, beliefs, and traditions of a child's culture as well as finding a "match" between the play therapy techniques and the child's cultural background (Kottman, 2009).

Selection of Materials

Landreth (1993) discussed the importance of selecting play materials that facilitate (1) exploration of real-life experiences, (2) expression of a wide range of feelings, (3) testing of limits, (4) expressive and exploratory play, (5) exploration and expression without verbalization, and (6) success without prescribed structure. This author warned against using mechanical or complex toys or materials that required the counselor's assistance to manipulate. Kottman (2009) suggested that toys should represent five different categories: family/nurturing toys, scary toys, aggressive toys, expressive toys, and pretend/fantasy toys. Kottman (2009) listed specific examples of toys to facilitate exploration of family/nurturing, including dolls of different ethnicities, dollhouses and furniture, play dishes, and soft blankets. Examples of scary toys, which help children express their fears and how to cope with them, include rubber snakes, monsters, insects, and fierce animal puppets. Dart guns, play swords and knives, toy soldiers, and a pounding board or bop bag were identified as toys that allowed children to express anger and aggression. Crayons, clay, paints, pipe cleaners, chalk, and newsprint were cited as examples of materials to facilitate creative expression. Pretend/fantasy toys that help children express their feelings and explore roles and behaviors include masks, costumes, hats, jewelry, telephones, magic wands, and people figures.

Toys selected should be in good condition. It is also important not to have so many toys that the room is cluttered and junky. The specific use of the toys depends on whether the approach is structured, where the counselor selects the toys to fit the child's problem, or nondirective, in which the child has more freedom to choose materials.

Games

Board games provide another way to establish rapport, facilitate verbalization, release feelings, and teach new behaviors (Vernon, 2002). Bradley et al., (2009) noted that games are familiar and non-threatening and have diagnostic value. Schaefer and Reid (2000) cited their usefulness in addressing specific topics in counseling. Games allow clients to gain a sense of mastery and receive positive feedback. For preadolescents and adolescents in particular, board games can make counseling more enjoyable and thus more productive.

Games such as checkers or chess generally work well in establishing rapport, as do other commercial board games. Once rapport has been established, the counselor may want to develop or select games that specifically address the concerns with which the child is working. The case of Stephanie illustrates this point.

Stephanie, a fourth-grader, was frequently upset because she made assumptions about what her peers were thinking and, therefore, assumed that they didn't like her, were upset with her, or didn't ever want to be her friend. To help her recognize how she upset herself by mistaking what she thought for factual information, the counselor engaged Stephanie in a game called "Fights with Friends" (Vernon, 2002, pp. 225–227). They took turns drawing assumption cards and coping strategies cards, identifying whether the child in the situation was thinking rationally (not making assumptions) and was demonstrating effective behavioral coping strategies. If not, Stephanie or the counselor had to identify what the assumptions or ineffective coping strategies were and discuss how to change them before putting an X (client) or O (counselor) on the game board (like tic-tac-toe).

After the game was completed, the counselor asked Stephanie to identify the difference between a fact and an assumption, and how making assumptions negatively affected her relationships with her friends. She then invited her client to make a set of new assumption and coping strategies cards to that pertained specifically to her situation. They were able to discuss Stephanie's tendency to mistake a fact ("My friend didn't sit by me in the lunchroom") from an assumption ("Because she didn't sit by me, there must be something wrong with me and she must not like me anymore"). The game was a concrete way of helping this fourth-grader work through her problem.

The value of play therapy is undisputed; research supports its use with a wide range of presenting problems (Johnson & Clark, 2001; Kottman, 2009; Malchiodi, 2005). Because the actual process of play therapy is complex and needs more explanation than this brief overview, the reader is encouraged to read *Play Therapy: Basics and Beyond* (Kottman, 2001), *The Play Therapy Primer* (O'Connor, 2000), or *Play Therapy Theory and Practice* by O'Connor and Braverman (2009).

SIDEBAR 10.5 Play and Games

Play is the natural language of children, so it is natural to incorporate play into counseling with children between the ages of 3 and 12. However, it can also be effective to use play with adolescents, especially those who are not very verbal. As a mental health therapist, I would sometimes play checkers with my clients, but before they could make a move, they had to draw a card out of a box and respond to it. The cards could be general get-acquainted topics or could be geared more specifically to a particular client's issues. For example, when Carrie wasn't very forthcoming about her feelings and thoughts about her parents' divorce, the checker game with cards asking specific questions about what this situation meant to her helped her to clarify and articulate what she was experiencing.

Imagery

The use of imagery, described as seeing with the mind's eye or has having an inner vision" (Gladding, 2011) has been defined as "perception that comes through any of the senses— sight, smell, touch, taste, hearing, and feeling "(Kanchier, 1997, p. 14, as cited in Gladding, 2011). The use of imagery is especially effective in helping people deal with life changes, and has increasingly been used in career counseling and life planning (Skovolt, Morgan, & Negron-Cunningham, 1989), as well as with children and adolescents (Gladding, 2011). It also has been used to help clients deal with post-traumatic stress (Smucker & Dancu, 1999), bulimia (Ohanian, 2002), physical pain (Pincus & Sheikh, 2009), marital issues (Morrison & Rasp, 2001), and couple communication (Hendrix, 2008). Witmer and Young (1987) noted that imagery facilitates awareness of personal values, emotions, goals, conflicts, and spiritual desires. Gladding (2011) emphasized that imagery is "a universal and natural modality for helping people engender, promote, or face change" (p. 63).

There is good rationale for using imagery in counseling. First of all, many clients already use imagery to help them learn new material or remember things (Gladding, 2011). Secondly, imagery can help people change behavior. Plummer (1999) noted that because the body cannot distinguish between a vivid mental experience and an actual physical experience, clients who use imagery may actually perform better. The use of imagery also teaches clients how to stimulate creativity and develop cognitive flexibility. In addition, because many client problems are connected to images of self and others, using imagery to change perspectives is helpful. Finally, imagery promotes a holistic approach (Gladding, 2011) and is especially effective with Native Americans, according to Dunn and Griggs (1995). Additionally, imagery can readily be incorporated into several different counseling theories, including Gestalt, rational emotive behavior therapy, behavioral therapy, and family therapy approaches.

Although free daydreams are often cited as one form of imagery, this section describes the use of guided imagery and concrete images to help a client re-conceptualize events and change behavior.

Guided Imagery

Guided imagery, which is sometimes called guided fantasy (Bradley et al., 2009), is a structured, directed activity designed to increase artistic expression, personal awareness, and concentration (Myrick & Myrick, 1993). In guided imagery, the counselor orchestrates a scenario for the client that consists of stimulus words or sounds to serve as a catalyst for creating a mental picture (Myrick & Myrick, 1993). The process involves inducing relaxation, the actual fantasy, and processing the fantasy (Skovholt et al., 1989). The use of relaxation is important because it helps bridge the gap between prior activities and the imagery experience to move the client's focus from external to internal.

Myrick and Myrick (1993) identified the following guidelines when using guided imagery:

1. Create a scripted story. This is particularly helpful because it allows the counselor to select words that connote vivid textures and other senses.
2. Introduce the concept of guided imagery, and instruct the client to sit or lie in a relaxed position, focusing on breathing.
3. Read the script slowly, using a quiet and soothing voice to help create vivid images.
4. Bring closure to the experience by stopping at a pleasant place accompanied by positive feelings. Inform the client that you are getting ready to stop, and as you count to three slowly, have the client open her or his eyes and stretch.
5. Invite the client to discuss the experience, focusing on positive aspects of the activity as well as his or her experiences with obstacles and how he or she overcame them.

The following script was used with a middle-aged woman who suffered from anxiety and procrastinated about completing housework and other chores. After being instructed to relax by imagining a peaceful scene and engaging in deep breathing to release tension, Jana was invited to involve herself in this imagery experience.

Setting: Imagine that it is next Monday (pause). You are waking up in the morning. What time is it? (pause) You get up and eat breakfast. Who is there? (pause) You finish breakfast. You don't have to leave for work until noon. What needs to be done? What do you do first? (pause) How do you see yourself doing this task, and how long does it take?

Is anyone helping you? If not, how are you feeling about that? (pause) You finish this activity. What do you do now? (pause) It is now time to get ready to leave for work. (pause) Work: You are now at work. Are you working alone, or are you interacting with others? What tasks are you doing? Are you enjoying them? (pause) Home: You have left work and are home again. Are you alone? (pause) If not, who is there? Do you interact with them? (pause) It is time to get dinner. Do you do this alone, or does anyone help you? (pause) Now it is after dinner. What do you do? Who is with you? (pause) Now it is time for bed. Tomorrow you will not work and will be at home all day. What will you do? How will you do it? (pause) End: You may open your eyes and we will discuss your experience.

In processing the imagery exercise, Jana said that it was not difficult to see what needed to be done, but it was hard to visualize what she would do first. Once she did select a task, it wasn't too difficult to see herself taking the necessary steps to complete it. She saw herself alone in doing the housework and resented that. She described the work portion of her day, where she had no trouble completing necessary tasks, as basically enjoyable.

In reflecting on the exercise, it seemed helpful for Jana to list the chores that needed to be done each day so she wouldn't become anxious about deciding what to do. It was also appropriate to begin teaching her some assertiveness skills so that she could negotiate for equality with the housework. The guided imagery effectively helped the counselor and client clarify issues and pinpoint target areas for goal setting and skill development.

Guided imagery has also been used successfully in career counseling where clients are asked to image "A Day in the Future"; "The Opposite Sex," growing up as the opposite sex and holding a job usually held by the opposite sex; or "Mid-Career Change or Retirement," focusing on shifting from the present career focus (Skovholt et al., 1989). Omizo, Omizo, and Kitaoka (1998) suggested using guided imagery with children to help clarify problems, reduce anxiety, enhance self-concept, and make behavioral changes. Bourne (1995) described its usefulness with athletes to achieve peak performance and as a part of a treatment program for various diseases, Pearson (2003) suggested using guided imagery to help counseling graduate students transition from student to professional, and Hendrix (2008) suggested the use of imagery to help couples overcome relationship blocks. As Hall and colleagues (2006) noted, there are many different ways to use imagery in counseling to address a variety of problems. It is a versatile approach that is culturally sensitive and appropriate for clients of all ages.

SIDEBAR 10.6 Guided Imagery

Have you ever participated in a guided imagery exercise? If so, was it effective for you? Think about a personal issue you are dealing with currently and try your hand at writing a guided imagery script similar to the one I developed for my client who became anxious when she procrastinated. It might also be useful for you to think about some examples of concrete images that would facilitate the counseling process. Jacobs (1992) used a rear view mirror to help clients focus on the present instead of the past, as well as an inflated beer bottle that he used to help clients see how alcohol got in the way of relationships. See if you can identify 5 concrete images that would be helpful to you or to clients.

Use of Concrete Images

Images can also be used therapeutically in isolation to help stimulate thinking that can lead to more productive behavior. When using images this way, the counselor tries to relate the image to something familiar to the client or something that conveys a type of metaphor, as in the following example.

Eighteen-year-old Nate was in counseling to help him deal with his depression. Irrational beliefs in the form of exaggerations, overgeneralizations, and awfulizations contributed to his depression. In the session when the image was introduced, Nate was discussing an incident with his girlfriend. He assumed that because she didn't call him every day, she didn't care about him. He said he couldn't stand it if she found someone else.

In previous sessions, the counselor had helped Nate dispute these irrational beliefs, but they continued to be quite prevalent. As Nate and the counselor were working on these irrational beliefs in the present session, the counselor glanced out the window and noticed a bug zapper. She called it to Nate's attention and asked him to watch the zapper and describe how it operated. The counselor explained to her client that he could image that his head was a zapper, too—when he started to think irrationally, he should visualize these irrational thoughts being deflected, just like the bugs were when they hit the zapper. Although this may seem simplistic, it helped Nate stop the irrational thinking more effectively because he could quickly recall the bug zapper image and use this to trigger his disputations before he felt the negative effects of the irrational beliefs. Not only did this particular client use this concrete image during adolescence, but also he used it as a college student, as a newly married man, and as a first-time father to help him think more clearly about things that were stressful.

In listening carefully to the client's problem, it is not difficult to think of helpful images. Children who have difficulty controlling impulsive behavior might be asked, when they start to feel out of control, to visualize a stop sign. Pairing the visualization with self-statements such as "I don't have to hit—I can walk away" increases the effectiveness of the image. A child who is reluctant to go to bed because she or he is afraid of monsters can visualize herself or himself in a scary Halloween costume, frightening away any monsters that might come into the room.

Gladding (2005; 2011) pointed out these benefits of imagery: it can be performed anywhere, it is an available resource that most clients already employ, it teaches clients how to use their imaginations to stimulate creative problem solving, it is a powerful type of mental practice, and it is holistic. In addition, many client problems, such as eating disorders, are connected to their images of self and others. Imagery helps clients learn about themselves, and although it might not work for everyone, it can be an extremely effective method to access information and resolve problems.

More Creative Approaches

The number of creative approaches used in a counseling session is endless. The only limiting factors are the counselor's own creative abilities to develop effective methods of helping the client resolve issues. I have found the following approaches helpful in the process of working with clients.

Props

Using props during a session can stimulate thinking or elicit emotion about a problem. Props are a way, other than words, to reach the client. For example, a woman who was constantly pessimistic was given a set of old eyeglasses and four round circles of paper—two grey and two pink. She was instructed to tape the grey paper on the glasses and talk about her day from a "doom and gloom" perspective. Next she was asked to substitute the pink paper and describe her day as if she were looking through "rose-colored glasses." She and the counselor then discussed the difference in the two perspectives and set some goals for developing a more optimistic perception of events.

In working with a young adult on her tendency to procrastinate, the counselor brought a pile of newspapers to the session. She invited her client to make a list of all the things she procrastinated about. Next, she asked her to lie on the floor and one by one, she read off the list of things about which the client procrastinated. As she read each one, she piled a bunch of newspapers on the client until the pile was quite high after all of the items on the list had been read. Next, they talked about how she felt with everything "all piled up," applying it to her personal experiences with procrastination. She then identified what she could do or say relative to each item on the list to help resolve the procrastination problems, and as she did so, the counselor lifted newspapers from the pile. This was a very graphic way to help this client remember that it is better not to let things pile up by procrastinating.

With another young client, using a tape recorder helped him become less dependent on the counselor and more skilled at solving his own problems. Adam had lots of worries, such as what he should do if someone teased him, what he should do if his mother wasn't home after school and what he should do if he didn't understand how to do his schoolwork.

Because Adam's father was concerned that Adam might be "inventing" some problems because he really liked coming to counseling, the counselor decided to teach Adam how to be his own counselor. When he arrived for his session, she asked Adam what was bothering him that week. He shared a situation about his friend teasing him, and the counselor helped Adam develop some tease tolerance techniques. Adam was to ask himself if he was what his friend said he was, if names could hurt him, and how he could handle the situation if he couldn't control what came out of the other person's mouth. Next the counselor said that she would pretend to be Adam and that Adam could be the counselor. As the counselor, Adam was asked to help solve a problem similar to his real one. After role-playing this, Adam was given a tape recorder and a blank tape. During the week, whenever he had a problem, he could use the tape recorder and first be the person who has the problem and then switch roles and pretend to be the counselor who helps him solve the problem. When Adam returned for his next session, he played the tape for the counselor. He had recorded several problems and had done a good job of helping himself deal with his problems.

Props were useful in a marriage counseling session when a rope helped a couple see the "tug of war" state of their marriage and to understand how they each felt controlled. Each person held one end of the rope, pulled on it, and verbalized one of the ways she or he felt controlled by the partner. The counselor wrote down each of the statements so the couple could also see what each other said. This simple activity was a good stimulus for mobilizing some energy and illuminating some of the issues that needed to be solved.

Use of Homework

To facilitate self-reliance, homework assignments can effectively extend the concepts dealt with during the counseling session. The following ideas can be adapted and expanded on, depending on the clients' age:

1. Have clients make a mad pillow which they decorate with pictures of things or people with whom they feel angry. When they experience anger, they can pound the pillow rather than act aggressively toward another person.

2. Suggest that when clients worry excessively about minor, as opposed to major problems, they can buy a bubble pipe. As they use it, they can visualize the minor problems blowing away.

3. Invite clients who are dealing with a lot of anger to write down on separate pieces of paper situations in which they have been angry. They should then collect as many rocks as they have slips of paper and go to a river or open field. As they throw the rocks away with force, they can yell out the name of the anger-provoking situation.

4. If clients have difficulty accomplishing tasks because they're overwhelmed with the amount of work to be done, invite them to buy a timer, set it for a given amount of time to work and a given amount of time to relax.

5. Recommend that clients make books of written text and/or illustrations to express their perceptions about a problem and their methods of solving it.

6. For clients who think that the "grass is greener on the other side of the fence" (i.e, spouses who think they would be better off single, adolescents who think they would be better off living with their friends' parents etc., have them interview people to find out more what it is "really like" on the other side.

Group Applications

The specialized individual counseling approaches previously described can usually be applied in a group context. Each of the approaches is discussed with a brief explanation of group applicability.

Art

To facilitate group cohesiveness, participants can make a collage to represent their group, using finger paint and scraps from fabric and paper. In a self-awareness group, members could tear a shape out of construction paper that tells something about themselves as a way to introduce themselves to the group. To teach cooperation, group participants could be given paper, tape, and magazines and instructions to design an object of beauty. Roles that members play in developing this project could then be discussed. In a group setting, members might take turns drawing symbols that they feel represent other group members as a way to provide feedback on how they come across to others.

Music

Musical activities facilitate self-awareness and interpersonal relationships. In a classroom setting, students can compose and perform their own compositions related to guidance topics: feelings, self-concept, decision making, friendship, or values. Newsome (2003) noted that music can be especially effective when a small group is nearing closure. She suggested that group members can use song lyrics to express what they had experienced in the group and then play portions of the songs for the others in the group. Music can also be used in classroom guidance as an energizer, to set the mood, or as a way of emphasizing the theme of a lesson.

Bowman (1987) described the "feelings ensemble." A group is divided into smaller groups of five or six, and each group is given a feeling word that becomes the title of their composition. They are instructed to make up and perform a song in front of the large group that describes their feeling word. They may use sound makers such as pencils or rulers, or the counselor can provide them with whistles, horns, harmonicas, or kazoos. After several minutes of planning, each group performs while other members attempt to guess what feeling they are expressing.

Music is also a good way to build group identity and cohesiveness. Group members can compose a song or select a recording that expresses who they are. An alternative activity is the musical collage. Each individual group member selects short segments of songs that have meaning, and tapes each of these segments to create a collage. After listening to each person's collage, group members discuss how the music represents that individual (Bowman, 1987).

Writing

Various forms of writing can be adapted for group use. Open-ended sentences can become a get-acquainted activity or prompt discussion and sharing. Questionnaires are also used this way, or they can be adapted to the specific focus of the group. For example, members of a stress management group might be given a questionnaire about ways they deal with stress. As responses are shared, members will benefit from hearing others' ideas.

In a classroom setting, students can be given journal topics related to self-awareness, clarification of values, or feelings about various issues. Examples of topics include

"Something I like best about myself is..."
"Something I feel strongly about is..."
"Something I'm good at doing is..."
"Something that I value highly is..."

Topics of this nature encourage self-exploration. Journal writing can be further shared in student dyads or triads to clarify responses. In such a situation, participants must feel comfortable with the sharing and have the option to pass if they wish.

Bibliotherapy

Borders and Paisley (1992) suggested that bibliotherapy be used not only in problem-centered interventions in individual or small-group counseling, but also with children in classroom guidance, to promote developmental growth. Their research indicated that the use of stories is an effective approach to help children solve problems and enhance personal growth.

Play

For younger children, particularly in a school setting, play can be highly effective in a small group of four or five children to improve socialization skills. One or two children in the group are selected as good models; the targeted individuals may need to develop cooperative versus competitive behavior, learn to control aggression, become more comfortable with group interaction, or learn to share.

In the group setting, the play is generally more structured and the toys used are selected to help children work on the desirable behaviors. For instance, if two of the children in the group have difficulty sharing, the counselor may have only one can of blocks for all group members to use. As the children play with the blocks, the counselor reflects on the interaction and involves the children in discussing how it feels when friends share or don't share, thus seeking to develop behaviors that will transfer to other situations.

Board games can also be developed for group use. A game called *Road to Achievement* (Vernon, 2002, p. 202) helps children identify effective study skills. *Stress Busters* (Vernon, 2009, p. 135) is a game similar to *Twister*, where children move around on a stress buster board and identify various ways to handle stressful situations. Another good game to use in small groups is *Stop or Go Behavior* (Vernon, 2009, p. 222), where children move match box cars around a game board and identify positive and negative behaviors.

Imagery

Guided imagery can be readily applied to a group setting. In a classroom or small group, students could be led in a guided imagery relative to test taking, task completion, stress management, or cooperative behavior with classmates. Guided imagery has also been used extensively in career development. Heppner, O'Brien, Hinkelman, & Humphrey (1994) described using guided imagery in life planning to spur the imagination of their clients. Jacobs (1992) used projective fantasies in a group setting where participants were encouraged to imagine themselves as a common object and to describe what their lives would be like if they were this object. As a result of this activity, they were able to see their lives differently.

Conclusion

As Carson and Becker (2004) noted, "The concept of creativity in counseling is not a novel one" (p. 150). Creative approaches to counseling enhance the counseling process in many ways and are enjoyable and self-motivating for clients. Gladding (2011) noted that approaches of this nature are "process-oriented, emotionally sensitive, socially directed, and awareness-focused" (preface) and can help clients from diverse backgrounds enhance their development. Culturally competent counselors will find that using art, music, literature, or play, as an adjunct or an alternative to traditional approaches may be the most meaningful way of engaging clients of all ages.

These creative arts approaches are not limited to the descriptions in this chapter. Movement, dance, drama, humor, and puppetry are other approaches that can meet client needs. No "universal" format exists for application, the creativity of the counselor and assessment of what would most effectively engage the client guide the implementation. The training needed to use these specialized approaches depends on whether they are used to supplement a verbal approach or constitute the major aspect of the counseling. As Nickerson and O'Laughlin (1982) noted, the issue is perhaps one of degree. In other words, a counselor does not have to be an artist to use some art with clients who are not able to express themselves verbally, but if art were the primary modality, further training would be needed.

Creative approaches have been used successfully with children and adolescents (Bradley et al., 2009; Gladding, 2011; Newsome, 2003; Vernon, 2002, 2009), the elderly (Gladding, 2011), clients with eating disorders (Robbins & Pehrsson, 2009; Sapp, 2000), children from violent homes (Malchiodi, 2005), and with Alzheimer's patients

(Forinash, 2005). They can be used to treat specific problems or can be applied preventively, particularly in school settings.

The diversity of specialized counseling approaches can help effectively address a wide range of client needs, including clients from diverse backgrounds. These methods move counseling beyond the mental arena, which relies on verbal techniques, to a more comprehensive orientation using a multitude of approaches.

SIDEBAR 10.7 Why Creativity?

Having read the chapter, reflect on what you learned and how you think incorporating creative arts interventions into the counseling process could enhance your performance as a counselor. Summarize your learnings in a creative way: make a collage, write a song or a limerick, paint or draw a picture, or write a short story about what you will do with this information. Or, you could imagine that you are an advocate for the use of creativity in counseling and are trying to convince stodgy counselors who only rely on traditional approaches why it would be valuable to consider these approaches. Think of creative ways you could do this!

Summary

Although counseling has traditionally been characterized by a verbal orientation, practitioners are now encouraged to explore other methods to help people cope with psychological problems. In this chapter, a variety of creative approaches to counseling were described. These approaches have been found to be effective for a variety of problems presented by both children and adults.

As discussed in this chapter, creative approaches to counseling can be adapted to fit the client's learning style. Art, imagery and writing were identified as appropriate strategies for clients of all ages. Specific ways to use music, bibliotherapy, and play were also described. Implementing approaches of this nature can enhance the counseling process because they combine theory and practice in flexible ways to focus on the unique aspects of the client and the problem.

The following websites provide additional information relating to chapter topics:

Useful Websites

www.arttherapy.com
www.selfesteembookshop.com
www.nadt.org
www.healingstory.org
www.mucictherapy.org
www.phototherapy-centre.com
www.impactpublishers.com

References

Allan, J. (1982). Social drawing: A therapeutic approach with young children. In E. T. Nickerson, & K. O'Laughlin (Eds.), *Helping through action: Action-oriented therapies* (pp. 25–32). Amherst, MA: Human Resource Development Press.

Allan, J. (2008). *Inscapes of the child's world*. New York: Continuum International Publishing Group.

Baikie, K. A., & Wilhem, K. (2005). Emotional and physical health benefits of expressive writing. *Advances in Psychiatric Treatment, 11*, 338–346.

Bates, M. (1993). Poetic responses to art: Summoning the adolescent voice. *Journal of Poetry Therapy, 3,* 149–156.

Bauer, M. S., & Balius, F. A. (1995). Storytelling: Integrating therapy and curriculum for students with serious emotional disturbances. *Teaching Exceptional Children, 27,* 24–29.

Borders, S., & Paisley, P. O. (1992). Children's literature as a source for classroom guidance. *Elementary School Guidance and Counseling, 27,* 131–139.

Bourne, E. J. (1995). *The anxiety and phobia workbook*. Oakland, CA: New Harbinger Publications.

Bowman, R. P. (1987). Approaches for counseling children through music. *Elementary School Guidance and Counseling, 21,* 284–291.

Bradley, L. J., Hendricks, C. B., & Crews, C. R. (2009). Expressive techniques: Counseling interventions for children and adolescents. In A. Vernon (Ed.), *Counseling children and adolescents* (4th ed., pp. 83–122). Denver, CO: Love Publishing.

Brems, C. (2002). *A comprehensive guide to child psychotherapy* (2nd ed.). Boston, MA: Allyn & Bacon.

Broder, M. S. (2002). *Can your relationship be saved?* Atascadero, CA: Impact Publishers.

Burnett, K. G. (2000). *Simon's hook: A story about teasing and put-downs*. Roseville, CA: GR Publishing.

Bush, J. (1997). *The handbook of school art therapy*. Springfield, IL: Charles C. Thomas Publisher, Ltd.

Carlson, N. (1992). *What if it never stops raining?* New York: Puffin Books.

Caron, J. C. (2005). DSM at the movies: Use of media in clinical or educational settings. In G. R. Walz, & R. K. Yep (Eds.), *VISTAS: Compelling perspectives on counseling 2005* (pp. 179–182). Alexandria, VA: American Counseling Association.

Carson, D. K., & Becker, K. W. (2003). *Creativity in mental health practice*. New York: Haworth.

Conley, D. (1994). *If you believe in you*. Coco Records: Treehouse Publishing.

Davis, W. B., Gfeller, K. E., & Thaut, M. H. (1999). *An introduction to music therapy: Theory and practice* (2nd ed.). Boston: McGraw-Hill.

Degges-White, S., & Davis, N. L. (2011). *Integrating the expressive arts into counseling practice: Theory-based interventions*. New York: Springer.

DeLucia-Waack, J. D. (2001). *Using music in children of divorce groups: A session by session manual for counselors*. Alexandria, VA: American Counseling Association.

DeLucia-Waack, J. L., & Gellman, R. A. (2007). The efficacy of using music in children of divorce groups: Impact on anxiety, depression, and irrational beliefs about divorce. *Group Dynamics: Theory, Research, and Practice, 11,* 272–282.

Doll, B., & Doll, C. (1997). *Bibliotherapy with young people*. Englewood, CA: Libraries Unlimited.

Duffey, T. (2007). *Creative interventions in grief and loss therapy: When the music stops, a dream dies*. Florence, KY: Taylor & Francis.

Dunn, R., & Griggs, S. A. (1995). *Multiculturalism and learning style*. Westport, CT: Praeger.

Forinash, M. (2005). Music therapy. In C. A. Malchiodi (Ed.), *Expressive therapies* (pp. 46–67). New York: Guilford Press.

Gladding, S. T. (1987). The poetics of a "check out" place: Preventing burnout and promoting self-renewal. *Journal of Poetry Therapy, 1,* 95–102.

Gladding, S. T. (1995). Creativity in counseling. *Counseling and Human Development, 28*(1), 1–12.

Gladding, S. T. (2005). *Counseling as an art: the creative arts in counseling* (3rd ed.). Alexandria, VA: American Counseling Association.

Gladding, S. T. (2011). *The creative arts in counseling* (4th ed.). Alexandria, VA: American Counseling Association.

Gladding, S. T., & Gladding, C. T. (1991). The ABC's of bibliotherapy. *The School Counselor, 39,* 7–13.

Gorelick, K. (2005). Poetry therapy. In C. A. Malchiodi (Ed.), *Expressive therapies* (pp. 117–140). New York: Guildford.

Griggs, S. A. (1985). Counseling for individual learning styles. *Journal of Counseling and Development, 64,* 202–205.

Griggs, S. A., Price, G. E., Kopel, S., & Swaine, W. (1984). The effects of group counseling on sixth-grade students with different learning styles. *California Journal of Counseling and Development, 5,* 28–35.

Guzzetta, C. E. (1991). A method for conducting improvised musical play with children both with and without developmental delays in preschool classrooms. *Music Therapy Perspectives, 9,* 46–51.

Hall, E., Hall, C., Stradlikng, P., & Young, D. (2006). *Guided imagery: Creative interventions in counseling and psychotherapy.* Thousand Oaks, CA: Sage.

Hendricks, P. B. (2000). A study of the use of music therapy techniques in a group for the treatment of adolescent depression. *Dissertation Abstracts International, 62,* 107.

Hendrix, H. (2008). *Getting the love you want: A guide for couples.* New York: Holt.

Heppner, M. J., O'Brien, K. M., Hindelman, J. M., & Humphrey, C. A. (1994). Shifting the paradigm: the use of creativity in career counseling. *Journal of Career Development, 21,* 77–86.

Higgens, J. A., & Dermer, S. (2001). The use of film in marriage and family counselor education. *Counselor Education and Superivison, 40,* 182–192.

Horden, P. (2000). *Music as medicine: The history of music therapy since antiquity.* Aldershot: Ashgate.

Hutchins, D. E., & Cole, C. G. (1992). *Helping relationships and strategies.* Pacific Grove, CA: Brooks/Cole.

Hynes, A. (1990). Poetry: An avenue into the spirit. *Journal of Poetry Therapy, 4,* 71–81.

Jackson, T. (2001). Using bibliotherapy with clients. *Journal of Individual Psychology, 57,* 289–297.

Jacobs, E. (1992). *Creative counseling techniques: An illustrated guide.* Odess, FL: Psychological Assessment Resources.

Jennings, B., & Vance, D. (2002). The short-term effects of music therapy on different types of agitation in adults with Alzheimer's. *Activities, Adaptation, and Aging, 26,* 27–33.

Johnson, S., & Clark, P. (2001). Play therapy with aggressive acting-out children. In G. Landreth (Ed.), *Innovations in play therapy: Issues, process, and special populations* (pp. 323–333). Philadelphia, PA: Taylor & Francis.

Joshua, J. M., & DiMenna, D. (2000). *Read two books and let's talk next week: Using bibliotherapy in clinical practice.* New York: John Wiley & Sons.

Kenny, A. (1987). An art activities approach: Counseling the gifted, creative and talented. *Gifted Child Today, 10,* 33–37.

Kottler, J. A. (2004). *Introduction to therapeutic counseling: Voices from the field.* Pacific Grove, CA: Brooks/Cole.

Kottman, T. (2001). *Play therapy: Basics and beyond.* Alexandria, VA: American Counseling Association.

Kottman, T. (2009). Play therapy. In A. Vernon (Ed.), *Counseling children and adolescents* (4th ed., pp. 123–146). Denver, CO: Love Publishing.

Kwiatowska, H. (2001). Family art therapy: Experiments with new techniques. *American Journal of Art Therapy, 40,* 27–39.

Landreth, G. L. (1993). Child-centered play therapy. *Elementary School Guidance and Counseling Journal, 28,* 17–29.

Lev-Weisel, R., & Daphna-Tekoha, S. (2000). The self-revelation through color technique: Understanding client's relationships with significant others through the use of color. *American Journal of Art Therapy, 39,* 35–41.

MacIntosh, H. B. (2003). Sounds of healing: Music in group work with survivors of sexual abuse. *Arts in Psychotherapy, 30,* 17–23.

Malchiodi, C. A. (2003). *Handbook of art therapy.* New York: Guilford Press.

Malchiodi, C. A. (Ed.). (2005). *Expressive therapies.* New York: Guilford Press.

Mercer, L. E. (1993). Self-healing through poetry writing. *Journal of Poetry Therapy, 6,* 161–168.

Morrison, N. C., & Rasp, R. R. (2001). The application of facilitated imagery to marital counseling. In B. J. Brothers (Ed.), *Couples, intimacy issues, and addiction* (pp. 131–151). New York: Haworth Press.

Myrick, R. D. (1997). *Developmental guidance and counseling: A practical approach.* Minneapolis, MN: Educational Media.

Myrick, R. D., & Myrick, L. S. (1993). Guided imagery: From mystical to practical. *Elementary School Guidance and Counseling, 28,* 62–70.

Newcomb, N. S. (1994). Music: A powerful resource for the elementary school counselor. *Elementary School Guidance and Counseling, 29,* 150–155.

Newsome, D. W. (2003). Counseling interventions using expressive arts. In B. T. Erford (Ed.), *Transforming the school counseling profession* (pp. 231–247). Upper Saddle River, NJ: Merrill Prentice Hall.

Nichols, M. (2010). *Family therapy: Concepts and methods* (9th ed.). Upper Saddle River, NJ: Pearson.

Nickerson, E. T., & O'Laughlin, K. (Eds.). (1982). *Helping through action: Action-oriented therapies.* Amherst, MA: Human Resource Development Press.

Nugent, S. A. (2000). Perfectionism: Its manifestations and classroom based interventions. *Journal of Secondary Gifted Education, 11,* 215–221.

O'Connor, K. (2000). *The play therapy primer* (2nd ed.). New York: Wiley.

O'Connor, K. J., & Braverman, L. M. (Eds.). (2009). *Play therapy theory and practice: Comparing theories and techniques* (2nd ed.). New York: Wiley.

Ohanian, V. (2002). Imagery rescripting within cognitive behavior therapy for bulimia nervosa: An illustrative case report. *International Journal of Eating Disorders, 31,* 352–357.

Omizo, M. M., Omizo, S. A., & Kitaoka, S. K. (1998). Guided affective and cognitive imagery to enhance self-esteem among Hawaiian children. *Journal of Multicultural Counseling and Development, 26,* 52–62.

Orton, G. L. (1997). *Strategies for counseling with children and their parents.* Pacific Grove, CA: Brooks/Cole.

Osterag, J. (2002). Unspoken stories: Music therapy with abused children. *Canadian Journal of Music Therapy, 9,* 10–29.

Pardeck, J. T. (1998). *Using books in clinical social work practice: A guide to bibliotherapy.* New York: The Haworth Press.

Parr, G., Haberstroh, S., & Kottler, J. (2000). Interactive journal writing as an adjunct in group work. *Journal for Specialists in Group Work, 25,* 229–242.

Pearson, Q. M. (2003). Polished rocks: A culminating guided imagery for counselor interns. *Journal of Humanistic Counseling, Education and Development, 42,* 116–120.

Pehrsson, D. E. (2006). Fictive bibliotherapy and therapeutic storytelling with children who hurt. *Journal of Creativity in Mental Health, 1,* 273–286.

Pehrsson, D. E., & McMillen, P. (2007). A bibliotherapy evaluation tool: Grounding counselors in the therapeutic use of literature. *Arts in Psychotherapy, 32,* 47–59.

Pehrsson, D. E., Allen, V. P., Folger, W. A., McMillen, P., & Lowe, I. (2007). Bibliotherapy with adolescents experiencing a divorce. *The Family Journal, 15,* 409–414.

Peters, J. S. (2000). *Music therapy: An introduction* (2nd ed.). Springfield, IL: Charles C. Thomas.

Pincus, D., & Sheikah, A. A. (2009). *Imagery for pain relief: A scientifically grounded guidebook for clinicians.* New York: Routledge.

Piper, W. (1986). *The little engine that could.* New York: Platt & Munk.

Plummer, D. (1999). *Using interactive imagework with children: Walking on the magic mountain.* Philadelphia: J. Kingsley.

Rio, R. (2002). Improvisation with the elderly: Moving from creative activities to process-oriented therapy. *Arts in Psychotherapy, 29,* 191–201.

Riordan, R. J., & Ketchum, S. B. (1996). Therapeutic correspondence: The usefulness of notes and letters in counseling. *Georgia Journal of Professional Counseling,* 31–40.

Robbins, J. M., & Pehrsson, D. E. (2009). Anorexia nervosa: A synthesis of poetic and narrative therapies in the outpatient treatment of young adult women. *Journal of Creativity in Mental Health, 4,* 42–56.

Rubin, J. A. (2010). *Introduction to art therapy: Sources and resources.* New York: Routledge.

Sapp, M. (2000). *Hypnosis, dissociation, and absorption: Theories, assessment, and treatment.* Springfield, IL: Charles C. Thomas.

Schaefer, C. E., & Reid, S. E. (2000). *Game play: Therapeutic use of childhood games.* New York: Wiley.

Scieszka, J. (1989). *The true story of the 3 little pigs!* New York: Scholastic.

Shallcross, L. (2011). Big screen therapy. *Counseling Today, 54,* 36–40.

Silver, R. (2001). *Art as language.* Lillington, NC: Edwards Brothers.

Silverman, D. (1991). Art psychotherapy: An approach to borderline adults. In H. B. Langarten, & D. Lubbers (Eds.), *Adult art psychotherapy.* New York: Brunner/Mazel.

Silverman, M. (2008). Nonverbal communication, music therapy, and autism: A review of literature and case example. *Journal of Creativity in Mental Health, 3,* 3–19.

Skovholt, T. M., Morgan, J. I., & Negron-Cunningham, H. (1989). Mental imagery in career counseling and life planning: A review of research and intervention methods. *Journal of Counseling and Development, 67,* 287–292.

Sloan, G. (2003). *Give them poetry!* New York: Teachers College Press.

Smucker, M. R., & Dancu, C.V. (1999). *Cognitive-behavioral treatment for adult survivors of childhood trauma: Imagery rescripting and reprocessing.* Northvale, N.J: Jason Aronson.

Stepakoff, S. (2009). From destruction to creation, from silence to speech: Poetry therapy principles and practices for working with suicide grief. *Arts in Psychotherapy, 36,* 105–113.

Stevens, R., & Spears, E. H. (2009). Incorporating photography as a therapeutic tool in counseling. *Journal of Creativity in Mental Health, 4,* 3–16.

Thaut, M. H. (1990). Neuropsychological processes in music relevance in music therapy. In R. F. Unkefer (Ed.), *Music therapy in treatment of adults with mental disorders: Theoretical bases and clinical interventions* (pp. 3–32). New York: Macmillan.

Thompson, C., Rudolph, L., & Henderson, D. (2004). *Counseling children.* Belmont, CA: Brooks/Cole.

Vernon, A. (2002). *What works when with children and adolescents: A handbook of individual counseling techniques.* Champaign, IL: Research Press.

Vernon, A. (2009). *More what works when with children and adolescents: A handbook of individual counseling techniques.* Champaign, IL: Research Press.

Vernon, A., & Clemente, R. (2005). *Assessment and intervention with children and adolescents: Developmental and multicultural considerations.* Alexandria, VA: American Counseling Association.

Vick, R. M. (2003). A brief history of art therapy. In C. A. Malchiodi (Ed.), *Handbook of art therapy* (pp. 5–15). New York: Guilford Press.

Vondracek, F. W., & Corneal, S. (1995). *Strategies for resolving individual and family problems.* Pacific Grove, CA: Brooks/Cole.

Wagner, W. G. (2003). *Counseling, psychology, and children.* Upper Saddle River, NJ: Merrill-Prentice Hall.

Welfel, E. R., & Patterson, L. E. (2005). *The counseling process: A multitheoretical integrative approach.* Belmont, CA: Thompson Brooks/Cole.

Wigram, T., Pedersen, I. N., & Bonde, L.-O. (2002). *A comprehensive guide to music therapy: Theory, clinical practice, research and training.* London: Jessica Kingsley.

White, V. E., & Murray, M. A. (2002). Passing notes: the use of therapeutic letter writing in counseling adolescents. *Journal of Mental Health Counseling, 24*(2), 166.

Winsor, R. M. (1993). Hypnosis-A neglected tool for client empowerment. *Social Work, 38,* 603–608.

Witmer, J. M., & Young, M. E. (1987). Imagery in counseling. *Elementary School Guidance and Counseling, 22,* 5–15.

Woytowich, J. M. (1994). The power of the poem in the counseling office. *School Counselor, 42,* 78–80.

Yarrow, P. (2000). *Don't laugh at me.* Los Angeles, CA: Warner Brothers Records.

11

ASSESSMENT PRACTICES IN COUNSELING

Linda H. Foster

Goldman (1971) proposed, in the introduction of his historically significant text *Using Tests in Counseling,* that assessment and counseling are inextricably linked. He wrote, "The types of tests used, and the ways in which assessment is conducted, differ to some extent, but all have in common a relationship between counselor and client in which the client's well-being, adjustment, and choices are paramount" (p. 1). Goldman's prophetic words continue to be relevant. Presently, counselors have ever increasing needs and demands for valid and reliable information about their clients in order to provide the most effective and empirically based treatment.

Assessment is an important part of the work of those in the helping professions and it requires substantive knowledge and well-honed counseling skills. The holistic process of gathering information about a client can help counselors define clients' problems and concerns, determine the frequency and intensity of these problems, and determine how clients and their families are being affected by these concerns. Additionally, assessment can help find clients' strengths and weaknesses and provide a roadmap for the treatment of clients and or their families. Assessment is much more than merely giving tests. A systematic approach using multiple methods, gathering as much information as possible from the client and from other sources, provides the client with the best possible information in order to make informed decisions for more effective living.

Unfortunately, some counselors have been reluctant to accept the suggestion that assessment is an integral part of counseling, instead viewing it as an unnecessary addition to their counseling practice. This perspective ignores the reality that counselors quite routinely, but usually subjectively, gather and interpret information from and about their clients. Effective counselors not only acknowledge that gathering and interpreting subjective information are important parts of counseling processes, but also recognize that objective assessment can facilitate and enhance achievement of counseling goals and the efficiency of their counseling.

What is Assessment?

Assessment is simply a systematic approach to collecting information about a client using a variety of sources and methods. Formal and informal methods of assessment can be used throughout the counseling process to gain understanding and insight for both the client and the counselor. Assessment often begins with the first contact with the client and may even occur during an initial telephone intake session. All information that is provided by the client and/or the client's family should be considered part of the assessment process, which is ongoing throughout the counseling process.

Some counselors' attitudes toward assessment may stem from confusion about semantics. Measurement, evaluation, assessment, appraisal and testing are sometimes used interchangeably; nevertheless, there are unique yet subtle differences. *Measurement* may be considered the assignment of numerical or categorical values to human attributes according to rules (Aiken & Groth-Marnat, 2006). *Assessment* includes measurement and also can be considered the data-gathering process or method (Drummond & Jones, 2010). *Evaluation* subsumes assessment and can be considered the interpretation and application of measurement data according to rules (Vacc & Loesch, 2000). *Appraisal* is sometimes considered synonymous to assessment (Vacc & Loesch, 2000), but more frequently linked with evaluation. Still sound confusing? This chapter focuses on assessment as an overall process and includes *testing* as a component of the entire assessment process, including collecting information through multiple methods (e.g., interviews, tests, observations). Multiple methods, both formal and informal, allow counselors to measure human concepts such as emotion, intelligence, personality, self-esteem, and aptitude (Naugle, 2009). There are various formal and informal instruments and strategies such as unstructured interviews, checklists, questionnaires, rating scales, projective testing instruments, and standardized tests (Drummond & Jones, 2010). Through observations and interviews, counselors can take note of client behaviors, both overt and covert. Whitson (2009) noted that tests only provide a sample of the clients' behaviors through their responses to test questions in a particular moment. Obtaining information from multiple sources may include the client, but can also include family members, spouses/partners, teachers, physicians, or other mental health professionals (Drummond & Jones, 2010). By including multiple sources, the counselor ensures that the assessment process will have breadth as well as depth (Neukrug & Fawcett, 2010).

Why Use It in Counseling?

Assessment is a vital part of the counseling process. Clients come to counseling for a variety of reasons, and sometimes without full awareness of their strengths or weaknesses. Counselors must assess the client's situation in order to conceptualize and help define the client's problem. By assessing the client's situation or problem in a holistic and comprehensive way, counselors can select and implement the most effective treatment. Additionally, assessment helps counselors to assess their own effectiveness and demonstrate their commitment to the client's well-being (Whitson, 2009).

Using assessment in counseling has several distinct advantages over other types of counselor interactions and data gathering with clients. First, assessment can provide a comprehensive and systematic way to gather information and gain insight all with the goal of promoting and improving the client's well-being. Second, assessment (in most cases) enables normative comparison of a client's personal data with that of similar persons, which can help to normalize client's concerns. Third, it typically results in a concise summary of client characteristics. Finally, assessment *may* "uncover" client characteristics about which the client is unaware. Thus, substantive information about clients' characteristics, behaviors, or problems can be gained quickly when assessment is used as a fundamental part of initial counseling activities (Drummond & Jones, 2010).

> Assessment can involve value judgments being made about measurement results, and, therefore, about people. For this reason, assessment sometimes has become equated with "labeling" people. Most counselors do not want to be viewed as "labeling" people because it suggests being judgmental. So, counselors often

complain about assessment based on a misunderstanding of what it really is. Counselors need to view assessment as an integral part of the counseling process in order to help clients with developmental issues rather than merely diagnosing pathology (Whitson, 2009). Diagnosis when accomplished through assessment should be more than assigning a "label" and should include information about a client's strengths, weaknesses, etiology, and the best choices for treatment planning.

(Gregory, 2007)

SIDEBAR 11.1 Case Study: Harry Gets a Label

Kristy and Samuel come to your office concerned about a referral from the school system about their 8-year-old son, Harry. Harry has had difficulties in school since kindergarten and the school believes that testing is required to determine if Harry has a learning disability. Your clients are anxious about their son being "diagnosed" and "labeled". Additionally, the parents mention they recently moved into a more affluent neighborhood and school system.

Testing in the educational setting causes high anxiety for parents and the children involved. Counselors are challenged to advocate for assessments that recognize the impact of culture including socioeconomic status. Counselors must advocate for socially marginalized populations and use caution to avoid "labeling". How can you help avoid the use of labels and share information with your clients in a non-judgmental manner? How can you incorporate social justice into your counseling practice? Finally, in what ways can you provide assessment that respects cultural identity of your client?

For counseling to be effective, counselors must gain accurate information about clients as quickly as possible. In fact, counselors may be required to create an effective treatment plan, and/ or provide a *diagnosis* soon after initial contact with their clients. Unfortunately, the term diagnosis is not used consistently in the counseling profession. In some contexts, it simply means "trying to find out what's going on with the client" (i.e., to determine rather general information about a client or the client's problem). In other contexts, it means to determine a specific mental health diagnosis based on the DSM-IV-TR. For example, Gregory (2007) wrote that, "Diagnosis consists of two intertwined tasks: determining the nature and source of a person's abnormal behavior, and classifying the behavior pattern within an accepted diagnostic system" (p. 38). However, in either case, one efficient means of gaining accurate information from which to understand a person's behavior is assessment.

SIDEBAR 11.2 Case Study: What Is Larry's Problem?

Larry, 59 year old, white male, comes to your office stating that he feels bad all the time. He is gainfully employed, reports being happily married, with adult children, but he states that he feels "uneasy all the time". He states that "nothing is really wrong" and is not sure he "needs" counseling. As the counselor how can you help Larry figure it out?

When clients come to counseling they may not know "what is really going on" and may be unaware of exactly what is contributing to their distress. As the counselor, how would you most efficiently find out about your client? What is the most effective source for determining the presenting problem? Is the client your only source for information? How can you develop trust and rapport and utilize assessment in a meaningful way?

Brief History of Assessment

Assessment provides an expedient way to gain information and insight for the client and the counselor, provide a diagnosis, and normalizes certain feelings and behaviors. While testing was used even in the time of Socrates and Plato to assess an individual's competences and vocational aptitude, and as early as 2200 B.C.E. by the Chinese for civil service employees, the testing movement did not begin in the United States until around the beginning of the 20th century (Drummond & Jones, 2010; Neukrug & Fawcett, 2010). The earliest rudimentary assessments were geared towards vocational and career interests. In France, however, during the 1800s, cognitive functioning began to be assessed forming the basis for intelligence testing (Neukrug & Fawcett, 2010). Esquirol and Sequin are thought to have been the first to examine verbal intelligence and performance intelligence respectively. As these cognitive development theories evolved, Charles Darwin (1809–1882) proposed his theory of evolution and thus began the curiosity and fascination with trying to understand human behavior. Darwin's cousin, Sir Frances Galton (1822–1911) began in earnest to examine the relationship between physical strength and intellectual capacity. During this time, investigation of human behavior and intellect expanded significantly as other researchers such as Wundt (1832–1920) and Cattell (1860–1944) established psychological testing and the term "mental test" was coined (Anastasi & Urbina, 1997). Finally, no historical review of assessment would be complete without mentioning Alfred Binet (1857–1911) and Lewis Terman (1877–1956) who were both instrumental in the further development of intellectual testing. Intelligence quotient (IQ), which is the ratio of chronological age to mental age, was created by Terman and is still used today as the formula to express intellectual ability (Neukrug & Fawcett, 2010).

Purpose of Testing

The purpose or reason for assessment is determined by the client and counselor together in order to enhance the counseling process and should be driven by the client's needs. The primary purposes for assessment can be educational, psychological or in the career area, providing a reliable and valid tool, again benefitting both the client and the counselor. Some of the purposes can include screening and selection, identification and diagnosis, treatment planning, and client progress. Assessment of ability, personality, interest, intelligence, achievement, and performance are human constructs which can be measured in order to provide a comprehensive picture of the client's situation and enhance the counseling process.

Selection or Screening

One useful purpose for testing includes the selection or screening process helping to identify persons who might benefit from counseling or who are eligible for counseling service. Screening instruments are typically brief assessments and may be used to decide whether more immediate or more intensive treatment is needed or to determine if further evaluation is warranted (Aiken & Groth-Marnat, 2006). In educational settings, large-scale assessment programs may be used to identify students whose scores appear as "outliers" and *may* suggest the need for special education services. Screening can also be used in employment situations to determine skills required to perform a certain job related task and essentially is used for selection purposes. Using test information for selection or screening usually involves measurement and evaluation of specific attributes helping to facilitate decision making in areas such as education, business/industry or employment, or counseling. Consequently, test results often are used to supplement subjective information (i.e., personal judgments) so that decision making is improved and more objective.

Placement and/or Planning

Counselors often use test results to help them determine the most appropriate situations (e.g., educational programs or occupational categories) in which to place people. This use of assessment is closely related to the selection or screening use, except that the focus of placement is typically narrower than that for a selection process. For example, determining assignment to a particular program of study within an institution of higher education is usually a narrower focus than determining eligibility for admission to the institution. Similarly, determining an applicant's appropriate job classification may be narrower in scope than determining the applicant's suitability for employment. Assessment for planning also usually involves the assessment of ability level or competency, and often the process is indistinguishable from that for placement. However, in this case, tests are used specifically to determine areas of functioning where increased competency is needed. Assessment for planning involves identifying the best methods to facilitate the necessary improvement for the client.

Facilitation of Self-Understanding

A primary reason clients seek counseling services is for the facilitation of self-understanding. One of the roles of the counselor in this regard is as an information gatherer, transmitter, and interpreter. This role necessitates the integration of both communication and assessment skills in order to provide clients with multiple sources of information. Whiston (2009) wrote that because assessment is an integral part of the counseling process, practitioners must become competent and skilled in the area of assessment. Counselors' effectiveness in this role is largely contingent upon clients' trust in the counselor. Clients must strongly trust their counselors before they will agree to exploration leading to self-understanding. This trust is difficult to achieve in early stages of the counseling process. However, assessment is one means by which counselors can obtain information which enhances feedback to clients. Using "objective" test information may then increase counselors' "credibility" with their clients.

Test results also may be used to normalize aspects tested, in turn leading to clients' self-understanding. For example, clients often wish to know how their characteristics, attributes, abilities, or behaviors compare with those of other people. Another possible use for clients in this regard is to use test results to identify specific aspects of themselves they may wish to change. Therefore, assessment facilitating self-understanding may help clients identify counseling goals.

The assessment process can focus on characteristic behaviors and many tests incorporate logical, systematic, and relatively "transparent" approaches to analysis of human behavior. Assessment may help clients discover new ways of evaluating themselves.

SIDEBAR 11.3 Self-Awareness: The Need for Assessment in Counseling

As you enter the counseling profession, have you participated in self-assessment? What information did you gain from engaging in self-assessment? Perhaps your experience with assessment has been more than merely a self-assessment. Through counseling, problems and concerns can be investigated and examined. Many times clients do not recognize the frequency and intensity of their problems and cannot find solutions. Using assessment in counseling can help find a client's strengths and weaknesses and provide solutions. A systematic approach using multiple sources helps the counselor and client enhance the therapeutic process. Have you utilized assessment as a student to gain information about yourself? What did you discover?

Assessment of Individual Progress

With increasing frequency and increased accountability demands, counselors are being required to demonstrate the effectiveness of their counseling activities to others, particularly others outside the counseling profession. Managed health care organizations, school boards and increasingly clients want evidence that counseling is effective and worth the cost (Whitson, 2009). Although there are a wide variety of ways that counselors can generate evidence of their counseling effectiveness, the use of tests is clearly one of the more accepted and expeditious methods. Effective counseling is synonymous with client change, which presumably is perceived by clients as positive. However, demonstration of client change is difficult if left to subjective interpretations by clients or counselors. The use of test data provides an objective way to document client change information. For example, pre- and post-counseling assessments of client characteristics, attributes, and/or behaviors can provide data for evaluating the degree of change.

Counselors also have a professional responsibility and ethical duty to demonstrate their effectiveness to their clients. Use of tests in this context may have an added, very subtle benefit. One of the more difficult aspects of counseling is maintaining a high level of client motivation throughout the counseling process, a difficulty that increases as the length of the counseling process increases. The counselor's provision of "encouraging" feedback, as well as client's self-monitoring, helps to maintain client motivation. However, again, these are subjective processes. Periodic use of tests that yield "objective" indications of client change can be a powerful reinforcement for client motivation. Moreover, counselor credibility is important and can add value, enhancing the counseling relationship through the counselor's knowledge and skills in the area of assessment (Whitson, 2009).

Basic Concepts in Assessment

There are many reasons for using assessment in counseling. Primarily, the reason for using assessment should be dictated by the needs of the client. The client's well-being and improvement in more effective living must remain at the core in deciding when and how to best use assessment in the counseling process. Tests used for counseling and related purposes are usually evaluated by three major attributes: validity, reliability, and appropriateness.

Validity

Validity is commonly defined as the extent to which a test measures what it purports to measure or in simpler terms, whether the test measures what it's supposed to measure (Aiken & Groth-Marnat, 2006; Drummond & Jones, 2010; Hood & Johnson, 2004; Kaplan & Saccuzzo, 2005; Neukrug & Fawcett, 2010). Validity can also be extended to whether inferences made from the test results are appropriate, meaningful and useful (Gregory, 2007). It also is the most important criterion upon which any test should be evaluated (Kaplan & Saccuzzo, 2005; Gregory, 2007).

Historically, validity was usually considered as a generalized characteristic of a test. The *Standards for Educational and Psychological Assessment* (AERA/APA/NCME, 1999) included a significant change in how validity was viewed, which in turn has significant implications for how it was established. Validity is now viewed as "contextual," meaning that the validity of a test must be specified *for a particular purpose and for use with a particular group of people*. Revision of these Standards is underway and it is expected that as a part of the "foundations" section, fundamental test issues such as validity, reliability and fairness will be updated and enhanced (http://www.apa.org/science/about/psa/2011/01/testing.aspx).

Three major types of validity typically have been discussed in most of the professional literature on assessment. *Content validity* refers to the extent to which a test is an adequate representation of a conceptual area which it is designed to question (Kaplan & Saccuzzo, 2005). Areas of interest to counselors include human attributes, characteristics, behaviors, attitudes, and abilities. Content validity evaluation is usually associated with measures of cognitive abilities. *Construct validity* is the accuracy with which test scores reflect levels or degrees of psychological concepts (Aiken & Groth-Marnat, 2006). Construct validity is particularly important for evaluating measures of personality dynamics, attitudes, or interests. *Criterion-related validity* refers to the extent to which test scores are predictably associated with other, often behavioral, criteria (Aiken & Groth-Marnat, 2006). Performance and competency measures in particular need to have criterion-related validity.

The newer interpretation of validity emphasizes the importance of substantive documentation and research to establish test validity for a particular use with a particular group of people. Within this perspective, a test's validity must be based on *evidence* of (a) representativeness of a content area, (b) appropriate response processes, (c) appropriate internal structure, or (d) appropriate relationships to other variables, or some combination of these types of evidence.

Reliability

The consistency of measurement in terms of accuracy, dependability, consistency or repeatability of test results is known as reliability (Kaplan & Saccuzzo, 2005). One example of reliability that has been used is comparing reliability to eating at the same restaurant over and over again. If it is a highly reliable restaurant, then the meals are always great … but if the taste of the food is inconsistent, or other factors influence the atmosphere, then perhaps it is not a reliably good restaurant (Neukrug & Fawcett, 2010). Similar to validity, three types of reliability are usually described in the literature. *Stability,* sometimes called test-retest reliability, indicates the likelihood of a group of people achieving the same or similar test scores if the test is administered on two or more occasions. *Equivalence,* sometimes called parallel forms, reliability indicates the extent to which two versions of a measure yield the same or essentially similar results. *Internal consistency* reliability indicates the extent to which items within a test (or subscale) correlate with one another (i.e., are internally consistent). The type of reliability deemed most important depends on the nature of the assessment situation (Gregory, 2007).

Appropriateness

A test is appropriate if performance or outcome on the test is not affected by factors extraneous to the purpose and nature of the test itself (e.g., size of print type used, assessment conditions, test delivery format, or reading level of test content). Validity, reliability, and appropriateness are interrelated but not necessarily interdependent. A valid test is necessarily reliable and appropriate. However, a test can produce reliable (i.e., consistent) but invalid results. Similarly, an inappropriate test (e.g., the response format is incorrect for the examinee) can produce reliable but not valid results. Some considerations for whether a test is appropriate include time, cost, format, readability, and ease of administration, scoring and interpretation (Neukrug & Fawcett, 2010). Time needed to administer a test should be considered along with the amount of time related to the attention span of the client. Cost is also an important fact in considering practicality. Insurance companies and third party reimbursement might play a role in considering the cost of various assessment instruments. Format and readability are issues that can certainly affect the choice of an appropriate instrument. Format issues such as print size, type of questions used (i.e., open-ended, multiple choice, essay) should be considered when choosing a test instrument. Readability is probably the most significant because if the client is unable to fully comprehend the assessment, results will be compromised. Finally, in order to practice within our area of competence, counselors must consider the ease of administration, scoring and interpretation. Interpretation is likely the most important aspect in ensuring quality delivery of results benefitting the client. Utilizing instruments that are easy to understand for the counselor and the client, non-complicated scoring for the counselor and interpretation of results that are useful to the client ensure that appropriate assessment instruments help clients to achieve their goals.

General Assessment Vocabulary

Tests have been characterized and/or differentiated through the use of a wide variety of terms. The following are brief clarifications of terms commonly used in the assessment literature.

Interpretation Basis

Norm-referenced and *criterion-referenced* are two terms commonly used to describe tests. The distinction between the two types of tests is usually made in regard to the interpretation of the results from each type (Gregory, 2007). In norm-referenced assessment, a client's test score is reported in comparison to performance on the same test by other persons. Percentiles, or other "standardized" scores such as T scores or deviation IQs (which are different from the original intelligence quotient which was defined as the person's mental age divided by the person's chronological age times 100), are commonly used to indicate *comparative* performance. For example, a person whose score is at the eighty fifth percentile is interpreted to have performed on the test at a level equal to or surpassing 85 percent of the persons in the "norm" group for the test. These persons presumably are similar to the client in important ways. Norm-referenced assessment necessitates establishment of normative data but not of specific behavioral criteria.

In criterion-referenced assessment, a client's test score is interpreted in comparison to some specified behavioral domain or criterion of proficiency. A client's score indicates how many criterion-specific tasks (i.e., items) the client completed successfully and, therefore, how many of the specific criteria (e.g., identified skills) the client has achieved. Criterion-referenced assessment involves the development of specific behavioral criteria and careful specification of the relationships of test items to those criteria.

Standardized Tests

Aiken and Groth-Marnat (2006) indicated that *standardized tests* usually are commercially prepared by measurement experts and incorporate uniform sets of items and administration and scoring procedures. In general, a test is "standardized" if it is used in the same way for all clients. Gregory (2007) also emphasized that "standardized" does not mean that the test *necessarily* accurately measures what it is intended to measure. So-called "nonstandardized" tests frequently are user-prepared and administration procedures may vary depending on the situation. The validity of standardized and nonstandardized tests must be evaluated on an individual basis; a test is not necessarily valid by its designation as standardized or invalid by its designation as nonstandardized.

Individual and Group Tests

Individual tests are designed and intended to be administered to one person at a time by a single administrator. These tests usually involve the administrator "tailoring" the assessment procedure (e.g., determining the time allowed for responding) to a specific client and/or assessment situation. A group test is one that is designed and intended to be administered to more than one person at a time.

Power and Speed Tests

In most types of assessment, maximum client performance is preferred. Therefore, assessment time allotments exceed time needed by most clients to complete the test. Such tests are called power tests. Intellectual ability, aptitude, and achievement tests are common examples of power tests. In contrast, speed tests involve speed of performance as a dynamic in the assessment process. Task completion tests (e.g., typing or other manual dexterity skills tests) are common examples of speed tests.

Vertical and Horizontal Tests

Tests that have different but conceptually and structurally related forms based on some hierarchy (e.g., age category, developmental level, or grade) are known as vertical tests. Horizontal tests are conceptually and structurally related and assess within a number of different domains simultaneously within a defined category (e.g., age group or grade level). Some tests, such as aptitude or achievement "test batteries" commonly used in schools, are both vertical and horizontal tests.

Structured and Unstructured Tests

Tests also differ by response task. In a structured test, the client is presented with a clear stimulus (e.g., an item stem) and instructed to select the appropriate response from those presented (e.g., response choices, sometimes known as distractors in a multiple-choice test). In an unstructured test, the client is presented with either a clear or an ambiguous stimulus and instructed to construct a response. This difference is evident in different types of personality inventories.

Computer-Based Tests

During the past two decades technology has exploded in many areas, not the least of which is assessment. Computer based assessments can be used in a wide variety of ways in counseling. First, the initial interview with a client can be used to create a computer generated report that describes the client's situation and can provide comprehensive description of assessment of legal issues, diagnosis, and even treatment recommendations (Neukrug & Fawcett, 2010). Computer based assessment can go beyond the traditional paper and pencil test instruments resulting in several benefits including reduced costs, immediate scoring, reduction of scoring errors, greater security, and the ability to include multimedia in testing.

Computer-based assessment clearly is the "method of choice" for the future. In particular, the increasing use of the Internet and advances in technology likely will increase dramatically both the nature and types of computer-based assessment. Assessment development, scoring procedures and interpretation will continue to increase in the future and there is already evidence that assessment in the traditional setting of the counselors' office is shifting to the client's home computer (Whitson, 2009). The proliferation of "online" assessments is staggering and clients may have a difficult time recognizing whether internet assessments have the reliability and validity needed to make essential life decisions. Computer based assessment will continue to be an important area for consideration by counselors and an area to be studied.

Paper-and-Pencil Tests

Currently, a majority of tests are "paper-and-pencil" tests, for example, wherein clients provide responses directly on tests, test booklets, or accompanying answer or response sheets. However, the connotation of the term "paper-and-pencil tests" has been broadened beyond the restrictive (literal) definition to encompass almost all structured tests, including some computer-based versions of those tests or at least computer scored tests.

Performance Tests

Tests that require clients to complete physical tasks to allow evaluation of skill or competence levels are known as performance tests. They also are sometimes referred to as "work sample" tests. Performance or work sample tests are used most frequently in the context of vocational or vocational rehabilitation counseling. However, they are increasingly becoming part of other assessment procedures. For example, the "in basket" technique used in the context of employee screening procedures calls for prospective employees to actually respond to a sample of what might be found in the person's "in basket" if hired (e.g., the potential employee could be asked to write a letter of response to a customer complaint or to write an informative memo to other employees). The responses of the potential employee are then evaluated by the employer.

High Stakes Assessment

Tests are increasingly being used as the bases for decisions about individuals' education and whether individuals may progress in an environment which utilizes "high standards". The assessment enterprise in this context is referred to as *high stakes* assessment. The most common example of high stakes assessment is statewide achievement assessment. For example, based on some of these assessment processes, students who do not perform well may be denied a diploma, their teachers' employment may not be continued or may be altered significantly, or their schools may receive differentiated funding. Credentialing and licensure examinations for counselors also fall in the realm of high stakes assessment because failure to achieve a minimum score may mean that an applicant is not be eligible to practice. Increasingly sophisticated assessment techniques in combination with increasing societal demand for performance-based evidence of competence is the driving force behind the rapidly increasing emphasis on high stakes assessment.

Additional Assessment Methods

The following are methods that may be thought of as tests because they yield information for evaluation purposes. However, these methods differ in that the information is not necessarily provided to the person for whom the records apply.

Structured and Unstructured Interviews

In a structured interview, the interviewer asks the interviewee a predetermined set of questions. Responses from the interviewee are classified (or coded) into predetermined potential response categories. Questions posed in an open-response interview are also predetermined, but categories of potential responses are not. Rather, *post hoc* analyses are made in the attempt to "sort out" client information.

Rating Scales

The use of rating scales involves a rater providing an indication of another person's *level or degree* of an attribute, attitude, or characteristic in terms of predetermined stimuli (e.g., items or criteria). Rating scales may be used to assess "live" behavior or through media (e.g., audiotape, videotape, or photographs) that record the behavior.

Behavior Observations

In making behavior observations, an observer views (sometimes on videotape) a person in a situation and records *frequencies* with which predetermined behaviors occur. Behavior observation and rating techniques are often used in the same contexts. For example, counselor trainees' verbal responses in counseling sessions are typically counted by type and rated for level of effectiveness by supervisors. Behavior observations also are used commonly in determination of a diagnostic classification.

Checklists

When used as assessment techniques, checklists contain either sets of behaviors or attributes. For behaviors, responses usually reflect *perceived* frequencies of occurrence. For attributes, responses usually reflect *perceived* presence or absence. Checklist responses can be self-reported, provided by another person (e.g., a counselor, teacher, or parent), or both.

Writing or Essay Examinations

In a composition (usually essay format) examination, clients are required to create responses to questions or other stimuli and to communicate their responses using written communication skills, including proper use of grammar, spelling, and information organization. These types of examinations have the advantage of allowing each client to develop a highly personalized response. However, they have the disadvantage of allowing significant variation in the responses given, which makes the determination of an effective or successful response to the question more challenging and in turn makes scoring difficult. Standardization in presentation of writing examinations and in "scoring" responses to them is increasingly being achieved through the use of computer-based assessments.

Assessment in Program Evaluation

Counselors should be familiar with the "counseling program evaluation literature." Assessment is an aspect of program evaluation, but an "assessment program" does not replace program evaluation. Program evaluation is a systematic assessment of a program or policy compared to a set of standards with the ultimate goal of contributing to the improvement of the program or policy. Program evaluation helps to find out what works and what does not work and provide future direction for programs. Effective program evaluation involves gathering a wide variety of both objective (empirical) and subjective information about program outcomes (Loesch, 2001). *Formative* and *summative* are the two major types of program evaluation processes. In formative program evaluation, data are gathered while the program is in progress so that process adjustments and modifications can be made to maximize the program's (eventual) effectiveness. Summative program evaluation involves gathering data at the conclusion of a program in order to determine the extent of the program's overall impact. Carefully and effectively designed program evaluation processes usually encompass both types.

SIDEBAR 11.4   Case Study: The Agency Needs to "Prove Its Worth"!

You were recently hired at a non-profit counseling center as a quality assurance counselor and as part of your role it is your responsibility to conduct a program evaluation. You are vaguely aware that you need to collect some data, but where to begin is the question. The goal of program evaluation is to create a systematic assessment which will work to improve the quality of services or the programs of the agency. The first step involves determining your goal and then creating a plan to collect objective and subjective information. There are several questions you must ask as you create the program evaluation. Who are your stakeholders? Are you focusing on specific programs with the agency? Are you going to utilize formative or summative evaluation? Would using test results be helpful? Will you utilize surveys, interviews, observations, or focus groups? Questions such as these guide the evaluation with the goal of accountability for the counseling profession.

There are a wide variety of approaches which can be used to evaluate programs that include multiple sources and all stakeholders. Surveys, interview, observations, focus groups and use of assessment data can provide helpful information. Program evaluation processes should be a part of counselors' accountability efforts because these processes reflect the full scope of services rendered by counselors.

Major Types of Tests

Specific tests are usually described according to their respective individual characteristics. More commonly, however, tests are grouped according to the general human dynamic being assessed. Therefore, counselors typically use five major types of standardized tests: achievement, aptitude, intelligence, interest, and personality.

Achievement Tests

Achievement tests are developed to measure the effects of relatively specific programs of instruction or training (Aiken & Groth-Marnat, 2006; Gregory, 2007; Kaplan & Saccuzzo, 2005). Accordingly, achievement tests are used widely in educational systems and are also used in business and industry settings to determine the need for or effects of "on the job" or other specialized training. In either case, achievement tests are designed to provide information about how much has been learned up to the date of assessment as a result of educational or training experiences.

SIDEBAR 11.5   Self-Awareness: Your Personal Assessment Journey

Assessment and testing have been an integral part of our educational journey. As a student, it is likely that you have been a test taker many times. What do you know about the types of tests that you have taken in your educational experience? Can you determine which test was "achievement" oriented or which one was "ability" oriented? Have you taken a "diagnostic" test? How was it different? Were the test results shared with you? How did the test results impact your education? Were you able to incorporate any of the information gained from taking these types of tests?

Structured or guided learning activities, such as school curricula, are intended to enable participants to learn the content of specific knowledge and skill areas. Achievement tests are developed related to those areas. Thus, content validity considerations are particularly important in evaluating achievement tests. Because achievement tests are generally administered one time, usually at the end of an instructional period, internal consistency reliability is a primary consideration in their evaluation.

Achievement tests typically are subdivided into three types: single-subject-matter, survey batteries, and diagnostic. The purpose of *single-subject-matter* achievement tests is to assess level of knowledge retention for a specifically defined content area. This type of test is most commonly used in schools. However, they are sometimes used in other specialized training programs such as construction or trade apprenticeship programs. *Survey battery* achievement tests are collections of single-subject-matter tests. Achievement test batteries contain subtests, each of which is designed to measure achievement in a specific area. Achievement test batteries have several advantages over a collection of single-subject-matter tests. Administration procedures are simplified by the format similarity in each subsection. Assessment costs often are less for achievement test batteries because printing, test booklet binding, answer sheet printing, and overall processing costs are usually minimized. The greatest advantage of achievement test batteries, however, is that all subtests in the battery have the same norm group. This commonality facilitates comparisons among a client's relative levels of achievement across areas tested. *Diagnostic* achievement tests are primarily concerned with identifying learning difficulties and deficits in a basic skill such as math, reading or writing. Subsequent instruction can be focused specifically upon the development of the deficit skills.

Clearly there is a continuing trend toward the development of criterion-referenced achievement tests paralleling the trend toward development of curricular competency objectives in schools. This latter trend should help clarify the objectives schools are trying to accomplish. However, it may result in greater tendencies to "teach to the test," particularly when curricular and test objectives and competencies are highly similar. Therefore, counselors using achievement tests should consider the instruction underlying results.

Aptitude Tests

Traditionally, aptitude tests have been defined as tests intended for the prediction of an individual's future behavior. For example, aptitude tests have been used to predict future performance in an academic curriculum area or in a specialized vocational activity. The traditionally used definition has the advantage of implying how the tests are to be used (i.e., for prediction). However, the definition does not clarify why aptitude tests have greater predictive power than other types of tests, or how they differ from other types of tests.

The physical formats of most aptitude tests are similar to other measures of cognitive functioning (e.g., intelligence or achievement tests). They frequently contain multiple-choice items, with a few tests containing manual or other dexterity tasks. The difference between aptitude and achievement tests lies in the criteria to which the items are theoretically related. Items in achievement tests are presumed to be related to academic and other learning experiences to which clients have been *previously* exposed. Items in aptitude tests are presumed to be related to learning or occupational tasks that clients will be *expected* to master or accomplish in the future.

Aptitude tests are usually categorized into either single-domain or multifactor batteries. The differentiation is the same as that for achievement tests. Single-domain aptitude tests focus upon a specific aspect of human performance such as a particular type of academic performance or job behavior. Aptitude (multifactor) test batteries are assemblies of single-domain tests having a common format, administration procedure, and norm group. Regardless of type, criterion-related validity (specifically *predictive* validity) is most important for aptitude tests. Similar to achievement tests, internal consistency reliability is the most important type for aptitude tests.

Counselors use aptitude test results primarily in academic and/or vocational counseling contexts. Because of the "faith" many people place in aptitude test results, it is imperative that counselors establish that aptitude tests have validity for the respective contexts in which predictions are made. Erroneous "predictions" of performance can have significant, long-term detrimental effects for clients.

Intelligence Tests

No area in assessment has resulted in more heated debate than the meaning and effective measurement of intelligence (Kaplan & Saccuzzo, 2005). Considerable interest exists among professionals in being able to evaluate an individual's "level of mental ability" because of the many significant implications that could be derived from such knowledge. However, while many of these implications serve the benefit of humankind, some can be construed as highly unethical. Therefore, it may be best that neither a definitive explanation nor a fully valid measurement of intelligence has yet been, or will be, conceived.

SIDEBAR 11.6 Self-Awareness: What Is Intelligence?

The definition of intelligence stirs controversy and debate. It seems like an elusive concept yet we continue to investigate and examine intelligence. Have you considered your own intellectual ability? Some have defined it as a single concept and others believe intelligence has many components. Verbal or nonverbal tests as well as performance tests are used in measuring intelligence. Have you taken an intelligence test? Did you agree with the results or not? When you think about your own intelligence quotient, what do you think are your strongest assets? As you define your own intelligence, is it single factor or is it multifactor? As you work with clients, think about your own experiences with assessment of intelligence. Can you help clients recognize their strengths when assessing intelligence?

The volume of literature on intelligence assessment prohibits more than cursory coverage of the topic. Therefore, only a few of the major concepts are addressed here. At the core of intelligence assessment is how intelligence is defined. Some, following the lead of Binet, conceive of intelligence as a *unitary* construct. In brief, they believe that intelligence is a single, generalized (likely inherited) human ability that underlies all human functioning. The most well-known example of a test based on this conceptualization is the Stanford-Binet Intelligence Test (S-B). In contrast, others, following the lead of Wechsler, believe that intelligence is the sum total of a large and diverse set of more specific (likely inherited) mental abilities. That is, they believe that intelligence is a *multifactor* construct. A variety of intelligence tests have been developed based on this conceptualization, such as the Wechsler Intelligence Scale for Children (WISC) or Wechsler Adult Intelligence Scale

(WAIS). Still others, such as the Kaufmans, believe that intelligence is multi-factored but inseparable from prior experiences and/or learning, and have developed tests such as the Kaufman Assessment Battery for Children (K-ABC) or Kaufman Adolescent and Adult Intelligence Test (KAIT) to reflect this "integrated" perspective. The pragmatic result is that different intelligence tests yield from one to twenty or more (subscale) scores depending on the definition used as the basis for the respective tests.

Intelligence tests also are classified as *group* or *individual* tests. Group intelligence tests are usually of the "paper-and-pencil" variety. They are heavily dependent on facility in use of language and are designed to be administered to large groups of persons during a single administration. As the name implies, individual intelligence tests are *designed* to be administered to one person at a time. Individual intelligence tests also typically include "performance" tasks to be completed by clients. The significant advantage of individual intelligence tests over group intelligence tests is that competent administrators can learn much about *how* a person responds to an assessment task (i.e., method of problem solving and/or affective reactions) by careful observation during the assessment session. The significant disadvantage of individual intelligence assessment is the cost of administering tests on an individual basis.

Intelligence tests (or subsections of them) also are described as verbal or nonverbal. A "verbal" intelligence test employs the use of language, such as providing definitions of words in a "vocabulary" subtest. In a "nonverbal" intelligence test, persons can respond without having to interpret written or spoken language. Traditionally, such tests have been composed of a variety of tasks involving figures, diagrams, symbols, or drawings (e.g., the Raven's Progressive Matrices). However, the term also has come to include "performance" tests (or subtests) in which clients physically manipulate objects (e.g., the Leiter International Performance Scale). Most well-accepted individual intelligence tests include both verbal and nonverbal subtests. Most group intelligence tests are verbal, although a few nonverbal ("culture-fair") group intelligence tests have been developed.

The immense general interest in intelligence assessment has subjected intelligence assessment to intense scrutiny, which has resulted in substantial criticism being aimed at intelligence tests. A common criticism is that intelligence tests are really "academic aptitude" tests; items in them seem closely related to the types of abilities needed to be successful in academic systems. The most significant criticism is that intelligence tests are culturally biased. Counselors should be aware of the challenges in addressing intelligence assessment for the increasing diversity of our client population. Counselors must also advocate for development of culturally acceptable intelligence assessments.

Interest Inventories

Interest inventories were developed as a means to assess a person's relative preferences for (i.e., feelings about) engaging in a variety of conceptually related activities (Drummond & Jones, 2010; Hood & Johnson, 2004; Kaplan & Saccuzzo, 2005). Among the most well-known interest inventories are the Strong Interest Inventory, Kuder Occupational Interest Survey, and Jackson Vocational Interest Survey. Although the vast majority of interest inventories focus upon assessment of vocational interests, leisure (or vocational) interest inventories are sometimes useful to counselors. However, the following discussion relates only to vocational interest inventories because of their predominance.

Vocational interest inventories are intended to provide information on a person's interests in various vocations or occupations. To achieve this goal, clients indicate their degree of preference on a scale with incremental values for each of a large set of activities. The activities that clients prefer are obtained and related to types of work activities that are characteristic of various occupations. Noteworthy is that activities for which preference information is obtained may not be obviously related to particular occupations. That is, clients typically do not know which activities are conceptually and/or empirically related to particular occupations.

Associations between activities and occupations are established by having persons who report being "satisfied" in an occupation indicate their preferences for a variety of activities. Activities that are most frequently preferred by "satisfied" workers become associated with the respective occupations. For counseling purposes, the basic assumption underlying interest assessment is that people are prone to engage in activities they prefer. Thus, a *very* simplistic view of "vocational" counseling is that of pairing people's interests with activities inherent in occupations, with interest assessment as a major component of the process. However, such a simplistic view belies the limitations of vocational interest assessment.

There are some limitations in using an interest inventory solely. A "high interest in" an occupation is not necessarily synonymous with "aptitude for" an occupation and, therefore, clients who are poorly counseled erroneously assume that interest and aptitude are equivalent, and may subsequently make misinformed decisions. Another limitation of interest inventories is susceptibility to respond in a socially acceptable way. Perhaps this explains why many young people "overselect" the "higher" professions as occupational goals although they do not have the requisite aptitudes for those professions. Reliability has been questioned in interest inventories because of the influences of life experience, maturation, social context, and/or economic need which affect interests. Finally, there is the potential for gender bias in interest assessment. Clearly gender roles and situations in the workplace have changed result. Therefore, the continuing possibility remains that vocational interest inventory results can be misinterpreted because of gender bias.

Despite these limitations, assessment of vocational interests is used frequently by counselors. Several reasons underlie this trend. One is that clients seek the most expedient means of finding satisfying and rewarding work. A second reason is that interest assessment is nonthreatening to clients; it is acceptable to lack interest in an area. A third is that clients view interest assessment as a way to understand themselves without fear of disclosing their "deficits." In summary, counselors and clients favor interest assessment because it provides information that is easily obtained and accepted in counseling processes.

Personality Inventories

A definition of personality assessment is difficult because of its multifaceted nature. However, in general, personality inventories are designed to yield information about a person's characteristics, traits, behaviors, attitudes, opinions, and/or emotions (Drummond & Jones, 2010; Kaplan & Saccuzzo, 2005; Whitson, 2009). Personality assessment is particularly relevant to the work of counselors, but it is the most complex type of assessment; counselors must be knowledgeable in both psychometric principles and personality theory. Additionally, they should have substantive supervised practice before using personality assessment instruments.

Personality inventories are classified as *structured* or *unstructured.* Structured personality inventories contain a set of items that are interpreted in the same way by all clients. These inventories also contain a set of potential item responses from among which a client selects one as most appropriate (i.e., pertinent to or characteristic of self). Structured personality inventories are sometimes referred to as self-report inventories (Kaplan & Saccuzzo, 2005). Responses are selected by clients, not made from the interpretations of administrators. Structured personality inventories yield quantitative scores based on predetermined scoring criteria. They are intended to be interpreted in comparison to normative data. The Myers-Briggs Type Inventory, Minnesota Multiphasic Personality Inventory—2, Sixteen Personality Factor Questionnaire, and California Psychological Inventory are among the more well-known self-report personality inventories.

Unstructured personality inventories contain stimuli that can be interpreted in different ways by different clients. Unstructured personality inventories are sometimes referred to as "projective" tests because in many of them clients are required to "project" thoughts or feelings onto the stimuli presented. The Rorschach Inkblot Test, Thematic Apperception Test, House-Tree-Person, and Kinetic Family Drawing Test are well-known examples of projective personality inventories. Although "scoring" procedures have been developed for some unstructured personality inventories, results are more commonly "clinical interpretations" of responses made.

Personality inventories have a number of limitations, many of which are similar to those for interest inventories. For example, personality inventories are susceptible to "faking." In these instances, clients subvert the validity of the assessment by providing responses they believe will make them "look good" or "look bad." Personality inventories also are susceptible to invalidity through contextual bias. What is a "perfectly normal" response in one context may be evaluated as an exceptionally deviant response in another (Drummond & Jones, 2010; Whiston, 2009). Clients also may perceive the use of personality inventories as threatening. While clients may be intrigued about the nature of their personalities, fear of "negative" attributes often outweighs curiosity-based motivation to respond openly and honestly.

The use of personality inventories can be beneficial in helping clients gain insights into their functioning. However, most counselors do not receive extensive training in personality assessment. Therefore, they should restrict the use of personality inventories to persons who are functioning normally, but who have areas of concern they want to address. In general, most counselors will derive most benefit from use of structured or self-report inventories.

Professional Issues

Credentialing and Licensure

Assessment has become a significant factor in many professional counselors' professional careers. A greatly increased emphasis on counselor credentialing and licensure in the past three decades has resulted in the development of several major national counselor certifications. In addition, counselor licensure laws now exist in all 50 states, the District of Columbia and Puerto Rico. All these procedures require some type of performance evaluation and most require successful performance on a credentialing examination. The examinations used encompass a variety of measurement formats including multiple-choice, essay, and simulation tests. Typically, counselors have to exceed a minimum criterion score on an examination to become certified and/or licensed and/or otherwise credentialed. Accordingly, the counseling profession has embraced assessment as an effective and efficient method for demonstrating professional identity.

Ethics

The American Counseling Association (ACA, 2005) specifically addresses assessment and offers guidelines for counselors beginning with the client's well-being and informed consent. Additionally, competency in the use and interpretation of assessment results is likewise mandated as ethical behavior for counselors. Other areas considered vital to ethical behavior with respect to assessment include proper diagnosis and sensitivity to culturally diverse populations. Finally, selection of appropriate instruments, administration, scoring and interpretation of results, distribution of results, as well as test security are outlined. Counselors should become very familiar with the measurement and evaluation sections of the ACA Code Ethics (http://www.counseling.org/Resources/CodeOfEthics/TP/Home/CT2.aspx). Ethical behavior of counselors with regard to assessment is an important professional issue for counselors as our commitment to client's well-being is demonstrated as well as our professional responsibility.

Training and Uses of Assessment in Counseling

The latest revision of the Council for Accreditation of Counseling and Related Educational Programs (CACREP) 2009 Standards includes specific standards to be used in the curriculum used for masters' level counseling students. Training in the use of assessment instruments begins at this level and must continue. CACREP specifically has included a mandate that the impact of social and cultural factors related to assessment and evaluation of individuals and groups be highlighted and that ethical strategies should be incorporated throughout the entire assessment process (http://www.cacrep.org/doc/2009%20Standards%20with%20cover.pdf).

Our professional association and our accreditation organizations demonstrate a commitment to thorough training in the use of assessment and strict adherence to ethical guidelines. There are many other organizations that likewise promote detailed guidelines and resources for counselors. The Association for Assessment in Counseling and Education (AACE) is a division of ACA that is comprised of "counselors, educators, and other professionals that advances the counseling profession by providing leadership, training, and research in the creation, development, production and use of assessment and diagnostic techniques" (http://www.theaaceonline.com/about.htm). AACE provides resources to assist educators, researchers and practitioners to promote effective and ethical assessment.

The Standards for Educational and Psychological Assessment (AERA/APA/NCME, 2000) were developed initially, and subsequently revised, through collaborative effort of the American Psychological Association (APA), American Educational Research Association (AERA), and National Council on Measurement in Education (NCME), and are now published by AERA (http://www.aera.net/publications/Default.aspx?menu_id=46&id=1407). The *Standards* are the recognized criteria against which tests, assessment procedures, test manuals, and other test information should be evaluated.

Another document of significance to counselors in using tests is the *Code of Fair Assessment Practices in Education* (http://www.apa.org/science/programs/testing/fair-testing.pdf). This non-copyrighted document was developed by the Joint Committee on Assessment Practices (JCTP) and included member representatives from a variety of professional organizations, notably including the ACA and AACE. The code is distinct in that it delineates responsibilities of both test users and test developers. Major sections of the code present guidelines for topics such as test development or selection, test score interpretation, fairness in assessment, and informing test takers of results.

One other document, Responsibilities of Users of Standardized Tests (RUST) (3rd edition), is currently undergoing a major revision. RUST was created to promote the accurate, fair, and responsible use of standardized tests by the counseling and education communities. The intent of the RUST statement is providing a concise statement useful in the ethical practice of testing (http://www.theaaceonline.com/rust.pdf).

Assessment with Diverse Populations

During the early 1990s, the AACE recognized the need for standards addressing a changing cultural diversity in our client population. Unique challenges exist for counselors in providing assessment that respects the effects of age, color, culture, ability, ethnic group, gender, race, religion, sexual orientation, linguistic background, socioeconomic status and other personal characteristics. (http://www.theaaceonline.com/multicultural.pdf.) Other professional groups (e.g., AERA, APA, and NCME) have also included social justice advocacy and published guidelines regarding assessment with diverse clients. No discussion of assessment with diverse clients would be complete without some reference to test bias. Test bias *appears* evident when at least two distinctly identifiable groups achieve different results on a test. These differences may be attributed to factors (e.g., gender, race, or physical condition) that, theoretically, *should not* be bases for the differences. It is important to note that while test bias is usually thought of as a characteristic of test items, the most significant (and usually detrimental) impact concerns interpretations of test data and the actions taken on the basis of those interpretations (Drummond & Jones, 2010).

A variety of methods have been developed to alleviate test bias, including empirical means. Test developers are conscientiously striving to produce nonbiased tests. Nonetheless, there remain some tests that are biased. Therefore, counselors must be sensitive to test results that may be biased and should strive to ensure that their interpretations of test results are not flawed by being based on biased data.

Advocacy in Assessment

Recently AACE has revised Standards for Multicultural Assessment (2012) in part due to the increased awareness of the impact and importance of cultural identity with regard to assessment and evaluation for our client population. Social justice advocacy in the field of assessment and diagnosis is an important topic, and the 2012 Standards address the importance of effectively selecting, administering, and interpreting assessments and diagnostic techniques by counselors addressing the increasing diversity of our client population. AACE hopes that the 2012 Standards for Multicultural Assessment (http://www.theaaceonline.com/multicultural.pdf) will raise awareness of the unique issues involved in assessment with diverse populations. There are also challenges that counselors must be aware of when using assessment for psychological screening, personnel selection, and placement with diverse populations. Counselor educators will also find the revised Standards helpful in training new professionals in the uses and development of culturally acceptable assessments. Assessment is both an individual and system intervention that is useful for client/student and community empowerment, advocacy, and collaboration designed to change systems, and inform public opinion and policy.

SIDEBAR 11.7 Self-Awareness: Advocacy in Assessment

Recognition of cultural diversity has been demonstrated by many professional counseling organizations. From the training perspective to counseling practice, cultural competency is acknowledged as a vital part of our professional responsibility. The field of assessment is not exempt from the mandates to address cultural identity and its impact on assessment of our clients. As counselors, we must recognize the unique challenges in using assessments that might be biased. Additionally, counselors can work to create assessments that recognize and value cultural identity. We must ensure that test results are not compromised by test bias. Through advocacy and efforts to promote social justice in assessment, counselors can create awareness of cross cultural fairness and the need for multicultural sensitivity in the assessment process. What can you do to promote cultural competency in assessment?

Advocacy in assessment should include a discussion of using assessment tools that are cross culturally fair (Neukrug & Fawcett, 2010). Awareness of cross cultural factors and their impact on test development, selection, administration and interpretation of results is a critical factor as the diversity in our population increases. Although laws exist to affirm the rights of marginalized populations in the area of assessment, it is incumbent on counselors to advocate for more development of culture-free assessments.

A particularly striking example of the need for multicultural sensitivity in assessment is evident when tests are used to support or confirm a diagnosis of mental illness. Obviously the "appropriateness" of behavioral reactions to life stressors is determined in part by the cultural context in which the reactions are evident. Being a culturally responsive counselor entails self-awareness, knowledge, and cultural competency in order to work effectively with diverse people (Lee & Chuang, 2005). If cultural identity is discounted, then how can an assessment be valid (Dana, 1993; Lee, 2001; Whiston, 2009)? As the demographics of the United States change, it is incumbent on the counseling profession to acknowledge the challenges and impact of a changing population. Clearly multicultural sensitivity must be incorporated into the assessment process.

Summary

Assessment is an integral and legitimate part of a counselor's professional functioning. However, counselors have a choice about the attitudes they adopt toward assessment. They can view it as a "necessary evil" and employ minimal effort toward assessment functions, or they can do what they need to do to gain understanding of psychometric principles, tests, and assessment processes and, therefore, reap the benefits of effective assessment practices. Counselors who adopt this latter perspective will find that assessment is a valuable resource, and one that enhances their counseling practice. The following websites provide additional information relating to the chapter topics.

Useful Websites

American Counseling Association: www.counseling.org
American Educational Research Association: www.aera.net

American Psychological Association: www.apa.org

Association for Assessment in Counseling and Education: http://www.theaaceonline.com/home.htm

Association of Test Publishers: www.testpublishers.org

ERIC Clearinghouse on Assessment: www.ericae.net

Fair Access Coalition on Assessment: www.fairaccess.org

International Test Commission: http://www.intestcom.org

National Council on Measurement in Education: www.ncme.org

Test Reviews Online: http://buros.unl.edu/buros/jsp/search.jsp

References

Aiken, L. R., & Groth-Marnat, G. (2006). *Psychological assessment and assessment* (12th ed.). Boston: Allyn and Bacon.

American Counseling Association. (2005). ACA code of ethics. Retrieved February 2, 2012 from http://www.counseling.org/Resources/CodeOfEthics/TP/Home/C"1"2.aspx.

Anastasi, A., & Urbina, S. (1997). Psychological assessment (7th ed.). New York: MacMillan.

Association for Assessment in Counseling and Education. (2011). Retrieved February 2, 2012 from http://www.theaaceonline.com/about.htm.

American Psychological Association. (2011*). Updated Standards for Educational and Psychological Testing.* Retrieved February 2, 2012 from http://www.apa.org/science/about/psa/2011/01/testing.aspx.

Council for the Accreditation of Counseling and Related Educational Programs. (2009). 2009 Standards retrieved February 2, 2012 from http://www.cacrep.org/doc/2009%20Standards%20with%20cover.pdf.

Dana, R. H. (1993). *Multicultural assessment perspectives for professional psychology.* Boston: Allyn and Bacon.

Drummond, R. J., & Jones, K. D. (2010). *Appraisal procedures for counselors and helping professionals* (6th ed.). Saddle River, NJ: Pearson Prentice Hall.

Goldman, L. (1971). *Using tests in counseling* (2nd ed.). New York: Appleton-Century-Crofts.

Gregory, R. J. (2007). *Psychological assessment history, principles, and applications* (5th ed.). Boston: Allyn and Bacon.

Hood, A. B., & Johnson, R. W. (2004). *Assessment in counseling: A guide to the use of psychological assessment procedures* (4th ed.). Alexandria, VA: American Counseling Association.

Kaplan, R. M., & Saccuzzo, D. P. (2005). *Psychological assessment: Principles, applications, and issues.* Thomson Wadsworth: Belmont, CA.

Lee, C. C. (2001). Assessing diverse populations. In G. R. Walz, & J. C. Bleuer (Eds.), *Assessment Issues and challenges for the new millennium* (pp.115–124). Greensboro, NC: ERIC/CAPS.

Lee, C. C., & Chaung, B. (2005). *Counseling people of color.* In D. Capuzzi, & D. R. Gross (Eds.), *Introduction to the Counseling Profession.* New York: Pearson Education, Inc.

Loesch, L. C. (2001). Counseling program evaluation inside and outside the box. In D. C. Locke, J. E. Myers, & E. L. Herr (Eds.), *The handbook of counseling* (pp. 513–525). Thousand Oaks, CA: Sage.

Naugle, K. A. (2009). Counseling and testing: What counselors need to know about state laws on assessment and testing. *Measurement and Evaluation in Counseling and Development, 42,* 31–45.

Neukrug, F. S., & Fawcett, R. C. (2010). Essentials of testing and assessment: A practical guide for counselors, social workers, and psychologists. (2nd ed.). Belmot: Brooks/Cole, Cengage.

Vacc, N. A., & Loesch, L. C. (2000). *The profession of counseling* (3rd ed.). Philadelphia: Taylor & Francis.

Whiston, S. C. (2009). *Principles and applications of assessment in counseling* (3rd ed.). Belmont, CA: Wadsworth.

12

DIAGNOSIS AND TREATMENT PLANNING

Elizabeth Christensen[1]

Sandra, 45 years old, is married with a daughter in her second year of college and a son about to finish high school. Within the past year or so, Sandra has been experiencing increasing anxiety and worry, but she can't pinpoint a cause. She has been able to keep up with her job as a librarian at the small branch library in her suburban town, but that has become increasingly difficult due to Sandra's restless sleep and daytime fatigue. Her husband believes that Sandra is experiencing "empty nest syndrome" but Sandra says he is trivializing her distress.

Jane is 40 years old and divorced. Her only child, Hannah, is about to go out of state to college. Jane has persistent yet vague fears that something bad will happen to her daughter, and Jane will be too far away to help. She worries about whether her daughter will be safe, if she will make friends, if she will be able to keep up academically—Jane knows that Hannah is a good student and makes friends easily, but this knowledge does nothing to ease her anxiety. These worries are interfering with Jane's ability to sleep and her concentration at work.

Ana is 9 years old. She attends a prestigious magnet school for gifted children. Lately, Ana has become increasingly nervous about giving presentations in class or participating in class discussions. At times, she has feigned minor illnesses such as laryngitis in order to delay having to give assigned presentations. This fear has begun to negatively impact her grades, and is threatening her eligibility for the magnet school program.

Bill is 35 years old, married with a seven-year-old son, and a veteran of the war in Iraq. Since his return from duty about a year ago, his wife has noticed substantial changes in him. She reports a kind of stiffness in his physical demeanor, and that his eyes dart around the room constantly. Whenever a sudden noise occurs, such as a slamming door or a clap of thunder, Bill seems overly startled. He refuses to talk about the war, or even to be honored at his son's "Hero Day" at school. He has yet to return to his previous job at his father's gun shop, and lately he has begun to drink regularly and, according to his wife, heavily.

All of the people described above are suffering from some variation of a common problem – anxiety. The brief descriptions of their situations are likely to be consistent with what you, as a counselor, might know about a client when going into your first session. Although the feeling of anxiety is something that virtually everyone has experienced, its expression may be quite different among people situated in different contexts, with different past experiences and systems of meaning, and with different coping abilities and social support systems. Because the feeling of anxiety is so common, and can be found at times in healthy, well-functioning people, it can be a daunting task to find a clear demarcation between "normal" anxiety and true anxiety disorders. How do we draw the line between normal and pathologic anxiety, and to what extent does that distinction influence our approach to counseling? How do we ensure that all clients in need of counseling for their anxiety or other types of distress have a way of receiving it?

The primary aim of this chapter is to provide an overview of the clinical strategies involved in mental health diagnosis, which is instrumental in planning and providing appropriate counseling and/or other mental health services. Another important goal is to familiarize readers with many of the assumptions underlying certain diagnoses, as well as diagnosis in general, and how those assumptions may differ among various mental health care professions. Third, we will introduce the socioeconomic, cultural, and political elements that have influenced, and continue to influence, the creation, application, and repercussions of mental health diagnosis. Finally, we will discuss the principles and practice of treatment planning.

The Process and the Product of Diagnosis

What Is Diagnosis?

Diagnosis is, in simple terms, the act of identifying and naming the nature of a problem, with the expectation that this naming will lead to a more informed and effective means of solving the problem. Diagnosis, then, is both the *process* of identifying and naming phenomena and the *product* of the name itself.

Diagnosis in counseling, as in most professional disciplines, relies on the use of a common language to identify the presence of an agreed-upon phenomenon, syndrome, or disorder, thus allowing the counselor and the client to choose a plan of treatment that is acceptable to both, and is based on established research and accepted standards of practice. The language of diagnosis should be clear and precise, because many of the concepts and experiences that are dealt with in counseling can have a range of meanings, depending on the perspectives of the people using the language, and the context in which the experience occurs.

A diagnosis is made based on client *signs* and *symptoms,* as well as other sources of data such as structured or non-structured interviews and psychological tests. A *sign* is a behavior or characteristic that can be seen, heard, or otherwise detected by others. Signs include pacing, crying, rapid or incoherent speech, unkempt personal appearance and hygiene, or muteness. A *symptom* is something that can be seen, heard, or felt only by the person experiencing it, such as anxiety, sadness, or hallucinations. Signs may be highly suggestive of symptoms; for example, the sign of crying suggests that the person feels intense sadness. But one should not automatically assume the meaning of a sign; for example, some people cry when they are angry or frustrated. The sign of pacing suggests the symptom of anxiety, but it may also stem from anger. It is important that counselors share their observations with clients, and ask for clients' explanation of the meanings behind their behaviors. This not only reduces the risk of making erroneous assumptions but also engages the client as a participant in the assessment process.

The most well-known and widely used system of diagnosis is the American Psychiatric Association (APA) publication, the *Diagnostic and Statistical Manual of Mental Disorders* (APA, 1952, 1968, 1980, 1987, 1994, 2000), commonly referred to as the *DSM.* This manual, first published in 1952 and having undergone several revisions and new editions, is expected to appear in a fifth edition (*DSM-5*) in the spring of 2013. As I write this manuscript, in early 2012, I am working without the benefit of having the fifth edition as a reference. Therefore, I will focus on the principles, concepts, assumptions, and professional worldviews that underlie diagnosis under the *DSM* system, and describe the specifics of the fourth edition, text revision (*DSM-IV-TR*), the most current version available to me, in less detail than did my predecessor in the previous edition of this text (Seligman, 2009). For brevity, I will use the generic "*DSM*" to refer to the series of manuals as a whole, and specify individual editions when that specification is necessary or useful.

The essence of the process of diagnosis is first to identify a client's experiences as belonging to a group or cluster based on similarities. In the cases described above, for example, the common element is the presence of anxiety. The next step in the process is to determine, as the assessment process continues, important differences among these experiences of distress. This assessment should include not only individual factors, but family, cultural, and other contextual factors as well.

SIDEBAR 12.1 Case Study: Where Do We begin?

Read over the four brief case vignettes at the beginning of this chapter. This limited amount of information is often all you will have when your first session begins. Think about the questions you might want to ask each of these clients as you begin the process of assessment.

Sandra's and Jane's situations seem to be quite similar. But look beyond the surface similarities and find the differences. How does the content of Jane's anxiety differ from Sandra's? What else do you want to know about each woman's life? What are the possible consequences of arriving at a quick diagnosis?

Ana is the only child in the group. What assumptions about her situation come to mind? How can you go about overcoming those assumptions and seeing Ana as an individual? What else would you like to know about Ana?

Finally, think about Bill. Again, the source of his problems seems obvious, but in order to counsel him effectively you will need to know a lot more specific information about his experiences both in the war and at home. What are some of the potential barriers to communication that might exist between you and Bill? How might you overcome them? What immediate concerns do you have regarding Bill?

The processes of clustering client problems (that is, they all are suffering from anxiety), and then differentiating them from each other by their salient characteristics (triggering events, intensity, and other factors) allows us to make *a differential diagnosis*. Only after we have thoroughly explored relevant elements of the client's experience though various methods should we begin the task of assigning a formal diagnosis. Arriving at an accurate diagnosis, or in some cases a group of diagnoses, allows us to set appropriate counseling goals, develop treatment plans based in research and well-established theory, and measure the client's movement toward those goals more effectively. If the client's signs and symptoms do not meet the criteria for a *DSM* diagnosis, this does not mean the client doesn't need, or won't benefit from, professional counseling. Many clients seek counseling for help with normal developmental needs, including career choices, relationships issues, and adaptation to life changes and challenges. These clients are not likely to be mentally ill, but can benefit from counseling.

Definition of a Mental Disorder

According to the *DSM-IV-TR* (APA, 2000), a mental disorder is "a clinically significant behavioral or psychological syndrome or pattern that occurs in an individual" (p. xxxi). Behaviors that are considered to be expected responses to an event or stressor of some sort, and behaviors that are sanctioned within the client's culture, such as certain religious practices or grieving rituals, are not considered to be mental disorders. In order for a diagnosis of mental disorder to be applied to a person, at least one of the following three features must be present: Either the person (a) is currently experiencing distress; (b) demonstrates impairment or disability in daily functioning; or (c) is at "a significantly increased risk of suffering death, pain, disability, or an important loss of freedom" (APA, p. xxxi).

The Expanding Role of Diagnosis in Counseling

As professional counseling has developed and expanded its presence in a wide variety of practice settings and with a diverse population of clients, the ability to recognize and accurately diagnose mental disorders has become increasingly important. The Council on Accreditation of Counseling and Related Educational Programs (CACREP) requires that certain accredited counselor education programs include coursework on the diagnosis, treatment, and prevention of mental disorders, specifically the ability to use the current edition of the *DSM* (CACREP, 2009). While counseling's professional identity emphasizes a strengths-based, wellness-oriented perspective, counselors must be able to recognize and appropriately work with people with mental illnesses, advocate for the proper use of diagnoses, and collaborate with other professionals. Doing so requires that counselors develop competency in using the diagnostic system most commonly in use, that is, the *DSM* system.

Diagnosis, like other elements of counseling, is a skill that requires significant educational preparation, supervised practice, and sound clinical judgment. The ability of professional counselors to accurately and appropriately diagnose mental disorders (as well as to recognize the *absence* of diagnosable disorders) is important for several reasons:

1. The development and use of a common diagnostic language enhances our ability to generate and share research and ideas both within the counseling profession and among other mental health professions, thus advancing professional counseling's contribution to the field of mental health and enhancing parity and mutuality among the various professions.
2. An accurate diagnosis is the foundation of appropriate treatment planning and using research-supported practices, which will be described later in this chapter.
3. Professional counselors are increasingly being recognized as primary providers of mental health care (that is, able to practice without a requirement of supervision by a psychologist or psychiatrist). This makes professional counselors eligible for third party payment, which usually requires that the treating professional provides the insurer with a formal diagnosis.
4. Professional counselors must recognize and practice within the boundaries of their scope of practice and their individual levels of experience, knowledge, and skill (American Counseling Association [ACA], 2005). Diagnosis permits the counselor to identify clients who would be better served by another practitioner or by a team

approach, for example, in coordination with a psychiatrist who can prescribe and monitor medications.

Potential Benefits and Risks of Diagnosis to the Client

The skillful and carefully communicated assignment of a diagnosis can offer benefits to the client; however, diagnosis, even when accurate and sensitively presented, creates potential risks as well. It is important that professional counselors understand these benefits and risks, and proceed in a manner that is in the best interests of the client.

Benefits of Diagnosis

Receiving a diagnosis may benefit the client in that it gives a name to the client's distress, and acknowledges that the client is not alone in his or her misery. Knowing that other people have the same or similar feelings and experiences can relieve the client of feeling alienated. Likewise, the client's family, if given information about the client's diagnosis, may be more understanding of the client's difficulties and thus be more supportive of the counseling process. Having a legitimate diagnosis might also facilitate the client's engagement in the counseling process, as well as activities such as reading about how to deal with the disorder or joining peer support groups or specialized counseling groups, again reducing the feelings of alienation, isolation, and shame that so often accompany the experience of having a mental disorder.

The accurate diagnosis of certain mental disorders may prompt the counselor to refer a client to another professional, such as a psychologist for more extensive testing, or a psychiatrist for further diagnosis and possibly medication. Ideally, the use of medications, such as antidepressants and mood stabilizers, allows the client's symptoms to improve enough that the client can engage more fully in the counseling process (Kaut, 2011). Finally, in purely practical terms, having a diagnosis often allows the client to receive insurance coverage for the cost of counseling and other mental health services, which might otherwise be prohibitive.

Risks of Diagnosis

The risks of assigning a formal diagnosis to a client's problems must also be acknowledged. Having a diagnosis of a mental disorder may, in some people, lead to a sense of hopelessness or futility, a feeling that the situation is outside of the client's control. Similarly, a client might use the diagnosis as a rationalization for irresponsible or destructive behaviors and a refusal to take responsibility for those behaviors. Another potential risk has to do with the stigma that accompanies many psychiatric diagnoses if that diagnosis becomes known to others (Johnstone, 2001). In some cases, having a diagnosis of a mental disorder may impede the person's ability to acquire health insurance or employment, and can follow the person for many years, perhaps for life (Dougherty, 2005).

Another risk of having a diagnosis of mental disorder is that it may, in effect, become the person's identity. Instead of thinking of themselves as simply *having* a disorder, for example, people may express their conditions by saying "I'm bipolar" or "I'm schizophrenic" and come to view all of their experiences and behaviors through the lens of those labels. In the context of the family, the individual with a diagnosed disorder may become the scapegoat for all of the family's problems and dysfunction. Alternatively, the person with a diagnosis of mental disorder might be overly coddled and protected by the family, ultimately limiting that person's capacity for an independent, healthy adult life. The person's strengths, talents, and abilities may be eclipsed by the diagnosis. An important value embedded in the counseling tradition is that of recognizing and building upon the client's strengths and abilities, even when disorders or disabilities are present as well. A formal psychiatric diagnosis may make it more difficult to live up to that value.

When a counselor focuses attention on arriving at a diagnosis, especially on doing so quickly, the counselor might selectively attend to client statements and behaviors sugges- tive of a diagnosis to the exclusion, or partial exclusion, of signs indicative of mental health (Tandos & Stukas, 2010). Finally, some diagnoses might divert the attention of the counselor and other mental health care providers away from recognizing and addressing cultural and systemic factors that contribute to, or even cause, individual distress (Vontress, Woodland, & Epp, 2007). This kind of shift in focus can, in some cases, take the form of blaming the victim. For example, victims of sexual or domestic abuse might be disparaged for the deep and complex problems with which they present, while many of those "problems" originally developed as mechanisms for coping with their abuse, a phenomenon described eloquently by Herman (1992).

Ethical Considerations in Diagnosis

Clearly, the process of assessing and diagnosing the client is a responsibility not to be taken lightly by the counselor. The ACA *Code of Ethics* (2005) states that clients have the right to receive information about the counseling process, and that process includes diag- nosis. Informed consent, which must be obtained from the client not only at the outset of counseling but throughout the counseling relationship, includes an understanding by the client of the potential risks and benefits of all aspects of counseling. Counselors are expected to respect the right of the client to choose whether to enter into, and remain in, the counseling relationship (Kress, Hoffman, & Eriksen, 2010). Only in situations of clear and substantial risk to the client or others is this freedom of choice overridden.

The *Code of Ethics* (ACA, 2005) also states that counselors and clients should collabo- rate in the development of a counseling plan. A diagnosis need not be purely a description of deficits or dysfunction. In addition to identifying *DSM* diagnosis, counselors can explore clients' strengths and resources, and develop counseling plans that capitalize on such strengths. This kind of collaborative approach, in which clients are empowered to be partners in their mental health care, is a core value of the counseling profession (Zalaquett, Fuerth, Stein, Ivey, & Ivey, 2008). Counseling plans will be discussed in more detail later in this chapter.

History and Overview of the *DSM*s

What is the DSM?

The *DSM-IV-TR* (APA, 2000) is a compilation of all mental disorders recognized by the APA, grouped according to shared characteristics, along with descriptions of the signs and symptoms that must be present in order for each diagnosis to be confirmed. These signs and symptoms are known as *diagnostic criteria*. The manual also provides informa- tion on the incidence of disorders, the usual age at onset, and expected course of the dis- orders. It includes issues that might interfere with the formulation of a correct differential diagnosis, and has a small amount of information regarding cultural considerations to be included in the diagnostic process. It intentionally does not offer information regarding the presumed causes of disorders or their most effective treatments. This theoretical neutrality was adopted in order to make the manual more accessible and relevant to practitioners from various theoretical schools (APA). However, many critics of the *DSMs* (e.g., Mayes & Horwitz, 2005; Mellsop, Menkes, & El-Badri, 2007) point out that the implicit message expressed in the manual by its structure and nomenclature is that mental disorders are analogous to physical illnesses, that is, that the *DSM* approach to mental and emotional distress follows what is commonly referred to as the *medical model*. This refers to the assumption that psychological distress is due to mental illness, analogous to physical diseases. The medical model focuses on the identification and treatment of pathology, rather than on wellness or the potential for wellness.

The *DSM* also provides numerical coding for each distinct disorder and subtypes of disorders. These codes are the consistent with those used in the *International Classification of Diseases (ICD)*, a product of the World Health Organization (WHO, 1990). These codes are required by most private insurers and by the federal Health Care Financing Administration (HCFA), which oversees Medicare and Medicaid reimbursement.

Revisions of the DSM over Time

The first and second editions of the *DSM*, published in 1952 and 1968 respectively, were produced to provide a structure for naming and coding mental disorders that would be compatible with the coding system used in the *ICD*. Like the *DSM*, the *ICD* has undergone revisions over the years as new diseases are discovered and differentiated. Part of the motivation behind the initial publication of the *DSM* was the desire for the relatively new medical specialty of psychiatry to be recognized and accepted by mainstream medicine, and to satisfy the demands of health insurance companies which were just beginning to include mental health care coverage in their policies. Because the dominant theoretical basis for psychiatry at the time was psychoanalytic theory, symptoms and syndromes were seen as manifestations of internal conflicts and, in and of themselves, relatively unimportant (Mayes & Horwitz, 2005).

Meanwhile, the profession of psychology was becoming a stronger force in the clinical mental health arena, and theories such as behaviorism, existentialism, and Gestalt were competing for the attention of professionals and the public as well. Social movements, including the civil rights movement for racial justice and the feminist movement, began to address social and cultural issues as germane to the emotional problems experienced by marginalized members of society. Activists both within and outside of mental health professions began to explore the effects of racism, poverty, lack of educational and employment opportunities, and the legacies of slavery on the mental health of African American individuals (Vontress, et. al., 2007). Likewise, feminist scholars and activists recognized that the disparity in social, economic, and political power between genders, as well as issues such as domestic and sexual violence and oppression, could lead to emotional problems in women (Chesler, 1972). Furthermore, normal and expectable responses to discrimination were, in the opinion of such activists, misinterpreted as mental illnesses or defects (Caplan & Cosgrove, 2004; Schwartz, Lent, & Geihsler, 2011). For people of color, normal expressions of anger or frustration could be interpreted by majority whites as acts of defiance, even to the point of criminality. In both groups, the true pathology often lay in the social structures that violated their liberties and thwarted their efforts at autonomy and self-fulfillment, yet psychiatric diagnoses would locate the problems as existing within the affected individuals; in other words, psychiatric diagnosis could have the effect of blaming the victims. Slowly and sporadically, racial, ethnic, and gender related injustices that had previously been considered, if at all, as sociologic issues, were being acknowledged as psychological forces as well.

SIDEBAR 12.2 Self-Awareness: Developing Multicultural Awareness

An important element of multicultural competence is the ability to recognize how people of various genders, ethnic backgrounds, and other cultural variables might respond to a given situation. For example, imagine that you are browsing in a clothing store located in a suburban mall. You notice that a man, dressed in regular street clothes, seems to be following your path as you meander through the store. What might you believe about this man and his intentions if you were:

- An African-American man in his 20s, dressed casually in jeans and a tee shirt?
- A 15-year-old White girl, dressed and made up in "Goth" fashion?
- A 27-year-old White woman who had been assaulted by a stranger 3 years ago?
- An 18-year-old African-American man wearing a high school letter jacket, with a leg cast and walking on crutches?
- A 70-year-old Asian-American woman, walking slowly with a cane?

How might someone outside of your culture, gender, age, or disability status interpret your responses to this situation?

As all of these factions staked their claims on the study of human emotional health and illness, it seemed to many observers (e.g., Mayes & Horwitz, 2005; Eriksen & Kress, 2005) that psychiatry had a strong motivation to secure its place as the ultimate authority on psychopathology. Finally, it was during this period from the late 1950s through the 1970s that effective psychotropic drugs became available, resulting in the release of many chronically mentally ill people from institutions to outpatient care. First-generation antipsychotic, antidepressants and mood stabilizer drugs required differential diagnosis in order to determine the appropriate drug regimen for each patient. From this cacophony of competing forces rose the *DSM-III*, which brought about a sea-change in the way psychiatric diagnoses were made and applied. It was then that the *DSMs* began to be referred to by many as the "psychiatric bible."

DSM-III: A Shift to the Medical Model

The third edition of *DSM* (APA, 1980) reflected a profound shift in the classification of mental disorders and the clinical and social implications of such change. Mayes and Horwitz (2005) described the creation of *DSM-III* as revolutionary in the way that it initiated a shift toward a biological model of mental disorders that not only persists, but has actually become stronger, today.

As the practice of psychiatry moved out of hospitals and institutions and into private practice and other outpatient settings, the consumers of psychiatric care changed from the severely disturbed to people with less extreme experiences of depression, anxiety, relationship problems, and the like. The fact of being in counseling or therapy was becoming more accepted in society, so people were more willing to seek help from psychiatrists as well as other mental health care providers such as psychologists, social workers, marriage and family therapists, and counselors. This resulted in a potential blurring of the line between normal and pathologic states, and thus the boundaries of psychiatry's domain of practice. Psychiatry's identity, legitimacy, and scientific basis for its professional domain were being threatened (Hale, 1995; Mayes & Horwitz, 2005).

The "antipsychiatry" movement led by psychiatrists such as R. D. Laing (1968, 1969, 1971, 1982; Laing & Esterson, 1971), Thomas Szasz (1972), and others, as well as nonprofessionals such as Ken Kesey, author of the 1962 novel *One Flew Over the Cuckoo's Nest*, constituted another powerful force threatening psychiatry's legitimacy. Supported by the influence of social constructivist philosophers such as Michel Foucalt (1965) and feminist scholars such as Phyllis Chesler (1972) and others, these writers reflected, as well as contributed to, a rising wave of doubt and dissatisfaction both within and outside of mainstream psychiatry (Chesler, Rothblum, & Cole, 1995).

The *DSM-III* (APA, 1980) presented a model of psychiatric nosology that was categorical and symptom-based. Suddenly, diagnosis moved from being a peripheral aspect of psychodynamic practice to the cornerstone of a new model of psychiatry, one based, at least implicitly, on a disease/biological model of mental illness. On the other hand, the *DSM-III* was the first edition to use a multiaxial system to capture psychosocial and other factors. The multiaxial system will be described later in this chapter.

DSM-IV *and* DSM-IV-TR

Subsequent editions of the *DSM* were created in response to the demands of the psychiatric profession, updates of the ICD codes, the advancement of knowledge in the mental health sciences, and changes in societal norms and values. The strong influence of social pressures, such as that which resulted in the removal of homosexuality from the list of mental disorders, has led many critics to contend that many disorders are based not on objective science but on a wide range of forces including political pressures, financial interests, and inter-professional turf battles. Another source of influence is the multibillion dollar pharmaceutical industry, which subsidizes research and profits from the "discovery" of diseases that can be treated with their products (Cosgrove, Krimsky, Vijayaraghavan, & Schneider, 2006).

DSM-IV (APA, 1994) was created, in part, in response to some of the criticisms already discussed. One well-recognized need was for the recognition of cultural diversity in the interpretation of behaviors and responses of different groups, rather than a monolithic white male orientation. The *DSM-IV* was developed by work groups consisting of psychiatrists (and, to a much lesser extent, psychologists) and each work group was assigned the task of reviewing the existing literature in order to solicit updated and more inclusive information as it applied to psychiatric diagnosis. A task force specifically for multicultural issues was included in the process. One member of the task force on multicultural issues, however, expressed some dismay that the information provided by the task force was not used as fully and in as meaningful a way as the task force members had hoped (Good, 1996). To the aforementioned source, multiculturalism was not taken as seriously as a central clinical, scientific, and ethical issue as it should have been. This lack of substantive attention to multicultural issues in diagnosis remains a major concern today (Caplan & Cosgrove, 2004; Cosgrove, 2005; Eriksen & Kress, 2005; Malik & Beutler, 2002). *DSM-IV-TR* (2000) included some revisions of the text, but no changes in the structure of the manual or diagnostic criteria.

Drug treatments for mental health problems have increased dramatically over the last several decades, not only as new drugs were rapidly developed, but as drug therapy allowed practitioners to demonstrate measurable improvement in clinical symptoms, even if the underlying problems remained unchanged. Drug treatments for milder forms of emotional distress were also being developed and marketed, including marketing directly to the consumers. The number of prescriptions for antidepressants, anti-anxiety drugs, sleeping pills, and even antipsychotics and mood stabilizers has soared in the past three decades, but their specificity in treating discrete diagnostic entities has actually decreased, leading to questions about the validity of *DSM* diagnoses as they currently exist (Mellsop, et. al., 2007).

Meanwhile, non-psychiatric practitioners, including counselors, psychologists and social workers, began to compete for the treatment of less severe emotional, behavioral, and relational distress, such as problems in adjustment, family issues, and milder forms of anxiety and mood problems. Since it could be convincingly argued that these professionals could effectively treat these problems without medical training and at less expense, these other professions began to push for third-party reimbursement for their services, a battle which is still being fought today with a great deal of success; however, reimbursement generally requires the use of a *DSM* diagnosis.

Overview of DSM-IV-TR

While a thorough description of the *DSM* is far beyond the scope of this chapter, it is useful for students to begin familiarizing themselves with the overall structure and focus of the *DSM*. As previously mentioned, at the time of this writing, *DSM-IV-TR* (APA, 2000) is the edition in use. *DSM-5* (note that the use of Roman numerals will be discontinued) is likely to retain much of the same overall character of the current edition. Some of the anticipated changes in the *DSM-5* will be covered later in this chapter.

Multiaxial Assessment

Five realms, or axes, of diagnostic information are assessed, interpreted, and recorded for each client. Whether or not the client has a mental disorder, a multiaxial diagnosis provides a means of organizing information regarding the client's symptoms as well as physical health, psychosocial/environmental factors, and the client's level of functioning in daily life. A multiaxial assessment creates a more complete picture of the client's situation and thus presents an opportunity to develop more comprehensive, holistic treatment planning.

Axis I addresses what the *DSM* calls "Clinical Disorders and Other Conditions That May Be a Focus of Clinical Attention." All disorders and conditions contained in the *DSM-IV-TR* are included in Axis I, except the Personality Disorders and both Mental Retardation and Borderline Intellectual Functioning, which are listed on Axis II. The Axis II disorders, particularly the personality disorders, must be very carefully considered before being assigned to a client, as these disorders are considered to be integral to the individual's personality structure and are expected to endure over time; thus by their nature they cannot be diagnosed hastily. Axis II disorders are often not covered under insurance policies, so they may impose a particularly heavy burden on the client and should be assigned with great care.

A person might have diagnoses or conditions on Axis I or Axis II, or neither, or both. Each diagnosis has a code number provided in the *DSM*. When a diagnosis is listed, both the name and the code number are specified (e.g., 307.51 Bulimia Nervosa). If the counselor has determined that no diagnosable disorders exist on either Axis I or II, they are coded as V71.09, No Diagnosis. If the counselor has insufficient evidence to apply a diagnosis on Axis I or II, it should be coded as 799.9, Diagnosis Deferred (which will, of course, be changed when a diagnosis is either identified or ruled out).

In addition, clinicians generally describe the severity of a mental disorder, using the terms *Mild, Moderate,* or *Severe*. Three additional specifiers describe disorders that the person had previously, but no longer meet the full criteria for the disorder. *In Partial Remission* describes symptoms that once met the criteria for a mental disorder but now are manifested in more limited ways. *In Full Remission* describes disorders in which the symptoms no longer are evident but that remain clinically relevant, perhaps because the person still receives medication for the disorder. *Prior History* characterizes past disorders, no longer treated or in evidence, but which remain noteworthy, perhaps because they have a tendency to recur under stress. Disorders characterized as Prior History would be one step removed from those described as In Full Remission, but both would be viewed as important to keep in mind. When more than one diagnosis is listed on an axis, they are listed in order of treatment priority. The *Principal Diagnosis* is assumed to be the first diagnosis on Axis I unless otherwise specified. The *DSM-IV-TR* also offers the optional use of the descriptor *Reason for Visit*, used if the presenting concern is not the principal diagnosis (APA, 2000).

When a client's clinical signs and symptoms are consistent with the characteristics of particular category of mental disorders, but do not fit into a specific diagnostic criteria set within that category, a designation of "[diagnostic category] *Disorder Not Otherwise Specified (NOS)*" may be used. When a clinician is uncertain about a diagnosis, perhaps because of incomplete or conflicting reports regarding the client's history or behaviors, a diagnosis may be labeled as *Provisional* until additional information is collected (APA, 2000).

Axis III is where General Medical Conditions, which may have a bearing on the client's emotional state, are noted. For example, a person with well-managed depression might experience an increase in depressive symptoms, including suicidal thoughts, after receiving a diagnosis of a potentially terminal illness. Or, some medical illnesses such as metabolic or hormonal disturbances can cause signs and symptoms that mimic emotional disorders. Because counselors are not qualified to diagnose medical conditions, they should state on Axis III that the medical symptoms and conditions are provided "by client report" until medical verification of the disorder is available.

Axis IV is where psychosocial and environmental problems that may have an impact on the client are listed. For instance, a client with a generalized anxiety disorder might find a significant increase in anxiety after being laid off from work or newly divorced. Counselors may use their own labels for these stressors, or they may organize them according to the *DSM* categories of stressors. Counselors generally list only stressors that have occurred within the past year, unless an earlier stressor is particularly relevant to the current diagnosis, such as combat experiences related to a diagnosis of Posttraumatic Stress Disorder.

A *Global Assessment of Functioning* rating on a scale ranging from 1–100 is recorded on Axis V. Here, counselors rate clients' current functioning, paying particular attention to symptoms associated with mental disorders and conditions listed on Axes I and II. GAF ratings below 50 reflect people who are suffering severe symptoms, and may need close monitoring, medication, and possibly even hospitalization. Moderate GAF scores are likely to describe clients who are being treated in a team approach, perhaps with psychiatric care and medication monitoring as an adjunct to counseling. Most people who are seen for counseling in outpatient settings have moderate to high GAF scores and are likely to posses some effective coping skills that can be capitalized upon in treatment planning. Such clients are likely to be more able to engage in a collaborative counselor-client relationship.

Yes/No Criterion-Based Approach

A feature of the *DSM-IV-TR* (APA, 2000) that has come under a good deal of criticism is the all-or-none nature of diagnostic criteria: either a person meets the criteria or they do not. Many critics would prefer a dimensional approach, in which the diagnostic criteria could be assessed and recorded as existing somewhere on a continuum. Dimensional criteria sets are expected to be introduced in *DSM-5*.

Recognition of "Culture-Bound" Syndromes and Minor Attention to Cultural Variations in Symptom Presentations and Meanings

As discussed earlier in this chapter, the lack of multicultural sensitivity and inclusion has been a criticism of the *DSM*s for quite some time. While *DSM-IV-TR* includes some attention to cultural variation in its descriptions of some diagnoses and their diagnostic criteria, it falls far short of what many people would consider appropriate. The *DSM-IV-TR* also describes certain culture-bound syndromes, which are conditions found exclusively in certain cultural groups, but these are relegated to an appendix rather than being integrated into the main text.

DSM-IV-TR *Categories of Mental Disorders*

The mental disorders and conditions described in the *DSM-IV-TR* are divided into 17 diagnostic categories, based upon similarities among the diagnoses in each category (for example, Anxiety Disorders or Mood Disorders), or by common etiologies (causes) of the disorders (such as Substance-Related Disorders or Mental Disorders Due to a General Medical Condition). This chapter is not designed to teach or interpret the *DSM*; students in CACREP-approved programs in Clinical Mental Health Counseling and Addiction Counseling will have a course in diagnosis, focusing on *DSM* diagnoses, in their curricula. Students in School Counseling programs would find it useful to be familiar with at least one *DSM* category, "Disorders Usually First Diagnosed in Infancy, Childhood, or Adolescence," and are required to be able to recognize the signs of substance abuse and the implications of disorders such as Attention Deficit-Hyperactivity Disorder in children and families. In all CACREP-approved programs, a focus on prevention and wellness is emphasized (CACREP, 2009).

Adjustment Disorders

One category of disorders that bears mentioning here is that of Adjustment Disorder. This diagnosis can be useful in working with people who are dealing with a significant stressor or group of stressors, and are responding with mild to moderate, but clinically significant, impairment within three months of the stressor. The type of Adjustment Disorder (e.g., With Depressed Mood, With Anxiety, With Disturbance of Conduct) is specified when the diagnosis is made. An example of Adjustment Disorder, in the experience of this author, is the distress experienced by many residents of the New Orleans area after hurricane Katrina. Many people were dealing with property destruction, displacement, job loss, separation from loved ones, and some were grieving the death of loved ones. The pain they were experiencing was commensurate with their losses, and most of them did not develop major mental illnesses as a result. But they were in terrible distress, many people experienced temporary disability, and they needed, among other kinds of help, the support and affirmation of counselors and other mental health professionals. In order for them to be eligible for services, some agencies required a diagnosis. The diagnosis of "Adjustment Disorder" was often the most appropriate for them.

According to the *DSM-IV-TR* (APA, 2000), this diagnosis can be maintained for a maximum of 6 months following the termination of the stressor (in the case of Katrina, the stressor lasted for months or even years after the actual storm for many victims). If symptoms persist beyond that time, the diagnosis must be changed; for example, diagnoses of PTSD and depressive disorders were not uncommon in some Katrina survivors. Adjustment disorders, among the mildest mental disorders found in the *DSM-IV-TR*, are common in people going through negative life experiences (e.g., a divorce, illness, being fired from a job), but also can be found in people experiencing positive life changes (e.g., marriage, the birth of a child, graduation). Adjustment disorders generally respond well to crisis intervention and solution-focused brief counseling.

The use of the diagnosis of Adjustment Disorder to describe the experiences of people who are working through stressful life events is, however, part of an ongoing debate regarding the use, and possible misuse, of the *DSM* in counseling. Daniels (2009) argues that the very notion of "mental disorder" implies an understanding of "order," the definition of which is elusive and somewhat nebulous. More importantly, it places the client on the precipice of being labeled as mentally ill, with only the passage of time serving as the line of demarcation. To many critics, this line is arbitrary and serves to increase the number of people that can be classified as mentally ill, while having no bearing or basis in the actual prevalence of mental illness. This argument, as well as others surrounding the *DSM*, can be further explored in the writings of Eriksen & Kress (2005), Kutchins and Kirk (1997), Wakefield (1992), and others.

V Codes

V Codes are used to note psychosocial or environmental circumstances that may be contributing to the client's distress. They can be used in conjunction with, or as an added explanation of, Adjustment Disorder, in which case they would be recorded on Axis IV, or they may stand alone. If a client is experiencing distress or dysfunction that is sufficient to require counseling but that does not rise to the level of a mental disorder, their distress can be listed on Axis I as a "V Code." V Codes are *not* mental illness or disorders but fall into the category of "Other Conditions That May be a Focus of Clinical Attention."

People may be given V Codes when they need help with situations such as grieving or phase of life problems. The case study of "Ana" at the beginning of this chapter could be coded on Axis I as V62.3, Academic Problem, because her grades are in jeopardy.

Take a moment to look a little deeper into Ana's case in Sidebar 12.3, and identify other factors that might be considered as V Codes.

SIDEBAR 12.3 Case Study: Another Look at Ana

Read over the case of Ana at the start of this chapter. Ana happens to be Hispanic American, and the children in her school are mostly White. Many children are anxious about giving presentations in class. How might Ana's cultural identity and the context of her difficulty affect this experience, if at all?

As you get to know Ana, you learn that she is the first-generation American born in her family and lives in a mostly Hispanic-American neighborhood. Her family and neighborhood friends speak Spanish, and Ana prefers to speak Spanish at home. She feels comfortable in her home and neighborhood, but feels out of place at school and has been the target of some teasing. Her parents want very much for Ana to have the best education available. Ana has told you, in private, that she would prefer to go to her neighborhood public school, which is more ethnically and socioeconomically diverse. She has not said this to her parents, and asks you not to tell them either. She does not want to disappoint them. How might an understanding of Ana's cultural, family, and school contexts inform your approach to counseling Ana?

Criticisms of the DSM Diagnostic Approach in Counseling

There are several areas of debate both within the counseling profession, and between different mental health professions, regarding the role of diagnosis in general and DSM diagnosis in particular in counseling. We have already discussed the risks and benefits to the client of receiving a DSM diagnosis. What follows is an admittedly brief and basic discussion of some of the major areas of contention, as well as the theoretical and philosophical underpinnings of some of these debates.

Categorical Criteria Sets and the Power to Name

First, the categorical (as opposed to dimensional) approach to listing and defining diagnostic criteria, first introduced in *DSM-III* (APA, 1980) increases psychiatric diagnoses' similarity to physical diagnosis. More importantly for the sake of this discussion, it creates a subjective and, some contend, somewhat arbitrary line of demarcation between "having" and not having a given symptom or, eventually, a disorder. The writers of *DSM-IV-TR* acknowledged this weakness, but stated that a dimensional rating scale would be unwieldy. As of the time of this writing, a dimensional approach is being designed and tested for inclusion in *DSM-5*.

Criterion-based diagnoses also contribute to the construction of statistically reliable diagnostic instruments, such as structured interviews, that can then be used to define desirable outcomes and thus support outcomes-based practice. However, reliability does not ensure construct validity (Eriksen & Kress, 2005). Experiences and phenomena that are classified as pathologic in a medical model may be seen as adaptive in a developmental model. Also, while the criteria sets used to make diagnostic decisions are designed to increase reliability (that is, the likelihood that several practitioners, given the same client case, will arrive at the same diagnosis), many of the criteria themselves are imprecise and subjective. Terms such as *frequent, excessive,* or *normal and expectable reaction* require a good deal of subjective judgment on the part of the practitioner, and may be strongly influenced by culture and gender.

The overwhelming dominance of the *DSM* system, however, eclipses alternate conceptualizations of mental health and mental dysfunction. The power to name and define a phenomenon carries with it the power to declare it as present, absent, controlled, or properly treated. In other words, the use of a categorical list of diagnostic criteria in the *DSM* gives psychiatry a greater claim to scientific objectivity as opposed to philosophical ideology. Professionals with different ideologies and guiding paradigms must scrutinize evidence-based practice in terms of how pathology and its absence are defined and operationalized, and by whom. Most importantly, how do a *DSM* diagnosis and its subsequent treatment benefit, or fail to benefit, the individual client?

The Increasing Number of Diagnosable Conditions

The criterion-based approach to diagnosis since the release of *DSM-III* contributed to the growing "medicalization" of psychiatry, coinciding with the explosive growth in the number of diagnoses, from 106 in *DSM*-I to 297 in *DSM-IV-TR* (Lopez et al., 2006) as well as medications being developed for specific diagnoses. This created a mutually beneficial relationship between the pharmaceutical industry, which needed discrete diagnoses for their products to treat, and psychiatry, which was the only mental health provider group with the authority to prescribe (Cosgrove et al., 2006). This shift toward a medical-biological focus also increased psychiatry's claim to third-party reimbursement for services under the medical insurance system, which had begun in the 1960s to increasingly include reimbursement for psychiatric care (Mayes & Horwitz, 2005).

Some critics have maintained that the effect of this explosive growth of *DSM* diagnosis has had the effect of "pathologizing" virtually all normal human distress, and artificially creating an overabundance of "mentally ill" people (e.g., Daniels, 2009). There is great debate over whether these increases represent a true discovery of heretofore unknown illnesses, or a construction of disorders based on social demand and consensus (Houts, 2002). This phenomenal growth in the number and variety of mental illnesses may have effects such as the overuse of psychotropic medications, which is of particular concern when applied to children (Graybar & Leonard, 2005), and runs the risk that those who are truly experiencing serious mental illness or emotional distress may become, in effect, lost in the crowd.

Lack of a Systemic Perspective

It is important to understand that implicit in the concept of a disorder is the assumption that the dysfunction is presumed to lie *within* the individual sufferer. This assumption is inconsistent with those of couples and family therapies, other systemic theories, and social/cultural and feminist theories of psychology, all of which consider the systems within which the individual operates as part of, and contributive to, individual distress. It is also inconsistent with the developmental and adaptational approaches to human experience as expressed in many counseling models (e.g., Ivy & Ivy, 1999; Zalaquett, et al., 2008), which interpret much of the emotional distress and dysfunction as reasonable responses to stressors or developmental demands to be mastered and integrated into a healthy life. Wellness orientation and strengths-based counseling are also inconsistent with the disease model in that, rather than focusing solely on pathology, they emphasize the person's abilities and resources for overcoming problems and becoming healthier (e.g., Davis-Gage, Kettmann, & Moel, 2010).

Diagnosis as a Requirement for Reimbursement or Access to Services

The dominance of the *DSM*s in mental health diagnosis is perhaps most apparent in the systems that determine who will be eligible for community mental health services and reimbursement by third-party payers such as insurance companies. This often means that if a person has a legitimate need for services but does not meet the criteria for inclusion in a *DSM* diagnostic category, they may be denied access to services or have to pay out-of-pocket for private counseling, which may be prohibitively costly for some. While there may be other options, such as counseling centers associated with colleges or private non-profit organizations, the absence of a *DSM* diagnosis may place an undue burden on the client.

The requirement for *DSM* diagnosis as a condition for services and/or reimbursement creates ethical quandaries for counselors as well. In many cases, the counselor must weigh the potential harm of assigning a diagnosis, and its attendant risks, to a person, thus qualifying that person for needed services against the potential harm of denying that person access to services (Danzinger & Welfel, 2001). Which is the lesser evil?

SIDEBAR 12.4 Self-Awareness: What Are Your Beliefs About *DSM* Diagnosis and the Counseling Profession?

Professional Counselors have a range of beliefs regarding the role of *DSM* diagnosis in counseling practice. At one end of the spectrum are those who readily engage in *DSM* diagnosis because they believe that doing so enhances counseling's professional status and improves client outcomes, as well as facilitates clients' access to care. On the other end are those who refrain from the use of *DSM* diagnoses (unless a serious mental illness is clearly present, in which case they refer the client out) and use other models of conceptualizing care because they think that the medical model is antithetical to counseling's values and guiding paradigms. These counselors often avoid seeking insurance reimbursement. In the middle of the spectrum are those who provide diagnoses with different degrees of comfort and try to make *DSM* diagnoses work with their own counseling models. Where on the spectrum do you think you lie? Why? How do you think your beliefs will influence your future counseling practice?

Diagnosis as a Tool for Collaborative Communication, Research, and Teaching

As mentioned earlier, the presence of a common language is critical to the advancement of knowledge and the communication between members of a profession. There is real value in having a single, agreed-upon definition of a term such as "major depressive disorder". This is true in terms of communicating about individual clients (for example, in supervision or consultation) as well as about groups of clients, such as in teaching or research.

However, there is a risk that diagnostic nomenclature can create an artificially narrow worldview for mental health professionals (Lopez et al., 2006). At the level of the individual client-counselor dyad, the expectation of arriving at a precise diagnosis may lead the counselor to selectively attend to information that supports the diagnosis and ignore or minimize information that might confound or contradict it, a process known as confirmatory bias. This has been shown to be true whether the practitioner is using structured diagnostic instruments such as questionnaires, or unstructured clinical interviews. The result is that the true nature of the client's situation may go unrecognized, or that the client will be "locked into" a diagnosis that is not valid. A classic example is the experiment conducted by Rosenhan in 1973, as described by Eriksen & Kress (2005) in which he and several co-researchers presented for treatment at psychiatric hospitals pretending to have a single symptom of psychosis, specifically, auditory hallucinations. Once the researchers were admitted to the hospital, they stopped feigning the symptom. However, the hospital staff continued to interpret their actions and responses as symptomatic of their presumed psychosis.

SIDEBAR 12.5 Case Study: Another Look at Sandra

Imagine that you have just been given the brief intake form containing the presenting problem of "Sandra," introduced at the beginning of this chapter. Another student, who is a year ahead of you in the counseling program, glances at it and says, "That looks easy – a V Code for 'phase of life problem' should be it. It sounds like the 'empty nest' idea is on target."

On further assessment, you come to the conclusion that Sandra's anxiety may be exacerbated by, but is not caused by, her children's transition into college. In fact, she meets the criteria for Generalized Anxiety Disorder. Based on the information you have, can you produce a multiaxial diagnosis for Sandra? What are the perils of arriving at an "instant" diagnosis? How might the appraisal of Sandra have been influenced by gender (both the client's and the counselor's)?

At the broader level, the use of diagnostic labeling may create or reinforce stereotypes that influence counselors' attitudes toward, and expectations for, a group of clients with that diagnosis. For example, clients diagnosed with personality disorders, particularly borderline personality disorders, are presumed to be manipulative and in need of an inordinate amount of emotional validation from their therapists. These clients, based solely on their diagnosis, may be pre-judged by mental health providers to be devious, manipulative, and unwilling to fully engage in the therapeutic process (Herman, 1992; Krawitz, 2004; Linehan, 1993).

Generating a Diagnosis and Developing a Counseling Treatment Plan

All problem-solving, as well as other endeavors in human development, should begin with a clear conceptualization of the nature of the problem to be solved or the goal to be reached. This simple statement seems to contradict the complexity and controversies in mental health diagnosis described thus far. But clarity of purpose does not imply simplicity in practice. Becoming proficient in diagnosis, whether within the *DSM* model or others, requires a substantial investment in education and supervised practice (Dougherty, 2005). While this chapter is not intended to provide the depth of understanding necessary for clinical practice in diagnosis and treatment planning, it is intended to present an introduction to the procedures and principles involved in that practice.

Generating an Appropriate Diagnosis

Diagnosis, like other aspects of the counseling process, should be done with the informed consent of, and in collaboration with, the client, as stated in ACA *Code of Ethics* (2005). This informed and collaborative approach has the benefits of promoting the engagement and investment of the client in the counseling relationship and process. As mentioned earlier, the client should be made aware of both the potential benefits and the potential risks of formal psychiatric diagnosis, and his or her freedom to engage in this process.

Diagnosis begins with gathering relevant information. Many counseling agencies have intake and assessment forms; these may provide a useful starting point. In other cases, an unstructured clinical interview may be used (Jones, 2010). The client should be asked to identify and describe the reason(s) for which counseling is being sought. The problems or symptoms identified by the client provide a platform for further assessment. For instance, the counselor should explore the duration of the problem, the presence of any event or situation that may have caused or triggered the problem, and situations or factors that seem to make the problem better or worse. The counselor should explore how the problem is affecting the client's daily life, such as work/school, relationships, enjoyment of activities, appetite, and sleep. The client's individual and family mental health history and current or recent stressors should also be identified. Finally, the counselor should inquire about the client's physical health and the use of any prescribed medications, alcohol and other substances. While the use of an intake form or assessment questionnaire can be helpful, it is important that the counselor remembers to truly *listen*, in an authentic and empathic way, to the client. The value of this kind of counselor-client connection is tremendous (Graybar & Leonard, 2005).

SIDEBAR 12.6 Case Study: Client Advocacy in the Diagnostic Process

Your client, Mary, has symptoms that would fit a diagnosis of dysthymia; however, as you take a careful history, you find that Mary has suffered an extraordinary series of traumatic losses over the past three years, including her son's suicide and the subsequent deaths of her mother and her husband. Now she is being laid off from her job and losing her health insurance. She knows that having a psychiatric diagnosis might jeopardize her ability to find a new job and insurance coverage. You believe that Mary is experiencing reasonable responses to an extraordinary set of circumstances and can benefit from counseling. Mary is not suicidal, and she is functioning reasonably well. If you give her a *DSM* diagnosis, she may qualify for psychiatric services, including medications, at a community clinic. Otherwise, she can continue to work with you on a sliding-scale fee basis at your college counseling center. Mary trusts you, and wants to know what you think is best. What would you do? What factors would you need to consider?

An assessment of the client's safety, and the safety of others, should be integral to the interview. Many initial assessment forms explicitly prompt the counselor to ask the client if he or she is having, or has had, thoughts of harming or killing self and/or others. Some beginning counselors are uncomfortable with asking about the risk of suicide or other dangers, and may believe that asking about suicide increases the client's risk. This is simply not so. Asking clients about suicidal or homicidal thoughts or intentions gives them permission to express thoughts and feelings that they may have otherwise considered taboo. It might be a great relief for clients to know that it is acceptable for them to talk about suicide, and students should learn to perform a suicide risk assessment (Schwartz & Rogers, 2004).

Based on the information obtained, the counselor can generate a broad list of potential diagnoses, then begin systematically begin narrowing the list (the process of differential diagnoses) by using various techniques. One popular, and fairly user-friendly, technique for differential diagnosis is the use of algorithms or decision trees, as described by Morrison (2007). The *DSM-IV-TR* (2000) also provides decision trees for differential diagnosis. Finally, social and cultural factors, whether or not they fit into the *DSM* paradigm, should be brought into the diagnostic picture.

Developing a Counseling Treatment Plan

The ACA *Code of Ethics* (2005) requires that counselors and their clients work collaboratively in the development of counseling plans that "offer reasonable promise of success and are consistent with abilities and circumstances of clients" (p. 4). Furthermore, counselors should periodically review counseling plans, again in collaboration with clients, in order to determine whether they are viable and effective. This provision, along with the principle of informed consent, should be guiding forces in the development and implementation of counseling treatment plans. The client has a right to accept or refuse to enter into, or continue, a counseling treatment plan except in situations of clear and foreseeable risk of harm to the client or others. Therefore, collaboration with the client is not only desirable, it is ethically mandated (Dougherty, 2005; Eriksen, Hoffman, & Kress, 2010).

A counseling treatment plan may be fairly simple—for example, a limited number of sessions of cognitive-behavioral interventions for a simple phobia—or quite complex, such as long-term counseling and psychiatric care for a person with a major depressive disorder. While the extent and severity of the client's problems are obvious factors in devising a treatment plan, so are other factors.

First, does the client want long-term counseling with the hope of resolving deeper issues that contribute to his or her distress, or does the client prefer short-term intervention for symptom management? Second, what kind of counseling or other treatment is the client capable of engaging in? This requires consideration not only of the client's current mental status, but of other resources as well, such as money, insurance coverage, and access to adequate social support. Finally, what kind of counseling are you able to offer the client, based on variables such as your agency or facility guidelines and your own level of experience and competence?

Prioritizing Problems

If a client has several problems, such as a formal diagnosis (or multiple diagnoses) as well as other problems such as relationship issues, threats to safety, employment problems, and physical health problems, where should you begin? A sound guiding principle in such a situation is to prioritize problems based on their degree of threat to the client and the extent to which the problem can be readily resolved. For example, a client with a long-standing history of schizophrenia who is currently homeless and without money for food needs a social services referral for emergency food and shelter before delving into his or her mental health issues.

Considering Individual Strengths and Resources in the Treatment Plan

The client's strengths, talents, and resources should be actively integrated into the counseling plan. For example, a client who likes art might use that modality as a means of emotional expression, especially for expressing feelings that are difficult to verbalize. A client who is open to approaches such as meditation and relaxation training will benefit more from these interventions than will someone who dismisses them as hocus-pocus. Family and community support, when appropriate and welcomed by the client, can contribute to the client's well-being and decrease the sense of isolation that often accompanies the experience of emotional distress.

Another facet of a strengths-based approach is in how we interpret the client's current symptoms as, perhaps, once-effective means of coping with challenges. For example, a woman who was sexually abused in childhood may have developed the ability to dissociate as a means of "escaping" a situation over which she had no control. As an adult, the dissociation is no longer useful and may be a source of problems, but can still be acknowledged and honored as a creative coping strategy. Unlinking responses such as dissociation from a disease framework can be very valuable in forging a mutually respectful and constructive client–counselor relationship.

Re-evaluation, Modification and Ongoing Evaluation of the Counseling Plan

A counseling treatment plan, however well-designed, must be re-evaluated periodically in order to evaluate its effectiveness and make modifications as indicated. As in the original plan, the client's collaboration and informed consent is central to the process.

Consultation and Referral

It is incumbent upon the counselor to recognize when a client's needs and problems fall outside of the counselor's scope of practice, qualifications, and experience. When this is the case, the counselor should consult with a supervisor or appropriate peer, and/or refer the client to the appropriate practitioner (ACA, 2005). In order to prevent misinterpretation on the part of the client, the counselor should be sure to explain that the reason for the referral is not to "get rid" of the client but to ensure the proper care.

SIDEBAR 12.7 Self-Awareness: Assessing Your Own Abilities

Imagine that you begin working with a client, Valerie, who has a history of childhood sexual abuse. At first, her symptoms of posttraumatic stress are within your comfort zone as a student counselor, and your clinical supervisor agrees. One day, the client arrives for a session wearing clothes and makeup that are very different from her usual style. She states that her name is Ginger, and that she has come in Valerie's place. She says that Valerie does not know about her, and that you are not to tell her. You suspect that Valerie has Dissociative Identity Disorder (DID), which you have never seen before. You are fascinated by Valerie's case and would like to continue to work with her in order to learn and gain this valuable experience. Your supervisor is also inexperienced in the area and would prefer that you refer Valerie to a provider with specialized experience in trauma and DID, but another professor in your program does have some experience in working with adult survivors of sexual trauma and people with dissociative disorders. What should you do?

Guidelines and Other Resources for Treatment Planning

Of course, not all diagnoses and treatment decisions are as clear-cut as the example provided above. Guidelines for treatment planning and prioritization are available in print and online; supervision and peer consultation are also helpful in developing appropriate intervention strategies. If you are working within certain agencies or managed care organizations (MCOs), you may be directed to use manual-based treatment plans for particular diagnoses. These plans may be referred to as "evidence-based treatments" or "best practices," although they are subject to criticism by those (e.g., Graybar & Leonard, 2005) who question whether they are designed to best serve the client or the health care provider. The individual counselor must decide if the prescribed treatment plan meets the wants and needs of the client, and respond appropriately (for example, advocating for more appropriate treatment for your client).

If a counselor is working outside of an agency setting and is interested in identifying evidence-based best practice, a literature search is often the most efficient means of gather such information. Articles such as literature reviews that present the cumulative knowledge gleaned from multiple studies is often most useful. For examples, see Couineau and Forbes (2011), Falzon, Davidson, and Bruns (2010), and Steinkuller and Rheineck (2009).

Looking Forward: The Upcoming DSM-5

It is likely that, as you read this chapter, the fifth edition of the *DSM* will have been released. The changes that are expected are currently being discussed and debated not only in professional journals but on the APA website (http://dsm5.org). As of this writing, it is anticipated that changes in the categorization of mental disorders, perhaps most notably the absorption of Axis II disorders into the domain of other (currently Axis I) disorders, and the use of dimensional rather than strictly categorical diagnostic criteria sets will be in use. Another expected change is the use of a lifespan development orientation in the presentation of categories, as well as diagnoses within categories. The extent to which *DSM-5* will affect your assessment and treatment planning in counseling practice will be ours to discover together.

Conclusion

The processes of diagnosis and treatment planning are integral to the overall practice of mental health counseling and are important elements of other areas of counseling practice.

While there is much debate within counseling as well as among other mental health disciplines regarding the validity of diagnostic systems, most famously of the *DSMs*, at this point the centrality of diagnosis in the accessibility, affordability, and therefore the delivery of counseling services cannot be denied. It is incumbent upon professional counselors to become proficient in the process of diagnosis, as well as to be cognizant of the counseling profession's traditions and values of wellness orientation, an emphasis on strengths, and the awareness and integration of cultural and social justice issues into the counseling process. The following websites provide additional information relating to the chapter topics.

Note

1 Author's note: I would like to acknowledge the work of the late Dr. Linda Seligman, who authored this chapter in the previous editions of this text and who contributed so much to the counseling profession, particularly in the areas of diagnosis and treatment planning.

Useful Websites

http://www.counseling.org/: This is the site for the American Counseling Association, with a link to the *Code of Ethics* and other information about the profession.

http://www.multiculturalcounseling.org/: This is the site for the Association for Multicultural Counseling and Development, and includes competencies for multicultural counseling.

http://www.apa5.org: This site, run by the American Psychiatric Association, provides updates on the progress of *DSM-5*.

http://www.samhsa.gov/: is the site for the Substance Abuse and Mental Health Services Administration, and includes some practice guidelines for mental health and substance abuse problems.

http://www.nimh.nih.gov/index.shtml: leads the user to the National Institute for Mental Health, which disseminates research on mental health topics.

References

American Counseling Association. (2005). *Code of ethics.* Alexandria, VA: Author.

American Psychiatric Association. (1952). *Diagnostic and statistical manual of mental disorders.* Washington, D.C.: Author.

American Psychiatric Association. (1968). *Diagnostic and statistical manual of menta disorders* (2nd ed.). Washington, D.C.: Author.

American Psychiatric Association. (1980). *Diagnostic and statistical manual of mental disorders* (3rd ed.). Washington, D.C.: Author.

American Psychiatric Association. (1987). *Diagnostic and statistical manual of mental disorders* (3rd ed., rev.). Washington, D.C.: Author.

American Psychiatric Association. (1994). *Diagnostic and statistical manual of mental disorders* (4th ed.). Washington, D.C.: Author.

American Psychiatric Association. (2000). *Diagnostic and statistical manual of mental disorders* (4th ed., text revision). Washington, D.C.: Author.

Caplan, L., & Cosgrove, L. (Eds.). (2004). *Bias in psychiatric diagnosis.* Lanham, MD: Jason Aronson.

Chesler, P. (1972). *Women and madness.* Garden City, NY: Doubleday.

Chesler, P., Rothblum, E. D., & Cole, E. (Eds.). (1995). *Feminist foremothers in women's studies, psychology, and mental health*. Binghamton, NY: Harrington Park Press.

Cosgrove, L. (2005). When labels mask oppression: Implications for teaching psychiatric taxonomy to mental health counselors. *Journal of Mental Health Counseling, 27*, 283–296.

Cosgrove, L., Krimsky, S., Vijayaraghavan, M., & Schneider, L. (2006). Financial ties between DSM-IV panel members and the pharmaceutical industry. *Psychotherapy and Psychosomatics, 75*, 154–160. doi: 0.1159/000091772

Council for Accreditation of Counseling and Related Educational Programs (2009). 2009 Standards. Retrieved online Jan 23, 2012. http://www.cacrep.org/doc/2009%20Standards%20 with%20cover.pdf.

Couineau, A., & Forbes, D. (2011). Using predictive models of behavior change to promote evidence-based treatment for PTSD. *Psychological Trauma: Theory, Research, Practice, and Policy, 2011*(3), 266–275. doi: 10.1037/a0024980

Daniels, J. (2009). The perils of "adjustment disorder" as a diagnostic category. *Journal of Humanistic Counseling, Education and Development, 48*, 77–90.

Danzinger, P. R., & Welfel, E. Z. (2001). The impact of managed care on mental health counselors: A survey of perceptions, practices, and compliance with ethical standards. *Journal of Mental Health Counseling, 23*, 137–150.

Davis-Gage, D., Kettmann, J. J., & Moel, J. (2010). Developmental transition of motherhood: Treating postpartum depression using a feminist approach. *Adultspan Journal, 9*, 117–126.

Dougherty, J. L. (2005). Ethics in case conceptualization and diagnosis: Incorporating a medical model into the developmental counseling tradition. *Counseling and Values, 49*, 132–140.

Eriksen, K., Hoffman, R. M., & Kress, V. (2010). Ethical dimensions of diagnosing: Considerations for clinical mental health counselors. *Counseling & Values, 55*, 101–112.

Eriksen, K., & Kress, V. (2005). *Beyond the DSM story: Ethical quandaries, challenges, and best practices*. Thousand Oaks, CA: Sage Publications.

Falzon, L., Davidson, K. W., & Bruns, D. (2010). Evidence searching for evidence-based psychology practice. *Professional Psychology: Research and Practice, 41*, 550–557. doi: 10.1037/a0021352

Foucault, M. (1965). *Madness and civilization: A history of insanity in an age of reason*. New York: Vintage Books.

Good, B. J. (1996). Culture and DSM-IV: Diagnosis, Knowledge, and Power. *Culture, Medicine, and Psychiatry, 20*, 127–132.

Graybar, S. R., & Leonard, L. M. (2005). In defense of listening. *American Journal of Psychotherapy, 59*, 1–18.

Hale, N. G. (1995). *The rise and crisis of psychoanalysis in the United States: Freud and the Americans, 1917–1985*. New York: Oxford University Press.

Herman, J. (1992). *Trauma and recovery*. New York: Basic Books.

Houts, A. C. (2002). Discovery, invention, and the expansion of the modern *Diagnostic and Statistical Manuals of Mental Disorders*. In L. E. Beutler, & M. L. Malik (Eds.), *Rethinking the DSM: A psychological perspective*. Washington, D.C.: American Psychological Association.

Ivy, A. E., & Ivy, M. B. (1999). Toward a developmental diagnostic and statistical manual: The vitality of a contextual framework. *Journal of Counseling & Development, 77*, 484–490.

Johnstone, M. (2001). Stigma, social justice, and the rights of the mentally ill: Challenging the status quo. *Australian and New Zealand Journal of Mental Health Nursing, 10*, 200–209.

Jones, K. D. (2010). The unstructured clinical interview. *Journal of Counseling & Development, 88*, 220–226.

Kaut, K. P. (2011). Psychopharmacology and mental health practice: An important alliance. *Journal of Mental Health Counseling, 33*, 196–222.

Kesey, K. (1962). *One flew over the cuckoo's nest*. New York: Viking Press.

Krawitz, R. (2004). Borderline personality disorder: Attitudinal change following training. *Australian and New Zealand Journal of Psychiatry, 38*, 554–559.

Kress, V. E., Hoffman, R. M., & Eriksen, K. (2010). Ethical dimensions of diagnosing: Considerations for mental health counselors. *Counseling and Values, 55,* 101–112.

Kutchins, H., & Kirk, S. A. (1997). *Making us crazy:* DSM: *The psychiatric bible and the creation of mental disorders.* New York: Free Press.

Laing, R. D. (1968). *The politics of experience.* New York: Ballantine Books.

Laing, R. D. (1969). *The divided self.* New York: Pantheon Books.

Laing, R. D. (1971). *Self and others.* Baltimore: Pelican Books.

Laing, R. D. (1982). *The voice of experience.* New York: Pantheon Books.

Laing, R. D., & Esterson, A. (1971). *Sanity, madness, and the family: Families of schizophrenics* (2nd ed.). New York: Basic Books.

Linehan, M. M. (1993). *Cognitive-behavioral treatment of borderline personality disorder.* New York: The Guilford Press.

Lopez, S. J., Edwards, L. M., Pedrotti, J. T., Prosser, E. C., LaRue, S., Spalitto, S. V., & Ulven, J. C. (2006). Beyond the *DSM-IV*: Assumptions, alternatives, and alterations. *Journal of Counseling & Development, 84,* 259–267.

Malik, M. L., & Beutler, L. E. (2002). The emergence of dissatisfaction with the DSM. In L. E. Beutler, & M. L. Malik (Eds.), *Rethinking the DSM: A psychological perspective.* Washington, D.C: American Psychological Association.

Mayes, R., & Horwitz, A. V. (2005). DSM-III and the revolution in the classification of mental illness. *Journal of the History of the Behavioral Sciences, 41,* 249–267. doi:10.1002/jhbs.20103

Mellsop, G., Menkes, D., & El-Badri, S. (2007). Releasing psychiatry from the constraints of categorical diagnosis. *Australian Psychiatry, 15,* 3–5. doi: 10.1080/10398560601083134

Morrison, J. (2007). *Diagnosis made easier.* New York: Guilford Press.

Schwartz, R. C., Lent, J., & Geihsler, J. (2011). Gender and diagnosis of mental disorders: Implication for mental health counseling. *Journal of Mental Health Counseling, 33,* 347–358.

Schwartz, R. C., & Rogers, J. R. (2004). Suicide assessment and evaluation strategies: A primer for counseling psychologists. *Counseling Psychology Quarterly, 17,* 89–97.

Seligman, L. (2009). Diagnosis in counseling. In D. Capuzzi, & D. R. Gross (Eds.), *Introduction to the counseling profession* (5th ed.) (pp.373–394). Upper Saddle River, NJ: Pearson.

Steinkuller, A., & Rheineck, J. E. (2009). A Review of evidence-based therapeutic interventions for bipolar disorder. *Journal of Mental Health Counseling, 31,* 338–350.

Szasz, T. (1972). *The myth of mental illness: Foundations of a theory of personal conduct.* New York: Harper & Row.

Tandos, J., & Stukas, A. A. (2010). Identity negotiation in psychotherapy: The influence of diagnostic and rapport-building strategies on the effects of clinical expectations. *Self &Identity, 9,* 241–256. doi: 10.1080/15298860902979331

Vontress, C. E., Woodland, C. E., & Epp, L. (2007). Cultural dysthymia: An unrecognized disorder among African Americans? *Journal of Multicultural Counseling & Development, 35,* 130–141.

Wakefield, J. C. (1992). The concept of mental disorder: On the boundary between medical facts and social values. *American Psychologist, 47,* 373–388.

World Health Organization. (1990). *International classification of diseases.* Geneva, Switzerland: Author.

Zalaquett, C. P., Fuerth, K. M., Stein, C., Ivey, A. E., & Ivey, M. B. (2008). Reframing the *DSM-IV-TR* from a multicultural/social justice perspective. *Journal of Counseling & Development, 86,* 364–371.

Part III

COUNSELING SPECIALIZATIONS

13

ADDICTIONS COUNSELING

Cynthia J. Osborn and Melanie M. Iarussi

Although addictions counseling is regarded as a specialization, addiction itself is a prevalent and pervasive concern, one that no counselor can avoid, regardless of practice setting. Indeed, West (2006) stated that addiction "is one of the most important concepts in behavioural and clinical science" (p. 9). Perhaps this explains in part the greater attention to addictions and substance use concerns in the current graduate education standards for counselors. For example, all counseling students enrolled in programs accredited by the Council for Accreditation of Counseling and Related Educational Programs (CACREP) must receive instruction in "theories and etiology of addictions and addictive behaviors, including strategies for prevention, intervention, and treatment" (CACREP *2009 Standards*, Section II.G.3.g.). This is a standard in the CACREP (2009) core curricular area of Human Growth and Development. There are additional standards related to addictions and substance use concerns for students enrolled in the specific program areas of Clinical Mental Health Counseling; Marriage, Couples, and Family Counseling; School Counseling; and Student Affairs and College Counseling. The newest program area, Addiction Counseling, is the most prominent example of a greater focus on addictions and substance use concerns in counselor preparation and in the counseling profession.

It is implied in the title of this chapter that there is not one kind or type of addiction. There are many. Depending on how addiction is defined, there could be a countless number of addictions. The most common throughout history is addiction to certain chemicals or substances, such as alcohol and other drugs. This form of addiction typically is associated with physiological dependence (i.e., tolerance, withdrawal) and involves a craving state or compulsive engagement, impaired control over substance-related behaviors, and continued engagement in substance-related behaviors despite adverse consequences (Saunders, 2006). Other types of addiction include gambling, sex, overeating, video gaming, physical exercise, and skin tanning. These are referred to as non-substance-related addictions, process addictions, or behavioral addictions. Behavioral addiction has been defined as the repetition of impulsive behaviors that do not involve the self-administration of a psychoactive substance (Saunders, 2006). It is the behavior, the activity itself, that has become addictive rather than an ingested substance. Behaviors associated with either chemical or non-chemical addictions supply mood-altering stimuli that produce pleasure or relieve pain.

Because addiction to alcohol and other drugs is the most common and most researched form of addiction, this chapter focuses on addiction to these substances. And although addiction is difficult to define and is not a term that appears in the current edition of the *Diagnostic and Statistical Manual of Mental Disorders* (DSM-IV-TR; American Psychiatric

Association, 2000), we use *addiction* in this chapter because it is (a) a generic term that encompasses a continuum of experiences, behaviors, and consequences of a range of substances used; (b) recognizable to professionals and laypersons alike; and (c) consistent with terminology used in the CACREP *2009 Standards*, specifically the name of the newest program area.

Foundations of Addictions Counseling

Problematic substance use is a common and widespread problem that is related to and is closely intertwined with many other problems (W. R. Miller, Forcehimes, & Zweben, 2011). These include physical and mental illnesses, crime, unemployment, violence, family disruption, vehicular accidents and fatalities, financial strain and poverty, malnutrition, trauma, homelessness, and suicide. An analysis of actual causes of death in 2000 in the United States revealed that substance use was responsible for almost one-half of all non-genetic or modifiable causes of death that year (Mokdad, Marks, Stroup, & Gerberding, 2004). In other words, nicotine, alcohol, and illicit drug use were responsible for approximately 46% of deaths not attributable to disease (e.g., heart disease, cancer, dementia), infection (e.g., pneumonia), or unintentional injuries. These preventable deaths include suicide. From 2005–6, alcohol intoxication was verified in 24% of all suicides tested for alcohol, the highest percentage (37%) being found in American Indian/Alaska Natives (Centers for Disease Control, 2009). Among U.S. Army soldiers, Kuehn (2010) reported that almost one-third of completed suicides and more than 45% of suicide attempts between 2003 and 2009 involved the use of alcohol and other drugs.

Although the majority of persons who use substances do not develop substance dependence (with the exception of nicotine use), substance use initiated prior to age 14 greatly increases the risk of developing substance dependence (Lopez-Quintero et al., 2011). This is compounded by experiencing various forms of adversity in childhood. Dube et al. (2006) found that any adverse childhood experience (ACE) was associated with a two- to three-fold increased likelihood of drinking alcohol by age 14. These ACEs included emotional, physical, and sexual abuse; parental discord/divorce; mental illness or substance abuse in the household; and having a battered mother or a household member incarcerated. It is estimated that between 60–80% of persons in the criminal justice system have a substance use problem, and that rates of past-month substance use, abuse, and dependence are almost two to three times higher among probationers and parolees than among those not in the criminal justice system (Feucht & Gfroerer, 2011).

The presence of a psychiatric illness also greatly enhances problematic substance use. Rates of co-occurrence or comorbidity (having a substance use disorder and a mental illness at the same time) vary widely in both the general population (10–50%) and in persons receiving clinical services (40–80%; Mueser, Drake, Turner, & McGovern, 2006). A recent report of the Substance Abuse and Mental Health Services Administration (SAMHSA, 2011a) indicates that in 2010, approximately 43% of all clients enrolled in substance abuse treatment were diagnosed with a co-occurring mental health disorder. Co-occurrence rates are higher for persons with more severe mental illnesses. Persons with schizophrenia, bipolar disorder, and antisocial personality disorder, for example, have co-occurrence rates of 47%, 56%, and 84%, respectively (Regier et al., 1990). Co-occurrence is therefore "a dominant clinical reality in most treatment settings" (Mueser et al., 2006, p. 116) and graduate training in mental health counseling *and* addictions counseling—referred to as "cross-training"—is warranted.

Unfortunately, "cross-trained" professionals remain the exception rather than the rule. This reflects the longstanding divide between mental health care and addictions treatment in the United States, due primarily to conceptions of addiction. For at least the past 200 years in U.S. history, problematic substance use (primarily alcohol) has been viewed as an immoral or sinful activity and addiction as a vague, nonspecific disease (Thombs, 2006). Although the disease model of addiction remains the most prominent belief system in U.S. treatment facilities today, it retains a moral connotation, leading Tracy (2005) to refer to it as a "hybrid medico-moral affliction" (p. 26). Recent advances in medicine and behavioral science have generated alternative explanations for or models of addiction (see W. R. Miller et al., 2011; Thombs, 2006; West, 2006). These include conditioning or behavior models, cognitive models (e.g., choice, expectancy, self-efficacy), sociocultural models, comorbidity models (e.g., secondary psychopathology, common factors), motivation-based models, and the biopsychosocial or public health model. The expansion of theories of addiction has ushered in a greater array of prevention and treatment services intended to provide relevant, engaging, individualized, and evidence-based or effective care. Examples of these practices can be found in SAMHSA's National Registry of Evidence-based Programs and Practices (NREPP) at http://nrepp.samhsa.gov. A few examples also are presented in Table 13.2 later in this chapter.

Although problematic substance use is often encountered in human services facilities (e.g., child protective services), school, correctional facilities (e.g., police department) or court settings, or medical settings (e.g., emergency department), persons employed in these settings remain ill prepared to address substance use problems directly. These include physicians, nurses, family therapists, and psychologists, all of whom, according to Doweiko (2012), have had little to no formal training in detecting and treating drug and alcohol problems. Certainly there are professionals trained in addictions in these service settings, but they remain in the minority. Denby, Brinson, and Ayala (2011) found that even "highly educated" clinicians who worked with children with co-occurring disorders lacked knowledge and skills in areas deemed essential for working with this client population. Areas of deficiency included assessing for trauma, defining the features of a major depressive episode, and understanding the prevalence of co-occurring mental health and substance use disorders.

SIDEBAR 13.1 Self-Awareness

Before you decided to become a counselor, what were your views of addiction and your perceptions of persons with addictions? What contributed to these views and perceptions? These might have included your direct experience with problematic substance use—your own, or that of a family member or close friend. Since enrolling in a graduate counseling program, how have those views and perceptions changed? What has contributed to these changes? How do the views and perceptions you hold today help you provide genuine and helpful counseling to clients who struggle with problematic substance use?

Only with a more educated workforce and astute leadership in the field can science or research findings be applied to routine counseling practice—a process referred to as technology transfer or diffusion of innovation (see P. M. Miller, 2009). In the counseling profession, this process has been mobilized in part by CACREP's more pronounced focus on addictions in its *2009 Standards*. This is a start. It also has been projected that starting in 2014, counselors in the addictions field will need to have earned a master's degree in order to comply with requirements of state Medicaid programs and private insurance (Knopf, 2011). These and other initiatives are needed to better equip professionals to work with persons with substance use problems and to better integrate addiction treatment with all aspects of care provision.

Addictions Counseling, Prevention, and Intervention

For persons with substance use problems, there remain many barriers to appropriate care. The lack of health care coverage and an inability to afford the cost of treatment is the most common reason given for not receiving treatment for problematic alcohol or drug use, even among persons 12 years old and older who recognize the need for treatment (SAMHSA, 2011b). This is followed by a lack of readiness to stop using, the belief that the problem can be managed without treatment, lack of transportation and other inconveniences (e.g., lack of child care), and the perception of negative repercussions (e.g., loss of job, stigmatized by neighbors and community). Addressing these barriers is essential for counselors, regardless of their practice setting. This begins with an understanding that substance use problems are common, intertwined with many other problems, and highly preventable and treatable, and that addiction is not a moral failure. Communicating these realities in an open, direct, and nonjudgmental manner to students, clients, and their families invites engagement, instills hope, and sets the stage for effective care. This type of dialogue and education also can take place with colleagues, administrators, and policy makers in an effort to change the system of care for persons with substance use problems. Although counselors may not be able to single-handedly change certain policies and procedures (e.g., making care more affordable), they can change the conversation. This means referring to substance use problems as maladaptive behaviors, not as character defects; defining addiction as a multifaceted and complex chronic condition, not as a simple or an easily defined disease resulting from willful misconduct, an absence or morals, or a loss of willpower; and describing the array of services available to effectively prevent, treat, and manage addiction. Conversations such as these can serve to lessen the stigma of addiction and to promote service access.

Evidence-Based Practices in Addictions Counseling

Addictions counseling in the United States continues its transition from being a rather ingrown, isolated, and loosely regulated practice that once relied primarily on personal evidence, subjective testimony, and the sufficiency of mutual support; to being a sophisticated practice informed by science, integrated into mainstream health care, and offering a menu of evidence-based practices (P. M. Miller, 2009). Whereas 28-day detoxification and inpatient treatment episodes, confrontation approaches, and staged family interventions were once the standards of care (see White & Miller, 2007), supportive and collaborative outpatient care provided in a number of different settings is now the norm. These include the four groupings of effective treatments described by Moos (2007): (a) motivational interviewing and motivational enhancement therapy, (b) twelve-step facilitation treatment, (c) cognitive-behavioral treatments and behavioral family counseling, and (d) contingency management and community reinforcement. Specific practices associated with these groups are recognized by NREPP. Four common

Table 13.1 Common components of evidence-based practices in addictions counseling

Common components or shared active ingredients	*Examples of targets and specific activities*
1. Support, structure, goal direction	a. Client-counselor cohesion
	b. Moderate structure
	c. Focus on moving toward achieving the personal milestones and objectives of clients
2. Rewards and rewarding activities	a. Use of extrinsic incentives or rewards (e.g., tangible prizes, vouchers redeemable for goods and services)
	b. Experience intrinsic rewards of sobriety
	c. Develop and participate in substance-free and rewarding social and service activities
3. Abstinence-oriented norms and models	a. Attend self-help group meetings
	b. Obtain feedback from non-substance using family and role models
	c. Reduce positive expectancies for substance use
4. Self-efficacy and coping skills	a. Affirm client's strengths and reinforce client's resources
	b. Elicit client's ideas about change
	c. Teach and develop specific coping skills

Source: Moos (2007)

components or the shared active ingredients of these practices that Moos (2007) identified are presented in Table 13.1.

Motivational Interviewing and Motivational Enhancement Therapy

Motivational interviewing (MI; W. R. Miller & Rollnick, 2002) is a method of communication intended to help clients mobilize their own internal resources for change. Its respectful and nonjudgmental approach makes it effective particularly for persons who do not think they need to change their substance use behavior, are ambivalent about changing, or are preparing to make certain changes. It is important to emphasize that MI is a therapeutic style not a collection of techniques. It uses fundamental listening and attending skills in a strategic, directive, or purposeful manner to guide clients through their own process of change. These skills are often referred to by the acronym OARS: asking Open-ended questions, providing sincere Affirmations, extending empathic Reflections, and periodically offering a Summary of content.

Chief among the OARS skills in MI is reflective listening. Reflections are statements not questions that make a guess about what the client is thinking or feeling. They are intended to cultivate client–counselor collaboration, keep the conversation going, and evoke the client's own reasons for change. Whereas questions have the potential to stall or at least interrupt the flow of conversation, well crafted reflections have the effect of furthering the conversation. The difference is similar to playing ping-pong or singles tennis compared to gliding on the ice with a skating partner: the first type of movement is a back-and-forth, stop-and-start pattern; whereas the second type is a side-by-side, in-step or in-sync pattern. Recent research has revealed that of the OARS skills, reflections in particular promote client talk about change, talk that can then lead to actual behavior change (Moyers, Martin, Houck, Christopher, & Tonigan, 2009).

Motivational enhancement therapy (MET) is a brief intervention and an adaptation of MI that provides students or clients with personalized and structured feedback. Feedback includes comparisons of student- or client-reported alcohol use relative to their peers and health information (e.g., maximum number of drinks per week recommended), and is presented in a candid and nonjudgmental manner. An example of MET is the Brief Alcohol Screening and Intervention for College Students (BASICS; Dimeff, Baer, Kivlahan, & Marlatt, 1999) that is conducted in two separate 50-minute sessions: an assessment session followed by a feedback session. Using the MI style or "spirit" of collaboration, honoring client autonomy and decision-making, and eliciting client resources and strengths, BASICS is intended to raise awareness of drinking behaviors in older teenagers and young adults. Once awareness has been enhanced and persons begin to talk about changing their behavior, they are encouraged in an affirming, collaborative, and non-confrontational manner to develop a personalized plan for healthy change.

Twelve-Step Facilitation Treatment

As its name suggests, twelve-step facilitation (TSF) is a treatment designed to help lients find and participate in Alcoholics Anonymous (AA) 12-step self-help fellowship meetings, and to internalize and endorse the philosophy of AA. Unlike AA, TSF is a treatment conducted by a professional counselor that can be delivered in individual sessions. TSF adheres to the concepts and beliefs of AA in the approved AA literature (Longabaugh et al., 2005). These include the belief that (a) alcoholism is a progressive illness that affects body, mind, and spirit; (b) alcoholism is characterized by a loss of control over drinking that can result in death if left untreated; and (c) the only effective remedy is total abstinence from alcohol. The TSF counselor reviews with clients (in individual or group formats) the 12 steps and the 12 traditions of AA, as well as other AA literature (available at www.aa.org); discusses protocol for AA meetings; prepares clients to know what to expect at meetings; reviews with clients their experiences at recent AA meetings; and encourages clients to sample a variety of meetings until they can find a fellowship to call "home." Consistent with AA philosophy, TSF promotes total abstinence, spiritual development (i.e., identifying a "higher power" as a source of hope and strength), and long-term recovery.

Research on TSF has generated compelling findings (see W. R. Miller et al., 2011, for a review), most notably, that clients enrolled in TSF are significantly more likely to achieve and maintain abstinence one year after treatment than clients in other types of treatment, such as MET and cognitive-behavioral therapy. Additional outcomes attributed to TSF when compared to other treatments include lower health care utilization, reduced cocaine and other drug use, and maintained abstinence (i.e., it is effective in preventing relapse). Because of these findings, it is recommended that all counselors encourage their clients who struggle with addiction to attend a variety of AA meetings (which are free and readily available in most communities) and then process with clients their experiences.

Cognitive-Behavioral Treatments and Behavioral Family Counseling

Cognitive-behavioral (CB) treatments represent an extensive collection of interventions that apply learning theory to observable behavior as well as to thoughts and emotions

(Barry & Petry, 2009). Principles of classical and operant conditioning are used, along with principles of social learning theory. CB treatments thus are developed and implemented on the assumption that substance using behaviors are learned through processes of conditioning, including observing others use substances. Pleasurable effects of substance use may not necessarily be the direct result of the pharmacologic properties of the substance used; the rewards of using—at least initially—may be social in nature such as prestige, acceptance, and belonging. Rewards also may be the absence or lessening of aversive stimuli, such as fear, loneliness, and lack of freedom. Once the association is made that using certain substances within a specific context (e.g., privacy of home, with admired peers or superiors, adventurous or high-risk activities) produces welcome and desired effects, a pattern of continued use may begin. Genetic influences explain to a certain degree the continuation of addictive behaviors despite experiencing over time a number of negative consequences related to substance use. This does not mean, however, that addictive behavior is not learned. Rather, it is learned within the context of genetic predisposition.

CB treatments involve learning to decrease or abstain from substance use by experiencing alternative rewards from substance-free activities, such as experiencing increased energy and reduced malaise from physical exercise or feeling understood and genuinely validated by a counselor. Because addiction generally does not develop quickly, learning to reduce using behavior and becoming sober takes time. A recent report suggests that when someone first enters treatment for a specific substance, an average of 15.6 years has elapsed from the time he or she first used that substance (SAMHSA, 2011c). This means in part that addictive behaviors often are firmly established when treatment begins. Counselors therefore must remain resolute yet patient in helping clients learn new ways of living. The highly structured format of CB treatments serves to counteract the "pull" of addictive behaviors but clearly not in a demeaning or abrasive manner. Scare tactics (e.g., "Scared Straight" programs for juvenile offenders) have no place in addictions counseling and actually have been found to cause more harm than good (see Norcross, Koocher, Fala, & Wexler, 2010). Specific and recommended CB treatments include (a) identifying stimuli associated with use (or triggers for using) through daily self-monitoring; (b) learning and practicing specific coping skills (e.g., mindfulness) to avoid triggers and reduce cravings; (c) identifying the costs and benefits of using, as well as the costs and benefits of not using (referred to as a cost/benefit analysis); and (d) learning to communicate more effectively with loved ones (e.g., practicing conflict resolution skills).

Involving family members in the prevention and treatment efforts of an adolescent or adult who is struggling with problematic substance use has become standard practice in the addictions (O'Farrell & Fals-Stewart, 2008). Its purpose is to engage the partner or other family members in a plan for systemic change, clarify and reinforce family roles and responsibilities (e.g., parental discipline), achieve and maintain abstinence, and improve relational dynamics and satisfaction. Behavioral approaches include (a) establishing and abiding by written recovery contracts among family members that promote substance-free and other healthy behaviors (e.g., attending self-help support groups together); (b) improving daily interactions, including participating in recreational activities; (c) increasing reciprocal positive exchanges; (d) teaching constructive communication and problem-solving skills; and (e) expanding a support network beyond the family unit. According to McCrady (2006), successful family-involved treatment is more likely when the family members do not have alcohol or drug problems themselves, the individual client is experiencing more severe alcohol or drug problems, there is a certain level of stability in social functioning (e.g., employment) and relational commitment (e.g., no threats of divorce or abandonment), and counseling has been initiated following a crisis (e.g., arrest for drug-related offense), especially when the stability of the family unit has been threatened. Clearly couples or family counseling is not appropriate when there has been significant domestic violence that has resulted in injury or the need for medical assistance.

Contingency Management and Community Reinforcement

Contingency management (CM; Higgins, Silverman, & Heil, 2008) and the community reinforcement approach (CRA; Meyers, Villanueva, & Smith, 2005) also are cognitive-behavioral treatments. They are very specialized practices specifically based on operant conditioning principles, such as positive and negative reinforcement. CM and CRA both use behavioral contracting to systematically reorganize a person's environment by increasing the rate of reinforcement for abstinent behavior and reducing or eliminating the rate of reinforcement for substance using behavior. Whereas CM makes use of contrived or tangible reinforcers (e.g., vouchers redeemable for such things as groceries and bus passes), CRA makes use of environmental or natural reinforcers (e.g., withdrawal of spousal affection, time spent with children). Although both are used together, CM is often implemented early in treatment to "jump start" the process of change and CRA is introduced once the change process has begun.

CM is considered a collection of interventions designed to shape behavior by rewarding non-substance use and concurrently withdrawing support or introducing aversive stimuli for substance-related behavior. Also known as voucher-based reinforcement therapy, prize-based CM, and prize or motivational incentives, these strategies all include the systematic dispensation of tangible items or privileges (e.g., family visits in inpatient programs) in return for the demonstration or evidence of abstinence-related behaviors or decreased substance use. For example, a pregnant woman who smokes 2 packs of cigarettes per day would be rewarded with baby items (e.g., diapers, formula) when her breath carbon monoxide reading is below a predetermined level. Similarly, someone who reports daily to a clinic to receive a dose of methadone (an opiate-like medication used to treat heroin and other opioid addiction) can receive take-home doses of methadone when urine screens are clean or negative for illicit drugs. To see a video of one treatment program's implementation of prize incentives, go to http://pami.nattc.org.

CRA is a multifaceted biopsychosocial approach designed to intentionally rearrange community or environmental influences such as employment and family relations so that sobriety is supported and substance use is no longer tolerated or rewarded. It is a flexible approach that can be used with a wide variety of clients in outpatient and inpatient settings. Components include sobriety sampling (e.g., a time-limited trial of abstinence), behavioral skills training, job skills, social and recreational counseling, and relationship counseling. An adaptation of CRA, Community Reinforcement and Family Training (CRAFT; Smith & Meyers, 2004), is for family members or friends of individuals with substance use problems who refuse to get treatment. CRAFT teaches skills to concerned significant others so they can influence the family member to enter treatment, help the family member reduce substance use, and make positive changes in their own lives whether or not the family member stops using or enters treatment.

SIDEBAR 13.2 Case Example

Gregg is beginning to realize that he needs to do something about his 6-year heroin addiction because he has seen the effects of infection (HIV, Hepatitis C) on fellow users (who have also used heroin by injection). He is not confident, however, that he can stay clean—or even *get* clean—on his own for a significant period of time, and he is really not even sure how to go about taking the first steps toward change. If you were the first professional Gregg met when he accessed care, what would be the first thing you would say to him? How would you encourage him in his efforts to initiate sobriety? Describe your style of interaction with him. How would you monitor his progress?

Common Practices and Formats in Addictions Counseling

There are common practices associated with addictions counseling whether or not specific evidence-based practices are implemented. These include recommending that clients attend and become involved in AA or other self-help support group meetings, consulting with the client's referral source as well as a collateral (i.e., family member, friend), and periodically screening for biological markers. This latter practice is briefly described in the Screening section later in this chapter.

Founded in 1935 in Akron, Ohio, Alcoholics Anonymous (AA) is now the largest self-help group in the world with over 2.1 million members. It is estimated that in the United States alone there are over 53,500 AA groups and over 1.2 million persons who belong to AA (based on 2007 AA Membership Survey, www.aa.org). Of the 4.1 million persons in the United States who reported receiving treatment for alcohol or drug use in 2010, the majority (56%) reported attending a self-help group (SAMHSA, 2011b). This is more than the number of persons who reported receiving outpatient or inpatient treatment for their substance use in that same year. Although AA is not treatment, it has proven to be a very effective adjunct to treatment, as mentioned earlier in the chapter in relation to TSF. Reasons that may explain the benefit of AA and other self-help groups are that they are free, widely available, and voluntary; anonymity and confidentiality are emphasized; and members have shared experiences and groups are self-governing (Doweiko, 2012). It is our belief that counselors who recommend AA to their clients must have attended AA meetings themselves. For counselors who are not in recovery from addiction, this means attending open meetings (i.e., open to all persons). Only by having experienced several different AA meetings first-hand do we believe counselors can adequately prepare clients for AA meetings and then effectively process those meetings with them.

Many persons who struggle with addictions do not decide to enter counseling on their own; they have accessed treatment services only because someone else has strongly recommended or required them to do so. As mentioned earlier in the chapter, addiction is not an isolated or a sequestered problem; it is intertwined with many other problems and "spills over" onto or affects many other persons beyond the person with an addiction. It is therefore recommended that counselors consult the referral source (e.g., physician, probation officer) and also a family member or friend, known as a collateral, and do so only after receiving the client's written permission. A collateral interview form is available at the Center on Alcoholism, Substance Abuse, and Addictions (http://casaa.unm.edu/inst/CIF.pdf). Additional questions might include the collateral's assessment of the client's strengths, as well as: "What do you value in your family member or friend?" "How do you hope counseling will be helpful for him or her?" and "What will convince you that he or she has made significant progress?" It is important for the collateral to know that his or her responses will be shared with the client. This information adds to the client's self-report and is used to help determine treatment goals. Consultation with the referral source clarifies the reasons for the referral and the contingencies involved, such as what is required for the client to regain custody of her children, to be reinstated for employment, or to get back his driver's license.

Groups remain the most common format of treatment for addiction mainly because they are practical and economical (W. R. Miller et al., 2011). Additional benefits of group counseling are that this format helps persons with addiction develop and reestablish connections with others, thereby lessening the isolation that addiction often precipitates. Groups also provide the context for learning new skills, especially interpersonal relation skills. Furthermore, it also may be easier for persons who have little respect for authority to receive feedback from their peers than from a counselor. Not all persons will respond well to a group format. This is particularly true for women when men are group members. Women who are addicted to substances often have experienced physical and sexual abuse. To be successful, groups must therefore be tailored to the specific needs and shared preferences of members. Clients also must have the option of individual counseling whether or not they participate in group counseling. For men and women with co-occurring mental health issues and histories of trauma, and for those who are in the very early stages of changing their substance use behavior or do not believe change is necessary, individual counseling is the recommended format. A caring and concerned counselor who conveys hope and acceptance and remains a stable force for the client who struggles through the cycles of addiction can serve as the catalyst for healthy and enduring change.

Although little is actually known about the specific effects of a group format on client outcomes in addictions treatment, it has been found that psychoeducational groups that make use of lectures and films to convey information about addiction are the least effective method for preventing or treating problematic alcohol use (W. R. Miller, Willbourne, & Hettema, 2003). Simply knowing about addiction and its harmful consequences does not translate into behavior change. Suggesting to a client that sobriety and recovery are simply a matter of a knowledge deficiency is not only demeaning, it is incorrect. What does facilitate the process of change in a group format is cultivating a culture of respect, safety, and predictability (e.g., norms or guidelines).

Determining Levels of Care

Since 1991, the American Society of Addiction Medicine (ASAM) has provided a comprehensive set of guidelines designed to enhance the use of multidimensional assessments in making decisions about matching patients or clients to appropriate levels of care. These remain the most widely used guidelines for professionals in the addictions field. Although initially focused on clients with only substance use concerns, the revised second edition of the *ASAM Patient Placement Criteria for the Treatment of Substance-Related Disorders* (*ASAM PPC-2R*; Mee-Lee, Shulman, Fishman, Gastfriend, & Griffith, 2001) incorporates criteria that address co-occurring disorders, including what are referred to as dual diagnosis capable programs (substance use remains primary concern) or dual diagnosis enhanced programs (designed for those with more unstable or disabling co-occurring mental disorders). Language used is consistent with the *DSM-IV*. It is noted that the guidelines are required in over 30 states (see www.asam.org/publications), and Mee-Lee and Gastfriend (2008) reported that these criteria have been adopted for use worldwide by the U.S. Department of Defense and by the U.S. Department of Veterans Affairs in its hospitals nationwide.

The *ASAM PPC-2R* assesses all clients (adults and adolescents) on six dimensions: (1) acute intoxication and/or withdrawal potential; (2) biomedical conditions/complications; (3) emotional, behavioral, or cognitive conditions/complications; (4) readiness to change; (5) relapse, continued use, or continued problem potential; and (6) recovery/living environment. Clients are then assigned to one of five basic levels of care that are on a continuum of increasing intensity: (1) early intervention (e.g., participating in a one-time educational session at a school or community center), (2) outpatient services, (3) intensive outpatient (9–19 hours/week of service provision) or partial hospitalization (20 or more hours/week of service provision), (4) residential/inpatient treatment (e.g., women's rehabilitation center), or (5) medically managed intensive inpatient treatment (i.e., 24/7 services provided in a hospital setting). Although presented as discrete levels, the five levels of care represent benchmarks that can be used to determine client progress. The process of matching clients to treatment setting and level of service is based on the principle of "clinical appropriateness" rather than "medical necessity." The former emphasizes quality and efficiency, in contrast to the latter, which is often associated with restrictions on utilization.

Diversity and Advocacy in Addictions Counseling

Counselors must be competent to work with diverse populations in order to practice ethically and to promote client welfare, and advocacy has become an increasingly emphasized role for professional counselors. Striving for multicultural competence by enhancing awareness, increasing knowledge, and learning specific skills related to working with diverse populations is considered essential for counselors (Arredondo et al., 1996). Diverse populations may have unique experiences or circumstances related to substance use and addiction, and it is important for counselors to be aware of and understand these differences in order to work effectively with clients and to advocate for them. We discuss in this section the prevalence of substance use among ethnically diverse populations and evidence-based practices used with diverse populations. We also address briefly issues pertaining to other specific populations such as adolescents, women, older adults, LGBT (lesbian, gay, bisexual, and transgender) populations, veterans, people with disabilities, and homeless individuals.

Ethnic and Racial Diversity

Cultural norms, practices, and beliefs—as well as environmental, social, and economic factors—all likely influence the substance use behaviors of persons of various cultures, races, and ethnicities. We present in this section trends in substance use in specific ethnic and racial groups in the United States. Primary sources of prevalence data are the 2010 National Survey on Drug Use and Health (NSDUH; SAMHSA, 2011b), a report of the National Institute on Drug Abuse (NIDA, 2003) on ethnic/racial minorities, and research conducted by Grant et al. (2006). Specific treatment considerations are also presented.

It is important to remember that cultural groups are heterogeneous and prevalence data should be used to inform counselors working with diverse populations and not to perpetuate stereotypes.

African Americans

According to the 2010 NSDUH, 8.2% of African Americans were classified with a substance use disorder and 19.8% reported engaging in binge drinking or heavy alcohol use, rates lower than European Americans (8.9% and 24% respectively. Between 1992 and 2002, the rate of alcohol abuse increased in the African American community for men (all age groups) and for women between the ages of 45 and 64, whereas the rates of alcohol dependence remained stable. In 2010, the rate of illicit drug use was 10.7%, a significant increase from 8.7% in 2003, a higher rate than that of European Americans (9.1%), Hispanic/Latino Americans (8.1%), and Asian Americans (3.5%), however, not statistically significantly so.

Asian Americans

Asian Americans have had the lowest reported rate of substance dependence or abuse among the five primary ethnical and racial groups in the United States. In regard to drug abuse, Asian Americans consistently have the lowest reported rate of using illicit drugs, and this group also has lower rates of alcohol use, including binge drinking and heavy alcohol use, compared to the other ethnic groups. However, statistically significant increases in alcohol abuse and dependence were found for Asian Americans between 1992 and 2002. Specifically, females between the ages of 18 and29 and both genders ages 65 and over showed increased rates of alcohol abuse and males aged 18–29 showed increased rates of alcohol dependence.

Hispanic/Latino Americans

In 2010, 9.7% of the Hispanic/Latino population was estimated to experience a substance use disorder. This rate is higher than that of European and African American populations (8.9% and 8.2% respectively), yet the rate of illicit drug use was lower comparatively (8.1% for Hispanic/Latino compared to 9.1% for European Americans and 10.7% for African Americans). Hispanic/Latino populations had a 41.8% alcohol use rate, with 20% engaging in binge drinking and 5.1% being heavy alcohol users. When examining Hispanic/Latino subgroups, Puerto Ricans had the highest rate of illicit drug use in the past month (approximately 10%), compared to Mexicans (less than 6%) and Central/South Americans and Cubans (approximately 4%). In general, Hispanic/Latino males have higher rates of alcohol abuse and dependence compared to females. Although Hispanic/Latino males showed a decrease in their rate of alcohol dependence between 1992 and 2002, the rate of alcohol abuse increased significantly for males between the ages of 18 and 29.

Native Americans

Rates of substance abuse or dependence were approximately 16% for Native Americans, the highest of the five primary ethnic/racial groups in the United States. Due to small sample sizes, reliable estimates of substance use have been difficult to obtain; however, it has been estimated that Native American populations have the highest rate of illicit drug use and heavy alcohol use (defined as 5 or more drinks on one occasion at least 5 days in one month) at 9.3% and 13.7% respectively. Between 1992 and 2002, rates of alcohol dependence remained stable, yet rates of alcohol abuse increased among Native American males aged 45–64.

Treatment

Research has shown that individuals from ethnic minority populations experience a higher rate of alcohol-related problems compared to European Americans (e.g., D'Avanzo, Dunn, Murdock, & Naegle, 2000), which suggests that ethnic minorities have more complex treatment needs (Schmidt, Greenfield, & Mulia, 2006). Limited employment opportunities, illiteracy or low education levels, and poverty and other unhealthy environmental conditions (e.g., high crime neighborhoods) can influence the rates of illegal drug use and associated problems experienced by specific population subgroups (Anthony & Helzer, 2002). Therefore, as Boyd, Phillips, and Dorsey (2003) stated, "Successful treatment must address [alcohol and other drug use] use within the context of the social, ecological environment. That means addressing poverty, violence, lack of health insurance, reluctance to seek treatment, and language barriers." (p. 254).

More and more research is being conducted on treatments developed for and/or implemented specifically with ethnically diverse populations. A sample of evidence-based practices from SAMHSA's NREPP (http://nrepp.samhsa.gov) that are appropriate for ethnic minority populations is presented in Table 13.2.

Specific Populations

Advocacy efforts have helped to increase awareness of the specific needs of additional groups of persons, leading to treatment practices for adolescents (e.g., SAMHSA, 2001), women (e.g., SAMHSA, 2011d, 2009a), older adults (e.g., SAMHSA, 2004), LGBT individuals (SAMHSA, 2009b), military persons and veterans (e.g., Department of Veterans Affairs, 2009), people with disabilities (e.g., SAMHSA, 1998), and homeless individuals (e.g., SAMHSA, 2010a). A brief overview is offered of some of the issues affecting each of these groups.

Adolescents

In 2010, 71% of high school students reported drinking alcohol, more than one-third of which had done so by the eighth grade, and rates of marijuana use increased from previous years (Johnston, O'Malley, Bachman, & Schulenberg, 2011). Considering their developmental stage, adolescents are especially influenced by their peers and family, and as such, the National Institute on Drug Abuse (2009) recommends that treatment for this group should emphasize healthy peer interactions and activities (e.g., athletics, school involvement) and incorporate parental involvement (e.g., increased monitoring). Substance-related treatment with adolescents should also take into account the developing nature of their neurocognitive and psychosocial functioning and co-occurring disorders (NIDA, 2009).

Table 13.2 Sample of evidence-based programs and practices for ethnic minority populations

Program or practice	Description/goals	Ethnic minority samples used in empirical studies
Brief Strategic Family Therapy	The objectives are to (1) prevent, reduce, and/or treat adolescent behavior problems (e.g., drug use, conduct problems); (2) improve prosocial behaviors (e.g., school attendance and performance); and (3) improve family functioning (e.g., effective parental leadership and management, positive parenting). Typically delivered in 12–16 family sessions.	*Study 1[a]: 100% Hispanic/ Latino* *Study 2[b]: 100% Hispanic/ Latino* *Study 3[c]: 84.4% Hispanic/ Latino, 15.6% African American/Black* *Study 4[d]: 76% Hispanic/ Latino, 24% African American/Black*
Contingency Management (CM)	Based on the principles of operant conditioning, or the use of consequences to modify behavior. Prizes are awarded for abstinence and treatment compliance. CM is added to services in community-based treatment settings. Over a period of 3 months, urine and breath samples are collected two or three times a week for at least the first 6 weeks and once or twice weekly thereafter.	*Study 1[e]: 45.5% Hispanic/ Latino, 35.1% African American/Black* *Study 2[f]: 64.2% African American/Black, 10% Hispanic/Latino* *Study 3[g]: 52.4% African American/Black, 11.2% Hispanic/Latino* *Study 4[h]: 35.9% African American/Black, 12.5% Hispanic/Latino*
Motivational Enhancement Therapy (MET)	An adaptation of motivational interviewing (MI) that includes one or more client feedback sessions in which normative feedback is presented and discussed in an explicitly nonconfrontational manner.	*Study 1[i]: 42.9% Hispanic/ Latino, 10.7% American Indian or Alaska Native, 7.1% African American/ Black*
Motivational Interviewing (MI)	A client-centered, goal-directed counseling style for facilitating behavioral change by helping clients to explore and resolve ambivalence. Often used as a brief intervention or as a general counseling style.	*Study 1[j]: 60% African American/Black, 22% Hispanic/Latino* *Study 2[k]: 12.8% African American/Black, 5.3% Asian, 2.1% Hispanic/Latino*
Project ASSERT (Alcohol and Substance Abuse Services, Education, and Referral to Treatment)	A model that includes screening, brief intervention (includes MI), and referral that was designed for use in health clinics or emergency departments (ED). Delivered by trained peers or ED staff to patients who have a positive drug screen. The intervention is typically conducted in 15 minutes and a 10-minute booster session is initiated 10 days following the intervention.	*Study 1[j]: 62% African American/Black, 23% Hispanic/Latino* *Study 2[l]: 37% African American/Black, 20% Hispanic/Latino* *Study 3[m]: 79% African American/Black, 15.7% Hispanic/Latino*

Table 13.2 Continued

Program or practice	Description/goals	Ethnic minority samples used in empirical studies
Project SUCEESS (Schools Using Coordinated Community Efforts to Strengthen Students)	The objectives are to prevent and reduce substance use among students age 12-18 identified as being high risk. Delivered in four main components: (a) eight sessions focused on alcohol and drug use prevention; (b) school-wide action to positively influence social norms; (c) parent education; and (d) individual and/or group counseling.	Study 1[n]: *65.6% African American/Black, 19.8% Hispanic/Latino* Study 2[o]: *41.5% African American/Black, 23.1% Hispanic/Latino*

Sources: [a]Santisteban et al. (1996). [b]Santisteban et al. (2003). [c]Santisteban et al. (1997). [d]Coatsworth, Santisteban, McBride, & Szapocznik (2001). [e]Petry, Martin, & Simcic, Jr. (2005). [f]Petry et al. (2004). [g]Petry, Alessi, & Hanson (2007). [h]Petry et al. (2005). [i]Brown & Miller (1993). [j]Bernstein et al. (2005). [k]Monti et al. (1999). [l]Academic ED SBIRT Research Collaborative. (2007). [m]Bernstein et al. (2009). [n]Morehouse & Tobler (2000). [o]Vaughan & Johnson (2007).

Women

The 2010 NSDUH (SAMHSA, 20011b) found that 6.8% of adult women used an illicit substance and an earlier report (SAMHSA, 2010b) identified 5.1% who were in need of treatment for alcohol use in 2008. Substance use among women increases the risk for physical and mental health problems as well as increases the likelihood that that a woman will be a victim of a violent crime or sexual assault. Although women consume smaller quantities of alcohol than men, they advance much more rapidly to alcohol dependence, a process described as a shortened or telescoped course. Furthermore, the National Institute on Alcohol Abuse and Alcoholism (NIAAA, 2008) warns that alcohol use among women can have severe detrimental effects on their families, such as fetal alcohol syndrome and child abuse or neglect. Women face multiple barriers (e.g., economic hardship, lack of transportation, family responsibilities) to accessing help and they are they less likely to seek treatment for substance use. Counselors are encouraged to address these barriers with female clients to enhance their motivation to engage in treatment (Brady & Randall, 1999).

Older Adults

Substance use among older adults often goes unidentified and unaddressed, although a number of factors explain the greater need for substance use treatment for this population. These include the aging of baby boomers who generally have more liberal attitudes about drug use and greater lifetime use than previous generations, and an increased use of prescription medications in general (NIDA, 2009). Changes that occur socially (e.g., death of peers, retirement) and physically (e.g., slowing metabolism, health conditions) may increase the vulnerability of older adults to the negative effects of substance use (Volkow, 2011), creating a need for prevention and treatment programs specific to the needs of this population.

SIDEBAR 13.3 Case Example

Delilah is a 32-year-old Native American/American Indian woman who works in one of the casinos on a reservation outside of Albuquerque, New Mexico. She has sought assistance at a local women's shelter at the urging of her coworkers because she confided in them that her boyfriend, Ray, who also works at the casino, had become increasingly abusive toward her. Delilah acknowledges to you, a counselor at the shelter, that she and Ray drink together at work and at home and just last week, after drinking quite a bit, he intentionally destroyed one of her son's favorite toys in front of her young son. Ray became angry with Delilah for defending her son and proceeded to hit her in front of her son. It was after this incident that Delilah decided to go to the shelter directly from work the next afternoon, after picking up her son from the babysitter's. First, describe the challenges Delilah faces. Second, explain how you would clarify the type and extent of her concerns. Third, describe the counseling approach or style that you would take in your work with Delilah.

LGBT

Accurate prevalence data for lesbian, gay, bisexual, and transgender (LGBT) individuals has been difficult to ascertain, but studies suggest that LGBT persons typically abuse substances more often than in the general population (SAMHSA, 2009b). For example, Woody and colleagues (1999) found that a sample of men who have sex with men were more likely to engage in use of inhalants, hallucinogens, stimulants, sedatives, marijuana, and tranquilizers compared to a general population sample of men, and Cochran and Mays (2000) found that lesbian women were more likely than heterosexual women to use alcohol at higher rates. However, research on LGBT persons has been questioned due to samples often being drawn from communities that involve substance use (e.g., "gay bars"), resulting in possible inflated prevalence data (Stevens & Smith, 2009). The LGBT population is a very diverse community with individuals from various ethnicities, ages, socioeconomic status, and genders. Specific concerns affecting this population include the coming out process, family of origin and relationship issues, legal problems and discrimination, and using substances as socializing agents (SAMHSA, 2009b; Stevens & Smith, 2009). Treatment specific to LGBT persons is developing and it is essential for counselors to be trained to work effectively with LGBT clients.

Veterans and Military Persons

Mental health and substance use concerns among veterans and military persons have received greater attention in recent years, and treatment services have been developed to meet the unique needs of persons who serve our country. The rates of prescription drug use and heavy alcohol use have increased among military persons (NIDA, 2011). According to the National Surveys on Drug Use and Health from 2004–2006, in the past year 7% of veterans experienced serious psychological distress, 7.1% experienced a substance use disorder, and 1.5% had co-occurring disorders, with younger veterans (between the ages of 18 and 25) being more likely to experience higher rates of these issues. Furthermore, veterans with annual incomes less than $20,000 were more likely than those with higher incomes to experience serious psychological distress, substance use disorders, or co-occurring disorders (SAMHSA, 2007). According to NIDA (2011), efforts "to contribute to the design and implementation of effective prevention and treatment interventions that can help safeguard the health and well-being of those who protect and serve our Nation" are underway.

Disabled Persons

Disabilities can be classified as physical, sensory, cognitive, or affective. Although chemical dependency is considered a disability according to the Americans with Disabilities Act (ADA), many people experience a co-occurring disability along with substance use. People with a disability are at a higher risk than the general population of experiencing a substance use disorder, yet they are less likely to initiate or complete treatment (SAMHSA, 1998). Counselors must make accommodations to enable and encourage people with disabilities to engage in appropriate treatment for substance-related concerns.

Homeless Persons

Finally, homeless populations can encompass a diverse group of people including youth, women, and mentally ill persons (Stevens & Smith, 2009). Alcohol and drug use often presents as a major impediment to ending homelessness as substance use may limit a person's eligibility for services and yet substance use may not be seen as a change priority. As W. R. Miller et al. (2011) explained, "A mother who is homeless is likely to be more urgently concerned with safety, shelter, and feeding her children than with abstaining from drugs" (p. 45). Barriers to treatment include a lack of transportation, and abstinence-only programs can deter homeless persons from entering treatment (Stevens & Smith, 2009).

Advocacy

Advocacy in the counseling profession emphasizes how counselors can "become active voices and conduits for social/political change at the macrolevel of intervention" (Lee & Rodgers, 2009, p. 285) as well as advocating for client empowerment at the individual and the systemic levels (Lewis, Arnold, House, & Toporek, 2002). Professional counselors who are competent in working with addictions are able to identify and assist individuals with addiction-related issues, regardless of their presenting concerns (e.g., depression, anxiety). In this way, counselors promote the welfare of each client by identifying when substance use is harmful and detrimental and by taking appropriate action such as conducting a comprehensive evaluation, ascribing a proper diagnosis, and offering appropriate interventions such as treatment or referral. On the other hand, counselors who fail to identify, acknowledge, or address addiction issues risk causing harm to or oppressing their clients.

Advocacy in addiction can be accomplished through various mediums. Being familiar with resources, such as Twelve-Step group meetings (e.g., AA), and treatment options for diverse persons (e.g., treatment specific for women, LGBT populations, people with co-occurring disorders) with varying means (e.g., insured and uninsured) can be a positive step in advocacy. For example, SAMHSA provides a Treatment Locator (www.samhsa.

Table 13.3 Advocacy resources

American Society of Addiction Medicine	www.asam.org/advocacy
National Association for Alcoholism and Drug Abuse Counselors	www.naadac.org/advocacy
Substance Abuse and Mental Health Services Administration	www.samhsa.gov/publicAwareness
National Coalition Against Prescription Drug Abuse	http://ncapda.org

gov/treatment) to enable easy access to treatment resources. Keeping abreast of current research and treatment practices for diverse populations is another form of advocacy in that it enables counselors to continue to provide quality care to clients. For example, NIAAA (www.niaaa.nih.gov), NIDA (www.nida.nih.gov), and SAMHSA (www.samhsa.gov) provide up-to-date publications and resources for public access. Involvement in professional organizations, such as the American Society of Addiction Medicine (ASAM; www.asam.org), the Association for Addiction Professionals (NAADAC; www.naadac.org), and the International Association of Addictions and Offender Counselors (IAAOC; a division of ACA; www.iaaoc.org), provides students and professionals with opportunities to receive current information related to research and trends in the area of addictions. By affiliating themselves with such organizations, counselors are exposed to information and a professional network to aid them in best helping their clientele.

Learning about the legislative and environmental issues that affect persons experiencing addictions is another positive step in advocacy. The goal of advocacy at this level is to influence public policy and legislation and enhance public awareness (Lewis et al., 2002). Becoming involved in organizations that emphasize advocating for legislative change and drawing attention to and educating the public about issues related to addictions can enable counselors to impact communities' understanding and responses to persons experiencing addictions. Table 13.3 presents a summary of organizations that emphasize advocacy in the addictions.

Evaluation Methods in Addictions Counseling

Counselors use various methods to evaluate clients' alcohol and drug use and related problems. Psychometric instruments are frequently used by counselors to help them determine whether or not a substance use problem exists, and if so, to what degree. Screening is often the first step in evaluating substance use. Results of screening instruments are typically categorical (e.g., "yes" or "no") and provide information to inform the question, "Does a substance use problem exist?" Assessments, on the other hand, are continuous in nature, have multiple dimensions, and help answer the question, "To what degree or extent is there a substance use problem?" A comprehensive substance use evaluation is essential in order for counselors to provide an accurate diagnosis and to recommend appropriate treatment.

Screening

In general, screening is used to help clinicians determine whether or not a substance use problem exists (Winters & Zenilman, 1994). Screening tools include sets of brief questions asked by the counselor during a conversation, hand-recorded or computer-based questionnaires completed by a client or prospective client, and biological measures.

The latter test for the presence of certain biologically active chemicals in the breath, hair follicles, urine, or blood and are used to corroborate self-reports (W. R. Miller et al., 2011). Clients who are required by their employer, a judge, or social service agency to attend counseling because of their substance use may need to supply periodically a urine sample, for example, to determine beyond their self-report or the counselor's report whether progress has been made. Not all practice settings are equipped to test for biological markers, and therefore clients may be sent to a local medical lab to provide a specimen.

The set of questions asked by the counselor and the questionnaires completed by clients that used for screening are typically brief, rely on self-reports, and provide information only about the construct that is under investigation (e.g., alcohol or drug use). It is important to remember that screening is a preliminary evaluation tool and should not be used in place of a comprehensive assessment. Information provided by screening tools alone is not sufficient to make a clinical diagnosis. As W. R. Miller and Feldstein (2007) state, "Properly used, a valid screening instrument signals the need for more careful evaluation and clinical confirmation of diagnosis, and does not itself serve or replace these functions" (p. 1003). Following screening, Winters and Zenilman (1994) suggest that clinicians engage in one of three subsequent actions: (a) recommend further evaluation (e.g., comprehensive assessment), (b) determine that further evaluation is unnecessary at this time, or (c) administer the screening again at a later time. We highlight five screening tools (i.e., clinical questions and questionnaires) that are often used.

CAGE

The CAGE (Ewing, 1984) is a brief, four-question screening tool that is typically administered verbally:

"Have you ever felt the need to *Cut* down on your drinking?"

"Have you ever felt *Annoyed* by someone criticizing your drinking?"

"Have you ever felt bad or *Guilty* about your drinking?"

"Have you ever had a drink first thing in the morning to steady your nerves and get rid of a hangover?"[*Eye-opener*]

A "yes" response to one of the above questions represents need to explore the client's drinking behaviors further. An affirmative response to two or three questions suggests an alcohol use problem is likely. Finally, clients who respond affirmatively to all four questions warrant further evaluation for alcohol dependence (O'Brien, 2008).

The CAGE is commonly used in primary care medical settings and is considered to be useful in detecting alcohol dependence; however, it does not inquire about current experiences (questions are phrased, "Have you ever…"), frequency of drinking, or quantity of alcohol consumed (Cooney, Kadden, & Steinberg, 2008; O'Brien, 2008). These may be considered limitations of this screening tool, but a strength of the CAGE is that it assesses the behavioral effects of alcohol use (O'Brien, 2008).

TWEAK

Based on the CAGE, the TWEAK (Russell, 1994) was developed to screen for alcohol use with pregnant women. It contains five questions:

T = How many drinks can you hold? [*Tolerance*]

W = Have close friends or relatives *Worried* or complained about your drinking in the past year?

E = Do you sometimes take a drink in the morning when you first get up? [*Eye-opener*]

A = Has a friend or family member ever told you about things you said or did while you were drinking that you could not remember? (*Amnesia* or blackouts)

K = Do you sometimes feel the need to *K/cut* down on your drinking?

The CAGE question about guilt was eliminated in the TWEAK and it was replaced with a question to assess for tolerance, and rather than asking about annoyance, the TWEAK inquires about amnesia or blackouts. Cherpitel (1997) reported that the TWEAK was more effective in correctly identifying individuals with alcohol problems than the CAGE.

MAST

The Michigan Alcohol Screening Test (MAST; Selzer, 1971) was one of the first alcohol use screening instruments available. It was developed in the 1960s and empirically tested in the 1970s. The MAST consists of 24–items that require a "yes" or "no" response, and the total possible score is 53. Scores of 5 or 6 suggest a possible alcohol problem and scores above 20 suggest a severe alcohol problem. Similar to the CAGE, the MAST is helpful in detecting alcohol dependence, but less likely to be helpful to those with less severe alcohol problems. Other limitations of the MAST include its (a) assessment of lifetime alcohol use rather than current use, (b) dichotomous classification (alcoholic or not), and (c) failure to assess binge drinking patterns (Doweiko, 2012).

SASSI

Another popular screening instrument is the Substance Abuse Subtle Screening Inventory (SASSI; G. A. Miller, 1999). The most recent version, the SASSI-3, was released in 1997. An adolescent version of the SASSI (SASSI-A2) and a Spanish language version are also available. The SASSI-3 requires about 15 minutes to complete and about two minutes to score, and the results indicate either a high or low probability of substance dependence disorder. It utilizes ten sub-scales, two of which are validity scales. The SASSI features indirect scales, which include items designed to detect problems with substance use despite the respondent's level of dishonesty or denial, as well as direct scales, which include items that are face-valid and obvious. Feldstein and Miller (2007) reported a number of concerns about the SASSI. First, no independent, peer-reviewed study has found the SASSI to have an advantage in accurately detecting substance use problems, regardless of the respondent's level of honesty or denial. Other reported concerns include that the indirect and validity scales have shown fair to poor internal consistency, lower test-retest reliability was found in studies than what is reported in the manual, and the indirect scales were found to be related to ethnicity, general stress, and social deviance, meaning that a positive screen for a substance use problem was more likely if the respondent was of an ethnic minority group, experiencing general distress, or had a higher level of social deviance (Feldstein & Miller, 2007).

AUDIT

The Alcohol Use Disorders Identification Test (AUDIT) was developed by the World Health Organization in 1992 to help detect alcohol problems with diverse populations (Saunders, Aasland, Babor, de la Fuente, & Grant, 1993). It consists of 10 questions: three that assess alcohol consumption, four that assess symptoms of alcohol dependence, and three that inquire about alcohol-related problems. The AUDIT is able to detect alcohol dependence and provides a framework for interventions with problem drinkers to reduce the probability of alcohol-related consequences (Babor, Higgins-Biddle, Saunders, & Monteiro, 2001). It may be administered in interview format or self-administered with pencil and paper.

Assessment

Assessment differs from screening in that assessments are continuous in nature and provide comprehensive information not only about the topic of concern, but also about multiple areas of the client's life (Winters & Zenilman, 1994). They often are referred to as "biopsychosocial" or "biopsychosocialcultural." The purpose of an assessment is to determine the degree or extent of the substance use problem, including whether or not a diagnosable disorder is present. Assessment also aims to help clinicians understand the multiple facets of a client's substance use, such as the negative consequences experienced from substance use (e.g., relationship problems, legal troubles, employment issues, physical and mental health concerns), the client's motivation for change, and client strengths and resources, including successful past behavior changes and social support (W. R. Miller et al., 2011). Clinical interviews are the preferred method to administer assessments (Doweiko, 2012). Compared to self-administered methods, clinical interviews allow for greater flexibility, facilitate rapport between client and counselor, allow the interviewer to ease a confused or distressed client, and give the interviewer an opportunity to monitor the client's nonverbal cues (Juhnke, 2002). Counselor actions resulting from an assessment include providing a diagnosis, making recommendations and providing referrals for treatment, developing a treatment plan, recommending additional assessments for specific concerns, and providing referrals for adjunctive services (e.g., job skills training, housing, entitlements; Winters & Zenilman, 1994).

The Addiction Severity Index (ASI; McLellan, Luborsky, Woody, & O'Brien, 1980) is a structured interview for adults lasting approximately one hour. It is not recommended to be self-administered as the dialogue that occurs in a clinical interview is important for the interviewer to formulate an assessment of substance use problems. The fifth edition of the ASI consists of 161 items and eight sub-scales plus a general information scale. The interviewer ascribes a severity rating score in each domain of the client's life (e.g., drug and alcohol use, medical, employment) indicating the intensity of the substance use problem and extent of related concerns. These scores are totaled and suggest the overall severity of the client's addiction.

The second edition of *Assessing Alcohol Problems: A Clinician's Guide for Clinicians and Researchers* (Allen & Wilson, 2003) offers information about how to introduce screening and assessment instruments to clients, the appropriate timing of evaluation, and helpful ways to provide clients with feedback from evaluation measures. This resource has been popular and helpful to clinicians working with clients who experience alcohol problems.

SIDEBAR 13.4 Case Example

Julie is working at an outpatient mental health agency when she receives a referral from an employee assistance program. When she meets with the client, Terrance, a 29 year-old biracial African American and Native American male who works at an automobile factory, she learns that he failed a random drug screen for marijuana at work last week. Terrance also admitted to being written up once previously for having alcohol on his breath while at work. What screening instruments and/or assessments might be helpful to Julie in her work with Terrance? What considerations might you have when deciding which instrument(s) to use? How would you proceed with informed consent with Terrance?

Diversity and Ethical Considerations

According to the American Counseling Association's (ACA) *ACA Code of Ethics* (2005), counselors must consider clients' personal and cultural contexts when evaluating substance use problems. It is helpful to remember that screening and assessment instruments are not a "one size fits all" phenomenon (Blume, Morera, & de la Cruz, 2005, p. 49), and counselors must consider the psychometric properties of such instruments prior to using them with diverse populations (ACA, 2005). Counselors must take into account discrepancies between the population with which the instrument was normed and the culture of the client, and whenever possible it is best to use instruments that have been designed for populations similar to the client's cultural context (Stauffer, Capuzzi, & Tanigoshi, 2008).

It also is important to consider how individuals from different cultural groups may react to evaluation. Because of the history of unethical testing practices with members of racial and ethnic minority groups, Blume et al. (2005) explained that these persons may have "a healthy mistrust of being tested, especially if the testing is conducted by people from outside the community" (p. 51). Therefore, prior to administering screening or assessment evaluations, it is important for counselors to provide a thorough informed consent with clients, including the nature and purposes of the assessment and the anticipated usefulness of the results (ACA, 2005).

In addition to ensuring that clients understand the purpose, process, and results of evaluation measures, it is essential that counselors are competent to administer and interpret the results of such instruments (ACA, 2005). Ethical practice involves only using

SIDEBAR 13.5 Self-Awareness

Recall a time when you were given a standardized test to take. What was the experience like for you? Was the purpose of the test clear to you? How did it feel to take the test? How were the results explained? What was the impact of the test? How did it affect you? Consider the similarities and differences between your experience and how clients may feel when completing assessment instruments in counseling. What might you do to help their experience be most comfortable and beneficial?

evaluation instruments for which the counselor has received specific training and is competent to use and interpret. Information taken from evaluation measures may be used to inform diagnoses; however, counselors must diagnose with care and be sensitive to cultural influences as well as historical and social prejudices that may lead to misdiagnosis (ACA, 2005).

Diagnosis in Addictions Counseling

In 2010, 8.7% of the population aged 12 and older in the United States (22.1 million people) were classified with substance abuse or dependence within the past year, an increase from 7.4% in 2008 (SAMHSA, 2011b). Of this population, 2.9 million were classified with abuse or dependence of both alcohol and an illicit drug. Currently, professional counselors use the American Psychiatric Association's (APA, 2000) *DSM-IV-TR* to classify mental health and substance use disorders. The fifth edition of the *DSM* is scheduled to be published in May 2013 (www.dsmv.org), and major revisions to the structure of substance-related diagnostic categories have been proposed.

SIDEBAR 13.6 Self-Awareness

Take a moment to consider how you feel about classifying or "labeling" people with diagnoses, such as "Substance Use Disorder." What are the benefits of diagnosis in addictions counseling? What are the potential drawbacks? Consider how you might explain substance-related diagnosis to a future client. What factors might influence your explanation?

The *DSM-IV-TR's* "Substance-Related Disorders" chapter includes two categories, "Substance Use Disorders" and "Substance-Induced Disorders." Substance Use Disorders includes Substance Dependence and Substance Abuse, whereas Substance-Induced Disorders includes Substance Intoxication and Substance Withdrawal as well as other disorders that occur as a result of substance use (e.g., Substance-Induced Mood Disorder, Substance-Induced Psychotic Disorder). Currently, the *DSM-IV-TR* uses a "bi-axial" diagnostic approach to Substance Use Disorders. On the first axis, diagnostic criteria for Substance Dependence describe biological (e.g., evidence of tolerance and withdrawal symptoms), behavioral (e.g., a great amount of time is spent using, obtaining, or recovering from substance use), and psychological (e.g. persistent desire to reduce substance use) manifestations of heavy substance use. On the second axis, Substance Abuse describes consequences incurred as a result of substance use (e.g., "failure to fulfill major role obligations at work, school, or home" (APA, 2000, p. 199).

Proposed changes for the *DSM-5* include combining the dichotomous diagnoses of Substance Dependence and Substance Abuse into a single, dimensional diagnosis labeled "Substance Use Disorder." The diagnostic criteria for Substance Use Disorder would include that of Substance Abuse *and* Substance Dependence from the *DSM-IV-TR*, as well as an added criterion that describes experiencing "craving or a strong urge to use a specific substance." At least two criteria must be present within a 12–month period to fulfill a diagnosis of Substance Use Disorder, and severity specifiers would be used to distinguish between moderate (2–3 criteria met) and severe (four or more criteria met) conditions. These diagnostic criteria would be used to determine if a Substance Use Disorder is present for persons who use substances in the following categories: alcohol; amphetamines; cannabis; cocaine; hallucinogens; inhalants; opioids; phencyclidine; sedative, hypnotic, or anxiolytic; tobacco; and other (or unknown) substances.

The *DSM-5's* proposed chapter, "Substance Use and Addictive Disorders," includes a range of Substance-Induced Disorders (e.g., Substance-Induced Psychotic Disorder, Substance-Induced Bipolar Disorder), Substance Intoxication, Substance Withdrawal, and Gambling Disorder. Gambling Disorder, which was labeled "Pathological Gambling" in the Impulse-Control Disorders chapter in the *DSM-IV*, is proposed to be relocated to the Substance Use and Addictive Disorders chapter in the *DSM-V*. As of this writing, Hypersexual Disorder has been proposed to be added as a new sexual disorder, placed outside of the Substance Use and Addictive Disorders chapter, but it is unclear whether it will be included.

Research in Addictions Counseling

The evolution of addictions counseling from intuitive practice to the emergence of evidence-based practice is simply astounding. This has occurred over the past 75 years in the United States. It is as if a veil of secrecy, misinformation, and suspicion has been removed, and a new kind of inquisitiveness about addiction and strategies to prevent and treat it has taken center stage. Certainly more needs to change with respect to general attitudes about addiction and providing greater access to varied services, but the transformation thus far is quite remarkable.

The dramatic shift in how addiction is talked about, understood, addressed, and studied makes this an exciting time to practice in the field. It also is a very hopeful time for persons who struggle with addictions. Burgeoning scientific discoveries in genetics, pharmacotherapy, and neuroscience have expanded the number of prevention and intervention options. For example, the medication buprenorphine, known by the trade names Subutex and Suboxone, is an alternative to methadone and is now used routinely to treat opiate addiction.

Professional counselors are in a prime position to provide leadership in and to advance the field of addictions counseling. This is true particularly for professional counselors from CACREP-accredited programs. For them, the master's degree has always been a requirement for licensure as a professional counselor. Their core curricular education also has included research, assessment, group work, and social and cultural diversity. Graduates of CACREP-accredited Clinical Mental Health Counseling or Addiction Counseling programs now have added and specialized training in diagnosis and treatment planning, as well as in counseling persons with addiction and co-occurring disorders (for graduates of Addiction Counseling programs, training in this latter area is understandably more extensive).

By comparison, substance abuse counselors or chemical dependency counselors are not necessarily required to have a graduate degree or to have received specialized clinical training (e.g., in diagnosis). Many have practiced over the years with only a bachelor's degree and the majority of persons in the addictions counseling workforce still do not have a master's degree (Rieckmann, Farentinos, Tillotson, Kocarnik, & McCarty, 2011). As mentioned earlier, beginning in 2014, at least a master's degree will likely be required for all persons who practice addictions counseling (Knopf, 2011).

Professional counselors who have specialized training in addictions and are eligible for dual licensure in their state (as mental health counselors and as substance abuse or chemical dependency counselors) may very well be the ones to further more sophisticated change in addictions counseling. This entails translating emerging research into routine counseling practice. The current emphasis on evidence-based practice has placed the spotlight not only on effective prevention and treatment approaches in the addictions (e.g., motivational interviewing), but also on ineffective and potentially harmful practices. These latter include the popular Drug Abuse Resistance Education (or DARE) conducted in many elementary and middle schools nationwide, planned interventions carried out by family members and friends (as is done on the television series "Intervention"), and confrontational counseling. All three of these have been rated by experts in the addictions field as discredited treatments (see Norcross et al., 2010). Professional counselors thus can assume a leadership role to correct misperceptions about appropriate services and highlight evidence-based practices, such as the ones described earlier in this chapter and recognized by NREPP.

Given the high rate of co-occurrence of mental health and substance use disorders, professional counselors can also be at the helm to further integrate treatment services. Proactive collaboration with other professionals (e.g., psychiatrists, social workers, nurses) will be essential. This may entail the professional counselor assuming leadership of a multidisciplinary treatment team, moving into an administrative role in the county's mental health and recovery board (and making decisions about funding allocation), and partnering with researchers at a local university to access additional funds for expanded prevention and treatment services. Furthermore, early detection and intervention (which may constitute preventive care), engaging persons with addiction in a system of care, and providing ongoing services throughout the person's recovery cycle (from treatment to relapse to treatment reengagement) all seem to be fundamental skills that comprise the professional counselor's repertoire. These skills must be maximized for the purpose of implementing more innovative, accessible, caring, and effective prevention and treatment services in addictions counseling.

Summary

Problematic substance use is not an isolated concern confined to certain groups of people. It is a public health issue that affects all Americans. This means that no counselor is immune to or can opt out of addressing the issue of addiction with clients and their families. It thus seems imperative that professional counselors obtain further and specialized training in theories of addiction beyond the disease model, screening and assessment methods, diagnosis of substance use disorders, and evidence-based prevention and treatment practices for persons with addictions and co-occurring disorders. Translating this training into routine counseling practice will advance the field, thereby improving access to services for the more than 20 million persons aged 12 and above in the United States who needed treatment for a substance use problem in 2010 but did not receive it (SAMHSA, 2011b). That this number represents the overwhelming majority (89%) of persons with a substance use problem indicates that significant changes are still needed in addictions service provision. Implementing evidence-based practices in addictions counseling also will improve the quality of care once persons access services. Professional counselors are in a prime position to develop and implement a truly integrative approach to addictions counseling, one that is, according to W. R. Miller et al. (2011), comprehensive and evidence-based, multidisciplinary, holistic, and collaborative.

References

Academic ED SBIRT Research Collaborative. (2007). The impact of screening, brief intervention, and referral for treatment on emergency department patients' alcohol use. *Annals of Emergency Medicine, 50*(6), 699–710.

Allen, J. P., & Wilson, V. B. (2003). *Assessing alcohol problems: A guide for clinicians and researchers* (2nd ed.). U.S. Department of Health and Human Services. (NIH Publication No. 03–3745). Bethesda, MD: National Institute on Alcohol Abuse and Alcoholism.

American Counseling Association. (2005). *ACA Code of Ethics.* Alexandria, VA: Author.

American Psychiatric Association. (2000). *Diagnostic and statistical manual of mental disorders* (4th ed., text rev.). Washington, DC: Author.

Anthony, J. C., & Helzer, J. E. (2002). Epidemiology of drug dependence. In M. T. Tsuang, & M. Tohen (Eds.), *Textbook in psychiatric epidemiology* (2nd ed.; pp. 479–561). New York: Wiley.

Arredondo, P., Toporek, M. S., Brown, S., Jones, J., Locke, D. C., Sanchez, J., & Stadler, H. (1996). *Operationalization of the Multicultural Counseling Competencies.* Alexandria, VA: Association for Multicultural Counseling & Development.

Babor, T. F., Higgins-Biddle, J. C., Saunders, J. B., & Monteiro, M. G. (2001). *AUDIT: The Alcohol Use Disorders Identification Test: Guidelines for primary care* (2nd ed). Geneva, Switzerland: World Health Organization: Department of Mental Health and Substance Dependence.

Barry, D., & Petry, N. M. (2009). Cognitive behavioral treatments for substance use disorders. In P. M. Miller (Ed.), *Evidence-based addiction treatment* (pp. 159–174). Burlington, MA: Academic Press

Bernstein, J., Bernstein, E., Tassiopoulos, K., Heeren, T., Levenson, S., & Hingson, R. (2005). Brief motivational intervention at a clinic visit reduces cocaine and heroin use. *Drug and Alcohol Dependence, 77*(1), 49–59.

Bernstein, E., Edwards, E., Dorfman, D., Heeren, T., Bliss, C., & Bernstein, J. (2009). Screening and brief intervention to reduce marijuana use among youth and young adults in a pediatric emergency department. *Academic Emergency Medicine, 16*(11), 1174–1185.

Blume, A. W., Morera, O. F., & de la Cruz, B. G. (2005). Assessment of addictive behaviors in ethnic-minority cultures. In D. M. Donovan, & G. A. Marlatt (Eds.), *Assessment of addictive behaviors* (2nd ed.; pp. 49–70). New York: Guilford.

Boyd, M. R., Phillips, K., & Dorsey, C. J. (2003). Alcohol and other drug disorders, comorbidity, and violence: Comparison of rural African American and Caucasian women. *Archives of Psychiatric Nursing, 17*(6), 249–258.

Brady, K. T., & Randall, C. L. (1999). Gender differences in substance use disorders. *The Psychiatric Clinics of North America, 22*(2), 241–252.

Brown, J. M., & Miller, W. R. (1993). Impact of motivational interviewing on participation and outcome in residential alcoholism treatment. *Psychology of Addictive Behaviors, 7,* 211–218.

Centers for Disease Control. (2009, June 18). Alcohol and suicide among racial/ethnic populations—17 states—2005–2006. *Morbidity and Mortality Weekly Report, 58*(23), 637–641. Retrieved from www.cdc.gov/mmwr/preview/mmwrhtml/mm5823a1.htm.

Cherpitel, C. J. (1997). Brief screening for alcohol problems. *Alcohol Health and Research World, 21*(4), 348–351.

Coatsworth, J. D., Santisteban, D. A., McBride, C. K., & Szapocznik, J. (2001). Brief Strategic Family Therapy versus community control: Engagement, retention, and an exploration of the moderating role of adolescent symptom severity. *Family Process, 40*(3), 313–332.

Cochran, S. D., & Mays, V. M. (2000). Relation between psychiatric syndromes and behaviorally defined sexual orientation in a sample of the U.S. population. *American Journal of Epidemiology, 151*(5), 516–523.

Cooney, N. L., Kadden, R. M., & Steinberg, H. R. (2005). Assessment of alcohol problems. In D. M. Donovan, & G. A. Marlatt (Eds.), *Assessment of addictive behaviors* (2nd ed.; pp. 71–112). New York: Guilford Press.

Council for Accreditation of Counseling and Related Educational Programs. (2009). *2009 Standards*. Alexandria, VA: Author.

D'Avanzo, D., Dunn, P., Murdock, J., & Naegle, M. (2000). Developing culturally informed strategies for substance related interventions. In M. Naegle, & D. D'Avanzo (Eds.), *Addictions and substance abuse: Strategies for advanced practice nursing* (pp. 59–104). Upper Saddle River, NJ: Prentice Hall.

Denby, R. W., Brinson, J. A., & Ayala, J. (2011). Adolescent co-occurring disorder treatment: Clinicians' attitudes, values, and knowledge. *Child & Youth Services, 32*, 56–74.

Department of Veterans Affairs. (2009). *VA/DoD clinical practice guideline for management of substance use disorders*. Retrieved from http://www.mentalhealth.va.gov/providers/sud/index.asp.

Dimeff, L. A., Baer, J. S., Kivlahan, D. R., & Marlatt, G. A. (1999). *Brief alcohol screening and intervention for college students: A harm reduction approach*. New York: Guilford.

Doweiko, H. E. (2012). *Concepts of chemical dependency* (8th ed.). Pacific Grove, CA: Brooks/Cole.

Dube, S. R., Miller, J. W., Brown, D. W., Giles, W. H., Felitti, V. J., Dong, M., & Anda, R. F. (2006). Adverse childhood experiences and the association with ever using alcohol and initiating alcohol use during adolescence. *Journal of Adolescent Health, 38*, 444.e1–444.e10.

Ewing, J. A. (1984). Detecting alcoholism: The CAGE questions. *JAMA, 252*, 1905–1907.

Feldstein, S. W., & Miller, W. R. (2007). Does subtle screening for substance abuse work? A review of the Substance Abuse Subtle Screening Inventory (SASSI). *Addiction, 102*, 41–50.

Feucht, T. E., & Gfroerer, J. (2011, Summer). Mental and substance use disorders among adult men on probation or parole: Some success against a persistent challenge. *Data Review*, a periodic publication of the National Institute of Justice, Substance Abuse and Mental Health Services Administration. Retrieved from http://nicic.gov/Library/025372.

Grant, B. F., Dawson, D. A., Stinson, F. S., Chou, S. P., Dufour, M. C., & Pickering, R. P. (2006). The 12–month prevalence and trends in DSM-IV alcohol abuse and dependence. *Alcohol Research & Health, 29*(1), 79–91.

Higgins, S. T., Silverman, K., & Heil, S. H. (Eds.). (2008). *Contingency management in substance abuse treatment*. New York: Guilford.

Johnston, L. D., O'Malley, P. M., Bachman, J. G., & Schulenberg, J. E. (2011). *Monitoring the Future: National results on adolescent drug use: Overview of key findings, 2010*. Ann Arbor, MI: Institute for Social Research, The University of Michigan.

Juhnke, G. A. (2002). *Substance abuse assessment and diagnosis*. New York: Brunner-Routledge.

Knopf, A. (2011, October 18). Compulsory education for counselors? Addiction counselors face *de facto* master's degree requirement in 2014. *Behavioral Healthcare* (publication of the National Association of Addiction Treatment Providers, www.behavioral.net).

Kuehn, B. M. (2010). Military probes epidemic of suicides: Mental health issues remain prevalent. *JAMA, 304*(13), 1427–1430.

Lee, C. C., & Rodgers, R. A. (2009). Counselor advocacy: Affecting systemic change in the public arena. *Journal of Counseling & Development, 87*, 284–287.

Lewis, J. A., Arnold, M. S., House, R., & Toporek, R. L. (2002). *ACA Advocacy Competencies*. Retrieved from www.counseling.org/Resources.

Longabaugh, R., Donovan, D. M., Karno, M. P., McCrady, B. S., Morgenstern, J., & Tonigan, J. S. (2005). Active ingredients: How and why evidence-based alcohol behavioral treatment interventions work. *Alcoholism: Clinical and Experimental Research, 29*, 235–247.

Lopez-Quintero, C., de los Cobos, J. P., Hasin, D. S., Okuda, M., Wang, S., Grant, B. F., & Blanco, C. (2011). Probability and predictors of transition from first use to dependence on nicotine, alcohol, cannabis, and cocaine: Results of the National Epidemiological Survey on Alcohol and Related Conditions (NESARC). *Drug and Alcohol Dependence, 115*, 120–130.

McLellan, A. T., Luborsky, L., Woody, G. E., & O'Brien, C. P. (1980). An improved diagnostic evaluation instrument for substance abuse patients: The Addiction Severity Index. *Journal of Nervous and Mental Disease, 168*(1), 26–33.

McCrady, B. S. (2006). Family and other close relationships. In W. R. Miller, & K. M. Carroll (Eds.), *Rethinking substance abuse: What the science shows, and what we should do about it* (pp. 166–181). New York: Guilford.

Mee-Lee, D., & Gastfriend, D. R. (2008). Patient placement criteria. In M. Galanter, & H. D. Kleber (Eds), *Textbook of substance abuse treatment* (4th ed.; pp. 79–91). Washington, DC: American Psychiatric Publishing.

Mee-Lee, D., Shulman, G. D., Fishman, M., Gastfriend, D. R., & Griffith, J. H. (Eds.). (2001). *ASAM patient placement criteria for the treatment of substance-related disorders* (2nd ed., revised). Chevy Chase, MD: American Society of Addiction Medicine.

Meyers, R. J., Villanueva, M., & Smith, J. E. (2005). The community reinforcement approach: History and new directions. *Journal of Cognitive Psychotherapy, 19*, 247–260.

Miller, G. A. (1985, 1999). *The Substance Abuse Subtle Screening Inventory (SASSI) Manual, Second Edition*. Springville, IN: The SASSI Institute.

Miller, P. M. (Ed.). (2009). *Evidence-based addiction treatment*. Burlington, MA: Academic Press.

Miller, W. R., & Feldstein, S. W. (2007). SASSI: A response to Lazowski & Miller. *Addiction, 102*, 1001–1004.

Miller, W. R., Forcehimes, A. A., & Zweben, A. (2011). *Treating addiction: A guide for professionals*. New York: Guilford.

Miller, W. R., & Rollnick, S. (2002). *Motivational interviewing: Preparing people to change addictive behavior* (2nd ed.). New York: Guilford.

Miller, W. R., Willbourne, P. L., & Hettema, J. (2003). What works?: A summary of alcohol treatment outcome research. In R. K. Hester, & W. R. Miller (Eds.), *Handbook of alcoholism treatment approaches: Effective alternatives* (3rd ed.; pp. 13–63). Boston: Allyn & Bacon.

Mokdad, A. H., Marks, J. S., Stroup, D. F., & Gerberding, J. L. (2004). Actual causes of death in the United States, 2000. *JAMA, 291*(10), 1238–1245.

Monti, P. M., Colby, S. M., Barnett, N. P., Spirito, A., Rohsenow, D. J., Myers, M., et al. (1999). Brief intervention for harm reduction with alcohol-positive older adolescents in a hospital emergency department. *Journal of Consulting and Clinical Psychology, 67*(6), 989–994.

Morehouse, E. R., & Tobler, N. S. (2000). *Project SUCCESS final report*: Grant number 4 HD1 SP07240. Report submitted January 26, 2000, to the Center for Substance Abuse Prevention, U.S. Department of Health and Human Services.

Moos, R. H. (2007). Theory-based active ingredients of effective treatments for substance use disorders. *Drug and Alcohol Dependence, 88*, 109–121.

Moyers, T. B., Martin, T., Houck, J. M., Christopher, P. J., & Tonigan, J. S. (2009). From in-session behaviours to drinking outcomes: A causal chain for motivational interviewing. *Journal of Consulting and Clinical Psychology, 77*, 1113–1124.

Mueser, K. T., Drake, R. E., Turner, W., & McGovern, M. (2006). Comorbid substance use disorders and psychiatric disorders. In W. R. Miller, & K. M. Carroll (Eds.), *Rethinking substance abuse: What the science shows, and what we should do about it* (pp. 115–133). New York: Guilford.

National Institute on Alcohol Abuse and Alcoholism. (2008). *Alcohol: A women's health issue*. (NIH Publication No. 03 4956). Washington, DC: U.S. Department of Health and Human Services.

National Institute on Drug Abuse. (2011). Substance abuse among the military, veterans, and their families: A research update from the National Institute on Drug Abuse. *Topics in Brief*. Retrieved from www.drugabuse.gov.

National Institute on Drug Abuse. (2009). *Principles of drug addiction treatment: A research-based guide* (2nd ed.). (NIH Publication No. 09–4180). Washington, DC: U.S. Department of Health and Human Services.

National Institute on Drug Abuse. (2003). *Drug use among racial/ethnic minorities,* (Rev. ed.). Bethesda, MD: U.S. Department of Health and Human Services.

Norcross, J. C., Koocher, G. P., Fala, N. C., & Wexler, H. K. (2010). What does not work? Expert consensus on discredited treatments in the addictions. *Journal of Addiction Medicine, 4*, 174–180.

O'Brien, C. P. (2008). The CAGE Questionnaire for Detection of Alcoholism. *JAMA, 300*(17), 2054–2056.

O'Farrell, T. J., & Fals-Stewart, W. (2008). Family therapy. In M. Galanter, & H. D. Kleber (Eds.), *Textbook of substance abuse* treatment (4th ed.; pp. 429–441). Arlington, VA: American Psychiatric Publishing.

Petry, N. M., Alessi, S. M., & Hanson, T. (2007). Contingency management improves abstinence and quality of life in cocaine abusers. *Journal of Consulting and Clinical Psychology, 75*(2), 307–315.

Petry, N. M., Martin, B., & Simcic, F., Jr. (2005). Prize reinforcement contingency management for cocaine dependence: Integration with group therapy in a methadone clinic. *Journal of Consulting and Clinical Psychology, 73*(2), 354–359.

Petry, N. M., Peirce, J. M., Stitzer, M. L., Blaine, J., Roll, J. M., Cohen, A., et al. (2005). Effect of prize-based incentives on outcomes in stimulant abusers in outpatient psychosocial treatment programs. A National Drug Abuse Treatment Clinical Trials Network study. *Archives of General Psychiatry, 62*(10), 1148–1156.

Petry, N. M., Tedford, J., Austin, M., Nich, C., Carroll, K. M., & Rounsaville, B. J. (2004). Prize reinforcement contingency management for treating cocaine users: How low can we go, and with whom? *Addiction, 99*(3), 349–360.

Regier, D. A., Farmer, M. E., Rae, D. S., Locke, B. Z., Keith, S. J., & Judd, L. L. (1990). Comorbidity of mental disorders with alcohol and other drug abuse: Results from the Epidemiologic Catchment Area (ECA) Study. *JAMA: Journal of the American Medical Association, 264*, 2511–2518.

Rieckmann, T., Farentinos, C., Tillotson, C. J., Kocarnik, J., & McCarty, D. (2011). The substance abuse counseling workforce: Education, preparation, and certification. *Substance Abuse, 32*, 180–190.

Russell, M. (1994). New assessment tools for drinking in pregnancy: T-ACE, TWEAK, and others. *Alcohol Health and Research World, 18*(1), 55–61.

Santisteban, D. A., Coatsworth, J. D., Perez-Vidal, A., Kurtines, W. M., Schwartz, S., LaPerriere, A., et al. (2003). The efficacy of Brief Strategic Family Therapy in modifying Hispanic adolescent behavior problems and substance use. *Journal of Family Psychology, 17*(1), 121–133.

Santisteban, D. A., Coatsworth, J. D., Perez-Vidal, A., Mitrani, V., Jean-Gilles, M., & Szapocznik, J. (1997). Brief Structural/Strategic Family Therapy with African American and Hispanic high-risk youth. *Journal of Community Psychology, 25*(5), 453–471.

Santisteban, D. A., Szapocznik, J., Perez-Vidal, A., Kurtines, W. M., Murray, E. J., & LaPerriere, A. (1996). Efficacy of intervention for engaging youth and families into treatment and some variables that may contribute to differential effectiveness. *Journal of Family Psychology, 10*, 35–44.

Saunders, J. B. (2006). Substance dependence and non-dependence in the Diagnostic and Statistical Manual of Mental Disorders (DSM) and the International Classification of Diseases (ICD): Can an identical conceptualization be achieved? *Addiction, 101* (Suppl. 1), 48–58.

Saunders, J. B., Aasland, O. G., Babor, T. F., de la Fuente, J. R., & Grant, M. (1993). Development of the Alcohol Use Disorders Identification Test (AUDIT): WHO collaborative project on early detection of persons with harmful alcohol consumption. *Addiction, 88*, 791–804.

Schmidt, L., Greenfield, T., & Mulia, N. (2006). Unequal treatment: Racial and ethnic disparities in alcohol treatment services. *Alcohol Research & Health, 29*(1), 49–54.

Selzer, M. L. (1971). The Michigan Alcoholism Screening Test (MAST): The quest for a new diagnostic instrument. *American Journal of Psychiatry, 127*, 1653–1658.

Smith, J. E., & Meyers, R. J. (2004). *Motivating substance abusers to enter treatment: Working with family members.* New York: Guilford.

Stauffer, M. D., Capuzzi, D., & Tanigoshi, H. (2008). Assessment: An overview. In D. Capuzzi, & M. D. Stauffer (Eds.), *Foundations of addiction counseling* (pp. 76–100). Boston: Pearson Education.

Stevens, P., & Smith, R. L. (2009). *Substance abuse counseling: Theory and practice* (4th ed.). Upper Saddle River, NJ: Pearson Education.

Substance Abuse and Mental Health Services Administration. (2011a). *National survey of substance abuse treatment services (N-SSATS): 2010. Data on substance abuse treatment facilities.* DASIS Series S-59, HHS Publication No. (SMA) 11–4665. Rockville, MD: Author.

Substance Abuse and Mental Health Services Administration. (2011b). *Results from the 2010 national survey on drug use and health: Summary of national findings.* NSDUH Series H-41, HHS Publication No. (SMA) 11–4658. Rockville, MD: Author.

Substance Abuse and Mental Health Services Administration. (2011c, September 29). *The TEDS report: Length of time from first use to adult treatment admission.* Rockville, MD: Author.

Substance Abuse and Mental Health Services Administration. (2011d). *Addressing the needs of women and girls: Developing core competencies for mental health and substance abuse service professionals.* HHS Pub. No. (SMA) 11–4657. Rockville, MD: Author.

Substance Abuse and Mental Health Services Administration (Producer). (2010a). *Homelessness and substance use disorder treatment: Recovery-oriented housing and achieving healthy lifestyles* [DVD]. Available from www.samhsa.gov.

Substance Abuse and Mental Health Services Administration, Office of Applied Studies. (2010b). *The TEDS Report: Trends in adult female substance abuse treatment admissions reporting primary alcohol abuse: 1992 to 2007.* Rockville, MD: Author.

Substance Abuse and Mental Health Services Administration. (2009a). *Substance abuse treatment: Addressing the specific needs of women.* Treatment Improvement Protocol (TIP) Series, No. 51. Rockville, MD: Author.

Substance Abuse and Mental Health Services Administration. (2009b). *A provider's introduction to substance abuse treatment for lesbian, gay, bisexual, and transgender individuals,* HHS Publication No. (SMA) 09–4104. Rockville, MD: Author.

Substance Abuse and Mental Health Services Administration, Office of Applied Studies. (2007). *The NSDUH report: Serious psychological distress and substance use disorder among veterans.* Rockville, MD: Author.

Substance Abuse and Mental Health Services Administration (Producer). (2004). *Rethinking the demographics of addiction: Helping older adults find recovery* [DVD]. Available from www.samhsa.gov.

Substance Abuse and Mental Health Services Administration. (2001). *Cannabis Youth Treatment (CYT) series.* Rockville, MD: Author.

Substance Abuse and Mental Health Services Administration. (1998). *Substance use disorder treatment for people with physical and cognitive disabilities treatment improvement protocol (TIP) series 29.* DHHS Publication No. (SMA) 98–3249. Rockville, MD: Author.

Thombs, D. L. (2006). *Introduction to addictive behaviors* (3rd ed.). New York: Guilford.

Tracy, S. W. (2005). *Alcoholism in America: From Reconstruction to Prohibition.* Baltimore, MD: The Johns Hopkins University Press.

Vaughan, R., & Johnson, P. (2007). *The effectiveness of Project SUCCESS (Schools Using Coordinated Community Efforts to Strengthen Students) in a regular secondary school setting.* Unpublished manuscript.

Volkow, N. D. (2011). Substance abuse among older adults. *NIDA Notes.* Retrieved from http://www.drugabuse.gov/news-events/nida-notes.

West, R. (2006). *Theory of addiction.* Oxford, UK: Blackwell.

White, W. L., & Miller, W. R. (2007). The use of confrontation in addiction treatment: History, science and time for change. *Counselor, 8*(4), 12–30.

Winters, K. C., & Zenilman, J. M. (1994). Simple screening instruments for outreach for alcohol and other drug abuse and infectious diseases. *Treatment Improvement Protocol Series 11.* Rockville, MD: U.S. Department of Health and Human Services.

Woody, G. E., Donnell, D., Seage, G. R., Metzger, D., Marmor, M., Koblin, B. A., Buchbinder, S., Gross, M., Stone, B., & Judson, F. N. (1999). Non-injection substance use correlates with risky sex among men having sex with men: Data from HIVNET. *Drug and Alcohol Dependence, 53,* 197–205.

14

CAREER COUNSELING

Abby Platt and Meredith Drew[1]

SIDEBAR 14.1 Does Sophia's Situation Have Any Significance for You?

I am so thankful for this job, Sophia thought to herself. It had been a long journey for Sophia to attain her position as a high school math teacher. She had worked her way through college, taking on various part-time jobs, most of which she disliked. At times she questioned whether it was worth it to continue with her education. She questioned if she could truly push through the psychological stress of balancing her work and school life. Now, as she sat with her friends talking about the many papers they all had to grade, students antics in the classroom, and what they had done over their weekends, she reflected on her journey to the classroom and thought, *it was all worth it.* As you review your educational struggles, can you relate to Sophia? Are you able to see the "light at the end of the educational tunnel?"

There are 24 hours in a day, 158 hours in a week. If we are lucky enough to spend 8 hours each evening sleeping, then that leaves 102 hours. After we work a conservative 40 hours per week, we are left with 62 hours, which is equivalent to 7.75 hours each day. This does not take into consideration commuting times, preparation, self-care (hygiene, nutrition, exercise, care of others) and the other daily chores; it then reduces that number significantly. Thinking of one's career in terms of numbers helps to understand the reality that many will spend most of their hours at work. Due to the amount of time spent at work, the idea of career satisfaction becomes even more essential. We often become friends with our co-workers and even meet significant others through work. Most will spend more than 40 hours a week there and experience a multitude of emotions at work—disappointments, excitement, sadness, happiness, anger, and fear. Sleep is possibly the one event that may compete with the hours spent working.

As a counselor reflecting on the reality of clients' working days, it becomes more important to be able to work with clients to help them determine the career that suits them best. It also reinforces the need for career counseling, which may be seen as the least interesting realm of counseling, but has one of the greatest needs. According to the Bureau for Labor Statistics (2012), 86% of men and 67% of women in the United States work more than 40 hours per week.

There is an understanding that one's professional self concept helps to create one's personal identity, it is something that needs time to be cultivated. At times mental health counselors do not put the effort into understanding the needs of their clients where career is concerned, but when counselors do, a clients' career choices can offer the counselor crucial information into the clients' self concept and worldview. When counselors begin their assessment process, clients will often begin by defining their identity with their roles and careers. Even stay-at-home parents, unemployed, and retired individuals will identify these roles as part of who they are. Since clients' sense of identity is tied to their career roles, it is important to understand, holistically, the role that it may play in clients' lives.

Gabriele (2008) found that higher levels of motivation that people experience in their career were correlated with a positive mood. When individuals feel positive in their career Gabriele also found it pushed them to learn and develop their skill set further. Satisfaction in one's work has been shown to be important and increases the level of output, as well as decreasing the amount of absences (Punnett, Duffy, Fox, Gregory, & Lituchy, 2007). Individuals who are satisfied in their careers have positive effects on their lives outside of work as well. People are less stressed at home when they are happier in their workplace. Since it is clear that more hours are spent at work, compared with at home, this is really important and something that most career counselors will strive to help clients achieve.

The purpose of this chapter is to introduce the concept of career counseling, and the theories, inventories, and interventions that are associated with it. It is important that mental health counselors have a sound understanding when it comes to career counseling because many clients will have career-related issues intertwined in other personal problems, regardless of the counselors' specialty.

Foundations

Career counseling has grown substantially from its historical roots, as the concepts covered in this short chapter will attest. From its roots in early American industrialization during the twentieth century, career counselors today work in a wide variety of

---

SIDEBAR 14.2 How Significant Are Job Motivation, Job Satisfaction, and Family Patterns in One's Career Choice?

Joe was a returning veteran, coming home after being deployed for three years during WWII. Before Joe left for service he was being mentored by his father into their family-owned mechanics business. Yet during his tour of duty, Joe lost his right hand. Joe came home and was able to utilize the GI Bill to go to his local college. Joe had been groomed his whole life to be a part of the family business, he had no idea what to major in, or what his long term career goals would be. Joe's professor sent him to see the newly hired vocational guidance counselor. The guidance counselor provides Joe with several different assessment tools that show he has an aptitude for calculus and mechanical drawing. Joe and his counselor discuss the results. Joe is left handed and feels that, despite his injury, he would excel at drafting. He also reveals to the counselor he has always wanted to draft for an architect. Joe's counselor sets him up with an apprenticeship with a local architecture firm. What part do you feel motivation and satisfaction will play in Joe's future career choice? What impact will his family's wishes play in his choice?

Stage 1: Placement Services (1890–1919). The United States moves from being an agriculturally based society to industrialization and growing urbanization. WWI veterans are returning home and find themselves displaced. Frank Parsons, often dubbed the father of career counseling, begins helping young people find employment. Parson's founds the Vocations Bureau in Boston and publishes "Choosing a Vocation" in 1909. During this stage Parson's develops his framework for helping individuals choose careers. Parsons advocated to create career counseling programs in schools. Parsons also introduced the use of psychometric testing to the career counseling field. The National Vocational Guidance Association (NVGA) (now the National Career Development Association) (NCDA) was founded in 1913.

Stage 2: Educational guidance (1920–1939). During this time period there is a growing student population along with a shift in the job market from the industrialization movement, it became more imperative for workers to become more educated. Many students would now seek out individual sessions with career counselors in effort to see where their skill set met with the possibilities of the job market.

Stage 3: Training for career counselor (1940–1959). Millions of WWII veterans are returning home and entering the job market. Many return to college as results of the G.I Bill of Rights. New theories and assessment tools for career counseling are developed. Several scholarly journals for career counseling are developed. The National Defense of Education Act of 1958 is passed.

Stage 4: Organizational Development (1960–1979). The Vietnam War and the Civil Rights movement inspired young people to seek careers that were more reflective of their values and added a dimension of meaning to their lives. Working conditions are continuing to improve. The Vocational Education Act of 1963 was passed.

Stage 5: Career counselors in private practice (1980–1989). The United States begins a shift in the job market from industrialization to information technology. Career counselors begin providing outplacement counseling for organizations lying off workers. There is a backlash against many of the social norms fought for in the previous two decades. During this time the importance of multicultural counseling and the implications of ethics are considered.

Stage 6: Technology and Diversity (1990-present). In 1990 the Americans with Disabilities Act (ADA) of 1990 is pasted. There is a greater focus on career development and theories for marginalized individuals. The demand for career counseling will continue to grow as the economy moves increasingly towards a globalized market and workers may hold several positions over the course of their lifespan (Pope, 1997).

Figure 14.1 Significant stages of carer counseling

private, public, educational and organizational settings. Once thought of as being a separate domain from personal development, there has been a shift in the career counseling profession that recognizes that an individual's career and personal concerns need to be viewed in a more holistic manner (Guindon, 2006, pp. 282–306). While the breadth of career counseling's historical roots is too extensive to cover within this chapter, a short summary is presented in figure 14.1. As seen in figure 14.1, career counseling has gone through significant stages of change that mirrored major societal shifts in the United States' history (Pope, 1997). Below, the reader will have an opportunity to become aware of career counseling's historical roots, philosophy and developing trends through learning about its diverse theoretical lenses.

Career Counseling Theories

Career counseling's rich history has lent itself to several different theoretical traditions. Each theory represents a lens that is reflective of the historical time period in which it was developed. The reader will find that many of the theoretical concepts and ideas have over arching themes. Shoffner (2006) states of John Krumbultz's work that, "a theory is an attempt to represent some aspect of behavior, much in the same way that a map is an attempt to represent some geographic territory" (Krumbultz, 1994, p. 9). As the reader examines the various theories in this chapter, she or he is encouraged to think about how each theory can provide a path or map for career counselors to follow with their clients. The beginning counselor is also encouraged to think about how each map or theory provides a different prospective and approach. Rigid adherence to one map or theory will keep the counselor and client from developing insights that can be developed from taking the road less traveled. It is important to note that the theories presented below are brief narratives. The reader is encouraged to develop a more comprehensive understanding of these theoretical works.

Frank Parsons

Frank Parsons (1909) is regarded as the founder of the vocational guidance movement and developer of the trait-and-factor approach. Frank Parsons developed his approach in response to the poverty many new immigrants were experiencing during the early 1900s. Despite being over a hundred years old, trait-and-factor theory continues to be a relevant approach for career counselors who are mapping out their approach for clients (Fouad, 1999). The foundation of Parsons' approach is that individuals are drawn to prospective careers due to their personality and variables that influenced their upbringing.

Parsons' approach consisted of three steps. These three steps included self-exploration including one's aptitudes, abilities, interests and limitations; having information about the current job market, and seeing what jobs make a good fit with that individual's strengths and weakness as well as the job market influences (Shoffner, 2006). The career counselor explores with the client what jobs may be a good fit based on this three-step process. Many of the concepts presented in Parsons' theory were incorporated into the theories that followed.

John Holland

John Holland's work is well known in the career counseling field and his contributions are numerous. There is a substantial body of research examining Holland's theory. Holland's work differed from his predecessors in that the focus of his theory has been on "why career choice occurs and the outcomes of that choice, rather than on how or why personality orientations develop" (Shoffner, 2006, p. 42). Holland's theory is based on six key ideas. These include:

1. In our culture, most people are one of six personality types: Realistic, Investigative, Artistic, Social, Enterprising, and Conventional.
2. People of the same personality tend to "flock together." For example, Artistic people are attracted to making friends and working with Artistic people.

3. People of the same personality type working together in a job create a work environ-ment that fits their type. For example, when Artistic persons are together on a job, they create a work environment that rewards creative thinking and behavior—an Artistic environment.
4. There are six basic types of work environments: Realistic, Investigative, Artistic, Social, Enterprising, and Conventional.
5. People who choose to work in an environment similar to their personality type are more likely to be successful and satisfied.

    For example, Artistic persons are more likely to be successful and satisfied if they choose a job that has an Artistic environment, like choosing to be a dance teacher in a dancing school—an environment "dominated" by Artistic type people where creative abilities and expression are highly valued.
6. How one acts and feels at work depends to a large extent on that individual's workplace environment (Career Key, 2011, p. 1).

Social Learning Theory

John Krumbultz developed the Social Learning Theory of Career Decision Making (SLTCDM). Krumbultz (1996) later refined the theory into the Learning Theory of Career Counseling (LTCC). LTCC examines cognitive behavioral approaches and outcomes for career counseling (Shoffner, 2006). LTCC and SLTCDM's foundations rest on the importance of learning the theories that people learn through experiential experiences and observations (Krumboltz, Mitchell, & Jones, 1976). Krumboltz identified four main factors that influence career development. These four main factors include one's genetics and special abilities (race, gender, physical characteristics, talents); environment (social, cultural, political, economic, climate, geographic); learning experience (instrumental and associative), and task approach skills (problem solving skills, work habits, emotional and cognitive processes) (Krumboltz, Mitchell, & Jones, 1976). Shoffner (2006) states, "learning through experience (both instrumental and associative) and human interaction are the primary focus of career development and decision making" (p. 55). Krumbultz believed that an individual's career decisions developed over the course of their life time.

Career counselors working from this model are often providing personal and career counseling. Krumboltz and Vosvick (1996) discuss how the clients' own distorted beliefs or schemas often influence their career decisions. Counselors may need to address these distorted beliefs or underlying schemas before the clients are ready to move into making decisions about their career concerns.

Social Cognitive Career Theory

Social cognitive career theory (SCCT) developed by Lent, Brown, and Hackett (1994) derives from Albert Bandura's social cognitive theory (1986, 1997). SCCT examines the interaction between the clients' environment and their belief systems. Heller, Watson & Illis (2004) found that the level of contentment clients feel with their career relates to their overall sense of well-being. This was one of the main rationales for the creation of the model. One of the main principles in SCCT is that one's self-efficacy (self efficacy meaning one's belief about his/her ability to succeed) affects one's self-concept, which in turn, affects one's career expectations and goals. One's self-concept and self-efficacy also influences one's ability to overcome any perceived or real barriers. SCCT also recognizes how a person's cultural background (for example, gender, race, ethnicity and contextual factors such as ones support systems) influences career choices and goals (Lent et al., 1994). Hackett and Betz's (1981) research speaks to the influence of environment and gender socialization on women's career choices; specifically, women's lack of representation in the math and science fields. While their research focusing on women's self efficacy in math and science is from 1981, today in 2012, there continues to be a lack of women represented in these fields. Kelly (2009) notes that Lent et al. (1994) worked to integrate common themes from other "career theorists such as person-environment correspondence personality typology, social learning, life span, life space and developmental theory" (p. 8). This theory is highly influential given its focus on the intersection of career choice, diversity and societal barriers.

Developmental Theories

Ginzberg, Ginsburg, Axelrad and Herma (1951) were theorists who were part of the paradigm shift in career counseling that began to explore the developmental process as it relates to career choice. Ginzberg et al. (1951) observed that people go through phases in their career decision making at different developmental stages of their life. For example, young children who are still in the fantasy stage speak of wanting to become famous singers, actresses and presidents. As children move into adolescence, they began to understand what is involved in these professional endeavors. Between the ages of 12 and 18 young adolescents are in the tentative stage where, along aside other important developmental milestones, adolescents begin to explore their interests as well as their level of self-efficacy with their interests. The third stage Ginzberg et al. (1951) recognized was the realistic stage. During this stage, career exploration has led to clear ideas about what individuals are gravitating towards in their career interests.

Donald Super

Around the same time that Ginzberg and his colleagues presented their developmental theory, Donald Super developed his highly influential developmental theory of careers. Super's theory is built on the foundation of Ginzberg and his associates. One of Super's (1990) major contributions to career counseling is how a person's developing self concept is affected by her/his life experiences. These life experiences and changes in self concept have a strong relationship in one's career decision making process. Super (1990) believed that most peoples' skill sets are varied and that they are qualified for more than one occupation. Super also recognized that occupational preferences and expertise change over the course of one's life span, thus, making choices and career adjustment an ongoing process. When a career counselor is working with clients, the career counselor takes into account not just the clients' skills and interests but where they are in their developmental process.

Super's developmental theory includes five stages. Super's five stages are: growth, exploration, establishment, maintenance (or management), and disengagement. From ages 0–14 Super recognized that children and young adolescents develop their self concept primarily through their interactions with the adults in their lives (Shoffner, 2006). During this time, children and young adolescents are developing interests, aptitudes and needs that are a reflection of their developing self-concept. The second stage, exploration, occurs from ages 15 to 24. During this developmental stage adolescents and young adults are narrowing down their career options as they relate to their developing self-concept. During this stage people have their first experience with working and thus are figuring out what occupations will prove satisfactory. These first experiences in the working world can be varied until a good fit is found between the suitable occupation and the individual's personality, interests and self-concept. Stage three, establishment, occurs from ages 25 to 44. During this stage, one is working to stabilize and advance his/her career. During this stage, one seeks out additional responsibility for promotion, often in hopes of further economic stability. In stage four, maintenance, from ages 45 to 64, one is continuing to advance and improve her/his career. While this can be an extremely busy time in one's career, it can also be a period of stagnation. The final stage, disengagement, occurs from ages 65 and above. During this time, one will begin to think about retirement from his/her career, and increase time spent on leisure activities and family. Super believed people filled a variety of roles over the course of their life time, for example, child, student, leisurite, citizen, worker and homemaker (Super, 1990). Super's Life-Career Rainbow provides a framework for understanding how these different roles influence career development across the lifespan. Another concept that Super developed is the idea of career maturity (Savickas & Super, 1996). Career maturity refers to the completion of the tasks one undertakes in each stage of development. Career counselors who are working to assess the client's stage of maturity, "may assess planfulness, exploratory attitudes, decision-making skills, realistic self appraisal, and the client's knowledge of developmental tasks and of occupations" (Shoffner, 2006, pp. 52–53). The therapist can decide which intervention would be most appropriate for the client based on the client's career maturity.

Linda Gottfredson

Gottfredson's (1981, 1996, 2002) theory is a developmental approach that examines the influences of socialization and cultural expectations. Children develop ideas about which career paths are acceptable to follow based on their early socialization. Of particular concern to Gottfredson is how sex roles and prestige affect career development. For example a young girl may feel that it is okay for her to become a teacher or a nurse, but not a policeperson or doctor. These ideas and beliefs are often modeled by the adults in the child's life. The child will rule out these options in a process she defined as circumscription.

In Gottfredson's theory there is a "zone of acceptable alternatives" that are reflective of the individual's worldview. Gottfredson believed that self concept is highly influenced by social class, intelligence and gender socialization. Gottfredson believed children progressed though four stages of development. The first stage, orientation to size and power, occurs between the ages of three and five. Children, during this time, develop schemas about being an adult and their occupation. The second stage of development, orientation to sex roles, occurs between the ages of six to eight years of age. Gottfredson notes that there is a substantial research base to support gender stereotyping during this time. This is when children develop ideas about which occupations are appropriate for which gender. The third stage of development, orientation to social valuation, occurs between nine and thirteen. During this time young adolescents develop an understanding of social class. Young adolescents try to emulate adults, who, in their view, society places a high value or prestige upon. The final and fourth stage of Gottfredson's model is orientation to the internal and unique self, which begins at age fourteen. During this stage, adolescents begin to develop self awareness and become increasingly aware of other perceptions of themselves. During this time individuals begin to explore their career aspirations within a cultural context. Gottfredson believed that when individuals decide they will have to compromise their career goals, they will first sacrifice their interests, then internal self, and finally prestige.

Diversity

As the field of multicultural counseling continues to evolve, counseling students should note that CACREP (2009), the Council for Accreditation of Counseling and Related Education Programs 2009 standards, emphasize the importance of multicultural competency in the career counseling relationship. Along with the CACREP's 2009 standards, counseling students should be aware of the American Counseling Association's (2005) Code of Ethics principles on providing culturally competent counseling services.

Americans with Disabilities Act

The Americans with Disabilities Act (ADA) of 1990 was implemented to protect the civil rights of individuals with disabilities. The legislation was important in many ways, including providing individuals with disabilities equal opportunity to employment (U.S. Department of Justice Civil Rights Division, 2001). The ADA also provided people with disabilities guarantees to services such as transportation, local and federal services, telephone services and places of public accommodation (U.S. Department of Justice Civil Rights Division, 2001). The act prohibits discriminatory practices such as barring employers from asking potential employees if they have a disability before making a job offer. It also states that employers must provide employees with disabilities "reasonable accommodations" (U.S. Department of Justice Civil Rights Division, 2001).

In order to practice competently, career counselors are required to be knowledgeable in the areas of policies, laws, and regulations as these relate to the ADA and career development (Council for Accreditation of Counseling and Related Educational Programs, CACREP, 2009; National Career Development Association, NCDA, 2007). Along with the career counseling competencies of CACREP and NCDA, it is imperative that career counselor be knowledgeable of the multicultural counseling competencies and applicable multi-cultural guidelines set forth in the Ethics Code for the American Counseling Association (2005).

Counseling, Prevention, and Intervention

Career counselors will find that clients come with a variety of decision making concerns. Olson, McWhirter, and Horan (1989) discuss four components in the decision making process for career counseling. The four components include conceptualization of the problem as one of choice, enlargement of the response repertoire, identification of discriminative stimuli, and response selection (Olson, McWhirter, & Horan, 1989).

Counselors can take many different approaches to the decision making process. For example, a counselor with a cognitive-behavioral theoretical orientation may ask clients to list the pros and cons in taking a particular course of action in their career development. The counselor may work with clients to explore the possible consequences

---

SIDEBAR 14.3 Are Decision Making Models Helpful in Career Exploration?

"It's the last semester of my Masters in education program, and I hate teaching."
"My parents want me to be an engineer, but I want to be a writer."
Career counselors walk their clients through a problem-solving process that includes weighing the pros and cons of their choices. Most importantly, they remind their clients that despite feeling "stuck" right now, and the client may have to make some tough decisions, the client does have choices. This process of exploring alternatives and weighing different courses of action teaches the client a decision making process that they can then apply to multiple situations. What other decision making models or processes are helpful for clients?

---

of changing career paths, going back to school to receive further training, or exploring the necessary steps to advance the clients' careers. The reader should note that the complexities of issues clients bring to the counseling session may make the clients feel "stuck" because they may have to choose between two undesirable choices. Yet, career counselors can empower their clients to explore resources and various social supports that can make this decision making process less hopeless than when they initially walked through the counselors' door.

For example, many adolescents aspire for careers that our society places prestige and ample financial rewards on, such as CEO of a Fortune 500 company, or becoming the next rock star. Counselors working with clients who are struggling with career making decisions will find they can more readily help clients through their decision making process with the use of various decision making models. Greenwood (2008) conducted a study following up on her career counseling clients and found that 65% of her clients had adhered to the program recommendation that was developed during their career counseling sessions. These clients were also noted to be significantly more committed to their careers (Greenwood, 2008).

Cultural competency is key when exploring the decision-making process with clients struggling with career concerns. Sue & Sue (2008) discuss the importance of recognizing various worldviews and their influence in the counselor–client relationship. Clients who were raised in westernized countries will place a higher value on making decisions that honor individual autonomy. For example, it is not uncommon for American college students to seek support in communicating to their families that they will be pursuing a career path their family may not have intended for the student. Yet, in many Eastern countries that have a collectivist orientation, college students follow career paths that their families have pre-determined for the student because they value an interdependent approach to decision making. Niles, Engels, and Lenz (2009) highlight career counseling training issues within a global context.

Whether a client's worldview is influenced by an independent or interdependent lens, an exploration of the client's values is important information for both the client and counselor. Clients may have few career options in their current geographical location. Yet the client may place a high value on their family or community ties, so moving to a new location would prove to be a less optimal choice for the client than exploring their generalizable skills that could expand their career opportunities in their current geographical location.

Yet many people do choose to relocate for career opportunities. This can present challenges for many clients, such as, acclimatizing to a new geographical and work place culture, building new social support systems, and balancing new responsibilities. There are also many decisions clients will be confronted with that are of a developmental nature. For example, clients who are newly divorced and struggling to balance their work and home responsibilities will need different supports than a client who is struggling with "empty nest syndrome". Some clients may be challenged with work environments that permit and sometimes encourage homophobia, sexism and racial and ethnic prejudice.

Clients can benefit from exploration and labeling of these various experiences. Many clients will walk into their counselors' office and may not know how to articulate the difficulties they are experiencing. In many cultures, symptoms of anxiety and depression may manifest themselves as physical ailments. Career counselors can support their clients in learning communication and assertiveness skills. This skill building can empower clients to label their experience when they are in discriminatory workplaces.

In addition to supporting clients in articulating their concerns both in session and in the clients' workplaces, the counselor can help provide their clients with behavioral techniques that can help to reduce stress and anxiety. Mindfulness based breathing exercises, meditative visualization practices, and self care behaviors such as physical exercise and good sleep hygiene can help clients to increase their distress tolerance. The beginning counselor is encouraged to help the client explore current and new support systems. For example, a client who is in recovery from drugs and alcohol and has recently moved to a new geographical area may need help connecting with local Alcoholics Anonymous groups.

Consultation in Career Counseling

Career counselors utilize their expertise to provide consultation in public, private, educational and organizational settings. For example, career counselors may be asked by their organizations to help design programs for employees struggling with addiction issues. Another example is a career counselor providing supervision to supervisees. Dougherty (2009) defines consultation as, "a process in which a human service professional assists a consultee with a work-related (or caretaking-related) problem with a client system, with the goal of helping both the consultee and the client system in some specified way" (pp. 3–4). As seen in the example of the career counselor helping their organization with employee substance dependence concerns, career counselors are often helping to facilitate a problem-solving process. The consultation process is a voluntary, nonjudgmental process in which the career counselor is providing indirect assistance by helping the consultees directly intervene with their clients (Dougherty, 2009). While there are many different models of consultation for the career counselor to draw from, Dougherty (2009) notes that there are three popularly applied models that counselors utilize—mental health, behavioral and organizational. No matter what model is used, the consultation process will involve "building relationships, defining problems, implementing and evaluating plans, and disengaging" (Dougherty, 2009, p. 6).

Diversity and Advocacy

Many of the early counseling theories were initially developed from a white male perspective (Sue et al., 1998). As career counseling clientele continues to diversify, it is an ethical mandate and professional requirement that career counselors be knowledgeable about a clients' worldview and cultural norms and whether they fit with the career counselors' theoretical biases. Career counselors should be able to choose a career theory and apply it to the client, providing best practices to meet the needs of clients regardless of their diverse backgrounds (Ethridge, Burnhill, & Dong, 2009). It is just as important to carefully select an intervention that meets the needs of the client, regardless of the personal preference as a career counselor. To make sure the career counselor's theoretical approach matches the needs of their client, the career counselor must obtain the client's informed consent before providing services to their clients. This does not mean the career counselors will not encounter ethical gray areas when working with a client who is culturally different than the counselor. The beginning career counselor is encouraged to consult the ACA Code of Ethics (2005) for best practices for working with multicultural clients. Beginning career counselors are also encouraged to have expertise in their state laws with regards to providing multicultural competent counseling.

SIDEBAR 14.4 What Part Does Multicultural Knowledge Play in Career Counseling?

Katherine is a 21-year-old junior nursing student whose family immigrated from Vietnam to the United States so that her brother, who is one year older than her, could pursue a degree in computer sciences. The brother has recently graduated with his degree and Katherine's father wants her to return with the family back to Vietnam so that she can care for her two younger siblings and aging grandparents. Katherine does not want to discontinue her academic pursuits, but does not want to upset her family either. The career counselor is shocked that she would consider not finishing her degree, as she is so close to completion. He urges her to push against her family's wishes and continue with her nursing program. Was this the correct approach for the career counselor to take with Katherine?

Career counselors need to have an awareness of workplace issues as they relate to various cultural groups. Mpofu and Harley (2006) note that it is critical for career counselors to have an awareness of the experience of discrimination and stigma for people of color in the work place. As career counselors develop their skills and competencies, it has been suggested that counselors seek out opportunities to work with a variety of cultures to become more culturally competent (Vespia et al., 2010). This provides extended opportunities for the counselor to become more competent and successful in meeting the needs of multiculturally diverse clients.

Social cognitive career theory has been identified as a theory that recognizes the inherent cultural differences of career counseling clients. It integrates a variety of factors that are a reality for women, ethnic minorities, LGBT community members, and people with disabilities in response to self-efficacy, discrimination issues, perceived barriers in the workplace, and environmental support (Lent, Brown, & Hackett, 1994).

While there has been increased research in the areas of diversity in career counseling, this still remains an area where continued research is needed. Issues that surround gender role stereotyping of occupations abound and gender stratification continues, and career counselors need to be aware of this discrimination. It has become important for career counselors to focus on diversity issues, but also on issues of gender and sexuality and the role these may play in the workplace for clients.

Information regarding diversity in career counseling has been slower to evolve, but "career counselors must take an active advocacy approach to working with all cultural minorities" (Ponterotto, et al., 2010, p. 740). Therefore, it places greater responsibility on career counselors to do additional research when working with clients with a cultural background with which they are unfamiliar. There are resources that are available, one being Leong's (1995) "Career Development and Vocational Behavior of Racial and Ethnic Minorities." Even with the awareness of diverse populations, Vespia et al. (2010) noted that the Lesbian, Gay, Transgendered, and Bisexual (LGTB) population, Asians, Native Americans and older adults appeared to be cultural groups in which career counselors showed weakness. Hunt, Jaques, Niles, and Wierzalis (2003) describe a variety of career issues and concerns relevant to individuals with HIV/AIDS. Gelberg and Chojnacki's (1995) discussion on the process of becoming gay, lesbian, and bisexual affirmative career counselors offers a realistic perspective on the challenges this endeavor represents.

The reality is that a counselor will not be familiar with all areas of multiculturalism. There are so many different cultural beliefs, religions, and traditions that it would be difficult to be an expert in all of these areas. But, it is the professional responsibility of the counselor to seek out resources to support clients who are culturally different from themselves. Each client is an individual and therefore, the beliefs that he/she holds are her/his own. It is the obligation of counselors to respect these differences and to understand them from the viewpoint of clients so that they are able to support them through the process of career counseling. Career counselors need to continue educating themselves through professional workshops, continuing education courses, consultation with experts in the field, current research and other means that allow for further understanding of clients. The obligation is carried through in the American Counseling Association Code of Ethics (2005), which outlines the requirements of counselors when working with diverse clients. Career counselors risk perpetuating disadvantages and discrimination when they fail to understand the dynamics of privilege and oppression, and the role of such environmental factors such as poverty and access to education and healthcare in the career development process (McWhirter, 1994, 2001; O'Ryan, 2003).

Assessment

Career counselors rely on the use of assessments in order to meet the needs of their clients. As with all counseling, assessment begins upon the first interactions with one's client. It is crucial to begin noting the nonverbal behaviors of the client (i.e. style of dress, facial behaviors, body language, eye contact), the way the client enters into the counseling session (i.e. appearing nervous or comfortable) and the verbal abilities of the client (i.e. language selection, verbal tracking). This initial assessment of verbal and nonverbal cues combined provides more knowledge than solely instrument assessments. In career counseling, there are times when feedback is necessary. As a counselor, there will be times when one has to present this information to one's client. The relationship between client and counselor needs to be developed; this takes time, so that the client is able to hear and

---

SIDEBAR 14.5 What Should the Career Counselor Know about Other Cultures Prior to Providing Counseling?

Asami was a third-year study abroad student who came to see the university career counselor because she was wanted to practice interviewing skills before she returned to Japan in the spring. The career counselor noticed that she would not maintain eye contact with her, and so continually brought it to Asami's attention. The career counselor noticed that when she called this to Asami's attention, she would exhibit a look of tension on her face. The career counselor asked Asami to come back for a second session to continue to practice her interviewing skills. Asami agreed. The next week however, Asami did not show. Shapiro (2012) has noted that Asian clients often do not maintain eye contact as a sign of respect for individuals with authority or status. If the career counselor had been aware of this, how might her assessment and approach with Asami have been different?

---

accept the feedback that is provided and ultimately make changes that are needed. It is important for clients to be aware of their body language and the messages that it can provide to prospective employers. Developing this awareness is an essential piece to the assessment process.

Career counselors, in their assessment process, still rely on the basic skills that provide the foundation of counselor identity. Career counselors need to be actively listening to their clients; this is conveyed through eye contact, posture, openness, verbal tracking and nonverbal responses. Career counselors need to maintain a nonjudgmental environment so that clients are comfortable disclosing issues and concerns. During the assessment process, clients will be sharing personal issues as they relate to their career development. Using counseling interviewing skills will be a crucial piece to developing this relationship (i.e. questioning, paraphrasing, reflection of feeling, restatements, confrontations and summarizations). These basic skills will also lead to defining the goals, an important part of the assessment process.

Before engaging in the assessment process, career counselors should provide the client with the opportunity to give their informed consent after explaining their approach and expectations. It is also important to discuss the expectations the client brings to the career counseling sessions. There may be an assumption by the client that the counselor will be directive in his/her approach. For example, the client may have the belief that the counselor will directly instruct the client in her/his career. The counselor is responsible for addressing these misconceptions. Career counselors do not direct clients as to what specific career they should work towards. It is a process of utilizing the counseling relationship that has been developed, along with various assessments that come together to provide the client with insight related to career decisions. At that point in counseling, clients are then able to make a determination as to what would work best in terms of their career path.

It is important to empower clients to make decisions that seem best for them and they will require help evaluating this information. For example, clients may see themselves as having nothing to offer to a potential employer. However, the career counselor may have a different perspective, noticing that the client is always on time, willing to work during the sessions and has an overall positive attitude. It is important for the client to receive this positive feedback from the career counselor. Providing positive feedback will continue to strengthen the counseling relationship while supporting clients to evaluate themselves and their future career endeavors. In addition, it is an ethical mandate that career counselors are well trained in diversity issues. Vespia, Fitzpatrick, Fouad, Kantamneni and Yung-Lung (2010) found that there still remained some areas of multicultural competences for career counselors that need to be developed further. Their suggestion is for career counselors entering the field to be exposed to environments that provide the opportunity to work with a wide range of clients. Vespia et al. (2010) noted that the Lesbian, Gay, Transgendered, and Bilingual (LGTB) population, Asians, Native Americans and older adults appeared to be cultural groups in which career counselors showed weakness. It is important for career counselors entering the field to be aware of the diversity that exists within clients and to seek out continued education, supervision or consultation to ensure that they continue to meet their needs effectively.

Building on the factors of initial assessment, interviewing skills, informed consent, empowerment, and dealing with diversity, career counseling can be approached from both a qualitative and objective perspective. Examples of these two approaches can be found in the following paragraphs.

Interests

Research suggests that clients relate directly to interests (Tracey & Hopkins, 2001). This information can help to assist clients in finding a rewarding career in which they feel a sense of connection. From a qualitative approach, the use of career genograms has been found to provide a visual diagram of family members' career history (Heppner, O'Brien, Hinkelman, & Humphrey, 1994; Okiishi, 1987). This information can then help support clients in developing their own personal career path that may be similar to family members who share their interests. Another qualitative approach to career counseling directs career counselors to spend time discussing and reviewing their clients' previous job history. While discussing the clients' career history, there needs to be a focus on the positive aspects of their former position. For example, clients may share that they enjoyed working with small children at a summer camp. It is important to determine what specifically about this position that they enjoyed. Clients may find the population of small children of interest to them; they may enjoy working outside each day, the different experiences of each day, or the supervisory responsibilities that they experienced. It is essential to clarify the aspects of the job to determine what was actually enjoyed and may be desired for the future. McMahon, Patton, and Wilson (2003) provide suggestions for career counselors to develop qualitative assessments for use with clients, as they have found that the use of assessments in career counseling is fundamental, but there is limited availability of this information in the literature. According to Goldman (1990), the advantages of qualitative assessment included a greater degree of adaptability with respect to individual characteristics such as gender and ethnicity.

Many times, qualitative approaches are used in conjunction with a more objective instrument. The career counselor, in providing informed consent, needs to make sure the client is clear regarding the purpose and use of the objective instrument. In addition to the client's having a role in deciding whether to utilize an instrument, it is also important for the counselor to be aware of some of the cultural limitations that many objective instruments may have. Some instruments have a history of gender and racial bias. The counselor needs to be assured of reliability and validity of the assessment tool. If an assessment needs to be translated into a different language to accommodate the needs of the client, it is important to understand that this may change the reliability and validity of the test instrument itself. There are many assessments that may already be translated into different languages that have strong reliability and validity. There are additional resources that are available to provide career counselors with insight into populations that are continually being developed (Gainor, 2001; Ward & Bingham, 2001). The creation of career counseling came from a White perspective (Sue, et al., 1998) and this may still be present in certain elements of career counseling. The following are examples of objective assessment approaches to gather information related to interests, aptitudes and values.

The Strong Interest Inventory

The Strong Interest Inventory (SII) is one of the most widely used interest inventories. Strong created the inventory in 1927 and it has been recently revised by Strong, Donnay, Morris, Schaubhut and Thompson (2004). The SII contains 291 items which measure six different areas: Occupations, Subject Areas, Activities, Leisure Activities, People, and Your Characteristics and then provides the user with an opportunity for further self-exploration of potential careers along with an educational assistance in making decisions (Case & Blackwell, 2008). The inventory is published by Consulting Psychological Press and available online. The results of this scale provide the user with insight into possible career options that would match the interest and personality of the user. The updated version continues to reflect the current trends of the occupational world. There are continued recommendations for the SII, specifically to create the inventory in a language other than English, which would allow counselors to utilize this tool with a greater number of clients (Case & Blackwell). There have been numerous studies that have looked at the validity of the SII. Rottinghaus, Lindley, Green, and Brogen (2002) found the General Occupational Themes to be predictive of work-related variables. Dirk and Hansen (2004) also noted that Occupational Scales have been demonstrated in research, showing their ability to predict occupations that people will eventually enter. Both of these studies show a practical use associated with the SII. While the SII has been limited in its cultural scope, the most recent version of the SII included a variety of cultural groups; non-White groups represented 30% of the sample, making it more representative of current society (Case & Blackwell, 2008). This inventory continues to be widely used in educational or counseling settings.

Self-Directed Search

The Self-Directed Search (SDS) was developed by John Holland to reflect his career theory, which has been the basis of many career inventories. The SDS is a self-administered tool with the intention of providing clients further insight into their career interests, activities, competencies and then provides a matching career path (Holland, 1994). The tool is easy to administer and provides a thorough analysis. The SDS is published by Psychological Assessment Resources and available online. The results of the SDS correspond to Holland's categories; Realistic, Investigative, Artistic, Social, Enterprising and Conventional and this also relates to the Dictionary of Occupational Titles (DOT). Chauvin, Miller, Godfrey, and Thomas (2010) found that as clients become more involved and motivated in the career counseling process they begin exploring and evaluating possible careers that may suit them. As a result of this involvement and motivation, Chauvin (et al., 2010) found that combining the SDS with the Myers-Briggs Inventory could provide even more insight into one's career preference, style, environment, and self-awareness of future career potential.

Kuder Occupational Interest Survey

The Kuder Occupational Interest Survey (KOIS) was developed by G. Frederic Kuder in 1966. The current Form DD evolved over the years from the research of Dr. Kuder that was continued by Zytowksi (1985). This inventory is published by National Career Assessment Services, Inc. (NCASI) and is available online. The KOIS is an inventory that compares interests with persons in a variety of occupations and college majors. This inventory has been found useful with high school students, college students and adult returning students. As careers and times continue to change, the KOIS was recently revised to become the Kuder Career Search Schedule (KCSS), which matches similar KOIS items to persons instead of samples (Dik, 2006).

Aptitudes

When understanding career assessment and how to help your clients find the career that matches who they are, it is also important to consider their aptitudes and skills. Working with clients to identify their strengths provides them with a connection to potential careers. If you were identifying skills that allowed clients to do well in school, these skills would need to be broken down into detailed areas. Since we know that grades are comprised of various assignments, it is important for clients to identify the specific components of the grade. Through this, their aptitude may be evident in the areas in which they are successful (i.e. essays, oral discussions/presentations, debates, group projects/activities, organization). It would be useful to review work evaluations that the client received to determine areas of higher ratings. In addition, when working with clients, discuss compliments, comments or feedback that they may have been given in the past at their places of employment; this may provide further information into areas of aptitude for the client. If this is a customer service field, it would be important to note direct feedback that customers may have provided to clients, as well as their supervisors. Some clients may struggle with this discussion. It is important to utilize your counseling skills here to work with the client and help them identify these pieces. This is an empowering process for clients that can help them to move forward in a direction in which they would like to go. There are times, when working with a client, when the verbal discussion does not provide enough of the needed information and you incorporate the use of aptitude testing to provide more information. The use of testing will provide more information for the career counselor and client to evaluate. One of the goals would be to provide insight into areas that the client has not considered before.

Differential Aptitude Test

(DAT) The Differential Aptitude Test Fifth Edition was published in 1990 and was developed by Bennet, Seashore, and Westman. The DAT is published by Pearson and is appropriate for students in grades 7th through 12th, as well as adults. This test provides further insight into areas that are key for a client in successful job performance. In addition to schools and colleges using this scale, many corporations provide this to potential employees to determine if they are appropriate for their positions. It does not predict occupational success or success in specific academic areas, but provides an overview of general areas of academic success potential.

General Aptitude Test Battery

The General Aptitude Test Battery (GATB) was developed and published by the U.S. Employment Service in 1947 and has undergone revisions since that time. The GATB provides a comparison with employees already in specific occupations in regards to nine aptitudes. The GATB is often used with the Occupational Outlook Handbook (OOH) to assist in exploration of possible job opportunities. The nine areas of the GATB are general learning ability, verbal ability, numerical ability, spatial ability, form perception, clerical ability, eye/hand coordination, finger dexterity, and manual dexterity (Sharf, 2010). It should be noted that the GATB measures on more levels than general aptitude tests and is able to provide a clearer picture for many clients.

Values

Values clarification is an important part of the career counseling assessment process. For example, a working mother may not be able to work in a business position that requires regular overnight travel, even if the position provides the recognition and financial security that she is seeking. Zytowski (1994) noted how this piece of career counseling is vital to the counselor's self-exploration as it provides a realistic viewpoint of the career and its relationship to the client.

Many clients who enter into career counseling do not realize the strong relationship that their values play in developing their desire for a career. Some clients have a clearer perspective of what will work for them in terms of their career desires; other clients will not have the same level of insight and will need further exploration with the counselor to develop a deeper understanding of these pieces. Career counselors need to be aware of the clients' cultural backgrounds and how this can affect the values clarification of clients. Hartung (2002) discusses the importance of career counselors examining cultural factors that influence values by working with the client to identify values that delineate the influence of broader cultural values on the individual and examine the individualistic/collectivistic cultural value orientations of the client.

Greenbank (2009) conducted in-depth personal interviews of undergraduate students who identified as part of the working class in order to understand the role of their perceived values in future decisions regarding careers. The initial assumption was that this population had low aspirations until Greenback (2009) discussed their values. It was determined that their level of apprehension was in utilizing resources, such as career counseling centers. Duffy and Sedlacek (2007) surveyed first-year college students to understand the factors they identify as most important in their career plans and found that career counselors need to place greater emphasis on work values in their career decision making.

Values Inventory

Super developed the Work Values Inventory which has 12 scales that address values in the workplace (i.e. prestige, lifestyle, income, independence, and creativity). This instrument is objective and assesses for work related values. In addition, there are other instruments that assess for values: Work Environment Preference Schedule, the Salience Inventory, The Study of Values and the Survey of Interpersonal Values. Some of these scales are able to explore the combination of work related values and personal values, which can be useful for certain clients.

The System of Interactive Guidance and Information (SIGI) is a computer system that works with clients in identifying and clarifying their values, and then the system is able to provide information on various careers directly based on their values. There are ten values that the system uses for the client to evaluate: income, prestige, independence, helping others, security, variety, leadership, interest field, leisure, and early entry. Peterson, Ryan-Jones, Sampson, and Reardon (1994) found that SIGI users report positive impact on their career exploration.

Research and Evaluation

While many career counselors are aware of the immediate outcomes of counseling, such as the choice of a college major or a reduction of job stress, in general practice, there is very little formal follow-up. In addition, it is good practice for counselors to end every counseling relationship with an evaluation of the process. Such an evaluation may be incorporated into one of the final sessions and may yield important information for both the counselor and the client. Potential closing topics to cover are similar to those of personal counseling: the relative helpfulness of the interventions, the degree of support experienced by the client throughout the process, the extent to which the client felt respected and understood, the extent to which the client felt like an active participant and collaborator, topics on which the client might have wanted to spend more or less time, and what the client might like to have done differently.

Feedback for clients might include the counselor's perceptions of their relevant strengths and weaknesses, changes and progress noted by the counselor, and suggestions for future directions.

There is also a need in career counseling for more formal evaluations of the relative effectiveness of various interventions. Surprisingly little is known about how various career interventions affect the vocational development process. Brown and Krane (2000) describe the results of several meta-analyses of the effects of career interventions and noted five specific intervention components that appear to be associated with positive career counseling outcomes: written exercises, individualized interpretation and feedback, world of work of information, modeling opportunities, and attention to building support within a social network. Their review is a promising step forward in understanding the complexity of career counseling and vocational choices. Greenwood (2008) did extensive follow up evaluation with career counseling clients to determine career satisfaction and enjoyment after attending career counseling and mapping out a program. This study was conducted over a period of time and provides insight to recognize the value in utilizing career counseling services.

Another area of competence key to career counseling is research methodology. The NCDA Code of Ethics (2007) in Section H calls upon career counselors to promote and engage in scholarly research to further the scope of knowledge and practice for career counselors. Section H provides the framework for engaging in ethical scholarly research. This framework includes informed consent, protecting the welfare of research participants, competencies, and overall responsibilities of the career counseling researcher

(National Career Development Association, 2007). Many in the career counseling field are drawn to the profession out of a passion for helping others through service. Understanding research methods applications are not seen by many counseling students as interesting or important to their practice with clients (Almeida, Brown, & Crace, 2006). Yet as Almeida, Brown, and Crace (2006) state, it is the most important element in providing effective counseling services free of personal biases and prejudices. This is true in any form of counseling; in order to be able to demonstrate competency, a career counselor needs to be aware of the research methods in the field and adhere to the ACA Code of Ethics (2005), which include diversity and competency in interventions employed.

There is an extensive research base in career development for career counseling to draw from in their practice, yet there continues to be a disconnect in career counseling *research* versus career counseling *practice*. Savickas (2003) asserts that despite extensive research on the development of interest inventories, there continue to be gaps in research on their usage in practice. Many private and public organizations who provide funding for counseling services are increasingly calling upon providers to show the effectiveness of their outcomes (Savickas, 2003; Niles, 2003). While many counselors considering engaging in formal research can become overwhelmed, career counselors can engage in practice-based approaches such as action research. Action research provides a framework for integrating theory and practice (Young, 1995), and these research methods allow career counselors to take an individualized approach with their client while contributing to research in the career counseling field.

SIDEBAR 14.6 Why Is Research Such a Big Hurdle for Many Students?

"I didn't go into career counseling to do research." Jen saw the research and statistics class for her program of study and froze. "I can't do stats!" She thought to herself. This section on research methodology focuses on an approach known as action research that many scholar-practitioners have found helpful in developing scholarly research. However there are many different types of research approaches. Below are some popularly utilized quantitative and qualitative approaches.

Quantitative: Experimental research designs include, between-group designs, With-in subject.

Quasi-Experimental design: Nonrandomized Pretest-Posttest Control Group Design, Cohort designs.

Single Subject: The AB design.

Descriptive designs: Survey research, Ex post facto designs.

Qualitative: Ethnography, grounded theory, case study, interview.

Based upon what is stated in the chapter, what might you do to change Jen's perception of research and her ability to handle it?

Diagnosis

Career development and personal identity development provide integral synergies to the career counseling process. There are many influences over the course of one's life that influence one's career goals. While many individuals think that career counseling is mainly about taking assessments and figuring out how they can guide the client's career aspirations, there are many contextual influences that affect client outcomes. Lewis (2001) notes that, "clients' career and personal concerns, including their emotional issues, are often interconnected" (as cited in Guindon & Smith, 2002, p. 74).

The World Health Organization (2002) notes that working in a supportive workplace environment leads to higher rates of production, less absenteeism, and lower rates of physical and psychological health concerns. While a healthy work environment can allow for lowered rates of mental health concerns and high rates of wellness, working in an unhealthy work environment can be damaging to one's mental health (World Health Organization, 2002). Poor working environments in which workers are asked to comprise their sense of self-worth and values can not only lead to psychological damage, but also exacerbate and compromise outcomes for career counselors working with these clients. In fact, much of the pathology clients present can be a direct result of working in an unhealthy working environment. Brooks and Brown (1985) note the importance of taking a thorough client history to examine whether the client's presenting concerns are related to their working environment or long-standing mental health issues. Many clients begin their careers believing that they can learn to "tolerate" unhealthy work environments for monetary rewards and job security (Dorn, 1992). Complicating this experience can be the stigma attached to such work, discrimination and systematic social barriers. For example, many career counselors working in substance abuse agencies with clients with legal histories often experience significant barriers helping clients find working environments that support recovery-oriented behaviors. Instability in our economy, balancing work and family roles, prejudice, and pre-existing mental health concerns can all be exasperated by unhealthy work environments.

Career counselors working with these at-risk populations need to be well versed and develop expertise in helping to empower these clients to confront social barriers such as prejudice in the work place. A veteran struggling with PTSD returning home and entering the job market for the first time in several years will need different supportive services and resources than an individual with a severe mental illness such as schizophrenia. All of these examples speak to the need for career counselors having expertise in treating both mental health and career development concerns.

Unemployment

Major shifts in the American economy have left many of our citizens dealing with the effects of long-term unemployment. Herr and Cramer (1992) note that, "the demoralization and despair associated with severe work or economic… problems triggers distress which has biological and physiological as well as psychological correlates" (as cited in Guindon & Smith, 2002, p. 93). Many unemployed workers will struggle with grief and depression related to the loss of their employment (Guindon & Smith, 2002). Career counselors who are aware of the stages of loss and grief that their client is experiencing due to unemployment are best prepared to support clients in accepting this experience and beginning the search for new employment opportunities (Guindon & Smith, 2002).

Program Promotion, Management, and Implementation

Career counselors provide services in a variety of different settings. In order to meet the needs of these different settings successfully, career counselors need skills in understanding how to manage people and systems, and in allocating resources (Schutt, 2006). Career counselors in management positions need to able to manage day-to-day operations while developing relationships and securing funding for their departments. Included in those daily operations is work in developing trainings, facilitating orientations, and evaluating staff performance (Schutt, 2006).

Many of the skills career counselors use in their individual sessions with clients are also needed to provide effective management. These include building rapport, self-awareness, understanding a multicultural perspective, reflective listening skills, conflict resolution, and understanding each individual's unique strengths.

Unfortunately many managers focus on developing technical abilities related to their specific careers, rather than learning and applying effective leadership models (Schutt, 2006). This can lead to high turnover rates and an unhealthy work environments. Pasmore (2011) captured the five top skills needed to engage in strong leadership, these include, "inspiring commitment, strategic planning, leading people, and resourcefulness and employee development" (p. 2). Boyatzis (2008) notes that "leadership development is an intentional process that engages one's emotional, social, or cognitive competencies" (p. 301). Career counselors who have been able to integrate a leadership model into practice are able to see themselves as those who they lead see them (Boyatzis, 2008). Regardless of the setting, career counselors managing career development programs in organizations will need to work on building relationships, organizing collaborative efforts, and team building. Career counselors are consistently working to examine the ways their organizational processes can improve through the use of strategic planning.

Once goals have been met using strategic planning, organizations use a variety of different program evaluation methods to measure whether these goals have been met. One example of a performance measure is a customer satisfaction survey (Schutt, 2006). This measure can be used to better meet the needs of the organizations' clients as well as improve processes and resource allocation (Schutt, 2006). Career counselors working in managerial roles will need to understand the needs of the organization and the individual members in order to provide services that focus their strategic planning. One way this is done is by administering a needs assessment. Needs assessments allow career counselors to focus their mission, core values, vision and organizational strategies (Schutt, 2006). Once career counselors have an understanding of the needs of their stakeholders and have

---

SIDEBAR 14.7 What Part Do Leadership Skills Play in the Role of Career Counselors?

Sheila was recently hired to be the new director of a human resource department for a large organization. Sheila could feel the tension in the air. She had heard from some of her new colleagues that the pervious supervisor had been "tough to deal with". When she held her first staff meeting, she asked her staff to provide feedback about the current state of the department. The feedback she received included the CEO of the company often trying to bully staff into providing confidential information on staff members, a consistent fear of job loss as the department had previously had a high turnover rate, difficulty communicating with other departments about employee concerns and a lack of personal and professional career development opportunities. How can Sheila utilize the leadership skills discussed in this chapter to address the above case study?

developed programming and interventions to meet these needs, they will need to market and promote their programming. While many considering a path in career counseling may not be enthused at the idea of having to engage in the business of marketing and promoting, it is an essential skill needed in order to secure funding and provide services. Promotion also allows clients to understand what services are offered, information about these services, and how to obtain these services (Hopkins, 1995). Hopkins (1995) notes that from this "we might begin to see marketing less as "selling" and more as "educating" (p. 1).

Information Resources

Career counselors often serve as gatekeepers to their clients by providing a variety of career related resources. For example, career counselors can inform their clients about a local job fair, or support clients in learning networking skills. Counselors of all types can help support their clients to learn how to use different online search engines for resume and cover letter writing. While no counselor can have knowledge of all the different career related resources available, it would behoove the beginning counselor to begin building a resource library that he/she can draw from in supporting her/his clients with career development concerns.

CACREP 2009 standards state the importance of experiential learning by requiring counseling students to engage in both a practicum and internship experience in order to obtain their degree (Council for Accreditation of Counseling and Related Educational Programs, 2009). Counselors can support their clients in researching their career aspirations by exploring opportunities for their client to talk with someone in the position they are looking to obtain. Clients should also be encouraged to explore their current social support systems. Career counselors might encourage their clients to network with their friends, family, neighbors, professional associations, online networking sites such as LinkedIn.com, and alumni groups. Career counselors can also encourage clients to volunteer and shadow professionals in similar positions the client is seeking. Many higher education institutions have resources in supporting their current and former students in their job seeking. Some colleges and universities also offer career counseling to members of their local community. Libraries can offer individuals an opportunity to explore career related journals as well as free or low cost access to internet job resources.

The Bureau of Labor Statistics offers their Occupational Outlook Handbook online at web address: http://www.bls.gov/ooh/. The handbook offers users profiles of different professions that include information on various work environments, what steps to take to move into specific career paths, and typical pay as well as many other facts about each profession the organization profiles. Another governmental resource clients can utilize is "O*NET" at the web address http://www.onetonline.org/. "O*NET" offers users descriptions of workplaces, assessment tools as well as career exploration tools. The site is updated regularly, offering users current job market information. There are many state specific job searches as well. The website Job Hunt at the web address http://www.job-hunt.org/jobs/states.shtml offers the user an opportunity to search their state's job resources. Career counselors should familiarize themselves with website resources before directing the client to the sites in question. Many clients who seek career support lack knowledge on how to navigate online resource websites. The U.S. Department of Labor (www.dol.gov) also offers many job seekers many valuable resources. It should also be noted that many employment seekers recognize the value of having a diverse work place environment and post on websites such as Hire Diversity (www.hirediversity.com). The internet is an invaluable tool for many job seekers. There are numerous job seeking websites that clients can utilize to search for career development materials.

Summary

The field of career counseling combines basic counseling skills, assessment, prevention, intervention, and diagnostic skills to work with the client. This chapter presented an overview of career counseling for beginning counselors. As new counselors embark on their professional journey, there remain many possibilities for both challenging and rewarding experiences. As a career counselor builds a strong foundation in the field of career development and intervention, it will enhance the counseling experience for both the client and counselor and allow for the exploration that is required. Resources that are available enhance the work that career counselors can do with their clients, providing for more positive outcomes. The area of career counseling is vital to the field of counseling.

Useful Websites

The following websites provide additional information relating to the chapter topics.
Career One Stop: http://www.acinet.org/
Code of Fair Testing Practices in Education: www.apa.og/science/faircode.html
Career Consulting Corner: http:/careercc.com/links
GLBT Central: www.glbtcentral.com/employment.html
Global Career Development Facilitators: http://www.cdf-global.org/index2.htm
National Career Development Association: http://ncda.org
O*Net: http://www.onetonline.org/
The Society for Human Resource Management: http:shrm.org
US Bureau of Labor Statistics: http://www.bls.gov/
www.hirediversity.com

Note

1   We wish to acknowledge the contributions made by Ellen Hawley McWhirter, Jeneka Joyce, and Christina L. Aranda in the 5th edition version of this chapter.

References

American Counseling Association. (2005). *ACA code of ethics*.

Almeida, L., Brown, D., & Crace, K. (2006). *Foundations of mental health counseling* (D. Borsos, A. Palmo, & W. Weikel, Eds.) (3rd ed.). Springfield, Illinois: Charles C. Thomas.

Bandura, A. (1986). Social foundations of thought and action: A social cognitive theory. Englewood Cliffs, NJ: Prentice-Hall.

Bandura, A. (1997). *Self-efficacy: The exercise of control*. New York: Freeman.

Boyatzis, R. (2008). Leadership development from a complexity perspective. *Consulting Psychology Journal: Practice and Research, 60*(4), 298–313.

Brooks, L., & Brown, D. (1985). Career counseling as a metal health intervention. *Professional Psychology: Research and Practice, 16*(6), 860–867.

Brown, S. D., & Krane, N. E. R. (2000). Four (or five) sessions and a cloud of dust: Old assumptions and new observations about career counseling. In S. D. Brown, & R. W. Lent (Eds.), *Handbook of counseling psychology* (3rd ed.). New York: Wiley.

Bureau for Labor Statistics. (2012). Retrieved on April 1, 2012 at www.bls.gov.

Career Key. (2011). *John Holland's theory of career choice*. Retrieved from http://www.careerkey.org/asp/your_personality/hollands_theory_of_career_choice.asp.

Case, J.C., & Blackwell, T.C. (2008). Strong Interest Inventory. *Rehabilitation Counseling Bulletin, 51*(2), 122–126.

Chauvin, I., Miller, M. J., Godfrey, E. L., & Thomas, D. (2010). Relationship between Holland's Vocational Typology and Myers-Brigg's Types: Implications for career counselors. *Psychology Journal, 7*(2), 61–66.

Council for Accreditation of Counseling and Related Educational Programs. (2009). *The 2009 Standards*. Alexandria, VA: Author. Retrieved February 1, 2012 from http://www.counseling.org/cacrep/2001standards700.htm.

Dik, Bryan J. (2006). Kuder Occupational Interest Survey. *Encyclopedia of Measurement and Statistics*.Thousand Oaks, CA: Sage.– *SAGE Reference Online*

Dirk, B. J., & Hansen, J. C. (2004). Development and validation of discriminant functions for the Strong Interest Inventory®. *Journal of Vocational Behavior, 64*(1), 182–197.

Dorn, F. (1992, December 1). Occupational wellness: The integration of career identity and personal identity. *Journal of Counseling & Development, 71*, 176–178.

Dougherty, A. (2009*). Casebook of psychological consultation and collaboration in school and community settings* (5th ed.). Belmont, Ca: Brooks/Cole.

Duffy, R.D., & Sedlacek, W. E. (2007). The work values of first-year college students: Exploring group differences. *Career Development Quarterly, 55*(4), 359–364.

Ethridge, G., Burnhill, D., & Dong, S. (2009). Career counseling across the life span. In I. Marini, & M. A. Stebnicki (Eds.), *The professional counselor's desk reference* (pp. 443–453). New York, NY: Springer.

Fouad, N. A. (Chair) (1999, August). Frank Parsons—contributions to vocational psychology 90 years later. Symposium conducted at the meeting of the American Psychological Association, Boston, MA.

Gabriele, R. (2008). Orientations to happiness: Do they make a difference in a student's educational life? *American Secondary Education, 36*(2), 88–101.

Gainor, K. A. (2001). Vocational assessment with culturally diverse populations. In L. A. Suzuki, J. G. Ponterotto, & P. J. Meller (Eds.), *Handbook of multicultural assessment: Clinical, psychological, and educational applications* (2nd ed.; pp. 169–189). San Francisco: Jossey-Bass.

Gelberg, S., & Chojnacki, J. T. (1995). Developmental transitions of gay/lesbian/bisexual-affirmative, heterosexual career counselors. *The Career Development Quarterly, 43*(3), 267–273.

Ginzberg, E., Ginsburg, S. W., Axelrad, S., & Henna, J. L. (1951). Occupational choice: An approach to a general theory. New York: Columbia University Press.

Goldman, L. (1990). Qualitative assessment. *The Counseling Psychologist, 18*, 205–213.

Gottfredson, L. S. (1981). Circumscription and compromise: A developmental theory of occupational aspirations. *Journal of Counseling Psychology, 28*(6), 545–579.

Gottfredson, L. S. (1996). Gottfredson's theory of circumscription and compromise. In D.Brown, L. Brooks, et al. (Eds.), *Career choice and development* (3rd ed.; pp. 179–232). San Francisco: Jossey-Bass.

Gottfredson, L. S. (2002). Gottfredson's theory of circumscription, compromise, and self-creation. In D. Brown, et al. (Eds.), *Career choice and development* (4th ed.; pp. 85–148). San Francisco: Jossey- Bass.

Greenback, P. (2009). An examination of the role of values in working-class students' career decision-making. *Journal of Further & higher Education, 33*(1), 33–44.

Greenwood, J. I. (2008). Validation of a multivariate career and educational counseling intervention model using long-term follow up. *Career Development Quarterly, 56*(4), 353–361.

Guidon, M. (2006). Career counseling in mental health and private practice settings. In D. Capuzzi, & M. Stauffer (Eds.), *Career counseling: Foundations, perspectives and applications* (pp. 282–306). New York: Pearson Education, Inc.

Guindon, M., & Smith, B. (2002, June). Emotional barriers to successful reemployment: Implications for counselors. *Journal of Employment Counseling, 39,* 73–82.

Hackett, G., & Betz, N. E. (1981). A self-efficacy approach to the career development of women. *Journal of Vocational Behavior, 18,* 326–339.

Hartung, P. J. (2002). Cultural context in career theory and practice: Role salience and values. *Career Development Quarterly, 51,* 12–25.

Heller, D., Watson, D., & Illies, R. (2004). The role of person versus situation in life satisfaction: A crtical examination. *Psychological Bulletin, 130,* 574–600.

Heppner, M. J., O'Brien, K. M., Hinkelman, J. M., & Humphrey, C. F. (1994). Shifting the paradigm: The use of creativity in career counseling. *Journal of Career Development, 21*(2), 77–86.

Herr, E. L., & Cramer, S. H. (1992). *Career guidance and counseling through the life span: Systematic approaches* (4th ed.). New York: HarperCollins.

Holland, J. L. (1994). *Self-Directed Search SDS Form R Assessment Booklet.* Lutz, FL: Psychological Assessment Resources.

Hopkins, S. (1995). *Marketing career counseling services: ERIC digest.* Retrieved from http://www.ericdigests.org/1998–2/marketing.htm.

Hunt, B., Jaques, J., Niles, S. G., & Wierzalis, E. (2003). Career concerns for people living with HIV/AIDS. *Journal of Counseling & Development, 81*(1), 55-60.

Kelly, M. (2009). *Social cognitive career theory as applied to the school-To-work transition* (Seton Hall University, 2009). Retrieved from http://scholarship.shu.edu/cgi/viewcontent.cgi?article=2438&context=dissertations.

Krumboltz, J. D. (1994). Improving career development theory from a social learning perspective. In M. L. Savickas, & R. W. Lent (Eds.), *Convergence in career development theories: Implications for science and practice* (pp. 9–31). Palo Alto, CA: CPP Books.

Krumboltz, J. D. (1996). A learning theory of career counseling. In M. L. Savickas & W. B. Walsh (Eds.), *Handbook of career counseling theory and practice* (pp. 55–80). Palo Alto, CA: Davies-Black.

Krumboltz, J. D., Mitchell, A., & Jones, G. (1976). A social learning theory of career selection. *The counseling psychologist, 6,* 71–81.

Krumboltz, J. D., & Vosvick, M. A. (1996). Career assessment and the career beliefs inventory. *Journal of Career Assessment, 4*(4), 345–361.

Lent, R. W., Brown, S. D., & Hackett, G. (1994). Toward a unifying social cognitive theory of career and academic interest, choice, and performance. *Journal Vocational Behavior, 45,* 79–122.

Leong, F. T. (Ed.). (1995). *Career development and vocational behavior of racial and ethnic minorities.* Hillsdale, NJ: Lawrence Erlbaum.

Lewis, J. (2001). Career and personal counseling: Comparing process and outcome. *Journal of Employment Counseling, 38,* 82–90.

McMahon, M., Patton, W., & Watson, M. (2003). Developing qualitative career assessment processes. *Career Development Quarterly, 51,* 194–202.

McWhirter, E. H. (1994). *Counseling for empowerment.* Alexandria, VA: American Counseling Association Press.

McWhirter, E. H. (2001, March). *Social action at the individual level: In pursuit of critical consciousness.* Invited keynote address, 5th Biennial Conference of the Society for Vocational Psychology, Houston, TX.

Mpofu, E., & Harley, D. (2006). Racial and disability identity: Implications for the career counseling of African Americans with disabilities. *Rehabilitation Counseling Bulletin, 50*(1), 14–23.

National Career Development Association. (2007). *Career Counseling Competencies.* Retrieved from http://ncda.org/about/polccc.html.

Niles, S. (2003, September). Career counselors confront a critical crossroads: A vision of the future. *The Career Development Quarterly, 52.*

Niles, S. G., Engels, D., & Lenz, J. (2009). Training career practitioners. *The Career Development Quarterly, 57*(4), 358–365.

Okiishi, R. W. (1987). The genogram as a tool in career counseling. *Journal of Counseling and Development, 66*(3), 139–143.

Olson, C., McWhirter, E. H., & Horan, J. J. (1989). A decision making model applied to career counseling. *Journal of Career Development, 16*(2), 19–23.

O'Ryan, L. (2003). Career counseling and social justice. *Counselors for Social Justice Newsletter, 4*(1), 1, 3.

Parsons, F. (1909). *Choosing a vocation.* Boston: Houghton-Mifflin.

Pasmore, W. (2011). *Developing a leadership strategy: A critical ingredient for organizational success* [Center for creative leadership]. Retrieved from http://www.ccl.org/leadership/pdf/research/LeadershipStrategy.pdf.

Peterson, G. W., Ryan-Jones, R. E., Sampson, J. P., & Reardon, R. C. (1994). A comparison of the effectiveness of three computer-assisted career guidance systems: Discover, SIGI, and SIGI PLUS. *Computers in Human Behavior, 10,* 189–198.

Ponterotto, J. G., Casas, J. M., Suzuki, L. A., & Alexander, C.M. (2010). *Handbook of Multicultural Counseling, Third Edition.* Thousand Oaks, CA: Sage Publications, Inc.

Pope, M. (1997). *History and development of career counseling in the USA.*

Pope, M. (2000, March). A brief history of career counseling in the united states. *The Career Development Quarterly,* 48.

Punnett, B. J., Duffy, J. A., Fox, S., Greogory, A., & Lituchy, T. (2007). Career success and satisfaction: A comparative study in nine countries. *Gender in Management, 22*(5), 371–390.

Rottinghaus, P. J., Lindley, L. D., Green, M. A., & Borgen, F. H. (2002). Educational aspirations: The contribution of personality, self-efficacy, and interests. *Journal of Vocational Behavior, 61,* 1–19.

Savickas, M. (2003, September). Advancing the career counseling profession: Objectives and strategies for the next decade. *The Career Development Quarterly, 52,* 87–96.

Schutt, D. (2006). Program promotion, management, and implementation. In D. Capuzzi, & M. Stauffer (Eds.), *Career counseling: Foundations, perspectives and applications* (pp. 204–229). United States of America: Pearson Education, Inc.

Shapiro, M. (2012). Asian culture brief: Vietnam (Culture Brief Series). Retrieved from http://www.ntac.hawall.edu/downloads/products/briefs/culture/pdf/ACVB-Vol12–Iss5–Vietnam.pdf.

Sharf, R. S. (2010). *Applying Career Development Theory to Counseling.* Belmont, CA: Brooks/Cole Cengage Learning.

Shoffer, M. (2006). Career counseling: Theoretical perspectives. In D. Capuzzi & M. Stauffer (Eds.), *Career counseling: Foundations, perspectives and applications* (pp. 40–68). United States: Pearson Education, Inc.

Strong, E. K., Jr., Donnay, D. A. C., Morris, M. L., Schaubhut, N. A., & Thompson, R. C. (2004). *Strong Interest Inventory®, Revised Edition.* Mountain View, CA: Consulting Psychologists Press, Inc.

Sue, D. W., Carter, R. T., Casas, J. M., Fouad, N. A., Ivey, A. E., Jensen, M., LaFromboise, T., Manese, J. E., Ponterotto, J. G., & Vazquez-Nutall, E. (1998). *Multicultural counseling competencies: Individual and organizational development.* Thousand Oaks, CA: Sage Publications, Inc.

Sue, D., & Sue, D. W. (2008). *Counseling the culturally diverse: Theory and practice* (5th ed.). Hoboken, New Jersey: John Wiley & Sons, Inc.

Super, D. E. (1990). A life span, life-space approach to career development. In D. Brown, L. Brooks, & Associates (Eds.), *Career choice and development: Applying contemporary theories to practice* (2nd ed.; pp. 197–261). San Francisco: Jossey-Bass.

Tracey, T. J. G., & Hopkins, N. (2001). Correspondence of interests and abilities with occupational choice. *Journal of Counseling Psychology, 48*(2), 178–189.

U.S. Department of Justice Civil Rights Division. (2001). *Americans with disabilities: Questions and answers.* Retrieved from http://www.ada.gov/qandaeng.htm.

Vespia, K. M., Fitzpatrick, M. E., Fouad, N. A., Kantamneni, N., & Yung-Lung, C. (2010). Multicultural career counseling: A national survey of competencies and practices. *Career Development Quarterly, 59*(1), 45–71.

Ward, C. M., & Bingham, R. P. (2001). Career assessment for African Americans. In W. B. Walsh, R. P. Bingham, M. T. Brown, & C. M. Ward (Eds.), *Career counseling for African Americans* (pp. 27–48). Mahwah, NJ: Erlbaum.

World Health Organization. (2002). *Mental health and work: Impact, issues and good practices.* Retrieved from http://www.who.int/mental_health/media/en/712.pdf.

Young, R. (1995). *An action approach to career counseling. Eric Digest, 95*(63).

Zytowski, D. G. (1985). *Kuder DD Occupational Interest Survey manual supplement.* Chicago, IL: Science Research Associates.

Zytowski, D. G. (1994). A super contribution to vocational theory: Work values. *Career Development Quarterly, 43*, 25–31.

15

COUNSELING IN CLINICAL MENTAL HEALTH AND PRIVATE PRACTICE SETTINGS

J. Kelly Coker and Savitri Dixon-Saxon[1]

Clinical mental health counseling describes those counseling services that take into account the "principles of psychotherapy, human development, learning theory, group dynamics, and the etiology of mental illness and dysfunctional behavior" (AMHCA, 2011, p. 2). The scope of practice of clinical mental health counselors ranges from prevention, intervention, consultation and treatment around problems of living to more pathological mental and emotional disorders. Mental health counselors are likely to work with diverse populations of individuals, families, and groups across the life span in clinics, private practice, non-profit agencies, group homes, schools, colleges and universities, and the workplace (AMHCA, 2011). Clients may deal with issues of a more severe nature requiring longer term counseling as well. Likewise, counselors in private practice may specialize in specific problems such as depression, anxiety, phobias, substance abuse, post-traumatic stress disorder (PTSD), eating disorders, or a particular population such as children with attention deficit disorder or gay, lesbian, bisexual, transgendered individuals.

Many counselors in training begin thinking about the setting in which they will work; particularly towards the end of their educational journey. Almost as important as the decision about the population of focus, theoretical orientation, and general counseling approach is the decision about where to practice, or the professional setting. Counseling has a rich history and counselors have worn multiple hats and worked within multiple environments. The purpose of this chapter is to explore the settings in which counselors work. Community based settings, for profit and non-profit settings, and inpatient settings and hospitals all represent locations where clinical mental health counseling takes place. The development of professional associations, standards of practice, and accreditation standards will also be discussed as well as the importance of cultural competence and advocacy in clinical mental health practice. Finally, future trends and new settings in which counseling takes place will be explored.

Foundations

Just as the practice of counseling has experienced an evolution; from vocational guidance to intensive psychotherapy to clinical mental health; so, too have the settings in which counseling takes place evolved. In the early 1900s pioneers like Beers, Parsons, and Davis were examining both the practice of counseling and the settings for counseling. Jesse B. Davis set up a systemized guidance program in public schools. Clifford Beers was a strong advocate for mental health reform and better facilities for working with the mentally ill. Frank Parson founded the Boston Vocational Bureau to aid adolescents and young adults in making career decisions (Gladding, 2007). Other factors that influenced the evolution of different settings in which counseling took place in the early part of the 20th century included the development of professional associations, the emergence of new theories of psychotherapy, and key legislation related to mental health counseling services.

The American Personnel and Guidance Association (APGA) was developed in the 1950s. Around the same time, Division 17 of the American Psychological Association to support counseling psychology as a practice was also established (Gladding, 2007). The continued involvement of mental health professionals in these two associations continued into the 1960s and 1970s. The 1970s also saw the development of the American Mental Health Counseling Association (AMHCA).

AMHCA was formed as an independent organization in 1976 when a group of practicing counselors recognized that there were a large number of masters or doctoral level counselors providing mental health services in private practice and mental health agencies similar to the services provided by psychologists, psychiatrists, and social workers. This was a notable departure from the activities endorsed by the larger group of professional counselors the American Personnel and Guidance Association, the precursor to the American Counseling Association (ACA), that was predominated by school and career counselors at the time (Colangelo, 2009). As members of the APGA, this collective group of agency counselors appealed to the organization in 1976 in hopes of becoming a division of APGA. Their attempt, however, was unsuccessful and resulted in the formation of AMHCA as an independent organization. In July of 1978, AMHCA became a division of APGA, but in 1998 it became a separate organization that retains its status as a division of ACA (AMHCA, 2011). Today the relationship between AMHCA and ACA is marked by independence and collaboration (Colangelo, 2009). AMHCA has advanced the practice of clinical mental health counseling by providing a definition of clinical mental health counseling; setting the standards for education, training, practice, and ethics; creating a credentialing system; and disseminating research and professional best practices in a professional journal (AMHCA, 2011).

During the 1960s and 1970s, as counselors began to look for professional opportunities in addition to the traditionally held positions in educational and career settings, they moved into various settings within the community. Initially, community counseling focused on the needs of individuals who were essentially healthy, but struggling with normal conflicts, uncertainties, or developmental transitions. Following the Community Mental Health Centers Act of 1963, counselors were employed to provide service to clients who had previously been hospitalized for various mental disorders. The last three decades of the twentieth century brought rapid and remarkable change to the practice of community mental health counseling (Browers, 2005). Carl Rogers, Albert Ellis, Frederick Perls, and Anna Freud are just a few of the names associated with new developments in theory in the early decades of the 1990s. New focuses on shorter-term therapy to address client issues took the place of traditional psychoanalysis, opening the door for a diversification of the settings in which counseling took place.

Today, professional clinical mental health counselors respond to clients facing a more complex world, a pluralistic society, changing views on families, and a shifting economic structure. Counselors work with a variety of people from diverse backgrounds. Counselors work as advocates and agents of social change. This chapter will discuss the wide variety of settings in which counselors work.

Professional mental health counselors hold master's degrees and may pursue a variety of professional credentials. In 50 states, counselors must have a license regulated by the state in order to be in private practice and to qualify for third-party payments. Many states are now requiring that counselors graduate from either a CACREP-accredited program or a program whose curriculum aligns with CACREP 2009 standards. Licensed professional counselors are sometimes called upon to testify in court, may receive contracts to conduct assessments and evaluations, provide consulting services in the schools, and consult with other mental health care professionals. Depending on areas of specialty, they may also be referral sources for physicians, other health care professionals, and managed health care systems. This chapter will provide an overview of the training required for clinical mental health counselors to work in different settings; the different settings in which clinical mental health counselor work including non-profit and for-profit environment; the professional identity of the practicing clinical mental health counselor; and other professional practice considerations including licensure, ethics, and new trends in counseling.

The training of counselors to serve a multitude of client issues has also gone through its own evolution. From the early days of counselor training, there has been a focus on needed competencies and outcomes (Hensley, Smith, and Thompson, 2003). The Council for the Accreditation of Counseling and Related Educational Programs (CACREP) was established in 1981 through partnership with the American Personnel and Guidance Association (APGA). CACREP was developed to provide national standards for counselor training. These standards have been revised several times through the years, and represent the accepted standard for counselor training. CACREP evaluates counselor education programs at the master's level in the areas of school counseling, mental health counseling, career counseling, addiction counseling, and marriage and family counseling. It also accredits doctoral-level programs in counselor education and supervision.

Although a voluntary process, the numbers of accredited counselor preparation programs are continuing to increase. As of February 2012 there were 601 individual programs accredited by CACREP for all categories (CACREP, 2009). In addition, there is a trend towards more private for profit programs and/or online counseling programs. Faculty and administrators recognize that CACREP accreditation is respected as a standard of excellence. In a study conducted by Adams (2005), students who graduate from CACREP programs scored higher on the *National Counselors Exam* (NCE) than those students who did not graduate from a CACREP accredited program.

In their most recent revision of standards, CACREP is putting additional emphasis on a program's ability to assess student learning outcomes (SLOs) and to demonstrate a systematic developmental assessment of all student progress (Urofsky, 2010). This change is noteworthy as it brings in to focus the importance of preparing all counselors in training to be able to demonstrate needed proficiencies throughout their time in the program to ensure their preparation for working with clients. Further, CACREP 2009 standards identify key areas of competence related to preparing professional counselors to work in different clinical settings.

Counseling, Prevention, and Intervention

Counseling professionals working in a variety of practice settings must be prepared to provide both intervention strategies for a wide range of identified issues and prevention strategies to guard against further development of identified issues. One distinction between counselors and other mental health professionals is that professional counselors focus more on prevention and wellness and less on pathology and diagnosis (Mellin,

Hunt, & Nichols, 2011). While it is important for professional counselors to be prepared to diagnose clients, develop treatment plans and intervention strategies, and identify observable and achievable goals for counseling, CACREP and counselor training programs tend to emphasize an orientation to wellness and prevention in the development of desired counseling goals (CACREP, 2009). Counselors working in private practice, clinical mental health, and other community-based settings rely more on strategies of collaboration, consultation, advocacy, empowerment, and prevention to assist clients (Mellin et al., 2011). Even with this focus, counselors must be prepared to work within the confines of the managed care system and clinical mental health agencies and be able to provide comprehensive assessment, diagnoses, and treatment strategies. Counselors' ability to provide prevention, intervention, and advocacy services to clients who might experience barriers is central to the role.

Assessment and Diagnosis

CACREP accredited programs preparing clinical mental health counselors must also demonstrate a focus on assessment and diagnosis as part of the curricular experiences of counseling students (CACREP, 2009). Some research suggests that confidence in counselors' ability to engage in assessment and diagnoses by clients and center directors is lacking (Fall et al., 2005; Ritchie, Partin, & Trivette,1998). Fall et al. conducted a study of perceptions of African American perceptions of mental health professionals. Fall and his colleagues found that perceptions of competency to address more complex (Axis II diagnosis) client issues was lower for masters-level Licensed Professional Counselors (LPC) than for their doctoral-level counterparts. Both doctoral-level and masters-level LPCs were generally ranked as lower in confidence when it came to addressing more severe clinical situations than either psychologists or psychiatrists.

Ritchie et al. examined agency director perceptions of licensed professional counselors in a 1998 study. Results of this survey of 203 mental health center directors showed that the ability to diagnose clients was ranked as the second-lowest observed skill among LPCs in their agencies. While this is an older study, it does highlight the ongoing need to ensure that professional counselors are adequately trained in assessment and diagnosis. The 2009 CACREP standards include more standards related to diagnosis and assessment for clinical mental health counselors, and more states are requiring this expertise for state licensure. Chapter 12 of this book focuses specifically on the process of diagnoses in the clinical mental health counseling field. Since a thorough discussion of concepts related to the counselor's role in diagnosis and treatment planning is addressed in chapter 12, a similar discussion is not repeated here.

SIDEBAR 15.1 CACREP Standards of Assessment and Diagnosis

Self-Reflection: As you examine your own masters counseling program's curriculum how well do you feel you and your peer are being prepared to provide accurate assessments of client concerns and diagnoses of mental disorders? How confident do you feel at this point in your training in your own ability to diagnose clients?

Research and Evaluation

In this era of managed care, there is increased emphasis on the ability of professional counselors to effectively evaluate their programs and services (Astramovich and Coker, 2007). Mental health counselors have not always identified program evaluation as a central and necessary skill in their work. This may be related to factors such as a lack of training, lack of resources to support this activity, and a lack of interest among counselors for conducting program evaluations (Whiston, 1996). A new focus on the ability to research and evaluate effective counseling strategies and interventions, however, is a central area of emphasis in the 2009 standards. This is in stark contrast to the emphasis placed on these skills in the CACREP 2001 standards for mental health counseling programs. The CACREP 2001 standards identified only one standard that had some relationship to research and evaluation of services and programs, compared to two entire sections of the clinical mental health counseling program standards in the 2009 standards (CACREP, 2001; 2009). According to Astramovich and Coker (2007), strong preparation in the ability to conduct assessments and program evaluations is central to the development of mental health counselor identity, the ability to demonstrate required outcomes to managed care entities and other stakeholders, and the need to provide empirically-based services to clients.

Diversity and Advocacy

The 2009 CACREP standards outline an infusion of advocacy for removing institutional and social barriers that impede access for clients throughout all curriculum standards. In addition, common core curricular experiences related to studies of social and cultural diversity must be included in CACREP accredited training programs. Specific training for clinical mental health counselors must also include knowledge and skills related to an understanding of the impact of discrimination, racism, sexism, and oppression on clients (CACREP, 2009).

In addition to the 2009 CACREP standards related to cultural competence and advocacy, the Association for Multicultural Counseling and Development (AMCD) developed multicultural competencies to guide professional counselors' work with diverse populations that were fully endorsed by the American Counseling Association in 2003 (Cartwright, Daniels, & Zhang, 2008). Counselors working in different clinical settings encounter clients from all racial, ethnic, religious, socio-economic, and sexual orientation backgrounds. Counselors' ability to provide prevention, intervention, diagnosis and assessment, and advocacy services to clients who might experience barriers is central to the role of professional counselors. A counselor's cultural competence has a direct impact on their work with diverse populations; particularly while serving as advocates and agents of social change. For this reason, more focus on this area of mental health counseling practice is provided below.

Cultural Competence, Advocacy, and Social Change

At this point, many school and work environments in the United States have had included some kind of diversity or cultural awareness training. However, for those who have had the opportunity to witness the evolution of diversity and cultural awareness activities over the last twenty to thirty years, one of the most notable aspects has been the move from awareness and appreciation to action. Like many other professions, the impetus for the counseling profession is no longer awareness, but cultural competence, advocacy, and social change that result in social justice. This new paradigm for cultural competence recognizes the importance of counselor self-awareness; counselor acceptance of the individual client, family or group as the authority; the counselor's recognition of the hierarchy of power and privilege; the counselor's awareness of his or her limitations in working with particular client groups; as well as the counselor's intentional efforts to gain competence in those areas. However, developing cultural competence and advocacy skills are processes that require an identifiable set of skills and behaviors. Cultural competence is a necessary to engage in advocacy and social change results from advocacy that employs specific strategies.

Cultural Competence

At this point, in the counseling profession, there is recognition that cultural competence is much more than being aware of other cultures. Cultural competence involves being self-aware enough to understand your own biases and cultural orientation; recognizing another person's cultural and values orientation as valid; and being able to employ the individual's cultural orientation as a resource for supporting and fostering healthy development and decision-making. The process of becoming culturally competent also involves understanding that the experience of an oppressed or marginalized individual is often the result of systematic and systemic inequalities for other people who are members of those groups.

In addition, cultural competence in the counseling profession is rooted in the understanding that much of the training counselors receive has a Eurocentric orientation, and the recognition that there are hierarchies of power and privilege that impact the way different groups of individuals experience the world. One such example of this hierarchy is white privilege in society. In 1988, Peggy McIntosh introduced a now classic work, describing the hierarchy associated with white privilege. White privilege describes the unearned privileges many European-Americans experience that result from being identified as White (Mindrup, Spray, & Lamberghini-West, 2011).

In 1992, Sue, Arredondo, and McDavis (Arredondo, 1999) presented a framework for multicultural competencies that focused on the counselor self-awareness; counselor's understanding of the worldview of others; and the counselor's ability to develop the culturally and contextually appropriate intervention strategies and techniques. Each of these areas were evaluated according to three dimensions: (a) beliefs and attitudes; (b) knowledge; and (c) skills (Arredondo, 1999).

It is a professional expectation that individual counselors commit to a life of developing cultural competence. Sections A and C of the American Counseling Association's Code of Ethics describe ethical practice of counselors related to cultural competence. The ACA code indicates that counselors should (a) communicate in ways that are culturally appropriate and in a language clients understand; (b) consider clients' cultural orientation towards informed consent; (c) recognize the role of family and support resources that may contribute to healthy development and progress for clients; (d) understand the limits of their ability to support clients and be able to identify culturally and contextually relevant support for clients; (e) understand that there is a history of cultural bias in diagnosis and treatment of groups; (f) identify treatments and assessments that are consider culture and context (American Counseling Association, 2005). Sections I of the AMHCA code of ethics also provide guidelines for ethical practice related to counselor competence (AMHCA, 2010). Chapter 3 of this book provides specific information related to cross cultural counseling, working with cultural competence, and working with diverse populations. The role of advocate is one that clinical mental health counselors also need to be aware of in their work with underrepresented and marginalized groups.

Advocacy

Counselors, because of their knowledge and skills, are able to advocate on behalf of individuals and groups to activate social change and consequently social justice. Advocacy requires counselors to be able to employ their knowledge and expertise in efforts to provide leadership, collaboration, and action to change systems and processes that limit access and opportunity for individual and groups of individuals. The goals of counselor advocacy are to empower clients and foster change that fulfills a client's needs (Toporek, Lewis, & Cretha, 2009).

The counseling profession's history of advocacy dates back to the days of Clifford Beers and Frank Parsons and in contemporary times, the American Counseling Association has supported the multicultural competence, advocacy, and social change agenda of counselors through the formation of the divisions the Association of Multicultural Counseling and Development; the Association of Lesbian, Gay, Bisexual, and Transgender Issues in Counseling; and Counselors for Social Justice. Each division has a mission of advocating for marginalized and underrepresented groups and disseminating training, research, and resources to counselors to create a better trained body of counselors equipped to effect social change (American Counseling Association, 2012). In addition, both the ACA and AMHCA codes of ethics offer principle or ethical guidelines for advocacy (American Counseling Association, 2005; American Mental Health Counselors Association, 2010).

Advocacy competence refers to an individual's ability to use his or her expertise and knowledge to effectively and ethically advocate (Toporek et al., 2009). Advocacy counseling involves the strategies counselors use to understand their client's lived experience in context in ways that are reflective of empathy, client empowerment, and social action (Green, McCollum, & Hays, 2008). In 2003, a set of advocacy competencies was adopted by the American Counseling Association (Toporek et al., 2009). Advocacy counselors (1) identify the impact of socio-political and economic systems on the identity development of individuals; (2) are self-aware and understand their personal identity and professional competence in intervening on behalf of their clients; and (3) are culturally competent and able to identify the culturally and contextually relevant advocacy strategies. (Toporek et al., 2009).

Social Change

The goal of advocacy is to effect social change in an effort to accomplish social justice for marginalized and oppressed groups in society. Social change is multidimensional and involves collaborating with clients in ways that empower clients to navigate and manipulate systems for their own welfare. The resulting change that takes place because of that advocacy results in greater access and opportunity for those clients and their communities (Toporek, Lewis, & Cretha, 2009). At the core of developing as an advocacy counselor who is able to contribute to social justice is counselor competence; the use of research and knowledge of resources to inform advocacy; the ability to recognize clients as the authorities in their own lives; and the ability to communicate the need for change and make recommend change to stakeholders and decision-makers.

The Need for Community-Based Mental Health Counseling

Professional mental health counselors face greater demands and have been challenged with more opportunities for practice in today's market. As more acute inpatient adult psychiatric facilities are closing, community-based mental health care providers are striving to serve the priorities of a broader client population who present with clinical issues of a more severe nature than a generation ago. While some agencies are responding to increasing budget demands and a reduction in crucial programs and services, community needs are not diminishing and it is clear that the necessity for competent and accessible mental health counseling services will continue to grow (Browers, 2005). In 2002, President George W. Bush appointed the New Freedom Commission on Mental Health to examine the services provided to people who were mentally ill in an effort to increase the quality of life of those people and to increase their opportunities to live and work in society. The president identified three barriers to that goal: (a) the stigma associated with mental illness; (b) people's lack of financial resources to pay for mental health services; and (c) fragmented delivery of mental health services. In 2003 the commission reported that there was a lack of services for children, the elderly, and seriously mentally ill. It also revealed that there was high unemployment for those with mental illness. The commission confirmed that many who suffer from mental health problems have unmet needs. While frequently referred to as mental health reform, the commission indicated that they were recommending transformation for mental health. Some hallmarks of the commission's report was a recommendation that mental health providers were better trained and specifically trained in culturally competent practice; that client or consumer treatment plans were evidence-based; that people in rural communities got better service; that more attention was paid to suicide risks in men, and that children receive better services in their communities as opposed to residential facilities. (Substance Abuse and Mental Health Services Administration, 2009). The commission maintained that no community is untouched by this mental illness, young or old, socioeconomic status, race, disability or sexual orientation (President's New Freedom Commission on Mental Health, 2003). Later in this chapter, you will learn about one of the most important aspects of the recommendations by the President's New Freedom commission. It was a recommendation that Medicaid funds be used to pay for community-based alternative treatments for children (Substance Abuse and Mental Health Services Administration, 2009).

The challenges are found in schools, homes, and the workplace. In a given year, according to the National Institute of Mental Health (NIMH, 2008) about 1 in 4 adults or 26.2% of the adult population suffer from a diagnosable mental disorder. Of those individuals, about 6% or 17 million people suffer from what is considered a serious mental illness. Statistics for children and adolescents (4–17 years) vary depending on age and gender. As reported by parent(s), from 2001 to 2004 the overall rate of emotional and behavioral difficulties rose from 5.1% to 5.4%. The percentage for males decreased from 6.2% to 5.8%, while females increased from 4.1% to 4.8%. Some differences were also evident when race was considered. Parents who identified as Hispanic reported the lowest incidences at 3.3% while both Blacks and Whites reported 6%. Family structure also appears to impact emotional and behavioral disturbances among children and

---

SIDEBAR 15.2 NIMH Statistics

Only about 14% of adults in the US seek out some kind of mental health services, but over 46% of adults will experience some kind of diagnosable mental disorder in their lifetime (NIMH, 2008). Reflect on these statistics and discuss with your peers possible reasons for this discrepancy.

---

adolescents. Statistics from 2004 indicate minors with two parents had an incidence rate of 4.4 % while children/adolescents with no parents had a rate around 9.4% (NIMH, 2008). Interestingly, only 14.4% of adults in the United States sought some kind of mental health treatment in 2008, even though about 46% of adults experience a diagnosable mental disorder across their lifetime. About 37% of adults with a diagnosable mental disorder sought some kind of treatment, and approximately half of the population of children and adolescents with a diagnosable mental disorder received some kind of treatment (NIMH, 2008).

For adults seeking mental health treatment, 40.5% of them do so in outpatient settings (NIMH, 2008). This means that for mental health counselors, providing opportunities for clients to access needed services in different communities is key.

Mental Health Counseling in Community Settings

The communities in which we live provide the most direct opportunities for services we seek. Our local grocer, hairdresser, and dentist are accessible and provide direct and needed services. Similarly, the services related to mental health treatment that are provided in communities provide direct and needed services for the families, couples, individuals, and children suffering from some kind of mental disorder. Counselors who work in community agencies gain experience working with very diverse client populations who present with problems from moderate to severe, and often enjoy the variety

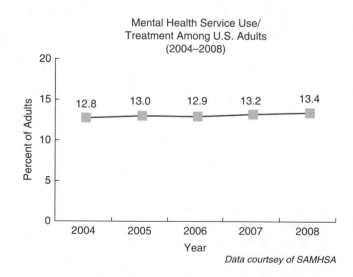

Figure 15.1 Percentage of adults seeking mental health service in the US (2004–2008)

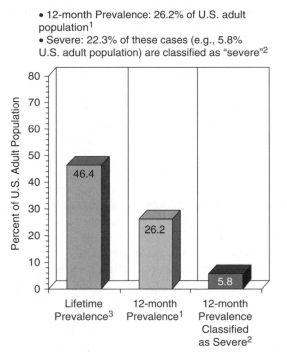

Figure 15.2 Prevalence of mental disorder

afforded them in such a setting. Because there are a significant number of clients with acute needs, counselors working in community agencies must be competent in diagnosis and treatment planning and must be knowledgeable about psychotropic medications (Nugent, 2000). The work is demanding, fast-paced, and challenging.

Most communities have a municipally funded mental health care facility. These agencies (whether broad-based or narrowly focused) may collaborate with a community system of care, may serve as referral sources, or may function completely independently of other programs within the community. The agency, by virtue of its location, its affiliation, or its source of funding, may serve particular population or community needs (e.g., county funded court diversion programs, county youth services, or a community halfway house). Counselors who have a specialty, or want to increase their experience in a specific area of practice, may work in one of these programs or agencies.

Non-Profit Agencies

Non-profit agencies do not have a goal to make a profit, but instead have as a goal to further a specific mission or purpose. Non-profit agencies generally receive their funding from local, state, or federal governments, individual contributors, corporate foundations, or endowments. The distinction is sometimes made between public and private non-profit organizations. Public non-profits are usually funded by local, state, or federal governments. A private non-profit is an organization that is incorporated under State law and whose purpose is not to make a profit, but rather to further a charitable, civic, religious, scientific, or other lawful purpose (NC Dept. of Health and Human Services, n.d.). Whether public or private, non-profit programs often function more independently and more autonomously, and, therefore, are sometimes not bound by institutional policies and restrictions. The number of non-profits continues to increase and, consequently, communities increasingly rely on non-profit organizations to provide much needed services to their citizens (Smith, 2010).

The current economic climate has resulted in fewer local government resources to serve citizens and has increased the need for services that non-profit agencies provide. However, while the federal government has committed more funds to non-profit agencies (Smith, 2010), the increased competition for available resources means that these organizations are experiencing strain on their financial resources (Kahnweiler, 2011). The current financial climate requires non-profit organizations to increase their level of accountability by evaluating their resources and demonstrating a need for their services. This is done through demonstration of the effectiveness of their services; evaluation of their financial model and identification of new funding sources (Katz, 2012). Non-profit entities also employ management strategies that not only serve the organization mission, but create efficiency and reduce waste and redundancy in organizations. Government funded or sponsored services tend to be multipurpose and available to the general public.

Even with the prevalence of a major publicly supported community mental health care center in most communities, mental health care services are found in many different programs scattered throughout the community and are not necessarily coordinated in the most efficient manner. These agencies are often work-driven and rely heavily on the volunteer human resources (Kahnweiler, 2011). Counselors in non-profit agencies often struggle for clear definition between the roles of trained professional counselors and the volunteers and professional counselors in public-non-profit agencies usually have salaries much lower than counselors in other environments. Those seeking services are likely to find different requirements for eligibility depending on their particular need, a diagnosis, their ability to pay, or limitations associated with insurance or managed care companies. Accessing counseling services can be a complicated and frustrating process at a time when the individual may have a diminished capacity to navigate the maze.

In spite of the obvious challenges to be overcome, there are some clear advantages to utilizing a community-based "system" of mental health care. Individuals seeking counseling will find many different areas of specialization available among practitioners in the community. Not only are different clinical needs addressed, but also an array of treatment options offered, different theoretical perspectives respected, flexible delivery systems utilized, and diverse counseling environments represented. Services may be interdisciplinary, or certain specialty areas are focused on that are not available elsewhere in community settings. Community mental health care agencies and counselors usually are strong advocates for their clients. Examples of community mental health services other than centralized community mental health centers include the following:

1. Drop-in crisis centers
2. Outpatient substance abuse treatment and support programs
3. Day treatment programs for severely and persistently mentally ill individuals
4. Support services for Alzheimer's patients and their caregivers
5. Counseling services aimed toward ethnic and culturally diverse communities
6. Child and family agencies

7. Homeless shelters
8. Anger management groups

For-Profit Mental Health Care

Whereas many services are provided through nonprofit agencies, a considerable number of others are accessed by clients from mental health counselors in private, for-profit settings. Clients receiving mental health counseling services pay a fee for service, either out of pocket, or through their insurance provider. The private agency or counselor in private practice intends to make a profit, and the fee structure is usually quite different from that of nonprofit services. An advantage of private practice includes the freedom to be as broad or as narrow in the services offered, or the clients served. According to Montoya (2006), profit status of health care providers is a significant predictor of the provision of those services. For-profit mental health services tend to provide more specialized services at a cost to the client. As a result, for-profit mental health providers often find themselves serving a narrower margin of the population for a specified issue.

Private Agencies

Services provided by professional counselors in private agencies range from individual, group, marital, or family counseling, to programs offered through contractual arrangements for other private companies, or occasionally, public institutions (Male, 1990). Types of services likely to be offered in for-profit settings include employee assistance programs (EAP), substance abuse treatment services, and general mental health services. Forensic evaluations are also often provided in private for-profit settings.

Probably the most common type of private for-profit service offered to clients outside of private practice is in the area of substance abuse treatment. For-profit and private substance abuse treatment services can occur in in-patient treatment facilities, therapeutic communities (TCs), and outpatient settings. The effectiveness of different kinds of substance abuse services (i.e., urine testing, group counseling, relapse prevention, mental health assessment, pharmacotherapy and aftercare) based on profit-status was examined by Montoya (2006). Findings indicated that profit status was not a key predictor in the number of overall services offered, but that some services were more likely to be provided by public, non-profit agencies than their for-profit counterparts. These included pharmacotherapy and case management.

For-profit mental health agencies and treatment centers, in general, cater to a narrower client base. The benefit of this is that clients with a clear diagnosis can target services designed to address that area of concern. The drawback could be that there is a lack of comprehensive services provided by for-profit mental health service providers. Another area of private mental health work that continues to be a key setting in which mental health counseling takes place is within the private practice arena.

Private Practice

Prior to the advent of insurance, third-party payment and managed care, counselors' professional lives in private practice was relatively simple (Gladding, 2007). Professional counselors in private practice may work independently, affiliate with other private practitioners to share administration and supervision services and costs, and may have part-time or full-time practices. It should be stressed that it is neither typical, nor advisable for mental health counselors to go into independent practice without significant postgraduate experience in working with a range of clients and counseling concerns. To do so without sufficient preparation is a violation of quite a few professional ethical standards, but most clearly would not meet the ACA standard (C.2.a.) that states, "Counselors practice only within the boundaries of their competence, based on their education, training, supervised experience, state and national professional credentials, and appropriate professional experience Counselors gain knowledge, personal awareness, sensitivity, and skills pertinent to working with a diverse client population" (ACA, 2005, p. 9).

In order to receive third-party payments through the managed care system and to practice independently, counselors need to have received the appropriate graduate degrees and state licensure credentials. Counselors in private practice are more successful when they establish a network of other professionals to serve as consultants, referral sources, and peer supervisors.

Depending on your point of view, mental health counselors in private practice have either maximum freedom and flexibility, or maximum limitations in their professional work. Gladding (2007) provided a brief overview of some advantages and difficulties in establishing a successful private practice. In addition to clinical proficiency, Gladding identified (a) strong business skills, (b) strong networking skills, and (c) the desire to donate services for the "public good" (p. 485). The benefits of private practice can be rewarding as well. According to Gladding, private practice provides a chance for counselors to be "specialists", provide flexibility and gain individual recognition for their quality of services. In the extreme, private practice affords the freedom of choosing to whom service will be provided, and the ability to work with those clients using whatever theoretically sound methods and interventions are considered most effective, without external influences on the format or duration of treatment. Some counselors feel when they are not dependent on third-party payment, they can be more responsive to the needs of the client, determining (with the client) how frequently to schedule appointments and the duration of the counseling process. It should be noted that mental health counselors who exercise this "maximum freedom" generally are limited to the white upper-middle class (Nugent, 2000; Nugent & Jones, 2005); although in theory, the independent counselor in private practice could offer services to the most diverse client population, depending on their range of competency and their flexibility in setting fees. Service fees should be determined judiciously and within the scope of the ACA *Code of Ethics* (2005). A fundamental area of focus in private practice work is being able to effectively manage a business. Making a private practice work ethically, legally, and profitably is central to its success. Counselor training programs lack a focus on preparing future counselors for working in this setting, as it requires knowledge of business. According to Zuckerman (2008), there is a need for both novice counselors and seasoned counselors in private practice to develop good professional habits around organization, paperwork, legal and ethical considerations, working with managed care, and effective procedures of practice. A thorough understanding and implementation of the Health Insurance Protability and Accountability Act (HIPAA), for example, is central to the private practitioner. As HIPAA offers no specific suggestions for language in explaining patient rights, it is up to the individual practitioner to tailor her or his communication to clients in ways that are HIPAA compliant but also fit their specific setting and practice.

Successful mental health counselors in private practice are more likely to be financially successful if they are eligible for third-party reimbursement (i.e., insurance payments) and are recognized as core providers by managed health care systems. There are identified advantages and disadvantages to working within this system for counseling private practitioners. Many counselors in private practice view the establishment of managed care for mental health diagnoses as an intrusion on the therapeutic process. Others may see the managed care system as a necessary part of the overall delivery of mental health services to best reach a wide range of clients (Patrick, 2007). Whatever the view, counselors can largely agree that working within a system of managed care means providing empirically-validated and shorter-term treatment to clients. For example, cognitive behavioral therapy is an accepted treatment modality by most managed care providers for treating a wide range of commonly-occurring diagnoses including depression and anxiety (Patrick, 2007). As private practitioners who choose to make managed care a part of their practice, mental health counselors must understand the process of obtaining professional licensure and professional liability insurance, ensuring their practice is HIPPA compliant, and going through the process of applying to be on various insurance panels as a recognized provider.

Counselors in private practice generally serve a wide range of client issues and concerns, but counselors in private practice may also specialize in one area or another. Professional mental health counselors who are trained in group counseling techniques may provide effective services and increase their income by offering counseling groups. In addition to a general practice, counseling specialties may include the following:

1. Marital and family counseling
2. Child and adolescent counseling
3. Treatment of eating disorders
4. Lesbian, gay, bisexual and transgendered clients
5. Gerontological counseling
6. Addictions and substance abuse counseling
7. Divorce mediation

Final Thoughts on Private Practice

The entrepreneurial opportunities afforded counselors who have a private practice are considerable. Counselors who work independently can create a practice that utilizes their own professional and personal strengths, allows them to respond to individuals and counseling and clinical issues which most interest them, and removes many of the restrictions associated with being part of a system of care.

Counselors working in private practice must be creative, energetic, and comfortable with risk taking. The ability to understand basic business practices, marketing, legal and ethical practice considerations, and effective written and oral communication are also keys to success. Because a private practice is a business, the mental health counselor in independent practice must be able to attend to the development and operating needs of the practice. In most cases, this means handling those responsibilities himself or herself. Like any other business, managing a private counseling practice means arranging for and maintaining office space, paying bills, and hiring and supervising any employees. Counselors promote their services, communicate with referral sources, consult with other professionals, and navigate the maze of insurance and managed health care systems.

Some responsibilities idiosyncratic to the counseling profession are maintaining client records, remaining current in therapeutic practice developments, and keeping abreast of frequently changing licensing, insurance, and tax regulations that affect the counselor and the client.

Professional mental health counselors who succeed in private practice enjoy the opportunity to be independent, find the tasks exciting, and especially enjoy the incredible variety that comes with the territory (Browers, 2005; Gladding, 2007).

SIDEBAR 15.3 Private Practice

Case Study: Jane is a recent graduate of a CACREP-accredited clinical mental health counseling program. She has been working at a community mental health agency under supervision to obtain her license. As she nears her license completion, she is considering starting her own private practice so she can specialize in working with children and adolescents. What specific steps does Jane need to take in embarking on this professional move? Is this a realistic endeavor for Jane? Why or why not?

Hospitals and Health Care Facilities

Although not strictly defined as community-based mental health care, community hospitals and other comprehensive health care facilities may operate as for-profit or as nonprofit, and may be private or public. They certainly interface with mental health services in the community and should be considered as a viable service under the community umbrella.

While the majority of the services are provided inpatient, some are provided on site or in communities. In either case, hospitals and health care facilities are a major component of most community health care systems—medical and psychological. Opportunities for counselors may be found in general hospitals, psychiatric facilities, Veteran's Administration facilities, rehabilitation centers and substance abuse treatment programs.

Residential treatment facilities/hospitals serve a variety of conditions and populations. Adult inpatient treatment can be acute (1–5 days) or specialized programs such as drug and alcohol rehabilitation. Specialized programs consist of more long-term treatment; often several weeks. Child and adolescent residential treatment consist of a variety of different services that include, but are not limited to, psychiatric residential treatment and group homes.

While some hospitals may not include any counseling programs, usually called behavioral medicine in hospital settings, many provide preventative and maintenance programs. Traditionally, medical care facilities relied on clinical psychologists, social workers, psychiatric nurses, and occupational therapists to address counseling and psychological needs of the patients in hospitals (Browers, 2005). In the past twenty or thirty years, hospitals and related health care facilities have expanded to include services to clients whose medical conditions may be complicated by psychological conditions, or conversely, whose medical diagnosis may cause or contribute to emotional problems. As a result, many mental health counselors are now finding employment in hospitals and medical settings where they collaborate with health care professionals to provide comprehensive treatment which includes counseling.

Counselors in hospital and health care settings focus on crisis work, preventative counseling, remediation, or supportive counseling with *patients* or clients (outside of medical settings, it is not considered appropriate to refer to clients as patients). Many health care facilities provide services to patients oriented toward wellness, especially for patients with cardiac disease, diabetes, injuries, and those who have had strokes. Counselors can effectively assist clients in identifying and changing behaviors or patterns of thinking, which may have complicated their medical concerns, and can contribute to their recovery. Additionally, counselors may assist clients in addressing the emotional issues of fear, anxiety, anger, or depression that often accompany or resulted from a medical diagnosis. This is especially relevant with older adults and the comorbidity of a physical ailment and psychological distress.

Other wellness and prevention programs found in hospitals, and employing mental health care counselors, are often available to patients in the hospital and open to the community as well. Those include programs and education focused on smoking cessation, nutrition, exercise, stress reduction, pain management, and sleep disorders.

SIDEBAR 15.4 Counselor Wellness

Just as counselors assist clients in obtaining optimal wellness, so too do they need to attend to their own wellbeing. Wellness is essentially a measure of a person's emotional, spiritual, physical, social, and professional health. Counselor burnout is one indication that a counselor is not well in at least one of these area, and this often results in clients not receiving the best services from their counselors (Lawson & Myers, 2011). Burnout can be the result of a number of things like over-taxed caseloads, ineffective or insufficient supervision, limited agency resources, lack of balance in personal and professional life, and compassion fatigue or vicarious trauma (Lee, Cho, Kissinger, & Ogle, 2010). What strategies can use you to prevent your burnout as a professional clinical mental health counselor?

Counselors have long been part of the medical team that provides counseling for clients or patients in treatment for alcohol and substance abuse and for eating disorders. More recently, health care facilities have begun to offer counseling and support services to patients, and their loved ones, who are critically or chronically ill, are facing or recovering from major surgery, or have a terminal illness.

Mental Health Counseling and Mental Health Counselors: A New Identity

A considerable amount of space in this chapter has been devoted to reviewing the likely settings where professional mental health counselors are providing services. Even a cursory reading of the material should make it very clear that the counseling profession has been in an evolutionary process and that professional mental health counselors have an important role in a cluster of disciplines that make up the professional community of mental health care providers. While the profession has been evolving, there have been profound changes in government policies and a restructuring of comprehensive health care delivery systems (including mental health care). Those changes make it clear that mental health counseling, while necessary and important, must be provided in ways that are compatible with current systems and structures. Current revisions in public policy influence the nature of the work of counselors, the client populations served, the counseling needs that can be addressed, and the settings where they work (Browers, 2005).

As a relatively young and dynamic profession clinical mental health counseling continues to evolve and be refined to accurately reflect the needs of the mental health community and the clients being served. As members of a profession, clinical mental health counselors should operate out of a common understanding of how counseling and the roles and responsibilities of counselors are defined.

Personal Counselor Identity

The professional clinical mental health counselor's identity is rooted in his or her continuous development as counselor across the life-span of the individual's professional career. This professional identity should evolve over time and become more informed as the counselor gains more clinical experience; gains more insight into the needs of his or her client population; gains more insight into his or her strengths and opportunities for development; and understands what he or she has to offer to the profession of counseling. There are several activities that allow a counselor to develop these understandings like regular supervision throughout training and professional work; and continuing education activities like courses, workshops, and literature reviews; professional service in state, regional, and national counseling organizations; certification and licensure activities. These are the activities that allow the counselor to develop competence and to stay current with best practices in the counseling profession; but most importantly, these are the activities that allow the counselor to provide effectiveness services to his or client population (Lawson & Myers, 2011).

Licensing and Certification for Mental Health Counselors

Licensure is a state regulated process, created by statute, and regulates the activities of the professional and occupational activities of the holder of the license. At the time of this writing, 50 states and the District of Columbia have licensing laws for professional counselors. Unfortunately, there is currently very little consistency in the licensing laws across the nation that regulate counseling. At least thirty-nine states and the District of Columbia have *practice acts or practice and title acts,* an act that does not permit one to practice as a counselor without holding a license. Several states have a *title act,* protecting only the title, and allowing anyone to practice counseling, as long as he or she does not represent themselves as licensed. For obvious reasons, a practice act is preferable; it assures a more professional community of mental health counselors and is a clearer designation for the community to understand. Although a license is not a guarantee of third-party reimbursement, it is highly unlikely that an unlicensed counselor would qualify for payment. In 1994, Glosoff and her colleagues made the case for conformity of state licensure laws through their discussion of model legislation for licensed professional counselors, the "1994 model" which incorporated standards of practice by the American Counseling Association, CACREP, the Council on Rehabilitation Education (CORE), and NBCC (Glosoff, Benshoff, Hosie & Maki, 1994). This effort was designed to create consistent licensure standards across the country by creating the possibility of licensure portability and state reciprocity. This work was preceded by Bloom and colleagues, who proposed the 1989 model legislation bill (Bloom, Gerstein, Tarvydas, Consaster, David,

Kater, Sherrard, & Esposito (1990). While both of these efforts identified best practices for licensed professional counselors, these efforts have yet to result in clear continuity of state licensure requirements for professional counselors.

Certification is a rather generic term or designation, potentially referring to a status granted by a state, an agency, a professional organization, or a professional board. Counselors can earn a variety of certifications, including designations that attest to their knowledge in areas of specialized practice. The most common and easily recognized certification in the counseling profession is available from the National Board for Certified Counselors (NBCC). Nationally certified counselors (NCCs) have earned masters or doctorate degrees that meet the academic requirements and have satisfied the experiential and supervision requirements designated by NBCC. Those seeking certification in a specialty area from NBCC may pursue a credential in the areas of mental health counseling, school counseling, career counseling, substance abuse counseling, and supervision.

One might ask, "Why seek a license and certification?" There are several good reasons. Like those who graduate from CACREP programs, nationally certified counselors experience some advantages should they seek a counselor's license in more than one state during the course of a new career. Many states having licensing laws that require the National Counselor Exam (NCE), or accept the NCE as partial fulfillment of the standards for obtaining a license. Professional certification is another means of demonstrating to the public that qualified counselors practice according to the high standards established by the counseling profession.

Those in the counseling profession have experienced increasing opportunities, and not so subtle pressure, to continually upgrade their professional status by seeking standard and specialized credentials. In the field of mental health care, professional credentials help to clearly identify the niche occupied by professional mental health counselors. The maintenance of credentials ensures the public that mental health counselors are continuing to upgrade their knowledge, collaborate with other professionals, and strictly adhere to the accepted standards of the profession.

New Dimensions in Counseling

Much change still lies ahead for the counseling profession. Individuals, partners, families, and communities will continue to struggle with experiences that are part of the human condition—loss, grief, transition, conflict, and self-doubt—and counselors will continue to respond to the emotional, psychological, and psychosocial needs that arise as a result. In some cases, the changes are a reflection of shifts in society, and in other cases may be a result of those changes. Mental health counselors can expect transitions in the profession that are philosophical in nature, some that are technical, a continuing evolution of mental health care delivery systems, and optimistically, growth in the understanding of how to best use counseling skills to assist others in improving their quality of life.

Trauma and Crisis Counseling

Events such as the Virginia Tech shootings (2007), Hurricane Katrina (2005) and the terrorist attacks on September 11, 2001 have become defining moments in how professional counselors are preparing and responding to trauma and crisis. These types of tragedies entail specialized training for both direct victims and indirect victims (i.e. family, friends, emergency responders). Diagnoses such as Acute Stress Disorder

(ASD) and Post Traumatic Stress Disorder (PTSD) may result from such experiences and counselors need to be prepared and trained to assess the unique symptomology and the critical needs of those affected.

Recognizing the vital role counselors play in national emergencies, CACREP was awarded a "historic first of its kind federal contract to consider establishing guidelines and standards that will prepare counselors to work with health care providers" (CACREP, 2007b). This initiative will implement a network of counseling professionals to create those standards and guidelines within educational programs training counselors.

Home-Based Counseling

The recommendations of the President's New Freedom Commission led to changes in how children, the elderly, and seriously mentally ill were cared for in communities. The commission recommended action designed to provide these groups with services that allowed them to remain with their families. As a result there has been an increase in the services provided to clients in their homes (Jeter, 2011). Increasingly clinical mental health counselors are providing these services to clients.

There are several benefits to home-based counseling. Counselors are able to observe family dynamics like communication and problem solving and use these for developing contextually relevant therapeutic strategies. Counselors are able to observe artifacts that depict the family system. Additionally, clients, many of whom may be distrustful of counselors, are more comfortable participating in counseling in their own environment (Lawson, 2005).

While there is an increase in the numbers of clinical mental health counselors who provide these services, many report that their training programs did not prepare them for the nuances of home-based counseling. One of the biggest considerations for home-based counseling is that it is difficult for counselors to manage the home environment in a way that maintains confidentiality and limits distractions. In addition, many counselors who provide in-home services report that one of their greatest concerns is for their safety. Another challenge to home counseling is that boundaries are not as clear as they would be if sessions were conducted in an office environment. It is not uncommon for clients

---

SIDEBAR 15.5 Home-Based Counseling (Case Study)

Dwana is a counselor trainee who is completing her internship with community agency that provides services mental health services to children in their homes. While Dwana is somewhat anxious about this work environment, she assumes it must be safe, otherwise her supervisor would not have agreed to the assignment. On her third visit with her ten year-old male client, she decides to have the counseling session outside in the backyard because there are at least eight other people in the one-bedroom house who are moving about. However, shortly after starting the session, her client's uncle comes to the backyard to sit and watch the session. He is holding a brown paper bag and appears to be drinking something from it. What steps could Dwana take to manage this counseling environment? What impact is her reaction to the uncle likely to have on the client? What kinds of support should Dwana ask for in the future and from whom?

---

and their families to ask personal questions of the counselor or ask for money or other favors. In addition to having to manage interpersonal boundaries, counselors frequently find that they need to manage boundaries of professional roles. Frequently, clients will confuse a home counselor's role with those of the case managing professional. For the novice home counselor, regular supervision is paramount to developing competence. Counselors who pursue these positions should be sure that regular supervision is available and that they are practicing in the roles for which they are competent.

Children and Counseling

Home-based counseling is frequently provided to children (Lawson, 2005), but there is a shortage of counselors adequately trained to work with the large population of children who need mental health services (Mellin, 2009). Some experts assert that one of the reasons that there has been such an increase in the numbers of children who are prescribed psychotropic medications is because there are so many community based mental health professionals who are not adequately trained to work with children (Mellin, 2009).

Most training programs provide students will knowledge and skills aimed at counseling interventions for adults and many counselors do not understand how to modify their counseling micro-skills to the needs of children. Children do not communicate in the same way that adults do, but their communication can be very revealing, particularly if the counselor understands how to track the child's behavior; interpret behavior and employ visual metaphors to overcome limits in communication or resistance; and set appropriate limits or boundaries with child clients (van Velsor, 2004). Additionally, many clinical mental health counseling programs have not sufficiently focused on the use of psychotropic drugs. Clinical Mental Health Counselors interested gaining proficiency in working with children would be well served to engage in specific training activities designed to support their development as counselors for children including training and education around psychopharmacology.

Technology and Counseling

As in other professions, computers and technology figure prominently in the work of mental health counselors. In recent years, many mental health counselors have become proficient in the use of computer assisted diagnostic programs. Community agencies and managed health care systems maintain some or all of clients' records in computer files. Counselors regularly go on-line to connect with other professionals, to access their professional organizations, and to search the Internet for the most current information and resources to better serve their clients.

Web-based on-line counseling is a reality and could become an important means of providing access to mental health services. This provides greater access to rural clients, those who may be housebound or disabled, and those with particular needs not available in their own community, such as non-English speakers. Recognizing the potential risks, the ACA established guidelines within its code of ethics governing the uses and restrictions of on-line counseling. The National Board of Certified Counselors (NBCC) also developed *The Practice of Internet Counseling* that encompasses electronic mail based, chat room based, and video based services (NBCC, n.d.). The standards for both address the issues of secured sites, confidentiality and its limits, record keeping, and the counseling relationship. NBCC describes a credential for *Distance Credentialed Counselor* offered by

Center for Credentialing Education. These credential holders meet requirements and standards of practice and the NBCC code of ethics for the purposes of providing delivery of counseling services to clients via electronic means including telephone counseling, e-mail communication, and video conferencing (Center for Credentialing and Education, n.d.). Counselors providing information or engaging in counseling and counseling-related activities via the Internet should seek appropriate legal, professional, and technical consultation to be certain that they are not in violation of any state, federal, or professional regulations or statutes, and to ensure that the activities are included in their liability coverage.

Summary

The counseling profession is at a crossroads. Graduate training assures a solid preparation for entry into the field, increased credentialing options define for the public what they can expect from mental health counseling, and professional counselors have gained recognition and status as professionals in mental health care. With a bright future, it is important to not lose touch with the rich history of the profession. First and foremost, counselors care about those they serve, respecting the dignity of each human being.

In a new age, those roots will serve the profession well. The nature of advocacy is descriptive of the challenges faced by counselors in a new century. The pluralistic nature of America makes it imperative that the profession be mindful of its own biases, increase the knowledge and understanding of differing systems (especially families), and broaden counseling approaches to be more useful to more of the community. Along the same lines, the counseling profession itself would be well served to increase the diversity within its own ranks.

The concept of advocacy expands to include the responsibility of speaking on behalf of the clients we serve and those we don't, seeking services and resources for those who may otherwise fall through the cracks. As economic diversity continues to create greater disparity between the "haves and the have-nots," professionals must lend their clout to improving the conditions of their communities.

Maintaining clinical competence is a professional, ethical, and in the case of the private practice, essential responsibility in order to be successful. Conditions may sometimes conspire to make those previously listed responsibilities difficult to meet. Professional mental health counselors must take responsibility for self-care and must take measures to remedy such a situation in order to provide competent counseling for their clients.

Mental health counselors have a specific role in the larger profession of counseling. The role has evolved out of a rich history and is supported by specific academic and clinical training. Mental health counselors collaborate with other mental health care professionals and have opportunities to practice counseling in many diverse settings. Some of these settings include community agencies (public and private), hospitals and health care facilities, government sponsored programs and services, and private practice. Some counselors have private practices.

Professional counselors have available to them many different professional credentials, which helps to define for the public what counselors do and increases their professional recognition in the mental health care community. Fifty states offer some form of professional counseling license and all counselors who qualify can seek certification as a *National Certified Counselor* (NCC). Some professional counselors hold credentials in counseling specialties.

Mental health counselors have made many advances during the relatively brief history of the counseling profession. That history reflects ongoing efforts to make sure the definition of counseling accurately reflects the competencies of counseling practitioners, as well as the roles fulfilled in the mental health profession.

SIDEBAR 15.6 Where Will You Serve?

Reflect on your personal areas of strength, your community's needs and resources, and your professional and personal goals. Describe the counseling environment you are interested in working in and describe how you will prepare for that specific counseling career.

The future of mental health counseling promises exciting challenges as mental health counselors use new resources in their work, gain greater access to managed health care systems, and engage with a more diverse society. The following websites provide additional information relating to the chapter topics:

1. American Counseling Association (ACA): www.counseling.org
2. American School Counselor Association (ASCA): www.schoolcounselor.org
3. American Mental Health Counselors Association (AMHCA): www.amhca.org
4. National Board of Certified Counselors (NBCC): www.nbcc.org
5. Council for Accreditation of Counseling and Related Educational Programs (CACREP): www.cacrep.org
6. National Institute of Mental Health (NIMH): www.nimh.nih.gov
7. Substance Abuse and Mental Health Services Administration (SAMHSA): www.samhsa.gov

Note

1   The authors wish to thank Dr. Jane Rheineck for work done on the previous edition of this chapter. We have updated the content significantly, but have retained much of Dr. Rheineck's original contributions to guide the framework of this chapter.

References

American Counseling Association. (2005). *ACA code of ethics*. Alexandria, VA: ACA Author.

American Mental Health Counselors Association. (2011). Standards for the practice of clinical mental health counseling. Retrieved February 21, 2012 from http://www.amhca.org/assets/content/AMHCA_Standards_1–26–2012.pdf.

American Mental Health Counselors Association. (2010). Principles for AMHCA code of ethics. Retrieved February 21, 2012 from https://www.amhca.org/assets/news/AMHCA_Code_of_Ethics_2010_w_pagination_cxd_51110.pdf.

Arredondo, P. (1999). Multicultural counseling competencies as tools to address oppression and racism. *Journal of Counseling & Development*, 77(1), 102.

Astramovich, R. L., and Coker, J. K. (2007). Program evaluation: The accountability bridge model for counselors. *Journal of Counseling and Development, 85,* 162–172.

Bloom, J., Gernstein, L., Tarvydas, V., Conaster, J., Davis, E., Kater, D., Sherrard, P., & Esposito, R. (1990). Model legislation for licensed professional counselors. *Journal of Counseling and Development, 68,* 511–523.

Browers, R. T. (2005). Counseling in mental health and private practice setting. In D. Capuzzi, & D. R. Gross (Eds.), *Introduction to the counseling profession* (4th ed.; pp. 309–330). Boston: Allyn and Bacon.

Cartwright, B. Y., Daniels, J., & Zhang, S. (2008). Assessing multicultural competence: Perceived versus demonstrated performance. *Journal of Counseling and Development, 86,* 318–322.

CACREP Accreditation Manual of the Council for Accreditation of Counseling and Related Educational Programs 2nd ed. (2001). Retrieved February 1, Alexandria, VA: Author.

Center for Credentialing and Education. (n.d.). Distance Credentialed Counselor. Retrieved February 24, 2012 from http://www.cce-global.org/DCC.

Colangelo, J. J. (2009). The American Mental Health Counselors Association: Reflection on 30 historic years. *Journal of Counseling & Development,* 87(2), 234–240.

Council for Accreditation of Counseling and Related Programs Standards. (2009). Retrieved February 1, 2012, from http://www.cacrep.org/doc/2009.

Fall, K. A., Levitov, J. E., Anderson, L., and Clay, H. (2005). African Americans' perceptions of mental health professions. *International Journal for the Advancement of Counselling,* 27(1), 47–56.

Gladding, S. T. (2007). *Counseling: A comprehensive profession* (5th ed.). Upper Saddle River, NJ: Prentice Hall.

Glosoff, H. L., Benshoff, J. M., Hosie, T. W., & Maki, D. R., (1994). The 1994 ACA model legislation for licensed professional counselors. *Journal of Counseling and Development, 74,* 209–220.

Green, E. J., McCollum, V. C., & Hays, D. G. (2008). Teaching advocacy counseling within a social justice framework: Implications for school counselors and educators. *Journal for Social Action In Counseling & Psychology,* 1(2), 14–30.

Hensley, L. G., Smith, S. B., Thompson, R. W. (2003). Assessing competencies of counselors-in-training: Complexities in evaluating personal and professional development. *Counselor Education and Supervision, 42,* 219–230.

Jeter, A. (2011, July 17). Medicaid pulls back on mental health for kids, teens. The Virginia Pilot [On-line]. Retrieved from http://hamptonroads.com/2011/07/medicaid-pulls-back-mental-health-kids-teens.

Kahnweiler, W. M. (2011). Non-profit organizations: A primer for OD researchers and practitioners. *Organization Development Journal,* 29(4), 81–89.

Katz, I. (2012, February 12). Reality time for human service organizations. *Stanford Social Innovation Review.* Retrieved from http://www.ssireview.org/blog/entry/reality_time_for_human_service_organizations.

Lawson, G. (2005). Special considerations for supervision of the home-based counselor. *The Family Journal, 13* (4), 437–444.

Lawson, G., & Myers, H. E. (2011). Wellness, professional quality of life, and career-sustaining behaviors: What keeps you well? *Journal of Counseling and Development,* 89(2), 163–171.

Male, R. A. (1990). Careers in public and private agencies. In B. B. Collison, & N. J. Garfield (Eds.), *Careers in counseling and human development* (pp. 81–89). Alexandria, VA: American Counseling Association.

Mellin, E. A. (2009). Responding to the crisis in children's mental health: Potential roles for the counseling profession. *Journal of Counseling & Development,* 87(4), 501–506.

Mellin, E. A., Hunt, B., & Nichols, L. M. (2011). Counselor professional identity: Findings and implications for counseling and interprofessional collaboration. *Journal of Counseling and Development, 89,* 140–147.

Mindrup, R. M., Spray, B. J., & Lamberghini-West, A. (2011). White privilege and multicultural counseling competence: The influence of field of study, sex, and racial/ethnic exposure. *Journal of Ethnic & Cultural Diversity in Social Work,* 20(1), 20–38. doi:10.1080/15313204.2011.545942.

Montoya, I. D. (2006). Differences in drug treatment services based on profit status. *Journal of Psychoactive Drugs, 38*(3), 219–228.

National Board of Certified Counselors (n.d.). Retrieved February 23, 2012, from http://www. nbcc.org.

National Institute of Mental Health (2008). *National institutes of health.* Retrieved February 23, 2012, from http://www.nimh.nih.gov.

North Carolina Department of Health and Human Services (n.d.). *County Attachment K.* Retrieved March 12, 2012, from http://www.ncdhhs.gov.

Nugent, F. A. (2000). *Introduction to the profession of counseling* (3rd ed.). Upper Saddle River, NJ: Prentice Hall.

Nugent, F. A., & Jones, K. D. (2005). *Introduction to the counseling profession* (4th ed.). Upper Saddle River, NJ: Prentice Hall.

Patrick, P. K. S. (2007). *Contemporary issues in counseling.* Boston: Allyn & Bacon. President's New Freedom Commission on Mental Health. (2003). Executive Summary. Retrieved February 24, 2012 from http://store.samhsa.gov/shin/content//SMA03-3831/SMA03-3831.pdf.

Reineck, J. E. (2009). Counseling in mental health and private practice settings. In D. Capuzzi, & D. R. Gross (Eds), *Introduction to Counseling* (5th ed.; pp. 421–444). Boston: Allyn & Bacon.

Ritchie, M., Partin, R., & Trivette, P. (1998). Mental health agency directors' acceptance and perceptions of licensed professional counselors. *American Mental Health Counselors Association Journal, 20*(3), 227–237.

Smith, S. R. (2010). Nonprofit organizations and government: Implications for policy and practice. *Journal of Policy Analysis and Management, 29*(3), 621–644.

Substance Abuse and Mental Health Services Administration. (2007). Retrieved May 20, 2007, from http://www.samhsa.gov.

Substance Abuse and Mental Health Services Administration. (2009). Transforming mental health care in America. Retrieved February 18, 2012 from http://www.samhsa.gov/Federalactionagenda/ NFC_execsum.aspx.

Toporek, R. L., Lewis, J. A., & Cretha, H. C. (2009). Promoting systemic change through the ACA advocacy competencies. *Journal Of Counseling & Development, 87*(3), 260–268.

Urofsky, R. I. (Spring 2010). Critical considerations for a 2009 self-study. *CACREP Connection.*

van Velsor, P. (2004). Revisiting basic counseling skills with children. *Journal Of Counseling and Development, 82*(3), 313–318.

Whiston, S. C. (1996). Accountability through action research: Research methods for practitioners. *Journal of Counseling & Development, 74,* 616-623.

Zuckerman, E. L. (2008). *The paper office* (4th ed). New York: The Guilford Press.

16

MARRIAGE, COUPLE, AND FAMILY COUNSELING

Cass Dykeman

Many counseling theories have been applied to treating families including behavior therapy (e.g., O'Farrell & Clement, 2012), cognitive behavior therapy (e.g., Dattilio, 2010), and gestalt therapy (e.g., Meneses & Greenberg, 2011). These individual-focused theories are detailed in other chapters of this text and thus will not be addressed by me. My attention here will be on the use of *interpersonal systems* to treat couples, marriages, and families. In this chapter I will use the term "family therapy" generically for all systems-focused couples and family treatment and the term "family therapist" generically for all mental health professionals who work with couples and families. Sidebar 16.1 contains some specialized systems terms.

Duncan Stanton (1988) stated, "Non-family therapists often view family therapy as (a) a modality, that (b) usually involves the nuclear family" (p. 8). He goes on to point out the inaccuracy of this conception, explaining that family therapy is based on a point of view that emphasizes the contextual nature of psychological problems.

> More fundamentally, it (family therapy) is a way of construing human problems that dictates certain actions for their alleviation. Its conceptual and data bases differ from most other (especially individually oriented) therapies in that the interpersonal context of a problem and the interplay between this context and the symptoms are of primary interest. An index patient is seen as responding to his or her social situation; those around the patient are noted to react to this response; the patient then reacts "back," and so on, in an on-going, give and take process. Interventions designed to alter this process derive from such interactional formulations. (p. 8)

It is, of course, possible for a counselor who is oriented to the treatment of individuals to interview the members of a client's family in the course of treatment. However, this rarely occurs, since the individual orientation places the source of dysfunction within the client rather than focusing on the context in which the symptoms occur.

With systems theory as a background, Wynne's (1988) definition of family therapy can be fully understood:

> Family therapy is a psychotherapeutic approach that focuses on altering interactions between a couple, within a nuclear family or extended family, or between a family and other interpersonal systems, with the goal of alleviating problems initially presented by individual family members, family subsystems, the family as a whole, or other referral sources. (pp. 250–251)

SIDEBAR 16.1 Personal Reflection and Integration: Specialized Systems Terms Used in Family Therapy (Adapted from Sieburg, 1985)

Fundamental Unity:

The universe is one system with infinite levels of subsystems; analysis at any level needs to consider the levels above and below. To understand the individual, it is essential to analyze both the inter-individual context and the intra-individual subsystems. A person's strange behavior may be due to dysfunctional family interactions or may be due to a chemical imbalance in the individual's blood.

System Change

Change in any part of a system will impact the whole system. If therapy with an individual is successful, the system of which the client is a part will be affected. Unfortunately, we will know of those changes only through the selective filter of our client, and our chances of success are diminished by the homeostatic drag of the system.

Recursive Causality

Inherent in the first two concepts is a nonlinear epistemology. Thus, our observation that A causes B is due only to our punctuation of a behavioral sequence that fails to see what follows from B or what preceded A. Every act (or nonaction) provokes feedback, which alters the nature of the next act. In a family, "does he drink because she nags?" (his punctuation); or "does she nag because he drinks?" (her punctuation).

Homeostasis

Systems use negative feedback to maintain a steady state; positive feedback creates change in the system. If one member of a family begins to change, perhaps as the result of individual therapy, the usual routine interactions of the family will be disrupted, and the family will send messages designed to bring the person in therapy back into line.

Viability

The viability of a system is based on order and structure; entropy is disorder. In addition to structure, which is a static quality, the system must also be open to new input if it is to be capable of accommodating to its changing environment. A family with young children needs a generational hierarchy, but the hierarchy must also be open to modification as the children mature.

To help you integrate these terms into your professional life, I would ask you to reflect on the following questions:

1. Did any of the terms make systems theory more alive and why?
2. Did any of the terms make systems theory more obscure and why?

Table 16.1 A comparison of family therapy approaches

	Strategic (Haley)	Structural (Minuchin)	Transgenerational (Bowen)	Experiential (Whitaker)	Conjoint (Satir)
Who is included in therapy?	Everyone involved in the problem	Whoever is involved and accessible	The most motivated family member(s)	Who he decides should come	The pattern is flexible
What is the theory of dysfunction?	Confused hierarchy; communication; rigid behavioral sequences	Boundaries (enmeshed or disengaged); stable coalitions; power	Fusion (emotions control; symbiosis with family of origin); anxiety; triangulation	Rigidity of thought and behavior	Low self-esteem; poor communication; triangulation
What are the goals of Therapy?	Solve the problem; restore hierarchy; introduce flexibility	Solve the problem; Change the structure; increase flexibility	Greater differentiation of self; reduced anxiety	Increase family creativity; greater sense of belonging and individuation	Improved communication; personal growth
What is the Method of Assessment?	Structured initial interview; intervene and observe the reaction; focus on the present	Joining the family to experience its process; chart the family structure; focus on the present	Detailed family history over several generations using the genogram; focus on the past	Informal; not separated from treatment; focus on both past and present	Family life chronology is used to take History and assess present functioning
What are the intervention procedures?	Directives are used to change behavior; they may be straightforward, paradoxical, or ordeals	Reframing is used to change the perception of the problem; structure is changed by unbalancing and increasing stress	Reducing anxiety by providing rational, untriangulated third party; coaching to aid in differentiation from family of origin	Increasing stress to force change; reframing symptoms as efforts at growth; affective confrontation	Modeling and coaching clear communication; family sculpting; guided interaction
What is the stance of the therapist?	Active, directive, but not self-revealing; planful, not spontaneous	Active, directive, personally involved; spontaneous; humorous	Interested but detached; reinforces calmness and rationality	Active, personally involved; encourages and models "craziness," co-therapy	Active, directive, matter-of-fact, nonjudgmental; models open communication

There are many approaches to family therapy that have emerged out of systems theory. Table 16.1 delineates these approaches. However, prominent family therapist researchers are now concentrating on integrating system-based approaches to leverage greater effectiveness (Breunlin, Pinof, Russell, & Lebow, 2011). I have taken this integrationist perspective in writing this chapter.

I will begin this chapter examining the foundations of a family systems perspective. Then I will turn to the pragmatic issues of (a) counseling, prevention, and intervention, (b) diversity and advocacy, and (c) assessment. Finally, I will address research and evaluation on family therapy.

Foundations

In this section I will discuss two key foundational aspects to family therapy. These aspects are: (a) history, and (b) specialization or profession.

History

The history of family therapy is relatively brief. It begins in the 1950s, with the seminal contributions of Nathan Ackerman, Theodore Lidz, Lyman Wynne, Murray Bowen, and Carl Whitaker. All of these psychiatrists, originally trained in the prevailing psychodynamic model, broke away from its restrictive influence and began to see that dysfunctional behavior was rooted in the individual's past and present family life. Each of these pioneers arrived at this insight relatively independently: Ackerman through his research on the mental health problems of the unemployed in Pennsylvania; Lidz studying the families of schizophrenics at Yale; Wynne treating patients with psychosis and ulcerative colitis in Massachusetts, and later doing research on the families of schizophrenics at the National Institute of Mental Health (NIMH); Bowen through his work with families at the Menninger Foundation and later with Wynne at NIMH; and Whitaker through seeing families at Oak Ridge and his later work with families with a schizophrenic member at Emory. In his preface to *The Psychodynamics of Family Life* (1958), the first book-length treatment of this point-of-view, Ackerman said:

> This approach attempts to correlate the dynamic psychological processes of individual behavior with family behavior in order to be able to place individual clinical diagnosis and therapy within the broader frame of family diagnosis and therapy. It has been necessary, therefore, to explore a series of interrelated themes: the interdependence of individual and family stability at every stage of growth from infancy to old age; the role of family in the emotional development of the child; the family as stabilizer of the mental health of the adult; the family as conveyor belt for anxiety and conflict and as a carrier of the contagion of mental illness; the interplay of conflict between family and community, conflict in family relationships, and conflict within individual family members; and breakdown in adaptation and illness as symptoms of the group pathology of the family. (p. viii)

With this statement he set the family therapy agenda for the next three decades.

During this same period, an unusual group of people assembled in Palo Alto to study the communication processes of schizophrenics. The project was headed by anthropologist Gregory Bateson. He hired Jay Haley (a recent graduate in communications theory),

Don Jackson (a psychiatrist), and John Weakland, (a chemical engineer). Early in the project, Haley began consulting with Milton Erickson who was known at that time primarily as a hypnotherapist. From this rich mixture emerged the beginnings of strategic family therapy. In 1959, Jackson founded the Mental Research Institute (MRI) in Palo Alto and invited Virginia Satir to join him. When the Bateson project ended in 1961, Haley and Weakland also joined the staff at MRI.

Satir diverged from the pragmatic approach of strategic therapy when she left MRI to join the human potential movement at the Esalen Institute. She established her own approach to family treatment. This approach incorporated MRI elements within a framework of Gestalt and experiential therapy.

Structural family therapy emerged on the east coast in the work of Salvador Minuchin and his colleagues at Wyltwick School and later the Philadelphia Child Guidance Clinic (PCGC). At Wyltwick, Minuchin worked with the families of delinquent boys and at PCGC he did research on families with a member who was psychosomatic. Each of these projects resulted in a book that enriched our understanding of family functioning (Minuchin et al., 1967; Minuchin, Rosman & Baker 1978). He was joined by Haley in 1967, and they worked together for ten years. As might be expected, the concepts of strategic and structural therapy have much in common. Haley, who met his second wife Cloe Madanes at the PCGC, left with her in 1977 to found the Family Therapy Institute of Washington, D.C.

Murray Bowen began his career at the Menninger Foundation and focused his research on families with a schizophrenic member. He continued this at the NIMH where, in 1954, he had the families of schizophrenic youngsters actually live in the hospital so that he could observe their interactions. In 1959, he moved to Georgetown University Medical Center where he worked for the rest of his career.

Last, but not least, is Carl Whitaker, who is often referred to as the "clown prince of family therapy." Whitaker began his career as a gynecologist, but soon switched to psychiatry. He was chief psychiatrist at Oak Ridge, Tennessee, where he first began bringing the family into treatment with his patients. He moved from Oak Ridge to the chair of the Department of Psychiatry at Emory University in 1946. The publication of his first book, *The Roots of Psychotherapy* (Whitaker & Malone, 1953), led to his dismissal, and he went into private practice for ten years. The book, which he co-authored with his colleague, Thomas Malone, challenged much of traditional psychodynamic thinking and was resoundingly condemned by the psychiatric establishment. In 1965, Whitaker began teaching at the University of Wisconsin. He would remain at this institution through the rest of his professional life. He referred to his work as Symbolic-Experiential Family Therapy.

Specialization or Profession?

At present there exists a strong debate as to whether family therapy is a professional specialization or a distinct profession (Gladding, 2010). Members of a number of different professions (i.e., psychiatry, nursing, psychology, counseling, and social work) practice family therapy as a professional specialization. In addition, there are mental health practitioners who practice family therapy exclusively and view this work as distinct from the activity of other professions. These practitioners go by the title of Marriage and Family Therapists (MFTs). Who is going to win the above noted debate? Wilcoxon, Remley, Gladding, & Huber (2012) suggested that this debate will be resolved as a

---

SIDEBAR 16.2 Personal Reflection and Integration: Specialization or Profession?

The profession/specialization debate occurs in many parts of the mental health world. Addiction counseling is one example. In terms of family therapy, where do you fall in the specialization or profession debate and why? Do you worry that a "both-and" solution might confuse funding agencies, governments, and consumers? Why or why not?

"both-and." That is, *both* MFTs and other mental health professionals will practice family therapy *and* Marriage and Family Therapy will be viewed as a distinct profession (See Sidebar 16.2).

Counseling, Prevention, and Intervention

The Initial Interview

In order to gain a better understanding of how family therapists work, let us look at how the initial interview is conducted. The following description owes a great deal to Jay Haley (1987), but also incorporates ideas from other therapists. The stages of the interview I will address are as follows: (a) pre-session planning, (b) joining, (c) problem statement, (d) interaction, (e) in-session conference, and (f) goal-setting.

Pre-session Planning

Whenever possible, the therapist should determine in advance who will attend the session, and have at least a general idea of the nature of the presenting problems. Whitaker and Bumberry (1988) call this the "battle for structure," and place great emphasis on the importance of the therapist determining who will attend the first session. It is their belief that if the therapist does not have control at this stage, therapeutic leverage is lost and the family is less likely to be helped. This may entail a pre-session telephone call or the use of an intake form. On the basis of the data derived from this initial contact, a pre-session plan should be developed that will include the therapist's hypotheses about the underlying basis of the presenting problem, areas of inquiry that must be addressed to reject or confirm the hypotheses, and a general plan for the session.

Joining

The most important task of the initial interview is to join with the family, accommodating to their affective tone, tempo, language, and family structure. This is done through mimesis (Walsh & McGraw, 2002). Mimesis is a therapeutic skill "used by the therapist to join with the family and become like family members in the manner or content of their communications" (Sauber et al., 1993, p. 255). Foreman and Cava (1993) advocate matching the family's style even to the extent of matching breathing, body movements, and representational system predicates (visual, auditory, kinesthetic). Care needs to be taken, however, that this matching does not cross the line into parody.

SIDEBAR 16.3 Case Study: Genogram

You are counseling the couple Anne and Susan. They have lived together for three years and came to you because of interpersonal strife between them. Anne complains that Susan is increasingly moody and irritable. Susan complains about Anne's growing neediness. Please review the genogram they provided.

What intergenerational patterns do you notice in the genogram? How might these patterns impact Susan and Anne's relationship and inform your work with them?

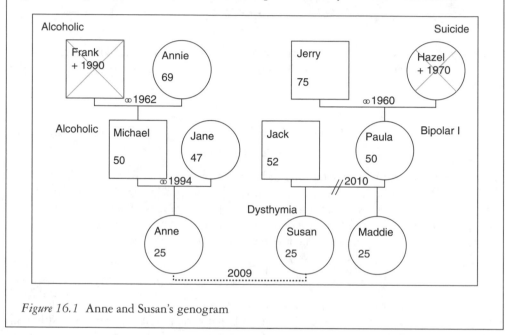

Figure 16.1 Anne and Susan's genogram

Tracking is another joining technique and consists of little more than Rogers-like "uh-huhs," reflection of content, and asking for clarification. During this time, the therapist should avoid comment or interpretation (Haley, 1987).

A third aspect of joining is maintenance. This aspect of joining refers to the therapist sensing the family's structure and acting in such a way as to be included within it (Minuchin & Nichols, 1993). If Dad acts as the "central switchboard" in this family, the therapist accommodates to that and contacts other members through him.

During the joining stage, the therapist should not allow the introduction of material related to the family problem. Only after some social contact has been made with every family member should the next stage begin (Haley, 1987). Joining, of course, is not finished at the end of this stage, but must be of concern throughout the therapy.

More structured approaches to joining include the use of family chronologies and genograms (McGoldrick, Gerson & Shellenberger 1999). Blanton (2005) shares valuable information on joining with Christian families. Both McGoldrick, Giordano & Garcia-Preto (2005) and Minuchin, Colapinto & Minuchin (2006) present a wealth of information on joining with economically and/or ethnically diverse families. Sidebar 16.3 contains an example of a genogram.

Problem Statement

When significant contact has been made with all family members in the social or joining stage, the therapist introduces the problem stage. During the joining stage, the therapist has learned something of the family structure and hierarchy and uses this information to decide to whom the first question should be directed. Haley (1987) recommends that "the adult who seems less involved with the problem be spoken to first, and the person with the most power to bring the family back be treated with the most concern and respect" (p. 22). He also says that, in general, it is unwise to begin with the identified patient (IP).

Don't attempt to force a mute member to speak. This member is often the IP who has lots of practice in resisting adult coercion. Instead, ask another family member, "What would Johnny say if he chose to talk?" This can be repeated in a round robin if necessary, and in most instances, the mute member will feel the need to defend himself or clarify his real feelings.

The second decision the therapist must make is how the problem question should be framed. Obviously, the question can be as vague as, "What brings you here today?" or as specific as "What is the problem for which you are seeking help?" It can also be framed to elicit etiologic information or be future-focused on the kinds of changes that are desired. I generally prefer ambiguity and a focus on the future: "When this therapy is successful, how will your family be different?"

Interaction

When the problem has been reasonably clarified or when it has become clear that the family is not in agreement regarding the nature of the problem, it is time for the therapist to introduce the interaction stage. During the earlier two stages, the therapist has maintained his or her centrality in the communication network, speaking in turn to each of the family members and blocking interruptions and attempts at dialogue between family members. This procedure tends to reduce tension and provide order and relatively clear communication, and establishes the therapist's power and leadership in the therapeutic process. The focus in the problem phase has been on clarifying how the family views the problem. In the interaction stage, the therapist's focus will be on determining the patterns of interaction that sustain the problem. In order to get this information, the therapist asks the family to "dance" in his or her presence (Kershaw, 1992).

This occurs most easily and naturally when the family is not in agreement regarding the problem. When this is true, the therapist can encourage them to discuss their differences and try to reach agreement. During this phase, it is crucial that the therapist abdicate the center of the communication network. All attempts to communicate with the therapist should be referred back to a family member. The therapist does not, however, completely abandon the leadership position; instead their role changes to being the director of the family drama, introducing a third party when two seem to reach an impasse, or asking family members to change their seating patterns to facilitate new encounters (Grove & Haley, 1993; Minuchin & Nichols, 1993).

If family members are in agreement regarding the problem that brings them to therapy (usually focusing on one person as the cause of the difficulty), then they can be asked to perform the problem. "When Johnny doesn't take out the garbage, what happens? Who is first to notice? Show me how it works." In order to get the family to act, rather

---

SIDEBAR 16.4 Case Study: Treatment of Maladaptive Coalitions, Boundaries, and Interactional Sequences Using Jose Szapocznik's Brief Structural Family Therapy (Szapocznik, Hervis & Schwartz, 2003)

Read the case of the Guerrero family (pp. 77–81) online: http://archives.drugabuse. gov/pdf/Manual5.pdf.

Imagine that you have been assigned to work with the Guerrero family. What would you specifically do to intervene on the following: (1) the *enmeshed* relationship between the mother and the son (i.e., the identified patient), (2) the *disengaged* relationship between mother and the son (i.e., the identified patient), and (3) the *disengaged* relationship between the parents?

---

than talk about the problem, it will be necessary for the therapist to get to his or her feet, help the family to build an appropriate stage set (in fantasy), and set the scene into action.

Interactions that are developed from the idiosyncratic information presented by the family are most likely to reveal the information needed to understand the problem. Unfortunately, some families are so uncommunicative that the therapist is unable to elicit enough information to stage an appropriate interaction. When this occurs, it is well to have a few preplanned interaction situations available. One that is often useful, particularly in families with young children, is to ask the family to enact a day in their lives. Establish who sleeps where, move them into the appropriate places, and then have the alarm go off. If it is to be successful, the therapist will need to coach this interaction, slowing it down and focusing on the most simple, concrete details of family life. In a large family, who has access to the bathroom at what time is often a major source of conflict. Care must also be taken to ensure that all family members become involved. Other generic interactions might be to plan a family vacation together, or decide how to spend a free Saturday. Or, using building blocks or crayon and paper, have the family draw their living quarters and discuss who spends the most time with whom in what part of the house.

The purpose of the interaction stage is to determine the family hierarchy, to reveal any stable coalitions, to locate diffuse or rigid boundaries between family subsystems, and hopefully to reveal the chronically repeating interactional sequence that sustains the problem behavior (A clinical example of the treatment of maladaptive coalitions, boundaries, and interactional sequences appears in Sidebar 16.4). When this information has been obtained, the therapist is in a position to develop the interventions that will lead to beneficial change.

In-session Conference

When the therapist is working with an observing team, or even when working alone, it is useful at this point to leave the family and take a few minutes to think about what has been observed in order to abstract from the concrete interactions the patterns that need correction. When working with an observing team, it is often true that the observers are more able to perceive these patterns than the therapist who is immersed in the hypnotic pull of the family dance. Moran et al. (1995) contains an excellent description of the use of such a team. The purpose of the in-session conference is to assess the accuracy of the pre-session hypotheses and to reformulate them in light of the new data gathered during the session. When this has been done, it is possible to design directives (homework) that will begin to change the family's dysfunctional interactions. In some instances the appropriate homework is not clear, but it is my contention that some homework should still be assigned. Family therapy, or any kind of therapy for that matter, is unlikely to be successful if the therapy is encapsulated in the therapeutic hour. The therapist needs to make an assignment that will establish an ongoing process that keeps the therapy salient throughout the week. When the therapist makes a homework assignment without being sure of its relevance, it is comforting to keep Jeff Zeig's dictum in mind. Zeig, who is an Ericksonian hypnotherapist, says his approach to therapy is "ready-shoot-aim" (Bourne, 1987). In other words, if you wait until you are sure of your interventions, therapy will be a long, drawn-out process. If you go with your hunches, and learn from the results, you will probably hit the bull's-eye much sooner.

Goal-Setting

As Haley (1987) has said, "If therapy is to end properly, it must begin properly—by negotiating a solvable problem and discovering the social situation that makes the problem necessary" (p. 8). The purpose of the goal-setting stage is to reach agreement with the family on a solvable problem and to initiate a process that will alter the social situation in such a way that the problem is no longer necessary. It is essential that the problem to be solved be stated in behavioral terms so that one will know when it has been solved. It is equally essential that the problem be one that the therapist believes is capable of solution. Often the process of operationalizing the complaint will be sufficient to produce a solvable problem. When a "rebellious child" problem is operationalized to "staying out after curfew," we have a specific concern upon which one can focus. However, some problems, and this would include most of the categories of the *DSM-IV-TR* (American Psychiatric Association, 2000), are not capable of solution. With ambiguous problems, the therapist must reframe the problem in such a way that it can be solved, and in such a way that the family will accept it. This is not an easy task and sometimes taxes the therapist's creative resources. A notable example would be a case in which Haley reframed a case of schizophrenia as "pseudo-schizophrenia" and then went on to help the family specify how the IP's behavior might be improved. It cannot be emphasized enough that the problem to be solved must be stated in behavioral terms (i.e., never negotiate to "improve communication," "raise self-esteem," or "make our family more cohesive").

When agreement has been reached regarding the problem, the therapist should assign homework that will have face validity with regard to the problem, but will also address the underlying structural or sequential changes that are necessary. In the case of "pseudo-schizophrenia" mentioned above, one might assume that the family is obsessively monitoring the patient, watching for abnormal behavior. An assignment that would utilize the obsessive nature of the family (i.e., pacing) and still institute a change would be to ask the family to keep an elaborate baseline measure of the "normal" behavior of the patient and bring it to the next session.

It is possible in a family with a daughter who is not keeping an assigned curfew that the rebelliousness is being secretly (and perhaps unconsciously) reinforced by the father. An intervention might be to put dad in charge of the daughter's behavior for a week, asking him during the session to negotiate with his daughter the expectations and consequences of noncompliance.

Initial sessions, particularly with large families, often cannot be conducted within the usual 50-minute hour. If it is not possible to schedule a longer session, it is likely that it will take more than one session to establish the therapeutic contract. When this is true, one should still attempt to give some kind of homework assignment that will increase the power of the therapy. When in doubt, asking family members to each keep a baseline of the behavior that they see as problematic is a good first step.

Key Therapy Techniques

In the preceding section, the focus was on the process of conducting the initial interview. In this section, I will focus on the techniques utilized by the family therapist throughout the course of treatment. The techniques offered here are derived from several therapeutic points of view and include: (a) circular questioning, (b) reframing, and (c) giving directives.

Circular Questioning

Following Bateson's dictum that "information is a difference; difference is a relationship (or a change in the relationship)," the Milan group developed a technique they refer to as circular questioning (Walsh & McGraw, 2002). The "circular" referred to here is epistemological; their questions are intended to uncover the complementarity of family relationships that make the presenting symptom necessary for family homeostasis. Each member of the family is invited to tell how he or she sees the relationship between two other family members; or between two different periods; or any other difference likely to be significant to the family. For example:

1. In terms of family relationships: "Tell us how you see the relationship between your sister and your mother."
2. In terms of specific interactive behaviors: "When your father gets mad at Bill, what does your mother do?"
3. In terms of differences in behavior: "Who gets most upset when Jimmy wets the bed, your father or your mother?"
4. In terms of ranking by various members of the family of a behavior or interaction: "Who is closest to your grandmother? Who is next, and next?"
5. In terms of change in the relationship before and after a precise event: "Did you and your sister fight more or less before your mother remarried?"
6. In terms of differences in respect to hypothetical circumstances: "If one of you kids should have to stay home, not get married, who would be best for your mother? Your father?" (Fleuridas, Nelson & Rosenthal 1986).

Perhaps it should be mentioned here, parenthetically, that this procedure would be anathema to some other therapists, including Virginia Satir, who specifically proscribe "gossiping" and "mind-reading." However, the Milan group has demonstrated that often more can be obtained by asking a person what he or she thinks about others than by asking questions that are more personal. When this is done in the family context, where all can hear and respond, the result is quite different than it would be in an interview with an individual.

Reframing

Haley (1987) says, "It cannot be emphasized enough that the problem the therapist settles on must be a problem which the family wants changed but which is put in a form that makes it solvable" (p. 38). While some problems presented by families lend themselves readily to therapeutic intervention, frequently it is necessary for the therapist to reframe the problem. Reframing may include the following:

1. *Operationalizing*: Casting the problem in observable, behavioral terms. The problem of "a child who is driving us crazy" is reframed by specifying the specific behaviors that are problematic and asking the parents to keep a record of their frequency of occurrence.
2. *Emphasizing complementarity*: Describing the problem in an interactional context, rather than as the property of one member of the family. A father who is depressed is asked, "Who makes you depressed?"
3. *Denominalizing*: Removing a reified diagnostic label and replacing it with a behavior that can be consciously controlled. Anorexia might be reframed as "a girl who refuses to eat."
4. *Positive connotation*: Describing the symptomatic behavior as positively motivated in the service of the family system. A defiant, delinquent boy is described as particularly sensitive to family conflict and his behavior as a sacrificial act designed to keep the parents from divorce.

Giving Directives

Giving directives refers to creating or selecting an intervention that will attack the hypothesized basis of the presenting problem. According to Haley (1987), giving directives has several purposes:

> ... the main goal of therapy is to get people to behave differently and so to have different subjective experiences. Directives are a way of making those changes happen.... directives are used to intensify the relationship with the therapist. By telling people what to do, the therapist gets involved in the action... directives are used to gather information. When a therapist tells people what to do, the ways they respond give information about them and about how they will respond to the changes wanted. Whether they do what the therapist asks, do not do it, forget to do it, or try and fail, the therapist has information she would not otherwise have. (p. 56)

Directives can be categorized as either (a) compliance-oriented or (b) defiance-oriented. Compliance-oriented directives are offered to families who may be expected to carry out the assignment as given. When the therapist wants the family to carry out the directive, the following should be considered:

1. The directive should be framed in such a way as to use the language and imagery of the family and be focused on solving the problem presented by the family.
2. Avoid asking the family not to do something; ask them to do something different.
3. Ask everyone to do something.

4. Be extremely concrete and repetitive (unless you have reason to be otherwise).
5. Arrange for concrete, specific feedback.
6. Practice the homework during the session, or at least ask the family to tell you in their own words what the assignment includes.
7. Anti-sabotage techniques: brainstorm reasons why they might not be able to comply; suggest probable problems that might interfere with compliance; discuss how they can overcome the problems.

Compliance-oriented directives can be either straightforward or paradoxical; the main idea is that you want them to be carried out. An example of a straightforward directive would be to ask Dad to be in charge of the discipline, and ask Mom to keep a record of problem behaviors and report them for his consideration. An example of a compliance-oriented paradoxical directive would be to prescribe the symptom to occur at a special time and place.

The following are some examples of compliance-oriented directives:

1. *Caring days*: Ask a hostile couple to act as if they care for each other by each daily performing five minor behaviors requested by his or her spouse (LeCroy et al., 1989). See Sidebar 16.5 for an example.
2. *Role reversal*: Ask a disengaged husband to give his enmeshed wife a vacation from responsibility for the children. He is to be responsible for the meting out of discipline; she may consult with him, but is not to be in charge.
3. *Safe practice*: Ask a man who is afraid of job interviews to apply for jobs that he would not take if they were offered.
4. *Surprise*: Ask a couple who are hostile and out of touch with each other to plan a surprise that will please the other, but would be so out of character that the other could never guess what it would be. Each should attempt to guess what the other will do, making a written record of his or her guesses.
5. *Symptom prescription*: Ask a single mother with two boys who are disrespectful to their mother and constantly fighting to hold a daily wrestling match where she is the referee and will enforce fair fighting; boys are to agree to reserve their fighting to these bouts. Mother is to insist on "the bouts" even if the boys are unwilling.

Defiance-oriented directives are offered to families whom one assumes to be resistant. The intention is to have the family defy the therapist in such a way as to eliminate the problem behavior. Defiance-oriented directives are always paradoxical. They should only be used by therapists who have considerable supervised experience with the use of such directives; they should never be used if there is a risk the family would be harmed if the directive was followed rather than defied.

When the therapist wants the family to defy her or his directives the following should be considered:

1. Do this only with families that have demonstrated their resistance.
2. Use this only after you have joined the family sufficiently to make noncompliance a significant issue. Your relationship to the family should be clearly defined as one of bringing about change.
3. The problem to be solved should be clearly defined and agreed on.

SIDEBAR 16.5 Case Study: Caring Days

Picture that you are the counselor for the clients discussed in Sidebar 16.3. You decide to disrupt the current strife-filled interpersonal patterns of Anne and Susan by having them complete a Caring Days intervention. After getting an agreement from them to do this task for two weeks, you give them the following instructions (Adapted from LeCroy et al., 1989; Stuart, 1980):

1. Susan and Anne, I would first like each of you to list nine behaviors that they would like to receive from your partner. These behaviors must be specific, positive, can be done daily, and not be related to the current issues in your relationship.
2. Now I would like you to share your list. Read your partner's list and select five behaviors you are willing to commit to doing daily whether or not your partner follows through on what they select.
3. Now each of you is going to make a chart with your partner's five behaviors in the first column and then 14 more columns to the right, one for each day of the two weeks. These charts should be placed in conspicuous places in your home. You should mark each time your partner performs a requested behavior.

Do you think this intervention will be successful with Anne and Susan? Why or why not? What challenges do you think you might encounter in administering this intervention. If you want more details about this intervention see either LeCroy et al. (1989) or Stuart (1980).

---

4. The rationale for the directive must utilize the family language and imagery and provide an acceptable rationale for the directive. Haley (1987) says that designing paradoxical directives is easy; you simply observe how the family members are behaving and ask them to continue. How you make the directive appear reasonable and how you react to changes that occur are the hard parts.
5. Give the directive and ask for a report.
6. When the family reports that they did not carry out the homework, condemn the noncompliance and be puzzled and surprised by the symptom reduction. Don't take credit for the change!
7. Repeat the directive and warn against relapse.

The following are some examples of defiance-oriented directives:

1. *Positive connotation*: Reframe the problem behavior in positive terms and indicate that it would be dangerous for the family to change.
2. *Symptom increase*: Recommend that the problem behavior be increased in order to get a better understanding of it.
3. *Restraining*: Recommend that the family slow down in its attempts to solve the problem.
4. *Symptom retention*: Advise the family to retain a certain percent of the problem in order to remember how awful it was.
5. *Prediction*: Predict relapse of a symptom that has been brought under control.

The techniques offered in the section above are, of course, only a brief introduction to the procedures used by various family therapists. Useful sources for family therapy techniques are the *Procedures in Marriage and Family Therapy* (Brock & Barnard, 1999), *101 Interventions in Family Therapy* (Nelson & Trepper, 1993), and *101 More Interventions in Family Therapy* (Nelson & Trepper, 1998).

Diversity and Advocacy

Cultural Competence

The International Association for Marriage and Family Counselors' ethical code (2005) highlights the need for marriage and family therapists to practice in a culturally competent manner. The first section of this code states: "Professional counselors realize their perspectives influence the conceptualization of problems, identification of clients, and implementation of possible solutions. Couple and family counselors examine personal biases and values. They actively attempt to understand and serve couples and families from diverse cultural backgrounds" (p. 3).

Taylor et al. (2006) stated that being a culturally competent marriage and family therapist involves more than the ability to repeat checklists of generalized norms for particular cultures. In their study on cultural competence in marriage and family therapists, these four researchers noted that cultural competence is derived from a therapist being aware of his/her own assumptions about a client's cultural narratives. They saw this awareness as the fundamental building block of cultural competence. They stated that "Cultural competence is not a global, measurable phenomenon but a socially constructed notion created by the therapeutic relationship that is influenced by the social locations of the therapist and clients which vary case by case. Family therapy...will become culturally competent as the therapist and client constantly strive to gain mutual understanding through the countless interactions that take place within the therapy session" (p. 444). In other words, Taylor et al. emphasized the particular over the general and the applied over the theoretical in describing cultural competence in marriage and family therapists. Thus, a family therapist operating unaware of his/her own cultural assumptions is unable to engage, from the start, any client in a profitable therapeutic relationship.

Narrow Rigid Beliefs and Self-Percepts

In a sense, this brings us full circle. To the extent that one's beliefs are narrow and unchanging, adaptation to the demands of a changing environment or the developmental demands of the family life cycle will be difficult and advocacy impossible. Milton Erickson held "... that individuals with a symptom were constricted by their own certainties, their own rules, whether these rules guided their belief system, their perceptions of self, their patterns of physiological response or relational habits, or their own ideas of contingency, (i.e., if A, then B)" (Ritterman, 1986, p. 37). The symptom, per se, is not the problem, but instead is "a metaphorical expression of a problem and attempt at resolution... the underlying problem is understood to be inflexibly patterned behavior resulting from internal and/or interactional rules that proscribe available choices and prevent the resolution of developmentally routine or unusual life dilemmas" (Ritterman, 1986, p. 36).

When an individual or a family is unable to resolve a difficulty, it is assumed that the conscious mind is imposing a narrow, restrictive mindset that does not allow the creative recovery of the resources necessary to solve the problem. From this point of view, the conscious, rational mind must be diverted to allow the creative potential of the unconscious to function. This is done through hypnosis or the use of indirect methods such as metaphor.

Assessment

In this section, we will examine the wide array of assessments that occur in family therapy. These include assessments of the following: (a) family dysfunction, (b) family life cycle, (c) family fusion (present or origin), (d) dysfunctional behavioral sequences, (e) hierarchy problems, (f) communication problems, and (g) family of origin struggles.

Family Dysfunction

Tolstoy said in the opening line of *Anna Karenina*, "All happy families resemble one another, but each unhappy family is unhappy in its own way." Family therapists tend to reverse this position, believing that good family functioning is based in diversity, while family dysfunction is due to narrowness and rigidity. Haley (1987) goes so far as to argue that therapies that have a picture of "ideal" functioning are in fact limiting, in that they impose "a narrow ideology, thus preventing the diversity that human beings naturally display. To put the matter simply, if the goal of therapy is to introduce more complexity, then imposing on clients psychological explanation of their own and other people's behavior is antitherapeutic" (p. 233).

When a system's orientation is applied to psychological problems, the diagnosis of the difficulty is very different from that presented in the *Diagnostic and Statistical Manual of Mental Disorders-IV-TR*. (American Psychiatric Association, 2000). Rather than focusing on the internal state of the individual, the family systems approach looks for pathology in the interactions that occur between people who have significance for each other.

Rather than adopting a linear model of causality, the family systems approach perceives causality as circular or recursive. It's not that a child is rebellious because his or her father is too authoritarian, or that the father is authoritarian because the child is rebellious, but that both are caught up in a chronic repetitive sequence of behavior: the "game without end."

Rather than focusing on the way people think or feel, the family systems therapist tends to focus on what they do. The purpose of family therapy is not insight, but behavior change.

Within the broad commonality of the systems orientation, each of the major family therapists has emphasized different aspects of human functioning as the source of symptomatic behavior. The following sections provide a compilation of the thinking of a number of family therapists regarding symptomatic behavior.

Family Life Cycle

Family dysfunction is often the result of a failure to accomplish the developmental tasks demanded by the family life cycle. The concept of the family life cycle dates from 1947 (Duvall & Hill, 1948). Evelyn Duvall's (1957) early delineation of this life cycle has influenced generations of family therapy theorists. Carter and McGoldrick's (1980) update is widely cited in the professional literature. Table 16.2 contains both of these historical delineations of the family life cycle as well as my contemporary one.

Inherent in the life cycle concept is the idea that there are certain developmental tasks that must be accomplished during periods of transition from one stage to another. Successful movement to the next development stage requires changes in the roles and structure of the family. Also, diversity re-shapes and nuances how families experience and negotiate these stages (Hancock, 2005). Finally, other potential life-cycle stages that can occur in families are (a) marital break-up, (b) single-parent living, and (3) remarriage (Nichols & Pace-Nichols 1993). If the family is unable to accommodate to the need for change, stress and symptomatology will occur.

The demand for change is a normal part of family development. It is not these normal difficulties that create the problem, but rather the chronic mishandling of them. It is the attempted solution that is the problem. Denying the need for change, treating a normal developmental change as if it were a problem, and striving for perfection are all likely to result in family distress. In general, the reaction of a dysfunctional family to a demand for change is met by doing "more of the same." For example, a girl becomes a teenager

Table 16.2 Stages of the family life cycle

Presence & type of children	Duvall (1957)	Carter & McGoldrick (1980)	Contemporary
None		Leaving home: young single adults	First residence permanently apart from parents
None	Beginning families	Joining of families through marriage: The new couple	Marriage, stable partnership, or committed singlehood
Oldest child, birth to 30 months	Childbearing families	Families with young children	Childbearing families
Oldest child, 2 ½ to 6 years	Families with preschool children		Families with pre-school children
Oldest child, 6 to 13 years	Families with school children		Families with schoolchildren
Oldest child, 10 to 12 years			Families with tweens
Oldest child, 13 to 18 years	Families with teenagers	Families with adolescents	Families with adolescents
First child's preliminary launch from home; oldest child, 19 to 22 years	Families as launching centers	Launching children and moving on	Families as trial launching environments
Adult children return home; oldest child, 23 to 30 years			Families with "boomerang" emerging adults
Adult children obtain stable separate residences	Families in the middle years	Families in later life	Families organized around middle adulthood tasks
Retirement to death	Aging family		Families in decay and closure

and exerts more autonomy; parents become concerned for her safety and morality; they introduce or increase their control over her behavior; the girl resents their attempt to control her autonomy and rebels; the parents increase their control; etc. (Gerson, 1995; Micucci, 1998). In a family with young children, a problem might arise when the grandparents have difficulty in giving up their parental role with their own children, thus interfering with the discipline of their new grandchildren.

The problems associated with family life cycle changes are exacerbated in remarried families. This exacerbation occurs because an individual's development is out of synchronization with the developmental stage of his or her family. For example, a newly remarried family is focused on issues of inclusion and forming of a viable entity; if that family contains an adolescent, he or she is focused on issues of separation and individuation.

Family Fusion (Present or Origin)

Bowen (1994) conceived a scale of differentiation of self from 0 to 100. At the low end of the scale, people are fused or enmeshed with their families to the extent that they are unable to think or act independently. Their lives are ruled by emotional reactivity. According to Bowen, people diagnosed as schizophrenic would be extremely fused.

At the upper end of the scale, people have achieved emotional separation from their families, are able to act autonomously, and can choose to be rational in emotionally charged situations. The individual's level of differentiation is closely related to the differentiation of his or her parents, and the process is transgenerational in nature. People with low levels of differentiation (fusion) are particularly reactive to environmental stressors and when under stress are likely to resolve it by (a) withdrawal, (b) conflict, (c) dysfunction of one spouse, or (d) triangulation of a child that results in dysfunction. When the latter occurs, that child, who is caught in the tug-of-war between the parents, will be even less differentiated than the parents. This is the basis of the intergenerational transmission of dysfunction (Bowen, 1991, 1994).

Boundary Problems

According to Minuchin, family boundaries are created by implicit rules that govern (a) who talks to whom, and (b) about what is discussed (Minuchin, Colapinto & Minuchin 2006; Minuchin& Fishman, 1990). When no rules exist, everyone is privy to everyone else's thoughts and feelings. Thus, family boundaries become diffuse and individuals become enmeshed (fused). When the rules are too strict and communication breaks down, the boundary is said to be rigid and the individuals disengaged. The preferred state is to have clear rules that allow for both individuation and togetherness. The similarity of this concept to Bowen's idea of differentiation of self is obvious, but Minuchin has developed it to refer to both extrafamilial boundaries and intrafamilial boundaries that separate subsystems (i.e., holons).

Family dysfunction can occur because the family is either disengaged from or enmeshed with the external environment. This is frequently a problem with remarried families where rules regarding contact with ex-spouses may be either rigid or lacking. Dysfunction can also occur when internal subsystems of the family are enmeshed or disengaged. The classic dysfunction in our culture is the mother who is enmeshed with a child (i.e., cross-generational coalition) and the father who is disengaged from both.

Dysfunctional Behavioral Sequences

Haley (1987) believes family dysfunction is often caused by behavioral sequences that are rigid, repetitive, and functionally autonomous. He describes such a sequence as follows:

1. One parent, usually the mother, is in an intense relationship with the child. By *intense* is meant a relationship that is both positive and negative and where the responses of each person are exaggeratedly important. The mother attempts to deal with the child with a mixture of affection and exasperation.
2. The child's symptomatic behavior becomes more extreme.
3. The mother, or the child, calls on the father for assistance in resolving their difficulty.
4. The father steps in to take charge and deal with the child.
5. Mother reacts against father, insisting that he is not dealing with the situation properly. Mother can react with an attack or with a threat to break off the relationship with father.
6. Father withdraws, giving up the attempt to disengage mother and child.
7. Mother and child deal with each other in a mixture of affection and exasperation until they reach a point where they are at an impasse. (pp. 121–122)

Such patterns can repeat ad infinitum unless some new behavior is introduced into the sequence. It perhaps needs to be pointed out that the dysfunctional behavior should not be "blamed" on any of the individuals; all are equally involved and each could change the sequence by introducing a new incompatible element. Unfortunately, the family members are not usually aware of the complete sequence and in any case punctuate the sequence in such a way as to hold themselves blameless.

Hierarchy Problems

Haley (1987) and Minuchin (Minuchin & Nichols, 1993) both stress the importance of hierarchy problems in family dysfunction. Problems can occur when the hierarchy is either absent, ambiguous, or culturally inappropriate; that is, when no one is in charge, when it is unclear who is in charge, or when the person wielding the power is not sanctioned by cultural mores. Dysfunction may also be due to coalitions that cut across generational boundaries. An example of the latter would be when a father and child collude to avoid what they feel are the mother's overly rigid rules. Another common example would be in a family where there is marital conflict and both parents try to enlist the children on their side of the argument.

Communication Problems

Virginia Satir (1983) placed special emphasis on the ways that people in a family communicate as a source of dysfunction. Communication may be inadequate owing to lack of clarity (e.g., information is deleted: "People get me down." Which people? How do they do that?). Communication can also be confusing because of a lack of topic continuity. This occurs when people are not really listening and their responses to the other become non-sequiturs. When people are unwilling to reveal themselves or commit themselves to a statement or request, communication falters (e.g., "I don't suppose you would like to go to my mother's with me?" rather than "I would like you to go with me to my mother's.").

Sometimes communication is problematic because it is incongruent; either the nonverbal behavior or vocal tone communicates a message that contradicts the verbal content. Such incongruency is often the basis for irony and humor, but when it is unintentional and the message is not clarified, the receiver does not know how to respond. In the extreme case, this is the classic "double bind," described by Bateson, Jackson, Haley & Weakland (1956). Satir (1983) describes this, and the effect that such incongruent communication can have on a child:

> How do mates unconsciously induce a child to behave in such a way that he eventually gets identified as a "patient?"... What conditions must be present for a child to experience the pressures associated with a double bind?
>
> a. First, the child must be exposed to double-level messages repeatedly and over a long period.
> b. Second, these must come from persons who have survival significance for him....
> c. Third, perhaps most important of all, he must be conditioned... from an early age not to ask, "Did you mean that or that?" but must accept his parents' conflicting messages in all their impossibility. He must be faced with the hopeless task of translating them into a single way of behaving. (pp. 45–46)

See Sidebar 16.6 for personal reflection questions concerning double-binds.

Family of Origin Struggles

Whitaker says, "We assume that dysfunction is related to the struggle over whose family of origin this new family is going to model itself after. One way to view etiology asserts there is no such thing as a marriage; it is merely two scapegoats sent out by families to perpetrate themselves" (Whitaker & Keith, 1981, p. 196). Young people who come from a common cultural background may be less likely to experience this problem, but in our multicultural society, the appropriate behaviors for "wife" or "husband" are often unclear, or represent role conflicts. When a child enters the picture before these roles are synchronized, the new roles of "mother" and "father" further complicate the picture. Often the young couple find themselves acting just like their parents, although they are reluctant to admit it.

SIDEBAR 16.6 Personal Reflection and Integration: Your Experience with Double-Binds

Think of an interpersonal double-bind that really sticks out in your mind and then answer the following questions:

1. What were your physical reactions when you experienced this double-bind?
2. What were your emotional reactions when you experienced this double-bind?
3. What cognitions were prompted by the experience of this double-bind?
4. Were you able to extricate yourself from this double-bind? If so, how? If not, why?

CASS DYKEMAN

Research and Evaluation
Background

The history of family therapy research is filled with contradictions. On one hand, this specialization/profession emerged from research projects such as Bateson's work on schizophrenia (Bateson et al., 1956). On the other hand, empirical research has been largely ignored in family therapy (Diamond, Serrano, Dickey, & Sonis 1996; Gladding, 2010; Lebow and Gurman (1995) Shields, Wynne, McDaniel, & Gawinsky 1994). In terms of family therapy research, two questions that any future professional counselor should address are: (1) Does family therapy work? and (2) What are the professional practice patterns of family therapists?

Does Family Therapy Work?

Research that examines whether an intervention works is known as *outcome* research. In family therapy, a dearth of outcome research left the above question unanswered until the late 1980s. Only at that time had a sufficient number of studies been published to allow researchers to conduct meta-analyses of the family therapy research literature. Meta-analysis is a research technique by which multiple individual studies can be grouped together to empirically analyze the overall effectiveness of a particular intervention approach. Hazelrigg, Cooper & Borduin (1987) conducted the first meta-analysis of family therapy outcome research. In their meta-analysis of 20 studies, they found that family therapy had a positive effect on clients when compared to either no treatment or an alternative treatment. Subsequent meta-analyses have confirmed that family therapy is indeed an efficacious mental health treatment approach (Baldwin, Christian, Berkelson, & Shadish 2012; Shadish & Baldwin, 2003).

In addition to knowledge concerning the overall effectiveness of family therapy, strong evidence exists in the research literature concerning the effectiveness of this type of therapy with a wide range of problems such as substance abuse, relationship discord, schizophrenia, anxiety and depression (Sprenkle, 2012). Overall, it is known that families treated with family-based interventions improved more than at least 67% of families treated with alternative treatments or no treatment (Diamond et al., 1996).

What Are the Professional Practice Patterns of Family Therapists?

Within the mental health service provider community, there exists a prejudice that family therapists do nothing more than "interminable marriage counseling for trivial problems" (Simmons & Doherty, 1995, p. 5). Surprisingly, little research on the practice patterns of family therapists has been conducted. Thus, research evidence that could challenge the above prejudice has not existed until recently. The research team of Bill Doherty and Deborah Simmons conducted the groundbreaking studies on this topic.

Doherty and Simmons (1996) studied the professional practice patterns of a random sample of MFTs drawn from 15 states. The practice variables they examined included (a) caseload, (b) presenting problem, (c) diagnosis, and (d) length of treatment. They found that MFTs, on average had 24 clients in their active caseload and completed 20 client contact hours per week. The clients served by the MFTs presented a multitude of problems at the commencement of treatment. These problems included (a) depression (44%), (b) marital problems (30%), (c) anxiety (21%), and (d) parent-child problems (13%).

Adjustment Disorder was the modal diagnostic category (25%). Other prevalent diagnostic categories included Depressive Disorder (23%) and Anxiety Disorders (14%). The median number of sessions per client was 12. Interestingly, almost one half (49.4%) of the treatments provided by the national sample of *marriage and family* therapists were in the form of individual counseling. Doherty and Simmons' research studies suggest that family therapists *do* serve clients with serious problems.

Summary

This chapter has attempted to introduce the reader to the contextual thinking that is the essence of family therapy. I have tried to illustrate this perspective through descriptions of family therapy diagnosis, interviewing, and treatment. In family therapy, diagnosis focuses on interpersonal rather than intrapersonal dysfunction. Sound family therapy interviewing follows a distinct process beginning with pre-session planning. Family therapy treatment is rich with powerful techniques. These techniques include circular questioning and giving directives among others. It is my hope that this brief introduction to the concepts and techniques of family therapy will whet the reader's appetite for further exploration. If that should prove to be the case, the references marked with an asterisk (*) are good starting points.

Useful Websites

The following Websites provide additional information relating to the chapter topics:
American Association for Marriage and Family Therapy: www.aamft.org
American Family Therapy Academy: www.afta.org
American Psychological Association, Family Psychology Division: http://www.apa.org/about/division/div43.aspx
National Council on Family Relations: www.ncfr.org
International Association for Marriage and Family Counselors: http://www.iamfconline.com/

References

Ackerman, N. W. (1958). *The psychodynamics of family life.* New York: Basic Books.

American Psychiatric Association. (2000). *Diagnostic and statistical manual of mental disorders* (4th ed.). *Text Revision.* Washington, DC: Author.

Baldwin, S. A., Christian, S., Berkeljon, A., & Shadish, W. R. (2012). The Effects of Family Therapies for Adolescent Delinquency and Substance Abuse: A Meta-analysis. *Journal of Marital and Family Therapy, 38,* 281–304. doi: 10.1111/j.1752–0606.2011.00248.x

Bateson, G., Jackson, D. D., Haley, J., & Weakland, J. (1956). Toward a theory of schizophrenia. *Behavioral Science, 1,* 251–264.

Blanton, P. G. (2005). How to talk to Christian clients about their spiritual lives: Insights from postmodern family therapy. *Pastoral Psychology, 54,* 93–101.

Bourne, M. G. (1987). Accessing inherent resources in individuals and families. *The American Journal of Family Therapy, 15,* 75–77. doi: 10.1080/01926188708251289

Bowen, M. (1991). Alcoholism as viewed through family systems theory and family psychotherapy. *Family Dynamics of Addiction Quarterly, 1,* 94–102.

*Bowen, M. (1994). *Family therapy in clinical practice.* New York: Aronson.

*Brock, G. W., & Barnard, C. P. (1999). *Procedures in marriage and family therapy.* Boston, MA: Allyn & Bacon.

Breunlin, D. C., Pinsof, W., Russell, W. P., & Lebow, J. (2011). *Integrative Problem-Centered Metaframeworks Therapy I: Core concepts and hypothesizing.* Family Process, 50, 293–313. doi: 10.1111/j.1545–5300.2011.01362.x

Carter, E. A., & McGoldrick, M. (1980). *The family life cycle: A framework for family therapy.* New York: Gardner Press.

Dattilio, F. M. (2010).*Cognitive-Behavioral Therapy with couples and families: A comprehensive guide for clinicians.* NY: Guilford.

Diamond, G. S., Serrano, A. C., Dickey, M., & Sonis, W. A. (1996). Current status of family-based outcome and process research. *Journal of the American Academy of Child and Psychiatry, 35,* 6–16.

Doherty, W. J., & Simmons, D. S. (1996). Clinical practice patterns of marriage and family therapists: A national survey of therapists and their clients. *Journal of Martial and Family Therapy, 22,* 9–25.

Duvall, E. M., & Hill, R. L. (1948). *Report of the committee on the dynamics of family interaction.* Washington, DC: National Conference on Family Life.

Duvall, E. R. M. (1957). *Family development.* Chicago: Lippincott.

Fleuridas, C., Nelson, T., & Rosenthal, D. (1986). The evolution of circular questions: Training family therapists. *Journal of Marital and Family Therapy, 12,* 113–127.

Foreman, B. D., & Cava, E. (1993). Neuro-linguistic programming in one-person family therapy. In T. S. Nelson, & T. S. Trepper (Eds.), *101 interventions in family therapy* (pp. 50–54). New York: Haworth Press.

Gerson, R. (1995). The family life cycle: Phases, stages and crises. In R. H. Mikesell, D. Lusterman, & S. H. McDaniel (Eds.), *Integrating family therapy* (pp. 91–112). Washington, DC: APA.

Gladding, S. T. (2010). *Family therapy: History, theory, and practice.* Upper Saddle River, NJ: Pearson.

Grove, D. R., & Haley, J. (1993). *Conversations on therapy.* New York: W. W. Norton.

*Haley, J. (1987). *Problem solving therapy* (2nd ed.). San Francisco: Jossey-Bass.

Hancock, T. U. (2005). Cultural competence in the assessment of poor Mexican families in the rural southeastern United States. *Child Welfare: Journal of Policy, Practice, and Program, 84,* 689–711.

Hazelrigg, M. D., Cooper, H. M., & Borduin, C. M. (1987). Evaluating the effectiveness of family therapies: An integrative review and analysis. *Psychological Bulletin, 101,* 428–442.

International Association of Marriage and Family Counselors. (2005). *Ethical code for the International Association of Marriage and Family Counselors.* Retrieved January 30, 2012 from http://www.iamfconline.com/PDFs/Ethical%20codes.pdf.

Kershaw, C. J. (1992). *The couple's hypnotic dance.* New York: Brunner/Mazel.

Lebow, J. L., & Gurman, A. S. (1995). Research assessing couple and family therapy. *Annual Review of Psychology, 46,* 27–57.

LeCroy, C. W., Carrol, P., Nelson-Becker, H., & Sturlaugson, P. (1989). An experimental evaluation of the Caring Days technique for marital enrichment. *Family Relations, 38,* 15–18. doi: 10.2307/583603

McGoldrick, M., Giordano, J., & Garcia-Preto, N. (2005). *Ethnicity and family therapy.* New York: Guilford.

McGoldrick, M., Gerson, R., & Shellenberger, S. (1999). *Genograms: Assessment and intervention.* New York: W. W. Norton.

Meneses, C. W., & Greenberg, L. S. (2011). The Construction of a Model of the Process of Couples' Forgiveness in Emotion-Focused Therapy for Couples. *Journal of Marital and Family Therapy, 37,* 491–502. doi: 10.1111/j.1752–0606.2011.00234.x

Micucci, J. A. (1998). *The adolescent in family therapy.* New York: Guilford.

Minuchin, P., Colapinto, J., &Minuchin, S. (2006). *Working with families of the poor* (2nd ed.). New York: Guilford.

*Minuchin, S., & Fishman, C. (1990). *Family therapy techniques.* Cambridge, MA: Harvard University Press.

Minuchin, S., Montalvo, B., Gurney, B., Rosman, B., & Schumer, F. (1967). *Families of the slums.* New York: Basic Books.

Minuchin, S., & Nichols, M. P. (1993). *Family healing.* New York: The Free Press.

Minuchin, S., Rosman, B., & Baker, L. (1978). *Psychosomatic families*. Cambridge, MA: Harvard University Press.

Moran, A., Brownlee, K., Gallant, P., Meyers, L., Farmer, F., & Taylor, S. (1995). The effectiveness of reflecting team supervision: A client's experience of receiving feedback from a distance. *Family Therapy, 22,* 31–47.

*Nelson, T. S., & Trepper, T. S. (Eds.). (1993). *101 interventions in family therapy*. New York: The Haworth Press.

*Nelson, T. S., & Trepper, T. S. (Eds.). (1998). *101 more interventions in family therapy*. New York: The Haworth Press.

Nichols, W. C., & Pace-Nichols, M. A. (1993). Developmental perspectives and family therapy: The marital life cycle. *Contemporary Family Therapy, 15,* 299–315. doi.org/10.1007/BF00897760

O'Farrell, T. J., & Clements, K. (2012). Review of Outcome Research on Marital and Family Therapy in Treatment for Alcoholism. *Journal of Marital and Family Therapy, 38,* 122–144. doi: 10.1111/j.1752–0606.2011.00242.x

Patten, C., Barnett, T., & Houlihan, D. (1991). Ethics in marital and family therapy: A review of the literature. *Professional Psychology: Research and Practice, 22,* 171–175.

Ritterman, M. (1986). Exploring relationships between Ericksonian hypnotherapy and family therapy. In S. de Shazer, & R. Kral (Eds.), *Indirect approaches in therapy* (pp. 35–47). Rockville, MD: Aspen Publications.

*Satir, V. (1983). *Conjoint family therapy* (3rd ed.).Palo Alto, CA: Science & Behavior Books.

Sauber, S. R., L'Abate, L., Weeks, G. R., & Buchanan, W. L. (1993). *The dictionary of family psychology and family therapy* (2nd ed.). Newbury Park, CA: SAGE.

Szapocznik, J., Hervis, O. E., & Schwartz, S. (2003). *Brief strategic family therapy for adolescent drug abuse* (NIH Publication No. 03–4751). NIDA Therapy Manuals for Drug Addiction. Rockville, MD: National Institute on Drug Abuse. Retrieved from: http://archives.drugabuse.gov/pdf/Manual5.pdf.

Shadish, W. R., & Baldwin, S. A. (2003). Meta-analysis of MFT interventions. *Journal of Marital & Family Therapy, 29,* 547–570.

Shields, C. G., Wynne, L. C., McDaniel, S. H., & Gawinski, B. A. (1994). The marginalization of family therapy: A historical and continuing problem. *Journal of Marital and Family Therapy, 20,* 117–138.

Sieburg, E. (1985). *Family communication*. New York: Gardner Press.

Simmons, D. S., & Doherty, W. J. (1995). Defining who we are and what we do: Clinical practice patterns of marriage and family therapists in Minnesota. *Journal of Marital and Family Therapy, 21,* 3–16.

Simmons, D. S., & Doherty, W. J. (1998). Defining who we are and what we do: Clinical practice patterns of marriage and family therapists in Minnesota. *Journal of Marital and Family Therapy, 24,* 321–336.

Sprenkle, D. H. (2012). Intervention Research in Couple and Family Therapy: A Methodological and Substantive Review and an Introduction to the Special Issue. *Journal of Marital and Family Therapy, 38,* 3–29. doi: 10.1111/j.1752–0606.2011.00271.x

Stanton, D. (1988). The lobster quadrille: Issues and dilemmas for family therapy research. In L. Wynne (Ed.), *The state of the art in family therapy research: Controversies and recommendations* (pp. 5–32). New York: Family Process Press.

Stuart, R. (1980). *Helping couples change: A social learning approach to marital therapy*. NY: Guilford Press.

Taylor, B. A., Gambourg, M. B., Rivera, M., & Laureano, D. (2006). Constructing cultural competence: Perspectives of family therapists working with Latino families. *The American Journal of Family Therapy, 34,* 429–445.

Walsh, W. M., & McGraw, J. A. (2002). *Essentials of family therapy*. Denver, CO: Love Publishing.

*Whitaker, C., & Bumberry, W. (1988). *Dancing with the family: A symbolic-experiential approach*. New York: Brunner/Mazel.

Whitaker, C., & Keith, D. (1981). Symbolic-experiential family therapy. In A. Gurman, & D. Kniskern (Eds.), *Handbook of family therapy* (pp. 187–225). New York: Brunner/Mazel.

Whitaker, C., & Malone, T. (1953). *The roots of psychotherapy*. New York: Blakiston.

Wilcoxon, S. A., Remley, T. P., Gladding, S. T., & Huber, C. H. (2012). *Ethical, legal, and professional issues in the practice of marriage and family therapy*. Boston: Pearson.

Wynne, L. (1988). An overview of the state of the art. In L. Wynne (Ed.), *The state of the art in family therapy research: Controversies and recommendations* (pp. 249–266). New York: Family Process Press.

17

SCHOOL COUNSELING

Tamara E. Davis

School counseling is a unique area in the field of counseling and offers an exciting way to integrate counseling and K-12 student academic success in the same setting. As a specialty area of counseling, school counseling differs from other areas in a variety of ways, and these differences will be discussed in this chapter. A brief history of significant events in school counseling is given, followed by a description of the current status of school counseling. Information from the American School Counselor Association (ASCA), the premier association for school counseling, will be shared throughout the chapter, and details will be given regarding the ASCA National Model for School Counseling Programs (ASCA, 2012) and other influential movements and documents in professional school counseling literature. Specific developmental issues of students and the role of the school counselor in addressing those issues will be explored. Further, the Council for the Accreditation of Counseling and Related Educational Programs (CACREP) has developed specific objectives in the area of school counseling (CACREP, 2009). These provide the rationale for many concepts about school counseling and the school counselor's role. These objectives are integrated throughout the chapter. Finally, credentials for becoming a school counselor will be presented and considerations for a career in school counseling will be offered.

The case of "Paul" in Sidebar 17.1 is an example of when a professional school counselor is needed. Often referred to as a *guidance counselor*, the professional school counselor has a unique and pivotal role in today's education system. A professional school counselor serves as a member of the educational team of qualified professionals whose specialty is the enhancement of students' academic, personal/social and career development as they experience their school life and beyond. Students do not leave their personal lives at the schoolhouse door; school counselors have the distinct opportunity to help students deal with issues that could hamper their academic progress. A counseling plan for Paul will be offered at the end of this chapter.

It should be noted that the term *school counselor* will be used to describe school personnel who are often referred to as *guidance counselors*. *Guidance* is a function of what school counselors do, but does not define who they are. Further, in most counseling fields, the persons receiving services are called *clients*. Because school counselors work in the school setting, the clients are students and will be referred to as *students*. Finally, any discussion of school counseling will refer to school counselors who work in K-12 school settings and will not include counseling in higher education.

School Counseling as a Specialty Area in Counseling

The role of school counselors has changed significantly over the years (Gysbers, 2010). School counseling as a specialty differs from other types of counseling in specific ways.

SIDEBAR 17.1 Case Study: What Would a School Counselor Do?

Everyone had noticed that Paul's behavior and academic performance at school had been deteriorating since the holiday break. The rumor was that Paul's parents had announced their intent to separate and divorce after the family had "gotten through Christmas." Paul's geometry teacher was especially concerned that he had not turned in any homework since returning from break. His swimming coach noted that Paul had been consistently late for practice and had even missed a swim meet with no excuse. Some students said that Paul had been hanging with a new group of friends (referred to as the "potheads") and that his moods were either depressed or almost manic. While the parental separation might explain some of this, there was great concern that Paul's downward spiral could cost him academically and ultimately affect his postsecondary plans. As a school counselor, how would you intervene? Identify the issues that you would address and how you might address them. Ideas for working with Paul will be offered later in this chapter.

One of those ways has already been mentioned—the setting in which counseling occurs (schools) and the clients being served (students). Another difference is the logistics of how, when, and where counseling is conducted. In agency or mental health counseling, most clients are seen by appointment, for a designated period of time, and then leave to go about their daily lives. For school counselors, most counseling occurs when students self-refer or are referred by a teacher, administrator, parent, or another student. There are rarely scheduled appointments due to the structure of the student's academic schedule. An advantage that school counselors have is the opportunity to see students on a daily basis, giving them ample time to follow up and check on students' progress. On the other hand, school counselors sometimes have difficulty meeting with students because pulling them from class interferes with their academic time-on-task.

The major goal of school counseling is to help students be in the best frame of mind to be effective lifelong learners. Other counseling professionals typically may not have a major goal in mind other than to help the client work through their presenting issue or concern. Because the focus of schools is on academic success, school counselors must also focus on student academic success and assist students in being in the best mental and emotional condition to learn. School counseling is *not* therapy in schools. However, it is difficult for students to focus and perform well on their algebra test if they are distraught and distracted because the police came to their house the night before to break up a parental dispute. The overarching goal of academic achievement is not typically found in other counseling specialty areas, although counselors in other settings often address academic concerns in their counseling.

A final difference between school counseling and other specialty areas of counseling is that school counselors are bound by external policies and the protocols of the school and school district. While external policies may also be present in other counseling settings, it may be more binding in the school setting. For example, if students come to the school counselors to talk about becoming sexually active and the school board's policy is that school personnel advocate for abstinence as the only sexual practice, school counselors are put in the position of deciding how to respond: Should they defy the policies of the school district (employer) and risk dismissal from their job or should they try to address the

---

SIDEBAR 17.2 Reflection & Self Awareness: Does School Counseling Appeal to You?

This section reveals the distinctive difference between school counseling and other areas of counseling. Based on this discussion, does counseling in schools appeal to you? Why or why not? If yes, what personal qualities or experiences have you had (perhaps with your own school counselor) that influence your thinking about being a school counselor?

---

students' needs without breaking school district policies? While there are ways to make decisions in compliance with policies or respond in ways that do not defy rules and regulations, being policed by a third party is another obstacle that school counselors face that may not be present in others counseling specialty areas.

More positively, school counseling also has some distinct advantages over other types of counseling: (1) there is a large group of students that can be served through counseling (a captive audience), (2) there tends to be support for counseling in schools since the ultimate goal is student success, and (3) the stigma that surrounds therapy in other areas of counseling may not be present for school counselors since school counseling programs are extensively offered in schools, which makes school counseling more familiar for the general population than other types of counseling. Because of the distinctive nature of counseling in schools, it is imperative that anyone considering a career in school counseling understand these important differences in order to avoid frustration or burnout early in their career.

Foundations in School Counseling: A Significant History

Chapter 1 provides a comprehensive history of the counseling field in general and CACREP requires that school counselors specifically "know history, philosophy, and trends in school counseling and educational systems" (CACREP, 2009, p. 40). School counseling grew out of the field of vocational counseling, which began in the early 1900s. Frank Parsons, often considered the "father of counseling" began the movement toward counseling by creating a bureau to help students get jobs. The purpose of counseling in this context was to help meet societal needs for trained, productive workers.

As World War I occurred and through the years of the Great Depression, the role of guidance personnel in schools began to include testing young men for the purposes of classification to serve in the armed forces. The emphasis on vocations was still the predominant role, but the war required placement of many young men in service to their country. One specific event that gave credence to school guidance personnel (as they were called at the time) was the advent of state certification for guidance counselors in 1924 (Baker & Gerler, 2008). The need for trained personnel to assist in placement for jobs or for service continued in the 1920's and 1930s.

Beginning in the 1940s, school counseling services were influenced by several events. Changes in support for school counseling have occurred, and the role of school counselors has been shifting with each decade until the present. Table 17.1 provides a snapshot of key events, legislation, and movements that influenced school counseling from the 1940s until the end of the 20th century.

The *ASCA National Model* (ASCA, 2012) is the document that currently guides school counseling programs and practices across the country and beyond. Its inception in 2003 (and revisions in 2005 and 2012) continues to drive the profession of school counseling today. For that reason, an overview of its components and elements is critical for those who seek to learn about current school counseling best practices.

The ASCA National Model for School Counseling Programs

Perhaps no document has affected school counseling more than the *ASCA National Model for School Counseling Programs* (2012) [hereafter referred to as the ASCA Model]. The ASCA Model has been identified as the predominant model for the profession of school counseling. CACREP emphasizes that school counselors must know "current models of school

Table 17.1 Events that influenced school counseling 1940–2010

Year/decade	Event	Impact on school counseling profession
Early 1940's	Books by Sigmund Freud and Carl Rogers are published.	The seminal works altered the public's perception of the counselor's role and promoted more personal counseling rather than vocational counseling.
1946	*George Barden Act* was passed.	This legislation supported the development and implementation of guidance and counseling activities in schools.
1953	The American School Counselor Association (ASCA) is chartered.	ASCA began as a small organization for school counselors; it has grown to more than 30,000 members.
1955	The Guidance and Personnel Services section of the U.S. Office of Education was reestablished (Schmidt, 2008).	The government begins to recognize the importance of professional school counselors in schools and created a department specifically to support guidance personnel.
1958	*National Defense Education Act (NDEA)* was passed.	The United States was threatened by the launching of Sputnik. NDEA mandated greater funding for academic programs and support services (like school counseling) in order to improve academic and vocational preparation of students.
1962	Gilbert Wrenn's *The Counselor in a Changing World* was published.	This book provided support for role refinement for school counselors and encouraged school counselors to respond to the needs of students in an ever-changing society.
1964	NDEA amended to include elementary school counselors.	Up until now, school counselors were only present at secondary levels. The amendment allowed for the hiring of elementary school counselors for the first time.
1975	*Education Act for All Handicapped Children* was passed.	While there were no specific implications for school counseling, the legislation focused on the need for individualized support services for all students, particularly those with challenging conditions.

Table 17.1 Continued

Year/decade	Event	Impact on school counseling profession
1983	A "Nation at Risk" report was published.	The report indicated the declining performance of American's students; as a result, school counselors were asked to be more accountable for their services and to provide more effective support services.
1996	The *Transforming School Counseling Initiative* (Education Trust, 1996) is funded through a grant initiative of the DeWitt Wallace-Reader's Digest fund and is implemented through the *Education Trust*.	The goal of the initiative was to refine school counselor training programs and current school counseling practices to expand to include competencies in advocacy, leadership, systemic change, teaming and collaboration, and use of data. The TSCI initiative partnered higher education institutions who were training school counselors with local school districts to improve the academic progress of all students.
1997	The *National Standards for School Counseling Programs* (Campbell & Dahir, 1997) are published.	The *Standards* are the first document to unify the profession by providing objectives for the academic, personal/social, and career development of all students.
2001	The *No Child Left Behind Act of 2001* (U.S. Department of Education, 2002) is endorsed by President George Bush.	While there is no specific mention of school counselors, this legislation involved school counselors in terms of greater accountability for student performance and closing the gap between the majority and the minority in terms of achievement.
2003	The *ASCA National Model for School Counseling Programs* is released; second edition released in 2005 and third edition released in 2012.	The *ASCA National Model* provides a framework for the development and implementation of effective, comprehensive school counseling programs. The document combined previous models and integrated them into one comprehensive model that would unite school counselors.
2004	RAMP begins	ASCA begins to award Recognized ASCA Model Program (RAMP) designations to school counseling programs that demonstrate effective school counseling programs and practices.

counseling programs" (p. 40) and specifically identifies the ASCA Model as an integral model. Figure 17.1 is the symbol of the ASCA Model: the "diamond" includes four quadrants that are the basis for the development of comprehensive school counseling programs.

The ASCA Model approaches counseling in schools from a systemic perspective rather than the individualistic model of traditional counseling. Walsh, Barrett, and DePaul (2007) described the shift and related it to other education reform movements:

> The shift in focus from providing services predominantly for individual students to working systematically to serve all students centralizes the role of school counselors in supporting the teaching and learning mission of schools and

Figure 17.1 American School Counselor Association. (2012) *The ASCA national model: A framework for school counseling programs* (3rd edition). Alexandria, VA: Author

> situates them as essential figures in the nation's goal to reform education and leave no child behind. (p. 377)

The ASCA Model (ASCA, 2012) is the professional framework that provides structure for what school counselors plan, implement, and produce in schools. Many of the tasks, particularly those in the Delivery System, involve direct work with students. Other components assist in the planning, organization, and evaluation of the school counseling program. The connection between the model and the role of school counselors is evident in the role statement of the school counselor (ASCA, 2009), and it is important to understand the role of professional school counselors in the context of the ASCA Model.

The Role of the Professional School Counselor: Alignment with the ASCA National Model

The ASCA Model (ASCA, 2012) offers a framework in which the school counseling program should be developed, implemented, sustained and improved. The Model (ASCA, 2012) contains four elements that are necessary for the creation of effective and comprehensive school counseling programs. The diagram indicates that the **Foundation** of the model contributes to the **Delivery** and **Management Systems**, which are connected to **Accountability.** Accountability then flows back to Foundation because the results of data collected about the school counseling program will ultimately influence the foundation of the program. An exploration of each component is critical to understanding the important work of professional school counselors.

Foundation

School counseling programs focus on the beliefs and philosophies about how students benefit from school counseling. According to ASCA (2009), these beliefs and philosophies "guide the development, implementation and evaluation of a culturally relevant and comprehensive school counseling program" (p. 1). Professional school counselors asks themselves: "What do I believe about student success? What is my philosophy of education student learning? What do I believe about students today?" These personal beliefs and philosophies are at the core of why people choose school counseling as a career and also impact the development of a mission statement for the school counseling program. The mission statement of the school counseling program should align with the school's mission statement and should encompass the ultimate goals of promoting student academic, personal/social, and career development. One way this is achieved is through the alignment of the school counseling program with state and national standards (Campbell & Dahir, 1997). Once these components are developed, the foundation for a comprehensive school counseling program is established.

Delivery System

The delivery system is how the school counseling program will be delivered or carried out and includes many roles for the school counselor. The delivery of counseling services is most likely the area in which most school counselors spend the majority of their time, and it consists of the school counseling curriculum, independent student planning, responsive services, consultation, and support services. The delivery system is divided into *direct* and *indirect services*. Direct services include the delivery of the school counseling curriculum and direct interaction with students. Indirect services include anything that has an impact on the student but may not include direct interaction, such as collaboration with teachers and parents (ASCA, 2012).

School Counseling Curriculum

The first component is the *school counseling curriculum* which is the means through which the counseling program is delivered. According to ASCA (2009): "The school guidance curriculum is delivered throughout the school's overall curriculum and is systematically presented by professional school counselors in collaboration with other professional educators in K-12 classroom and group activities" (p. 1). Classroom guidance, which is the teaching of lessons in the classroom or large-group setting, is a unique feature of

---

SIDEBAR 17.3 Reflection & Self Awareness: Beliefs and Philosophy

What do you believe about students and learning? What do you believe that schools should provide for students?

Table 17.2 Developmental classroom guidance topics for each level

Elementary	Middle	High
Developing Friendships	Friendship Issues	SAT/ACT Prep Strategies
Bully Prevention	Peer Pressure	Post-secondary Options
Conflict Resolution Skills	Academic Planning	Applying for Scholarships
Test-taking Strategies	Relationship Issues	Relationship Issues (family,
Character Education	Bullying/Harassment	dating)
Uniqueness/Differences	Fitting In	Academic Planning (yearly)
Responses to Peer Pressure	Test Preparation Skills	Career Decision-making
Career Awareness	Career Exploration	

school counseling. The teaching component of school counseling may be intimidating for school counselors who do not have teaching experience. However, teaching or speaking in front of large groups is a reality in school counseling, so many counseling preparation programs provide training specific to classroom instruction, such as classroom management strategies. CACREP (2009) requires that school counselors "understand curriculum design, lesson plan development, classroom management strategies, and differentiated instructional strategies for teaching counseling- and guidance-related material" (p. 44). While these roles are not traditionally thought of when one thinks of counseling, the nature of counseling in schools includes these various tasks.

Classroom guidance topics for school counselors at each level may vary due to the development needs of students. For example, elementary school classroom guidance lessons tend to be more preventive in nature, whereas middle and high school topics may be more instructional. Table 17.2 lists topics that may be addressed at each school level.

Individual Student Planning

One of the reasons that people select a career in school counseling is the opportunity to have an influence on students on an individual basis. Individual student planning is often conducted through individual counseling sessions and, while planning may be academic in nature, often includes addressing personal and social needs of students. As students begin to plan for their futures, there are often issues or concerns that may arise. Family issues, personal issues, or other external concerns may become barriers to the student's academic progress. Individual planning includes important actions such as establishing goals and planning for the future while addressing personal/social issues. The developmental nature of education-career planning across levels is indicated by Trusty, Niles, and Carney (2005): "Ideally, students get a solid introduction to education-career planning at

---

SIDEBAR 17.4 Individual Student Planning: Self-Reflection

Think about your own academic experience. Were there times in your development that you could have used the support of school counselor? What do you remember about the issues that arise that are specific to each level (elementary, middle, high)? What value do you see in having support from a school counselor during these experiences?

---

the elementary school; planning becomes increasingly specific and involved through middle school, resulting in appropriate plans for high school" (p. 142). Further, CACREP (2009) states that school counselors know "strategies for helping students identify strengths and cope with environmental and developmental problems" (p. 41).

Responsive Services

In most schools, the majority of the school counselor's day is spent responding to the needs of students, faculty, parents, and community. According to ASCA (2009), the roles of the school counselor in responsive services include: "individual or group counseling, consultation with parents, teachers, and other educators, referrals to other school support services or community resources, peer helping, [providing] and intervention and advocacy at the systemic level" (p. 1). CACREP also emphasizes that it is best practice for school counselors to provide "individual and group counseling and classroom guidance to promote the academic, career, and personal/social development of students" (p. 41). Addressing the issues that students may encounter in their educational careers is a key responsibility of the school counselor.

Individual and small group counseling is often the role that attracts people to the school counseling profession. Individual counseling may be on-going or may be a drop in, brief encounter with a student. A distinction between individual counseling in schools and in community or agency counseling is that school counselors rarely keep students in a session for long periods of time. Because most individual counseling occurs during the school day, it is critical to keep students in class when possible. The time issues involved in school counseling have facilitated more frequent use of solution-focused brief counseling interventions, because counseling must be efficient as well as effective and solution-focused strategies have proven to be effective in school counseling (Birdsall & Miller, 2002; Cook & Kaffenberger, 2003; Schmidt, 2008).

Small group counseling typically involves the gathering of smaller groups (usually 6–8 students) to work on specific skills. Two specific types of groups in schools are *remedial* and *support groups* (Davis, 2005). Remedial groups may include topics such as study skills, social skills, anger management, and behavior management and will include activities that provide skill development to address issues. Support groups focus more on personal issues such as changing families, grief, or life transitions. School counselors solicit referrals for group counseling from teachers, parents, or student self-referrals. Parent consent for participation is secured and small groups typically last from 6–8 weeks, although some school counselors have support groups (such as "Girls Group" or "Relationship Issues Group") on an on-going basis with changing student membership each session. Research supports the efficacy of small group counseling in schools (Bostick & Anderson, 2009; Bruce, Getch, & Ziomek-Daigle, 2009; Glaser & Shoffner, 2001; Kayler & Sherman, 2009).

Collaboration & Consultation

An indirect role for school counselors is consultation with parents, teachers, other educators and school personnel, and community members. The school counselor is often a consultant for teachers who are seeking help with students. "Counselors often handle situations by meeting with the student, calling a parent, or establishing a working alliance with the teacher to help meet the needs of the student" (Davis, 2005, p. 82).

Consultation with parents is another common role for school counselors, and school counselors are often the first to be contacted when parents have a concern about their child. The school counselor becomes the facilitator for action that is taken to address parent concerns or student needs. Finally, the school counselor serves as a consultant and liaison to the community. The consultative and collaborative role of the school counselor is a primary objective of CACREP (2009), which states that school counselors must know strategies and be able to work with parents, teachers, staff, and community "to act on behalf of" students and "to promote student academic, career, and personal/social development" (p. 45). The school counselor must be accessible, available, and willing to serve as a consultant to others and has a crucial role to play in the development of strategies and solutions for concerns that are expressed.

When school counselors are not sure how to respond to a situation or do not have the expertise needed to address a problem, they have an ethical obligation to refer the student or person to other school personnel services or community resources. CACREP (2009) also supports the view that the school counselors must "....recognize his or her limitations as a school counselor and to seek supervision or refer clients when appropriate" (p. 41). The school counselor may need to coordinate or facilitate the connection between the school and the community. Coordination of services is another key role of school counselors and requires organization, knowledge, and the ability to connect constituents with the services they need. Research supports creating partnerships to address the barriers that hinder economically disadvantaged students and families from having access to the services that they need (Steen & Noguera, 2010).

Management

An important role for school counselors is the overall management and organization of the school counseling program. The Management System (ASCA, 2012) includes (1) agreement with administrators in terms of school counseling services and service delivery, (2) the development of an advisory council to provide input and feedback to the school counseling program, (3) using student data to make decisions regarding the counseling services that are needed to effectively meet student needs, (4) developing action plans to address student needs, and (5) using master and weekly calendars to keep others informed of the activities and events in the school counseling program (pp. 47–56). The management of the school counseling program requires organizational skills as well as effective communication in order to facilitate the implementation of the school counseling program.

Because management responsibilities can be time-consuming, school counselors must be careful that their management duties do not undermine the delivery of counseling services. ASCA (2012) recommends that 80 percent of the school counselor's time is devoted to direct service (i.e. counseling, consultation) with students. Further, ASCA also recommends a student to school counselor ratio of 250:1 (ASCA, 2012). The management tasks and responsibilities should enhance the delivery of counseling services, not replace them.

Accountability

As education has become increasingly standards-based, the emphasis on high-stakes testing has also affected school counseling. School counseling services are often considered ancillary to the education program and school personnel are reluctant to allow school counselors to pull students from class. School counselors may find themselves in a position where they need to rationalize or *prove* that school counseling programs make a difference in student success. According to Whiston (2002), "School counselors may believe they make a difference, but without 'hard data' to support these claims, school counselors run the risks of losing their positions" (p. 153). A special issue of the *Professional School Counseling* journal focused on action research in school counseling and included articles that "highlight the power of evidence-based programming... and specific types of interventions that result in successful changes for students" (Kaffenberger & Davis, 2009, p. 393).

Current research practices in school counseling include action research (Rowell, 2006) and the development of assessment instruments that can reflect the results of school counseling programs and interventions (Studer, Oberman, & Womack, 2006). The development of the National School Counseling Research Center (Sabella, 2006) and the National Center for School Counseling Research (Carey & Dimmitt, 2006) is evidence of the shift toward greater accountability in school counseling programs. The following is an example of how a school counselor might use data to support the efficacy of the school counseling program.

Mr. Ledford, a middle school counselor, was concerned about having so many students on the D/F grade list for English during the first nine weeks. In his caseload alone, there were 20 students already at risk of failing for the semester if things did not improve. Mr. Ledford decided he would implement a variety of counseling services to support these students. His plan included: (1) small group counseling sessions with the students to work on study skills such as time management, organization, and study skills; (2) individual counseling or "check ins" with students weekly; (3) consultation with teachers of the students at risk of failure; and (4) contact with parents to enlist their help in making sure homework was completed and returned. He implemented this plan for the second nine-week grading period. Mr. Ledford also conducted a pre-test survey to see if students could name three effective strategies for help with studying (12 students could identify three strategies).

At the end of the second nine weeks, Mr. Ledford checked the students' grades and found that 15 out of 20 had successfully raised their grades to at least a "C" in English. Mr. Ledford could conclude that 75% of the students had improved their grade after counseling interventions were implemented to specifically address areas of weakness. Mr. Ledford also completed a post-test survey and found a 50% increase in the number of students who could identify three successful study strategies (18 students could identify three study strategies).

Mr. Ledford can feel good about his success! However, his role as a professional school counselor does not end with his findings. He should let others know of his success with these students. All educational stakeholders need to know that allowing students to participate in counseling services can positively impact student success.

SIDEBAR 17.5 Accountability: Consider

Most people would not consider accountability and data collection as a critical role for school counselors. However, there has been an increase in the emphasis on results-based data in school counseling. How do you feel about collecting data to support the effectiveness of counseling programs? Does it make sense to see if programs are making a difference with children or does it go against the nature of counseling to "objectify" results? Explain your response.

Foundations in School Counseling: The ASCA Ethical Standards

An important resource for school counselors is an ethical code written specifically for school counselors (*Ethical Standards for School Counselors*, ASCA, 2010). The ethical standards for school counselors are applicable to situations and circumstances that are relevant in the school setting and serve as a guide for school counselors as they work with students, parents, peers, administrators, and community members. CACREP (2009) requires that school counselors "demonstrate the ability to apply and adhere to ethical and legal standards in school counseling" (p. 40).

Ethical dilemmas can be challenging in schools, based on limits to confidentiality and school board policies. For example, the ASCA Ethical standards support maintaining the confidentiality of students, however, the standards become complicated when the school board has a policy that challenges or contradicts the ethical standards of the profession. The best advice offered when faced with an ethical dilemma is to respond in the way *any reasonable counselor would respond* and to follow ethical decision-making steps (Stone, 2001, as cited in ASCA, 2010). While there are many issues that are clear-cut and decisions are black and white, there are other issues that emerge in schools that are not so clear. Consulting the ASCA ethical standards and consulting with colleagues is best practice for an ethically responsible school counselor.

Counseling, Prevention, & Intervention: The Role of the School Counselor

The role of the school counselor that most attracts people to the school counseling field is the opportunity to affect and enhance the lives of young people. As has been mentioned, the school counselor assists in the academic, personal/social, and career development of students. School counselor programs and services may be prevention-oriented (such as a school-wide bullying prevention program) or focused on intervention (such as a study skills small group for students who have not passed a standardized test). This section explores counseling elementary and secondary students and will provide insight into the comprehensive role of K-12 school counselors.

SIDEBAR 17.6 An Ethical Dilemma

Mr. Starr is a high school counselor. One of his students comes to him and tells him that she thinks her friend is pregnant. When he confronts the friend, she begins to cry but does not admit that she is pregnant. Mr. Starr knows that the school district has a Board policy regarding confidentiality and student sexual activity (i.e., the counselor is supposed to call the parent or guardian). The student has admitted nothing but is visibly upset by whatever is going on.

What should Mr. Starr do? What ethical issues are evident in this case?

Licensure and Accreditation

First and foremost, school counselors are committed to helping students become effective, lifelong learners (Davis, 2005). Because school counseling occurs within the school environment, it makes sense that academic success (the goal of education) is also the goal of school counseling. CACREP (2009) states it is critical that the school counselor "understands the relationship of the school counseling program to the academic mission of the school" (p. 44). At the elementary level, the school counselor contributes to the development of effective study skills and student appreciation for learning. Early intervention programs are necessary so that students make the connection between academic success and postsecondary options and opportunities (CACREP, 2009, p. 44). Classroom guidance that focuses on study skills or test-taking strategies can help students perform better on academic tasks. At both elementary and secondary levels, individual and small group counseling often address specific learning problems, provide strategies to facilitate learning, and encourage goal-setting for academic progress. School counselors may also provide school-wide programs that create a positive climate for learning, such as award programs for academic achievement, school attendance, or good citizenship.

Research supports the effectiveness of school counselor interventions on academic performance such as improved test scores (Bruce, Getch, & Ziomek-Daigle, 2009), and improved academic performance (Brigman, Webb, & Campbell, 2007; Steen, 2011). This evidence reinforces the critical role of the school counselor in student academic development.

Personal/Social Development

One of the barriers to student academic achievement is the effect of personal/social events that occur in the students' lives that often overwhelm them to the point of distraction and, often, result in apathy regarding their academic progress. Student issues run the gamut from family issues (divorce, poverty, moving, abuse, etc.) to social issues (friendships, dating, peer pressure, etc.) and these may even result in destructive behaviors such as eating disorders and self-mutilation (e.g., cutting).

Regardless of their severity, the impact of life events is a reality for students, regardless of age. School counselors are uniquely trained to help students process their feelings about their personal and social circumstances with the ultimate goal of assisting the student in being in the best frame of mind to be successful in class. This may be accomplished through individual counseling, small group counseling, and, in some situations, classroom guidance is the appropriate delivery service. Counseling may also include consultation and collaboration with parents and teachers in order to provide a network of support for students. Davis (2005) provides some general guidelines for counseling students around personal/social issues:

- Listen to the story: Students need to be heard.
- Help students identify their concerns: What are the major issues or concerns?
- Meet the student where the student is: Empathize with his/her issues.
- Help the student set goals: What the student would like to have happen?
- Consider challenges to achieving goals: What are the consequences of acting toward the goals?
- Be available and check in with the student: Provide support and follow-up.
- Consider referral: Recognize the extent of professional knowledge and expertise and refer if necessary (pp. 119–120).

The counseling role of school counselors is critical and school counselors must possess the knowledge and skills to know how to appropriately intervene (CACREP, 2009). Research supports the role of the school counselor in facilitating the personal/social development of students. Individual, small group, and school-wide interventions may include programs that promote student resiliency and empowerment (Rose, Miller, & Martinez, 2009; Wyatt, 2009; Young et al., 2009).

Career Development

Because school counseling foundations began in the career and vocational arena, it seems appropriate that career development is still a primary focus of school counseling. Career counseling involves helping students with post-secondary planning, whether students are headed for college or planning to enter the world of work. ASCA (2006) posited: "Professional school counselors collaborate with administrators, teachers, staff, parents, and the community to ensure that all students have the opportunity to design a rigorous and relevant academic and career program" (p. 1). Recent school reform movements have increased the emphasis on college and career readiness and hold schools accountable for making sure students are prepared to enter post-secondary education or career options. Therefore, academic and career planning naturally falls under the career development umbrella of the school counselor.

The National Office for School Counselor Advocacy (College Board, 2010) identifies components that provide a K-12 systemic approach for school counselors to "inspire all students to, and prepare them for, college success and opportunity—especially students from underrepresented populations" (p. 2). Further, the College Board identifies school counselors as the school professionals that "provide information, tools and perspective to parents, students, schools and their communities that build college and career readiness for all students" (p. 2). These activities may range from Career Days in elementary school to College Fairs in high school; the school counselor is the catalyst for career development K-12.

At the elementary level, school counselors perform career counseling by promoting *awareness* of the world of work. Students learn that there is a connection between getting an education and getting a job. School counselors may help coordinate a career day where professionals from a variety of jobs come to share their careers with students. Also, class-room guidance lessons may focus on interests and skills as they are related to specific careers.

Middle school counselors focus more on career *exploration* and typically spend time learning about a variety of careers. Middle school counselors may use technology and career exploration programs that are available via the internet. Career lessons might include interest inventories or skill assessments so that students may begin to consider careers of interest. Also, middle school may be the first time that a student's course selection might influence post-secondary plans and decisions about the type of diploma or course of study might be affected by decisions of the middle school student. School counselors may facilitate important sessions with students as they consider their academic plans.

As one might expect, career *decision-making* is most necessary for high school students. Many high schools have a Career Center that is dedicated specifically to the process of helping students explore and decide on post-secondary options. Even though the Career Center may have personnel available for students, this does not take away the important role of career counseling from school counselors.

Diversity & Advocacy

Advocacy in school counseling is necessary at many levels. Davis (2005) identified areas of *student advocacy*, *program advocacy*, and *educational advocacy* as required roles of school counselors. Table 17.3 summarizes the types of advocacy that are necessary roles of school counselors.

Research supports the need for school counselor advocacy to maximize the student learning experience (Davis, 2005; Erford, 2007), but perhaps the best definition is offered by Kuranz (2002):

> A good advocate listens, communicates, embraces different points of view, sets goals, develops strategies, provides feedback, works with people no matter who is in charge, thinks on his or her feet, coordinates, mediates, juggles more than one job at a time, identifies resources, and sticks with a task until a solution is found. (p. 178)

School counselor advocacy efforts often focus on student groups that are underrepresented or underserved by academic programs in school and many of those groups include diverse students. Historically, diversity has often been associated with differences in ethnicity. However, diversity must be considered in a much broader context when considering the varied composition of students in schools. School counselors must "understand the cultural, ethical, legal, and political issues surrounding diversity, equity, and excellence in terms of student learning" (CACREP, 2009, p. 42). Programs and services that address closing the gap and equity issues are critical to facilitating student success. Equality involves offering the same opportunity to all; equity is making sure there is not a disproportionate representation of one group more or less than any other. This section will look at diversity as it relates to minority groups of students, students with special needs, and LGBT students; while there are certainly other student groups that will need the advocacy efforts of school counselors, the three groups discussed indicate the critical role of school counselors as an advocate.

Table 17.3 Advocacy roles of school counselors

Advocacy area	Examples
Student Advocacy – supporting the academic, personal/social, and career development of students.	Educating students about their personal and educational rights; representing students in administrative hearings of meetings, testifying in court on behalf of a student; representing students in decisions that affect their student life.
Program Advocacy – providing evidence that the school counseling program is effective and essential to student success.	Distributing newsletters or brochures that highlight current and future school counseling programs and services; developing accountability reports that demonstrate the efficacy of school counseling programs and sharing the reports with key stakeholders.
Educational Advocacy – supporting the goals of education and ascertaining that the educational program benefits students.	Learning how the school and school system work; becoming aware of protocol for reporting concerns about the educational program; supporting curricular or program decisions that benefit students.

Multicultural/Minority Students

The changing demographics of student populations certainly impacts programs and services in schools. Racial and ethnic diversity has grown dramatically in the last three decades and is projected to continue current trends in the future (Federal Interagency on Child and Family Statistics, 2012). According to the National Center for Education Statistics (NCES, 2011), in 2009, the percentage of school-age children who spoke a language other than English at home and spoke English with difficulty at school varied by demographic characteristics such as race/ethnicity and poverty status. It is definitely not appropriate to use a "one size fits all" approach to promoting student development. Capuzzi and Gross (2007) identified areas such as language, identity, generational difference, cultural customs, geography, family history and traditions as issues that school counselors (and all school personnel) face in schools. School counselors must be prepared to deal with the myriad of issues that often surface around multiculturalism and to advocate for students who may otherwise fall through the cracks of the education system.

Lee (2001) recommended that culturally responsive schools take a "salad bowl" approach when considering multiculturalism in schools; that is, school counselors should consider diverse student groups as a separate but necessary part of the student body (p. 258). It is imperative that school counselors develop multicultural competence in order to work with students from various cultural backgrounds. In a global sense, school counselors must "advocate for school policies, programs, and services that enhance a positive school climate and are equitable and responsive to multicultural student populations" (CACREP, 2009, p. 42). Providing counseling services for students, such as support groups, transition groups, and individual counseling are ways that the school counselor supports minority students. "Advocacy activities also can take the form of educating other school personnel about the importance in fostering culturally supportive environments so that youth of color can attain personal and academic success" (Shin, Daly, & Vera, 2007, p. 386). Research supports that school counseling services aimed at closing the achievement gap and addressing cultural barriers to achievement can be successful advocacy tools that support students (Goh, Wahl, McDonald, Brissett, & Yoon, 2007; Schellenberg & Grothaus, 2011).

Students with Special Needs

For the purposes of this discussion, *special needs* will refer to students who qualify for special education services under the Individuals with Disabilities Education Act (2004). According to the NCES (2011), students with special needs comprising 13.2 percent of children aged 3 to 21 years are being served in federally supported programs for the disabled, with the highest percentage being those identified with specific learning disabilities. School counselors may have a variety of roles in working with students with special needs: individual counseling, group counseling, collaboration and consultation with parents of students with special needs, and serving on the multidisciplinary team that makes decisions about special education services. Because special education has legal implications, it is important for the school counselor to become familiar with the state and federal laws that pertain to serving students with special needs. According to ASCA (2004):

Professional school counselors work with students with special needs both in special class settings and in the regular classroom and are a key component in assisting with transitions to post-secondary options. It is particularly important that the professional school counselor's role in these procedures is clearly defined and is in compliance with laws and local policies. (p. 1).

Student advocacy is a primary role for school counselors who work with students with special needs. In addition, school counselors help parents and families of students with special needs as they seek to adapt to the unique needs of their children. Persons who are pursuing school counseling jobs would benefit from coursework specific to students with special needs in order to become familiar with special needs categories as well as the laws around special needs services.

Sexual Minority Youth

Other diversity issues, such as working with sexual minority youth, are also part of the educational setting. School counselors, especially those in middle and high school, will be working with students as they develop their sexual identity and begin to explore dating relationships. For sexual minority youth, the consequences of coming out may include harassment, parental rejection, and dealing with homophobia. Research supports the school counselor's role in working with sexual minority youth (Byrd & Hayes, 2012). The school counselor is also an integral person to help create a climate of tolerance for all students, regardless of sexual orientation. ASCA (2007) asserted that:

Professional school counselors promote affirmation, respect and equal opportunity for all individuals regardless of sexual orientation or gender identity. Professional school counselors also promote awareness of issues related to sexual orientation/gender identity among students, teachers, administrators, parents and the community...work to eliminate barriers that impede student development and achievement and are committed to the academic, career and personal/social development of all students. (p. 1).

There are many student populations in schools that need the assistance of school counselors to address issues and situations that occur naturally in schools; only two were discussed here. Professional school counselors strive to meet the needs of *all* student populations in order to provide equitable access to educational and counseling services.

Assessment

There is often the misconception that school counselors conduct student assessments in schools, such as intelligence testing and psychological testing. The fact is that it is the school psychologist who is typically responsible for this type of assessment. This does not mean that school counselors do not conduct assessments; in fact, CACREP (2009) requires that school counselors know assessment strategies and analyze assessment information to help when evaluating a student's needs or "assessing the effectiveness of educational programs" (p. 43). In addition, assessment can also mean evaluating whether or not a student issue or concern might be better served by other helping professionals. For example, if a student is exhibiting severe anxiety and engages in self-destructive behaviors such as cutting, school counselors may realize they may not be the best resource for the student or the family. In that case, they might make a referral to a mental health specialist outside the school setting.

CACREP (2009) emphasizes that school counselors must be knowledgeable about and skilled in dealing with many factors and student issues that affect student functioning. Factors such as eating disorders, substance abuse, and attention issues often impede academic and personal/social development. In addition, Eppler and Weir (2009) advocate for school counselors "to employ a wide variety of techniques to ensure equitable distribution of services to all students and their families" (p. 501). The school counselor's ability to assess a student's situation, identify his/her unique needs, and then connect the student and family to programs and services to address those needs is the role of the school counselor in assessment.

Research and Evaluation

Successful school counseling programs and interventions have been cited in research throughout this chapter. Action research in school counseling has been growing in the last decade. Dahir & Stone (2009) provided a summary of studies that used accountability practices to reach school improvement goals with elementary, middle, and high school students. With the emphasis on results-based programs and accountability in school reform, school counselors must join the movement and show their impact on student success through action research and outcome data (Rowell, 2006). Reporting that students feel better after seeing the school counselor is no longer enough. "It is now apparent that school counselors must add a workable accountability skill set to their daily practice in order for their school improvement leadership activities to be sustainable over time" (Sink, 2009, p. 69).

Research and evaluation in school counseling may look slightly different than research in other counseling arenas. School counseling research includes program evaluation, methods that inform decision making, and evaluating counseling outcomes (CACREP, 2009, p. 43). The ability to collect, analyze and use data to enhance school counseling programs are necessary skills for school counselors. This is often a surprise to those who pursue school counseling because they think that school counseling means conducting therapy sessions in school; the reality is that school counselors must show how their programs affect student attendance, behavior, and achievement. If programs do not show an impact in one of those three areas, then school counselors are often seen as ancillary to student success. The question is "How are students different as a result of the school counseling program?" (ASCA, 2005). Perhaps it is stated most succinctly by Dimmitt (2009): "Ultimately, evaluation helps us do our best work, with the greatest impact, most efficiently" (p. 395).

Consultation & Collaboration

The role of consultation and collaboration was discussed briefly under the *Delivery System* of the ASCA National Model. School counselors spend a majority of their time in consultation or collaboration with many groups affiliated with students. The groups that school counselors most often interface with, however, are other school personnel and parents.

Collaborating with School Personnel

The nature of counseling in schools is that there are many other people with whom the counselor may interface on a daily basis. Collaboration with others in the school and also outside the school (parents, community members) is an important role for school counselors. Building relationships with school personnel and working as a team in the best interest of students is a primary goal for school counselors. While school counselors primarily support students, they are also in a unique position to provide support for colleagues (teachers and administrators). Effective communication skills with school personnel will forge connections that will ultimately benefit students as everyone works together to ensure student success.

School counselors may work with a variety of school personnel, depending on the need to be involved with student situations. It is not unusual for the school counselor to work closely with administrators (Dahir, Burnham, Stone, & Cobb, 2010), the school psychologist (Simcox, Nuijens, & Lee, 2006), the school social worker, the school nurse, or the student resource office (a police officer in the school). Because school counselors become acquainted with a large number of students, it makes sense that they are involved with personnel who interact with these students. The forging of these relationships will ultimately benefit students. As Davis (2005) concluded:

> In order to provide effective and comprehensive services to students, which may require the input and expertise of many school professionals, school counselors should initiate dialogue and interactions that will benefit students. It is only through…effective working relationships and team efforts toward student development and success that everyone wins. (p. 193).

Collaborating with Parents/Families/Guardians

Parents are an integral part of student academic success and, therefore, should be involved in their children's education. School counselors build positive relationships with parents by being available, accessible, and flexible. Often, parents do not participate in a student's education program due to a variety of reasons such as work schedules or avoidance due to a negative educational experiences in their own past. School counselors should try to connect with parents and emphasize that everyone wants the same goal—the academic success of the student.

School counselors can provide support for parents in a variety of ways, such as parent education programs, parenting skills workshops, and developing a parenting resource library. In addition, participating in parent–teacher conferences on behalf of the student can also help alleviate some of the anxiety that parents may experience in consultation with teachers. Supporting parents is necessary as they focus on supporting their child in school. School counselors develop important relationships with parents in order to effectively bridge the gap between home and school.

Obviously, school counselors have many roles to play as they facilitate the academic, personal/social, and career development of students. Recent research in family–school–community collaboration has supported the effectiveness of a comprehensive, multifaceted approach to work effectively with students (Epstein & Van Voorhis, 2010; Griffin & Steen, 2010; Stinchfield & Zyromski, 2010). Because each student brings his/her unique stories to the school setting, school counselors have to be prepared to guide students through their school careers and help facilitate healthy and positive growth toward life goals.

Leadership

The roles of advocacy and leadership in school counseling go hand-in-hand. Most people who think about school counseling do not consider leadership an obvious role. However, school counselors have opportunities to be included in important decisions that benefit students. It is necessary for the school counselor to know "the qualities, principles, skills, and styles of effective leadership" (CACREP, 2009, p. 45). This includes participation on school curriculum and advisory committees in order to advocate for student well-being.

Brown and Trusty (2005) discuss leadership in school counseling in terms of *power*. In particular, they refer to *expert power* (the school counselor possesses the knowledge and skills to achieve goals), *referent power* (the school counselor possesses professional characteristics that others would like to emulate), and *informational power* (the school counselor can identify and deliver critical information to teachers and others) (pp. 211–213). School counselors who possess these qualities are inherently prone to leadership and can gain respect for their roles.

SIDEBAR 17.7 Is this School Counselor a Leader?

Mrs. Jackson has been a school counselor for 2 years. Her principal approaches her to work on the advisory committee for the new math materials that are going to be used in the school district. Her initial reaction is: "Why would I be involved with math materials? It has nothing to do with counseling." Do you think Mrs. Jackson's response is reasonable? Would there be any benefit to her serving on this curriculum committee? If so, what?

School counselors lead by involvement and example. For example, involvement on curriculum and/or discipline committees gives school counselors the opportunity to have a voice in school programs and activities (Ryan, Kaffenberger, & Carroll, 2011). Effective leadership includes being visible, being an advocate, and being around the table in important conversations that involve decision-making about educational programs and school climate. Further, leadership involves implementing a comprehensive school counseling program that aligns with the mission of the school and school improvement goals (Mason, 2010). Leadership in school counseling includes participating in important conversations about student development, being visible so that people know who the school counselor is and what school counseling is about, and getting involved in all areas of student development.

Academic Development

A professional school counselor typically has a graduate degree in school counseling although some states allow counselors with degrees in related counseling fields to be given a license in school counseling. Each state has different criteria for licensure/certification as a school counselor; information by state may be found on the ASCA website (listed at the end of this chapter) or information is also provided on each state's Department of Education website.

Many school counseling graduate programs are accredited by the Council for the Accreditation of Counseling and Related Education Programs [CACREP] (2009). These standards have been integrated throughout this chapter. Coursework in CACREP-accredited school counseling graduate programs must meet objectives in the core areas in addition to school counseling-specific standards. School counselor preparation programs that are CACREP-accredited are typically 60 credits. It is best to consult with university preparation programs to see what requirements are needed to complete a graduate degree in school counseling and also consult state department of education websites to see what other experience or criteria are required.

Most states do not require teaching experience to be a school counselor, but some do. Also, some states require that candidates take a standardized test such as the *Praxis* before being licensed as a school counselor. Again, consulting with the state department of education is the best way to determine what licensure as a school counselor in that state requires.

Considerations for a Career as a Professional School Counselor

With recent events across our country and in the world, the need for school counselors is evident. Schools are a constant in our society and youth, by virtue of being students in schools, will bring many issues, concerns, and joys into the education setting. School counselors are specifically trained in counseling skills that will help provide mental health services for students in schools. While professional school counselors are not *therapists* in schools, they are trained to begin to address the mental, physical, social, and emotional health of students as they pursue their academic goals.

When considering a school as a school counselor, one must consider the personal and professional challenges that might arise. Consider the following case example:

Samantha was completing her undergraduate degree in psychology. The looming question that haunted her as graduation approached was "What next?" Samantha had been examining graduate programs in several specialties of counseling. One of the areas she was strongly considering was becoming a professional school counselor. When weighing the feasibility of this career, Samantha wrote a list of pros and cons about being a school counselor.

Pros	Cons
I enjoy working with kids.	*Not sure if I want to only work with kids.*
I had a positive school experience.	*Will I be stifled by the structure of schools?*
I would like to help students achieve academic and career goals.	*How much personal counseling will I get to do?*
I enjoy working in a collaborative environment.	*I don't like confrontation; how will I handle an irate parent?*

The effective school counselor is able to balance the personal qualities and goals of helping students and the political and structural nature of schools. School counseling is a profession in which each day is different; planned events may go by the wayside because of a crisis or emergency that must be addressed immediately. Professional school counselors must be flexible and also be able to respond to crises in appropriate ways. Being able to multitask and keep informed about many student situations at one time are other qualities of effective school counselors.

Perhaps one of the biggest stressors for school counselors is being unable to leave student problems and issues at school when it is time to go home. Often, school counselors will emotionally burn out because they spend both working and non-working hours concerned about students. Siebert (2002) offered the following advice about developing *caregiver resiliency.*

> As a school counselor, a big part of your job is that of caregiver. You provide people in need with a shoulder to cry on, someone to listen to their concerns and advise on how to deal with adversity. However, it can be a fine line to walk between helping others with their problems and letting others' problems have a negative impact on your own mental health. You not only owe it to yourself but to your students to be a role model for resiliency. (p. 11)

While the rewards of being a professional school counselor are many, the challenge is meeting the daily demands of students, parents, peers, and administrators who often believe that the school counselor is the remedy for many issues. This challenge, while often exhausting, is exhilarating as the school counselor has the capacity to forever influence the healthy development and success of students.

Summary

The world of professional school counseling is one of great opportunity and challenge. Unlike other specialty areas in counseling, professional school counselors have, as an ultimate goal, the academic success of students. The role of professional school counselors is multifaceted and includes many activities related to providing services for students, parents, and other school personnel. The school counseling profession continues to respond to the needs of a diverse and ever-changing society. Issues related to diverse student populations, equitable access to education, technology, and role definition of the school counselor will continue to permeate the profession (Jones & Granello, 2002). Outcome-based program evaluation and finding time for counseling in an age of testing and accountability also challenge school counselors. However, the professional school counselor will confront these challenges head on and continue the positive course of recent events in school counseling that show the impact of school counseling programs and services on the academic success of students.

So, how would a professional school counselor work with Paul, the struggling student in Sidebar 17.1? First, the school counselor might consult with Paul's teachers to try to understand what specific behaviors Paul has been demonstrating in class and what changes they have observed in his school performance. Second, the school counselor would conduct individual counseling with Paul to assess his perspective on what is going on in his life. Using effective counseling skills, the school counselor would try to get Paul to be open about his life situation and the effect his home life might be having on his school performance. The school counselor would encourage Paul to express his feelings about things and then ask what Paul would like to have happen. In this session, the school counselor is also going to address Paul's decline in academic performance and help generate strategies to provide support for him at school. If necessary, the school counselor will help Paul identify resources that he can use to improve his academic performance. Finally, the school counselor would seek Paul's consent to speak with his parents so that everyone can be informed about the impact of the family situation on his academic progress. If Paul gives consent, the school counselor would arrange a meeting with the parents (with Paul present if he wishes) and perhaps include teachers as well so that everyone is collaborating about helping Paul experience success at school. A comprehensive school counseling plan, involving the roles of counseling, consultation, and coordination of services as well as monitoring and assessment of the effectiveness of interventions will highly increase Paul's chances of school and personal success.

The following websites provide additional information relating to the chapter topics.

Useful Websites

www.schoolcounselor.org: American School Counselor Association (some information is member protected)

http://nosca.collegeboard.org/: National Office for School Counselor Advocacy (College Board)

http://www.edtrust.org/dc/tsc: National Center for Transforming School Counseling - Education Trust

www.umass.edu/schoolcounseling: National Center for School Counseling Outcome Research

www.nces.ed.gov: National Center for Education Statistics

References

American School Counselor Association. (2012). *The ASCA national model for school counseling programs* (3rd ed.). Alexandria, VA: Author.

American School Counselor Association. (2010). *Ethical standards for school counselors.* Retrieved from http://www.schoolcounselor.org/files/EthicalStandards2010.pdf.

American School Counselor Association. (2009). *The role of the professional school counselor.* Retrieved from http://ascatemp.membershipsoftware.org/files/RoleStatement.pdf.

American School Counselor Association. (2007). *The professional school counselor and LGBTQ youth.* Retrieved from http://www.schoolcounselor.org/files/PS_LGBTQ.pdf.

American School Counselor Association. (2006). *The professional school counselor and academic and career planning.* Retrieved from http://www.schoolcounselor.org/files/PS_Academic%20and%20Career%20Planning.pdf.

American School Counselor Association. (2004). *The professional school counselor and students with special needs.* Retrieved from http://www.schoolcounselor.org/files/Special%20Needs.pdf.

Baker, S. B., & Gerler, E. R. (2008). *School counseling for the twenty-first century* (5th ed.). Upper Saddle River, NJ: Merrill/Prentice Hall.

Birdsall, B. A., & Miller, L. D. (2002). Brief counseling in the schools: A solution-focused approach for school counselors. *Counseling and Human Development, 35,* 1–10.

Bostick, D., & Anderson, R. (2009). Evaluating a small group counseling program: A model for program planning and improvement in the elementary setting. *Professional School Counseling, 12,* 428–433.

Brigman, G., Webb, L. D., & Campbell, C. (2007). Building skills for school success: Improving the academic and social competence of students. *Professional School Counseling, 10,* 279–288.

Brown, D., & Trusty, J. (2005). *Designing and leading comprehensive school counseling programs: Promoting student competence and meeting student needs.* Belmont, CA: Brooks/Cole.

Bruce, A. M., Getch, Y. Q., & Ziomek-Daigle, J. (2009). Closing the gap: A group counseling approach to improve test performance of African-American students. *Professional School Counseling, 12,* 450–457.

Byrd, R., & Hays, D. G. (2012). School counselor competency and lesbian, gay, bisexual, transgender, and questioning (LGBTQ) youth. *Journal of School Counseling, 10*(3). Retrieved from http://www.jsc.montana.edu/articles/v10n3.pdf.

Campbell, C. A., & Dahir, C. A. (1997). *National standards for school counseling programs.* Alexandria, VA: American School Counselor Association.

Capuzzi, D., & Gross, D. R. (2007). *Counseling and psychotherapy: Theories and Interventions* (4th ed.). Upper Saddle River, NJ: Merrill Prentice Hall.

Carey, J. C., & Dimmitt, C. (2006). Resources for school counselors and counselor educators: The Center for School Counseling Outcome Research. *Professional School Counseling, 9,* 416–420.

College Board, National Office for School Counselor Advocacy. (2010). *Eight components of college and career readiness counseling.* Washington, D.C.: Author.

Cook, J. B., & Kaffenberger, C. J. (2003). Solution shop: A solution-focused counseling and study skills program for middle school. *Professional School Counseling, 7,* 116–123.

Council for the Accreditation of Counseling and Related Educational Programs [CACREP]. (2009). *2009 standards.* Retrieved from http://www.cacrep.org/doc/2009%20Standards%20 with%20cover.pdf.

Dahir, C. A., Burnham, J. J., Stone, C. B., & Cobb, N. (2010). Principals as partners: Counselors as collaborators. *NASSP Bulletin, 94,* 286–305. doi: 10.1177/0192636511399899

Dahir, C. A., & Stone, C. B. (2009). School counselor accountability: The path to social justice and systemic change. *Journal of Counseling and Development, 87,* 12–20.

Davis, T. E. (2005). *Exploring school counseling: Professional practices and perspectives.* Boston, MA: Lahaska Press/Houghton Mifflin.

Dimmit, C. (2009). Why evaluation matters: Determining effective school counseling practices. *Professional School Counseling, 12,* 395–399.

Education Trust. (1996). *Transforming school counseling initiative.* Retrieved June 13, 2007 from http://www2.edtrust.org/EdTrust/Transforming+School+Counseling/main.

Eppler, C., & Weir, S. (2009). Family assessment in K-12 settings: Understanding family systems to provide effective collaborative services. *Psychology in Schools, 46,* 501–514.

Epstein, J. L., & Van Voorhis, F. L. (2010). School counselors' roles in developing partnerships with families and communities for student success. *Professional School Counseling, 14,* 1–14.

Erford, B.T. (Ed.). (2007). *Transforming the school counseling profession* (2nd ed.). Upper Saddle River, NJ: Merrill Prentice Hall.

Federal Interagency Forum on Child and Family Statistics. (2012). *America's children: Key national indicators of well-being, 2011.* Retrieved from http://www.childstats.gov/americaschildren/demo.asp.

Glaser, J. S., & Shoffner, M. F. (2001). Adventure-based counseling in schools. *Professional School Counseling, 5,* 42–48.

Goh, M., Wahl, K. H., McDonald, J. K., Brissett, A. A., & Yoon, E. (2007). Working with immigrant students in schools: The role of school counselors in building cross-cultural bridges. *Journal of Multicultural Counseling and Development, 35,* 66–79.

Griffin, D., & Steen, S. (2010). School-Family-Community partnerships: Applying Epstein's Theory of the six types of involvement to school counselor practice. *Professional School Counseling, 13,* 218–226.

Gysbers, N.C. (2010). *School counseling principles: Remembering the past, shaping the future.* Alexandria, VA: American School Counselor Association.

Individuals with Disabilities Education Act. (2004). *Building the legacy: IDEA 2004.* Retrieved from http://idea.ed.gov/.

Jones, S., & Granello, D. H. (2002). School counseling now and in the future: A reaction. *Professional School Counseling, 5,* 164–171.

Kaffenberger, C., & Davis, T. (2009). Introduction to special issue: A call for practitioner research. *Professional School Counseling, 12,* 392–393.

Kayler, H., & Sherman, J. (2009). At-risk ninth-grade students: A psychoeducational group approach to increase study skills and grade point average. *Professional School Counseling, 12,* 434–439.

Kuranz, M. (2002). Cultivating student potential. *Professional School Counseling, 5,* 172–179.

Lee, C. C. (2001). Culturally responsive school counselors and programs: Addressing the needs of all students. *Professional School Counseling, 4,* 257–261.

Mason, E. (2010). Leadership practices of school counselors and counseling program implementation. *NASSP Bulletin, 94,* 274–285.

National Center for Education Statistics. (2011). *Fast facts.* Retrieved from http://nces.ed.gov.

Rose, H., Miller, L., & Martinez, Y. (2009). FRIENDS for life: The results of a resilience-building, anxiety-prevention program in a Canadian elementary school. *Professional School Counseling, 12,* 400–407.

Rowell, L. L. (2006). Action research and school counseling: Closing the gap between research and practice. *Professional School Counseling, 9,* 376–384.

Ryan, T., Kaffenberger, C. J., & Caroll, A. G. (2011). Response to intervention: An opportunity for school counselor leadership. *Professional School Counseling, 14,* 211–221.

Sabella, R. A. (2006). The ASCA national school counseling research center: A brief history and agenda. *Professional School Counseling, 9,* 412–415.

Schellenberg, R., & Grothaus, T. (2011). Using culturally competent responsive services to improve student achievement and behavior. *Professional School Counseling, 14,* 222–230.

Schmidt, J. J. (2008). *Counseling in schools: Comprehensive programs of responsive services for all students* (5th ed.). Boston, MA: Allyn & Bacon.

Shin, R., Daly, B., & Vera, E. (2007). The relationships of peer norms, ethnic identity, and peer support to school engagement in urban youth. *Professional School Counseling, 10,* 379–388.

Siebert, A. (2002). Caregiver resiliency. *ASCA School Counselor, 39,* 10–13.

Simcox, A. G., Nuijens, K. L., & Lee, C.C. (2006). School counselors and school psychologists: Collaborative partners in promoting culturally competent schools. *Professional School Counseling, 9,* 272–277.

Sink, C. A. (2009). School counselors as accountability leaders: Another call for action. *Professional School Counseling, 13,* 68–74.

Steen, S. (2011). Academic and personal development through group work: An exploratory study. *The Journal for Specialists in Group Work, 36,* 129–143.

Steen, S., & Noguera, P. A. (2010). A broader and bolder approach to school reform: Expanded partnership roles for school counselors. *Professional School Counseling, 14,* 42–52.

Stinchfield, T. A., & Zyromski, B. (2010). A training model for school, family, and community collaboration. *The Family Journal: Counseling and Therapy for Couples and Families, 18,* 263–268.

Studer, J. R., Oberman, A. H., & Womack, R. H. (2006). Producing evidence to show counseling effectiveness in the schools. *Professional School Counseling, 9,* 385–391.

Trusty, J., Niles, S. G., & Carney, J. V. (2005). Education-career planning and middle school counselors. *Professional School Counseling, 9,* 136–142.

U.S. Department of Education. (2002). *No child left behind: A desk reference.* Washington, D.C.: Office of Elementary and Secondary Education.

Walsh, M. E., Barrett, J. G., & DePaul, J. (2007). Day-to-day activities of school counselors: Alignment with new directions in the field and the ASCA national model. *Professional School Counseling, 10,* 370–378.

Whiston, S. C. (2002). Response to the past, present, and future of school counseling: Raising some issues. *Professional School Counseling, 5,* 148–155.

Wrenn, C. G. (1962). *The counselor in a changing world.* Washington, D.C.: American Personnel and Guidance Association.

Wyatt, S. (2009). The Brotherhood: Empowering adolescent African-American males toward excellence. *Professional School Counseling, 12,* 463–470.

Young, A., Hardy, V., Hamilton, C., Biernesser, K., Sun, L., & Niebergall, S. (2009). Empowering students: Using data to transform a bullying prevention and intervention program. *Professional School Counseling, 12,* 413–420.

18

COLLEGE COUNSELING
AND STUDENT AFFAIRS

Theodore P. Remley, Jr. and Brian M. Shaw

Introduction

For counseling and student affairs professionals who have enjoyed being students most of their lives and love being in an academic environment, choosing a career in college counseling or student affairs could be a satisfying and rewarding decision. Depending on the type of college or university in which counselors and student affairs professionals are employed, work days are spent interacting with students whose ages generally range from 18 to 28. However, students arrive in college at all ages. In fact, the oldest person to ever graduate from college was Allan Stewart who earned his bachelor of law degree when he was 91 from the University of New England in New South Wales, Australia in 2006 (Guinness World Records, 2012a). And the youngest college graduate was Michael Kearney who in 1994 at age 10 received his bachelor's degree in Anthropology at the University of South Alabama (Guinness World Records, 2012b). To illustrate the variety of tasks within college and university counseling and student affairs, it is likely that professionals provided services to the 91-year-old Mr. Stewart near the end of his bachelor's degree program and to the 6 year old Mr. Kearney as he began his college studies. Despite these record breaking old and young students, colleges and universities primary serve young adults, and college students are becoming younger. The percentage of 18 to 24 year old college students rose from 36% to 41% between 1999 and 2009 (National Center for Education Statistics, 2012). Some colleges and universities primarily educate students who are from 18 to 22 years old, while others (such as community colleges) tend to cater to older students who might be in their 30s, 40s, or 50s.

College and university counselors and student affairs professionals usually hold a master's degree. Those who earn master's degrees in counseling are qualified for jobs that require that counseling services be provided to students. However many with counseling degrees take student affairs jobs in colleges or universities that might be counseling-related, but not specifically focused on individual or group counseling, choosing to utilize the counseling skills from their degree programs through student development and programming activities rather than through traditional counseling services.

Those who have master's degrees in student affairs or in higher education usually do not hold counseling positions and generally do not have jobs in which the word *counselor* is in the position title. Student affairs professionals work in a variety of offices on campuses that serve students. In some states, statutes exist that require that individuals who render counseling services be licensed by the state as counselors or some other type of mental health professional. However, in most states, public and non-profit institutions are exempt from the requirements of counselor or mental health professional licensure

(American Counseling Association, 2010). In most college and university settings, there is a tendency to hire only individuals who hold counseling master's degrees or higher in positions that require that students be counseled or that include the job title of counselor. Professional counselors usually advocate that the word *counselor* be changed to *advisor* or some other non-counselor word for position titles such as *financial aid counselor, admissions counselor,* and *residence hall counselor.*

SIDEBAR 18.1 Do I Want to be a College Counselor or a College Student Affairs Professional?

While college and university student affairs professionals usually take an introductory counseling course and perhaps a few other counseling-related courses, the curriculum for student affairs or higher education master's degrees is strongly oriented toward college student development theories, understanding colleges and university settings, providing psychoeducational experience for students, preparing students for leadership positions, and performing administrative tasks.

Do you think you would be most satisfied working primarily in the role of counselor or in the role of student affairs professional on a college or university campus?

Until about 50 years ago, colleges and universities operated under a legal doctrine known as *in loco parentis.* This Latin phrase meant that college and university faculty, administrators, and staff members took the place of parents to young people who lived away from home usually for the first time. Higher education officials were parent substitutes and often set strict living rules that included dress codes, curfews in the evening, separation of the sexes, and close oversight of students' activities inside and outside the classroom. However, with the lowering of the age of majority in the United States to 18, which makes traditionally-aged students legally adults by the time they enter college or at least by the end of their freshman year, courts have removed the duty of parental oversight of students from colleges and universities (Higher Education Center, 2011). Of course, parents and guardians who send their children off to college expect that they will have a safe and supportive environment in which to learn and develop, but there is much less oversight of student behavior than there was 200 years ago when public college education began in the United States.

What makes careers in college counseling unique from the careers of other counselors is that college counselors serve adult students who are working toward earning college or university degrees. School counselors also work with students, but their students are usually under the age of 18, which requires school counselors to often take on the role of parent substitute and also requires them to interact regularly with the parents or guardians of their students. Since most college and university students are above the age of 18 (and therefore are legally adults), college counselors and student affairs professionals are seldom in the role of parent substitute and interact with the parents and guardians of their adult students less often. However, a common complaint of college counselors and student affairs professionals are the annoying *helicopter parents* who hover over their children while they are in college and often treat their adult children as if they still are children (Gibbs, 2009). Unlike mental health counselors who work in community agencies or private practices, college counselors and student affairs professionals provide their services in a college or university setting in which the education of their clients is the primary focus, as opposed to the mental health issues of their clients (although counselors in college and university counseling centers certainly are called upon to address the mental health needs of students).

Like the rest of American society, diversity is increasing on college and university campuses. It is estimated that by the year 2018, on college and university campuses, Hispanic student enrollment will increase by 38% and African-Americans enrollment will increase by 26%, while overall enrollment will increase by only 13% (Brainard, 2009). Even the most traditional colleges and universities in the United States are becoming more diverse. As a result, all contemporary college and university counselors and student affairs professionals are called upon to be culturally competent and multiculturally sensitive (American Counseling Association, 2012).

Many people who think of college counselors have images only of counselors who deal with students' emotional and mental issues who work in a counseling center or mental health clinic on campus. While most colleges and universities do have traditional counseling centers that serve the mental health needs of their student populations, there are numerous other offices on campuses that employ counselors and student affairs professionals. Counselors might be found in college and university programs that serve students with disabilities, international students, student athletes, students who are culturally different from the majority of the students on campus, and students who are nontraditional in some way (such as first-generation college students, students who enter college with low test scores or low high school grade point averages, female students seeking to enter traditionally male careers, or students who work full-time and study part-time). In addition, many counselors and student affairs professionals work in career development and job placement centers and campus residence hall programs. Student affairs professionals might also hold professional positions in areas such as academic advising, financial aid, student success, student activities, admissions, or recreation and intramural sports.

An example of a college or university counseling program located outside a traditional counseling center would be an office that provides counseling services to student athletes (Hack, 2007). As early as 1998, Miller and Wooten called for the development of a new specialty of sports counseling. Watson (2007) conducted a study in which athletes and non-athletes in colleges were asked about their attitudes toward seeking counseling services. Athletes in this study were found to have less positive attitudes toward seeking counseling services than their non-athlete peers.

Butte College (2012), a two-year community college located in Oroville, California, has described a student success program for student athletes. The program served about 200 student athletes who participate in football, basketball, soccer, golf, baseball, softball, volleyball, track, and cross country. Student athletes who had been identified as needing assistance spent at least three hours a week in the college's Center for Academic Success participating in study activities, tutorial support, and skills workshops. The goal of the program was for student athletes to internalize positive study habits that would result in a successful academic future. The supervisor of the program, Bobby Bernal-Wood, played football for the Butte College team and was later a wide receiver for the University of Idaho football team. He was named to the First Team All-Sun Belt Conference and received a bachelor's degree in communications from the university. He spent 20 hours a week supervising the student success program and was an assistant coach for the Butte College football and track teams.

The University of Notre Dame (2012), a university known for its top-level collegiate sports, has described a program entitled Academic Services for Student Athletes. The program included a staff of eight and academic counselors were key staff members. All athletes on scholarship were required to participate in the program. As they entered the university, student athletes were given an orientation to the services provided to them that included advising, referral, tutoring, and support. A goal of the orientation was to "Assess transition from high school, adjustment, progress, and overall academic, personal, and social well being."

Another example of specialized counseling programs within universities was found at the University of Kentucky in a residence hall set aside specifically for first generation college students (Johnson, 2011). After realizing that only 40% of first generation college students were graduating at the end of six years (compared to their peers who were graduating at the rate of 61%), administrators created a program for first generation college students that included being housed in a residence hall together. Participants were encouraged to celebrate their uniqueness and support each other rather than feeling stigmatized because their parents were not college educated. The initial program, which enrolled 42 students, included on-site tutoring, weekly seminars about adjusting to college life, and special field trips to help students get to know one another. Freshmen participants also had to enroll in a semester-long course intended to help them transition successfully from high school to college. Similar support programs for first generation college students existed at the University of Cincinnati and the University of North Carolina at Charlotte.

The actual day-to-day work of counselors and student affairs professionals on college and university campuses varies considerably depending on the office in which they are employed. While counselors in traditional college or university counseling centers might see clients for individual or group counseling most of each day, student affairs professionals who are residence hall managers may spend most of their day providing training for residence hall assistants, attending meetings with other student affairs professionals on campus, planning programs, and dealing with crises that arise from time to time. Almost all college and university counselors and student affairs professionals spend most of their time talking with other people. They counsel students, consult with others, interact with faculty members and administrators, plan with other student affairs professionals, deliver training workshops, and perform administrative tasks such as developing schedules, writing reports, constructing and monitoring budgets, and evaluating the performance of students and other staff members who report to them. As mentioned earlier, those who are counselors and who have received master's degrees in counseling tend to render counseling services to students, while those who are student affairs professionals and who hold master's degrees in student affairs or in higher education tend to hold jobs that are not counseling focused and usually perform tasks that are advising, educational, or administrative in nature.

In addition to the traditional functions outlined above, today's counselors and student affairs professionals are facing new challenges. On top of paying attention to students' mental health concerns and areas such as career development, job placement, needs of special groups of students, academic success, and recreational activities and sports, contemporary counselors and student affairs professionals on college and university campuses now are involved in a host of new activities. It is not unusual for counselors and student affairs professionals to be involved in enrollment management (does the institute have enough students?), campus safety, the stress experienced by college students,

SIDEBAR 18.2 Self-Awareness: Pros and Cons of Being a College or University Counselor or Student Affairs Professional

Choosing a career as a college or university counselor or student affairs professional requires reflection upon the job and an understanding of its specific requirements. Listed below are some distinct features of college counseling and student affairs positions that some professionals in the field consider to be advantages (pros). Also listed are some of the complaints people have sometimes voiced about being in a career as a college or university counselor or student affairs professional (cons).

Pros:

1. Being in an academic environment for a career is comfortable after having been a student most of my life.
2. I like the rhythm of the academic year that includes celebrations of holidays, breaks between semesters and summer terms, "seasons" of sporting events, and the excitement each year of students entering in the fall and graduating in the spring.
3. The varied duties of college or university counselors including individual counseling, group counseling, psychoeducation, testing, and consultation appeal to me. Or alternatively, the varied duties of college or university student affairs professionals including fostering the personal development of students, serving their needs outside the classroom, and developing and administering programs for students appeal to me.
4. The range of issues college students bring to counseling sessions and bring to meetings with student affairs professionals seem challenging and interesting.

Cons:

1. Beginning school counselors and community mental health counselors and administrators in business and industry seem to make higher salaries than college and university counselors and student affairs professionals.
2. College and university counselors and student affairs professionals usually have 12-month contracts and usually have to work while students are on break or are on vacations.
3. College and university faculty members and administrators appear to have all the power on campus, which means counselors and student affairs professionals often feel like second-class citizens, and have little influence in campus decision-making.
4. There is not enough time in an eight-hour work day to do all the duties college and university counselors and student affairs professionals are expected to do.

Can you add two or three Pros and two or three Cons to these lists?

Which of these aspects in these lists are important to you?

Overall, does being a college or university counselor or student affairs professional seem like a good career choice to you?

managing serious mental health problems of students, suicide prevention, and helping young people develop leadership skills.

Similar to schools and community mental health settings, counselors and students affairs professionals in higher education, after a few years of direct service to students, usually assume supervisory responsibility over others and take jobs administering offices, programs, or units within universities. Along with the increased authority of administrative posts come requirements that counselors and student affairs professionals manage budgets, hire new staff members, evaluate subordinates, and assume responsibility for the effectiveness of the programs the administer. Skills including leadership, administrative supervision, budgeting, program evaluation, and program accountability are required at this stage of their careers (Waple, 2006). It is incumbent upon counselors and student affairs professionals who become administrators to develop the necessary skills during the time they are preparing for leadership positions, because these skills generally are not taught in the courses they take as graduate students.

SIDEBAR 18.3 Case Study: Helping Students Become Leaders

At a staff meeting with the Vice President of Student Affairs at a medium-sized state university, several department heads indicate that the students with whom they work need help in developing leadership skills. The Sorority and Fraternity Advisor says that officers of the organizations often make errors of judgment that lead to problems for Greek organizations. The Student Government Advisor says that most elected officers do not know how to delegate tasks to others and then monitor their work. The Residence Hall Director says that resident advisors and hall advisors have difficulty understanding their responsibilities and duties and often do not consult with others when they should.

You are the Dean of Students and the Vice President asks you to develop a comprehensive leadership training program that will address the concerns that have been raised in these campus student affairs units. How would you go about determining what type of leadership development is needed and then organizing a leadership development program for students?

The Council for the Advancement of Standards in Higher Education (2012) has published standards for student development programs in colleges and universities. Standards have been published in the following 41 areas to promote high quality student learning and development programs in colleges and universities: Academic Advising; Admission Programs; Adult Learner Programs; Alcohol, Tobacco, and Other Drug Programs; Assessment Services; Auxiliary Services; Campus Activities Programs; Campus Information and Visitor Services; Campus Religious & Spiritual Programs; Career Services; Clinical Health Services; College Honor Societies; College Unions; Commuter and Off-Campus Living Programs; Conference and Events Programs; Counseling Services; Dining Services; Disability Support Services; Distance Education Programs; Education Abroad Programs and Services; Financial Aid; Fraternity and Sorority Advising Programs; Graduate and Professional Student Programs; Health Promotion Services; Housing and residential Life Programs; International Student Programs; Internship Programs; Learning Assistance Programs; Lesbian, Gay, Bisexual, and Transgender Programs;

Master's Level Student Affairs Administration Preparation Programs; Multicultural Student Programs and Services; Orientation Programs; Parent and Family Programs; Recreational Sports Programs; Registrar Programs and Services; Service-Learning Programs; Student Conduct Programs; Student Leadership Programs; TRIO and Other Educational Opportunity Programs; Undergraduate Research Programs; and Women Student Programs.

An overview of duties and responsibilities of college and university counselors and student affairs professionals has been provided. The remainder of this chapter will review important elements of the specialization of college counseling and student affairs. The major college student development and adult development theories will be highlighted. Some of the professional functions associated with these theories will be discussed as well. Leadership theories and learning theories will also be addressed as they relate to counselors and student affairs professionals who work in higher education. The role of counselors in providing counseling services, developing and managing programs that are prevention-focused, and intervening in crisis situations will be addressed. Differences in counselors' roles depending on the type of institution of higher education they work in will also be discussed. Diversity and advocacy for students who are members of minority groups on campus will be reviewed. Assessment and testing on college and university campuses will be discussed. A review will be provided of research and program evaluation requirements of college and university counselors and student affairs professionals.

Foundations

It is essential that counselors and student affairs professionals in colleges and universities understand theories associated with several fields including the following: counseling (Corey, 2013); college student development (Evans, Forney, Guido, Patton, & Renn, 2009); adult development (Stevens-Long & Michaud, 2002); leadership (Komives, Dugan, Owen, Slack, & Wagner, 2011); and learning (Merriam, Caffarella, & Baumgartner, 2007). By studying theories, those who provide services to college students can understand why their work with students is important. Theories provide a solid foundation for developing and implementing programs for the benefit of students.

College Student Development Theories

Various theories have given rise to concepts within college and university counseling and student affairs that have become accepted throughout the field. These concepts include the following: (1) college and university student development programs (including counseling services) should be supportive of the overall goals of the institution of higher education in which they are found; (2) student affairs staff members must form partnerships with faculty members, administrators, and other staff members within the institution and with professionals in organizations outside the institution for the benefit of the students who are being served; (3) student development programs must be tailored to fit the unique student population for whom they have been developed; (4) student development programs must be established with clear goals and include measureable objectives that can be evaluated; (5) sensitivity to diversity of students must be included in all student development programs; and (6) advocacy for students is important and must be accomplished within the structure of the college and university where the student development program is located.

Institutional Goals

Each college and university in the United States is unique. Even though there are categories of higher education institutes such as large state research universities, technical colleges, small private liberal arts colleges, community colleges, colleges affiliated with religious groups, for-profit, on-line universities, etc., individual institutions within each category are different due to many factors. The size of the college or university, the location, the profile of the students who attend, the history, the resources available, and even the buildings themselves (if there are any) have an impact on counseling and other student services that are offered by a particular college or university.

For counseling or student affairs programs to be successful, the programs must be in sync with their institutions' purpose, vision, mission, goals, and stated objectives. For example, a successful counseling program on the rural campus of a seminary college that has about 100 full-time residential students will look totally different from a successful counseling program on the campus of a community college in an urban setting with 15,000 students who are mostly part-time. To receive long-term administrative support, counseling and student services programs must advance the goals of the college or university in which the programs is located.

An example of a university with a unique focus is the Massachusetts Institute of Technology (MIT), which is known as perhaps the best science and technology university in the world (Times Higher Education, 2012). The university is a major research institution and admission is highly competitive. The university has a reputation as being a stressful academic environment for the high-achieving students who are admitted. The university's Medical Mental Health Services (2012) office has published a brochure for faculty entitled, *How to Help Students in Distress*. In response to the unique nature of MIT, the university has established an office of Student Support Services (2012) that focuses on helping students who experience serious academic pressure. Five professional mental health staff members worked in the office in 2012. In their profiles, the following comments were included: "At MIT, David sees students whose personal circumstances are intersecting with their academic life in challenging ways;" "Arnold is committed to assisting and supporting students during their challenging years at MIT;" and "Miri supports students around personal and academic matters, helping them to use their inherent strengths to meet their challenges." Universities such as MIT often create counseling and student affairs programs that meet the unique needs of their students because of their unusual mission.

Partnerships

To effectively serve students, counselors and student affairs professionals must work with other people on their campuses and within their communities. A modern student development office on a college or university campus that is insular and distanced from the people and services students need to be successful will not last very long.

Within the college or university, counselors and student affairs professionals must make efforts to be viewed by the faculty as being supportive of their academic work with students. Participating in institutional committees or task forces that include faculty members is an excellent way to build relationships and connections that will be meaningful if student needs or concerns later must be addressed with a particular faculty member. Assuming that faculty members have the best interests of students in mind as they teach their courses is an important assumption to make. Deferring to faculty members' judgment regarding academic matters is also essential. If a faculty member does appear to be biased, unreasonable, or unfair, and students determine it is impossible to resolve the problem through direct interaction with the faculty member, then students should address the issues with the administrators to whom faculty members report. Counselors or student affairs professionals should not try to act on behalf of students. Of course counselors and student affairs professionals should support students as they attempt to resolve any problems they have with faculty members.

SIDEBAR 18.4 A Racially Prejudiced Professor Complaint

You are one of six academic advisors for the College of Engineering in a large state university. An African-American 20-year-old male student tells you that he is certain one of his engineering professors is racially biased. The student tells you that the professor asks him questions in class much more frequently than he asks questions of White students and the student believes the professor is asking the questions purposefully to embarrass him. The student also tells you that he believes his papers receive lower grades on essay exams than the grades of White students even though his answers are almost identical to those of the White students. The student claims that many of his friends in the class who are White have told him they believe the professor is biased against him because of his race. You ask the student if he has spoken to the professor directly about his concerns and the student tells you he has not because he is afraid it will make the professor even more biased against him if the professor sees his concerns as a criticism. You ask the student if he has any specific instances of interchanges with the professor or grades received from the professor that would indicate racial bias on the part of the professor. The student says he can't think of any offhand. You ask the student if he is willing to talk with the professor's department chair about his concerns and the student says he would never do that because if the professor finds out he did that, the professor would be even more biased against him. How would you handle this situation?

Counselors and student affairs professionals should assist students in dealing with problems with administrators or offices within the college or university, and support students as they attempt to resolve issues, but should avoid acting on behalf of students.

Outside the university, there are many resources that might be helpful to students. For example, local healthcare facilities, law enforcement agencies, municipal offices, and social service agencies might be used by students from time to time. Counselors and student affairs professionals who establish connections with the people who work in these off-campus agencies can be very helpful to students if they need to seek services outside the university.

Programs Tailored for Unique Student Populations

Groups of students in a particular college or university are unique. Even though there are profiles of students who attend community colleges, for example, clearly the students in a small rural community college in the far west are much different from the students in a large community college located in New York City. Colleges and universities in the Southwestern part of the United States tend to have large Hispanic populations (Martin & Meyer, 2010) and institutions of higher education in California often include many students who are of Japanese descent (Jaschik, 2005). Some colleges emphasize art courses and degrees (e.g., The University of the Arts in Philadelphia, Pennsylvania), while others require students to study the Great Books (e.g., St. John's College in Annapolis, Maryland and Santa Fe, New Mexico). The location of colleges or universities, their academic focus, their history, and many other factors affect the nature of the student populations who attend. Counseling and student development programs must be designed to meet the needs of the students in the colleges and universities where they are located.

Diversity and Student Advocacy

A later section of this chapter discusses the importance of sensitivity to diversity and advocacy. Counselor and student affairs professionals must be culturally competent and respect the differences inherent in the students they serve. Counselors and student affairs professionals must also understand their role as student advocates and perform that role within the structures of the institutions of higher education in which they work.

Counseling, Prevention, and Intervention

College and university counseling centers today can vary significantly in the roles and functions they serve and the student needs they address. The most common role of counseling centers, and the role reported as one of the most important to directors and administrators, is the provision of individual counseling services (Boyd et al., 2003; Gallagher, 2009). Counselors in college and university counseling centers may provide counseling for a variety of personal, academic, and career needs; however most priority and time is given to personal needs (Cooper & Archer, 2002). A study of directors reported that counselors spend 80.7% of their time on personal counseling, 4.7% on academic counseling, and 2.8% on career counseling (Gallagher, 2009).

While taking up less time, crisis intervention and consulting with faculty and staff are also important roles of college counselors (Boyd et al., 2003; DeStefano, Petersen, Skwerer, & Bickel, 2001; Gallagher, 2001). Counselors intervene in situations where there are mental health emergencies on campus, in particular where students are at risk of harm to themselves or others. Most counseling centers also require counselors to share responsibility for after-hours and weekend coverage in order to provide 24 hour on-call availability for students facing mental health emergencies. Faculty and staff may also seek help from counselors when they have concerns about a student or are otherwise seeking a counselor's help in remediating a situation.

Presenting Issues of Students

College counseling centers sometimes get the reputation of being "relationship clinics," and people with this view are likely speaking to the prevalence of relationship issues for which many students seek counseling services. However, relationships constitute only one of many issues for which college students seek help, and this characterization masks the severity of issues college counselors encounter. In an annual survey of college counseling centers (Gallagher, 2009), directors reported that 48.4% of their clients have severe psychological problems. One classification model developed for college student presenting concerns groups problems into 13 areas: Relationship difficulties, career uncertainty, self-esteem issues, existential concerns, academic concerns, depression, anxiety, eating disorders, substance abuse, sexual abuse or harassment, stress and psychosomatic symptoms, sexual dysfunction, and unusual behavior (Chandler & Gallagher, 1996). In this classification, unusual behavior refers to confused thinking, hallucinations, social isolation, paranoid ideation, and borderline personality. Clearly, there are many issues facing college students besides relationships! Indeed, even relationship issues may involve more serious mental health concerns such as depression and suicidal risk.

Statistics from a 2011 survey conducted by the American College Health Association (ACHA, 2011) of 105,781 students across 129 colleges and universities in the U.S. illuminates the prevalence of major mental health issues on college campuses. Students indicated that in the last 12 months 50.6% felt overwhelming anxiety, 31.3% felt "so depressed it was difficult to function," 6.4% seriously considered suicide, 5.2% intentionally cut, burnt, bruised, or otherwise injured themselves, and 4.4% indicated problems with alcohol use. In the same 12-month period, 0.9% indicated having been diagnosed or treated by a mental health professional for anorexia, 0.8% for bulimia, and 1.4% for bipolar disorder. While some students needing specialized or longer-term treatment may be referred outside the college or university to community resources, college counselors at a minimum need the ability to identify and assess for more severe psychological and substance abuse issues.

An annual survey of college counseling center directors has consistently suggested that the demand for counseling services and the severity of mental health issues for which students present are increasing. In 2009, 66.2% of college counseling center directors indicated a major concern for their counseling centers was dealing with an increase in demand for services without a corresponding increase in staffing and 93.4% perceived an increase in the severity of issues in recent years (Gallagher, 2009). While it has been difficult to prove conclusively that the severity of client issues has increased due to a lack of consistent definitions and measures used over time in data collected on college counseling centers (Sharkin & Coulter, 2005), those who support this claim point have suggested that an increase could be due to modern psychotropic medications enabling more individuals with severe mental health issues to attend college (Kitzrow, 2003).

Role of Outreach in Prevention

Prevention is an important role of counselors in any setting, but it difficult to imagine a setting where the opportunities and needs for prevention are greater than on college campuses. Traditional aged college students are in a developmental period when many mental health issues emerge and, for most students, college is a high stress environment putting students at greater risk for mental health problems. At the same time, only approximately 10% of college students will use the counseling center in a given year (Gallagher, 2009). Thus, a role of counselors working in most counseling centers is to participate in outreach to the campus community to make contact with the broader student population. Outreach can be particularly important for targeting populations that underutilize counseling services.

At its most basic level, outreach may involve visiting classrooms to talk about counseling services that are available to students and describe reasons that students often seek counseling. Counselors may also provide psychoeducational programs on various topics relevant to college students to help improve their experience at college and act as a preventative measure against mental health issues. Some common examples of outreach program topics include:

- Making the adjustment to college life
- Stress management
- Time management
- Relaxation training
- Overcoming test anxiety
- Sexual assault and relationship violence prevention
- Communication and assertiveness skills

Outreach may also involve counselors being present for emotional support at campus events, such as at memorial services for students who have died, or at campus events of a sensitive nature, such as presentations addressing gender or racial issues.

While outreach may sound as if it involved situations in which counselors would spend most of their time in order to maximize their utility to the campus community, in reality outreach is a role valued less than other activities by directors (Gallagher, 2001). Part of the reason may be that when counselor center resources are limited, preventative efforts are viewed as a lower priority than more pressing needs such as crisis counseling.

Small Colleges and Community Colleges

While many factors may influence the services offered by counseling centers, small colleges and community colleges present distinct differences from their larger 4-year counterparts. In counseling literature, the term small college typically refers to 4-year institutions with a maximum of between 2,500 and 5,000 full-time students (Vespia, 2007). Colleges with fewer than 5,000 full-time students represent approximately 75% of higher education institutions in the U.S., though they contain only approximately 23% of total enrolled students (National Center for Educational Statistics, 2010a). Community college refers primarily to 2-year institutions of higher education that grant associate degrees and certificates, although increasingly some community colleges grant 4-year baccalaureate degrees. Community college students account for 44% of all undergraduate students in the U.S. (American Association of Community Colleges, 2011).

Small Colleges

A major difference between small and large colleges and universities is that small colleges often have fewer resources for counseling. Practically, this means counseling centers at small colleges on average employee fewer full time mental health professionals, employ more master's level as opposed to doctoral level mental health professionals, and are less likely to offer on-campus psychiatric services (Vespia, 2007). As an example, 57% of counseling centers in small colleges report employing 0 or 1 full-time counselors (Vespia, 2007). Working alone can present challenges as counselors have more difficulty obtaining consultation on cases and do not have the benefit of another counselor on campus to whom to refer students should ethical issues arise.

Of the difference in psychiatric services, 32.9% of colleges with fewer than 2,500 students reported having psychiatric services compared to 71.4% for institutions with 2,500 or more students (Gallagher, 2009). Another study, which utilized a larger sample of small colleges, found this number to be much lower at 9% for small colleges with between 500 and 4,000 enrolled students (Vespia, 2007). Sampling bias in the former survey likely accounts for most of the difference in results, but both studies point to a significant disparity in services.

Despite a lack of resources, counseling centers in small colleges are less likely to impose session limits or to refer students to off-campus agencies or private practitioners for long-term counseling than their larger counterparts, even when encountering students with more severe mental health issues (Vespia, 2007). One explanation for this seemingly contradictory finding may be that small colleges are more likely to take on an in loco parentis role (Vespia, 2007). In support of this explanation, counselors working in counseling centers at small colleges were more likely to follow up on students who were referred to off campus services and were more likely to notify parents if a student attempted suicide (Vespia, 2007).

Community Colleges

In contrast to small colleges, community colleges can range in size from a few thousand to over 30,000 students (American College Counseling Association, 2011). The mean age of community college students is 28 years with 45% of students between the ages of 22 and 39 (American Association of Community Colleges, 2011). Many community college students are balancing work and family obligations in addition to school, with 80% of full time students enrolled in community college reporting working at least part-time and 21% reporting working full-time (American Association of Community Colleges, 2011). Unlike 4-year colleges and university, few students live on-campus with only 27% of community colleges providing access to on campus housing for students (American Association of Community Colleges, 2011).

Similar to small colleges, resources for mental health services are restricted at community colleges. For this reason, many community colleges lack a separate counseling services department and college counselors serve multiple roles in addition to personal counseling (American College Counseling Association, 2011; Bundy & Benshoff, 2000). In addition to personal counseling, 78.8% of community counselors responding to a survey indicated involvement in committee work, 70% indicated providing academic advising, and 68.2% indicated providing career counseling (American College Counseling Association, 2011). A lesser, but significant percentage were involved in other duties including 41.9% teaching and 35.5% providing disability services. Serving in these multiple roles can complicate interactions with students and administrators and increase the likelihood of ethical conflicts related to confidentiality and dual roles (Bundy & Benshoff, 2000). As a consequence of having more roles, community college counselors on average have smaller weekly caseloads for personal counseling and see a smaller percentage of the student body for personal counseling (American College Counseling Association, 2011). Of additional note, only about 13% of community colleges reported having on campus psychiatric services and only 12.4% indicated providing after-hours emergency crisis services (American College Counseling Association, 2011).

Diversity and Advocacy

Today's college student is anything but "typical." In recent decades, college campuses have become increasingly diverse settings. In 2009, racial/ethnic minority students accounted for 34.3% of students enrolled in degree granting post-secondary institutions (National Center for Educational Statistics, 2010b). In the same year, 39.1% of students were over the age of 25 (National Center for Educational Statistics, 2010c). Additional examples of diversity and special populations on college campuses include international students, sexual minority students, student athletes, students with disabilities, graduate students, transfer students, victims of sexual assault, and veterans (Fauman & Hopkinson, 2010).

Given this diversity, it is important that counselors who work in college settings have training to increase their sensitivity in working with diverse populations. Diversity sensitivity training can help counselors be more attentive to issues facing different groups of students. For example, counselors need to be aware of discrimination issues that ethnic/ cultural minority students and sexual minority students face and the ways these issues may have a negative impact on their academic goals (Lucas & Berkel, 2005; Write, 2000). Additionally, non-traditional students may require special assistance in balancing academic demands against employment and family obligations, and may have difficulty accessing services that are only offered during typical business hours (Bundy & Benshoff, 2000). Awareness of these differences can help counselors better target services to meet the needs of all students.

Diversity training also helps counselors advocate for student needs across the campus. This advocacy includes intervening in situations where there are potential issues of discrimination and mediating conflicts that occur among students related to diversity issues. As a preventative measure, counselors may also conduct training sessions to raise the awareness and responsiveness to needs of minority populations. A popular training related to LGBTQ issues is the Safe Zone/Safe Space Allies Training that raises awareness of LGBTQ issues and fosters a network of faculty and staff supportive of the needs of LGBTQ students (Evans, 2002).

Offices and Organizations Serving Minority Students

Numerous campus offices exist to serve diverse student groups on college campuses with which counselors may be involved. Generally, these offices serve to create community among minority students, promote diversity awareness issues on campus, provide advocacy for students who face discrimination, and connect students to relevant services that will benefit them. The table below represents a sampling of some offices that are present at colleges, although offerings will vary by college and may differ in name and stated mission.

Multiple student organizations also exist to support the needs of diverse student groups. Examples include groups supporting LGBTQ students, organizations focused on racial/cultural minorities such as the National Association for Advancement of Colored People (NAACP), and fraternities and sororities targeting special populations. At a minimum, counselors working in colleges and universities should be aware of these groups as they may serve as resources in support of students. Additionally, counselors working in student affairs and counseling positions may serve as liaisons or advisors to these groups.

Table 18.1 Examples of offices serving minority students and special populations

Office of college	*Description*
Office of Multicultural Relations	This office serves to create an inclusive campus environment for all minority students, to promote understanding across the campus of multicultural issues, to aid in prevention of discrimination and harassment, and to provide programming directed towards minority students.
Women's Center	A women's center serves to provide support for gender issues with a focus on promoting gender equity and supporting victims of partner violence, sexual assault, and sexual harassment.
Disability Services	Disability Services provides support for students with disabilities, which includes helping students obtain accommodations, providing resources for students with disabilities, and mediating between students and faculty/staff with conflicts that arise related to accommodating students with disabilities.
International Student Services	International Student Services are focused on supporting needs of international students and include helping students manage issues with visas, obtain assistance with housing, transportation, and employment.

SIDEBAR 18.5 Serving Specialized Groups of Students

Make a list of all the offices on your campus that have physical space or a staff member devoted to serving a specific subgroup of students. How many are there? Enough or too many? Can you think of other offices that should be established on your campus?

Assessment

From the admissions process to the day of graduation, colleges and universities are continually engaged in using assessment to collect information about students. At an academic level, assessment instruments are used in measuring potential of applicants to aid colleges in making admissions decisions and measuring the performance of enrolled students to track their progress toward graduation.

When students experience academic difficulty, counselors may refer students for formal testing to collect information regarding psychological factors or learning disabilities that may hinder student achievement. This information can provide support for the provision of accommodations such as additional testing time for students diagnosed with Attention

Deficit Hyperactivity Disorder. For students who face difficulty with major and career selection, counselors use assessments to gather information that will help aid in decision-making (Eichler & Schwartz, 2010).

In counseling centers, counselors use assessments to aid in the diagnosis and treatment of mental health issues, to evaluate the effectiveness of treatment provided, and to screen for suicidal and homicidal risk (Eichler & Schwartz, 2010; Whiston, 2008). Across these diverse areas, assessment serves to help counselors identify problems, understand more about students, assist in decision making, and demonstrate the effectiveness of services provided (Whiston, 2008). The following list provides examples of assessment instruments that are used by counselors working in college settings.

Assessments Used in Counseling Centers

- Intake Interviews
- Personality Inventories
- Symptom Checklists
- Screening for Alcohol/Substance Abuse
- Screening for Suicidal Risk
- Assessment for Depression and Anxiety
- Minnesota Multiphasic Personality Inventory (MMPI)
- Beck's Depression Inventory (BDI)
- Counseling Center Assessment of Psychological Symptoms (CCAPS)
- Alcohol Use Disorders Identification Test (AUDIT)
- Mental Status Exam (MSE)

Assessments Used in Career Services

- Interest and Skill Inventories
- Personality Inventories
- Strong Interest Inventory
- Campbell Interest and Skills Survey
- Self-Directed Search
- Myers-Brigg Type Inventory

Assessments Used in Academic Testing and Disability Services

- ADHD screening
- Intelligence Testing
- Achievement Testing
- Neuropsychological Testing
- Conner's Adult ADHD Rating Scale (CAARS)
- Wechsler Adult Intelligence Scale (WAIS-R)
- Stanford-Binet Intelligence Scales
- Woodcock-Johnson-III Tests of Achievement (WJ-III-ACH)

Counselors may not administer some of these assessments, but college counselors are often in positions that require knowledge about them.

Needs Assessment

A needs assessment is a common tool counselors use on college campuses to better understand the needs of the students they are serving and to guide the development of programs. It helps counselors better understand problems, identify opportunities, and build relationships among stakeholders (Gupta, Sleezer, & Russ-Eft, 2007). Specifically, counselors use assessments to evaluate the needs of students and the extent to which existing services and programs of the university are meeting those needs. The gap between these two becomes the focus of future planning and action.

In conducting a needs assessment, counselors collect information by using a combination of individual interviews, focus groups, surveys, observations, and archival data (Gupta et al., 2007). Archival data are data that were previously collected prior to conducting the needs assessment, such as data collected previously by other offices at the institution. Some examples of needs assessments on college campuses include a needs assessment to learn about the mental health needs of graduate students (Hyun, Quinn, Madon, & Lustig, 2006) or a needs assessment to learn about the academic and career needs of international students (Leong & Sedlacek, 1989).

SIDEBAR 18.6 Case Study: Conducting a Needs Assessment

As a counselor, you have been asked to facilitate a group of students who are on academic probation. Your supervisor states that the purpose of this group is to increase student retention and that the group will meet weekly for one semester. You decide to conduct a needs assessment to gain information that will help in designing your program for the group.

1. What are some questions that you would want to ask to aid in planning the group?
2. What are some sources you might use to gain this information?
3. How might your group plan be affected if you were to discover that most of the students who would be in your group were first generation college students? Transfer students? Minority students?

Issues with the Use of Assessments

While assessment provides a resource for gaining information about students, it also presents some risks and challenges for those who use them. Specifically, counselors must use discretion in the choice of assessment instruments and in the ways the results of assessment instruments are used. For example, assessments may discriminate against minorities or pathologize cultural factors (Whiston, 2008).

Additionally, Eichsler and Schwartz (2010) have warned of the danger of relying on a single test result in lieu of a complete assessment. They provide an example of a college student receiving a test result that indicates his reading comprehension is at a ninth grade level. "This single finding may simply reflect overall intellectual endowment; or it could be indicative of a learning disability, or of a lack of adequate past instruction, or of a poor command of English if English is a second language; or it may reflect a highly idiosyncratic interpretation of reality consistent with serious mental illness; or problems in concentration, which in turn may be secondary to trauma, depression, substance abuse, or a primary attention deficit" (p. 83).

These issues of assessments have become central in arguments regarding the use of standardized testing in admissions decisions for colleges, where opponents of their use have viewed them as unfair at best and discriminatory at worst (Zwick, 2007). Counselors working in college settings related to admissions need to be able to competently make decisions regarding the administration, usage, and interpretation of academic assessment instruments to best mitigate these risks (Zwick, 2007).

Research and Evaluation

Colleges and universities are increasingly being called upon to demonstrate that their programs and services are effective (Bishop & Trembley, 1987; Schuh, 2011). Part of this demand comes from business pressures as institutions compete for students and funding. Public institutions must also answer to taxpayers supporting them, who want to know that the money they are spending is being used wisely and producing results. Demand also comes from accrediting bodies for higher education that mandate accountability in order for colleges to demonstrate that they are meeting acceptable standards. Together, research and evaluation serve as the foundation of quality assurance in college and university settings and answer this call for accountability.

Use of Research in Counseling and Student Affairs Positions

Within counseling and student affairs positions, ensuring quality begins by using research to guide the development of programs and services. A wealth of existing research provides a source of information for counselors to learn more about common characteristics of students, concerns, and issues students face within college settings, and models of student development (Brownson, 2010; Layton, Sandeen, & Baker, 1971). Published research can also provide information on the outcome of programs and approaches that have been implemented in other colleges and universities, allowing counselors to learn from others' experiences.

Research is of particular importance to counselors working in counseling services (Boyd et al., 2003). Beyond fostering a greater understanding of the mental health needs of students, counselors are required by ethical standards to "engage in counseling practices that are based on rigorous research methodologies" (American Counseling Association, 2005). Thus, research justifies the approaches counselors use to work with students.

Because the characteristics of students and the college environment continue to change, it is important that counselors stay up-to-date with current research findings. A primary source of research is through professional journals, such as *The Journal of College Student Development*, the *Journal of College Counseling*, the *Journal of College Student Psychotherapy*, and the *Journal of Student Affairs Research and Practice*. Other relevant sources of information include the *Annual Survey of College Counseling Center Directors* (Gallagher, 2009) and the *National College Health Assessment* conducted bi-annually by the American College Health Association (ACHA, 2011). These surveys provide information on national statistics, trends, and practices on college and university campuses regarding student health issues.

Beyond being consumers of research, many counselors will also have a role in producing research. Results from research may be used solely at a local level to provide helpful information about students to the greater college or university community, or may be further disseminated to contribute to broader professional knowledge (Cooper & Archer, 2002, Minami et al., 2009). A significant amount of research that has occurred in college counseling centers has been beneficial not only to college counseling knowledge but to the broader mental health field (Minami et al., 2009).

A recent example of a large-scale research effort in college counseling centers is a project being coordinated through the Center for Collegiate Mental Health (CCMH). CCMH coordinates the collection of standardized data from approximately 150 college and university counseling centers in the U.S. While in its infancy, research using this data is likely to contribute significant knowledge to guide the future practice of counseling services on college campuses. As an example of research that has utilized this data, multiple studies have addressed questions about the utilization of counseling services by minority students (Hayes, Locke, & Castonguay, 2011).

SIDEBAR 18.7 Being a Consumer and Producer of Research

To what extent do you desire research to be a part of your career as a counselor? Do you wish to be involved as a producer and not just a consumer of research? Counselor training programs typically include a course in research and a course in statistics. If you desire to be more involved in producing research, what are some opportunities you could use in your training program to gain additional skills that would help you to become a better researcher?

Evaluation in Counseling and Student Affairs Programs and Services

In addition to producing and utilizing research, counselors working in college settings are often responsible for conducting evaluations of the services they provide. At its core, evaluation serves to provide feedback on the merit of programs. Patton (2008) described evaluation as answering questions of: what? so what? and now what?; examining what was intended versus what was implemented; determining which outcomes were achieved; understanding the meaning of outcomes, and planning future actions that will be taken based on findings.

For counseling and student affairs programs, evaluations can be distinguished into outcome and process evaluations. Outcome evaluation focuses on the extent to which intended goals and objectives are met. Examples of questions asked as part of outcome evaluations include: What results were achieved by the program? How effective is the program? Did the program make a difference? What needs of students were met? (Colton & Covert, 2007; Patton, 2008). Increasingly in colleges and universities, goals and objectives must connect to larger institutional goals and objectives and ultimately to the mission statement of the college or university (Schuh, 2011). In some areas, counselors may be able to find ways that services directly have an impact on institutional goals. Such is the case with a common institutional goal of student retention, for which studies have found counseling has a positive impact (Sharkin, 2004). In other cases, counselors may need to look at indirect ways that services and programs contribute to institutional goals such as through increasing student satisfaction and adjustment to college, which are factors that may contribute to increasing student retention. Counselors may also look to learning outcomes that promote out-of-classroom student development such as promoting civic responsibility. By demonstrating how programs and services contribute to the ultimate goals of the university, counselors provide justification for the resources that are spent on the services they provide to colleges and universities (Schuh, 2011).

In contrast to outcome evaluation, process evaluation focuses on the implementation details of programs and services provided rather than on the end outcomes, answering questions—such as When? Where? How often? How much?—regarding programs and services (Colton & Covert, 2007; Patton, 2008). While many colleges and universities focus on outcome evaluation, process evaluation is important in that it promotes a better understanding of how a program was implemented and how it works. As such, process evaluation may be useful in college and universities for evaluating the efficiency of services and for better understanding contributing factors to the successes and failures of programs (Patton, 2008; Schuh, 2011).

A number of sources of information may be useful for both process and outcome evaluations in colleges and universities. Most colleges and universities collect data on the number and demographics of people utilizing services and attending programs. Another common tool is using questionnaires to solicit subjective data from students on their experiences of programs and services and the benefit they derive from them. For more objective evaluations, counselors will often need access to college or university data collected by other departments such that they can evaluate the effect of programs and services against factors such as academic performance and retention data. While important, these evaluations will often require greater coordination with other departments, and counselors will need to be aware of additional potential ethical and legal issues that may arise (Brownson, 2010; Schuh, 2011).

Specific to college counseling centers, students are often asked to complete follow up surveys where students report on their satisfaction with services and the extent to which they felt they met their goals and were helped by counseling. A more objective measure used in college counseling centers is through comparing the results of standardized assessments at intake and following termination. A common assessment used for this purpose is the Counseling Center Assessment of Psychological Symptoms (CCAPS), which is available for college counseling centers to use free and assesses students across factors of depression, anxiety, eating concerns, alcohol use, hostility, family distress, social anxiety, and academic distress (Hayes, Locke, & Castonguay, 2011). Counseling centers that use the *Diagnostic and Statistical Manual of Mental Health* (American Psychiatric Association, 2000) may also base evaluation on changes to the diagnoses of students over the course of counseling services.

Regardless of what is being evaluated, a key part of the evaluation cycle is using information that is gained as feedback to guide future changes to programs and services.

SIDEBAR 18.8 Evaluating a New Campus Program

Your university established a new program in the admissions office two years ago to recruit African American applicants and enroll more students. What data might you collect to determine whether the new program has been successful?

Relevant questions include: How might what was learned from the program be used to improve it in the future? Is there a need for increasing or decreasing funding based on findings? How might findings from the evaluation be applicable to other programs and services? College counselors focused on quality are committed to continuous improvement, conducting regular evaluations, and making appropriate changes to increase the value and quality of programs and services offered.

Conclusion

College counseling or college student affairs are career options for those who hold master's degrees in counseling and college student development. Jobs in colleges and universities are varied and range from positions as counselors in traditional college counseling centers where clients are seen in individual sessions, to positions in financial aid or admissions where little activity takes place that might be considered counseling. The setting of the college or university has a significant impact on the jobs master's level counselors might find. Working in a small residential liberal arts college that has 100 undergraduate students is much different from having a professional position in a multi-campus urban community college that has 100,000 freshman and sophomore students, or being a counselor in a large state university with 80,000 students who are both undergraduates and graduate students.

Graduate students who plan to be counselors or student affairs professionals in colleges or universities should join and be active members of the American Counseling Association (ACA) and its division, the American College Counseling Association (ACCA). They should also consider being members of the American College Personnel Association (ACPA). If they are oriented toward administration, they should also join the NASPA: Student Affairs Administrators in Higher Education. Once they become professionals, to ensure they have current information in the field, college counselors and student affairs professionals should maintain active memberships in appropriate professional associations.

References

American Association of Community Colleges. (2011). *American Association of Community Colleges 2011 community college fast facts*. Retrieved from http://www.aacc.nche.edu/AboutCC/Documents/FactSheet2011.pdf.

American College Health Association. (2011). *National college health assessment: Reference group executive summary spring 2011*. Retrieved from http://www.acha-ncha.org/docs/ACHA-NCHA-II_ReferenceGroup_ExecutiveSummary_Spring2011.pdf.

American College Counseling Association. (2011). *Survey of community/2 year college counseling services*. Retrieved from http://www.collegecounseling.org/docs/ACCA-CCTF-2011SurveyBooklet.pdf.

American Counseling Association. (2005). *ACA Code of Ethics and Standards of Practice*. Alexandria, VA: Author.

American Counseling Association. (2010). *Licensure requirements for professional counselors*. Alexandria, VA: Author.

American Counseling Association. (2012). AMCA *Multicultural Counseling Competencies*. Alexandria, VA: Author. Retrieved from http://www.counseling.org/Resources/Competencies/Multcultural_Competencies.pdf.

American Psychiatric Association. (2000). *Diagnostic and statistical manual of mental disorders* (4th ed., text rev.). Washington, DC: Author.

Bishop, J. B., & Trembley, E. L. (1987). Counseling centers and accountability: Immovable objects, irresistible forces. *Journal of Counseling & Development, 65*, 491–494.

Boyd, V., Hattauer, E., Brandel, I. W., Buckles, N., Davidshofer, C., Deakin, S., & Steel, C. M. (2003). Accreditation standards for university and college counseling centers. *Journal of Counseling & Development, 81*, 168–177.

Brainard, J. (September 15, 2009). College enrollments will be more diverse over next decade, report says. *The Chronicle of Higher Education.* Retrieved from http://chronicle.com/article/College-Enrollments-Will-Be/48414.

Brownson, C. (2010). Conducting research in college and university counseling centers. In J. Kay, & V. Schwartz (Eds.), *Mental health care in the college community* (pp. 325–342). Hoboken, NJ: John Wiley & Sons.

Bundy, A. P., & Benshoff, J. M. (2000). Research: Students' perceptions of need for personal counseling services in community colleges. *Journal of College Counseling, 3*, 92–99. doi: 10.1002/j.2161–1882.2000.tb00169.x

Butte College. (2012). *Student athlete success program.* Oroville, CA: Author. Retrieved from http://www.butte.edu/athletics/student_athlete_success_program.html.

Chandler, L. A., & Gallagher, R. P. (1996). Developing a taxonomy for problems seen at a university counseling center. *Measurement & Evaluation in Counseling & Development, 29*, 4–12.

Colton, D., & Covert, R. W. (2007). *Designing and constructing instruments for social research and Evaluation.* San Francisco, CA: Jossey-Bass.

Cooper, S. E., & Archer, J. A., Jr. (2002). Evaluation and research in college counseling center contexts. *Journal of College Counseling, 5*, 50–59.

Corey, G. (2013). *Theory and practice of counseling and psychotherapy* (9th ed.). Belmont, CA: Brooks/Cole.

Council for the Advancement of Standards in Higher Education. (2012). *CAS professional standards for higher education* (8th ed.). Washington, DC: Author. Retrieved from http://www.cas.edu.

DeStefano, T. J., Petersen, J., Skwerer, L., & Bickel, S. (2001, March). *Key stakeholder perceptions of the role and functions of college counseling centers.* Paper presented at the Annual Conference of the National Association of Student Personnel Administrators, Seattle, WA.

Eichler, R. J., & Schwartz, V. (2010). Essential Services in College Counseling. In J. Kay, & V. Schwartz (Eds.), *Mental health care in the college community* (pp. 57–93). Hoboken, NJ: Wiley-Blackwell.

Evans, N. J. (2002). The impact of an LGBT safe zone project on campus climate. *Journal of College Student Development, 43*, 522–538.

Evans, N. J., Forney, D. S., Guido, F. M., Patton, L. D., & Renn, K. A. (2009). *Student development in college: Theory, research, and practice* (2nd ed.). San Francisco: Jossey-Bass.

Fauman, B. J., & Hopkinson, M. J. (2010). Special population. In J. Kay, & V. Schwartz (Eds.), *Mental health care in the college community* (pp. 247–263). Hoboken, NJ: Wiley-Blackwell.

Gallagher, R. P. (2001). *National survey of counseling center directors.* Alexandria, VA: International Association of Counseling Services.

Gallagher, R. P. (2009). *National survey of counseling center directors.* Alexandria, VA: International Association of Counseling Services.

Gibbs, N. (November 20, 2009). The growing backlash against overparenting. Time. Retrieved from http://www.time.com/time/magazine/article/0,9171,1940697,00.html.

Guinness World Records. (2012a). *Oldest Graduate.* Retrieved from http://www.guinnessworldrecords.com/world-records/3000/oldest-graduate.

Guinness World Records. (2012b). *Youngest undergraduate.* Retrieved from http://www.guinnessworldrecords.com/world-records/11000/youngest-undergraduate.

Gupta, K., Sleezer, C. M., & Russ-Eft, D. F. (2007). *A practical guide to needs assessment* (2nd ed.). San Francisco: John Wiley & Sons.

Hack, B. (2007). The development and delivery of sport psychology services within a university sports medicine department. *Journal of Clinical Sport Psychology, 1*, 247–260.

Hayes, J. A., Locke, B. D., & Castonguay, L. G. (2011). The Center for Collegiate Mental Health: Practice and research working together. *Journal of College Counseling, 14*, 101–104.

Higher Education Center. (2011). *Q&A with William Auvenshine.* Washington, DC: United States Department of Education. Retrieved from http://www.higheredcenter.org/about/messages/qa-william-auvenshine.

Hyun, J. K., Quinn, B. C., Madon, T., & Lustig, S. (2006). Graduate student mental health: Needs assessment and utilization of counseling services. *Journal of College Student Development, 47*, 247–266. doi:10.1353/csd.2006.0030

Jaschik, S. (February 17, 2005). From concentration camp to campus. *Inside Higher Ed.* Retrieved from http://www.insidehighered.com/news/2005/02/17/japanese2_17.

Johnson, L. (December 4, 2011). First generation freshmen get a residence of their own. *The Chronicle of Higher Education.* Retrieved from http://chronicle.com.

Kitzrow, M. A. (2003). The mental health needs of today's college students: Challenges and recommendations. *NASPA Journal, 41*(1), 165–179.

Komives, S. R., Dugan, J. P., Owen, J. E., Slack, C., & Wagner, W. (2011). *The handbook for student leadership development* (2nd ed.). San Francisco: Jossey-Bass.

Layton, W. L., Sandeen, A., & Baker, R. D. (1971). Student development and counseling. *Annual Review of Psychology, 22*, 533–564.

Leong, F. T. L., & Sedlacek, W. E. (1989). Academic and career needs of international and United States college students. *Journal of College Student Development, 30*, 106–111.

Lucas, M. S., & Berkel, L. A. (2005). Counseling needs of students who seek help at a university counseling center: A closer look at gender and multicultural issues. *Journal of College Student Development, 46*, 251–266. doi:10.1353/csd.2005.0029

Martin, N. K., & Meyer, K. (2010). Efforts to improve undergraduate student retention rates at a Hispanic service institution: Building collaborative relationships for the common good. *College and University, 85*(3), 40–49.

Minami, T., Davies, D. R., Tierney, S. C., Bettmann, J. E., McAward, S. M., Averill, L. A., & Wampold, B. E. (2009). Preliminary evidence on the effectiveness of psychological treatments delivered at a university counseling center. *Journal of Counseling Psychology, 56*, 306–320. doi:10.1037/a0015398

Medical Mental Health Services. (2012). *How to help students in distress.* Cambridge, MA: Massachusetts Institute of Technology.

Merriam, S. B., Caffarella, R. S., & Baumgartner, L. M. (2007). *Learning in adulthood: A comprehensive guide* (3rd ed.). Hoboken, NJ: John Wiley & Sons.

Miller, G. M., & Wooten, H. R., Jr. (1998). Sports counseling: A new counseling specialty area. *Journal of Counseling and Development, 74*, 172–173.

National Center for Education Statistics. (2010a). *Digest of educational statistics, 2010, Table 244, Number of degree-granting institutions and enrollment in these institutions, by size, type, and control of institution: Fall 2009.* Retrieved from http://nces.ed.gov/programs/digest/d10/tables/dt10_244.asp.

National Center for Education Statistics. (2010b). *Digest of educational statistics, 2010, Table 235, Total fall enrollment in degree-granting institutions, by race/ethnicity, sex, attendance status, and level of student: Selected years, 1976 through 2009.* Retrieved from http://nces.ed.gov/programs/digest/d10/tables/dt10_235.asp.

National Center for Education Statistics. (2010c). *Digest of educational statistics, 2010, Table 200, Total fall enrollment in degree-granting institutions, by level of enrollment, sex, age, and attendance status of student: 2007 and 2009.* Retrieved from http://nces.ed.gov/programs/digest/d10/tables/dt10_200.asp.

National Center for Education Statistics. (2012). *Fast facts.* Washington, DC: Author. Retrieved from http://nces.ed.gov.

Patton, M. Q. (2008). *Utilization-focused evaluation* (4th ed.). Thousand Oaks, CA: Sage.

Schuh, J. H. (2011). *Assessment methods for student affairs.* San Francisco, CA: Jossey-Bass.

Sharkin, B. S. (2004). College counseling and student retention: Research findings and implications for counseling centers. *Journal of College Counseling, 7*, 99–108.

Sharkin, B. S., & Coulter, L. P. (2005). Empirically supporting the increasing severity of college counseling center client problems: Why is it so challenging? *Journal of College Counseling, 8*, 165–171.

Stevens-Long, J., & Michaud, G. (2002). Theory in adult development: The new paradigm and the problem of direction. In J. Demick, & C. Andreoletti (Eds.), *Handbook of adult development* (pp. 3–22). New York: Springer.

Student Support Services. (2012). Staff members. Cambridge, MA: Massachusetts Institute of Technology. Retrieved from http://web.mit.edu/uaap/s3/about/staff.html.

Times Higher Education. (2012). *The Times higher education world university rankings 2011–2012.* London: Author. Retrieved from http://www.timeshighereducation.co.uk/world-university-rankings.

University of Notre Dame. (2012). *Academic services for student athletes.* South Bend, IN: Author. Retrieved from http://www.nd.edu/ assa/index.html.

Vespia, K. M. (2007). A national survey of small college counseling centers: Successes, issues, and challenges. *Journal of College Student Psychotherapy, 22*, 17–40. doi:10.1300/J035v22n01_03

Waple, J. N. (2006). An assessment of skills and competencies necessary for entry-level student affairs work. *Journal of Student Affairs Research and Practice, 43*(1).

Watson, J. C. (2007). College student athletes' attitudes toward help-seeking behavior and expectations of counseling services. *Journal of College Student Development, 46*, 442–459. doi: 10.1353/csd.2005.0044

Whiston, S. C. (2008). *Principles and applications of assessment in counseling* (3rd ed.). Belmont, CA: Thompson, Brooks Cole.

Write, D. J. (2000). College counseling and the needs of multicultural students. In D. C. Davis, & K. M. Humphrey (Eds.), *College counseling: Issues and strategies for a new millennium* (pp. 153–168). Alexandria, VA: American Counseling Association.

Zwick, R. (2007). *College admission testing.* Arlington, VA: National Association for College Admission Counseling.

INDEX